SQL
FUNDAMENTALS
Third Edition

SQL
FUNDAMENTALS
Third Edition

John J. Patrick

PRENTICE
HALL

Upper Saddle River, NJ • Boston • Indianapolis • San Francisco
New York • Toronto • Montreal • London • Munich • Paris • Madrid
Capetown • Sydney • Tokyo • Singapore • Mexico City

The publisher offers excellent discounts on this book when ordered in quantity for bulk purchases or special sales, which may include electronic versions and/or custom covers and content particular to your business, training goals, marketing focus, and branding interests. For more information, please contact:

U.S. Corporate and Government Sales
(800) 382-3419
corpsales@pearsontechgroup.com

For sales outside the United States, please contact:

International Sales
international@pearsoned.com

Visit us on the Web: informit.com/ph

Library of Congress Cataloging-in-Publication Data

Patrick, John J.
  SQL fundamentals / John J. Patrick. — 3rd ed.
     p. cm.
  Includes indexes.
  ISBN 978-0-13-712602-6 (pbk. : alk. paper) 1. SQL (Computer program language) 2. Oracle. 3. Microsoft Access.
I. Title.
  QA76.73.S67P38 2008
  005.75'65—dc22

                                        2008024745

ISBN-13: 978-0-13-712602-6
ISBN-10:   0-13-712602-6
Text printed in the United States on recycled paper at Courier in Stoughton, Massachusetts.
First printing, August 2008

Dedicated to four wonderful teachers

    Seymour Hayden, who taught me mathematics
    Stanley Sultan, who taught me Irish literature
    Jim Seibolt, who taught me computers
    Scot Stoney, who taught me databases

and to all my students.

CONTENTS AT A GLANCE

CONTENTS

PREFACE

SQL is one of the most important computer languages. It is the language of databases. Whenever you search for the information you need in a large library of information, the code that performs the search is likely to be using SQL. Many applications in which you share information to coordinate with other people also use SQL.

It is used in more than 100 software products, and new ones are being added all the time. This book shows you how to get the most out of the databases you use. It explains how to use SQL to solve practical problems, using the most widely used SQL products, Oracle and Microsoft Access. Oracle and Access are both widely used, easily available, and run on personal computers. By learning these two products in detail, you will have all the basic skills to use any of the many products based on SQL.

How the Topics Are Presented

This book uses an informal conversational style to take you on a tour of SQL topics. Oracle and Access are placed side by side doing the same tasks, so you can see their similarities and differences. Most topics are illustrated with an example of SQL code. I have intentionally kept the tables small in these examples, which makes them easy to check and understand.

Each example of SQL code begins by setting a task. Then the SQL code is given that performs that task. Whenever possible, I wrote the SQL code so that it works in both Oracle and Access. However, sometimes I could not do that, so I wrote one version of SQL code for Oracle and a different version for Access.

To make this book easier to read, each example of SQL shows the beginning and ending data table(s). This allows you to check that you understand what the SQL is doing. I have tried to make these examples small so they are easy to check.

Each example is often followed by notes to explain any subtle points about the SQL code or the data tables.

Finally, I give you a problem to solve to check your understanding of the topic. You can decide if you want to do these problems or not. Usually they are fairly easy and require only a small modification of the SQL code in the example. If you decide to do a problem, the Web site will allow you to determine if your solution is correct.

Each example of SQL code in this book is designed to be independent and stand on its own, without needing any changes performed in previous sections. This allows you to skip around in the book and read the sections in any order you want. Some people may want to read the book from beginning to end, but it is not necessary to do this.

Be sure to look at the appendices for practical tips on how to run Oracle and Access. The database files and the code for all the examples are available from the Web site. In several places throughout this book, I have expressed opinions about computer technology, something that many other technical books avoid doing. These opinions are my own and I take full responsibility for them. I also reserve the right to change my mind. If I do so, I will put my revised opinion, and the reasons that have caused me to change my thinking, on the Web site for this book.

The Companion Web Site

The companion Web site for this book is a Google group called "sqlfun." The group Web address is:

`http://groups.google.com/group/sqlfun`

You can also send e-mail to me at:

`sqlfun@gmail.com`

This Web site contains:

- Oracle SQL code to build all the data tables used in this book.
- Access databases with all the data tables used in this book. Databases are available for several versions of Access.
- Ways to check your answers to problems in the book.
- A list of corrections, if there are any.
- An open area for discussions, your comments, and questions you want me to answer.

I invite you to come visit the Web site!

Acknowledgments

Many people contributed greatly to this book. I would like to thank them for all the support they have given me during the time I was writing it. Their ideas and feedback have improved the quality of the material and the way I present it. In particular, I want to thank the following people for their suggestions and help with this third edition:

- Dejang Liu
- Alma Lynn Bane

People who helped with the previous editions include:

- Anila Manning, for much help in writing the second edition.
- Paul Reavis, who taught this course with me at UC Berkeley Extension.

- Todd Matson, who reviewed the Access material.

- Faysal Shaarani and Bill Allaway, who reviewed the Oracle material.

- Spencer Brucker and the UC Berkeley Extension, who have supported me in teaching the SQL Fundamentals course and developing the material in this book.

- All the folks at Prentice Hall, especially Bernard Goodwin, editor; Vanessa Moore, Moore Media, Inc., production editor; Michael Meehan and Jeffery Pepper, the original editors for this book; and the many other people with whom I never worked directly.

- Thanks especially to my mom, Jean Praninskas, and to my son, Richard Watts, who also reviewed this book.

Thanks also to Brian Akitoye, Mehran Ansari, Asa Ashraf, Anne Bester, Sandra Bush, Connie Chong, Patricia Cleveland, Robert D'Antony, Gan Davnarrain, Bruce Douglass, James Drummond, Ron Duckworth, Dean Evans, Steve Fajardo, Earl Gardner, Wolday Gebremichael, Neelam Hasni, Reda Ismail, Marques Junior, John Karsnak, Allyson Kinney, Gladys Lattier, Brian Lester, Mahen Luximan, Alex McDougall, E. Muljadi, Satyendra Narayan, Bade Oyebamiji, Stefan Pantazi, Todd Perchert, Oxana Rakova, Jacob Relles, Ricardo Ribeiro, Cindy Roberts, John Rusk, Ty Seward, Gary Shapiro, David Smith, Kenneth Smith, Joan Spasyk, Patricia Warfel, and William White.

chapter 1

STORING INFORMATION IN TABLES

In relational databases, all the data is stored in tables and all the results are expressed in tables. In this chapter, we examine tables in detail.

Introduction

1-1   What is SQL?

The name SQL stands for Structured Query Language. It is pronounced "S-Q-L" and can also be pronounced "sequel."

SQL is a computer language designed to get information from data that is stored in a relational database. In a moment, I discuss what a relational database is. For now, you can think of it as one method of organizing a large amount of data on a computer. SQL allows you to find the information you want from a vast collection of data. The purpose of this book is to show you how to get the information you want from a database.

SQL is different from most other computer languages. With SQL, you describe the type of information you want. The computer then determines the best procedure to use to obtain it and runs that procedure. This is called a *declarative* computer language because the focus is on the result: You specify what the result should look like. The computer is allowed to use any method of processing as long as it obtains the correct result.

Most other computer languages are *procedural*. These are languages like C, Cobol, Java, Assembler, Fortran, Visual Basic, and others. In these languages, you describe the procedure that will be applied to the data; you do not describe the result. The result is whatever emerges from applying the procedure to the data.

Let me use an analogy to compare these two approaches. Suppose I go to a coffee shop in the morning. With the declarative approach, used by SQL, I can say *what* I want: "I would like a cup of coffee and a donut." With the procedural approach, I cannot say that. I have to say *how* the result can be obtained and give a specific procedure for it. That is, I have to say how to make a cup of coffee and how to make a donut. So, for the coffee, I have to say, "Grind up some roasted coffee beans, add boiling water to them, allow the coffee to brew, pour it into a cup, and give it to me." For the donut, I will have to read from a cookbook. Clearly, the declarative approach is much closer to the way we usually speak and it is much easier for most people to use.

The fact that SQL is easy to use, relative to most other computer languages, is the main reason it is so popular and important. The claim is often made that anyone can learn SQL in a day or two. I think that claim is more a wish than a reality. After all, SQL is a computer language, and computers are not as easy to use as telephones — at least not yet.

Nonetheless, SQL is easy to use. With one day of training, most people can learn to obtain much useful information. That includes people who are not programmers. People throughout an organization, from secretaries to vice presidents, can use SQL to obtain the information they need to make business decisions. That is the hope and, to a large extent, it has been proven true.

Information is not powerful by itself. It only becomes powerful when it is available to people throughout an organization when they need to use it. SQL is a tool for delivering that information.

Notes about SQL

- SQL is the designated language for getting information from a relational database.

- SQL says **what** information to get, rather than **how** to get it.

- Basic SQL is easy to learn.

- SQL empowers people by giving them control over information.

- SQL allows people to handle information in new ways.

- SQL makes information powerful by bringing it to people when they need it.

1-2   What is a relational database and why would you use one?

A **relational database** is one way to organize data in a computer. There are other ways to organize it, but in this book, we do not discuss these other ways, except to say that each method has some strengths and some drawbacks. For now, we look only at the advantages a relational database has to offer.

SQL is one of the main reasons to organize data into a relational database. Using SQL, information can be obtained from the data fairly easily by people throughout the organization. That is very important.

Another reason is that data in a relational database can be used by many people at the same time. Sometimes hundreds or thousands of people can all share the data in a database. All the people can see the data and change the data (if they have the authority to do so). From a business perspective, this provides a way to coordinate all the employees and have everybody working from the same body of information.

A third reason is that a relational database is designed with the expectation that your information requirements may change over time. You might need to reorganize the information you have or add new pieces of information to it. Relational databases are designed to make this type of change easy. Most other computer systems are difficult to change. They assume that you know what all the requirements will be before you start to construct them. My experience is that people are not very good at predicting the future, even when they say they can, but here I am showing my own bias toward relational databases.

From the perspective of a computer programmer, the flexibility of a relational database and the availability of SQL make it possible to develop new computer applications much more rapidly than with traditional techniques. Some organizations take advantage of this; others do not.

The idea of a relational database was first developed in the early 1970s to handle very large amounts of data — millions of records. At first, the relational database was thought of as a back-end processor that would provide information to a computer application written in a procedural language such as C or Cobol. Even now, relational databases bear some of the traits of that heritage.

Today, however, the ideas have been so successful that entire information systems are often constructed as relational databases, without much need for procedural code (except to support input forms). That is, the ideas that were originally developed to play a supporting role for procedural code have now taken center stage. Much of the procedural code is no longer needed.

In relational databases, all the data is kept in tables, which are two-dimensional structures with columns and rows. I describe tables in detail later in this chapter. After you work with them for a while, you will find that tables provide a very useful structure for handling data. They adapt easily to changes, they share data with all users at the same time, and SQL can be run on the data in a table. Many people start thinking of their data in terms of tables. Tables have become the metaphor of choice when working with data.

Today, people use small personal databases to keep their address books, catalog their music, organize their libraries, or track their finances. Business applications are also built as relational databases. Many people prefer to have their data in a database, even if it has only a few records in it.

The beginning of relational databases

- Relational databases were originally developed in the 1970s to organize large amounts of information in a consistent and coherent manner.

- They allowed thousands of people to work with the same information at the same time.

- They kept the information current and consistent at all times.

- They made information easily available to people at all levels of an organization, from secretaries to vice presidents. They used SQL, forms, standardized reports, and ad-hoc reports to deliver information to people in a timely manner.

- They were designed to work as an information server back end. This means that most people would not work directly with the database; instead, they would work with another layer of software. This other software would get the information from the database and then adapt it to the needs of each person.

- They empowered people by making current information available to them when they needed to use it.

Today — How relational databases have changed

- In addition to the large databases described already, now there are also many smaller databases that handle much smaller amounts of information. These databases can be used by a single person or shared by a few people.

- Databases have been so successful and are so easy to use that they are now employed for a wider range of applications than they were originally designed for.

- Many people now work directly with a database instead of through another layer of software.

- Many people prefer to keep their data in databases. They feel that relational databases provide a useful and efficient framework for handling all types of data.

1-3   Why learn SQL?

SQL is used in more than 100 software products. Once you learn SQL, you will be able to use all of these products. Of course, each one will require a little study of its special features, but you will soon feel at home with it and know how to use it. You can use this one set of skills over and over again.

Major SQL Products	Other SQL Products (and Products Based on SQL)
Oracle	4th Dimension
Microsoft SQL Server	SQLBase
Microsoft Access	CSQL
MySQL	FileMaker PRO
DB2 (IBM Data Server)	Helix Database
Informix	ODBC
PostgreSQL	Ingres
Sybase	MonetDB
Microsoft Visual FoxPro	H2
NonStop SQL	MaxDB
Dataphor	VMDS
Teradata	TimesTen
	Openbase
	eXtremeDB
	Interbase
	OpenEdge ABL
	SmallSQL
	Linter SQL DMBS
	Derby
	Adabas D
	Greenplum Database
	HSQLDB
	Alpha_Five
	One$DB
	ScimoreDB
	Pervasive PSQL
	Gladius DB
	Daffodil database
	solidDB
	(and many more)

There are reasons SQL is used so much. One reason is that it is easy to learn, relative to many other computer languages. Another reason is that it opens the door to relational databases and the many advantages they offer. Some people say that SQL is the best feature of relational databases and it is what makes them successful. Other people say that relational databases make SQL successful. Most people agree that together they are a winning team.

SQL is the most successful declarative computer language — a language with which you say what you want rather than how to get it. There are some other declarative languages and report-generation tools, but most of them are much more limited in what they can do. SQL is more powerful and can be applied in more situations.

SQL can help you get information from a database that may not be available to people who do not know SQL. It can help you learn and understand the many products that are based on it.

Finally (don't tell your boss), learning SQL can be enjoyable and fun. It can stretch your mind and give you new tools with which to think. You might start to view some things from a new perspective.

1-4   What is in this book?

The subject of this book

This book shows you how to use SQL to get information from a relational database. It begins with simple queries that retrieve selected data from a single table. It progresses step by step to advanced queries that summarize the data, combine it with data from other tables, or display the data in specialized ways. It goes beyond the basics and shows you how to get the information you need from the databases you have.

Who should read this book?

Anyone with an interest in getting information from a database can read this book. It can be a first book about databases for people who are new to the subject. You do not need to be a computer programmer. The discussion begins at the beginning and it does not assume any prior knowledge about databases. The only thing you need is the persistence to work through the examples and a little prior experience working with your own computer.

Professional programmers can also use this book. The techniques shown here can help them find solutions to many problems. Whether you are a novice or a professional, an end user or a manager, the SQL skills you learn will be useful to you over and over again.

Organization of this book

This book discusses the practical realities of getting information from a database. A series of specific tasks are accomplished and discussed. Each concept is presented with an example.

The tasks are designed and arranged to show the most important aspects of the subject. Each topic is discussed thoroughly and in an organized manner. All the major features and surprising aspects of each topic are shown.

Why compare two different implementations of SQL — Oracle and Access?

If a book discusses only the theory of SQL, and no particular product that implements it, the reader will be left with no practical skills. He or she will be able to think about the concepts, but might have difficulty writing code that works.

If a book discusses only one implementation of SQL, it is easy to get distracted by the quirks and special features it has. You also lose sight of the fact that SQL is used in many products, although in slightly different ways.

This book compares Oracle and Access because they are two of the most widely used SQL products and because they both run on a PC. They are somewhat different. You will see them side by side. Oracle is used mostly for larger business applications. Access is used mostly for personal database applications and smaller business applications.

The Parts of a Table

SQL always deals with data that is in tables. You probably understand tables already on an informal level. The tables used in a relational database have a few unusual features. Because computers need precise definitions, the description of a table must be formalized. In this section, I define what a table is and what its parts are.

1-5   Data is stored in tables

In a relational database, all the data is stored in tables. A table is a two-dimensional structure that has **columns** and **rows**. Using more traditional computer terminology, the columns are called **fields** and the rows are called **records**. You can use either terminology.

Most people are familiar with seeing information in tables. Bus schedules are usually presented in tables. Newspapers use tables to list stock values. We all know how to use these tables. They are a good way to present a lot of information in a very condensed format. The tables in a relational database are very similar to these tables, which we all understand and use every day.

All the information in a relational database is kept in tables. There is no other type of container to keep it in — there are no other data structures. Even the most complex information is stored in tables. Someone once said that there are three types of data structures in a relational database: tables, tables, and tables. In a relational database, we have nothing but tables; there are no numbers, no words, no letters, and no dates unless they are stored in a table.

You might think that this restricts what a relational database can do and the data it can represent. Is it a limitation? The answer is no. All data is capable of being represented in this format. Sometimes you have to do some work to put it in this format. It doesn't always just fall into this format by itself. But you can always succeed at putting data into tables, no matter how complex the data is. This has been proven in mathematics. The proof is long and complex and I do not show it to you here, but you can have confidence that tables are versatile enough to handle all types of data.

The following two depictions show a basic table structure and how a table might store information.

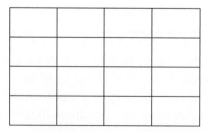

A conceptual diagram of a table.

First Name	Last Name	Age	Gender	Favorite Game
Nancy	Jones	1	F	Peek-a-boo
Paula	Jacobs	5	F	Acting
Deborah	Kahn	4	F	Dolls
Howard	Green	7	M	Baseball
Jack	Lee	5	M	Trucks
Cathy	Rider	6	F	Monsters

An example of a table that stores information about children.

Each row contains information about one child. Each column contains one type of information for all the children. As always, this table contains only a limited amount of information about each child. It does not say, for instance, how much each child weighs.

Notes

- In a relational database, all the data is stored in tables.
- A table has two dimensions called columns and rows.
- Tables can hold even the most complex information.
- All operations begin with tables and end with tables. All the data is represented in tables.

1-6   A row represents an object and the information about it

Each row of a table represents one object, event, or relationship. I call them all objects for now, so I do not have to keep repeating the phrase "object, event, or relationship."

All the rows within a table represent the same type of object. If you have 100 doctors in a hospital, you might keep all the information about them in a single table. If you also want to keep information about 1,000 patients who are in the hospital, you would use a separate table for that information.

The tables in a relational database may contain hundreds or thousands of rows. Some tables even contain many millions of rows. In theory, there is no limit to the number of rows a table can have. In practice, your computer will limit the number of rows you can have. Today, business databases running on large computers sometimes reach billions of rows.

There are also some tables with only one row of data. You can even have an empty table with no rows of data in it. This is something like an empty box. Usually, a table is only empty when you first build it. After it is created, you start to put rows of data into it.

In a relational database, the rows of a table are considered to be in no particular order so they are an unordered set. This is different from the tables most people are familiar with. In a bus schedule, the rows are in a definite and logical order. They are not scrambled in a random order.

Database administrators (DBAs) are allowed to change the order of the rows in a table to make the computer more efficient. In some products, such as Access, this can be done automatically by the computer. As a result, you, the end user seeking information, cannot count on the rows being in a particular order.

A conceptual diagram of a row.

Notes

- A row contains data for one object, event, or relationship.
- All the rows in a table contain data for similar objects, events, or relationships.
- A table may contain hundreds or thousands of rows.
- The rows of a table are not in a predictable order.

1-7   A column represents one type of information

A column contains one particular type of information that is kept about all the rows in the table. A column cannot, or should not, contain one type of information for one row and another type for another row. Each column usually contains a separate type of information.

Each column has a name, for instance "favorite game," and a datatype. We discuss datatypes in chapter 6, but for now let's keep it simple. There are three main datatypes: text, numbers, and dates. This means that there are three types of columns: columns containing text, columns containing numbers, and columns containing dates.

Some columns allow nulls, which are unknown values. Other columns do not allow them. If a column does not allow nulls, then data is required in the column for every row of the table. This means it is a required field. When a column does allow nulls, the field is optional.

Most tables contain 5 to 40 columns. A table can contain more columns, 250 or more, depending on the relational database product you are using, but this is unusual.

Each column has a position within the table. That is, the columns are an ordered set. This contrasts with the rows, which have no fixed order.

Information about the columns — their names, datatypes, positions, and whether they accept nulls — is all considered to be part of the definition of the table itself. In contrast, information about the rows is considered to be part of the data and not part of the definition of the table.

A conceptual diagram of a column.

Notes

- A column contains one type of data about each row of the table.

- Each column has a name.

- Each column has a datatype. The most important datatypes are:

  - Text

  - Numbers

  - Dates with times

- Some columns accept nulls, and others do not. A null is an unknown value.

- Each column has a position within the table. In contrast to rows, the columns of a table form an ordered set. There is a first column and a last column.

- Most tables have 40 columns or fewer.

1-8   A cell is the smallest part of a table

A **cell** occurs where one row meets with one column. It is the smallest part of a table and it cannot be broken down into smaller parts.

A cell contains one single piece of data, a single unit of information. At least that is the way it is in theory, and this is how you should begin to think about it. In practice, sometimes a cell can contain several pieces of information. In some applications a cell can contain an entire sentence, a paragraph, or an entire document with hundreds of pages. For now we will consider that a cell can contain one of the following:

- One word

- One letter

- One number

- One date, which includes the time

- A null, which indicates that there is no data in the cell

For the first few chapters of this book, we consider the information in a cell to be **atomic**, which means that it is a single indivisible unit of information. We gather and arrange information from a table by manipulating its cells. We either use all the information within a cell or we do not use that cell at all. Later, when we discuss row functions, you will see how to use only part of the data from a cell.

A column is a collection of cells. These cells have the same datatype and represent the same type of information. A row is a collection of cells. Together, they represent information about the same object, event, or relationship.

A conceptual diagram of a cell.

Notes

- A cell contains a single piece of data, a single unit of information.
- Usually a cell contains one of the following types of data:
  - Text, sometimes one word, or sometimes a one-letter code, such as M for male or F for female
  - A number
  - A date and time
  - A null, which is an unknown value (some people call this an empty cell, or missing data)
- All the cells in a column contain the same type of information.
- All the cells in a row contain data about the same object, event, or relationship.

1-9   Each cell should express just one thing

Each cell expresses just one thing — one piece of information. That is the intent of the theory of relational databases. In practice, it is not always clear what this means. The problem, partly, is that English and other spoken languages do not always express information clearly. Another part of the problem is that information does not always come in separate units.

Let's examine one case in detail. A person in America usually has two names — a first name and a last name. Now that is a bit of a problem to me when I want to put information in the computer. There is one person, but there are two names. How should I identify the person? Should I put both names together in one cell? Should I put the names into two separate cells? The answer is not clear.

Both methods are valid. The designers of the database usually decide questions like this. If the database designers think that both names will always be used together, they will usually put both names in a single cell. But if they think that the names will be used separately, they will put each name in a separate cell.

The problem with this is that the way a database is used may change over time, so even if a decision is correct when it is made, it might become incorrect later on.

Full Name
Susan Riley

(A)

First Name	Last Name
Susan	Riley

(B)

Two ways to show the name of a person in a table. (A) One column for the name. Both the first and last names are put in a single cell. (B) Two separate columns: one for the first name and another for the last name. Each cell contains a single word.

Notes

- Both methods are equally valid.

- The first method emphasizes that Susan Riley is one person, even though the English language uses two separate words to express her name. It implies that we will usually call her "Susan Riley," using both her names together as a single unit.

- The second method emphasizes the English words. It implies that we will want to use several different variations of her name, calling her "Susan" or "Susan Riley" or "Miss Riley." The words "Susan" or "Riley" can come from the table in the database. Any other words must be supplied by some other means.

- The database design intends each cell to be used in whole or not used at all. In theory, you should not need to subdivide the data in a cell. However, in practice that is sometimes required.

1-10 Primary key columns identify each row

Most tables contain a *primary key* that identifies each row in the table and gives it a name. Each row must have its own identity, so no two rows are allowed to have the same primary key.

The primary key consists of several columns of the table. By convention, these are usually the first few columns. The primary key may be one column or more than one. We say that there is only one primary key, even when it consists of several columns, so it is the collection of these columns, taken as a single unit, that is the primary key and serves to identify each row.

The primary key is like a noun because it names the object of each row. The other columns are like adjectives because they give additional information about the object.

A table can only contain a single primary key, even if it consists of several columns. This makes sense because there is no point in identifying a row twice — those identities could conflict with each other. Suppose, for example, that we have a table of employees. Each employee can be identified by an employee number or a Social Security number. The database designers would need to choose which column to make the primary key of the table. They could choose either one to be the primary key of the table, or they could choose to use both together to make a primary key. However, they are not allowed to say that each column by itself is a primary key.

The name of a column is considered to be part of the definition of the table. In contrast, the name of a row, which is the primary key of the row, is considered to be part of the data in the table.

There are two rules that regulate the columns of the primary key of a table:

1. None of the columns of the primary key can contain a null. This makes sense because a null is an unknown value. Therefore, a null in any part of the primary key would mean we do not know the identity of the object or the row. In databases, we do not want to enter information about unidentified rows.

2. Each row must have an identity that is different from every other row in the table. That is, no two rows can have the same identity — the same values in all the columns of the primary key. For any two rows of the table, there must be at least one column of the primary key where the values are different.

Primary Key

A			
B			
C			
D			

The first column is usually the primary key of the table.

Primary Key

A	1		
A	2		
B	1		
B	2		

Sometimes the primary key is the first several columns of the table.

Notes

- Most tables have primary keys.

- Usually, the primary key consists of the first column or the first several columns of the table.

- The primary key names the object, event, or relationship the row represents. In grammatical terms, it is a noun because it is the subject of all the information in the row.

- The other columns of the table make statements about the primary key. In grammatical terms, they are adjectives or adverbs that describe the object named by the primary key and give additional information about it.

1-11 Most tables are tall and thin

Many books on SQL give the impression that tables are usually square — that they have about the same number of rows as they have columns. This false impression is left because the tables in most SQL books are approximately square. In any book, the tables must be kept small. In a book, when you run SQL code you must be able to examine the results in full detail.

However, the tables that are used in real production systems usually have a different shape. They are tall and thin. They may have 30 columns, but 1,000,000 rows.

Not all tables have this shape, but most do. Some tables have only one row.

I tell you this because I like to visualize the data and the tables I am working with. If you like to visualize them, too, then at least I have provided you with the correct picture. If you are not inclined to visualize these things, do not worry about it. Just go on to the next page.

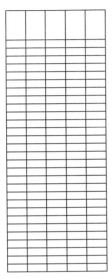

Most tables have many more rows than columns.

Examples of Tables

Up to now, we have discussed the theory of tables, but you have not seen any real ones. In the following sections you will see some actual tables. We look at a table to see how it looks in both Oracle and Access. We discuss some of the design decisions that are used in constructing many tables. We also examine the tables of the Lunches database, which is used in many of the examples throughout this book.

1-12 An example of a table in Oracle and Access

This section shows the same table in both Oracle and Access. This is our first opportunity to examine how Oracle and Access compare.

You will have to decide for yourself how similar they are and how different they are. To me, this example shows that they are about 90 percent similar and about 10 percent different. Of course, this is just one example. You might ask yourself which percentages you would use to describe this.

Oracle tables can be shown in two formats that are very similar, but have a few slight differences. To keep things simple here, I am only showing you one of those formats. The following Oracle table was obtained using the "SQL Command Line" environment. The other Oracle format occurs in the "Database Home Page" environment. I will discuss it briefly in the notes at the end of this section.

1_employees table: Oracle format

```
EMPLOYEE                          DEPT                  CREDIT  PHONE   MANAGER
      ID  FIRST_NAME  LAST_NAME   CODE  HIRE_DATE       LIMIT   NUMBER       ID
--------  ----------  ---------   ----  ------------    -------  ------  -------
     201  SUSAN       BROWN       EXE   01-JUN-1998     $30.00  3484    (null)
     202  JIM         KERN        SAL   16-AUG-1999     $25.00  8722       201
     203  MARTHA      WOODS       SHP   02-FEB-2009     $25.00  7591       201
     204  ELLEN       OWENS       SAL   01-JUL-2008     $15.00  6830       202
     205  HENRY       PERKINS     SAL   01-MAR-2006     $25.00  5286       202
     206  CAROL       ROSE        ACT   (null)          (null)  (null)  (null)
     207  DAN         SMITH       SHP   01-DEC-2008     $25.00  2259       203
     208  FRED        CAMPBELL    SHP   01-APR-2008     $25.00  1752       203
     209  PAULA       JACOBS      MKT   17-MAR-1999     $15.00  3357       201
     210  NANCY       HOFFMAN     SAL   16-FEB-2007     $25.00  2974       203
```

1_employees table: Access format

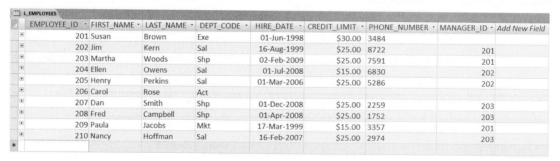

Similarities between Oracle and Access

- Column names are printed at the top of the column. The column names are part of the structure of the table, not part of the data in the table.

- Sometimes the column names shown in the column headings are truncated. This is a slight problem. You are given tools to deal with it.

- Columns containing text data are justified to the left.

- Columns containing numbers are justified to the right.

- Columns containing dates often display only the date. The format for displaying the date is not part of the data. The value of the date is stored in the table, but the format of the date is specified separately. The date actually contains both a date and a time, but the time is often not displayed.

- Columns displaying currency amounts are actually stored as numbers, and use a format to put in the dollar signs and decimal points.

Differences between Oracle and Access

- **Display framework:** Oracle displays lines of character data. Access uses graphical techniques to display the data in a grid and color the borders of the grid.

- **Case:** The Oracle table is shown all in uppercase. The Access table uses uppercase only for the first letter. It is a common convention to set the databases up this way. Mixed-case data can be put into an Oracle table, but this makes the data more difficult to handle, so Oracle data is usually either all uppercase or all lowercase. Access data is handled as if it were all uppercase, although it is displayed in mixed case. This makes it look nicer, but sometimes it can also be deceiving. In Access, the data appears to be mixed case, but the data behaves as if it were in uppercase. For instance, `John` and `jOhn` appear different in Access, but they are handled as if they are the same.

- **Column headings:** Oracle can use several lines for a column heading. Access displays the heading on a single line.

- **Date formats:** The dates above show Oracle and Access using the same date format. I made that happen here because I wanted Oracle and Access to look similar. However, on your computer the dates will probably use different formats.

  Oracle and Access can both display dates in a variety of formats. Each has a default format to use for dates when no other format is specified. However, Oracle uses one method to specify this default format for dates and Access uses a different method.

- **Date alignment:** Oracle aligns dates to the left, whereas Access aligns them to the right.

- **Nulls:** In this book, I have set up Oracle to always display nulls as `(null)` in all the columns of every table. This cannot easily be done in Access.

- **Position pointer:** The Access table contains a record selector and a pointer to a particular field within that record, which allows you to modify the data. The Oracle table does not contain these.

- **Ability to add data:** In Access, a blank row at the bottom of a table indicates that new rows of data can be entered into the table. Also an extra column is displayed called "Add New Field". This is not done in Oracle.

Notes

The other Oracle format is used in the "Database Home Page" environment. It has several technical differences, but none that will challenge your understanding of what is going on. Here are a few of these differences:

- Tables are displayed on pages in your Web browser.
- Column headings are never truncated.
- All fields are justified to the left.
- Nulls are shown with dashes
- Dollar amounts are not automatically formatted.

1-13 Some design decisions in the `1_employees` table

The `1_employees` table contains some design decisions that I want to point out to you because they reflect some common practices within relational databases. Like all design decisions, they could have been made in other ways. This is not the only way to design the table. It might not even be the best way. But you may often encounter these design decisions and you need to be aware of them.

1_employees table

EMPLOYEE ID	FIRST_NAME	LAST_NAME	DEPT CODE	HIRE_DATE	CREDIT LIMIT	PHONE NUMBER	MANAGER ID
201	SUSAN	BROWN	EXE	01-JUN-1998	$30.00	3484	(null)
202	JIM	KERN	SAL	16-AUG-1999	$25.00	8722	201
203	MARTHA	WOODS	SHP	02-FEB-2009	$25.00	7591	201
204	ELLEN	OWENS	SAL	01-JUL-2008	$15.00	6830	202
205	HENRY	PERKINS	SAL	01-MAR-2006	$25.00	5286	202
206	CAROL	ROSE	ACT	(null)	(null)	(null)	(null)
207	DAN	SMITH	SHP	01-DEC-2008	$25.00	2259	203
208	FRED	CAMPBELL	SHP	01-APR-2008	$25.00	1752	203
209	PAULA	JACOBS	MKT	17-MAR-1999	$15.00	3357	201
210	NANCY	HOFFMAN	SAL	16-FEB-2007	$25.00	2974	203

Design decisions to be aware of

- The `phone_number` column contains text data, not numbers. Although the data look like numbers, and the column name says number, it actually has a text datatype. You can tell this by its alignment, which is to the left. The reason the table is set up this way is that the phone number data will never be used for arithmetic. You never add two phone numbers together or multiply them. You only use them the way they are, as a text field. So this table stores them as text.

- The `employee_id` column contains numbers. You can tell this by its alignment, which is to the right. Now, we do not do arithmetic with employee IDs, we never add them together, so why isn't this a text field, too? The answer is that numbers are often used for primary key columns even when no arithmetic will be performed on them. This can allow the computer to handle the table more quickly.

- The `manager_id` column contains numbers, but it is not a primary key column. So why doesn't it contain text? This column is intended to match with the `employee_id` column, so it has been given the same datatype as that column. This improves the speed of matching the two columns.

- The name of the table, `1_employees`, might seem strange. The 1 indicates that this table is part of a group of tables. The names of all the tables in the group start with the same letter(s). In this case it shows that the table is part of the `Lunches` database. (Here I use the term *database* to mean a collection of related tables.)

- The people who design databases put a considerable amount of work into the consistent naming of objects, using standard prefixes, suffixes, abbreviations, and column names. This makes the whole model easier to understand and more usable for the code that is developed for each database.

1-14 The Lunches **database**

Most of the examples of SQL code in this book are based on the `Lunches` database. You can get a complete listing of this database from the Web site. To read this book, you will need to understand the story and the data, so here is the basic story.

There is a small company with ten employees. This company will serve lunch to its employees on three occasions. Each employee can attend as many of these lunches as his or her schedule permits. When employees register to attend a lunch, they get to pick what they want to eat. They may choose from among the ten foods available to them. They can decide to have a single portion or a double portion of any of these foods. The Lunches database keeps track of all this information.

That is the story. Now let's look at the data. When I call this a database, I mean that it is a collection of related tables. The set of tables, taken together, tell the story. There are seven tables in this database:

- Employees (1_employees)

- Departments (1_departments)

- Constants (1_constants)

- Lunches (1_lunches)

- Foods (1_foods)

- Suppliers (1_suppliers)

- Lunch Items (1_lunch_items)

To show that these tables are all related to each other and to distinguish them from other tables we may use, the names of these tables are all prefixed with the letter 1. When there are multiple words, such as lunch_items, the spaces are replaced with underscore characters. This helps the computer understand that the two words together are a single name.

1_employees table

EMPLOYEE ID	FIRST_NAME	LAST_NAME	DEPT CODE	HIRE_DATE	CREDIT LIMIT	PHONE NUMBER	MANAGER ID
201	SUSAN	BROWN	EXE	01-JUN-1998	$30.00	3484	(null)
202	JIM	KERN	SAL	16-AUG-1999	$25.00	8722	201
203	MARTHA	WOODS	SHP	02-FEB-2009	$25.00	7591	201
204	ELLEN	OWENS	SAL	01-JUL-2008	$15.00	6830	202
205	HENRY	PERKINS	SAL	01-MAR-2006	$25.00	5286	202
206	CAROL	ROSE	ACT	(null)	(null)	(null)	(null)
207	DAN	SMITH	SHP	01-DEC-2008	$25.00	2259	203
208	FRED	CAMPBELL	SHP	01-APR-2008	$25.00	1752	203
209	PAULA	JACOBS	MKT	17-MAR-1999	$15.00	3357	201
210	NANCY	HOFFMAN	SAL	16-FEB-2007	$25.00	2974	203

The `1_employees` table lists all the employees. Each employee can be identified by an employee ID, which is a number assigned to him or her. This allows the company to hire two people with the same name. The primary key is the `employee_id` column.

Each employee has a manager, who is also an employee of the company. The manager is identified by his or her employee ID. For instance, the `manager_id` column shows that Jim Kern is managed by employee 201. Employee 201 is Susan Brown.

Susan Brown and Carol Rose are the only employees without a manager. You can tell this because there is a null in the `manager_id` columns. However, these nulls mean different things.

Susan Brown is the head of the company. The null in this case does not mean that we do not know who her manager is. Rather, it means that she does not have a manager.

Carol Rose is a new hire. The null in her `manager_id` column could mean that she has not yet been assigned to a manager or it could mean that the information has not yet been entered into the database.

`1_departments` table

```
DEPT
CODE  DEPARTMENT_NAME
----  ------------------------------
ACT   ACCOUNTING
EXE   EXECUTIVE
MKT   MARKETING
PER   PERSONNEL
SAL   SALES
SHP   SHIPPING
```

Each employee works for one department. The department code is shown in the `1_employees` table. The full name of each department is shown in the `1_departments` table. The primary key of this table is `dept_code`.

These tables can be linked together by matching the `dept_code` columns. For example, the `1_employees` table shows us that employee 202, Jim Kern, has a department code of `SAL`. The `1_departments` table says that the sales department uses the department code `SAL`. This tells us that Jim Kern works in the sales department.

1_constants table

BUSINESS_NAME	BUSINESS START_DATE	LUNCH_BUDGET	OWNER_NAME
CITYWIDE UNIFORMS	01-JUN-1998	$200.00	SUSAN BROWN

The 1_constants table contains some constant values and has only one row. We use these values with the other tables of the database. These values are expected to change infrequently, if at all. Storing them in a separate table keeps the SQL code flexible by providing an alternative to hard-coding these values into SQL. Because the table of constants has only one row, it does not need a primary key.

1_lunches table

LUNCH_ID	LUNCH_DATE	EMPLOYEE_ID	DATE_ENTERE
1	16-NOV-2011	201	13-OCT-2011
2	16-NOV-2011	207	13-OCT-2011
3	16-NOV-2011	203	13-OCT-2011
4	16-NOV-2011	204	13-OCT-2011
6	16-NOV-2011	202	13-OCT-2011
7	16-NOV-2011	210	13-OCT-2011
8	25-NOV-2011	201	14-OCT-2011
9	25-NOV-2011	208	14-OCT-2011
12	25-NOV-2011	204	14-OCT-2011
13	25-NOV-2011	207	18-OCT-2011
15	25-NOV-2011	205	21-OCT-2011
16	05-DEC-2011	201	21-OCT-2011
17	05-DEC-2011	210	21-OCT-2011
20	05-DEC-2011	205	24-OCT-2011
21	05-DEC-2011	203	24-OCT-2011
22	05-DEC-2011	208	24-OCT-2011

The 1_lunches table registers an employee to attend a lunch. It assigns a lunch ID to each lunch that will be served. For example, employee 207, Dan Smith, will attend a lunch on November 16, 2011. His lunch is identified as lunch_id = 2.

The lunch_id column is the primary key of this table. This is an example of a **surrogate key**, which is also called a **meaningless primary key**. Each row is assigned a unique number, but there is no intrinsic meaning to that number. It is just a convenient name to use for the row, or the object that the row represents — in this case, a lunch.

The `1_lunches` table shows the most common way to use a surrogate key. Usually a single column is the primary key. That column has a different value in every row.

Some database designers like to use surrogate keys because they can improve the efficiency of queries within the database. Surrogate keys are used especially to replace a primary key that would have many columns, and when a table is often joined to many other tables.

Other designers do not like surrogate keys because they prefer to have each column contain meaningful data. This is an area of debate among database designers, with many pros and cons on each side. People who use databases need only be aware that these columns are meaningless numbers used to join one table to another.

1_foods table

SUPPLIER ID	PRODUCT CODE	MENU ITEM	DESCRIPTION	PRICE	PRICE INCREASE
ASP	FS	1	FRESH SALAD	$2.00	$0.25
ASP	SP	2	SOUP OF THE DAY	$1.50	(null)
ASP	SW	3	SANDWICH	$3.50	$0.40
CBC	GS	4	GRILLED STEAK	$6.00	$0.70
CBC	SW	5	HAMBURGER	$2.50	$0.30
FRV	BR	6	BROCCOLI	$1.00	$0.05
FRV	FF	7	FRENCH FRIES	$1.50	(null)
JBR	AS	8	SODA	$1.25	$0.25
JBR	VR	9	COFFEE	$0.85	$0.15
VSB	AS	10	DESSERT	$3.00	$0.50

The `1_foods` table lists the foods an employee can choose for his or her lunch. Each food is identified by a supplier ID and a product code. Together, these two columns form the primary key. The product codes belong to the suppliers. It is possible for two suppliers to use the same product code for different foods. In fact, the product code AS has two different meanings. Supplier JBR uses this product code for soda, but supplier VSB uses it for dessert.

The price increases are proposed, but are not yet in effect. The nulls in the `price_increase` column mean that there will not be a price increase for those food items.

1_suppliers table

```
SUPPLIER
ID         SUPPLIER_NAME
--------   ------------------------------
ARR        ALICE & RAY'S RESTAURANT
ASP        A SOUP PLACE
CBC        CERTIFIED BEEF COMPANY
FRV        FRANK REED'S VEGETABLES
FSN        FRANK & SONS
JBR        JUST BEVERAGES
JPS        JIM PARKER'S SHOP
VSB        VIRGINIA STREET BAKERY
```

The `1_suppliers` table shows the full names for the suppliers of the foods. For example, the `1_foods` table shows that french fries will be obtained from supplier ID FRV. The `1_suppliers` table shows that Frank Reed's Vegetables is the full name of this supplier. The primary key of these tables is the supplier ID.

1_lunch_items table

```
                        SUPPLIER  PRODUCT
 LUNCH_ID  ITEM_NUMBER  ID        CODE     QUANTITY
 --------  -----------  --------  -------  ---------
        1            1  ASP       FS               1
        1            2  ASP       SW               2
        1            3  JBR       VR               2
        2            1  ASP       SW               2
        2            2  FRV       FF               1
        2            3  JBR       VR               2
        2            4  VSB       AS               1
        3            1  ASP       FS               1
        3            2  CBC       GS               1
        3            3  FRV       FF               1
        3            4  JBR       VR               1
        3            5  JBR       AS               1
 (and many more rows)
```

When you look at the `1_lunch_items` table you need to be aware that the data in the `item_number` column is aligned to the right because it is a column of numbers. The data in the `supplier_id` column is aligned to the left because it is a column of text. So when you look at the first row, `1 ASP` is not a single piece of data. Instead, the `item_number` value is `1` and the `supplier_id` value is ASP.

The `l_lunch_items` table shows which foods each employee has chosen for his or her lunch. It also shows whether they want a single or a double portion. For example, look at `lunch_id 2`, which we already know to be Dan Smith's lunch on November 16. It consists of four items. The first item is identified as `ASP-SW`. Here I am putting the `supplier_id` and the `product_code` column data together separated by a hyphen. Looking in the `l_foods` table, we find this is a sandwich. The `l_lunch_items` table says he wants two of them, which is shown in the `quantity` column. See if you can figure out all the foods he wants for his lunch.

The correct answer is:

    2 sandwiches

    1 order of french fries

    2 cups of coffee

    1 dessert

The primary key of this table consists of the first two columns of the table, `lunch_id` and `item_number`. The `item_number` column is a **tie-breaker column**, which is another type of meaningless primary key. In this design, I wanted to use the lunch ID to identify each food within a lunch. However, most lunches have several foods. So I cannot use the lunch ID by itself as a primary key, because that would create several rows in the table with the same value in the primary key, which is not allowed. I needed a way for each row to have a different value in the primary key. That is what a tie-breaker column does. The `item_number` column numbers the items within each lunch. Therefore, the combination of lunch ID and item number provides a unique identity for each row of the table and can serve as the primary key. A primary key of this sort, containing more than one column, is sometimes called a **composite key**.

Challenging features of the Lunches database

Most SQL books have you work with a database that is tame and contains no challenges. This book is different. I have intentionally put some features in the Lunches database that could cause you to get the wrong result if you do not handle them properly. I show you how to become aware of these situations and how to deal with them. Many real business databases contain similar challenges. Here are a few of them:

- Two employees are not attending any of the lunches — employee 209, Paula Jacobs, and employee 206, Carol Rose.

- One food has not been ordered in any of the lunches — broccoli.

- One of the departments is not yet staffed with any employees — the personnel department.

Key Points

- In this book we assume that the database has already been built and you just need to learn how to use it. By analogy, this book shows you how to drive a car without trying to show you how to build one.

- Databases are used in many businesses and SQL is used in many software products, so the skills you learn will help you in many different situations.

- Tables are the main construct of a database. All data is kept in tables. Also any data that is given to you will be given in the form of a table. Tables have columns and rows. Usually there are many more rows than columns.

- Most tables have a primary key. This gives a name to each row of the table and prevents the table from having any two rows that are identical.

- There are a few differences between Oracle and Access, but there are many more similarities.

- Oracle is mostly used in businesses with large databases. Hundreds of people may be using the database at the same time. The database can help coordinate all the people in a business and keep them working together.

- Access is mostly used by individuals with small personal databases. Usually only one person is using the database at any given time. Access is also used in some business situations.

chapter 2

GETTING INFORMATION FROM A TABLE

This chapter explains the basic technique for getting the information you want from a table when you do not want to make any changes to the data and when all the information is in one table. The table might be very large and you might only want a small amount of data from it.

The Select Statement

In SQL, the `select` statement is used to get information from a table. Much of this book is concerned with the `select` statement. This chapter explains its four basic clauses and the options available for three of these clauses.

2-1 The goal: Get a few columns and rows from a table

Our goal is to get the data we want from a table. The table may be large and contain a lot of data. We only want a small part of it and we do not want to change the data in any way. The `select` statement allows us to retrieve a few columns and a few rows of data from the table.

Let's put some numbers on this. The particular numbers are not important, but they draw the picture more clearly. Suppose that printing all the data in the table would take 1,000 pages, and suppose we want only two pages of data from it. The `select` statement allows us to get just the two pages of data we want.

It is as if we want to read an article on redwood trees from an encyclopedia. We only want to see that one article. We do not want to read the entire encyclopedia from beginning to end. The `select` statement allows us to find the particular article we want to read.

The following diagram shows a large table of data. A small amount of that data is being retrieved into the result of the `select` statement. In this diagram, the data we want is scattered throughout the table in various columns and rows. It is collected together by the `select` statement.

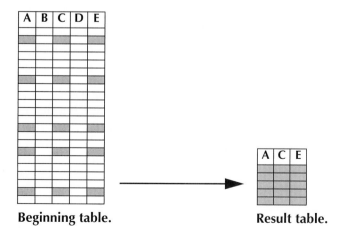

Beginning table.   **Result table.**

Handling small tables of data

If a table of data is small, there might not be much reason to write a `select` statement. For instance, if we can print the entire table on two pages, then why not print it completely and let people work to find the information they want? In many situations, this approach makes the most sense.

In this book, we use small tables as learning tools. With tables this size, there is not much reason to use `select` statements. However, these tables are being used as examples to show how the `select` statement works when it is used with larger tables.

2-2   Overview of the `select` statement

The `select` statement is used to get some of the data from a table. It has six clauses:

`select`	Which columns of data to get
`from`	Which table has the data
`where`	Which rows of data to get
`group by`	(Described in chapter 12)
`having`	(Described in chapter 12)
`order by`	Which columns are used to sort the result

They must be written in this order. `Group by` and `having` are used in summarizing data, and we examine them later.

This chapter discusses the options available for the `select`, `where`, and `order by` clauses. For now, the `from` clause will always list only one table.

A `select` statement is often called a **query**. These two terms are used interchangeably. The term "`select` statement" emphasizes the syntax of the SQL command. The term "query" emphasizes the purpose of the command.

Task

Show an example of a `select` statement that uses all of the clauses just listed. Show the `employee_id`, `last_name`, and `credit_limit` columns from the `1_employees` table of the `Lunches` database. Show only the employees who have a credit limit greater than $20.00. Sort the rows of the result by the last name of the employee.

Oracle & Access SQL

```
select employee_id, ❶
       last_name,
       credit_limit
from 1_employees ❷
where credit_limit > 20.00 ❸
order by last_name; ❹
```

Beginning table (1_employees table)

EMPLOYEE ID	FIRST_NAME	LAST_NAME	DEPT CODE	HIRE_DATE	CREDIT LIMIT	PHONE NUMBER	MANAGER ID
201	SUSAN	BROWN	EXE	01-JUN-1998	$30.00	3484	(null)
202	JIM	KERN	SAL	16-AUG-1999	$25.00	8722	201
203	MARTHA	WOODS	SHP	02-FEB-2009	$25.00	7591	201
204	ELLEN	OWENS	SAL	01-JUL-2008	$15.00	6830	202
205	HENRY	PERKINS	SAL	01-MAR-2006	$25.00	5286	202
206	CAROL	ROSE	ACT	(null)	(null)	(null)	(null)
207	DAN	SMITH	SHP	01-DEC-2008	$25.00	2259	203
208	FRED	CAMPBELL	SHP	01-APR-2008	$25.00	1752	203
209	PAULA	JACOBS	MKT	17-MAR-1999	$15.00	3357	201
210	NANCY	HOFFMAN	SAL	16-FEB-2007	$25.00	2974	203

Result table ❺

EMPLOYEE ID	LAST_NAME	CREDIT LIMIT
201	BROWN	$30.00
208	CAMPBELL	$25.00
210	HOFFMAN	$25.00
202	KERN	$25.00
205	PERKINS	$25.00
207	SMITH	$25.00
203	WOODS	$25.00

Notes

❶ The `select` clause lists the columns you want to show in the result table. They can be listed in any order. Their order in the `select` clause determines their order within the result table. When the computer sees a column name that is not followed by a comma it expects to see the next clause, the `from` clause.

Also, note that the names of these columns do not contain spaces. Access allows this, but I do not recommend it because a space is usually used as a delimiter. The underscore character (_) is usually used instead of a space to separate the words in the name of each column. By typing `last_name` with an underscore, you are telling the computer that this is the name of a single column. If you typed `last name` with a space, the computer would try to find a column named `last` and it would not find any column with that name. This would cause an error and the computer would not process the `select` statement. Chapter 3 discusses the issue of using spaces in column names in more detail.

❷ The `from` clause names the table that the data comes from — the `l_employees` table of the `Lunches` database. In the naming scheme used here, the prefix "l_" indicates that the `employees` table is part of the `Lunches` database. This table is shown as the beginning table.

❸ The `where` clause indicates which rows to show in the result table. The condition `where credit_limit > 20.00` eliminates the rows for employees 204 and 209 because they have a $15.00 credit limit, and employee 206, which has a null value.

Note that the dollar amount is written without the dollar sign. It must also be written without any commas. The decimal point is acceptable, but not required. The condition could also be written as follows: `where credit_limit > 20`. In this SQL code here, I put two zeros after the decimal point to make it look more like a currency value. This has no effect on the result of the query.

❹ The `order by` clause specifies that the rows of the result table should be sorted in alphabetical order by the `last_name` column. A semicolon marks the end of the SQL statement. In Oracle, this statement will not run without the semicolon. In Access, it is optional. In Oracle, you could put a slash (/) on the next line as an alternative to the semicolon. Because using a semicolon is valid within both products, in this book I use a semicolon at the end of every SQL statement.

❺ Some people would call this a **query result listing**. This name has some merit, because it is not a table. It is the result of running a query or a `select` statement. In Oracle, these results are shown on the screen as a Web page within your browser. In Access, they are shown on the screen as if they are in a table, with some interactive elements, in datasheet view. In other books you may find the terms **derived table** and **virtual table**.

I call this a **result table** because according to relational database theory, tables are the only database structure. The input to a query is a table, and the output of a query is a table. This result table appears only on the screen. It is not stored on the disk.

The Select Clause

The `select` clause is the first part of a query. The `select` clause says which columns of information you want, what order you want them in, and what you want them to be called. Do not confuse the `select` clause with the `select` statement.

2-3   Overview of the `select` clause

There are three forms of the `select` clause. The following pages show an example of each of these.

`select` **a list of columns**

- Get only the columns listed.
- Put them in the order they are listed.
- You can rename them.

`select *`
or `select` **table_name**.*

- Get all the columns of the table.
- Put them in the same order they are in the table.
- You cannot rename them in SQL. (Within some products, you can rename them in other ways.)
- When any additional columns are listed, besides those of one table, the table name is required before the asterisk. A period is placed between the table name and the asterisk, so the command reads as follows: `select` **table_name**.*

`select distinct` **a list of columns**

- Get only the columns listed.
- Put them in the order they are listed.
- You can rename them.
- Eliminate duplicate rows from the result.

The first form, `select` *a list of columns*, gets only the columns that are listed. It can rename these columns, giving them a *column alias*. It also specifies the order in which the columns are to be listed.

The second form, `select *`, gets all the columns of a table. This does not list the columns individually, so it cannot give the columns an alias or specify an order for the columns. The columns are listed in the order in which they appear in the table.

The third form, `select distinct` *a list of columns*, is similar to the first form, but it includes the word `distinct`. This eliminates all the duplicate rows from the result table. Two rows are duplicates if they have identical values in every column of the result table. If even one column is different, they do not match and they are not duplicates.

The only required clauses are the `select` clause and the `from` clause. You can write a `select` statement with only these two clauses. The following query lists all the columns and all the rows of the `l_employees` table.

```
select *
from l_employees;
```

2-4   Use a `select` clause to get a list of some of the columns

This section shows an example of a `select` clause that is used to get a list of columns. Only the columns listed in the `select` clause appear in the result table. The other columns of the beginning table are omitted.

The order of the columns within the `select` clause determines their order within the result table. This can be different from their order within the beginning table.

It is possible for the same column to be listed two or more times. This is sometimes useful when different formatting or functions are applied to the column. Chapter 7 discusses formatting. Functions are covered in chapters 9 and 10.

A literal value can be included in the `select` clause. That value will then appear in every row of the result table. If the literal value is text, it must be enclosed in single quotes. If it is a number, no quotes are used. In the example for this section, the text literal "excellent worker" is enclosed in single quotes, but there are no quotes around the numeric literal 10.

A column can be renamed by giving it a column alias. This changes the heading that appears in the result table. It does not have any permanent effect on the table or the database. To assign a column alias, use this syntax:

`column_name AS alias_name`

The word "as" is optional in Oracle and required in Access. I recommend that you use it because it makes the `select` statement easier to read and understand. Usually you should avoid using spaces within the name of the column alias. A common convention is to replace the spaces with underscore characters. In the example for this section, four columns are given new names.

In the result table you might sometimes see the column heading truncated. This is done to save space and make the result table fit better on the page. Instead of showing the full column name or column alias, only the beginning part is shown. This is done in both Access and the older interface of Oracle that uses the SQL command line. The newer interface of Oracle, the Database Home Page environment, does not have this problem.

In Access, if you want to see the full column heading, use the mouse to make the column wider. This can be done after SQL has been run.

Task

Get the following three columns from the `1_employees` table:

```
employee_id
phone_number
last_name
```

Display them in that order. Change the name of the `employee_id` column to `employee_number` and the name of the `phone_number` column to `extension`. Also create two new columns: `evaluation` and `rating`. Give every employee an evaluation of "excellent worker" and a rating of 10.

Oracle & Access SQL

```
select employee_id as employee_number, ❶
       phone_number as extension,
       last_name,
       'EXCELLENT WORKER' as evaluation, ❷
       10 as rating ❸
from 1_employees;
```

Beginning table (1_employees table)

```
EMPLOYEE                        DEPT                  CREDIT PHONE   MANAGER
      ID FIRST_NAME LAST_NAME  CODE HIRE_DATE         LIMIT  NUMBER      ID
-------- ---------- ---------  ---- -----------       ------ ------  -------
     201 SUSAN      BROWN      EXE  01-JUN-1998       $30.00 3484    (null)
     202 JIM        KERN       SAL  16-AUG-1999       $25.00 8722       201
     203 MARTHA     WOODS      SHP  02-FEB-2009       $25.00 7591       201
     204 ELLEN      OWENS      SAL  01-JUL-2008       $15.00 6830       202
     205 HENRY      PERKINS    SAL  01-MAR-2006       $25.00 5286       202
     206 CAROL      ROSE       ACT  (null)            (null) (null)  (null)
     207 DAN        SMITH      SHP  01-DEC-2008       $25.00 2259       203
     208 FRED       CAMPBELL   SHP  01-APR-2008       $25.00 1752       203
     209 PAULA      JACOBS     MKT  17-MAR-1999       $15.00 3357       201
     210 NANCY      HOFFMAN    SAL  16-FEB-2007       $25.00 2974       203
```

Result table

```
EMPLOYEE_NUMBER EXTENSION   LAST_NAME   EVALUATION          RATING
--------------- ----------  ----------  -----------------   ---------
            201 3484        BROWN       EXCELLENT WORKER         10
            202 8722        KERN        EXCELLENT WORKER         10
            203 7591        WOODS       EXCELLENT WORKER         10
            204 6830        OWENS       EXCELLENT WORKER         10
            205 5286        PERKINS     EXCELLENT WORKER         10
            206 (null)      ROSE        EXCELLENT WORKER         10
            207 2259        SMITH       EXCELLENT WORKER         10
            208 1752        CAMPBELL    EXCELLENT WORKER         10
            209 3357        JACOBS      EXCELLENT WORKER         10
            210 2974        HOFFMAN     EXCELLENT WORKER         10
```

Notes

❶ The `employee_id` column is being renamed `employee_number`. This new name, the column alias, is the column heading in the result table. An underscore character is used to join the words "employee" and "number." This makes the column alias a single word, as it contains no spaces. My reason for doing this is that Oracle and Access SQL are the same as long as the column alias does not contain spaces.

Both Oracle and Access allow spaces in the column alias. However, the code is written with a slight difference. In Oracle, **_double quotes_** must be used around a column alias that contains a space, whereas in Access, **_square brackets_** are used:

Oracle: **select employee_id as "employee number"**
Access: **select employee_id as [employee number]**

❷ The text 'EXCELLENT WORKER' is added to every row of the result table in a column called evaluation. This is an example of placing a literal value in a select statement. Here, the literal value is text, so it is enclosed in single quotes.

I used uppercase letters within the single quotes because I wanted to have uppercase letters in the result table. If I had used lowercase letters in the select statement, the result table would show this text in lowercase letters.

❸ Here the literal value is a number, so it is not enclosed in quotes.

Check your understanding

List the description and price of all the foods. Change the name of the description column to food_item and the name of the price column to cost.

2-5   Use a select clause to get a list of all of the columns

Here is an example of a select clause that gets all the columns of a table and lists them in the same order in which they occur within the beginning table. In this example, there is no where clause, so the result table contains all the columns and all the rows of the beginning table. This means that the beginning table and the result table are identical.

This is the simplest select statement that you can write. The select clause and the from clause are required in any select statement. All other clauses are optional.

This method of showing the contents of a table gives you a good guess about the following:

- The number of columns in the table

- The number of rows in the table, unless there are too many rows to list conveniently

- The names of the columns

However this information is not always accurate. Sometimes a table has been set up so that certain columns or rows are hidden from you. Sometimes the column names shown here can be different from the column names used in the actual table.

Task

Get the entire `l_employees` table, all the columns and all the rows. Display all the columns in the same order as they are defined in the table.

Oracle & Access SQL

```
select *
from l_employees;
```

Beginning table (1_employees table)

EMPLOYEE ID	FIRST_NAME	LAST_NAME	DEPT CODE	HIRE_DATE	CREDIT LIMIT	PHONE NUMBER	MANAGER ID
201	SUSAN	BROWN	EXE	01-JUN-1998	$30.00	3484	(null)
202	JIM	KERN	SAL	16-AUG-1999	$25.00	8722	201
203	MARTHA	WOODS	SHP	02-FEB-2009	$25.00	7591	201
204	ELLEN	OWENS	SAL	01-JUL-2008	$15.00	6830	202
205	HENRY	PERKINS	SAL	01-MAR-2006	$25.00	5286	202
206	CAROL	ROSE	ACT	(null)	(null)	(null)	(null)
207	DAN	SMITH	SHP	01-DEC-2008	$25.00	2259	203
208	FRED	CAMPBELL	SHP	01-APR-2008	$25.00	1752	203
209	PAULA	JACOBS	MKT	17-MAR-1999	$15.00	3357	201
210	NANCY	HOFFMAN	SAL	16-FEB-2007	$25.00	2974	203

Result table ❶

EMPLOYEE ID	FIRST_NAME	LAST_NAME	DEPT CODE	HIRE_DATE	CREDIT LIMIT	PHONE NUMBER	MANAGER ID
201	SUSAN	BROWN	EXE	01-JUN-1998	$30.00	3484	(null)
202	JIM	KERN	SAL	16-AUG-1999	$25.00	8722	201
203	MARTHA	WOODS	SHP	02-FEB-2009	$25.00	7591	201
204	ELLEN	OWENS	SAL	01-JUL-2008	$15.00	6830	202
205	HENRY	PERKINS	SAL	01-MAR-2006	$25.00	5286	202
206	CAROL	ROSE	ACT	(null)	(null)	(null)	(null)
207	DAN	SMITH	SHP	01-DEC-2008	$25.00	2259	203
208	FRED	CAMPBELL	SHP	01-APR-2008	$25.00	1752	203
209	PAULA	JACOBS	MKT	17-MAR-1999	$15.00	3357	201
210	NANCY	HOFFMAN	SAL	16-FEB-2007	$25.00	2974	203

Notes

❶ The result table is identical to the beginning table, except possibly for the order of the rows. In the listings here, the rows are in exactly the same order. I did this to make the example easy to understand. In theory, however, the rows of both tables are unordered sets, so the rows in the result table could appear in a different order.

Oracle & Access SQL: Variation 1 — Adding a where clause

If a `where` clause is added to the `select` statement, the result table can contain only some of the rows of the beginning table. For example:

```
select *
from l_employees
where manager_id is null;
```

This lists the two rows for employees 201 and 206.

Result table: Variation 1

EMPLOYEE ID	FIRST_NAME	LAST_NAME	DEPT CODE	HIRE_DATE	CREDIT LIMIT	PHONE NUMBER	MANAGER ID
201	SUSAN	BROWN	EXE	01-JUN-1998	$30.00	3484	(null)
206	CAROL	ROSE	ACT	(null)	(null)	(null)	(null)

Oracle & Access SQL: Variation 2 — Adding an order by clause

If an `order by` clause is added to the `select` statement, the rows of the result table may be sorted in a different order. For example, you could sort them by `hire_date`. When there is no `order by` clause, the computer is allowed to list the rows of the result table in any order. To control the order and ensure that the rows are sorted by the value in the `employee_id` column, it is necessary to write:

```
select *
from l_employees
order by last_name;
```

Result table: Variation 2

EMPLOYEE ID	FIRST_NAME	LAST_NAME	DEPT CODE	HIRE_DATE	CREDIT LIMIT	PHONE NUMBER	MANAGER ID
201	SUSAN	BROWN	EXE	01-JUN-1998	$30.00	3484	(null)
208	FRED	CAMPBELL	SHP	01-APR-2008	$25.00	1752	203
210	NANCY	HOFFMAN	SAL	16-FEB-2007	$25.00	2974	203
209	PAULA	JACOBS	MKT	17-MAR-1999	$15.00	3357	201
202	JIM	KERN	SAL	16-AUG-1999	$25.00	8722	201
204	ELLEN	OWENS	SAL	01-JUL-2008	$15.00	6830	202
205	HENRY	PERKINS	SAL	01-MAR-2006	$25.00	5286	202
206	CAROL	ROSE	ACT	(null)	(null)	(null)	(null)
207	DAN	SMITH	SHP	01-DEC-2008	$25.00	2259	203
203	MARTHA	WOODS	SHP	02-FEB-2009	$25.00	7591	201

Displaying the data in any table

If you know the name of any table, you can display all the data in it with the `select` statement:

```
select *
from table_name;
```

You replace `table_name` with the name of your table.

Check your understanding

List all the columns and all the rows of the foods table. How many columns are in this table? How many rows? What are the names of the columns?

2-6   Use a `select` clause to get the distinct values in one column

This section shows an example of using `select distinct` on one column to find all of its values and list each of them only once. This is particularly useful when you are working with a column that contains codes, such as the `dept_code` column. In this example, we apply `select distinct` to the `manager_id` column. In the result table, manager ID 201 is displayed only once, even though there are three rows of the beginning table with this value. The duplicate values are removed.

Notice that the null value does appear in the result table. Here we see that `select distinct` treats nulls as it treats any other data in the table. If there were several nulls in the `manager_id` column of the beginning table, the result table would still contain only a single null.

In Access, to use `select distinct` you need to write the SQL yourself. The tools to help you write a query in Access will not write a `select distinct` query for you.

Task

Get a list of all the different values in the `manager_id` column of the `1_employees` table.

Oracle & Access SQL

```
select distinct manager_id
from 1_employees;
```

Beginning table (1_employees table)

EMPLOYEE ID	FIRST_NAME	LAST_NAME	DEPT CODE	HIRE_DATE	CREDIT LIMIT	PHONE NUMBER	MANAGER ID
201	SUSAN	BROWN	EXE	01-JUN-1998	$30.00	3484	(null)
202	JIM	KERN	SAL	16-AUG-1999	$25.00	8722	201
203	MARTHA	WOODS	SHP	02-FEB-2009	$25.00	7591	201
204	ELLEN	OWENS	SAL	01-JUL-2008	$15.00	6830	202
205	HENRY	PERKINS	SAL	01-MAR-2006	$25.00	5286	202
206	CAROL	ROSE	ACT	(null)	(null)	(null)	(null)
207	DAN	SMITH	SHP	01-DEC-2008	$25.00	2259	203
208	FRED	CAMPBELL	SHP	01-APR-2008	$25.00	1752	203
209	PAULA	JACOBS	MKT	17-MAR-1999	$15.00	3357	201
210	NANCY	HOFFMAN	SAL	16-FEB-2007	$25.00	2974	203

Result table

MANAGER ID
201
202
203
(null)

Where nulls are placed in the sort order — A difference between Oracle and Access

In Oracle, nulls are placed at the bottom of the sort order. In Access they are placed at the top. This is not a big difference. It causes a slight difference in the appearance of the result, although the rows in the result are the same in both cases.

Everyone agrees on the sort order for the numbers 0 to 9 and for the letters A to Z. However, there is no such agreement about how nulls fit into the sort order. In the absence of a common agreement, the developers of Oracle decided to resolve the issue one way and the developers of Access decided to resolve it another way.

The result table shown next shows the null at the bottom. This is the Oracle method. People using Access will find the null at the top. In Access, the null appears as a blank.

In this example, one could argue that because the select statement contains no order by clause, the rows of the result table are allowed to be in any order. In theory, the null can appear in any position within the result table. In practice, when select distinct is used, a sort is performed as part of the process of eliminating duplicates. Therefore, the rows of the result table are presented in sorted order, even though no order by clause is used. In this case, the sort is performed on the manager_id column.

Oracle & Access SQL:
Variation 1 — Adding a where clause to select distinct

Select distinct may be used with a where clause to limit the number of rows in the result table. The where clause is processed first, which removes some rows from the beginning table. Then the select distinct clause is processed. Here is an example:

```
select distinct manager_id
from l_employees
where employee_id in (201, 208, 210);
```

Result table: Variation 1

```
MANAGER
     ID
-------
    203
(null)
```

Oracle & Access SQL:
Variation 2 — Adding an `order by` clause to `select distinct`

`Select distinct` may be used with an `order by` clause to sort the rows of the result table in either an ascending or a descending order.

```
select distinct manager_id
from l_employees
order by manager_id desc;
```

Result table: Variation 2

```
MANAGER
     ID
-------
(null)
    203
    202
    201
```

Oracle & Access SQL:
Variation 3 — What happens if you eliminate the word `distinct`?

If the word `distinct` is removed from the `select` statement, the result table will be the same as the `manager_id` column of the beginning table. The value 201 will appear three times. No duplicate values will be removed, nor will any sort occur. The rows might appear in the same order as in the beginning table, or they could appear in some completely different order. Here is an example:

```
select manager_id
from l_employees;
```

Result table: Variation 3

```
MANAGER
     ID
-------
(null)
    201
    201
    202
    202
(null)
    203
    203
    201
    203
```

Check your understanding

List all the different `supplier_id` values from the `1_foods` table.

2-7   Use a `select` clause to get the distinct values in two columns

This section shows an example of using `select distinct` with two columns. The same technique can be used when there are three or more columns. We want to get a list of the distinct values when all these columns are combined together as a single unit.

The SQL code is similar to the code in the previous section. Here a second column, the `credit_limit` column, is added to the `select distinct` clause. The result table shows all the different combinations of values in the two columns, `manager_id` and `credit_limit`.

When `select distinct` is used with several columns, the result table shows a single instance of each valid combination of the columns. In other words, no two rows of the result table are the same. Any two rows must differ in the values of one or more columns.

You should pay attention to the way that nulls are handled by `select distinct`. SQL makes a point in saying in most circumstances that a null is an unknown value. Therefore we are not allowed to say that that one null is equal to another null. We have to assume that they might have different values.

However, there are some exceptions to this rule and `select distinct` is one of them. Here all the nulls within a single column are treated as if they have the same value, the value of "missing data."

When data is being summarized, as it is here, it is common for nulls to be handled this way.

Task

Get a list of all the different values in the `manager_id` and `credit_limit` columns of the `1_employees` table.

Oracle & Access SQL

```
select distinct manager_id,
                credit_limit
from l_employees;
```

Beginning table (l_employees table)

EMPLOYEE ID	FIRST_NAME	LAST_NAME	DEPT CODE	HIRE_DATE	CREDIT LIMIT	PHONE NUMBER	MANAGER ID
201	SUSAN	BROWN	EXE	01-JUN-1998	$30.00	3484	(null)
202	JIM	KERN	SAL	16-AUG-1999	$25.00	8722	201
203	MARTHA	WOODS	SHP	02-FEB-2009	$25.00	7591	201
204	ELLEN	OWENS	SAL	01-JUL-2008	$15.00	6830	202
205	HENRY	PERKINS	SAL	01-MAR-2006	$25.00	5286	202
206	CAROL	ROSE	ACT	(null)	(null)	(null)	(null)
207	DAN	SMITH	SHP	01-DEC-2008	$25.00	2259	203
208	FRED	CAMPBELL	SHP	01-APR-2008	$25.00	1752	203
209	PAULA	JACOBS	MKT	17-MAR-1999	$15.00	3357	201
210	NANCY	HOFFMAN	SAL	16-FEB-2007	$25.00	2974	203

Result table

MANAGER ID	CREDIT LIMIT
201	$15.00
201	$25.00
202	$15.00
202	$25.00
203	$25.00
(null)	$30.00
(null)	(null)

What it means to eliminate duplicate rows from the result

The result table here contains two rows with a manager ID of 201. In section 2-6, there was only one such row. What is the difference?

There is another column in the result, the credit_limit column. The two rows in which manager ID equals 201 have different values in the credit_limit column, $15.00 and $25.00. Two **rows** of the result are distinct as long as there is at least one column in which they differ. In section 2-6, the credit limit was not part of the result, so the difference between these rows is not in the result. That is why these two occurrences of 201 are condensed into a single row.

The beginning table contains three rows with a manager ID of 201. Two rows have a $25.00 credit limit and one has a $15.00 credit limit. The result table shows only one row for each of these combinations.

In the result table, each **_row_** is distinct. You can think of this as a three-step process. First, all the columns in each row of the result table are concatenated together into a single unit of data, then these units are sorted. Last, all the duplicate units are removed.

Check your understanding

List all the different values in columns A and B of the sec0207 table.

The Where Clause

The where clause is used to choose which rows of data you want to retrieve. Because a table can have thousands of rows, this clause must be flexible enough to specify many different conditions. This makes it more complex than the other clauses we examine in this chapter.

2-8   Overview of the where clause

The where clause specifies a condition that is true for all the rows you want in the result table. For all other rows the condition is false or unknown. The following table summarizes the conditions you can use. All of these conditions can be used with any of the main types of data — text, numbers, and dates.

Each condition has both a positive form and a negative form. The negative form is always the exact opposite of the positive form. For example, the is not null condition is true for every row for which the is null condition is false. The not between condition is true for every row where the between condition is false.

Comparison conditions that can be used in the where clause.

Condition	Meaning	Examples
EQUAL — and other comparison tests		

=	equal	with numbers: `credit_limit = 25.00`
		with text: `first_name = 'SUE'`
		with dates:
		    Oracle: `hire_date = '01-JUN-2010'`
		    Access: `hire_date = #01-JUN-2010#`

<	less than	`credit_limit < 25.00`
<=	less than or equal	`first_name <= 'M'`
>	greater than	Oracle: `hire_date > '01-JUN-2010'` Access: `hire_date > #01-JUN-2010#`
>=	greater than or equal	`credit_limit >= 30.00`
<> and others	not equal	`first_name <> 'ALICE'`
SET INCLUSION TEST — a list of specific values		
`in`	in a set	`credit_limit in (15.00, 25.00)`
`not in`	not in a set	`dept_code not in ('EXE', 'MKT', 'ACT')`
RANGE TEST — anywhere between two values		
`between`	in a range	`credit_limit between 21.00 and 27.00`
`not between`	not within a range	`dept_code not between 'ACT' and 'SAL'`
PATTERN MATCHING TEST — using wildcard characters		
`like`	matches a pattern	`phone_number like '%48%'`
`not like`	does not match a pattern	`dept_code not like '%A%'`
NULL TEST — find nulls		
`is null`	is a null value	`manager_id is null`
`is not null`	is not a null value	`manager_id is not null`
BOOLEAN CONNECTORS — joining simple conditions together		
`and`	both of the conditions are true	`(credit_limit = 25.00)` `and (first_name = 'SUE')`
`or`	one of the conditions is true	`(credit_limit = 25.00)` `or (first_name = 'SUE')`
`not`	the condition is false	`not (credit_limit = 25.00)`

2-9   Using an Equal condition in the `where` clause

This section shows a query in which the `where` clause uses an Equal (=) condition. I will show you four examples of this.

In the first example, the Equal condition is used with a number. No quotes are used around the number. All the rows from the beginning table that have `manager_id` values equal to 203 are shown in the result table.

Note that the employees who have a null value in the `manager_id` column are not shown. This affects employees 201 and 206. The null value means that the value is missing in the database. The value could be equal to 203, but we do not know this, so the row for the employee is not shown in the result table.

In the second example, the Equal condition is used with text. The text must be enclosed in single quotes.

Task for example 1

For all employees who report to employee 203, Martha Woods, list the following:

```
employee_id
first_name
last_name
manager_id
hire_date
```

Oracle & Access SQL

```
select  employee_id, ❶
        first_name,
        last_name,
        manager_id,
        hire_date
from 1_employees
where manager_id = 203; ❷
```

Beginning table (1_employees table)

EMPLOYEE ID	FIRST_NAME	LAST_NAME	DEPT CODE	HIRE_DATE	CREDIT LIMIT	PHONE NUMBER	MANAGER ID
201	SUSAN	BROWN	EXE	01-JUN-1998	$30.00	3484	(null)
202	JIM	KERN	SAL	16-AUG-1999	$25.00	8722	201
203	MARTHA	WOODS	SHP	02-FEB-2009	$25.00	7591	201
204	ELLEN	OWENS	SAL	01-JUL-2008	$15.00	6830	202
205	HENRY	PERKINS	SAL	01-MAR-2006	$25.00	5286	202
206	CAROL	ROSE	ACT	(null)	(null)	(null)	(null)
207	DAN	SMITH	SHP	01-DEC-2008	$25.00	2259	203
208	FRED	CAMPBELL	SHP	01-APR-2008	$25.00	1752	203
209	PAULA	JACOBS	MKT	17-MAR-1999	$15.00	3357	201
210	NANCY	HOFFMAN	SAL	16-FEB-2007	$25.00	2974	203

Result table: Example 1

EMPLOYEE ID	FIRST_NAME	LAST_NAME	MANAGER ID	HIRE_DATE
207	DAN	SMITH	203	01-DEC-2008
208	FRED	CAMPBELL	203	01-APR-2008
210	NANCY	HOFFMAN	203	16-FEB-2007

Notes

❶ The select clause lists five columns, and the result table shows these five columns in the order in which they are listed.

❷ The where clause contains only one condition:

```
manager_id = 203
```

Three rows of the beginning table satisfy this condition, and the result table shows all these rows.

Task for example 2

For all the employees whose first name is Henry, list the same columns as before.

Oracle & Access SQL

```
select employee_id,
       first_name,
       last_name,
       manager_id,
       hire_date
from l_employees
where first_name = 'HENRY'; ❸
```

Result table: Example 2

```
EMPLOYEE                        MANAGER
      ID FIRST_NAME LAST_NAME       ID HIRE_DATE
-------- ---------- ---------- ------- -----------
     205 HENRY      PERKINS        202 01-MAR-2006
```

Notes

❸ A text value must be enclosed in single quotes. It must be in uppercase to match the data in the table.

Task for example 3

For all the employees who were hired on July 1, 2008, list the same columns as before.

Oracle SQL

```
select employee_id,
       first_name,
       last_name,
       manager_id,
       hire_date
from l_employees
where hire_date = '01-JUL-2008'; ❹
```

Access SQL

```
select employee_id,
       first_name,
       last_name,
       manager_id,
       hire_date
from 1_employees
where hire_date = #01-JUL-2008#;  ❺
```

Result table: Example 3

```
EMPLOYEE                         MANAGER
      ID FIRST_NAME LAST_NAME         ID HIRE_DATE
-------- ---------- ---------- ------- ------------
     204 ELLEN      OWENS          202 01-JUL-2008
```

Notes

❹ In Oracle, date values must be enclosed in single quotes.

❺ In Access, date values must be enclosed in pound signs.

Task for example 4

For all the employees whose first name is Paula, list the same columns as before. Change the name of the first_name column to given_name.

Oracle & Access SQL

```
select employee_id,
       first_name as given_name,
       last_name,
       manager_id,
       hire_date
from 1_employees
where first_name = 'PAULA';  ❻
```

Result table: Example 4

```
EMPLOYEE                         MANAGER
      ID GIVEN_NAME LAST_NAME         ID HIRE_DATE
-------- ---------- ---------- ------- ------------
     209 PAULA      JACOBS         201 17-MAR-1999
```

Notes

❻ In the `where` clause you must use the original name of the column, `first_name`, even though the `first_name` column has been renamed to `given_name` in the `select` clause.

Check your understanding

List the first name and last name of the employees with the first name of Nancy.

2-10 Using a Less Than condition in the `where` clause

This section shows an example of a query that uses a Less Than (<) condition in the `where` clause. If there were rows with a null value in the `credit_limit` column, they would not be included in the result table.

In place of the < sign, in this example you could write any of these:

<=	(less than or equal to)
>	(greater than)
>=	(greater than or equal to)

Task for example 1

List all employees who have a credit limit less than $17.50. Show the columns:

```
employee_id
first_name
last_name
credit_limit
```

Oracle & Access SQL

```
select employee_id,
       first_name,
       last_name,
       credit_limit
from l_employees
where credit_limit < 17.50; ❶
```

Beginning table (1_employees table)

EMPLOYEE ID	FIRST_NAME	LAST_NAME	DEPT CODE	HIRE_DATE	CREDIT LIMIT	PHONE NUMBER	MANAGER ID
201	SUSAN	BROWN	EXE	01-JUN-1998	$30.00	3484	(null)
202	JIM	KERN	SAL	16-AUG-1999	$25.00	8722	201
203	MARTHA	WOODS	SHP	02-FEB-2009	$25.00	7591	201
204	ELLEN	OWENS	SAL	01-JUL-2008	$15.00	6830	202
205	HENRY	PERKINS	SAL	01-MAR-2006	$25.00	5286	202
206	CAROL	ROSE	ACT	(null)	(null)	(null)	(null)
207	DAN	SMITH	SHP	01-DEC-2008	$25.00	2259	203
208	FRED	CAMPBELL	SHP	01-APR-2008	$25.00	1752	203
209	PAULA	JACOBS	MKT	17-MAR-1999	$15.00	3357	201
210	NANCY	HOFFMAN	SAL	16-FEB-2007	$25.00	2974	203

Result table: Example 1

EMPLOYEE ID	FIRST_NAME	LAST_NAME	CREDIT LIMIT
204	ELLEN	OWENS	$15.00
209	PAULA	JACOBS	$15.00

Notes

❶ The where clause contains only one condition:

```
where credit_limit < 17.50
```

This condition uses the less than (<) sign. The numeric value in the SQL code, 17.50, cannot contain a dollar sign or a comma. This can be confusing because often dollar signs and commas are displayed when you see the data in a table. The beginning table has two rows that satisfy this condition. The result table shows those two rows.

Task for example 2

Show another way to write this query, using the greater than or equal to (>=) sign and negating the condition with a Boolean not.

Oracle & Access SQL

```
select employee_id,
       first_name,
       last_name,
       credit_limit
from l_employees
where not (credit_limit >= 17.50); ❷
```

Result table: Example 2 — Same as previous result table

Notes

❷ This is another way to write the Less Than condition.

Check your understanding

List the first name and last name of the employees with `employee_id` greater than or equal to 205.

2-11 Using a Not Equal condition in the `where` clause

This section shows an example of a query that uses a Not Equal condition in its `where` clause.

Most SQL products support several ways to write the Not Equal condition. Unfortunately, some of the ways that work in one product may not work in another product. I prefer the method shown here because it works in all products and it is easy for both people and computers to understand.

When possible, it is best to avoid using a Not Equal condition because it is much less efficient for the computer to process than conditions such as Equal (=) or `between`.

Task

List all employees who do not report to employee 203, Martha Woods.
Show the following columns:

```
employee_id
first_name
last_name
manager_id
```

Oracle & Access SQL

```
select  employee_id,
        first_name,
        last_name,
        manager_id
from l_employees
where not (manager_id = 203);  ❶
```

Beginning table (l_employees table)

EMPLOYEE ID	FIRST_NAME	LAST_NAME	DEPT CODE	HIRE_DATE	CREDIT LIMIT	PHONE NUMBER	MANAGER ID
201	SUSAN	BROWN	EXE	01-JUN-1998	$30.00	3484	(null)
202	JIM	KERN	SAL	16-AUG-1999	$25.00	8722	201
203	MARTHA	WOODS	SHP	02-FEB-2009	$25.00	7591	201
204	ELLEN	OWENS	SAL	01-JUL-2008	$15.00	6830	202
205	HENRY	PERKINS	SAL	01-MAR-2006	$25.00	5286	202
206	CAROL	ROSE	ACT	(null)	(null)	(null)	(null)
207	DAN	SMITH	SHP	01-DEC-2008	$25.00	2259	203
208	FRED	CAMPBELL	SHP	01-APR-2008	$25.00	1752	203
209	PAULA	JACOBS	MKT	17-MAR-1999	$15.00	3357	201
210	NANCY	HOFFMAN	SAL	16-FEB-2007	$25.00	2974	203

Result table

EMPLOYEE ID	FIRST_NAME	LAST_NAME	MANAGER ID
202	JIM	KERN	201
203	MARTHA	WOODS	201
204	ELLEN	OWENS	202
205	HENRY	PERKINS	202
209	PAULA	JACOBS	201

Notes

❶ The Boolean `not` reverses the meaning of the condition that follows it. It only applies to that one condition. Here it changes the Equal condition into the Not Equal condition.

Variations

Some other ways to write the Not Equal condition are as follows:

```
where manager_id <> 203
```

```
where not manager_id = 203
```

```
where manager_id != 203
```

```
where manager_id ^= 203
```

You might find these variations in code you inherit, or you might prefer to use some of them yourself.

SQL uses three-valued logic

The result table in this section does not show the rows that have a null value in the `manager_id` column. To show all the rows from the beginning table, we need to consider three different conditions:

```
where manager_id = 203
```

```
where not (manager_id = 203)
```

```
where manager_id is null
```

This is an example of what we mean when we say that SQL uses three-valued logic. Chapter 3 discusses this in more detail.

Check your understanding

List the first name and last name of the employees with employee id not equal to 205. Write this in three different ways that all work in the version of SQL you are currently using,

2-12 Using the `in` condition in the `where` clause

This section shows an example of a query that uses an `in` condition in its `where` clause. The `in` condition is used to show membership in a set. It is used when there is a list of discrete values that satisfy the condition. The set of all these valid values is placed in parentheses as a comma-delimited list.

All the values must have the same datatype — numbers, text, or dates. All the values can be numbers, or they can all be text, or they can all be dates. It does not make sense to mix these categories. More specifically, the values must have the same datatype as the column being tested.

It would not make sense to include null in the list of valid values because the `in` condition is never satisfied by a null in the data.

Sometimes in production code an `in` condition checks for 10 to 50 different values. In this situation it is much more efficient to write the code using an `in` condition rather than many Equal conditions. The examples in this book do not show this efficiency because they check for only two or three values.

Task for example 1

List all employees who report to employees 202 or 203, Jim Kern or Martha Woods. Show the following columns:

```
employee_id
first_name
last_name
manager_id
```

Oracle & Access SQL

```
select employee_id,
       first_name,
       last_name,
       manager_id
from l_employees
where manager_id in (202, 203);  ❶
```

Beginning table (1_employees table)

EMPLOYEE ID	FIRST_NAME	LAST_NAME	DEPT CODE	HIRE_DATE	CREDIT LIMIT	PHONE NUMBER	MANAGER ID
201	SUSAN	BROWN	EXE	01-JUN-1998	$30.00	3484	(null)
202	JIM	KERN	SAL	16-AUG-1999	$25.00	8722	201
203	MARTHA	WOODS	SHP	02-FEB-2009	$25.00	7591	201
204	ELLEN	OWENS	SAL	01-JUL-2008	$15.00	6830	202
205	HENRY	PERKINS	SAL	01-MAR-2006	$25.00	5286	202
206	CAROL	ROSE	ACT	(null)	(null)	(null)	(null)
207	DAN	SMITH	SHP	01-DEC-2008	$25.00	2259	203
208	FRED	CAMPBELL	SHP	01-APR-2008	$25.00	1752	203
209	PAULA	JACOBS	MKT	17-MAR-1999	$15.00	3357	201
210	NANCY	HOFFMAN	SAL	16-FEB-2007	$25.00	2974	203

Result table: Example 1

EMPLOYEE ID	FIRST_NAME	LAST_NAME	MANAGER ID
204	ELLEN	OWENS	202
205	HENRY	PERKINS	202
207	DAN	SMITH	203
208	FRED	CAMPBELL	203
210	NANCY	HOFFMAN	203

Notes

❶ This condition means that the `manager_id` column is equal to either 202 or 203.

Task for example 2

Show another way to write the same query. Use two Equal conditions combined together with a Boolean `or`.

Oracle & Access SQL variation: Using Equal conditions

```
select employee_id,
       first_name,
       last_name,
       manager_id
from 1_employees
where manager_id = 202
      or manager_id = 203; ❷
```

Notes

❷ You must repeat the column name, `manager_id`, within each Equal condition.

Result table: Example 2 — Same as previous result table

Check your understanding

List the first name, last name, and department code of the employees that have department codes `sal`, `shp`, and `act`. Do this using an `in` condition.

2-13 Using the `between` condition in the `where` clause

This section shows an example of a query that uses the `between` condition in its `where` clause. Note that the endpoints, August 16, 1999, and July 1, 2003, are both included in the result table. Some people prefer not to use the `between` condition with dates because a date can also contain a time, which can create some confusion.

The `between` condition can be applied to numbers, text, and dates. In this example, it is applied to dates. In Oracle, dates must be enclosed in single quotes (`' '`). In Access, they must be enclosed in pound signs (`##`). That is the only difference between the Oracle SQL and the Access SQL in this example.

Task for example 1

List all employees hired between August 16, 1999, and July 1, 2008. Show the following columns:

```
employee_id
first_name
last_name
hire_date
```

Oracle SQL

```
select employee_id,
       first_name,
       last_name,
       hire_date
from l_employees
where hire_date between '16-AUG-1999'
                    and '01-JUL-2008';
```

Access SQL

```
select employee_id,
       first_name,
       last_name,
       hire_date
from l_employees
where hire_date between #16-AUG-1999#
                   and #01-JUL-2008#;
```

Beginning table (1_employees table)

EMPLOYEE ID	FIRST_NAME	LAST_NAME	DEPT CODE	HIRE_DATE	CREDIT LIMIT	PHONE NUMBER	MANAGER ID
201	SUSAN	BROWN	EXE	01-JUN-1998	$30.00	3484	(null)
202	JIM	KERN	SAL	16-AUG-1999	$25.00	8722	201
203	MARTHA	WOODS	SHP	02-FEB-2009	$25.00	7591	201
204	ELLEN	OWENS	SAL	01-JUL-2008	$15.00	6830	202
205	HENRY	PERKINS	SAL	01-MAR-2006	$25.00	5286	202
206	CAROL	ROSE	ACT	(null)	(null)	(null)	(null)
207	DAN	SMITH	SHP	01-DEC-2008	$25.00	2259	203
208	FRED	CAMPBELL	SHP	01-APR-2008	$25.00	1752	203
209	PAULA	JACOBS	MKT	17-MAR-1999	$15.00	3357	201
210	NANCY	HOFFMAN	SAL	16-FEB-2007	$25.00	2974	203

Result table: Example 1

EMPLOYEE ID	FIRST_NAME	LAST_NAME	HIRE_DATE
202	JIM	KERN	16-AUG-1999
204	ELLEN	OWENS	01-JUL-2008
205	HENRY	PERKINS	01-MAR-2006
208	FRED	CAMPBELL	01-APR-2008
210	NANCY	HOFFMAN	16-FEB-2007

Task for example 2

Write the same query as in the preceding task with an `in` condition. This requires you to write about 3,300 dates and demonstrates the usefulness of the `between` condition. Even when the code can be written in another way, the code is more compact and less prone to errors when the `between` condition is used.

Oracle SQL variation: Using an `in` condition

```
select employee_id,
       first_name,
       last_name,
       hire_date
from l_employees
where hire_date in ('16-aug-1999',
                    '17-aug-1999',
                    '18-aug-1999',
```
(about 3,300 more dates)
```
                    '29-jun-2008',
                    '30-jun-2008',
                    '01-JUL-2008');
```

Access SQL variation: Using an `in` condition

```
select employee_id,
       first_name,
       last_name,
       hire_date
from l_employees
where hire_date in (#16-aug-1999#,
                    #17-aug-1999#,
                    #18-aug-1999#,
```
(about 3,300 more dates)
```
                    #29-jun-2008#,
                    #30-jun-2008#,
                    #01-JUL-2008#);
```

Result table: Example 2 — Same as previous result table

Notes on the dates in this variation

Actually, these two methods of writing the code are not quite equivalent. A date in SQL always includes a time, although often the time is not shown when the data is displayed. With the SQL code using the `between` condition, all the times of all the dates are included. But with the code using the `in` condition, the time must be midnight on the dates listed. `Between` always specifies a range and `in` always specifies a series of points.

Check your understanding

List the employee ID, first name, and last name of the employees that have an employee ID between 201 and 205.

2-14 Using the `like` condition in the `where` clause

This section shows an example of a query that uses the `like` condition in its `where` clause. The `like` condition is used for finding patterns in the data. Patterns are specified using wildcard characters, which are used only with the `like` condition. When the same characters are used with another condition, such as the `between` condition, they are no longer wildcards. A column of any of the major datatypes — text, number, or date — can be searched with a pattern. Case sensitivity is often an issue, but here I have turned it off. For details, see sections 3-9 to 3-13.

In both Oracle and Access SQL, the pattern specification should be enclosed in single quotes. Patterns are specified differently in Oracle than they are in Access. Access allows a greater variety of patterns than Oracle. The wildcard characters are different. These wildcard characters are shown in the following table.

Wildcard characters and their meanings.

Oracle	Access	Meaning
% (percent sign)	* (asterisk)	A string of characters of any length, or possibly no characters at all (a zero-length string).
_ (underscore)	? (question mark)	One character.
(not available)	# (pound sign)	One digit (numeric character).
(not available) ❶	[c-m] (square brackets with a dash)	Range of characters. (The characters must be in ascending order. [a-z] is correct; [z-a] is not.)
(not available) ❷	[!c-m]	Outside a range of characters.
\% or _ (backslash) ❸	[*] or [?] or [#] (square brackets)	In Access, putting a character in square brackets means to take it literally, rather than using it as a wildcard character.

The following table shows some examples of patterns.

Examples of wildcard patterns.

Pattern	Oracle	Access	Examples

Text string beginning with an n	`'N%'`	`'N*'`	`'NONE'`
			`'N123'`
			`'NO CREDIT'`
			`'N'`

Four characters ending with an e	`'_ _ _ E'`	`'???E'`	`'NONE'`
			`'123E'`
			`'1  3E'`

Starting with a letter between a and g, followed by two digits	(not available)	`'[A-G]##'`	`'A47'` `'B82'`

Notes

❶ Sometimes this code can be used: `'c' <= value and 'm' > value`

❷ Sometimes this code can be used: `'c' > value or 'm' <= value`

❸ In Oracle, you can set up the backslash to be an Escape character. Any character placed after it is treated as a literal value rather than given a special meaning. To activate the backslash as an Escape character, use the SQL*Plus command:

```
set escape \;
```

Task

List all employees who have the letter n in their last name. Show the following columns:

```
employee_id
first_name
last_name
```

Oracle SQL

```
select employee_id,
       first_name,
       last_name
from l_employees
where last_name like '%N%';
```

Access SQL

```
select employee_id,
       first_name,
       last_name
from l_employees
where last_name like '*N*';
```

Beginning table (l_employees table)

```
EMPLOYEE                        DEPT                    CREDIT  PHONE   MANAGER
      ID FIRST_NAME LAST_NAME  CODE HIRE_DATE           LIMIT   NUMBER       ID
-------- ---------- ---------- ---- ------------        ------- ------  -------
     201 SUSAN      BROWN      EXE  01-JUN-1998         $30.00  3484    (null)
     202 JIM        KERN       SAL  16-AUG-1999         $25.00  8722       201
     203 MARTHA     WOODS      SHP  02-FEB-2009         $25.00  7591       201
     204 ELLEN      OWENS      SAL  01-JUL-2008         $15.00  6830       202
     205 HENRY      PERKINS    SAL  01-MAR-2006         $25.00  5286       202
     206 CAROL      ROSE       ACT  (null)              (null)  (null)  (null)
     207 DAN        SMITH      SHP  01-DEC-2008         $25.00  2259       203
     208 FRED       CAMPBELL   SHP  01-APR-2008         $25.00  1752       203
     209 PAULA      JACOBS     MKT  17-MAR-1999         $15.00  3357       201
     210 NANCY      HOFFMAN    SAL  16-FEB-2007         $25.00  2974       203
```

Result table

```
EMPLOYEE
      ID FIRST_NAME LAST_NAME
-------- ---------- ----------
     201 SUSAN      BROWN
     202 JIM        KERN
     204 ELLEN      OWENS
     205 HENRY      PERKINS
     210 NANCY      HOFFMAN
```

Check your understanding

List the employee ID, first name, and last name of the employees that have an employee ID that contains a number 1.

2-15 Using the `is null` condition in the `where` clause

This section shows an example of a query that uses an `is null` condition in its `where` clause. A null means the data value is missing from the database. This can happen under several different conditions:

- When the data value is unknown

- When it would never make sense to put data in that field

- When someone knows the data value, but it has not yet been entered into the database

Note that you must write this condition "`is  null`," rather than "`= null`." This is to remind you that a null is missing data and it is not like any other value in the table, because it does not have a particular value.

Nulls receive special treatment in several situations within a database. Throughout this book I point out when they are treated differently from other data.

Task

List all employees who have a null in the `manager_id` column. Show the following columns:

```
employee_id
first_name
last_name
manager_id
```

Oracle & Access SQL

```
select employee_id,
       first_name,
       last_name,
       manager_id
from l_employees
where manager_id is null;
```

Beginning table (1_employees table)

EMPLOYEE ID	FIRST_NAME	LAST_NAME	DEPT CODE	HIRE_DATE	CREDIT LIMIT	PHONE NUMBER	MANAGER ID
201	SUSAN	BROWN	EXE	01-JUN-1998	$30.00	3484	(null)
202	JIM	KERN	SAL	16-AUG-1999	$25.00	8722	201
203	MARTHA	WOODS	SHP	02-FEB-2009	$25.00	7591	201
204	ELLEN	OWENS	SAL	01-JUL-2008	$15.00	6830	202
205	HENRY	PERKINS	SAL	01-MAR-2006	$25.00	5286	202
206	CAROL	ROSE	ACT	(null)	(null)	(null)	(null)
207	DAN	SMITH	SHP	01-DEC-2008	$25.00	2259	203
208	FRED	CAMPBELL	SHP	01-APR-2008	$25.00	1752	203
209	PAULA	JACOBS	MKT	17-MAR-1999	$15.00	3357	201
210	NANCY	HOFFMAN	SAL	16-FEB-2007	$25.00	2974	203

Result table

EMPLOYEE ID	FIRST_NAME	LAST_NAME	MANAGER ID
201	SUSAN	BROWN	(null)
206	CAROL	ROSE	(null)

Why databases use nulls

Before nulls were invented, computer systems often used spaces or special values, such as 99, to designate that data was missing. This caused two problems.

One problem was a lack of uniformity. Each computer system used different values to designate missing data. Often a single application used three of these special values: one for numbers, one for text, and one for date fields.

The special values for numbers were often all 9s, but one application might use 999, whereas another used 999999. Sometimes the various fields within a single application would use different numbers of digits.

The special values for text were often spaces. However, some applications used a single space. Others would fill the field with spaces. The computer would not always consider these to be equal. Some applications even used a zero-length string, which just confused things even more.

For date fields, January 1, 1900 often designated missing data, but some applications used other dates.

The second problem was that these special data values were sometimes processed as if they were actual data. This could lead to errors that were difficult to detect, particularly if some calculation was done that changed the values of these fields.

To solve these problems, nulls were created to designate missing data. A rigid distinction is made between nulls and other types of data. Nulls do not have datatypes, meaning there is no distinction between a null in a numeric column and one in a text or date column.

Check your understanding

List all the columns of the employee table for rows that contain a null in the `manager_ID` column.

The Order By Clause

The `order by` clause determines how the rows of the result table are sorted when they are printed or displayed on the screen. If you leave out the `order by` clause, you are saying that you do not care about this order and you are giving the computer permission to display the rows of the result in any order.

2-16 Overview of the `order by` clause

In working with most of the tables in this book, you can get acceptable results even if you do not write an `order by` clause because most of the tables are small. They contain only a few rows. However, when you work with larger tables, it is essential to use an `order by` clause.

This section shows the syntax of the `order by` clause and a few examples of it. The clause contains a list of columns and a specification for each of these columns to sort them in either ascending or descending order.

The first column listed in the `order by` clause is the primary sort order. The columns that are listed after the first one are used only when two rows have identical values in the first column. This rule applies to all the columns. For example, the third column is only used to sort the rows that have identical values in the first two columns of the `order by` clause.

Ascending order is the default. It is usually not specified. To sort on a column in descending order, `desc` must always be specified.

Columns are usually specified by their names. Another method is to specify a number — this is the position of the column within the `select` clause. This is an older method that is being phased out. Some brands of SQL allow you to use a column alias in an `order by` clause. Oracle allows this, but Access does not.

A column can sometimes be listed in the `order by` clause without listing it in the `select` clause. However, it is good programming practice to list in the `select` clause all the columns used in the `order by` clause.

In Oracle, nulls are sorted at the bottom. In Access, they are sorted at the top. Other slight differences in the sort order can occur depending on a variety of factors, such as:

- Which SQL product you are using
- Whether you are using a small computer or a large computer
- Whether you are using a special alphabet
- Options set by your DBA

Syntax of the `order by` clause

`order by` *a list of column names*	You may specify a sort order for each column (see below).
`order by` *a list of numbers*	You may specify a sort order for each column (see below).

Sort order options for each column

`asc`	Means ascending order (default).
`desc`	Means descending order.

Examples of an `order by` clause

```
order by employee_id

order by last_name, first_name

order by hire_date desc,
         last_name,
         first_name
```

2-17 Sorting the rows by one column in ascending order

This section shows a query with one column in its order by clause. The rows of the result table are sorted by the values in that column. The default order is ascending order. There are two methods to write this:

- The first method uses the name of the column within the data table. This method is usually best because it is easiest for people to read and understand. If this column has been renamed, you must still use the old name within the order by clause.

- The second method uses a number instead of a column name. This number is the position of the column within the select clause.

Task

List the last name and first name of all the employees in the l_employees table. Rename the last_name column to family_name. Sort the rows by the last_name column in ascending order. Show how to do this using the two methods of specifying the column to sort on.

Oracle & Access SQL: Use the column name to specify the sort order

```
select last_name as family_name,
       first_name
from l_employees
order by last_name; ❶
```

Oracle & Access SQL: Use the column number to specify the sort order

```
select last_name as family_name,
       first_name
from l_employees
order by 1; ❷
```

Beginning table (1_employees table)

```
EMPLOYEE                       DEPT                CREDIT PHONE  MANAGER
      ID FIRST_NAME LAST_NAME CODE HIRE_DATE       LIMIT NUMBER      ID
-------- ---------- --------- ---- ------------  ------- ------ -------
     201 SUSAN      BROWN      EXE  01-JUN-1998    $30.00 3484   (null)
     202 JIM        KERN       SAL  16-AUG-1999    $25.00 8722      201
     203 MARTHA     WOODS      SHP  02-FEB-2009    $25.00 7591      201
     204 ELLEN      OWENS      SAL  01-JUL-2008    $15.00 6830      202
     205 HENRY      PERKINS    SAL  01-MAR-2006    $25.00 5286      202
     206 CAROL      ROSE       ACT  (null)        (null) (null) (null)
     207 DAN        SMITH      SHP  01-DEC-2008    $25.00 2259      203
     208 FRED       CAMPBELL   SHP  01-APR-2008    $25.00 1752      203
     209 PAULA      JACOBS     MKT  17-MAR-1999    $15.00 3357      201
     210 NANCY      HOFFMAN    SAL  16-FEB-2007    $25.00 2974      203
```

Result table

```
FAMILY_NAME FIRST_NAME
----------- -----------
BROWN       SUSAN
CAMPBELL    FRED
HOFFMAN     NANCY
JACOBS      PAULA
KERN        JIM
OWENS       ELLEN
PERKINS     HENRY
ROSE        CAROL
SMITH       DAN
WOODS       MARTHA
```

Notes

❶ The last_name column has been renamed to family_name in the select clause. However, in the order by clause, you must still use its original name from the beginning table, which is last_name.

❷ The number 1 here means that the rows of the result table will be sorted by the first column in the select clause, which is also the first column of the result table.

Check your understanding

List the department name column from the departments table. Give this column a new name of dept. Put the rows in ascending order. Write this SQL in two different ways.

2-18 Sorting the rows by several columns in ascending order

This section shows a query with two columns in its order by clause, both of which are sorted in ascending order.

Task

List the department codes and last names of all the employees, except for employee 209. Sort the rows of the result table on both columns in ascending order.

Oracle & Access SQL

```
select dept_code,
       last_name
from 1_employees
where not (employee_id = 209)
order by dept_code,   ❶
         last_name;   ❷
```

Beginning table (1_employees table)

EMPLOYEE ID	FIRST_NAME	LAST_NAME	DEPT CODE	HIRE_DATE	CREDIT LIMIT	PHONE NUMBER	MANAGER ID
201	SUSAN	BROWN	EXE	01-JUN-1998	$30.00	3484	(null)
202	JIM	KERN	SAL	16-AUG-1999	$25.00	8722	201
203	MARTHA	WOODS	SHP	02-FEB-2009	$25.00	7591	201
204	ELLEN	OWENS	SAL	01-JUL-2008	$15.00	6830	202
205	HENRY	PERKINS	SAL	01-MAR-2006	$25.00	5286	202
206	CAROL	ROSE	ACT	(null)	(null)	(null)	(null)
207	DAN	SMITH	SHP	01-DEC-2008	$25.00	2259	203
208	FRED	CAMPBELL	SHP	01-APR-2008	$25.00	1752	203
209	PAULA	JACOBS	MKT	17-MAR-1999	$15.00	3357	201
210	NANCY	HOFFMAN	SAL	16-FEB-2007	$25.00	2974	203

Result table

```
DEPT
CODE  LAST_NAME
----  ----------
ACT   ROSE
EXE   BROWN
SAL   HOFFMAN
SAL   KERN
SAL   OWENS
SAL   PERKINS
SHP   CAMPBELL  ❸
SHP   SMITH     ❸
SHP   WOODS     ❸
```

Notes

❶ The rows of the result table are sorted first and primarily on the dept_code column. For instance, all four rows with a dept_code of SAL are sorted before the three rows with SHP.

❷ The rows with identical values in the dept_code column are then sorted on the last_name column. Within the SAL department code, the last names are put in ascending alphabetical order. Within the SHP department code, the names are put in a separate ascending alphabetical order.

❸ Note the order of these rows in the result table. Here, for the employees within any particular department, the last names are in ascending order. In the next section, we change the order and place the last names in descending order.

Check your understanding

The table sec0218 has two columns named A and B. Each column contains the numbers 1, 2, and 3. The table has nine rows showing all the combinations of values.

List all the columns of this table. Sort the rows in two ways:

1. First by column A, then by column B.

2. First by column B, then by column A.

Observe the difference in the result.

2-19 Sorting the rows by several columns in various orders

This shows the same query as in the previous section, except that the sort on the last_name column is in descending order. The contrast with the result table in the previous section shows the difference.

Task

List the department codes and last names of all the employees, except for employee 209. Sort the rows of the result table in ascending order on the dept_code column and in descending order on the last_name column.

Oracle & Access SQL

```
select dept_code,
       last_name
from 1_employees
where not (employee_id = 209)
order by dept_code, ❶
         last_name desc; ❷
```

Beginning table (1_employees table)

EMPLOYEE ID	FIRST_NAME	LAST_NAME	DEPT CODE	HIRE_DATE	CREDIT LIMIT	PHONE NUMBER	MANAGER ID
201	SUSAN	BROWN	EXE	01-JUN-1998	$30.00	3484	(null)
202	JIM	KERN	SAL	16-AUG-1999	$25.00	8722	201
203	MARTHA	WOODS	SHP	02-FEB-2009	$25.00	7591	201
204	ELLEN	OWENS	SAL	01-JUL-2008	$15.00	6830	202
205	HENRY	PERKINS	SAL	01-MAR-2006	$25.00	5286	202
206	CAROL	ROSE	ACT	(null)	(null)	(null)	(null)
207	DAN	SMITH	SHP	01-DEC-2008	$25.00	2259	203
208	FRED	CAMPBELL	SHP	01-APR-2008	$25.00	1752	203
209	PAULA	JACOBS	MKT	17-MAR-1999	$15.00	3357	201
210	NANCY	HOFFMAN	SAL	16-FEB-2007	$25.00	2974	203

Result table

```
DEPT
CODE  LAST_NAME
----  ----------
ACT   ROSE
EXE   BROWN
SAL   PERKINS
SAL   OWENS
SAL   KERN
SAL   HOFFMAN
SHP   WOODS    ❸
SHP   SMITH    ❸
SHP   CAMPBELL ❸
```

Notes

❶ The rows of the result table are sorted first and primarily on the dept_code column.

❷ All the rows with the same value in the dept_code column are sorted on the last_name column in descending order. This is applied twice, once with the SAL department codes and again with the SHP ones.

❸ Note the order of these rows. Compare the order here with the order shown in the previous result table.

Check your understanding

The table sec0219 has three columns named A, B, and C. Each column contains the numbers 1, 2, and 3. There are 27 rows, one for each combination of values.

List all the columns of this table. Sort the rows first by column A, second by column B in reverse order, and third by column C in reverse order.

2-20 The whole process so far

Here is a quick summary of the process a select statement describes. Note that clauses of the select statement are processed in a different order than they are written.

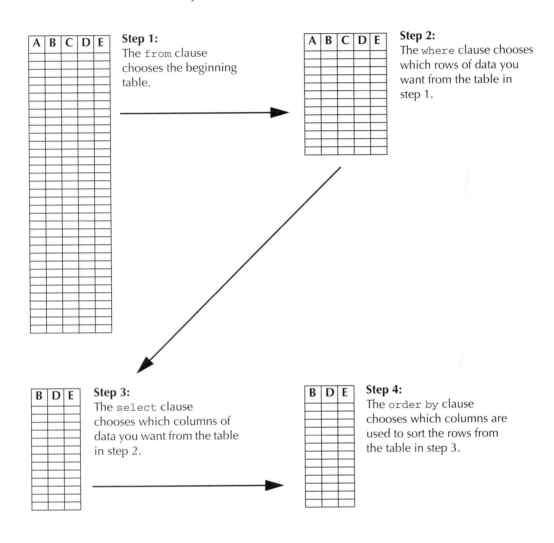

Step 1:
The from clause chooses the beginning table.

Step 2:
The where clause chooses which rows of data you want from the table in step 1.

Step 3:
The select clause chooses which columns of data you want from the table in step 2.

Step 4:
The order by clause chooses which columns are used to sort the rows from the table in step 3.

Key Points

- A `select` statement allows you to get the data you want from a table. Usually you will only want a few columns and rows from a large table. The basic `select` statement has four clauses:

  - The `select` clause says which columns you want.

  - The `from` clause says what table you are getting the data from.

  - The `where` clause says which rows you want.

  - The `order by` clause says how to sort the final result.

  There are two more clauses used to summarize data. You will learn about them in chapters 11 and 12.

- In the `select` clause you can choose the columns you want, specify the order in which you want them, and give them new names. Optionally you can tell SQL to eliminate any duplicate rows from the result. Another variation of the `select` clause gives you all the rows of the table.

- In the `from` clause you name the table that contains the data. For several chapters you will get all the data from a single table. In chapters 13 and 14 you will learn how to get data from several tables.

- In the `where` clause you can choose the rows you want. Often there are many rows to choose from, so you need to be sure to specify just the ones you want. Some of the relations you can use in the `where` clause are:

  - Equal

  - Less Than

  - Greater Than

  - Not Equal

  - In

  - Between

  - Like

  - Is null

  You can also combine these together with And, Or, and Not. Chapter 3 shows you how to do this.

- In the order by clause you can specify the order in which you want the rows of the result table to be sorted. If you do not include an order by clause, the rows of the result table could be in a random order, so it is a good practice to always write an order by clause in your select statement.

- A null represents data that is missing from the database table. It could be missing permanently because no data would make sense there, or it could be missing temporarily because the data is not known or it has not been entered into the table yet.

- Most of the time, the same SQL code that works in Oracle also works in Access.

chapter 3

Compound Conditions in the Where Clause

In chapter 2, we used fairly simple conditions in the where clause. In this chapter, we discuss how to combine several of these simple conditions into a compound condition. This is particularly important when we are handling tables with many rows. It allows us to specify the particular set of rows we want.

This chapter also discusses several other important topics. You should read this chapter quickly and make sure you do not get bogged down in any part of it. The topics themselves are not really part of SQL. Rather, these are general programming topics that could trip you up along the way if you are not aware of them.

If your main goal is to learn SQL, I recommend that you read the chapter once and then move quickly onto the next chapter. This chapter is not meant to be studied. You can come back to it later if you find you need to.

Compound Conditions in the Where Clause

This group of sections deals with the Boolean connectors and, or, and not. It shows how to place complex conditions in the where clause into standard form. Along the way, it shows you the rules you need to know to work with these Boolean connectors.

If you handle large tables, with a million or more rows, you may need to use very complex conditions in the where clause to specify the set of rows you want in the result. To keep this complexity to a reasonable level, these conditions are often put into standard form.

The standard form is discussed in section 3-3. You should read this sections over once, but do not worry if you have difficulty with it. This material is not needed in the rest of the book, but the details are here if you need them later when you are working with very large tables.

3-1   Using a compound condition in the where clause

Compound conditions can be formed using the three Boolean connectors: and, or, and not. And and or combine two conditions to form a single compound condition. They can be applied repeatedly, thus combining many conditions into a single compound condition. Not is applied to a single condition and reverses its meaning.

Definition of and

> The statement "A and B" is true only when both A and B are true.

Definition of or

> The statement "A or B" is true when either A or B is true.

Definition of not

> The statement "not A" is true when A is false.

In the preceding definitions, A and B stand for any statement, such as employee_id < 500 or first_name = 'Mary'.

The way the words and, or, and not are used in computer languages is not quite the same as the way they are used in spoken and written English. They are sometimes used in a loose and casual way in English, but they are always used in a precise way in computer languages.

In English the word "not" is often misplaced and misused. Here is an example:

"All that glitters is not gold."
— Shakespeare

I think Shakespeare is completely wrong in this statement. I think he meant to say "Not all that glitters is gold" or perhaps "Some things that glitter are not gold." The point is that the word NOT is often misused in English.

In English the words "and" and "or" are sometimes used in a way that makes them interchangeable. They are never interchangeable in computer languages. Here is an example:

"Please make the seats near each doorway available to seniors or disabled persons."
— a sign in the San Francisco BART subway system

Would it make any difference if the word "or" was changed to "and"? Would the meaning change or would it stay the same?

Within a complex condition, when several Boolean connectors are being used, parentheses should be used liberally. Even if you think they are not needed by the computer, they are needed to make the statement easy for people to read and understand. If you leave out some of the parentheses, the computer may understand the statement one way, but many people might interpret it in another way.

The example in this section shows a query that has a `where` clause that uses a compound condition. It shows how to include the null values when using a Not Equal condition. You must explicitly ask for the nulls if you want them to appear in the result table.

Task

List all employees who do not report to employee 203, Martha Woods. Include rows with a null value in the `manager_id` column. Show the following columns: `employee_id`, `first_name`, `last_name`, and `manager_id`.

Oracle & Access SQL

```
select employee_id,
       first_name,
       last_name,
       manager_id
from l_employees
where not (manager_id = 203) ❶
   or manager_id is null; ❷
```

Beginning table (`1_employees` table)

```
EMPLOYEE                         DEPT                   CREDIT  PHONE   MANAGER
      ID FIRST_NAME  LAST_NAME  CODE  HIRE_DATE         LIMIT   NUMBER       ID
-------- ----------  ---------  ----  ------------      -------  ------  -------
     201 SUSAN       BROWN      EXE   01-JUN-1998       $30.00  3484    (null)
     202 JIM         KERN       SAL   16-AUG-1999       $25.00  8722       201
     203 MARTHA      WOODS      SHP   02-FEB-2009       $25.00  7591       201
     204 ELLEN       OWENS      SAL   01-JUL-2008       $15.00  6830       202
     205 HENRY       PERKINS    SAL   01-MAR-2006       $25.00  5286       202
     206 CAROL       ROSE       ACT   (null)           (null)  (null)  (null)
     207 DAN         SMITH      SHP   01-DEC-2008       $25.00  2259       203
     208 FRED        CAMPBELL   SHP   01-APR-2008       $25.00  1752       203
     209 PAULA       JACOBS     MKT   17-MAR-1999       $15.00  3357       201
     210 NANCY       HOFFMAN    SAL   16-FEB-2007       $25.00  2974       203
```

Result table

```
EMPLOYEE                        MANAGER
      ID FIRST_NAME  LAST_NAME       ID
-------- ----------  ----------  -------
     201 SUSAN       BROWN       (null)
     202 JIM         KERN           201
     203 MARTHA      WOODS          201
     204 ELLEN       OWENS          202
     205 HENRY       PERKINS        202
     206 CAROL       ROSE        (null)
     209 PAULA       JACOBS         201
```

Notes

❶ Not is used to reverse the meaning of "`manager_id = 203`" to create the meaning "`manager_id` is not equal to 203." The parentheses are optional. I used them here to make the meaning clearer to people who read the SQL code.

❷ Or is used to combine the two conditions:

```
not (manager_id = 203)   and   manager_id is null
```

This forms a single compound condition:

```
not (manager_id = 203)   or   manager_id is null
```

Check your understanding

List all the rows of the `1_foods` table that have a price less than $1.00 or greater than $5.00.

3-2   Using not with in, between, like, and is null

This section shows the word not can be used in two different ways with the following conditions: in, between, like, and is null. The meanings are exactly the same.

Version 1 will show the word not used as part of the condition test. There is one condition test called in and there is another condition test called not in. The same applies to all these conditions:

```
in              not in
between         not between
like            not like
is null         is not null
```

Version 2 will show the word not used as a Boolean connector modifying an entire condition. In the first line of the where clause, not is applied to the condition:

dept_code in ('act', 'mkt')

This condition is then written with an additional set of parentheses:

not (dept_code in ('act', 'mkt'))

The computer also understands this without the additional set of parentheses:

not dept_code in ('act', 'mkt')

However, this can be more confusing to most people, so I do not recommend it.

In the following code, you will notice that the patterns used with the like condition differ in Oracle and in Access. We discussed this in section 2-14.

Task

Show the employee_id, first_name, last_name, and manager_id of the employees having all of the following conditions:

- dept_code is not act or mkt
- last_name does not begin with any letter from J to M
- last_name does not end with S
- manager_id is not a null value

Oracle & Access SQL: Version 1 — Using not within the condition

```
select employee_id,
       first_name,
       last_name,
       manager_id
from l_employees
where dept_code not in ('ACT', 'MKT')
  and last_name not between 'J' and 'M'
  and last_name not like '%S'        (Oracle)
  and last_name not like '*S'        (Access)
  and manager_id is not null;
```

Oracle & Access SQL: Version 2 — Using a Boolean not

```
select employee_id,
       first_name,
       last_name,
       manager_id
from l_employees
where not (dept_code in ('ACT', 'MKT'))
  and not (last_name between 'J' and 'M')
  and not (last_name like '%S')       (Oracle)
  and not (last_name like '*S')       (Access)
  and not (manager_id is null);
```

Beginning table (1_employees table)

EMPLOYEE ID	FIRST_NAME	LAST_NAME	DEPT CODE	HIRE_DATE	CREDIT LIMIT	PHONE NUMBER	MANAGER ID
201	SUSAN	BROWN	EXE	01-JUN-1998	$30.00	3484	(null)
202	JIM	KERN	SAL	16-AUG-1999	$25.00	8722	201
203	MARTHA	WOODS	SHP	02-FEB-2009	$25.00	7591	201
204	ELLEN	OWENS	SAL	01-JUL-2008	$15.00	6830	202
205	HENRY	PERKINS	SAL	01-MAR-2006	$25.00	5286	202
206	CAROL	ROSE	ACT	(null)	(null)	(null)	(null)
207	DAN	SMITH	SHP	01-DEC-2008	$25.00	2259	203
208	FRED	CAMPBELL	SHP	01-APR-2008	$25.00	1752	203
209	PAULA	JACOBS	MKT	17-MAR-1999	$15.00	3357	201
210	NANCY	HOFFMAN	SAL	16-FEB-2007	$25.00	2974	203

Result table

EMPLOYEE ID	FIRST_NAME	LAST_NAME	MANAGER ID
207	DAN	SMITH	203
208	FRED	CAMPBELL	203
210	NANCY	HOFFMAN	203

Check your understanding

List all the foods from the `1_foods` table that do not have a null in the `price_increase` column.

3-3   The standard form of a complex condition in the `where` clause

This section shows an example of a query with a very complex condition in its `where` clause. You might need to use a condition of this sort when you are dealing with a large table that has many millions of rows. As a general rule, as a table gets larger the `where` clause gets more complex. Additional conditions are required to select the rows you want. Also, sometimes the logic within a query needs to be quite complex.

The purpose of this example is to show a condition in the `where` clause that is organized in the standard form of a Boolean expression. With a little effort, any complex condition can be written in this form. Writing a condition in this way can make it easy for people to read, understand, and work with. Complex conditions that are not in standard form are prone to errors. So, part of the debugging effort of a `select` statement can be working with the condition in the `where` clause to put it into standard form. Here I am using the term **standard form** to mean that the expression is placed in a standardized format.

The example in this section is a bit contrived. You really do not need complexity on this scale when you are dealing with tables as small and simple as the ones in this book. However, I want to show you the principle.

Definition of standard form in the `where` clause

The three Boolean connectors `and`, `or`, and `not` are strictly controlled:

- `Not` is applied only to simple conditions. It is not applied to compound conditions that include an `and` or an `or`.
- `And` is used to combine simple conditions and conditions involving `not`. None of these conditions are allowed to contain an `or`. Many conditions can be combined together with `and`. If there is more than one `and`, the conditions can be combined in any order and no parentheses are required. Each of these compound conditions is usually enclosed in parentheses.
- `Or` is the top-level connector. It combines all the compound conditions using `and` and `not`. If there is more than one `or`, the compound conditions can be combined in any order and no parentheses are required.

Task

Show an example of a select statement that has a where clause in standard form. The following example shows the format. It does run, but it is not intended to make much sense.

Oracle & Access SQL

```
select employee_id,
       first_name,
       last_name
from 1_employees
where (manager_id is null ❶
       and first_name = 'SUSAN'
       and credit_limit = 30.00)
   or ❷
     (not (hire_date is null) ❸
      and credit_limit between 10.00 and 50.00 ❹
      and last_name in ('SMITH', 'JACOBS', 'PATRICK')
      and not (dept_code = 'SHP'))
   or
     (credit_limit > 22.00
      and hire_date is null)
   or
     (employee_id > 700
      and dept_code in ('SAL', 'MKT')
      and manager_id = 400);
```

Beginning table (1_employees table)

EMPLOYEE ID	FIRST_NAME	LAST_NAME	DEPT CODE	HIRE_DATE	CREDIT LIMIT	PHONE NUMBER	MANAGER ID
201	SUSAN	BROWN	EXE	01-JUN-1998	$30.00	3484	(null)
202	JIM	KERN	SAL	16-AUG-1999	$25.00	8722	201
203	MARTHA	WOODS	SHP	02-FEB-2009	$25.00	7591	201
204	ELLEN	OWENS	SAL	01-JUL-2008	$15.00	6830	202
205	HENRY	PERKINS	SAL	01-MAR-2006	$25.00	5286	202
206	CAROL	ROSE	ACT	(null)	(null)	(null)	(null)
207	DAN	SMITH	SHP	01-DEC-2008	$25.00	2259	203
208	FRED	CAMPBELL	SHP	01-APR-2008	$25.00	1752	203
209	PAULA	JACOBS	MKT	17-MAR-1999	$15.00	3357	201
210	NANCY	HOFFMAN	SAL	16-FEB-2007	$25.00	2974	203

Result table ❺

EMPLOYEE ID	FIRST_NAME	LAST_NAME
201	SUSAN	BROWN
209	PAULA	JACOBS

Notes

❶ This line and the next two lines are a compound condition joined together with and. The parentheses enclosing these three lines are optional, but make the condition easier to read.

❷ This is an or joining together the compound conditions formed with and.

❸ This shows a Boolean not applied to a simple condition that does not contain any and or or.

❹ The and on this line is part of the between condition. It is not a Boolean and connector.

❺ The result table shows that this code actually runs. In this example, it is not important to follow the precise logic.

Check your understanding

Put the following where clause into standard form:

```
select *
from 1_employees
where not ((first_name = 'JIM' or first_name = 'DAN')
and (last_name = 'BROWN' or last_name = 'SMITH'))
```

3-4   A common mistake

This section shows a common mistake that people make when they write a complex condition in the where clause and they do not specify enough parentheses. In this example, most people understand that the first three conditions of the where clause are related because they all involve the same column, employee_id. Placing a pair of parentheses around the first three conditions can represent the understanding that most people have.

To a computer, however, or is always a higher level connector than and when parentheses do not say otherwise. So the computer understands the statement differently. To the computer, there are three clusters joined together by or.

Task

Of the employees whose employee IDs are 203, 204, or 205, list only the ones in the sales department.

Beginning table (1_employees table)

```
EMPLOYEE                        DEPT                    CREDIT PHONE   MANAGER
      ID FIRST_NAME LAST_NAME  CODE HIRE_DATE           LIMIT  NUMBER       ID
-------- ---------- ---------  ---- -----------        ------- ------  -------
     201 SUSAN      BROWN      EXE  01-JUN-1998        $30.00  3484    (null)
     202 JIM        KERN       SAL  16-AUG-1999        $25.00  8722       201
     203 MARTHA     WOODS      SHP  02-FEB-2009        $25.00  7591       201
     204 ELLEN      OWENS      SAL  01-JUL-2008        $15.00  6830       202
     205 HENRY      PERKINS    SAL  01-MAR-2006        $25.00  5286       202
     206 CAROL      ROSE       ACT  (null)             (null)  (null)  (null)
     207 DAN        SMITH      SHP  01-DEC-2008        $25.00  2259       203
     208 FRED       CAMPBELL   SHP  01-APR-2008        $25.00  1752       203
     209 PAULA      JACOBS     MKT  17-MAR-1999        $15.00  3357       201
     210 NANCY      HOFFMAN    SAL  16-FEB-2007        $25.00  2974       203
```

Oracle & Access SQL: Parentheses are missing — A common mistake

```
select *
from 1_employees
where employee_id = 203 ❶
   or employee_id = 204
   or employee_id = 205
  and dept_code = 'SAL';
```

Notes

❶ This where clause does not contain enough parentheses to control the way that the individual conditions are combined. Most people will understand it to mean one thing, but the computer will understand it to mean something else.

Oracle & Access SQL: How people often misunderstand this code

```
select *
from 1_employees
where (    employee_id = 203 ❷
       or employee_id = 204
       or employee_id = 205)
  and dept_code = 'SAL';
```

Result table that people often expect from this code

```
EMPLOYEE                            DEPT                    CREDIT  PHONE   MANAGER
      ID FIRST_NAME LAST_NAME  CODE HIRE_DATE         LIMIT  NUMBER       ID
-------- ---------- ---------  ---- -----------    -------  ------ -------
     204 ELLEN      OWENS      SAL  01-JUL-2008     $15.00 6830        202
     205 HENRY      PERKINS    SAL  01-MAR-2006     $25.00 5286        202
```

Notes

❷ The pair of parentheses here shows how most people understand the code in ❶.

Oracle & Access SQL: How a computer understands this code

```
select *
from l_employees
where (employee_id = 203) ❸
   or
      (employee_id = 204)
   or
      (employee_id = 205
       and dept_code = 'SAL');
```

Result table that the computer produces ❹

```
EMPLOYEE                            DEPT                    CREDIT  PHONE   MANAGER
      ID FIRST_NAME LAST_NAME  CODE HIRE_DATE         LIMIT  NUMBER       ID
-------- ---------- ---------  ---- -----------    -------  ------ -------
     203 MARTHA     WOODS      SHP  02-FEB-2009     $25.00 7591        201
     204 ELLEN      OWENS      SAL  01-JUL-2008     $15.00 6830        202
     205 HENRY      PERKINS    SAL  01-MAR-2006     $25.00 5286        202
```

Notes

❸ The pairs of parentheses here show the way that the computer understands the code in ❶. The computer combines phrases with and before combining phrases with or.

❹ This table contains the row from `employee_id` 203, Martha Woods, who is in the shipping department. This occurred because a mistake was made when writing the code in ❶. The mistake was in leaving out a pair of parentheses. If you don't want this row in your result table, you must write the code in ❷.

Check your understanding

Add parentheses to the following `select` statement to prevent it from making a common mistake.

```
select *
from l_foods
where description = 'FRESH SALAD'
   or description = 'SANDWICH'
   or description = 'DESSERT'
  and price <= 2.50
  and price_increase <= 0.25;
```

Constant Values

On the level of data in a table, a **constant value** is a column that contains the same value in every row. Usually there is no reason to place a column like this in a table. Two other techniques can be used instead. One technique places a literal value into the `select` clause as a hard-coded value. This works well when you have only a few `select` statements. However, when you have a large number of `select` statements, this technique can make the code inflexible. This means that the code cannot easily be changed to adapt to changing requirements.

The other technique places the constant values in a separate table, which I call a **table of constants.** This is defined as a table that has only one row. It has a separate column for each distinct constant value. The names of these columns are usually designed so they are unique and are not identical to the column names in any other table. After this table has been created, it can be used in coding `select` statements with any other table.

This technique is used primarily when you have 20 or more `select` statements that all use the same set of constants. For instance, I once became responsible for a set of quarterly reports someone else had written. The beginning date and ending date of the quarter was hard-coded into each `select` statement. Each time I wanted to run these reports I had to change the beginning date and ending date in all of the code. This took most of a day, and there would always be some errors to find and correct, so the whole process took about two days. After doing this a few times, I got tired of it and I changed the code to get the dates from a table of constants. It would then take me only a few minutes to run all the reports.

3-5   Using a constant value in the `select` clause

This section shows constant values hard-coded within a `select` clause. This example shows all the different types of data that can be coded as constant values — text, numbers, and nulls. The column that appears to be a date is actually a text field, where the text represents a date.

You will understand this comment about dates better when we discuss the Date datatype and the formatting of dates in chapters 6 and 7. Data with a Date datatype can be stored in a table, but cannot be printed directly. Dates must be printed as text. So when a date appears in a `select` clause, it must appear as text.

Beginning table   **Literals in `select` clause**

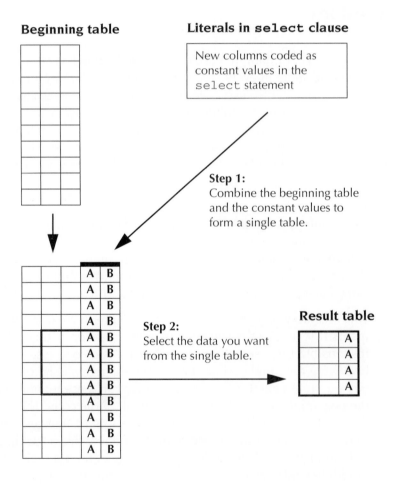

New columns coded as constant values in the `select` statement

Step 1:
Combine the beginning table and the constant values to form a single table.

Step 2:
Select the data you want from the single table.

Result table

The preceding diagram shows what happens on a conceptual level when a constant value is used within a `select` clause. It is as if a new column was added to the beginning table. This new column contains the same value in every row and it can be given a column alias, a temporary name, just like any other column. The syntax is the same here as it is for a column. The syntax is:

constant_value AS column_alias

This is parallel to:

column_name AS column_alias

Task

Show a query that contains hard-coded values in the `select` clause. Show a text value, a numeric value, a date value, and a null value.

Oracle & Access SQL

```
select employee_id,
       last_name,
       'EXCELLENT WORKER' as evaluation, ❶
       10 as rating, ❷
       '01-JAN-2011' as eval_date, ❸
       null as next_eval ❹
from 1_employees
order by employee_id;
```

Beginning table (1_employees table)

EMPLOYEE ID	FIRST_NAME	LAST_NAME	DEPT CODE	HIRE_DATE	CREDIT LIMIT	PHONE NUMBER	MANAGER ID
201	SUSAN	BROWN	EXE	01-JUN-1998	$30.00	3484	(null)
202	JIM	KERN	SAL	16-AUG-1999	$25.00	8722	201
203	MARTHA	WOODS	SHP	02-FEB-2009	$25.00	7591	201
204	ELLEN	OWENS	SAL	01-JUL-2008	$15.00	6830	202
205	HENRY	PERKINS	SAL	01-MAR-2006	$25.00	5286	202
206	CAROL	ROSE	ACT	(null)	(null)	(null)	(null)
207	DAN	SMITH	SHP	01-DEC-2008	$25.00	2259	203
208	FRED	CAMPBELL	SHP	01-APR-2008	$25.00	1752	203
209	PAULA	JACOBS	MKT	17-MAR-1999	$15.00	3357	201
210	NANCY	HOFFMAN	SAL	16-FEB-2007	$25.00	2974	203

Result table

```
EMPLOYEE                                                     NEXT
      ID LAST_NAME   EVALUATION            RATING EVAL_DATE   EVAL
-------- ---------- ------------------- --------- ----------- ------
     201 BROWN       EXCELLENT  WORKER         10 01-JAN-2011 (null)
     202 KERN        EXCELLENT  WORKER         10 01-JAN-2011 (null)
     203 WOODS       EXCELLENT  WORKER         10 01-JAN-2011 (null)
     204 OWENS       EXCELLENT  WORKER         10 01-JAN-2011 (null)
     205 PERKINS     EXCELLENT  WORKER         10 01-JAN-2011 (null)
     206 ROSE        EXCELLENT  WORKER         10 01-JAN-2011 (null)
     207 SMITH       EXCELLENT  WORKER         10 01-JAN-2011 (null)
     208 CAMPBELL    EXCELLENT  WORKER         10 01-JAN-2011 (null)
     209 JACOBS      EXCELLENT  WORKER         10 01-JAN-2011 (null)
     210 HOFFMAN     EXCELLENT  WORKER         10 01-JAN-2011 (null)
```

Notes

❶ This constant value is a text field. Although it is a hard-coded literal within the `select` clause, it behaves as if it had created a new column within the beginning table.

❷ This constant value is a numeric field.

❸ This constant value is a text field that represents a date.

❹ This constant value is a null. You must not put quotes around the word `null`.

3-6   Using a table of constants

Here are some of the benefits of using a table of constants:

- It adds flexibility to your SQL code. Your `select` statements can change easily if the value of any of these constants ever changes.

- It guarantees consistency. You are sure that all the `select` statements are using the same values for these constants.

This section shows an example of a `select` statement that uses a table of constants. To do this, the `from` clause needs to list two tables: the table of constants and another table of data. All the other clauses of the `select` statement can refer to the columns of either table. No relationship between the two tables is required. The fact that a table of constants has only one row ensures that all the constant values will be copied into every row of the other table.

For this technique to work, the names of the columns in the table of constants must all be different from any column name in the other table. When this is not true, you need to use other techniques discussed in chapter 13.

The following diagram shows what happens on a conceptual level when a table of constants is used with another table in a `select` statement. It is as if new columns have been added to the other table. These new columns contain the same value in every row.

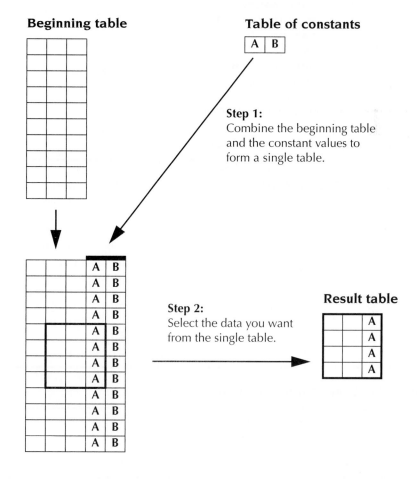

Beginning table

Table of constants

Step 1:
Combine the beginning table and the constant values to form a single table.

Step 2:
Select the data you want from the single table.

Result table

Task

Code the `select` statement from the previous section using a table of constants instead of hard-coded literals.

Oracle & Access SQL

```
select employee_id,
       last_name,
       evaluation, ❶
       rating, ❶
       eval_date, ❶
       next_eval ❶
from l_employees,
       sec0306_constants
order by employee_id;
```

Beginning table 1 (l_employees table)

EMPLOYEE ID	FIRST_NAME	LAST_NAME	DEPT CODE	HIRE_DATE	CREDIT LIMIT	PHONE NUMBER	MANAGER ID
201	SUSAN	BROWN	EXE	01-JUN-1998	$30.00	3484	(null)
202	JIM	KERN	SAL	16-AUG-1999	$25.00	8722	201
203	MARTHA	WOODS	SHP	02-FEB-2009	$25.00	7591	201
204	ELLEN	OWENS	SAL	01-JUL-2008	$15.00	6830	202
205	HENRY	PERKINS	SAL	01-MAR-2006	$25.00	5286	202
206	CAROL	ROSE	ACT	(null)	(null)	(null)	(null)
207	DAN	SMITH	SHP	01-DEC-2008	$25.00	2259	203
208	FRED	CAMPBELL	SHP	01-APR-2008	$25.00	1752	203
209	PAULA	JACOBS	MKT	17-MAR-1999	$15.00	3357	201
210	NANCY	HOFFMAN	SAL	16-FEB-2007	$25.00	2974	203

Beginning table 2 (sec0306_constants table)

EVALUATION	RATING	EVAL_DATE	NEXT EVAL
EXCELLENT WORKER	10	01-JAN-2011	(null)

Result table

```
EMPLOYEE  LAST                                             NEXT
      ID  NAME      EVALUATION         RATING  EVAL_DATE    EVAL
--------  --------  ----------------   ------- -----------  ------
     201  BROWN     EXCELLENT WORKER        10 01-JAN-2011  (null)
     202  KERN      EXCELLENT WORKER        10 01-JAN-2011  (null)
     203  WOODS     EXCELLENT WORKER        10 01-JAN-2011  (null)
     204  OWENS     EXCELLENT WORKER        10 01-JAN-2011  (null)
     205  PERKINS   EXCELLENT WORKER        10 01-JAN-2011  (null)
     206  ROSE      EXCELLENT WORKER        10 01-JAN-2011  (null)
     207  SMITH     EXCELLENT WORKER        10 01-JAN-2011  (null)
     208  CAMPBELL  EXCELLENT WORKER        10 01-JAN-2011  (null)
     209  JACOBS    EXCELLENT WORKER        10 01-JAN-2011  (null)
     210  HOFFMAN   EXCELLENT WORKER        10 01-JAN-2011  (null)
```

Notes

❶ This column now comes from the table of constants instead of being hard-coded as a literal into the `select` clause.

Check your understanding

Modify the following `select` statement to remove the hard-coded values $1.00 and $2.00 from the code and place them in a table of constants.

The table `sec0306_price_constants` is already set up for you. The `min_price` field = 1.00 and the `max_price` field = 2.00.

When I make a change like this, in addition to replacing the hard-coded values, I often put those values in the `select` clause so I can see exactly what the values are whenever I run the SQL code.

```
select description
from l_foods
where price between 1.00 and 2.00
order by description;
```

Punctuation Matters

It is almost embarrassing to talk in detail about punctuation . Small problems, like the one in the previous sentence, are often ignored. (Did you notice that there is a space before the period?) People usually focus on the words first and then expect the punctuation to be easy. However, computers focus on the punctuation first and then look at the words. Any mistake in punctuation can completely confuse the computer. More than half the errors most people make while learning SQL are errors in punctuation.

This is made more difficult because punctuation has additional meanings in SQL that it does not have in English or any other spoken language. Also, Oracle and Access use punctuation somewhat differently.

Section 3-7 contains the minimum you need to know about punctuation. Section 3-8 contains a more detailed discussion of punctuation. You might want to skim this section for now and refer to it later.

3-7   Punctuation you need to know right now

This section contains short explanations about punctuation. I only tell you enough here to keep you out of trouble and tell you about the best practices. More detailed explanations are presented in the next section.

Spaces in names — Avoid them when you can

It is best to avoid using a space in any name — table names, column names, and the names of any other database objects. Use an underscore character instead of a space. For example, do not name a column `hire date`, which has a space between the e of hire and the d of date. Name it `hire_date`.

Commas

Commas separate the items of a list. A list cannot end with a comma. If the last item of a list is removed, the comma preceding it must also be removed. The following example shows a common error:

```
select first_name,
       last_name,
from l_employees;
```

Do not use commas or dollar signs when entering numbers. Decimal points are the only punctuation allowed within numbers.

Single quotes

If you are going to use single quotes, make sure you are using a text editor, such as Notepad, that will use "straight quotes." Some word processing programs substitute "curly quotes" for straight quotes. Usually curly quotes are not acceptable in SQL code.

In Oracle, you should use only single quotes to surround text strings and dates. Do not use quotes around numbers. See the following examples:

```
select *
from l_employees
where dept_code in ('SAL', 'SHP')
   or hire_date > '01-JAN-2003'
   or employee_id = 201;
```

In Access, like in Oracle, text strings must be enclosed in quotes and numbers must not be enclosed in them. However, dates are punctuated differently in Access than they are in Oracle. In Access, dates are enclosed in pound signs, not in quotes:

```
select *
from l_employees
where dept_code in ('SAL', 'SHP')
   or hire_date > #01-JAN-2003#
   or employee_id = 201;
```

Double quotes

If you are going to use double quotes, make sure you are using a text editor, such as Notepad, that will use "straight quotes." Some word processing programs substitute "curly quotes" for straight quotes. Usually curly quotes are not acceptable in SQL code.

In Oracle, single quotes and double quotes have different meanings. You should almost always use single quotes, except in two special situations, which are explained in the next section.

In Access, single quotes and double quotes have the same meaning, so you can use double quotes anywhere you can use single quotes. In this book I mostly use single quotes because I want the same code to work in both Oracle and Access.

Pound signs

Access uses pound signs to enclose dates. See the previous example.

Semicolons

A semicolon marks the end of an SQL statement.

Reserved words — Avoid them

SQL uses some reserved words. In general, you should avoid using any word you think might be reserved. For example, do not try to name a column `from` or `date`. Few reserved words contain an underscore, so adding an underscore is a way to avoid using a reserved word. In the example, it would be acceptable to name a column `from_` or `date_`.

Task

List the names of all the suppliers that have an apostrophe or an ampersand in their names. Use the `l_suppliers` table.

Oracle SQL

```
select supplier_name
from l_suppliers
where supplier_name like '%''%' ❶
   or supplier_name like '%&%'
order by supplier_name;
```

Access SQL

```
select supplier_name
from l_suppliers
where supplier_name like "*'*" ❷
   or supplier_name like "*&*"
order by supplier_name;
```
or
```
select supplier_name
from l_suppliers
where supplier_name like '*''*' ❶
   or supplier_name like '*&*'
order by supplier_name;
```

Beginning table (1_suppliers table)

```
SUPPLIER
ID        SUPPLIER_NAME
--------  --------------------------
ARR       ALICE & RAY'S RESTAURANT
ASP       A SOUP PLACE
CBC       CERTIFIED BEEF COMPANY
FRV       FRANK REED'S VEGETABLES
FSN       FRANK & SONS
JBR       JUST BEVERAGES
JPS       JIM PARKER'S SHOP
VSB       VIRGINIA STREET BAKERY
```

Result table

```
SUPPLIER_NAME
--------------------------
ALICE & RAY'S RESTAURANT
FRANK & SONS
FRANK REED'S VEGETABLES
JIM PARKER'S SHOP
```

Notes

❶ Use two single quotes in succession to express a single apostrophe when it occurs within single quotes.

❷ Use only one single quote to express a single apostrophe when it occurs within double quotes.

Check your understanding

Find and correct the error in the following:

```
select *
from 1_suppliers
where supplier_name = 'frank reed's vegetables';
```

3-8   Punctuation reference section

This is a reference for the most common types of punctuation required by Oracle and Access. It includes the previous section. This section covers punctuation you can learn later. You do not need to read it now.

How to avoid having spaces in names

It is best to avoid using spaces in the names of database objects or column names. Traditionally with computers, spaces have been used as a separator character and you are simply asking for trouble if you start to use a space in any other way.

There are two methods that are often used to eliminate spaces. One method replaces the spaces with underscore characters. The other method uses mostly lowercase letters, except each word begins with one uppercase letter. The spaces are removed. Here is an example of both methods:

```
Name with spaces:   hire date
Method 1:           hire_date
Method 2:           HireDate
```

In this book I use the first method. To me, this makes the code easier to read, but this is a matter of taste, so you can use the other method if you prefer it.

How to handle spaces in names

Sometimes you cannot avoid having spaces in names, usually because the system is already set up before you arrive. Then you just have to deal with them. Both Oracle and Access provide a way to handle this situation. In Oracle, you enclose the name in double quotes. In Access, you enclose the name in square brackets. For example:

```
Name with spaces:   hire date
Oracle method:      "hire date"
Access method:      [hire date]
```

Commas

Commas separate the items of a list. A list cannot end with a comma. If the last item of a list is removed, the comma preceding it must also be removed.

This example shows a common error:

```
select first_name,
       last_name,
from l_employees;
```

Do not use commas or dollar signs when entering numbers. Decimal points are the only punctuation allowed within numbers.

Single quotes

In Oracle, character strings and dates must be enclosed in single quotes. The terms **character string** and **text string** mean the same thing. In Access, they can be enclosed in either single quotes or double quotes.

Two single quotes next to each other can be used to code an apostrophe. For details, see the discussion of apostrophes.

Double quotes

In Access, double quotes and single quotes mean the same thing, so text strings can be enclosed in either single quotes or double quotes.

In Oracle, double quotes are used around any column alias. In particular, they are needed around a column alias that contains a special character or a space. After the column alias is created in the `select` clause, it can be used in the `order by` clause, but it must still be in double quotes. For example:

```
select first_name as "FIRST NAME"
from l_employees
order by "FIRST NAME";
```

In Oracle, double quotes are also used to put text into date formats. We discuss date formats in chapter 7. Here is an example:

```
select employee_id,
to_char(hire_date, '"HIRED IN THE YEAR " yyyy')
from l_employees;
```

Apostrophes

An apostrophe can be written as two single quotes next to each other. To find the names of all the suppliers with an apostrophe in their names, you can write as follows.

Oracle SQL

```
select *
from l_suppliers
where supplier_name like '%''%';
```

Access SQL method 1

```
select *
from 1_suppliers
where supplier_name like '*''*';
```

Access SQL method 2

An easier method to write an apostrophe in Access encloses a single quote in a pair of double quotes:

```
select *
from 1_suppliers
where supplier_name like "*'*";
```

Pound signs

Access uses the pound sign to enclose dates:

```
select *
from 1_employees
where hire_date = #16-FEB-2007#;
```

Oracle encloses dates in single quotes:

```
where hire_date = '16-FEB-2007';
```

SQL can be written in free format

Most of the SQL in this book is written in a highly structured way. I recommend using this format. However, this formatting is not required. The code can all be written on one line, or you can get creative and write it in some fancy shape.

The clauses of the `select` statement must always be written in a specified order. However, you can run the lines together in any way you wish. You can write as follows:

```
select *
from 1_employees;
```

or

```
select * from 1_employees;
```

or

```
select
   *   from

            1_employees
  ;
```

There are two exceptions to this. A bug in Oracle at one time did not allow any completely blank lines in the middle of an SQL statement. This issue has mostly been fixed now. However, when you run the Oracle SQL Command Line environment, you may have to use an SQL*Plus command to allow them.

Access allows blank lines, but it does not allow any characters after the semicolon that marks the end of the SQL statement.

Double dashes (comment line)

In Oracle and most other SQL products, any text written after two dashes is a comment. The dashes can be written at the beginning of the line or in the middle:

```
-- This is a comment line
```

or

```
select first_name, last_name   -- this is a comment
```

Access does not allow comments in the SQL window. So, when you write SQL for both Oracle and Access, you cannot put comments into it.

Periods and exclamation marks

In both Oracle and Access, a period is often used between a table name and a column name to indicate that the column is part of that particular table:

```
select l_employees.first_name
from l_employees;
```

In Access, an exclamation mark can sometimes be used to mean the same:

```
select l_employees!first_name
from l_employees;
```

Oracle can use a period in a column alias. Access cannot. The following SQL works in Oracle, but not in Access:

```
select first_name as "AND SO MUCH MORE ..."
from l_employees;
```

Ampersands

In Oracle, when you use the SQL Command Line environment, the ampersand is often used to indicate a variable. For instance, &fox could be a variable. A slightly different type of variable is &&fox. You will be asked to supply a value for &fox each time it occurs in an Oracle script file. With &&fox you will only be asked to supply a value the first time it occurs.

If you want to use an ampersand as an ordinary character, you should turn this feature off. To do this, run the following command:

`set define off`

This is an SQL*Plus command, not an SQL command. It sets the environment in which SQL runs in Oracle.

In Access, an ampersand is used for concatenation. For example:

`"sweet" & "heart" = "sweetheart"`

Vertical bars

The vertical bar or double bar is the uppercase symbol above the back-slash. The key usually shows two short lines, one above the other. However, many printers display it as a single line.

Oracle, in the SQL Command Line environment, uses a vertical bar to divide a column heading into two or more lines. This is done within the `column` command. For example:

`column first_name heading 'FIRST | NAME'`

Oracle also uses two consecutive double bars for the concatenation function. For example:

`'SUN' || 'SHINE' = 'SUNSHINE'`

Semicolons

A semicolon marks the end of an SQL statement. This tells the computer that the statement is complete and may now be processed. Oracle requires a semicolon to end a statement. Oracle also accepts a forward slash as another method of statement termination. In Access, the semicolon is optional.

Colons

Oracle, in the Database Home Page environment, uses a colon as the first character of a variable name. An example is `:fox`. The user will be asked for the value of this variable at the time that the `select` statement is run.

Numbers — Commas, decimal points, and dollar signs

When you are using a number within SQL code, do not use commas or dollar signs. Decimal points may be used.

Square brackets

In Access, square brackets are used to enclose names that contain spaces:

```
select [employee ID],
       [first name],
       [last name]
from [employees table of the lunches database];
```

Asterisks

In both Oracle and Access, `select *` means "select all the columns." `Count(*)` means "count all the rows." An asterisk is also used as a sign for multiplication. In Access patterns, it is a wildcard character meaning "any number of characters, or possibly no characters at all."

Forward slashes

In Oracle, a forward slash can be used to terminate an SQL statement. More precisely it means "run the SQL code that is now in the buffer."

A different meaning in both Oracle and Access uses a forward slash for division of numbers.

Multiline comments

In Oracle, you can enter a multiline comment by beginning it with `/*` and putting `*/` at the end. For example:

```
/*
this is the beginning of the comment,
then you add as many lines as you want ...
and keep on adding more lines
You end the comment this way
*/
```

Not Equal conditions

The Not Equal condition can be shown in several ways. To exclude an `employee_id` of `201`, you may write any of the following:

`where employee_id != 201`	Oracle only
`where employee_id ^= 201`	Oracle only
`where employee_id <> 201`	Oracle & Access
`where not employee_id = 201`	Oracle & Access
`where not (employee_id = 201)`	Oracle & Access

Wildcards

Wildcards are used in a `where` clause with a `like` condition.

In Oracle

% (percent)	Used to mean any number of characters, or possibly no characters at all.
_ (underscore)	Used to mean exactly one unknown character.

In Access

* (asterisk)	Used to mean any number of characters or possibly no characters at all.
? (question mark)	Used to mean exactly one unknown character.
# (pound sign)	Used to mean exactly one digit, 0 to 9.
[a-d] (square brackets)	Used to mean a range of characters, in this case from a to d.
[*] (square brackets around a wildcard character)	Means the character itself, without its wildcard properties.

Regular expressions

Oracle can now use regular expressions. They are a more powerful alternative to using wildcard expressions. I am not going to try to explain them in this book. They come from the Perl language. Here is an example of a regular expression:

```
select regexp_replace(number_with_format_1,
        '([[:digit:]]{3})\.([[:digit:]]{5})\.
        ([[:digit:]]{4})\.([[:digit:]]{7})',
        '+\1-\3-\3-\4') as number_with_format_2
from my_table;
```

Note how complex this is and how much punctuation there is in it. Also note that three different types of parentheses are used, each with its own special meaning. In this code, lines 2 and 3 must be put on a single line, otherwise the code runs but gives the wrong results.

If you want to know more about the use of regular expressions in Oracle, see chapter 3 of the *Two Day Developer Guide* in the Oracle documentation.

Case Sensitivity

3-9 Case sensitivity in Oracle

Many Oracle databases are case sensitive. That means that the data held in the tables distinguishes between uppercase letters, such as "A", and lowercase letters, such as "a". Some fields may be in mixed case. The data often looks better that way.

Unfortunately, it can also mean that sometimes you need to remember for each column in which case the data is coded. For instance "JOHN", "john", and "John" are all different. If you look for data but you use the wrong case, you will not find it. There are two ways to deal with this.

First, the only parts of SQL code that are case sensitive are the parts between quotation marks, so that is the only part where you need to be concerned about uppercase versus lowercase. Now let us assume for this discussion that the data in the `first_name` column is actually "John", where the first letter is uppercase and the remaining letters are lowercase.

One strategy is to actually remember which case the data is written in. If you remember this you can use your knowledge when you write the literal values (the part between quotation marks) in your SQL code. Here is an example:

```
select *
from employees
where first_name = 'John';
```

The other strategy is to use a row function to convert the `first_name` column in the `where` clause to be in a particular case. There are two row functions you can use to do this: upper and lower. They can convert the `first_name` column to uppercase letters or lowercase letters, respectively. Using this strategy, you can write the SQL code:

```
select *
from employees
where upper(first_name) = 'JOHN';
```

A common compromise in an Oracle database is to put most of the data in uppercase and have only a few fields that are exceptions to this. Then people simply remember that most text between quotes should be in uppercase. I am using that compromise in this book.

Task for example 1

Show that the demonstration database distributed with Oracle XE is a case-sensitive database.

Procedure

1. Start Oracle by going to the Database Home Page.

   Start > All Programs > Oracle Database 10g Express Edition
   > Go To Database Home Page

2. Log on as userID `hr`. The password is `hr` if you followed the directions in the "Getting Started Guide" for Oracle Database Express Edition; otherwise the password is whatever you set it to when you unlocked this account.

3. Click the SQL icon, then the SQL Commands icon.

4. Change Display to 200.

5. In the top part of the screen enter:

   select * from employees;

   and click the Run button.

6. Note that the data in the `first_name` and `last_name` columns is mixed case, but the data in the `email` and `job_id` columns is in uppercase. This shows you that this is a case-sensitive database.

Oracle result table 1 (first few rows, shows this table uses mixed case)

EMPLOYEE_ID	FIRST_NAME	LAST_NAME	EMAIL	PHONE_NUMBER	HIRE_DATE	JOB_ID	SALARY
100	Steven	King	SKING	515.123.4567	17-JUN-87	AD_PRES	24000
101	Neena	Kochhar	NKOCHHAR	515.123.4568	21-SEP-89	AD_VP	17000
102	Lex	De Haan	LDEHAAN	515.123.4569	13-JAN-93	AD_VP	17000
103	Alexander	Hunold	AHUNOLD	590.423.4567	03-JAN-90	IT_PROG	9000
104	Bruce	Ernst	BERNST	590.423.4568	21-MAY-91	IT_PROG	6000
105	David	Austin	DAUSTIN	590.423.4569	25-JUN-97	IT_PROG	4800

Task for example 2

Show the problem in dealing with a case-sensitive database.

Oracle SQL: This does not work

Enter this code in the top part of the screen and click the Run button:

```
select *
from employees
where first_name = 'john';
```

Oracle result for example 2: a message

no data found

Task for example 3

Show one method to deal with case sensitivity.

Oracle SQL: Using the case that matches the data

```
select *
from employees
where first_name = 'John';
```

Oracle result table 3

EMPLOYEE_ID	FIRST_NAME	LAST_NAME	EMAIL	PHONE_NUMBER	HIRE_DATE	JOB_ID	SALARY
110	John	Chen	JCHEN	515.124.4269	28-SEP-97	FI_ACCOUNT	8200
139	John	Seo	JSEO	650.121.2019	12-FEB-98	ST_CLERK	2700
145	John	Russell	JRUSSEL	011.44.1344.429268	01-OCT-96	SA_MAN	14000

3 rows returned in 0.17 seconds   CSV Export

Warning

If you use this method, you could often get the wrong results. There are two reasons for this:

- You might not know exactly what case is used in the data.
- The data in the table may be entered in an inconsistent way.

Task for example 4

Show the other method to deal with case sensitivity.

Oracle SQL: Using a row function

```
select *
from employees
where lower(first_name) = 'john';
```

Oracle result table 4

Same as result 3

EMPLOYEE_ID	FIRST_NAME	LAST_NAME	EMAIL	PHONE_NUMBER	HIRE_DATE	JOB_ID	SALARY
110	John	Chen	JCHEN	515.124.4269	28-SEP-97	FI_ACCOUNT	8200
139	John	Seo	JSEO	650.121.2019	12-FEB-98	ST_CLERK	2700
145	John	Russell	JRUSSEL	011.44.1344.429268	01-OCT-96	SA_MAN	14000

3 rows returned in 0.17 seconds   CSV Export

Task for example 5

Show SQL code that uses the common compromise to put all literals in uppercase.

Oracle SQL: A common compromise, using uppercase for most fields

```
select *
from employees
where email = 'SKING';
```

Oracle result table 5

EMPLOYEE_ID	FIRST_NAME	LAST_NAME	EMAIL	PHONE_NUMBER	HIRE_DATE	JOB_ID	SALARY
100	Steven	King	SKING	515.123.4567	17-JUN-87	AD_PRES	24000

1 rows returned in 0.17 seconds   CSV Export

Check your understanding

Add the word "upper" to the following code to make it work regardless of how the name is capitalized in the data.

```
select *
from employees
where last_name = 'de haan';
```

3-10 The debate about case sensitivity in SQL

Actually, there is not much of a debate about case sensitivity in SQL. Rather there are two camps of people. Each camp believes that it is entirely right and everyone else is entirely wrong, so this is more like a religion than a debate. I find I can get along with either group as long as I pretend that I believe the same way they do.

The issue is whether a database should be case sensitive or not. Some people believe that making it non-case-sensitive makes it easier to use and therefore a more useful and reliable tool. Other people believe that case sensitivity is just a fact of life; it is not such a big deal, and everyone should be able to handle it.

The original designers of the SQL language believed that non-case-sensitivity is best. You can still see traces of this in the SQL language itself. For instance, table names and column names are not allowed to be case sensitive. If you already have a table named "employees", you are not allowed to create a new table named "EMPLOYEES", because each table is required to have its own name and these two names are considered to be the same.

3-11 You have a choice

When you use Oracle, you can choose whether you prefer to work with a case-sensitive or a non-case-sensitive database. If you start Oracle by going to the Database Home Page, then you will be operating in a case-sensitive environment.

However, if you prefer to use a non-case-sensitive environment, that is also available to you. Just start Oracle by going to the SQL Command Line.

The next section explains how to turn off case sensitivity in the SQL Command Line environment.

3-12 You can turn off case sensitivity in the Oracle SQL Command Line environment

Some people prefer to use a non-case-sensitive database. This allows them to focus on learning SQL without having an additional nagging concern about uppercase versus lowercase.

Two steps are required to do this. First, the data must be stored in the Oracle database using uppercase letters. In the Oracle database for this book I have already done this. There are no mixed case fields or lowercase fields outside of this chapter. By contrast, the Access data is usually in mixed case.

Second, you can use the SQL*Plus command:

```
set sqlcase upper;
```

SQL*Plus is the environment in which Oracle SQL is run when you start Oracle with the "Run SQL command line" interface. This command causes SQL*Plus to translate every SQL command into uppercase letters. For example, when you enter

```
select * from employees where first_name = 'john';
```

the SQL*Plus environment changes this to

```
SELECT * FROM EMPLOYEES WHERE FIRST_NAME = 'JOHN';
```

before the command is run.

3-13 Case sensitivity in Access

Access deals with the case sensitivity issue in an entirely different way. Access stores data in the database in exactly the way you enter it, using uppercase and lowercase letters. Oracle does this, too. But when Access compares two values to see if they are the same, Access uses a non-case sensitive method of comparing them.

This means that every Access database is non-case-sensitive. When you write SQL code for an Access database, you do not have to worry whether the literal values need to be uppercase or lowercase letters. The case in the literal value does not need to match the case of the data in the database.

Usually in this book I try to show you that Oracle SQL and Access SQL are similar. In this section I am going to do something different because I want to show you that they handle the case sensitivity issue in different ways. I am going to write one SQL statement that does not even involve literals of any sort. You will see that I get one result when I run it in Oracle and a different result when I run it in Access.

Task

Show that Oracle and Access handle case sensitivity in different ways and that this can affect the result of running an SQL statement.

Oracle & Access SQL

```
select *
from sec0313_case_sensitivity
where name1 = name2
order by row_id;
```

Beginning table (sec0313_case_sensitivity table)

```
    ROW_ID NAME1       NAME2
---------- ---------- ----------
         1 john        john
         2 John        John
         3 JOHN        JOHN
         4 john        JOHN
```

Oracle result table

```
    ROW_ID NAME1       NAME2
---------- ---------- ----------
         1 john        john
         2 John        John
         3 JOHN        JOHN
```

Access result table

Notes

Note that these tables are different. The result in Oracle has three rows and the Access result has four rows.

Three-Valued Logic

3-14 SQL uses three-valued logic

Many people know the statement that SQL uses three-valued logic, but some people are not sure what it means. The meaning is very simple. Take any logical statement that you could put in a `where` clause, let's call it A. It could be

`first_name = 'JOHN'`

or

`supplier_id = 'FV' and product_code = 'AS'`

or

many other logical conditions.

The point is we can think that our logical condition is either true or not true for each row of any table.

Actually, that way of thinking is incorrect. That would be correct if there were two alternatives: Either the statement is true or it is false. However, there is a third possibility. It could be unknown, which means that we do not know if it is correct or not. There could be a null in one of the columns we are testing. The term *three-valued logic* refers to this third possibility. It is another way to say that there could be some nulls in the data.

There is also another way to think of this. If you take any table, you can separate its rows into three separate groups. One group will be all the rows where condition A is true. One group will be all the rows where condition A is false. The third group will be all the rows where we do not know whether condition A is true or not.

Task

Show that the logical condition

`"the price increase is greater than 20 cents"`

divides rows of the `1_foods` table into three separate parts:

- The rows where it is a true statement
- The rows where it is a false statement
- The rows where where we do not yet know if the statement is true or false

Oracle & Access SQL

1. Show the rows where the statement is true.

```
select *
from l_foods
where price_increase > 0.20
order by menu_item;
```

2. Show the rows where the statement is false.

```
select *
from l_foods
where not(price_increase > 0.20)
order by menu_item;
```

3. Show the rows where the truth of the statement is unknown.

```
select *
from l_foods
where price_increase is null
order by menu_item;
```

Beginning table (1_foods table)

SUPPLIER ID	PRODUCT CODE	MENU ITEM	DESCRIPTION	PRICE	PRICE INCREASE
ASP	FS	1	FRESH SALAD	$2.00	$0.25
ASP	SP	2	SOUP OF THE DAY	$1.50	(null)
ASP	SW	3	SANDWICH	$3.50	$0.40
CBC	GS	4	GRILLED STEAK	$6.00	$0.70
CBC	SW	5	HAMBURGER	$2.50	$0.30
FRV	BR	6	BROCCOLI	$1.00	$0.05
FRV	FF	7	FRENCH FRIES	$1.50	(null)
JBR	AS	8	SODA	$1.25	$0.25
JBR	VR	9	COFFEE	$0.85	$0.15
VSB	AS	10	DESSERT	$3.00	$0.50

Result table 1 (The rows where the statement is true)

SUPPLIER ID	PRODUCT CODE	MENU ITEM	DESCRIPTION	PRICE	PRICE INCREASE
ASP	FS	1	FRESH SALAD	$2.00	$0.25
ASP	SW	3	SANDWICH	$3.50	$0.40
CBC	GS	4	GRILLED STEAK	$6.00	$0.70
CBC	SW	5	HAMBURGER	$2.50	$0.30
JBR	AS	8	SODA	$1.25	$0.25
VSB	AS	10	DESSERT	$3.00	$0.50

Result table 2 (The rows where the statement is false)

SUPPLIER ID	PRODUCT CODE	MENU ITEM	DESCRIPTION	PRICE	PRICE INCREASE
FRV	BR	6	BROCCOLI	$1.00	$0.05
JBR	VR	9	COFFEE	$0.85	$0.15

Result table 3 (The rows where the truth of the statement is unknown)

SUPPLIER ID	PRODUCT CODE	MENU ITEM	DESCRIPTION	PRICE	PRICE INCREASE
ASP	SP	2	SOUP OF THE DAY	$1.50	(null)
FRV	FF	7	FRENCH FRIES	$1.50	(null)

Error Messages

3-15 Error messages are often wrong

One of the major challenges in dealing with computer software of any type is that the error messages are often wrong. This can drive you crazy at times. The message is usually correct in saying there is an error. There usually is an error of some kind. However, identifying the error and telling you how you can correct it is the part that is often wrong. Many people want to know why.

The short answer is that when the computer encounters an error, it can become genuinely confused. It doesn't have anything to fall back on. It doesn't understand your thinking, motivation, or intent. It does not have an overall understanding of what you are trying to accomplish. It does not even have another level of code to give it some guidance. In short, it was totally dependent on your code and your code did not work.

The best that many error messages can do is point out the location of the error. That can help you guess what might be wrong, but sometimes the error actually occurs before the place that the message indicates. If the error points to the end of your code, then it is not telling you much. As you get more experience with computers, you become better at guessing what the problems could be.

Because I know of this problem with error messages, I am not a big fan of computer systems that try to give you several error messages at a time. I think that if a computer encounters an error it should show you one error message, indicate the location as best it can, and then stop. Most computer software does this today.

I remember the first COBOL program I wrote. COBOL is not used much today, but there are still some programs written in it. In theory, this language would tell you all your errors in one compile. It would not just stop at the first error.

My program was about 20 pages long. The output of my first compile was 50 pages of error messages. That was very shocking and discouraging. However, I sat down determined to go through every one of those messages. I knew that they were all supposed to be valuable information.

When I finished the process of going through all the error messages, I had found one word that was spelled incorrectly and one period that was missing. These problems were indicated in the first two messages. All the other messages were total rubbish because the computer was completely confused before it got to that point

Task

Show the error messages produced by the code:

```
select first_name,
       last_name,
from l_employees;
```

The problem with this code is that there is a comma after `last_name`.

Oracle error message

ORA-00936 missing expression

Access error message

Check your understanding

Start with any `select` statement that works. On purpose, change it so that it does not work anymore. See how well the error messages can tell you what the problem is.

Some Exercises Solved for You

Here are some exercises I have solved for you. The problems might look simple, but they are actually a bit tricky. I chose to solve these exercises because they illustrate many of the fine points in the topics we have already discussed.

3-16 Exercise 1

Task

List the employees who have last names starting with H through P.

Oracle & Access SQL: First attempt — INCORRECT

```
select employee_id,
       first_name,
       last_name
from l_employees
where last_name between 'H' and 'P'
order by employee_id;
```

Beginning table (l_employees table)

EMPLOYEE ID	FIRST_NAME	LAST_NAME	DEPT CODE	HIRE_DATE	CREDIT LIMIT	PHONE NUMBER	MANAGER ID
201	SUSAN	BROWN	EXE	01-JUN-1998	$30.00	3484	(null)
202	JIM	KERN	SAL	16-AUG-1999	$25.00	8722	201
203	MARTHA	WOODS	SHP	02-FEB-2009	$25.00	7591	201
204	ELLEN	OWENS	SAL	01-JUL-2008	$15.00	6830	202
205	HENRY	PERKINS	SAL	01-MAR-2006	$25.00	5286	202
206	CAROL	ROSE	ACT	(null)	(null)	(null)	(null)
207	DAN	SMITH	SHP	01-DEC-2008	$25.00	2259	203
208	FRED	CAMPBELL	SHP	01-APR-2008	$25.00	1752	203
209	PAULA	JACOBS	MKT	17-MAR-1999	$15.00	3357	201
210	NANCY	HOFFMAN	SAL	16-FEB-2007	$25.00	2974	203

Result table ❶

```
EMPLOYEE
      ID FIRST_NAME LAST_NAME
-------- ---------- ----------
     202 JIM        KERN
     204 ELLEN      OWENS
     209 PAULA      JACOBS
     210 NANCY      HOFFMAN
```

Notes

❶ Henry Perkins is not listed in the result table. The problem is that P means "P followed by a space" in this context, and PE comes after P followed by a space.

Oracle SQL: Second attempt — INCORRECT

```
select employee_id,
       first_name,
       last_name
from l_employees
where last_name between 'H' and 'P%' ❷
order by employee_id;
```

Access SQL: Second attempt — INCORRECT

```
select employee_id,
       first_name,
       last_name
from l_employees
where last_name between 'H' and 'P*' ❷
order by employee_id;
```

Result table

```
EMPLOYEE
      ID FIRST_NAME LAST_NAME
-------- ---------- ----------
     202 JIM        KERN
     204 ELLEN      OWENS
     209 PAULA      JACOBS
     210 NANCY      HOFFMAN
```

Notes

❷ Here we are trying to use a wildcard character after the P to mean "P followed by any other character." The code runs, but Henry Perkins is still missing from the result.

Only the `like` condition supports wildcard characters. When these characters are used with the `between` condition, they are considered to be regular characters instead of wildcard characters. So here the percent sign and the asterisk are regular characters. PE comes after P% and P*, so Perkins is not included in the result.

Oracle & Access SQL: Third attempt — CORRECT

```
select employee_id,
       first_name,
       last_name
from l_employees
where last_name between 'H' and 'PZZ' ❸
order by employee_id;
```

Result table

```
EMPLOYEE
      ID FIRST_NAME LAST_NAME
-------- ---------- ----------
     202 JIM        KERN
     204 ELLEN      OWENS
     205 HENRY      PERKINS
     209 PAULA      JACOBS
     210 NANCY      HOFFMAN
```

Notes

❸ This stretches the `between` condition to the end of the Ps. Of course, it assumes there will not be any data between PZZ and Q.

Oracle & Access SQL: Fourth attempt — CORRECT

```
select employee_id,
       first_name,
       last_name
from l_employees
where last_name between 'H' and 'Q' ❹
order by employee_id;
```

Notes

❹ This is another way to stretch the range of the `between` condition to include all words beginning with P. Of course, if someone has Q as their last name, then that row would also be included in the result table. (There is a jazz musician whose last name is Q.)

Access SQL: Fifth attempt — CORRECT

```
select employee_id,
       first_name,
       last_name
from l_employees
where last_name like '[H-P]*'  ❺
order by employee_id;
```

Notes

❺ In this solution we are using the `like` condition instead of the `between` condition. We can do this in Access, but not in Oracle, because Access supports a greater variety of patterns than Oracle does.

Oracle & Access SQL: Sixth attempt — CORRECT (the best solution)

```
select employee_id,
       first_name,
       last_name
from l_employees
where last_name >= 'H'
  and last_name < 'Q'
order by employee_id;
```

3-17 Exercise 2

In the `l_suppliers` table, list the row for Alice & Ray's Restaurant.

Oracle & Access SQL: First attempt — INCORRECT

```
select *
from l_suppliers
where supplier_name = 'ALICE & RAY'S RESTAURANT';  ❶
```

Result — An error message

Oracle & Access SQL: Second attempt — CORRECT

```
select *
from l_suppliers
where supplier_name = 'ALICE & RAY''S RESTAURANT';  ❷
```

Access SQL: Third attempt — CORRECT

```
select *
from l_suppliers
where supplier_name = "ALICE & RAY'S RESTAURANT";  ❸
```

Part of the beginning table (1_suppliers table)

```
SUPPLIER
ID        SUPPLIER_NAME
--------  --------------------------
ARR       ALICE & RAY'S RESTAURANT
ASP       A SOUP PLACE
```

Result table

```
SUPPLIER
ID        SUPPLIER_NAME
--------  --------------------------
ARR       ALICE & RAY'S RESTAURANT
```

Notes

❶ The supplier name contains an apostrophe, which confuses the computer.

❷ Use two consecutive single quotes to code an apostrophe in a text string that is enclosed in single quotes.

❸ In Access, we can enclose a text string in double quotes. When we do this, the apostrophe in the name does not cause a problem.

3-18 Exercise 3

List the employee_id, first_name, last_name, and hire_date of all the employees hired in the year 2008.

Oracle & Access SQL: First attempt — INCORRECT

```
select employee_id,
       first_name,
       last_name,
       hire_date
from l_employees
where hire_date = '2008';        (Oracle) ❶

where hire_date = #2008#;        (Access)
```

Result — An error message

Oracle & Access SQL: Second attempt — CORRECT

```
select employee_id,
       first_name,
       last_name,
       hire_date
from l_employees
where hire_date between '01-JAN-2008'        (Oracle) ❷
                   and '31-DEC-2008';        (Oracle)

where hire_date between #01-JAN-2008#        (Access)
                   and #31-DEC-2008#;        (Access)
```

Beginning table (l_employees table)

EMPLOYEE ID	FIRST_NAME	LAST_NAME	DEPT CODE	HIRE_DATE	CREDIT LIMIT	PHONE NUMBER	MANAGER ID
201	SUSAN	BROWN	EXE	01-JUN-1998	$30.00	3484	(null)
202	JIM	KERN	SAL	16-AUG-1999	$25.00	8722	201
203	MARTHA	WOODS	SHP	02-FEB-2009	$25.00	7591	201
204	ELLEN	OWENS	SAL	01-JUL-2008	$15.00	6830	202
205	HENRY	PERKINS	SAL	01-MAR-2006	$25.00	5286	202
206	CAROL	ROSE	ACT	(null)	(null)	(null)	(null)
207	DAN	SMITH	SHP	01-DEC-2008	$25.00	2259	203
208	FRED	CAMPBELL	SHP	01-APR-2008	$25.00	1752	203
209	PAULA	JACOBS	MKT	17-MAR-1999	$15.00	3357	201
210	NANCY	HOFFMAN	SAL	16-FEB-2007	$25.00	2974	203

Result table

```
EMPLOYEE
      ID FIRST_NAME LAST_NAME   HIRE_DATE
-------- ---------- ----------  ------------
     204 ELLEN      OWENS       01-JUL-2008
     207 DAN        SMITH       01-DEC-2008
     208 FRED       CAMPBELL    01-APR-2008
```

Notes

❶ When we specify a date, we cannot only give the year.

❷ To specify a year, we must say that the date is between January 1 and December 31 of that year.

Oracle SQL: Another solution, using features we have not covered yet

```
select employee_id,
       first_name,
       last_name,
       hire_date
from l_employees
where to_char(hire_date, 'yyyy') = '2008'; ❸
```

Access SQL: Another solution, using features we have not covered yet

```
select employee_id,
       first_name,
       last_name,
       hire_date
from l_employees
where year(hire_date) = 2008; ❹
```

Notes

❸ In Oracle, the to_char function can specify the format of a date. For more details, see section 7-2.

❹ In Access, the year function shows only the year part of a date, and it shows this as an integer. Here the hire_date is 2008, which is an integer and not a date so it is not enclosed within pound signs.

Key Points

- Computers use the words `and`, `or`, and `not` in a precise way that is a little different that the way they are sometimes used in English.

- When you write a `select` statement, you may sometimes want to hardcode some values into the statement you are writing. You can make your code more flexible by using a table of constants instead.

- Punctuation is very important in all computer languages, including SQL.

- Some databases are case sensitive and others are not. You need to know if the database you are using is case sensitive or not.

- SQL uses three-valued logic. This is another way to say that there can be nulls in the data.

- Error messages are not always completely correct. This applies to all computer software.

chapter 4

SAVING YOUR RESULTS

The result table of a query has columns and rows. It is a table and it can be handled like any other table. This chapter shows you how to save the results of a query in a new table and make modifications to the data.

Saving Your Results in a New Table or View

All the queries you have written so far display their results on the screen. After the computer is turned off, the results are gone. This chapter shows how to save the results in a table. Alternatively, they can be saved in a view, which is similar to a table.

To see the data in your table or view, you must use:

```
select * from new_table or view;
```

4-1 Create a new table from the result of a `select` statement

This section shows how to create a new table from the results of a `select` statement. Both Oracle and Access can perform this operation, but they specify it with different syntax. Oracle follows the SQL standard, but Access has created its own nonstandard expression.

You are the owner of the new table and have complete control over it. The new table is private and can only be seen and used by you unless you decide to share it with other people. You can modify the data in this table by adding new rows, changing rows, or deleting rows.

There are two tasks in this section. In the first task we create a new table from a `select` statement. In the second task you create your own copy of an existing table so you can modify it and change its data without affecting the original table.

Description of the process

Begin with any `select` statement. In Oracle, one new line is added before the `select` clause. This line says `create table`, and then gives the name of the new table, followed by the word `as`.

In Access, a new clause is added right after the `select` clause. This clause says `into` followed by the name of the new table. Except for this one change, the original `select` statement does not need to be changed. However, there are some special considerations about the `order by` clause.

In old versions of SQL, you could not include an `order by` clause. If the original `select` statement included this clause, you had to delete it. The reasoning was that the rows of a table are, in theory, an unordered set, so when you created a new table, you were not allowed to specify an order for its rows.

Now this has changed. The newer versions of Oracle and Access do allow you to use an `order by` clause in a `create table` statement. However, in theory, the rows of the table are still an unordered set, which means that the `order by` clause is being ignored. For that reason I do not usually use it in this book.

In both Oracle and Access, I recommend that the name of the new table be a name that is not already used by any other object in the database. Both Oracle and Access allow some exceptions to this rule, but you are inviting confusion and trouble if you have two objects with the same name. Each table must have a unique name. If a name is already being used, you will receive an error message and your SQL statement will not be processed.

In Access, when you create a new table from a `select` statement, you must click the Run button on the Ribbon in the upper left corner of the screen. This might be a little different from your usual procedure to run a query. I often run a query by clicking the View Datasheet button in the bottom right corner of the screen. However, if you click that button the `select` statement will run and you will see the results, but the results will not be saved in a new table.

The Run button you need to click is not always available to you on the Ribbon; that is, it is context sensitive. To see it you need to create a query. To do this you can:

1. Click the Create tab.

2. Click Query Design in the Other group.

3. Close the Show Table window.

4. Click SQL View.

5. Enter a `select` statement SQL query or create it.

The Run button appears within the Results group of the Design tab within the Query Tools context.

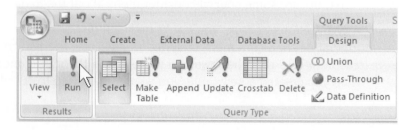

Task: Create a new table from a `select` statement

Save the result table of the following `select` statement. Create a new permanent table. Show how to change a `select` statement so that the result is saved in a new table, instead of being displayed on the screen. Name the new table `sec0401_sales_staff`.

```
select employee_id, ❶
       first_name,
       last_name,
       dept_code
from l_employees
where dept_code = 'SAL'
order by employee_id; ❷
```

Oracle SQL: Modified `select` statement — Save results in a table

```
create table sec0401_sales_staff as ❸
select employee_id,
       first_name,
       last_name,
       dept_code
from l_employees
where dept_code = 'SAL';
```

Access SQL: Modified `select` statement — Save results in a table

```
select employee_id,
       first_name,
       last_name,
       dept_code
into sec0401_sales_staff ❹
from l_employees
where dept_code = 'SAL';
```

Oracle & Access SQL: Show the table you created ❺

```
select *
from sec0401_sales_staff ❻
order by employee_id; ❼
```

Beginning table (1_employees table)

EMPLOYEE ID	FIRST_NAME	LAST_NAME	DEPT CODE	HIRE_DATE	CREDIT LIMIT	PHONE NUMBER	MANAGER ID
201	SUSAN	BROWN	EXE	01-JUN-1998	$30.00	3484	(null)
202	JIM	KERN	SAL	16-AUG-1999	$25.00	8722	201
203	MARTHA	WOODS	SHP	02-FEB-2009	$25.00	7591	201
204	ELLEN	OWENS	SAL	01-JUL-2008	$15.00	6830	202
205	HENRY	PERKINS	SAL	01-MAR-2006	$25.00	5286	202
206	CAROL	ROSE	ACT	(null)	(null)	(null)	(null)
207	DAN	SMITH	SHP	01-DEC-2008	$25.00	2259	203
208	FRED	CAMPBELL	SHP	01-APR-2008	$25.00	1752	203
209	PAULA	JACOBS	MKT	17-MAR-1999	$15.00	3357	201
210	NANCY	HOFFMAN	SAL	16-FEB-2007	$25.00	2974	203

New table (sec0401_sales_staff table)

EMPLOYEE ID	FIRST_NAME	LAST_NAME	DEPT CODE
202	JIM	KERN	SAL
204	ELLEN	OWENS	SAL
205	HENRY	PERKINS	SAL
210	NANCY	HOFFMAN	SAL

Notes

❶ You can begin with any `select` statement.

❷ Removing the `order by` clause is optional. You are allowed to use it when you create a table. However, this is just allowed for convenience in writing the SQL statement. The rows of the table will still be an unordered set. The meaning of the `order by` clause will be ignored.

❸ In Oracle, you add a `create table` clause before the `select` clause.

❹ In Access, you add an `into` clause after the end of the `select` clause and before the `from` clause.

❺ After you create a new table, you can write any `select` statement using the data from the new table. To see the data in the new table you created, you need to use the following:

```
select * from sec0401_sales_staff;
```

❻ The `from` clause here names the new table.

❼ The `order by` clause here does put the rows of the result table in a specific order.

Check your understanding

Create a copy of the `l_employees` table. Name it `sec0401_employees`.

Here is the reason you might want to do this. Later in this chapter you will learn how to change the data in a table. However, you should not make any changes to the data in the `l_employees` table because many of the examples in this book are based on it. If you make a change to the data in this table, the examples in the book might not work correctly.

Instead, you can make a new copy of the table and then you can change the data in the new copy. This allows you to practice changing the data and still keep the `l_employees` table unchanged so it works in all the examples from the book.

4-2 Creating a new view from the results of a `select` statement

This section shows another way to save the results of a query. Here the results are saved in a view rather than a table. A view is very much like a table. The next two sections discuss the similarities and differences between a view and a table, but for now, you can think of a view as a special type of table.

Access uses the term *saved query* instead of the term *view*. However, they both mean the same thing. Standard SQL calls it a view.

After the new view is created, it can be used like a table. It can be used in the `from` clause of any `select` statement. You are the owner of this view and have complete control over it. You are the only person who can use it, unless you decide to share it with other people.

In the previous section I showed you how to create your own personal copy of a table, so in this section you might expect me to show you how to create your own personal copy of a view. However, that is usually not necessary. Just use your own initials at the beginning of the name of the view. That usually gives you all the ownership you need.

Description of the process

Begin with any `select` statement. In Oracle, one new line is added before the `select` clause. This line says `create view`, and then gives the name of the new view, followed by the word `as`.

In Access you use a graphical user interface (GUI) method to create a saved query. After you enter the query, press CTRL + S or click the Save icon near the Microsoft Office button. Then enter the query name in the Save as window. The name of the view, just like the name of a table, must be unique.

In older versions of SQL, the `order by` clause had to be dropped when you created a view. However, the current versions of both Oracle and Access allow you to keep the `order by` clause in the `select` statement that defines the view.

Task

Save the result table of the following `select` statement. Here we are getting a few rows and a few columns from a table. Create a new view from this `select` statement and name it `sec0402_sales_staff_view`.

```
select employee_id, ❶
       first_name,
       last_name,
       dept_code
from 1_employees
where dept_code = 'SAL'
order by employee_id; ❷
```

Oracle SQL:
Modified `select` statement — Save the results in a view

```
create view sec0402_sales_staff_view as ❸
select employee_id,
       first_name,
       last_name,
       dept_code
from 1_employees
where dept_code = 'SAL'
order by employee_id;
```

After you create this view, you can look at it with:

```
select * from sec0402_sales_staff_view; ❹
```

This is not available in Access as an SQL command that runs within the SQL view.

Access GUI method: Save the results in a saved query ❺

Step 1: Enter the `select` statement in the SQL window:

```
select employee_id,
       first_name,
       last_name,
       dept_code
from l_employees
where dept_code = 'SAL'
order by employee_id;
```

Step 2: Run the query by clicking the Run button on the Ribbon or the View Datasheet button. You do this to make sure that the query runs.

Step 3: Save the `select` statement. One way to do this is with CTRL + S.

Step 4: Enter a name for the query in the Save As window, as shown here.

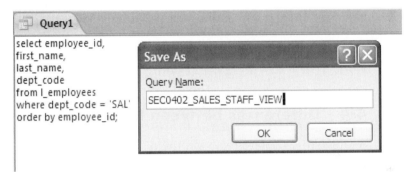

Beginning table and result table — Same as in the previous section

Notes

❶ Begin with any `select` statement.

❷ The `order by` clause is allowed in Oracle and Access.

❸ In Oracle, you add a `create view` clause before the `select` clause.

❹ You can always use a `select *` query to see the view you have created.

❺ Access does not have an SQL command to create a view, at least not on the SQL window level. Instead, it uses a GUI method to create a saved query.

Check your understanding

Create a view of the `l_employees` table. Name it `sec0402_employees_view`.

4-3   Similarities between tables and views

Tables and views are very similar. They look alike. They both are two-dimensional structures that can contain the same types of data. They both have columns, rows, and cells. They can both be used as a source of data in the `from` clause of a `select` statement.

Most of the time there is no need to distinguish between them. Often when I use the word *table* I mean a view or a table. When I want to differentiate a table from a view, I usually call the table a *base table* or a *data table*.

Check your understanding

Show that you can use the table and view created in the previous sections as a source of data for a query. Run these `select` statements:

```
select *
from sec0401_employees;
```

```
select *
from sec0402_employees_view;
```

4-4   Differences between tables and views

A table stores data directly on the disk. A view stores a `select` statement on the disk, but does not store any data. When SQL uses a view in the `from` clause of a query, it runs the `select` statement that defines the view. The result table of this `select` statement is the data of the view. On a basic level, tables store the data that is in a database. A view displays a presentation of the data that is already in the tables.

A table always requires much more disk space than a view. A table can contain thousands or even millions of rows, which can require a substantial amount of disk space. A view needs very little disk space because it is only storing a `select` statement.

A table is static, but a view is dynamic. If you want stability to be sure the data will not change unless you explicitly make changes to it, you should store your data in a table. On the other hand, if you want the latest information that shows all the recent changes to the data in the database, you should use a view.

Whenever you use a view, SQL runs the `select` statement that defines the view. The data is drawn from the underlying tables at that time, so the data in a view can change although no commands have been issued to explicitly change it.

The differences between a table and a view.

Table	View
Stores the data in the database on the disk drive.	Stores the `select` statement that defines the view. It has no data of its own.
Uses a lot of disk space for a large table.	Uses very little disk space.
The data belongs to the table.	The data does not belong to the view. It belongs to the tables used in the `select` statement that defines the view.
The data in a table is stable and does not change by itself.	The data in a view is dynamic and changes when the data in the underlying tables is changed.

Should you use a table or a view?

Use a table when you want to store data that does not exist anywhere else in the database. Use a view when you want to present the data in a new way. The underlying data must already be present in the tables of the database. Also use a view if you want the data to change dynamically as other people make changes to the tables in the database.

4-5   Deleting a table

Now that you know how to create new tables, you also need to know how to delete them. Otherwise, you will eventually have more of them than you want.

In both Oracle and Access, you can delete a table with the SQL command `drop table`, followed by the name of the table. This gets rid of the table entirely. It deletes the data in the table, the table structure, and the definitions of the columns. The name of the table is no longer reserved.

Task

Delete the table named `sec0405_sales_staff`.

Oracle & Access SQL

```
drop table sec0405_sales_staff;
```

Access GUI method alternative

In Access, you can also use a GUI method to delete a table.

Step 1: Click the Tables tab.

Step 2: Highlight the name of the table, as shown here.

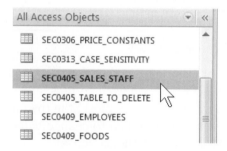

Step 3: Press the Delete key.

Beginning table (`sec0405_sales_staff` table)

```
EMPLOYEE                        DEPT
      ID FIRST_NAME LAST_NAME   CODE
-------- ---------- ----------  ----
     202 JIM        KERN        SAL
     204 ELLEN      OWENS       SAL
     205 HENRY      PERKINS     SAL
     210 NANCY      HOFFMAN     SAL
```

Result — No table

Check your understanding

Delete the table `sec0405_table_to_delete`.

4-6 Deleting a view

In Oracle, there is an SQL command to delete a view. In Access, you must use a GUI method. Except for this difference, deleting a view is like deleting a table.

Task

Delete the view named sec0406_sales_staff_view.

Oracle SQL

```
drop view sec0406_sales_staff_view;
```

Access GUI method

Step 1: Highlight the name of the saved query, as shown here.

Step 2: Press the Delete key.

Beginning view (sec0406_sales_staff_view)

```
EMPLOYEE                          DEPT
      ID FIRST_NAME  LAST_NAME    CODE
-------- ----------  ----------   ----
     202 JIM         KERN         SAL
     204 ELLEN       OWENS        SAL
     205 HENRY       PERKINS      SAL
     210 NANCY       HOFFMAN      SAL
```

Result — No view

Check your understanding

Delete the view sec0406_view_to_delete.

4-7   One view can be built on top of another view

A view can be defined from another view. This is similar to defining a view from a base table. In the `select` statement that defines a view, the `from` clause can name either a base table or another view.

Why would you want to do this? Why not just define each view directly from base tables? There are two reasons. One reason is to control complexity. A very complex query can often be replaced by a series of simple queries built on top of each other. This produces code that is easier for people to understand. The code can be verified and debugged more easily, and it is more likely to be correct.

The other reason is to coordinate two parts of a computer application. This can tie the parts together, so that if one part is changed, the other part is changed automatically to maintain a specific relationship with the first part.

An important feature of views is that they run automatically. If a higher level view is used in the `from` clause of a `select` statement, then all the views it depends on are also run. This can be quite a lot of processing. The important point is that you do not need to run the lower level views yourself. SQL takes care of this for you.

There are layers of views

Circular definitions are not allowed in views. When one view is built from another view, care must be taken to ensure that there are no *circles* in the definition. A circle would occur if `view_1` is defined, directly or indirectly, from `view_2` and `view_2` is defined, directly or indirectly, from `view_1`. The computer must always be able to find the base tables for every view. It could not do this if circles were allowed in the definitions.

Because of this, the views can be thought of as being organized into layers. Views built directly from base tables are the first layer, views built from these are the second layer, and so on.

What happens when an underlying base table or view is deleted?

In some SQL products, if you delete a base table or a view, all the other views that are built on top of that table or view are also deleted. This is a cascaded delete. Dropping any base table or view can automatically trigger the dropping of many other views. In this situation, you must be very cautious before you drop any base table or view.

In other SQL products, including Oracle and Access, the higher level views are inactivated, but they are not entirely deleted. This means that the definition of the higher level view is retained even though it does not work currently. If, at a later time, the base table or lower level view is restored, the higher level view will work again.

An example of building one view on top of another view

In this section I build two views. The first view, sec0407_sales_staff_view1, is built directly on the 1_employees table. The second view, sec0407_sales_staff_view2, is built on top of the first view. I want to keep this example clear and simple, so I am trying to avoid any unnecessary complexity. That is why this example does not show the level of complexity being reduced.

In this example, the sec0407_sales_staff_view2 view could have been defined directly from the 1_employees table. This view is so simple that there is no particular reason to define it in two steps, except to show the technique of building one view from another view.

Now let's return to the discussion of the effects of deleting one of these objects. If the 1_employees table is deleted, both of the views would be disabled until a new table or view named 1_employees is built again. If sec0407_sales_staff_view1 is deleted, only sec0407_sales_staff_view2 would be disabled. If sec0407_sales_staff_view2 is deleted, this would have no effect on either the table or the other view.

Task

Create a view, named sec0407_sales_staff_view1, that lists the employees in the sales department. Show the following columns: employee_id, first_name, last_name, and dept_code.

Then create another view, named sec0407_sales_staff_view2, from the first view. Use all the rows from the sec0407_sales_staff_view1, except the ones with employee_id greater than 208. Use all the columns from the sec0407_sales_staff_view1 except dept_code.

Oracle SQL: Step 1 — Create the first view from a base table ❶

```
create view sec0407_sales_staff_view1 as
select employee_id,
       first_name,
       last_name,
       dept_code
from l_employees
where dept_code = 'SAL';
```

Access GUI method: Step 1 — Create the first view from a base table ❶

Step 1, Part 1: Enter this query in the SQL window:

```
select employee_id,
       first_name,
       last_name,
       dept_code
from l_employees
where dept_code = 'sal';
```

Step 1, Part 2: Save the query. Name it sec0407_sales_staff_view1.

Result of Step 1 — sec0407_sales_staff_view1

```
EMPLOYEE                       DEPT
      ID FIRST_NAME LAST_NAME  CODE
-------- ---------- ---------- ----
     202 JIM        KERN       SAL
     204 ELLEN      OWENS      SAL
     205 HENRY      PERKINS    SAL
     210 NANCY      HOFFMAN    SAL
```

Oracle SQL: Step 2 — Create a second view from the first one ❷

```
create view sec0407_sales_staff_view2 as
select employee_id,
       first_name,
       last_name
from sec0407_sales_staff_view1 ❸
where employee_id <= 208;
```

Access GUI method: Step 2 — Create a second view from the first one ❷

Step 2, Part 1: Enter this query in the SQL window:

```
select employee_id,
       first_name,
       last_name
from sec0407_sales_staff_view1 ❸
where employee_id <= 208;
```

Step 2, Part 2: Save the query. Name it sec0407_sales_staff_view2.

Result of Step 2 — sec0407_sales_staff_view2

```
EMPLOYEE
      ID FIRST_NAME LAST_NAME
-------- ---------- ----------
     202 JIM        KERN
     204 ELLEN      OWENS
     205 HENRY      PERKINS
```

Notes

❶ This shows how the view sec0407_sales_staff_view1 is created. In the select statement that defines this view, the from clause refers to a base table, 1_employees.

❷ This shows how the view sec0407_sales_staff_view2 is created. It is built on top of the view sec0407_sales_staff_view1.

❸ The from clause refers to the first view, sec0407_sales_staff_view1, rather than to a base table.

4-8   Preventative delete

A *preventative delete* drops the previous version of a table or view before it creates the new version. This ensures that the name will be available within the database for the new table or view you want to create. People use this coding technique when they are in the process of developing new code, and they need to try several versions before they get it correct. Preventative deletes are also used to ensure that the following create table or create view statement will run without the error of the name being unavailable.

It is called a preventative delete because it prevents an error from occurring. Often, we do not expect that anything will actually be deleted. There may be no such object to delete. The delete is done to prevent a possible problem.

A preventative delete can be used in Oracle. In Access you could follow the same procedure, but you would have to do it manually as a two-step process. This would not save you any work, so usually it is not done.

Coding a preventative delete

For tables, a preventative delete can be coded by putting a `drop table` statement before a `create table` statement. In Oracle this is usually done within a script file, where several commands are run as a single unit. If the object does not currently exist, the `drop` command will fail and issue an error message. However, the Oracle script will continue to run.

For views, Oracle has a special option to support preventative deletes. You can say `create or replace view`, instead of `create view`. This is not part of standard SQL. It is an extension to the standard that is special to Oracle. Oracle does not have a similar feature for tables. This is probably because it would be too "dangerous" to encourage the use of preventative deletes with tables.

In Access, you get a warning message if the table or view already exists. You are given the option to replace the previous object. This makes preventative deletes less important in Access than they are in Oracle

Task

Show how to code a preventative delete. List all the columns of the `1_employees` table.

Oracle SQL: A preventative delete for a table

```
drop table sec0408_sales_staff;   ❶
create table sec0408_sales_staff as
select *
from 1_employees
where dept_code = 'SAL';
```

Access issues a warning message if you try to use the same name twice in the database.

Oracle SQL: Method 1 — A preventative delete for a view

```
drop view sec0408_sales_staff_view;   ❷
create view sec0408_sales_staff_view as
select *
from 1_employees
where dept_code = 'SAL';
```

Oracle SQL: Method 2 — A preventative delete for a view

```
create or replace view sec0408_sales_staff_view as  ❸
select *
from l_employees
where dept_code = 'SAL';
```

This feature is not available in Access.

Notes

❶ This `drop table` statement is a preventative delete. It is placed directly before the table is created.

❷ This `drop view` statement is a preventative delete.

❸ `Create or replace view` is a special feature available in Oracle.

Modifying the Data in a Table with SQL

After you have created a new table, you may want to put some rows of data in it. For tables that already contain data, you may want to add new rows, change the data in a few columns of an existing row, or delete some rows entirely. This section shows you how to do these things.

4-9   Adding one new row to a table

This section shows how to add a single new row to a table. There are two methods to do this. Both are versions of the `insert` statement, and begin with `insert into` followed by the name of the table. They both have the word `values` followed by a list of values in parentheses. The value put into any column must always match the datatype of that column: text, number, or date.

Method 1 specifies a value for each column of the table. The list of values must contain an entry for every column of the table and be listed in the same order as the columns of the table. The columns of a table always have a specific order. The information in the table is not affected by the order of the columns. However, the order of the columns does affect the syntax of some SQL statements, such as this one.

If you want to put a null in a column using this method, you must code the value `null` without quotes. SQL does not allow you to code two commas in a row to produce a null.

Method 2 puts values in only some of the columns of the table. These columns are listed after the name of the table in the SQL command. Nulls are placed in all the columns that are not listed. The list of values must contain an entry for each column in the list. The values must be listed in the same order as the columns.

When you use this method, you must include every column of the primary key in the list of columns. Otherwise, nulls would be entered in the columns of the primary key, which is not allowed. You receive an error message if you forget to list any of the columns of the primary key.

Method 2 is the standard in many shops. It is more specific even if it is a little more trouble to write. If a new column is added to a table, code written using the first method will no longer work, but code written using the second method will run.

Task

Add two new rows to the sec0409_foods table. Show the two methods of adding a single row.

Oracle & Access SQL:
Method 1 — Putting data in all the columns

```
insert into sec0409_foods ❶
values ('ARR', 'AP', 11, 'APPLE PIE', 1.50, null); ❷
```

Oracle & Access SQL:
Method 2 — Putting data in only some columns

```
insert into sec0409_foods
(product_code, description, supplier_id, price) ❸
values ('BP', 'BLUEBERRY PIE', 'ARR', 1.60); ❹
```

Table before the changes (`sec0409_foods` table)

SUPPLIER ID	PRODUCT CODE	MENU ITEM	DESCRIPTION	PRICE	PRICE INCREASE
ASP	FS	1	FRESH SALAD	$2.00	$0.25
ASP	SP	2	SOUP OF THE DAY	$1.50	(null)
ASP	SW	3	SANDWICH	$3.50	$0.40
CBC	GS	4	GRILLED STEAK	$6.00	$0.70
CBC	SW	5	HAMBURGER	$2.50	$0.30
FRV	BR	6	BROCCOLI	$1.00	$0.05
FRV	FF	7	FRENCH FRIES	$1.50	(null)
JBR	AS	8	SODA	$1.25	$0.25
JBR	VR	9	COFFEE	$0.85	$0.15
VSB	AS	10	DESSERT	$3.00	$0.50

Table after the changes

SUPPLIER ID	PRODUCT CODE	MENU ITEM	DESCRIPTION	PRICE	PRICE INCREASE	
ASP	FS	1	FRESH SALAD	$2.00	$0.25	
ASP	SP	2	SOUP OF THE DAY	$1.50	(null)	
ASP	SW	3	SANDWICH	$3.50	$0.40	
CBC	GS	4	GRILLED STEAK	$6.00	$0.70	
CBC	SW	5	HAMBURGER	$2.50	$0.30	
FRV	BR	6	BROCCOLI	$1.00	$0.05	
FRV	FF	7	FRENCH FRIES	$1.50	(null)	
JBR	AS	8	SODA	$1.25	$0.25	
JBR	VR	9	COFFEE	$0.85	$0.15	
VSB	AS	10	DESSERT	$3.00	$0.50	
ARR	AP	11	APPLE PIE	$1.50	(null)	❺
ARR	BP	(null)	BLUEBERRY PIE	$1.60	(null)	❻

Notes

❶ There is no list of columns following the table name. This means that values will be entered in all the columns of the table.

❷ A value is given for every column of the table. The last column contains a null, and this must be coded as `null` without quotes.

❸ The four columns listed after the table name are the only columns in which data can be entered. All other columns will be null.

❹ The values must be listed in the same order as the columns are listed in ❸. If any of these columns is null, the word `null`, without quotes, must be coded in the list of values.

❺ The first `insert` statement, using method 1, added this row.

❻ The second `insert` statement, using method 2, added this row.

Warning: Text fields may be silently truncated

Text is sometimes truncated by the `insert` statement. For example, if you try to put a 20-character text string into a 5-character field, only the first 5 characters are kept. The remaining 15 characters are thrown away.

Worse, when this happens, there is no warning message to tell you it happened. There is no message at all! So you might only find out when you see that some of your data is missing.

Each text field is limited to some maximum length. This limitation may not be obvious to you, but it is always present behind the scenes.

Check your understanding

Add a new row to the `sec0409_employees` table. Use the data:

```
employee_id = 301
first_name = Ellen
last_name = Perkins
dept_code = IT
hire_date = March 9, 2009
credit_limit = $20.00
phone_number = null
manager_id = 201
```

4-10 Adding many new rows to a table

This section shows you how to add several new rows to a table using a `select` statement. This can only be done when the data is already in the database in some form. You cannot enter data that is completely new using this method.

This is another variation on the command to enter a single row of data. The format of the SQL statement is as follows:

Method 1

```
INSERT INTO table_name
select_statement;
```

Method 2

```
INSERT INTO table_name (list_of_columns)
select_statement;
```

It is best to write the `select` statement that creates the new rows without an `order by` clause. If it does contain an `order by` clause, the statement will still run, but the ordering will be ignored.

The result table from the `select` statement must have the correct number of columns, in the correct order, and those columns must have the correct datatypes. It is as if each row of the result table provides a list of values to be inserted into the table (see section 4-9).

Task

In the `sec0410_foods` table, duplicate all the rows from supplier ASP and change the supplier to ARR. Put nulls in the `price` and `price_increase` columns of the new rows.

You might do this if you are unhappy with supplier ASP and you are now going to get all those products from supplier ARR. This task would be the first step. The next step would be to delete all the rows for supplier ASP.

So that you can run both versions of this code, method 1 and method 2 use two different copies of the `1_foods` table.

Oracle SQL: Method 1 — Putting data in all the columns

```
insert into sec0410_foods ❶
select 'ARR', ❷
       product_code,
       menu_item,
       description,
       null,
       null
from sec0410_foods ❸
where supplier_id = 'ASP'; ❹ ❺
```

Access does not support this syntax. Use method 2 instead.

Oracle & Access SQL: Method 2 — Putting data in only some columns

```
insert into sec0410a_foods
(supplier_id, product_code, menu_item, description) ❻
select 'ARR', ❼
       product_code,
       menu_item,
       description
from sec0410_foods
where supplier_id = 'ASP';
```

Table sec0410_foods and sec0410a_foods after the changes

```
SUPPLIER PRODUCT    MENU                                     PRICE
ID       CODE       ITEM DESCRIPTION              PRICE   INCREASE
-------- -------    ------- --------------------  -------- --------
ASP      FS              1 FRESH  SALAD            $2.00    $0.25
ASP      SP              2 SOUP  OF  THE  DAY      $1.50   (null)
ASP      SW              3 SANDWICH                $3.50    $0.40
CBC      GS              4 GRILLED  STEAK          $6.00    $0.70
CBC      HB              5 HAMBURGER               $2.50    $0.30
FRV      BR              6 BROCCOLI                $1.00    $0.05
FRV      FF              7 FRENCH  FRIES           $1.50   (null)
JBR      AS              8 SODA                    $1.25    $0.25
JBR      VR              9 COFFEE                  $0.85    $0.15
VSB      AS             10 DESSERT                 $3.00    $0.50
ARR      FS              1 FRESH  SALAD           (null)   (null)    ❽
ARR      SP              2 SOUP  OF  THE  DAY     (null)   (null)    ❽
ARR      SW              3 SANDWICH               (null)   (null)    ❽
```

Notes

❶ The sec0410_foods table will receive the new rows of data. Because no columns are listed after the table name, the select statement must create a value for every column of the table.

❷ There are six columns in the table receiving the data, so there must be six columns listed in the select clause. Note that the last two columns are explicitly coded as the word null, without quotes. The 'ARR' is a literal that is hard-coded into this select statement. Here it sets the supplier_id column to the value ARR in all the new rows of the result table.

❸ The data will be retrieved from the sec0410_foods table. This is the same table that is receiving the new rows of data. This is an unusual situation, but it works without any problems.

❹ The where clause limits the data that is taken from the table named in the from clause in ❸.

❺ The select statement does not contain an order by clause.

❻ A list of columns follows the name of the table receiving the data. Only these columns can receive data. All the other columns will be null.

❼ Four columns are listed after the table name in ❻, so the select clause must contain four columns in the same order.

❽ These three rows have been added to the table by a single insert statement. Either the method 1 or the method 2 SQL statement can add all three of these rows.

Check your understanding

Tables sec0410_data2 and sec0410_data1 have the same record structure. Each row has three columns: a number column, a text column, and a date column. Write an insert statement that puts all the rows of table sec0410_data2 into table sec0410_data1.

4-11 Changing data in the rows already in a table

This section shows you how to change data in rows that are already in the table. You can modify the values in one column or several columns. Usually, the data in only a few columns is modified at a time. If you want to modify the data in all the columns, it might be easier to add a new row to the table and delete the old row.

The format of the SQL statement is as follows:

```
UPDATE table_name
SET column_1 = value_1,
    column_2 = value_2
WHERE condition;
```

The values of any number of columns can be changed in one statement.

The syntax here is easier to read and work with than in the insert command. The name of the column is aligned with its value. You do not need to correlate two separate lists. However, this comes at a price. The names of the columns must be explicitly stated in each update statement.

The value can be a fixed value, a function, an expression, or even a subquery. In later chapters we discuss row functions and subqueries in detail.

Some people would call the functions in this example *expressions* because of the form in which they are written, with the plus sign in the middle, like "price + .10". They would call it a function if the plus sign were written first, like "+(price, .10)". I do not find this distinction to be very significant and I call them both functions.

The where clause is critical, because it indicates which rows of the table should be changed. Without it, all the rows of the table are changed. Data is changed only in the rows that satisfy the where condition. Other rows remain unchanged.

If you want to change the data in a single row, it is best to specify the values of the primary key columns in the where clause.

Task

In the sec0411_foods table, add 10 cents to both the price and the price increases for all the foods supplied by JBR and FRV.

Oracle & Access SQL

```
update sec0411_foods ❶
set price = price + 0.10, ❷
    price_increase = price_increase + 0.10 ❸
where supplier_id in ('JBR', 'FRV'); ❹
```

Table before the changes (sec0411_foods table)

SUPPLIER ID	PRODUCT CODE	MENU ITEM	DESCRIPTION	PRICE	PRICE INCREASE
ASP	FS	1	FRESH SALAD	$2.00	$0.25
ASP	SP	2	SOUP OF THE DAY	$1.50	(null)
ASP	SW	3	SANDWICH	$3.50	$0.40
CBC	GS	4	GRILLED STEAK	$6.00	$0.70
CBC	SW	5	HAMBURGER	$2.50	$0.30
FRV	BR	6	BROCCOLI	$1.00	$0.05
FRV	FF	7	FRENCH FRIES	$1.50	(null)
JBR	AS	8	SODA	$1.25	$0.25
JBR	VR	9	COFFEE	$0.85	$0.15
VSB	AS	10	DESSERT	$3.00	$0.50

Table sec0411_foods after the changes

SUPPLIER ID	PRODUCT CODE	MENU ITEM	DESCRIPTION	PRICE	PRICE INCREASE	
ASP	FS	1	FRESH SALAD	$2.00	$0.25	
ASP	SP	2	SOUP OF THE DAY	$1.50	(null)	
ASP	SW	3	SANDWICH	$3.50	$0.40	
CBC	GS	4	GRILLED STEAK	$6.00	$0.70	
CBC	SW	5	HAMBURGER	$2.50	$0.30	
FRV	BR	6	BROCCOLI	$1.10	$0.15	❹
FRV	FF	7	FRENCH FRIES	$1.60	(null)	❹❺
JBR	AS	8	SODA	$1.35	$0.35	❹
JBR	VR	9	COFFEE	$0.95	$0.25	❹
VSB	AS	10	DESSERT	$3.00	$0.50	

Notes

❶ The data will be changed in the `sec0411_foods` table.

❷ Ten cents is added to the `price` column, then the result is placed back in the `price` column. The comma at the end of the line shows that there is another column with a value that will be changed.

❸ Ten cents is added to the `price_increase` column, then the result is placed in the `price_increase` column. Because there is no comma at the end of this line, there are no more columns being changed. Also note that there is no `from` clause.

❹ The `where` clause limits the rows that are changed. There are only four rows that satisfy the following condition:

```
supplier_id in ('JBR', 'FRV')
```

These are the only rows that are changed.

❺ The price increase value is null in the result table because it is null in the beginning table.

Check your understanding

In the `sec0411_employees` table, change the credit limit to $27.00 for all the employees who currently have a credit limit of $15.00 and also for any employee who has a null in the credit limit field.

4-12 Deleting rows from a table

This section shows how to delete rows from a table. You can delete one row or several rows. The SQL statement format is as follows:

```
DELETE FROM table_name
WHERE condition;
```

The `where` condition is critical here, as in the `update` statement. Without it, all the rows of the table are deleted. The table structure remains and the table itself still exists, but it has no data in it.

The `where` clause controls which rows are deleted. It sets a condition that can be like any of the ones we used in the `where` clause of a `select` statement. All the rows for which the condition is true are deleted.

Task

Delete all the rows with `supplier_id` values of `cbc` and `jbr` from the `sec0412_foods` table.

Oracle & Access SQL

```
delete from sec0412_foods ❶
where supplier_id in ('CBC', 'JBR'); ❷
```

Table before the changes (sec0412_foods table)

SUPPLIER ID	PRODUCT CODE	MENU ITEM	DESCRIPTION	PRICE	PRICE INCREASE	
ASP	FS	1	FRESH SALAD	$2.00	$0.25	
ASP	SP	2	SOUP OF THE DAY	$1.50	(null)	
ASP	SW	3	SANDWICH	$3.50	$0.40	
CBC	GS	4	GRILLED STEAK	$6.00	$0.70	❸
CBC	SW	5	HAMBURGER	$2.50	$0.30	❸
FRV	BR	6	BROCCOLI	$1.00	$0.05	
FRV	FF	7	FRENCH FRIES	$1.50	(null)	
JBR	AS	8	SODA	$1.25	$0.25	❸
JBR	VR	9	COFFEE	$0.85	$0.15	❸
VSB	AS	10	DESSERT	$3.00	$0.50	

Table after the changes

SUPPLIER ID	PRODUCT CODE	MENU ITEM	DESCRIPTION	PRICE	PRICE INCREASE
ASP	FS	1	FRESH SALAD	$2.00	$0.25
ASP	SP	2	SOUP OF THE DAY	$1.50	(null)
ASP	SW	3	SANDWICH	$3.50	$0.40
FRV	BR	6	BROCCOLI	$1.00	$0.05
FRV	FF	7	FRENCH FRIES	$1.50	(null)
VSB	AS	10	DESSERT	$3.00	$0.50

Notes

❶ Rows of data will be deleted from the sec0412_foods table.

❷ Delete all the rows where the supplier_id value is cbc or jbr.

❸ These rows will be deleted.

Check your understanding

In the sec0412_employees table, delete the rows with employee_id between 202 and 205.

Modifying the Data in a Table with the GUI

Both Oracle and Access allow you to use the GUI to change the data in a table. This is often more convenient than using SQL commands. It can feel more immediate and more direct, as if there is less of a barrier between you and the data.

However, this convenience comes at a price. It works best when you are the only person using the database and you do not need an audit trail for the changes you are making to the data. Probably you are in that situation right now, while you are reading this book.

Part of the price is that the Oracle GUI is different than the Access GUI, so that the skills you develop in one product do not immediately carry over to working with the other product. Also some SQL products do not offer this function through a GUI at all.

Another problem occurs when you are sharing the database with many other people. The GUI might not handle potential conflicts as well as the SQL commands would handle them. These conflicts could occur if you are trying to change a row at the same time that another person is changing it.

You cannot use the GUI if you are using another programming language, such as Java, to access the database. Program interfaces to the database generally use the SQL commands: `insert`, `update`, and `delete`.

Also the GUI will not give you an audit trail of your changes. If you need an audit trail, one of the best methods is to create a file of your changes using an editor such as Notepad. That file can then be used to make the actual changes to the database and if you save the file, it can act as your audit trail.

To sum up, you should use SQL commands, not the GUI, to make changes to the data in the following circumstances:

- Many people are using the database at the same time.

- You are using a program interface to access the database.

- You need an audit trail of your changes.

4-13 Using the Oracle GUI to change data in a table

In the Oracle GUI you can use the Object Browser to change the data in a table. Click the arrow on the right side of the Object Browser icon, then select:

Browse > Tables

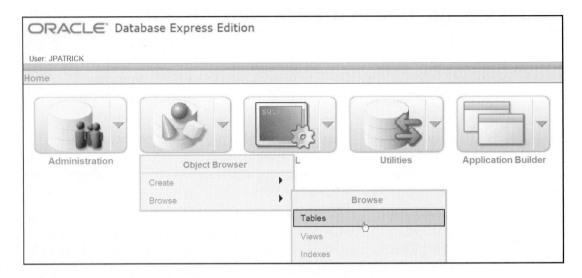

Then select the table and click Data.

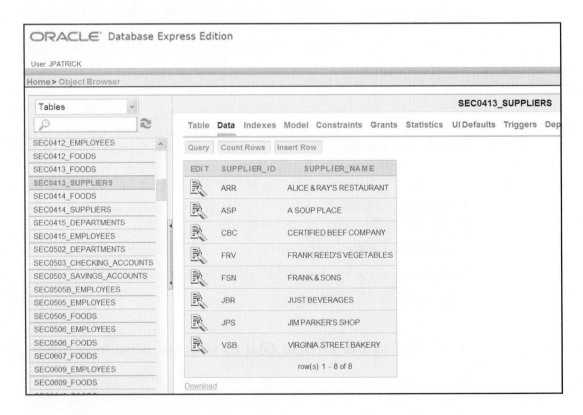

Task

Use the `sec0413_suppliers` table to show how the Oracle GUI can:

- Add a new row to the table.
- Change the data in some fields within a row already in the table.
- Delete a row from the table.

Adding a new row

To add a new row to the table, click the Insert Row button. You will get a new screen that shows you all the fields of the row and gives you a space to enter the new data.

To add this one row, click the Create button. To add additional rows after this one, click the Create and Create Another button.

Changing the data in a row already in the table

To change the value of a field within a row already in the table, click the Edit icon on the left of the row you want to change. This opens a new screen that shows you all the fields of that row. Then you can enter new values in any of the fields you want to change.

When you have entered all your changes, press the Apply Changes button to change the data in the row.

Deleting a row

To delete a row of data, click the Edit icon on the left of the row you want to delete. This opens a new screen that shows you all the fields of that row. Then click the Delete button.

Check your understanding

Use the Oracle GUI to change the following data in the sec0413_foods table:

- Add a new row to the table for "Irish stew" or one of your favorite foods.

- Change "broccoli" to "peas".

- Delete the row for the food you like the least.

4-14 Using the Access GUI to change the data in a table

In the Access GUI you essentially type your changes into the table as if it were a Word document. This gives a very direct experience of being in control of the data, without any extra buttons to push or other complexities of the interface.

To select a table to change, double-click the name of the table in the Navigation Bar.

Task

Use the `sec0414_suppliers` table to show how the Access GUI can:

- Add a new row to the table.
- Change the data in some fields within a row already in the table.
- Delete a row from the table.

Beginning table (`sec0414_suppliers` table)

SUPPLIER_ID	SUPPLIER_NAME	Add New Field
Arr	Alice & Ray's Restaurant	
Asp	A Soup Place	
Cbc	Certified Beef Company	
Frv	Frank Reed's Vegetables	
Fsn	Frank & Sons	
Jbr	Just Beverages	
Jps	Jim Parker's Shop	
Vsb	Virginia Street Bakery	
*		

Adding a new row

To add a new row to the table, type the data into the blank row at the bottom of the table — the one with the asterisk beside it. As soon as you start to enter data in the new row, the icon of the row you are entering changes to a pencil to show that this is the row that is being written at this moment.

As soon as you start to enter data into one new row, another new row is added to the bottom of the table with an asterisk for an icon. This gives you a place to add another row if you wish to do so.

SUPPLIER_ID	SUPPLIER_NAME	Add New Field
Arr	Alice & Ray's Restaurant	
Asp	A Soup Place	
Cbc	Certified Beef Company	
Frv	Frank Reed's Vegetables	
Fsn	Frank & Sons	
Jbr	Just Beverages	
Jps	Jim Parker's Shop	
Vsb	Virginia Street Bakery	
NEW	NEW SUPPLIER	
*		

Changing the data in a row already in the table

To change data in rows already in the table, type over the value that is there.

SUPPLIER_ID	SUPPLIER_NAME	Add New Field
Arr	Alice & Ray's Restaurant	
Asp	A Soup Place	
Cbc	CHANGED NAME	
Frv	Frank Reed's Vegetables	
Fsn	Frank & Sons	
Jbr	Just Beverages	
Jps	Jim Parker's Shop	
Vsb	Virginia Street Bakery	

SEC0414_SUPPLIERS

Deleting a row

To delete a row of data, highlight the row by clicking on the left margin, then press the Delete key.

SUPPLIER_ID	SUPPLIER_NAME	Add New Field
Arr	Alice & Ray's Restaurant	
Asp	A Soup Place	
Cbc	Certified Beef Company	
Frv	Frank Reed's Vegetables	
Fsn	Frank & Sons	
Jbr	Just Beverages	
Jps	Jim Parker's Shop	
Vsb	Virginia Street Bakery	

SEC0414_SUPPLIERS

Check your understanding

Use the Access GUI to change the following data in the sec0414_foods table:

- Add a new row to the table for "Irish stew" or one of your favorite foods.

- Change "broccoli" to "peas".

- Delete the row for the food you like the least.

Restrictions on Modifying the Data in a Table

4-15 Constraints with `insert`, `update`, and `delete`

Sometimes you can enter a perfectly correct `insert`, `update`, or `delete` statement and it will not work. Instead, you will get an error message. Many tables have restrictions on what data can be put into them. These restrictions are called **constraints**. We discuss them further in chapter 8.

If you try to modify the data in a table in a way that the constraints do not allow, you will get an error message but the data will not be changed.

For instance, suppose you want to change the data in a table that has a primary key. The primary key is a type of constraint. It does not allow nulls in any of the columns that are part of the primary key. Also, no two rows can have the same values in all the columns of the primary key. You will receive an error message if you try to put data in the table that violates these constraints.

Task

Show an `update` statement that is valid when it is applied to one table, but gives an error when it is applied to another similar table because of a constraint on the second table.

The `1_employees` table has a constraint that each person must have a different phone number. If you try to change a phone number in some row and that number is already being used by another person, you will not be allowed to make the change.

The `sec0415_employees` table is similar to the `1_employees` table. It has all the same columns, all the same rows, and all the same data, but it does not have any constraint on the phone number column.

Show an `update` statement that changes the phone number for Jim Kern to be the same as the phone number for Susan Brown. Show that this `update` statement works when it is applied to the `sec0415_employees` table. Show that this same `update` statement gives an error when it is applied to the `1_employees` table.

Oracle & Access SQL: This works

```
update sec0415_employees
set phone_number = '3484'
where employee_id = 202;
```

Oracle & Access SQL: This gives an error because it violates a constraint

```
update l_employees
set phone_number = '3484'
where employee_id = 202;
```

Beginning table (`sec0415_employees` table and `l_employees` table)

EMPLOYEE ID	FIRST_NAME	LAST_NAME	DEPT CODE	HIRE_DATE	CREDIT LIMIT	PHONE NUMBER	MANAGER ID
201	SUSAN	BROWN	EXE	01-JUN-1998	$30.00	3484	(null)
202	JIM	KERN	SAL	16-AUG-1999	$25.00	8722	201
203	MARTHA	WOODS	SHP	02-FEB-2009	$25.00	7591	201
204	ELLEN	OWENS	SAL	01-JUL-2008	$15.00	6830	202
205	HENRY	PERKINS	SAL	01-MAR-2006	$25.00	5286	202
206	CAROL	ROSE	ACT	(null)	(null)	(null)	(null)
207	DAN	SMITH	SHP	01-DEC-2008	$25.00	2259	203
208	FRED	CAMPBELL	SHP	01-APR-2008	$25.00	1752	203
209	PAULA	JACOBS	MKT	17-MAR-1999	$15.00	3357	201
210	NANCY	HOFFMAN	SAL	16-FEB-2007	$25.00	2974	203

Result after the `update` statement is applied to the `sec0415_employees` table

EMPLOYEE ID	FIRST_NAME	LAST_NAME	DEPT CODE	HIRE_DATE	CREDIT LIMIT	PHONE NUMBER	MANAGER ID
201	SUSAN	BROWN	EXE	01-JUN-1998	$30.00	3484	(null)
202	JIM	KERN	SAL	16-AUG-1999	$25.00	3484	201
203	MARTHA	WOODS	SHP	02-FEB-2009	$25.00	7591	201
204	ELLEN	OWENS	SAL	01-JUL-2008	$15.00	6830	202
205	HENRY	PERKINS	SAL	01-MAR-2006	$25.00	5286	202
206	CAROL	ROSE	ACT	(null)	(null)	(null)	(null)
207	DAN	SMITH	SHP	01-DEC-2008	$25.00	2259	203
208	FRED	CAMPBELL	SHP	01-APR-2008	$25.00	1752	203
209	PAULA	JACOBS	MKT	17-MAR-1999	$15.00	3357	201
210	NANCY	HOFFMAN	SAL	16-FEB-2007	$25.00	2974	203

**Result after the `update` statement is applied to the `1_employees` table —
Oracle error message (Access shows a different error message)**

```
ORA-00001:unique constraint (JPATRICK.UNIQUE_EMP_PHONE_NUM) violated ❶
```

Notes

❶ The word "constraint" in this error message tells us there is a rule restricting the data that can be placed in this table. In this case the rule says that no two employees can have the same phone number. That rule caused this `update` statement to be rejected.

Check your understanding

Write SQL to delete the Sales Department (`SAL`) from the `sec0415_departments` table. This should work. Then apply the same SQL statement to the `1_departments` table. This time you will get an error message.

4-16 Security restrictions

In addition to constraints, there may also be security restrictions that limit the modifications you can make to the data in a table. Constraints are like business rules that are enforced on the data by the database. You can usually find a way to satisfy a constraint.

Security restrictions are meant to keep you out of private areas or impose limitations on what you can do. They are the guard rails that keep everyone safe and keep the database operating smoothly. Usually you will encounter security restrictions only when you are sharing a large database with many other people.

Relational databases have a large variety of security restrictions that can be imposed. Some tables may contain private or confidential information and you may not be able to see those tables at all. Other tables might have restrictions on which rows and which columns you can see. Sometimes you are allowed to see data, but you are not allowed to change it.

When you bump up against a security restriction, you might want to ask your DBA about it, just to be sure you understand what is going on. Then it is usually best to just accept the restriction and find another way to accomplish whatever you are trying to do.

Key Points

- You can save the result of any `select` statement in a table or view. A table saves the actual data as it is at one particular moment in time. A view saves the `select` statement and runs it again whenever you use the view.

- A table contains fixed data, unless you change it.

- A view contains data that is constantly updated.

- One view can be built from another view. Both views will run automatically each time you use them.

- You can delete a table or view.

- `Insert` adds one new row to a table. When `insert` is used with a `select` statement, it can add many new rows to a table.

- `Update` makes changes to rows that are already in the table.

- `Delete` removes rows from the table.

- You can change the data in a table using the GUI. The effect is the same as using the SQL commands: `insert`, `update`, and `delete`.

- Sometimes you are not allowed to make certain changes to the data in a table because of constraints or security restrictions.

chapter 5

THE DATA DICTIONARY AND OTHER ORACLE TOPICS

This chapter expands on the topics we discussed in chapter 4. In this chapter, we discuss transactions and modifying data through a view. We also discuss the SQL Commands page, which Oracle uses to run an SQL command. You learn how to find information about the tables and views we have created and the ones that have already been created for us.

Commit, Rollback, and Transactions

5-1   The `commit` and `rollback` commands

When you make a change to the data in a table, at first the change is made in a temporary way. Later, you can make the change permanent or reverse it. `Commit` makes the change permanent. It is a save command on the SQL level. `Rollback` throws out the changes. It is an undo command on the SQL level. `Rollback` goes back to the last `commit` point.

As an analogy, when you make changes to a word processing document, at first your changes are only temporary; they are held in memory. To make them permanent you must save them. That is like doing a `commit`. To throw out your changes, you close the document without saving the changes. That is like doing a `rollback`.

`Commit` also has another effect: It makes your changes public. When you first enter your changes, they are private and only you can see them. If other people are using the database table you are changing, they will not see your changes until you `commit` them.

Oracle supports `commit` and `rollback`, as they are actual commands within Oracle. Most other SQL products also support them. However, Access does not support them. Access uses a different mechanism to provide the same ability — the UseTransaction property. Because this property is used primarily on the Visual Basic level within Access, I do not discuss it further. To keep this book to a reasonable size, I am not discussing the Visual Basic level of Access.

Oracle SQL: To save your changes permanently and make them public

Issue one or more commands to change the data — `insert`, `update`, `delete`.

```
commit;
```

Oracle SQL: To undo your changes

Issue one or more commands to change the data — `insert`, `update`, `delete`.

```
rollback;
```

Access does not support `commit` and `rollback` on the level of the SQL window.

5-2   The Autocommit option

In chapter 4 you used the `insert`, `update`, and `delete` commands. The changes you made to the data were permanent even though you did not `commit` them. How did that happen?

Actually, your changes were committed automatically by the database. That is why you did not have to issue the `commit` command yourself.

Most SQL products have an option that allows the database engine to issue a `commit` command right after every `insert`, `update`, and `delete` command. This option is often called Autocommit.

In the Oracle Database Home Page environment, on the SQL Commands screen, there is a checkbox that allows you to turn Autocommit on or off:

ORACLE Database Express Edition

User: SQLFUN

Home > SQL > SQL Commands

☑ Autocommit   Display   10 ▾

When the checkbox is selected, the results of the `insert`, `update`, and `delete` commands are saved automatically and immediately by Oracle with a `commit` command. This is often convenient, but it prevents you from performing transactions.

When the checkbox is cleared, you are able to perform transactions. However, you must issue the `commit` and `rollback` commands yourself.

In Access, the Autocommit option is always on by default when you enter code through the SQL view. If you use Macros or Visual Basic modules then there are ways you can turn it off and create transactions.

Check your understanding

1. Turn off the Autocommit option:

   - If you are using the Home Page environment, clear the Autocommit checkbox.

   - If you are using the SQL Command Line environment, issue the SQL*Plus command:

     ```
     set autocommit off;
     ```

2. Add a new row to a copy of the `departments` table:

```
insert into sec0502_departments
values('IT', 'INFORMATION TECHNOLOGY');
```

3. Save this change by issuing a `commit` command:

```
commit;
```

4. Add another new row to the copy of the `departments` table:

```
insert into sec0502_departments
values('LAW', 'LEGAL DEPARTMENT');
```

5. Undo this change by issuing a `rollback` command:

```
rollback;
```

6. List all the rows in the copy of the `departments` table:

```
select *
from sec0502_departments;
```

7. Confirm that the table has the row for the `IT` department and that it does not have the row for the `LAW` department.

5-3 **Transactions**

A transaction can only occur when the `autocommit` option is turned off. A transaction allows you to bundle several changes together. These changes can affect several different tables and they can be a mixture of `insert`, `update`, and `delete` commands.

The most important thing about a transaction is that all the changes will go into the database together. There are two options:

- All of the updates are successful and they will all go into the database together at the same time with a single `commit` command.

- If any one of the updates fails for any reason, then none of the changes will be made to the database. All of the changes will be rolled back.

Often transactions are programmed and controlled by another level of software that is issuing SQL commands to the database. But you can use transactions yourself by issuing your own `commit` and `rollback` commands.

A transaction occurs between two commit points. You can begin a transaction by issuing a `commit` or `rollback` command. This finalizes any changes to the database that are already pending and establishes the point you will return to if you issue a rollback command. Sometimes you do not need to issue this initial `commit` or `rollback` command because the computer automatically does it for you.

The transaction consists of all the `insert`, `update`, and `delete` statements done after one `commit` or `rollback` and before the next one.

A transaction is used to ensure that the data in the database stays consistent. Sometimes the data in several tables needs to be changed in a coordinated way. By placing all these changes within a transaction, you can be sure that the tables will not become corrupted if some of the changes succeed and others fail.

Here is an example that uses a transaction. Suppose you have been saving to buy a new car. You have been putting money in your savings account and now you have $5,000 to use for a down payment on the car you want. You need to transfer the money from your savings account to your checking account so you can write a check to the car dealer.

The bank keeps information about its savings accounts in one table and information about its checking accounts in another table. Both of these tables need to be changed in a coordinated way. You want to take $5,000 out of your savings account and put $5,000 into your checking account. These two changes should be put into a transaction so they both succeed or they both fail. The code to do this follows.

Task

Take $5,000 from the savings account of Amy Johnson and put $5,000 into her checking account. Wrap these two changes in a single transaction.

Oracle SQL

```
commit; ❶
```

```
update sec0503_savings_accounts ❷
  set balance = balance - 5000
where customer = 'AMY JOHNSON';
```

If you get an error message, do a `rollback` and stop entering this transaction.

```
update sec0503_checking_accounts ❸
  set balance = balance + 5000
where customer = 'AMY JOHNSON';
```

If you get an error message, do a `rollback` and stop entering this transaction.

If both `update` statements succeed, `commit` the changes.

```
commit; ❹
```

Table before changes 1 (`sec0503_savings_accounts` table)

S_ACCOUNT_ID	CUSTOMER	BALANCE
5926	FRED BOYD	15642.33
6197	AMY JOHNSON	5280.25
5926	VALERIE SHAW	35159.64

Table before changes 2 (`sec0503_checking_accounts` table)

C_ACCOUNT_ID	CUSTOMER	BALANCE
2741	BOB WILKINS	1567.35
3852	AMY JOHNSON	357.26
8954	JUDY SPENCER	6296.54

Commit is performed . . .

Table after changes 1 (`sec0503_saving_accounts` table)

S_ACCOUNT_ID	CUSTOMER	BALANCE
5926	FRED BOYD	15642.33
6197	AMY JOHNSON	280.25
5926	VALERIE SHAW	35159.64

Table after changes 2 (`sec0503_checking_accounts` table)

C_ACCOUNT_ID	CUSTOMER	BALANCE
2741	BOB WILKINS	1567.35
3852	AMY JOHNSON	5357.26
8954	JUDY SPENCER	6296.54

Notes

❶ The first `commit` makes sure that there are no unsaved changes already present. It guarentees that we are starting off with a clean slate. If later you decide to do a `rollback`, this is the point to which you will return.

❷ The first statement to modify the data begins the transaction.

❸ All subsequent changes that modify the data are part of the transaction that is already started.

❹ The final `commit` statement ends the transaction and makes the changes permanent.

Transactions are important

Transactions are a powerful and important feature of SQL. However, they are usually used in a more complex setting than the database we are using in this book. For that reason, I do not discuss them any further.

Check your understanding 1

Use the tables for checking accounts and savings accounts in this section. Use a transaction to delete the checking account for Bob Wilkins and transfer all his money to a new savings account. The ID of the new savings account is 5678.

To do this you can follow these steps:

1. Turn off the `autocommit` option.
2. Delete the checking account.
3. Create the savings account.
4. Verify that your changes are okay.
5. Commit your changes.

Check your understanding 2

Again, use the tables for this section. Use a transaction to transfer $20,000 for Fred Boyd from his savings account to his checking account.

To do this you can follow these steps:

1. Update the amount of money in his savings account.
2. Update the amount of money in his checking account.
3. Verify that your changes are okay. In particular, verify the amount of money left in his savings account. If this is a negative number, then the change is not okay.
4. Roll back the changes.

Modifying Data through a View

Up to now, when we used an `insert`, `update`, or `delete` statement, that statement always named the table in which the data would be changed. For example, the word `insert` is followed by the name of the table that will receive the new row.

It is also possible to follow the word `insert` with the name of a view, instead of a table. You might wonder what this means because a view is only a `select` statement and it does not contain any data. It means to add a new row to the underlying table on which the view is based.

Here is an analogy: Picture yourself standing outside a house in the garden. Inside the house there is a large table with many things on it. You can reach through an open window to manipulate some of the things on the table. Other things on the table are beyond your reach. In this analogy, the view is the open window. You can manipulate the data in the table by reaching through the view.

If you are the only person using a database, you will probably change the data directly in a table, rather than using a view. It is simpler to do it that way. However, it is a common practice to change the data through a view when you are working with a large database that many people are using at the same time.

This is partly a matter of how large databases are managed and administered. Usually, only the DBAs are allowed to work directly with the tables. Everyone else who changes the data must use a view. The purpose of this rule is to allow the DBAs to make changes to the tables, such as adding a new column, at the same time that other people are modifying the data. DBAs and the other users are separated so they have a minimal impact on each other. Each can work separately without concern about what the other person is doing.

A view can also be used for security. It can limit the data a user can change, allowing changes to only certain columns and rows.

5-4   Changing data through a view

When you change data through a view, only some of the data in the table can be changed. In general, you can only change the data that can be seen through the view. Here are two exceptions to this rule:

1. You can only delete rows that can be seen through the view. When you delete a row, you delete the entire row, which includes all the columns, even those that cannot be seen through the view.

2. You can insert a new row even if it cannot be seen through the view. If the view is defined With Check Option, then you can only insert rows that can be seen through the view. See section 5-6 for details.

The following table summarizes these exceptions.

Exceptions to `insert`, `update`, and `delete`.

	Rows restricted to the ones in the view	Columns restricted to the ones in the view
Insert	No	Yes
Update	Yes	Yes
Delete	Yes	No

Only certain views can be used for changing data. These are called **updateable views**. A view is updateable when the following apply:

1. It only contains data from one table.

2. It contains some or all of the columns and rows from the table.

3. It does not summarize the data or condense it by using `select distinct`. The data in each cell of the view comes from the data in only one cell of the table.

Both Oracle and Access allow a few more views to be updateable. However, this is the usual set of updateable views within most SQL products. In Access, it is easy to tell whether a view is updateable. If it is, a blank row is shown at the bottom of the view where you can enter new rows of data.

The following diagram shows a conceptual picture of a view and its underlying table.

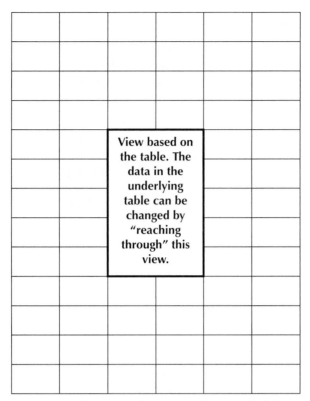

View based on the table. The data in the underlying table can be changed by "reaching through" this view.

Conceptual diagram of a view and its underlying table.

5-5 Example of changing data through a view

This section shows how to change the data in a table, using a process that changes it through a view. Part 1 shows all the components of this process. Parts 2 and 3 show data actually being changed.

This looks more complicated than changing the data directly in the table. However, from the user's perspective, the difference is very small. The user issues the same `insert`, `update`, and `delete` commands. The only difference is that these commands name a view instead of naming a base table.

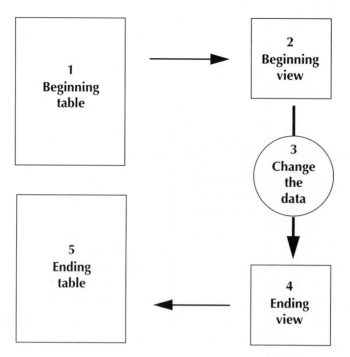

Conceptual diagram of changing data through a view.

The components of the process in the conceptual diagram

1. The first component is the beginning table. This is where the data is actually stored.

2. The second component is the beginning view. This is derived from the beginning table by applying the `select` statement that defines the view. The view definition is not shown separately in this diagram.

3. The data is changed through the view using an `insert`, `update`, or `delete` command. An `update` command can only work on the data that appears in the beginning view. It cannot change the data in any column or row that does not appear in the beginning view.

    The `insert` command can add rows to the table that do not appear in the view, but it can only place data in the columns that appear in the view. All other columns are set to null.

    The `delete` command can only delete rows from the table if they appear in the view. However, it deletes entire rows from the table, including columns that do not appear in the view.

4. The fourth component is the ending view. The illustration shows this from the user's perspective. From the computer's perspective, the changes are made directly to the ending table. The ending view is then derived from the ending table.

5. The last component is the ending table. This shows all the changes made to the data, regardless of whether they appear in the ending view.

In Access, if you are changing the data using the GUI environment, the ending view does not appear immediately. Access provides a stable working environment for making the changes. It shows you the beginning view and your changes as a working document called a **datasheet**. To see the ending view, you must close the view and then open it again.

This section shows two examples of changing data through a view. Here is the definition of that view.

Oracle SQL: `shipping_dept_view`

```
create or replace view sec0505_shipping_dept_view as
select employee_id,
       first_name,
       last_name,
       dept_code,
       credit_limit
from sec0505_employees
where dept_code = 'SHP';
```

Access SQL: `shipping_dept_view`

Step 1: Delete the saved query `shipping_dept_view` if it already exists.

Step 2: Enter this query in the SQL window:

```
select employee_id,
       first_name,
       last_name,
       dept_code,
       credit_limit
from sec0505_employees
where dept_code = 'SHP';
```

Step 3: Save the query. Name it `sec0505_shipping_dept_view`.

Beginning table (sec0505_employees table)

EMPLOYEE ID	FIRST_NAME	LAST_NAME	DEPT CODE	HIRE_DATE	CREDIT LIMIT	PHONE NUMBER	MANAGER ID
201	SUSAN	BROWN	EXE	01-JUN-1998	$30.00	3484	(null)
202	JIM	KERN	SAL	16-AUG-1999	$25.00	8722	201
203	MARTHA	WOODS	SHP	02-FEB-2009	$25.00	7591	201
204	ELLEN	OWENS	SAL	01-JUL-2008	$15.00	6830	202
205	HENRY	PERKINS	SAL	01-MAR-2006	$25.00	5286	202
206	CAROL	ROSE	ACT	(null)	(null)	(null)	(null)
207	DAN	SMITH	SHP	01-DEC-2008	$25.00	2259	203
208	FRED	CAMPBELL	SHP	01-APR-2008	$25.00	1752	203
209	PAULA	JACOBS	MKT	17-MAR-1999	$15.00	3357	201
210	NANCY	HOFFMAN	SAL	16-FEB-2007	$25.00	2974	203

Task for example 1

Add a new employee, John Patrick, with a credit limit of $25.00, to the shipping department. Increase Martha Woods' credit limit to $35.00 and delete the row for Fred Campbell. Make these changes through the sec0505_shipping_dept_view.

Notes

❶ You can make changes to any of the data that appears in the columns and rows of this view.

❷ Make all command changes through the sec0505_shipping_dept_view.

❸ All the changes are reflected in the ending view.

❹ All the changes are reflected in the ending table.

Ending table (sec0505_employees table) ❹

EMPLOYEE ID	FIRST_NAME	LAST_NAME	DEPT CODE	HIRE_DATE	CREDIT LIMIT	PHONE NUMBER	MANAGER ID
201	SUSAN	BROWN	EXE	01-JUN-1998	$30.00	3484	(null)
202	JIM	KERN	SAL	16-AUG-1999	$25.00	8722	201
203	MARTHA	WOODS	SHP	02-FEB-2009	$35.00	7591	201
204	ELLEN	OWENS	SAL	01-JUL-2008	$15.00	6830	202
205	HENRY	PERKINS	SAL	01-MAR-2006	$25.00	5286	202
206	CAROL	ROSE	ACT	(null)	(null)	(null)	(null)
207	DAN	SMITH	SHP	01-DEC-2008	$25.00	2259	203
209	PAULA	JACOBS	MKT	17-MAR-1999	$15.00	3357	201
210	NANCY	HOFFMAN	SAL	16-FEB-2007	$25.00	2974	203
212	JOHN	PATRICK	SHP	(null)	$25.00	(null)	(null)

Beginning view (sec0505_shipping_dept_view) ❶

```
EMPLOYEE                           DEPT   CREDIT
      ID FIRST_NAME  LAST_NAME     CODE    LIMIT
-------- ----------- ----------- ----   -------
     203 MARTHA      WOODS         SHP    $25.00
     207 DAN         SMITH         SHP    $25.00
     208 FRED        CAMPBELL      SHP    $25.00
```

Oracle & Access SQL: Change the data through the view ❷

These changes can be seen in the ending view, so this code runs whether or not the view is defined With Check Option.

```
insert into sec0505_shipping_dept_view
values (212, 'JOHN', 'PATRICK', 'SHP', 25.00);

update sec0505_shipping_dept_view
  set credit_limit = 35.00
where employee_id = 203;

delete from sec0505_shipping_dept_view
where employee_id = 208;
```

Ending view (sec0505_shipping_dept_view) ❸

```
EMPLOYEE                           DEPT   CREDIT
      ID FIRST_NAME  LAST_NAME     CODE    LIMIT
-------- ----------- ----------- ----   -------
     203 MARTHA      WOODS         SHP    $35.00
     207 DAN         SMITH         SHP    $25.00
     212 JOHN        PATRICK       SHP    $25.00
```

Beginning table (sec0505b_employees table) ❶

```
EMPLOYEE                          DEPT                     CREDIT PHONE   MANAGER
      ID FIRST_NAME LAST_NAME     CODE HIRE_DATE            LIMIT NUMBER       ID
-------- ---------- ----------    ---- ------------        ------- ------  -------
     201 SUSAN      BROWN         EXE  01-JUN-1998         $30.00 3484     (null)
     202 JIM        KERN          SAL  16-AUG-1999         $25.00 8722        201
     203 MARTHA     WOODS         SHP  02-FEB-2009         $25.00 7591        201
     204 ELLEN      OWENS         SAL  01-JUL-2008         $15.00 6830        202
     205 HENRY      PERKINS       SAL  01-MAR-2006         $25.00 5286        202
     206 CAROL      ROSE          ACT  (null)              (null) (null)   (null)
     207 DAN        SMITH         SHP  01-DEC-2008         $25.00 2259        203
     208 FRED       CAMPBELL      SHP  01-APR-2008         $25.00 1752        203
     209 PAULA      JACOBS        MKT  17-MAR-1999         $15.00 3357        201
     210 NANCY      HOFFMAN       SAL  16-FEB-2007         $25.00 2974        203
```

Task for example 2

From the sec0505b_employees table, transfer Dan Smith from shipping to marketing and add Susan Manning as a new executive.

Notes

❶ The beginning table shows Dan Smith in the shipping department, and there is no row for Susan Manning.

❷ Make the sec0505b_shipping_dept_view from the sec0505b_employees table.

❸ The update and insert statements make changes through the sec0505b_shipping_dept_view.

❹ You cannot verify that the changes were made correctly. The ending view does not contain a record for either Dan Smith or Susan Manning.

❺ Only in the ending table, the sec0505b_employees table, can you verify that Dan Smith is now in the marketing department and Susan Manning is now an executive.

Ending table (sec0505b_employees table) ❺

```
EMPLOYEE                          DEPT                     CREDIT PHONE   MANAGER
      ID FIRST_NAME LAST_NAME     CODE HIRE_DATE            LIMIT NUMBER       ID
-------- ---------- ----------    ---- ------------        ------- ------  -------
     201 SUSAN      BROWN         EXE  01-JUN-1998         $30.00 3484     (null)
     202 JIM        KERN          SAL  16-AUG-1999         $25.00 8722        201
     203 MARTHA     WOODS         SHP  02-FEB-2009         $25.00 7591        201
     204 ELLEN      OWENS         SAL  01-JUL-2008         $15.00 6830        202
     205 HENRY      PERKINS       SAL  01-MAR-2006         $25.00 5286        202
     206 CAROL      ROSE          ACT  (null)              (null) (null)   (null)
     207 DAN        SMITH         MKT  01-DEC-2008         $25.00 2259        203
     208 FRED       CAMPBELL      SHP  01-APR-2008         $25.00 1752        203
     209 PAULA      JACOBS        MKT  17-MAR-1999         $15.00 3357        201
     210 NANCY      HOFFMAN       SAL  16-FEB-2007         $25.00 2974        203
     211 SUSAN      MANNING       EXE  (null)              $50.00 (null)   (null)
```

Beginning view (sec0505b_shipping_dept_view) ❷

```
EMPLOYEE                               DEPT   CREDIT
      ID FIRST_NAME LAST_NAME          CODE    LIMIT
-------- ---------- ----------         ----   -------
     203 MARTHA     WOODS              SHP    $25.00
     207 DAN        SMITH              SHP    $25.00
     208 FRED       CAMPBELL           SHP    $25.00
```

Oracle & Access SQL: Change the data through the view ❸

These changes can only be seen in the ending table, not in the ending view, so this code runs only if the view is not defined With Check Option.

```
update sec0505b_shipping_dept_view
set dept_code = 'MKT'
where employee_id = 207;

insert into sec0505b_shipping_dept_view
values (211, 'SUSAN', 'MANNING', 'EXE', 50.00);
```

Ending view (sec0505b_shipping_dept_view) ❹

```
EMPLOYEE                               DEPT   CREDIT
      ID FIRST_NAME LAST_NAME          CODE    LIMIT
-------- ---------- ----------         ----   -------
     203 MARTHA     WOODS              SHP    $25.00
     208 FRED       CAMPBELL           SHP    $25.00
```

Check your understanding

Change the following SQL code to create your own example that shows you can modify the data in a table by making changes to a view based on that table.

In this example, the view you create will include all the columns and all the rows of the underlying table. This is the easiest and most straightforward case. It is also the way that this feature is used most often.

1. List all the columns and rows of the `foods` table. This shows what data is in the table before you make any changes to it.

   ```
   select *
   from sec0505_foods;
   ```

2. Create a view of the `foods` table. Include all the columns and rows in the view.

   ```
   create or replace view sec0505_foods_view as
   select *
   from sec0505_foods;
   ```

3. Show that you can use an `insert` statement with this view.

   ```
   insert into sec0505_foods_view
   values('ABC', 'DEF', 51, 'BLUEBERRY PIE', 2.99, null);
   ```

4. Show that you can use an `update` statement with this view.

   ```
   update sec0505_foods_view
   set menu_item = 20,
       description = 'CARROTS'
   where description = 'BROCCOLI';
   ```

5. Show that you can use a `delete` statement with this view.

   ```
   delete from sec0505_foods_view
   where description = 'DESSERT';
   ```

6. List all the columns and rows of the underlying table. Show that all the changes you made to the view actually affected the data in the underlying table.

   ```
   select *
   from sec0505_foods;
   ```

5-6   Views using With Check Option

In the previous section we saw that a change can be made to the data through a view, even if the new or modified row does not appear in the ending view. In particular, an `insert` command can insert a new row even if that row does not appear in the ending view. Also, an `update` command can make a change to a row so that it does not appear in the ending view.

Sometimes we do not want to allow such changes. We can prevent them by defining the view With Check Option. This can be done in Oracle and most other types of SQL. However, Access does not support this option.

When the view is defined With Check Option, you are only permitted to use `insert` or `update` when the resulting row will appear in the ending view. You can still delete any row that appears in the beginning view. In effect, this says that you can only make changes when you can see the result of those changes and verify that they are correct. You are not allowed to make changes you cannot see.

In the example of the previous section, we would not be allowed to change the department for Dan Smith. We would also not be allowed to add Susan Manning, because she will not work in the shipping department.

Task

Create the `sec0506a_shipping_dept_view` without using With Check Option. Then show how to modify this code to create the `sec0506b_shipping_dept_view` that uses With Check Option.

Oracle SQL: Create the `sec0506a_shipping_dept_view` without using With Check Option

```
create or replace view sec0506a_shipping_dept_view as
select employee_id,
       first_name,
       last_name,
       dept_code,
       credit_limit
from sec0506_employees
where dept_code = 'SHP';
```

Oracle SQL: Create the `sec0506b_shipping_dept_view` using With Check Option

```
create or replace view sec0506b_shipping_dept_view as
select employee_id,
       first_name,
       last_name,
       dept_code,
       credit_limit
from sec0506_employees
where dept_code = 'SHP'
with check option; ❶
```

Access does not support With Check Option.

Notes

❶ To code with check option, place it at the end of the select statement that defines the view.

Check your understanding

Change the following SQL code to create your own example that shows the effect of using With Check Option when you define a view.

In this example, the view you create will include all the columns of the underlying table, but only some of its rows. A few rows cannot be seen through this view.

1. List all the columns and rows of the foods table. This shows what data is in the table before you make any changes to it.

```
select *
from sec0506_foods;
```

2. Create a view of the copy of the foods table. Include all the columns and most of the rows in the view. Use With Check Option when you define the view.

```
create or replace view sec0506_foods_view as
select *
from sec0506_foods
where price <= 2.00
with check option;
```

3. Show that you can use an `insert` statement to add a new row that will appear in this view.

```
insert into sec0506_foods_view
values('ABC', 'DEF', 61, 'CHICKEN SOUP', 1.99, null);
```

4. Show that you cannot use an `insert` statement to add a new row that will not appear in this view.

```
insert into sec0506_foods_view
values('ABC', 'DEF', 61, 'BEEF SOUP', 2.01, null);
```

5. Show that you can use an `update` statement to change a row that appears in this view, if the changed row will also appear in the view.

```
update sec0506_foods_view
set price = 1.50
where description = 'SODA';
```

6. Show that you cannot use an `update` statement to change a row that appears in this view, if the changed row will not appear in the view.

```
update sec0506_foods_view
set price = 3.00
where description = 'COFFEE';
```

7. Show that you cannot use an `update` statement to change a row that does not appear in this view, even if the changed row would appear in the view.

```
update sec0506_foods_view
set price = 1.50
where description = 'GRILLED STEAK';
```

8. Show that you can use a `delete` statement to delete a row that appears in this view.

```
delete from sec0506_foods_view
where description = 'FRENCH FRIES';
```

9. Show that you cannot use a `delete` statement to delete a row that does not appear in this view.

```
delete from sec0506_foods_view
where description = 'DESSERT';
```

10. List all the columns and rows of the underlying table. Verify that the data has changed in the way you expected.

```
select *
from sec0506_foods;
```

The SQL Commands Page in Oracle

When you run a single SQL command in the Oracle Home Page environment, you use the SQL Commands page. Appendix B shows you the basic technique of using this page. Here we examine in greater detail all the various features and options that are available on this page.

5-7   Overview of the SQL Commands page

Here is what the SQL Commands page looks like before any SQL command is entered into it:

The features available on this page are:

- Home link — Use this to go back to your home page.

- Logout link — Use this to log out of the database.

- Help link — Use this to get help with the SQL Commands page.

- User Identification — This shows the userID that is currently logged on.

- Home > SQL > SQL Commands — This shows you where you are in relationship to your home page. For example, here we are currently on the SQL Commands page. We got here from our home page via the SQL page. If you click on "Home" or "SQL," you will go back to those pages.

- Autocommit checkbox — See section 5-8.

- Display drop-down list — The maximum number of rows to display of the result table.

- Save button — Click this button to save an SQL command that you will want to run many times in the future. When you save an SQL command this way, you will be able to give it a name and enter a description of what it does.

- Run button — Click this button to run an SQL command.

- Area to enter an SQL command — Usually you enter one SQL command here. You can also enter several SQL commands, then select and highlight the one you want to run.

- Results option — Select this option to run an SQL command and see the result table.

- CSV Export — This option appears at the bottom of the result table when you run an SQL query. It exports the result table in CSV format, which is Comma-Separated Values format.

- Explain option — See section 5-9.

- Describe option — "Describe" is an Oracle command that shows you the definitions of the columns of any table or view. This shows you the datatype, length, and other information about each column.

- Saved SQL option — This shows you a list of all the SQL commands you saved by clicking the Save button. Each of these SQL commands is identified with a name and a description.

- History option — This shows you a list of all the SQL commands you have ever run. You can click on an SQL command to copy it back to the command area and you can modify it there. A Find box is available to help you search for the particular SQL command you want.

- Results area — This is the area that shows the results.

5-8   The Autocommit option

When the Autocommit checkbox is checked, here is what that means:

- An SQL `commit` command runs automatically after each change to the data in a table or view. That is, it runs after any `insert`, `update`, or `delete` command. This `commit` command causes the change to become permanent immediately.

- The `commit` and `rollback` SQL commands are disabled and have no effect.

- All other people who are using the database will immediately see any changes you make to the data in the tables or view of the database.

When the Autocommit checkbox is unchecked, here is what that means:

- An SQL `commit` command is not run automatically after each change to the data in a table or view. This causes all your changes to the data to be in a temporary status until you issue a `commit` or a `rollback` command.

- You can make changes to the data in several tables and they will all be temporary changes until you issue a `commit` or `rollback` command. This allows you to batch several changes together in a "transaction." Then you can either accept the batch and make all those changes permanent or you can reject the batch and reject all of those changes.

- The `commit` SQL command makes permanent all your temporary changes to the data. After your changes have become permanent all other people who are using the database will immediately see your changes.

- The `rollback` SQL command rejects and discards all the temporary changes you have made.

5-9   The Explain option

The Explain option is used to estimate how long a query will take to process. This is an advanced option that is used mostly when there is a lot of data in the database and when the queries are quite complex.

If you have an advanced query and you want to estimate whether it will take one hour to run or ten hours, then you might run the Explain option.

If you have SQL code that will run many times, maybe once a week or more, then you might want to write several versions of the SQL code to try to find the one that is most efficient. You might use the Explain option to compare these different versions of the SQL query.

A DBA might use the Explain option with an SQL query that is run many times to determine which indexes are being used to process the query. This might lead the DBA to conclude that some new indexes need to be built to make the database process more efficiently.

Using the Oracle Data Dictionary — Part 1

This section describes how to find information about the tables and views in a database. The database needs to keep track of all the tables and views for its own processing. This information is available to everyone who uses the database.

5-10 Overview of the Data Dictionary

The **Data Dictionary** is a set of tables that contains all the information about the structure of the database. It contains the names of all the tables, their columns, their primary keys, the names of the views, the select statements that define the views, and much more. The Data Dictionary is sometimes called the **System Catalog**. Most SQL products have a Data Dictionary.

These tables are created and maintained by the database system itself. They contain all the information the database system needs to support its own processing, its self-knowledge. Because this information is stored in tables, you can use select statements to get information from it. These tables are like any other tables. This may seem natural, but it is actually a big step forward. Often in software, the "inner knowledge" is in a completely different format than the "outer knowledge."

The details of the Data Dictionary differ for each SQL product. They even differ slightly from one version of a product to the next. The differences are in the names of the Data Dictionary tables, what columns they contain, and what codes are used.

These details are tied very closely to the inner workings of the database engine itself, the Database Management System (DBMS). When new capabilities are added to the DBMS, new information is often added to the Data

Dictionary. Much of this information is meant only for the DBAs and can be ignored by other people. However, you can use a lot of the information that can be found there. Almost anything you might want to know about the database is contained in the Data Dictionary.

Oracle Data Dictionary

Oracle has a Data Dictionary. This set of tables contains complete information about all the database tables, views, and other objects. For now, I focus on obtaining information from it about the database objects we have discussed so far: tables, views, and primary keys.

The Oracle Data Dictionary: Information about tables and views.

Information to Get	Data Dictionary Table	Data Dictionary Columns
Table names	user_tables or all_tables	table_name
View names	user_views or all_views	view_name
View definition	user_views or all_views	text
Columns of tables and views	user_tab_columns or all_tab_columns	column_name
Primary keys of tables	user_constraints and user_cons_columns or all_constraints and all_cons_columns	(see section 5-15)

Note that user_tables are limited to information about the database objects that you own; all_tables may also include information about database objects that are owned by other people, but only if they have decided to share them with you.

Access uses the GUI to show this information

Access does not have a Data Dictionary. This is unusual for an SQL product. Instead, it can show you information about your table, views, and primary key by using the GUI.

Having this information available via the GUI is not always as good as having it in tables. If you simply want to look up the information by hand, the GUI method is fine, but if you want to write `select` statements that make use of this information, it is much better to have the information available in tables.

5-11 How to find the names of all the tables

When I start to work with any database, the first thing I want to know is the names of the tables. All the data is contained in tables. They are the basic building blocks for everything else in the database. Once I know the name of a table, I can examine its data by using the following command:

```
SELECT *
FROM table_name;
```

In the Oracle Data Dictionary, the table named `user_tables` contains the names of all the tables you own. It has many columns and most of them will not interest you — they are for the DBAs. The column called `table_name` contains the name of every table.

The table named `all_tables` contains the names of all the tables you are allowed to access. This includes tables owned by other groups or people in addition to the tables you own.

In Oracle, the table names and the view names are contained in different Data Dictionary tables. In some other SQL products, the information about the tables and views is kept together in a single table.

Task for example 1

Find the names of all the tables you own.

Oracle SQL — List all the tables you own

```
select table_name
from user_tables;
```

Oracle result table

```
TABLE_NAME
----------------
L_CONSTANTS
L_DEPARTMENTS
L_EMPLOYEES
L_FOODS
L_LUNCHES
L_LUNCH_ITEMS
L_SUPPLIERS
NUMBERS_0_TO_9
(and many others)
```

Task for example 2

Find the names of all the tables you are permitted to use.

Oracle SQL — List all the tables you are permitted to use

```
select table_name
from all_tables;
```

The result is the same as before because I am the only user of my database.

Access GUI method: Find the names of all the tables and views

In Access, all the tables and views (queries) are shown in the navigation pane.

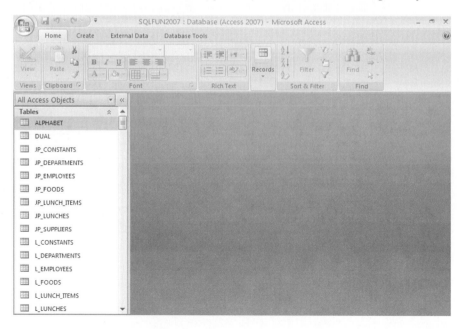

Check your understanding

List the names of all the tables you own.

5-12 How to find the names of all the views

This section shows how to find the names of all your views, which are another important part of a database. In the Oracle Data Dictionary, the table named `user_views` contains information about all the views owned by your userID. The `view_name` column is the only one you need right now.

Task

Find the names of all the views you own.

Oracle SQL

```
select view_name
from user_views;
```

Oracle result table ❶

```
VIEW_NAME
------------------
ALL_LUNCHES
NUMBERS_0_TO_99
SALES_STAFF_1
SALES_STAFF_2
SHIPPING_DEPT

(and many more)
```

Notes

❶ Your results may be different if you have not run all the Oracle SQL in the book so far.

Check your understanding

List the names of all the views you own.

5-13 How to find the `select` statement that defines a view

This section shows how to find the `select` statement that defines a particular view. You get the `text` column from the `user_views` table. You can use the `where` clause to specify which view definition you want.

Oracle retains the format of the `select` statement the way you enter it, but Access does not. Access uses its own formatting. Sometimes it rewrites the `select` statement entirely. In this example, the Access format is easy to read, but sometimes the format is difficult because it is written to be read by computers, not people.

Task

Find the `select` statement that defines the sec0513_shipping_dept_view.

Oracle SQL

```
select view_name,
       text
from user_views
where view_name = 'SEC0513_SHIPPING_DEPT_VIEW'; ❶
```

Oracle result table

```
VIEW_NAME                          TEXT
------------------------------     ------------------------------
SEC0513_SHIPPING_DEPT_VIEW         SELECT  EMPLOYEE_ID,
                                           FIRST_NAME,
                                           LAST_NAME,
                                           DEPT_CODE,
                                           CREDIT_LIMIT
                                   FROM L_EMPLOYEES
                                   WHERE DEPT_CODE = 'SHP'
                                   WITH CHECK OPTION
```

Notes

❶ The `where` clause limits the information to a single view.

Access GUI method: Find the definition of a view

Step 1: Find the view in the Navigation Pane and right-click on it.

Step 2: Choose Design View.

```
SEC0513_SHIPPING_DEPT_VIEW

SELECT employee_id, first_name, last_name, dept_code, credit_limit
FROM l_employees
WHERE dept_code = 'SHP';
```

Check your understanding

Find the `select` statement that defines the `numbers_0_to_99` view.

5-14 How to find the names of the columns in a table or view

This section shows you how to get the names of the columns to use in coding a `select` statement. When you look at a table, the column names seem to be displayed above each column. These names are meant to help a person read and understand the table, but they are not always the actual names you need to use to write a `select` statement. They can be truncated or they can be changed entirely by the SQL select statement.

Oracle has two different methods to obtain this information. One method uses the `describe` command followed by the name of the table. This is a command that only works in Oracle.

The other method uses the Oracle Data Dictionary. A `select` statement gets the `column_name` column from the `user_tab_columns` table. This table contains information about the columns of both tables and views. The name of this table should be pronounced "User Table Columns," but in the spelling, the word "Table" is truncated.

A `where` clause is needed to limit the result to the columns of a single table or view. If you do not use a `where` clause you will get the names of all the columns of all your tables and views, which might be an overwhelming amount of information. In this `where` clause, `table_name` is set equal to the name of either a table or a view. The order of the columns within the table is contained in the `column_id` column.

Task

Find the full names of all the columns of the `l_employees` table. List these columns in their order within the table.

Describe command in Oracle

```
describe l_employees;
```

Oracle response from the SQL Commands page of the Database Home Page environment. (This does not work in an SQL Script file.)

Table	Column	Data Type	Length	Precision	Scale	Primary Key	Nullable	Default	Comment
L_EMPLOYEES	EMPLOYEE_ID	Number	-	3	0	1	-	-	-
	FIRST_NAME	Varchar2	10	-	-	-	✓	-	-
	LAST_NAME	Varchar2	20	-	-	-	✓	-	-
	DEPT_CODE	Varchar2	3	-	-	-	✓	-	-
	HIRE_DATE	Date	7	-	-	-	✓	-	-
	CREDIT_LIMIT	Number	-	4	2	-	✓	-	-
	PHONE_NUMBER	Varchar2	4	-	-	-	✓	-	-
	MANAGER_ID	Number	-	3	0	-	✓	-	-

1 - 8

Oracle SQL: Column names of tables and views

```
select table_name,
       column_name,
       column_id
from user_tab_columns
where table_name = 'L_EMPLOYEES'
order by column_id;
```

Result table

```
TABLE_NAME                        COLUMN_NAME                     COLUMN_ID
------------------------------    ----------------------------    ---------
L_EMPLOYEES                       EMPLOYEE_ID                             1
L_EMPLOYEES                       FIRST_NAME                              2
L_EMPLOYEES                       LAST_NAME                               3
L_EMPLOYEES                       DEPT_CODE                               4
L_EMPLOYEES                       HIRE_DATE                               5
L_EMPLOYEES                       CREDIT_LIMIT                            6
L_EMPLOYEES                       PHONE_NUMBER                            7
L_EMPLOYEES                       MANAGER_ID                              8
```

Access GUI method: Column names for tables, but not for views

Step 1: Find the table in the Navigation Pane and right-click on it.

Step 2: Choose Design View.

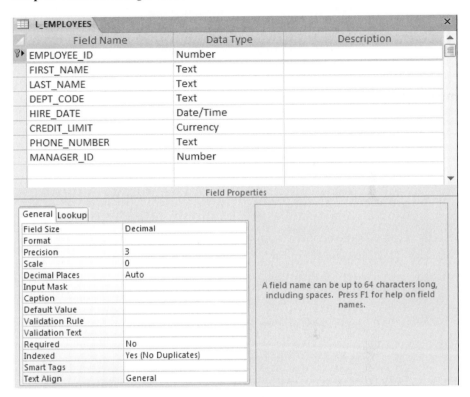

Check your understanding

Use the Data Dictionary to find the names of all the columns of the `l_employees` table.

5-15 How to find the primary key of a table

This section shows how to find the primary key of a table. The primary key can consist of several columns, but is considered to be a single unit. A view does not have a primary key.

To find information about primary keys in the Oracle Data Dictionary, you need to know that a primary key is one type of constraint. A **constraint** is any rule that restricts the data that can be entered into a column. We discuss constraints in more detail in chapter 8. A primary key is a constraint because the data that can be entered into its columns is restricted by the following rules:

1. Nulls are not allowed in primary key columns.

2. No two rows can have the same value in all the primary key columns.

For now, you must use a two-step process to find this information in the Oracle Data Dictionary. In section 13-18 I will show you how to combine these steps and get this information with a single `select` statement.

The goal of the first step is to find the exact name of the constraint from the `user_constraints` table. In the following example, the `select` statement lists all the constraints on the `l_foods` table. There are three of them. The primary key constraint is the one with a value of `P` in the `constraint_type` column, so the name of this constraint is `pk_l_foods`. If you have put `pk_` in the names of all the primary key constraints, this first step may not be necessary.

The second step finds all the columns involved with the constraint. It uses the `user_cons_columns` table. The name of this table is pronounced "User Constraint Columns," but in the spelling, the word "Constraint" is truncated. In the example, the `pk_l_foods` constraint is listed with two columns: `supplier_id` and `product_code`. You already know that this is the correct answer from the design of the `Lunches` database.

Task

Find all the columns in the primary key of the `l_foods` table.

Oracle SQL: Step 1

```
select table_name,
       constraint_type,
       constraint_name
from user_constraints
where table_name = 'L_FOODS';  ❶
```

Result table: Step 1 ❷

TABLE_NAME	C	CONSTRAINT_NAME
L_FOODS	P	PK_L_FOODS
L_FOODS	R	FK_FOODS_SUPPLIER_ID
L_FOODS	C	FOODS_MAX_PRICE

Oracle SQL: Step 2

```
select *
from user_cons_columns
where table_name = 'L_FOODS'; ❶
```

Result table: Step 2

OWNER	CONSTRAINT_NAME	TABLE_NAME	COLUMN_NAME	POSITION	
SQLFUN	FK_FOODS_SUPPLIER_ID	L_FOODS	SUPPLIER_ID	1	
SQLFUN	FOODS_MAX_PRICE	L_FOODS	PRICE	(null)	
SQLFUN	PK_L_FOODS	L_FOODS	SUPPLIER_ID	1	❸
SQLFUN	PK_L_FOODS	L_FOODS	PRODUCT_CODE	2	❸

Notes

❶ This `where` clause limits the result to the constraints on one table. This is what you want. Otherwise the result can become confusing to read.

❷ The `constraint_type` column contains the following codes:

    P — Primary key

    R — Referential Integrity, foreign key

    C — Check constraint

    U — Uniqueness constraint

Constraints are discussed in chapter 8.

❸ The `constraint_name`, `pk_l_foods`, shows you which rows you want from this table. The `position` says that `supplier_id` is the first column in the primary key, and `product_code` is the second column.

Access GUI method: Find the primary key of a table ❹

Step 1: Find the table in the Navigation Pane and right-click it.

Step 2: Choose Design View.

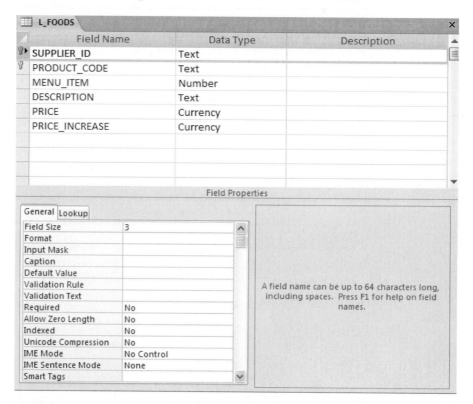

Notes

❹ In Access, the columns of the primary key are shown with the key symbol to the left of the column names.

Check your understanding

Use the Data Dictionary to find the primary key of the l_employees table.

Key Points

Transactions:

- A transaction is an SQL structure that allows you to group several database changes together so either they will all succeed or they will all fail.

- The `commit` command ends a transaction by saving all the changes.

- The `rollback` command ends a transaction by deleting all the changes. It restores the tables to the way they were when the last commit occurred.

- The `autocommit` option automatically performs a commit after every `insert`, `update`, and `delete` statement.

Modifying data through a view:

- When many people are using a database at the same time, you might be required to make changes to the data in a table by modifying the data through a view. This is also sometimes required when additional layers of software are involved.

- Some views are updateable and others are not.

- When you modify data through a view, you are really changing the data in the table that the view is based on.

Oracle SQL Commands page:

- The SQL Commands page contains features to save your SQL queries, control the maximum number of rows of the output, export the result table, and control whether autocommit is on or off.

Oracle Data Dictionary:

- The Data Dictionary is a set of tables that contain all the information about objects in the database. These tables are used by the RDBMS (Relational DataBase Management System) itself to control the database. You can also use them, like any other tables, to find information about the database.

chapter 6

CREATING YOUR OWN TABLES

In this chapter, you learn how to create your own tables in a way that provides maximum control over every aspect of the tables. In chapter 4, you created new tables from other tables. Here, you create tables from the beginning, without relying on other tables.

Creating Tables

A table can be created with an SQL command, giving you precise control over every part of the table.

6-1   The `create table` command

The `create table` statement creates a new table. When it is first created, this table will not have any rows of data in it. This command has the following format:

```
CREATE TABLE table_name
(column_name_1    data_type_1,
 column_name_2    data_type_2,
 ...);
```

This is the simplest form of the command. Many other options can be specified in this command or added later. All the columns of the table must be listed.

This method of creating a table allows the greatest control over all its elements. A table consists of the following:

- A table name

- Names of the columns

- Datatypes of the columns

- A sequence to the columns

People sometimes think of a table as consisting of data, but this is incorrect. The table is a container, like a box. The data are held in a table.

The list of datatypes in Oracle is a little different from the one for Access. Each SQL product supports datatypes that differ slightly from other SQL products. Because the datatypes are named in this command, the SQL statement for Oracle is different from the one for Access.

Primary keys and many other options can be specified when the table is first created or they can be specified after it is already built. They can even be specified after the table has data in it. The `alter table` statement is used to add a primary key to a table after it has been created. We discuss this in section 6-9.

In the following example, the `create table` statements are the same for Oracle and Access, except for the names of the datatypes.

Task

Create a new table similar to the `1_foods` table by defining its columns with a `create table` statement. Move the position of the `menu_item` column to make it the first column.

Oracle SQL

```
create table sec0601_foods
(menu_item          number(2),
 supplier_id        varchar2(3),
 product_code       varchar2(2),
 description        varchar2(20),
 price              number(4,2),
 price_increase     number(4,2) );
```

Access SQL

```
create table sec0601_foods
(menu_item          byte,
 supplier_id        varchar(3),
 product_code       varchar(2),
 description        varchar(20),
 price              money,
 price_increase     money );
```

Result — An empty table with no data in it

When a table is created, at first it does not contain any data, so you cannot see it with a `select` statement. In Oracle you can see this table in Object Builder or by looking in the Data Dictionary. In Access, you can see the table in the Navigation Pane.

6-2   Datatypes in Oracle and Access

What is a datatype? Data is represented inside the computer as a pattern of 1s and 0s. Only certain patterns are meaningful — all others are nonsense. These meaningful patterns are called **datatypes**.

Oracle uses a different set of meaningful patterns than Access does. For instance, each use a different pattern of 1s and 0s to represent the date January 1, 2010. The meaning of the data is the same, but the binary representation of it is different. In short, they use different datatypes. Each SQL product has its own set of datatypes. Each one assigns slightly different meanings to patterns of binary digits.

For the most part, the meanings are the same, even though they are represented differently on a binary level. The differences show up mostly at the extremes. Consider dates. Both Oracle and Access can handle dates between 100 AD and 9999 AD. That is a greater range of dates than I have ever needed to use.

However, Oracle dates and Access dates do have some differences because of the different patterns of 1s and 0s that represent them. In particular, Oracle can handle dates between 4712 BC and 100 AD, but Access cannot.

The main point here is that the datatypes for Oracle and Access are very similar, but they differ in the small details. Also, the names of these datatypes are different, so the `create table` statements are different.

The following table shows the similarities and differences between the datatypes used in Oracle and Access. The datatypes for text, date/time, and storage are very similar. Access has a one-bit datatype for Yes/No and True/False, which Oracle does not have. Oracle might use an entire byte of data to represent this. Usually, that is acceptable.

Another difference is the numbers. Access uses many datatypes for numbers. This is the traditional approach and most computer products follow it. Oracle combines decimal numbers and floating-point numbers together in a single datatype.

The datatypes for storage are used for binary data such as pictures, sound clips, video clips, and compiled programs. These are not active elements within the database — you cannot search, sort, index, or apply functions to them.

The use of storage datatypes in databases is currently in the process of change. It is changing in two opposite directions at the same time. From one perspective, their use is being phased out in favor of storing files within the operating system, rather than in a database, and only placing a pointer to them in the database itself. From another perspective, their use is increasing to support object-oriented concepts.

The names of the datatypes given here are the ***internal*** names for the elements of the database engines. For Access they are the names used by the JET engine. The GUI graphical presentation layer of Access sometimes uses slightly different names.

Many of these datatypes also have **synonyms** or **external** names. These are intended to make one SQL product compatible with another. This is an attempt to map the datatypes of one product to the datatypes of another.

Main Oracle and Access datatypes.

Oracle	Access	Comments
CHARACTER DATATYPES		
`varchar2(Size)` (when size is 1 to 255)	`varchar(Size)` or `text(Size)`	Variable-length character string. `Size` is the maximum length of the column. `Size` can be from 1 to 255. In Oracle, the size can be larger but columns more than 255 bytes long are ***long strings***. They have restricted capabilities and behave differently.
`char(Size)`	`char(Size)`	Fixed-length character strings. `Size` is the maximum length of the column. `Size` can be from 1 to 255.
DATE/TIME DATATYPES		
`date`	`datetime`	A date and time. Oracle: from 4712 BC to 9999 AD. Access: from 100 AD to 9999 AD.
NUMERIC DATATYPES		
`number(P,S)`		`Number`: Either integers, decimals, or scientific notation (floating-point) numbers. `P`: Precision, is the total number of digits other than zeros. From 1 to 38. `S`: Scale, is the number of digits to the right of the decimal point. From 0 to 130. Examples: 1234.56 has type `number(6,2)` 0.0000123 has type `number(3,7)` 1230000. has type `number(7,0)` Valid numbers: From .00...01 (129 zeros after the decimal point), which has type `number(1,130)` To 99...9900...00 (38 nines followed by 88 zeros), which has type `number(38,0)`

Main Oracle and Access datatypes. *(continued)*

Oracle	Access	Comments
NUMERIC DATATYPES *(continued)*		
	`byte`	Integer, from 0 to 255.
	`smallint`	Integer, from about −32,000 to 32,000.
	`integer` or `number`	Integer, from about −2,000,000,000 to 2,000,000,000.
	`money` or `currency`	Integer and four decimal places. Plus or minus about 900,000,000,000,000 Automatically formatted as `currency`.
	`real`	Floating-point number (positive or negative). From about 1.4E−45 to 3.4E38.
	`float`	Floating-point number (positive or negative). From about 4.9E−324 to 1.8E308.

Additional Oracle and Access datatypes.

Oracle	Access	Comments
STORAGE DATATYPES (You cannot sort, search, or index them)		
`clob`	`memo`	Character data. CLOB is a Character Large OBject. Maximum length is 2 GB or more.
`varchar2(Size)` (when size is 256 to 4,000)		Character data.
`raw(Size)`	`binary`	Binary data: pictures, sound. Oracle: up to 2,000 bytes long Access: up to 255 bytes long.
`blob`	`image` or `OLE object`	Binary data: pictures, video, sound, compiled programs, multimedia. BLOB is a Binary Large OBject. Maximum length is 2 GB or more.

Additional Oracle and Access datatypes. *(continued)*

Oracle	Access	Comments
BIT DATATYPES		

	`bit`
	or
	`yesno`
		Any binary choice.
		For instance: yes or no, true or false.

PSEUDO DATATYPES		
	`counter`	Automatically numbers the rows in a table. Access GUI calls this `autonumber`.
`rowid`		Address of a row within its table. Each row has a different address.
`rownum`		Sequential number assigned to each row.
`bfile`	`OLE object`	Locator for a large binary file stored outside the database. This is a type of pointer. It points to a file, which is stored by the operating system.
SPECIALIZED TIME/DATE DATATYPES		
`timestamp(P)`		Point of time. Used to show the sequence of events within the computer. Year, month, day, hour, minute, second, and fraction of a second. P: Precision, is the number of digits in the fractional part of a second. From 0 to 9.
`interval year(P) to month`		Period of time in years and months. P: Precision, is the number of digits in the year.
`interval day(D) to second(S)`		Period of time in days, hours, minutes, and seconds. D: Number of digits in the day. S: Number of digits in the fractional part of a second.

6-3   Text datatypes

The most important datatypes for storing text are:

- Variable length strings
- Fixed length strings
- Long strings

Here the word "string" is short for the phrase "string of characters." Those characters can be letters of the alphabet, numerals, punctuation marks, or spaces, which are all 8-bit characters.

There are also strings for 16-bit unicode characters that are used for Chinese and other languages, but that is another topic, which I do not discuss now.

Variable length strings

Variable length strings are the most frequently used datatype for text. They are used for short text, up to about 250 characters long. If you want to store entire documents of text, usually you would use a different datatype.

In a column of variable length strings, each string can have a different length. There is a maximum limit to what that length can be.

Strings up to that maximum length are accepted. Strings that are longer than the maximum length are sometimes truncated to the maximum length and sometimes cause the row to be rejected entirely.

Strings that are shorter than the maximum length are stored completely, except for any spaces on the end of the string. Let me go over that again. If there are spaces at the beginning or middle of the string, they are stored in the field. Only spaces at the end of the string are truncated. This is done to save storage space on the disk drive.

Often, each variable length string begins with a hidden field that states its actual length. However, the particular method of storing variable length strings can vary from one SQL product to another.

Here is an example. Suppose I try to store "   good dog " in a variable length string with a maximum length greater than 10. The characters I enter are:

space - space - g - o - o - d - space - d - o - g - space

What is actually stored in the string is:

10 - space - space - g - o - o - d - space - d - o - g

In this example, 10 is the hidden length indicator.

Fixed length strings

Fixed length strings are mostly used for high-performance databases. Fixed length strings can process more quickly than variable length strings.

In a column of fixed length strings, all the strings are the same length. Shorter strings entered into the field are padded with spaces on the end. Longer strings are truncated or rejected entirely.

Continuing the earlier example, suppose I store "   good dog   " in a fixed length string of length 13.

What is actually stored in the string is:

　space - space - g - o - o - d - space - d - o - g - space - space - space

Long strings

Long strings are used to store large amounts of text data, such as entire books or other documents. Sometimes they are considered to be a storage datatype, rather than a text datatype.

It used to be that any string longer than 255 characters was considered to be a long string. Long strings had reduced functionality within SQL. For instance, you could not search for a long string or use a long string in a where clause.

Now, however, many of these restrictions have been reduced. Some SQL products, including Oracle, allow you to use much longer strings with full SQL functionality.

In Oracle, long strings are an older feature of databases and they are not used much anymore. They have been mostly replaced by newer features that are sometimes called LOBs (for Large OBjects) for binary data, or CLOBs for character data.

In Access, the Memo datatype is used for long strings. A memo field can hold up to two gigabytes of data and allows rich text formatting.

Task

Create a table with columns that show all the text datatypes. Put some data in it and test it.

Oracle SQL ❶

```
create table sec0603_text_datatypes
(row_id                    varchar2(3),
 variable_length_string    varchar2(3),
 fixed_length_string       char(3),
 long_string               varchar2(1000) );

-- These insert statements will work correctly
insert into sec0603_text_datatypes
values ('A', '1', '1', '1');

insert into sec0603_text_datatypes
values ('B', '22', '22', rpad('2', 1000, '2'));

insert into sec0603_text_datatypes
values ('C', '333', '333', rpad('3', 1000, '3'));

-- The next insert statements reject with an error message
-- Because the data in one of the fields is too long

-- The error message says that the data in the second field
-- is too long.
-- The variable-length-string field has a maximum length
-- of 3 characters.
-- But the data in the insert statement is 4 characters.
-- This causes the insert statement to reject.
insert into sec0603_text_datatypes
values ('D', '4444', '22', rpad('2', 1000, '2'));

-- The error message says that the data in the third field
-- is too long.
-- The fixed-length-string field has a maximum length
-- of 3 characters.
-- But the data in the insert statement is 4 characters.
-- This causes the insert statement to reject.
insert into sec0603_text_datatypes
values ('E', '22', '4444', rpad('2', 1000, '2'));

-- The error message says that the data in the fourth field
-- is too long.
-- The long-string field has a maximum length
-- of 1000 characters.
-- But the data in the insert statement is 1001 characters.
-- This causes the insert statement to reject.
insert into sec0603_text_datatypes
values ('F', '22', '22', rpad('4' ,1001, '4'));
```

```
-- Show the result
select row_id,
    length(variable_length_string) as length_of_vl_string,
    length(fixed_length_string) as length_of_fl_string,
    length(long_string) as length_of_long_string
from sec0603_text_datatypes;
```

Oracle result table

ROW_ID	LENGTH_OF_VL_STRING	LENGTH_OF_FL_STRING	LENGTH_OF_LONG_STRING
A	1	3	1
B	2	3	1000
C	3	3	1000

Access SQL ❶

```
create table sec0603_text_datatypes
(row_id      varchar(3),
 variable_length_string  varchar(3),
 fixed_length_string  char(3),
 long_string  memo);

-- These insert statements will work correctly
insert into sec0603_text_datatypes
values ('A', '1', '1', '1');

insert into sec0603_text_datatypes
values ('B', '22', '22', string(1000, '2'));

insert into sec0603_text_datatypes
values ('C', '333', '333', string(1000, '3'));

-- The next two insert statements actually run
-- But they run incorrectly and silently change the data.
-- The data is truncated to the maximum length of the field
-- But there is no error message or warning message.
-- YOU DO NOT WANT THIS TO OCCUR
-- THIS IS A BAD FEATURE

-- In this insert statement, the second field is too long.
-- The data in the variable length string is changed
-- silently to '444'.
insert into sec0603_text_datatypes
values ('D', '4444', '22', string(1000, '2'));
```

```
-- In this insert statement, the third field is too long.
-- The data in the fixed length string is changed
-- silently to '444'.
insert into sec0603_text_datatypes
values ('E', '22', '4444', string(1000, '2'));

-- In this insert statement, there is a problem with
-- the fourth field.
-- The fourth field has a memo datatype.
-- This datatype can hold up to 2 gigabytes of characters.
-- However, you may hit many limitations before you can
-- create a string of that size.
-- In this example, I hit the limitation of the amount
-- of memory installed in my computer.
-- This causes the String function to fail.
-- The error message I get is: system resources exceeded
-- Then the failure of the String function causes the
-- Insert statement to also fail.
-- That is what you want to happen.
insert into sec0603_text_datatypes
values ('F', '22', '22', string(1000000, '2'));

-- Show the result
select row_id,
       len(variable_length_string) as length_of_vl_string,
       len(fixed_length_string) as length_of_fl_string,
       len(long_string) as length_of_long_string
from sec0603_text_datatypes;
```

Access result table

row_id	length_of_vl_string	length_of_fl_string	length_of_long_string
A	1	3	1
B	2	3	1000
C	3	3	1000
D	3	3	1000
E	2	3	1000

Notes

❶ I know that this code contains row functions that we haven't discussed yet, but just let me do the work here so you can observe the text datatypes. These row functions are discussed in chapter 9.

6-4   Numeric datatypes

Access has many different types of numbers. It makes a distinction between precise numbers and floating-point (approximate) numbers. It also has different categories of numbers according to the number of bits they can use.

Oracle has integrated all these different types of numbers into one datatype, so you do not need to wonder which type of number to use in Oracle because there is only one possibility.

6-5   Date/time datatypes

A field with a date/time datatype always contains both a date and a time. If you enter only the time, usually the date will be set to today's date. If you enter only the date, usually the time is automatically set to midnight. In most SQL products, the date/time data is kept to an accuracy of one second.

When greater accuracy is needed, the timestamp datatype is used. This is used mostly for timing and sequencing events within the computer itself. Oracle supports this datatype, but Access does not.

Oracle also has a datatype, called interval, to express lengths of time rather than specific points of time. For example "26 minutes" is a length of time, but "January 1, 2000 at 12:01" is a point of time.

In Access, lengths of time are expressed as numbers with an implied unit. In the preceding example, Access would just store the number 26 in the data. The unit of "minutes" would be implied.

6-6   Other datatypes

Most of the other datatypes are used for specialized purposes such as:

- Storage
- HTML data (Web pages)
- XML data
- Spatial data

Several datatypes are available for storage. The types of data that can be stored includes pictures, spreadsheets, compiled programs, and the entire text of books.

Sometimes a database will store a set of objects, such as a set of pictures, in a table as a way of organizing them. Then additional columns are added to the table to describe each object. SQL does not do much with the objects themselves, but SQL can be useful in manipulating the table using the descriptive columns.

HTML and XML data are important for Web applications. In the past few years there has been a lot of growth in the uses of XML.

Some SQL products have special datatypes to handle spatial data. This functionality is used in medical imaging, engineering, city planning, and architecture.

6-7 Putting data into a new table

When we first create a table by defining its columns, the table itself is just an empty structure. There is no data in it.

In section 6-1 we created a new version of the 1_foods table with the columns rearranged to make the menu_item column be the first column. Here we continue that example. The new table has already been built. Now we want to put data in it.

We have discussed two ways to put data in a table. One way uses an insert statement with literal values and adds one row at a time (see section 4-9). The other way uses an insert statement with a select statement and can add many rows at once (see section 4-10).

In this example we use an insert with a select statement because all of the data is already in the original version of the table and it just needs to be copied into the new table.

Task

Copy all the data from the 1_foods table to the sec0607_foods table.

Oracle & Access SQL

```
insert into sec0607_foods
select menu_item,
       supplier_id,
       product_code,
       description,
       price,
       price_increase
from 1_foods;
```

The `sec0607_foods` table with data loaded into it

```
   MENU  SUPPLIER  PRODUCT                                          PRICE
   ITEM  ID        CODE     DESCRIPTION           PRICE  INCREASE
 -------  --------  -------  --------------------  --------  --------
       1  ASP       FS       FRESH SALAD            $2.00     $0.25
       2  ASP       SP       SOUP OF THE DAY        $1.50    (null)
       3  ASP       SW       SANDWICH               $3.50     $0.40
       4  CBC       GS       GRILLED STEAK          $6.00     $0.70
       5  CBC       SW       HAMBURGER              $2.50     $0.30
       6  FRV       BR       BROCCOLI               $1.00     $0.05
       7  FRV       FF       FRENCH FRIES           $1.50    (null)
       8  JBR       AS       SODA                   $1.25     $0.25
       9  JBR       VR       COFFEE                 $0.85     $0.15
      10  VSB       AS       DESSERT                $3.00     $0.50
```

Check your understanding

Use a `create table` statement to create a new copy of the `1_employees` table, with a new name of course. Then use an `insert` statement with a `select` clause to copy all the data from the `1_employees` table to your new copy of the table.

6-8　Creating the `1_employees` table in Oracle

It is time for you to look at some real code instead of simplified examples. In this section I want to show you the Oracle code I wrote to create the `1_employees` table of the `Lunches` database. The notes explain what the code is doing. You might understand most of this already, but there are a few parts of the code that we haven't covered yet.

This code is from the SQLFUN_BUILD_ORACLE_TABLES.TXT script you ran to create the tables for this book. After you read this section, you might want to try to read the rest of this script to see how the other tables are built.

The type of punctuation used in this example is what I consider to be the most "natural" type of punctuation. Sometimes you might see SQL code like this written with a very stylized method of punctuation, such as:

```
CREATE TABLE L_EMPLOYEES
(   EMPLOYEE_ID     NUMBER(3)
,   FIRST_NAME      VARCHAR2(10)
,   LAST_NAME       VARCHAR2(20)
);
```

Task

Show the Oracle code that creates the `l_employees` table.

Oracle SQL

```
-- CREATE THE L_EMPLOYEES TABLE   ❶
CREATE TABLE L_EMPLOYEES   ❷
(EMPLOYEE_ID      NUMBER(3),
FIRST_NAME        VARCHAR2(10),
LAST_NAME         VARCHAR2(20),
DEPT_CODE         VARCHAR2(3),
HIRE_DATE         DATE,
CREDIT_LIMIT      NUMBER(4,2),
PHONE_NUMBER      VARCHAR2(4),
MANAGER_ID        NUMBER(3));

ALTER TABLE L_EMPLOYEES   ❸
ADD CONSTRAINT PK_L_EMPLOYEES
PRIMARY KEY (EMPLOYEE_ID);


INSERT INTO L_EMPLOYEES VALUES   ❹
  (201, 'SUSAN', 'BROWN', 'EXE', '01-JUN-1998', 30, '3484',
  NULL );
INSERT INTO L_EMPLOYEES VALUES
  (202, 'JIM', 'KERN', 'SAL', '16-AUG-1999', 25, '8722',
  201);
INSERT INTO L_EMPLOYEES VALUES
  (203, 'MARTHA', 'WOODS', 'SHP', '02-FEB-2009', 25,
  '7591', 201);
INSERT INTO L_EMPLOYEES VALUES
  (204, 'ELLEN', 'OWENS', 'SAL', '01-JUL-2008', 15, '6830',
  202);
INSERT INTO L_EMPLOYEES VALUES
  (205, 'HENRY', 'PERKINS', 'SAL', '01-MAR-2006', 25,
  '5286', 202);
INSERT INTO L_EMPLOYEES VALUES
  (206, 'CAROL', 'ROSE', 'ACT', NULL, NULL, NULL, NULL);
INSERT INTO L_EMPLOYEES VALUES
  (207, 'DAN', 'SMITH', 'SHP', '01-DEC-2008', 25, '2259',
  203);
INSERT INTO L_EMPLOYEES VALUES
  (208, 'FRED', 'CAMPBELL', 'SHP', '01-APR-2008', 25,
  '1752', 203);
INSERT INTO L_EMPLOYEES VALUES
  (209, 'PAULA', 'JACOBS', 'MKT', '17-MAR-1999', 15,
  '3357', 201);
```

```
INSERT INTO L_EMPLOYEES VALUES
  (210, 'NANCY', 'HOFFMAN', 'SAL', '16-FEB-2007', 25,
  '2974', 203);
COMMIT;

ANALYZE TABLE L_EMPLOYEES COMPUTE STATISTICS;   ❺

CREATE SEQUENCE SEQ_EMPLOYEE_ID   ❻
START WITH 211
INCREMENT BY 1;
```

Notes

❶ This code begins with a brief comment that says what the code does. In Oracle and most other SQL products, a comment line begins with two dashes usually followed by a space.

❷ Set up the structure of the table. Define the names of the columns, their datatypes, and their sequence.

❸ This `alter table` command makes the `employee_id` column the primary key of the table.

❹ These `insert` statements put the data into the table.

❺ You should run the `analyze table` command after you create a new table and load data into it. You should also run this command after you add a substantial amount of data to any table. The command puts information about the table, such as its size and other characteristics, into the Data Dictionary.

❻ This `create sequence` command sets up a sequence that can be used to automatically set the next value for the `employee_id` column.

Changing Tables

The structure of a table is not cast in concrete and fixed forever. A table can be changed in many ways, even after it contains data. The `alter table` statement is especially designed to make changes to tables. It can make several types of changes. A few examples of this command are given in these sections.

6-9   Adding a primary key to a table

This section shows how to add a primary key to a table, even after the table contains many rows of data. The syntax is:

```
ALTER TABLE table_name
ADD CONSTRAINT name_of_the_constraint
PRIMARY KEY (list_of_columns_in_the_primary_key);
```

A primary key is one type of constraint, which is a rule that restricts the data that can be entered into the table. This is discussed in section 5-15. The preceding command adds a constraint to a table and the type of constraint it adds is a ***primary key constraint***.

When you create a new table by saving the results of a `select` statement, as we did in chapter 4, the new table is created without a primary key. If you want to have a primary key on one of these tables, you must create it yourself.

If the table already contains data, that data must conform to the restrictions of a primary key. Otherwise, this command will fail and you will get an error message. A primary key cannot be put on a table if the data in the table does not support it. The data must not have two rows with the same values in all of the primary key columns, or nulls in any of the columns of the primary key.

A table is only allowed to have one primary key, although this key may consist of a combination of several columns.

It is not necessary to issue a `commit` command after an `alter table` command. Changes made by the `alter table` command are immediately made in a permanent way. Actually, a `commit` is never needed after a Data Definition Language (DDL) command, which creates a database object or changes the structure of an object. `Commit` is only needed after the Data Modification Language (DML) commands, such as `insert`, `update`, and `delete`, which change the data in a table.

Task

Add a primary key to the `sec0609_foods` table. The primary key of this table will consist of the two columns, `supplier_id` and `product_code`.

Oracle & Access SQL: Add a primary key to a table

```
alter table sec0609_foods ❶
add constraint pk_sec0609_foods ❷
primary key (supplier_id, product_code); ❸
```

Notes

❶ The table `sec0609_foods` will be changed by this command.

❷ This gives a name to the constraint. In this case, the name is `pk_sec0609_foods`. It combines `pk_`, meaning primary key, with the name of the table. This is my own naming convention. You can name it something else.

The name of the constraint is used mostly in error messages and in a few operations such as deleting the constraint or temporarily disabling it. It is not referred to directly in any `select` statement. The name should suggest the purpose of the constraint.

❸ The words `primary key` specify that this is a primary key constraint. The list of columns that follows includes the columns that will form the primary key. This list can contain any number of columns, even all the columns in the table, but it is usually limited to one or two.

Check your understanding

Add a primary key to a copy of the employees table, `sec0609_employees`.

6-10 Changing the primary key of a table

This section shows you how to change the primary key of a table. A table can have only one primary key, so you must delete the old primary key before you can create a new one. Often when you do this, the new primary key adds more columns to the old one.

Task

Change the primary key of the `sec0610_foods` table. Make the `menu_item` column the new primary key of this table. Show two ways to drop the primary key of a table.

Oracle & Access SQL:
Method 1 — Using the name of the constraint to drop it

```
alter table sec0610_foods
drop constraint pk_sec0610_foods;  ❶

alter table sec0610_foods
add constraint pk_sec0610_foods
primary key (menu_item);
```

Oracle SQL:
Method 2 — Not using the name of the constraint to drop it

```
alter table sec0610b_foods
drop primary key; ❷

alter table sec0610b_foods
add constraint pk_sec0610b_foods
primary key (menu_item);
```

Access does not support this syntax.

Notes

❶ On this line, `pk_sec0610_foods` is the name of the constraint. The name of a constraint is easy to forget. You might need to find the name of the constraint in the Data Dictionary to delete the primary key.

❷ Using this format for the `alter table` statement, you do not need to know the name of the constraint to delete the primary key.

6-11 Adding a new column to a table

This section shows you how to add a new column to a table. The table may already have many rows of data in it. The new column is always positioned at the end of the table. Initially it contains only nulls. Later you will have the task of putting data into it.

The SQL code to add a new column is different in Oracle than it is in Access. This is partly because they must use their own datatypes in this command. Another reason is that Access uses the words `add column` where Oracle only uses `add`.

In Access, the GUI always shows a table with "Add New Field" positioned at the end of the table. This is done to remind you that you can always add a new column to a table.

Task

Add a new column to the `sec0613_foods` table. Name the new column `date_introduced` and give it a datatype of `date`.

Oracle SQL

```
alter table sec0611_foods
add date_introduced date; ❶
```

Access SQL

```
alter table sec0611_foods
add column date_introduced datetime; ❷
```

Beginning table (sec0611_foods table)

MENU ITEM	SUPPLIER ID	PRODUCT CODE	DESCRIPTION	PRICE	PRICE INCREASE
1	ASP	FS	FRESH SALAD	$2.00	$0.25
2	ASP	SP	SOUP OF THE DAY	$1.50	(null)
3	ASP	SW	SANDWICH	$3.50	$0.40
4	CBC	GS	GRILLED STEAK	$6.00	$0.70
5	CBC	SW	HAMBURGER	$2.50	$0.30
6	FRV	BR	BROCCOLI	$1.00	$0.05
7	FRV	FF	FRENCH FRIES	$1.50	(null)
8	JBR	AS	SODA	$1.25	$0.25
9	JBR	VR	COFFEE	$0.85	$0.15
10	VSB	AS	DESSERT	$3.00	$0.50

Ending table ❸

MENU ITEM	SUPPLIER ID	PRODUCT CODE	DESCRIPTION	PRICE	PRICE INCREASE	DATE_INTR
1	ASP	FS	FRESH SALAD	$2.00	$0.25	(null)
2	ASP	SP	SOUP OF THE DAY	$1.50	(null)	(null)
3	ASP	SW	SANDWICH	$3.50	$0.40	(null)
4	CBC	GS	GRILLED STEAK	$6.00	$0.70	(null)
5	CBC	SW	HAMBURGER	$2.50	$0.30	(null)
6	FRV	BR	BROCCOLI	$1.00	$0.05	(null)
7	FRV	FF	FRENCH FRIES	$1.50	(null)	(null)
8	JBR	AS	SODA	$1.25	$0.25	(null)
9	JBR	VR	COFFEE	$0.85	$0.15	(null)
10	VSB	AS	DESSERT	$3.00	$0.50	(null)

Notes

❶ In Oracle, the `date_introduced` column is given the Oracle datatype `date`. Notice that the word `add` is followed by the column name. The implication is that a new column is being added.

❷ In Access, the `date_introduced` column is given the Access datatype `datetime`. Notice that the word `add` is followed by the word `column`.

❸ Initially, the new column contains nulls. After you define this column, you need to put data into it. The new column is always the last column in the table. Within most SQL products, you have no control over the placement of the column.

Check your understanding

Add two new columns to a copy of the departments table, `sec0611_departments`. One new column, a text column, will be for the name of the manager of the department. The other new column, a numeric column, is for the annual budget of the department.

6-12 Expanding the length of a column

This section shows you how to expand the length of a column in Oracle by changing its datatype. A text column must remain a text column, but you can change its maximum length and switch between a fixed length character string and a variable length character string.

A numeric column must remain a numeric column, but you can change the maximum number of digits it can contain or the number of digits after the decimal point. These changes are useful when you receive data that is too big to put into the columns you have defined.

All dates have the same datatype, so it does not make sense to change the datatype of a date column.

Task

Change the datatype of the `description` column of the `sec0612_foods` table. It is currently defined as a variable length character string with a maximum length of 20 characters. Change it to a character string with a length of 25 characters.

In Oracle, change the price column of this table. It is currently defined as a number with a maximum of four digits, two of which come after the decimal point. Change it to have a maximum of seven digits total — five before the decimal and two after. In Access, this change is not needed because the price column already has a datatype of currency, so it can already handle large numbers.

Oracle SQL

```
alter table sec0612_foods
modify description varchar2(25);

alter table sec0612_foods
modify price number(7,2);
```

Access SQL ❶

```
alter table sec0612_foods
alter column description varchar(25);
```

Result table — The table does not show any difference

Notes

❶ In Access you can make similar changes on the GUI level using the Design view of the table.

Check your understanding

Expand the length of the last_name column of a copy of the employees table, sec0612_employees. Expand it to a length of 50 letters so people with hyphenated last names can be hired by the company.

6-13 Deleting a column from a table

This section shows you how to delete a column from a table. The early versions of Oracle did not support this option, but now it does. It was added to Oracle version 8. New options continue to be added to the alter table command.

Task

Delete the `price_increase` column from the new version of the `sec0613_foods` table.

Oracle & Access SQL

```
alter table sec0613_foods
drop column price_increase;
```

Beginning table (sec0613_foods table)

```
 MENU SUPPLIER PRODUCT                                     PRICE
 ITEM ID       CODE    DESCRIPTION           PRICE INCREASE DATE_INTR
------- -------- ------- ---------------------- -------- -------- ---------
      1 ASP      FS      FRESH SALAD           $2.00    $0.25 (null)
      2 ASP      SP      SOUP OF THE DAY       $1.50  (null)   (null)
      3 ASP      SW      SANDWICH              $3.50    $0.40 (null)
      4 CBC      GS      GRILLED STEAK         $6.00    $0.70 (null)
      5 CBC      SW      HAMBURGER             $2.50    $0.30 (null)
      6 FRV      BR      BROCCOLI              $1.00    $0.05 (null)
      7 FRV      FF      FRENCH FRIES          $1.50  (null)   (null)
      8 JBR      AS      SODA                  $1.25    $0.25 (null)
      9 JBR      VR      COFFEE                $0.85    $0.15 (null)
     10 VSB      AS      DESSERT               $3.00    $0.50 (null)
```

Ending table

```
 MENU SUPPLIER PRODUCT
 ITEM ID       CODE    DESCRIPTION            PRICE DATE_INTR
------- -------- ------- ---------------------- -------- ---------
      1 ASP      FS      FRESH SALAD           $2.00 (null)
      2 ASP      SP      SOUP OF THE DAY       $1.50 (null)
      3 ASP      SW      SANDWICH              $3.50 (null)
      4 CBC      GS      GRILLED STEAK         $6.00 (null)
      5 CBC      SW      HAMBURGER             $2.50 (null)
      6 FRV      BR      BROCCOLI              $1.00 (null)
      7 FRV      FF      FRENCH FRIES          $1.50 (null)
      8 JBR      AS      SODA                  $1.25 (null)
      9 JBR      VR      COFFEE                $0.85 (null)
     10 VSB      AS      DESSERT               $3.00 (null)
```

Check your understanding

Delete the `phone_number` column from a copy of the employees table, `sec0613_employees`.

6-14 Making other changes to tables

This section shows a method of making changes to a table that does not use the `alter table` command. You already know this method, but I want to remind you of it here, in the context of the present discussion. This method can make almost any change you can think of. It is very flexible, but it is less efficient than the `alter table` command. Efficiency is usually important only when you are working with very large tables.

Here are some of the changes you can make to any table:

- Add new columns.

- Delete columns.

- Delete rows.

- Rename columns.

- Change the data in columns.

- Change the datatype of columns.

- Reorder columns.

- Delete a primary key.

This gives you nearly total control over every aspect of a table. Adding a primary key is the only change that requires the `alter table` command.

This technique uses a `create table` statement with a `select` statement, which we used in section 4-1.

Task

Create the `sec0614_phone_list` table from the `l_employees` table. Include the columns `last_name`, `first_name`, and `phone_number`.

- Rename the `phone_number` column to `ext`.

- Change the order of the `first_name` and `last_name` columns.

- Delete many columns from the beginning table.

- Add a new column for `notes` and leave it blank.

- Change the phone number for Woods to 9408.

Oracle SQL ❶

```
create table sec0614_phone_list as
select last_name,
       first_name,
       phone_number as ext,
       '               ' as notes ❸
from 1_employees
where employee_id between 203 and 206;

update sec0614_phone_list
set ext = '9408' ❹
where last_name = 'WOODS';
```

Access SQL ❷

```
select last_name,
       first_name,
       phone_number as ext,
       '               ' as notes ❸
into sec0614_phone_list
from 1_employees
where employee_id between 203 and 206;

update sec0614_phone_list
set ext = '9408'
where last_name = 'WOODS';
```

Beginning table (1_employees table)

EMPLOYEE ID	FIRST NAME	LAST NAME	DEPT CODE	HIRE_DATE	CREDIT LIMIT	PHONE NUMBER	MANAGER ID
201	SUSAN	BROWN	EXE	01-JUN-1998	$30.00	3484	(null)
202	JIM	KERN	SAL	16-AUG-1999	$25.00	8722	201
203	MARTHA	WOODS	SHP	02-FEB-2009	$25.00	7591	201
204	ELLEN	OWENS	SAL	01-JUL-2008	$15.00	6830	202
205	HENRY	PERKINS	SAL	01-MAR-2006	$25.00	5286	202
206	CAROL	ROSE	ACT	(null)	(null)	(null)	(null)
207	DAN	SMITH	SHP	01-DEC-2008	$25.00	2259	203
208	FRED	CAMPBELL	SHP	01-APR-2008	$25.00	1752	203
209	PAULA	JACOBS	MKT	17-MAR-1999	$15.00	3357	201
210	NANCY	HOFFMAN	SAL	16-FEB-2007	$25.00	2974	203

New table created in this section (`sec0614_phone_list` table) ❺

```
LAST_NAME    FIRST_NAME  EXT   NOTES
----------   ----------  ----  -------------
WOODS        MARTHA      9408
OWENS        ELLEN       6830
PERKINS      HENRY       5286
ROSE         CAROL       (null)
```

Notes

❶ In Oracle, the `create table` command and the `update` command can be put into a single script and run as a single unit.

❷ In Access, the `create table` command must be run first. Then the `update` command can be run. The SQL window in Access only allows us to run one command at a time.

❸ This adds a new column to the table and names it `notes`. There are 13 spaces between the beginning quote and the ending quote. In Oracle this makes the column a fixed length character string with a length of 13 characters. In Access the 13 spaces are not needed, and you can use two quotes with one space between them. Spaces, not nulls, are put in this field.

❹ In the `update` statement, the `phone_number` must be referred to by its new name, `ext`.

❺ Here is the procedure you would follow if you wanted to name this new table `l_employees`, so that it would replace the beginning table. Do not do this now.

```
drop table l_employees;
create table l_employees as
select * from sec0614_phone_list;
```

Tables with Duplicate Rows

In a relational database you are allowed to create tables with duplicate rows. That is, you can have two or more rows that have the same values in every column. Usually you want to avoid duplicate rows in your tables. When a table has a primary key, no duplicate rows are allowed. That is one of the purposes of a primary key.

6-15 The problem with duplicate rows

This section discusses when you may want to avoid duplicate rows and when you may want to allow them.

When to avoid duplicate rows

If you are going to share a table with someone else, or give it to them, the table should have a primary key, which will ensure that it does not have any duplicate rows. Such rows are avoided because it is usually unclear what they mean. Two different interpretations are possible:

1. Each row represents a separate object.

2. These rows are redundant representations of the same object.

To prevent confusion, you should not allow duplicate rows in tables that are made public.

When to allow duplicate rows

If you are the only person using a table, you might want to allow duplicate rows. You may allow them especially if the table is part of an intermediate step of some process, rather than a final result. The idea is that you will know what the duplicate rows mean in your own tables, even if nobody else knows.

Why duplicate rows are allowed in tables

Duplicate rows are allowed in tables for convenience. It is always better not to have duplicate rows in your tables, but it often requires extra effort to avoid them. You do not always have to make that effort.

For example, when you use a `select` statement to get a result table, two of the rows of the result table may be identical. That might or might not be a problem. It is a problem if you are showing the results to others and they do not know the meaning of these duplicate rows. It is not a problem if you are the only person seeing these results and you do know their meaning.

Example of duplicate rows that represent separate objects

In this example, the duplicate rows in a table represent distinct objects, events, or relationships. You are using a database to track your expenses. To keep things simple, you have decided to keep two pieces of data: the object you bought and the price. On Monday, you buy a hamburger for $2.00 and eat it. On Tuesday, you buy another hamburger for $2.00 and eat it. In your table of expenses these are duplicate rows. The duplicate row means that there is really another object. Together, the two rows mean that you bought two hamburgers and spent $4.00.

This example may seem artificial because if you also entered the date of the purchase, the rows would not be duplicates. They are only duplicates because you have not recorded all the data. However, we are always in this situation, whether we are aware of it or not. Our tables contain what we consider to be the most significant pieces of information, but there is always some information that is left out.

The two duplicate rows are two different pieces of information (sec0615a table)

```
OBJECT_BOUGHT            PRICE
--------------------  --------
NEWSPAPER                $0.75
COFFEE                   $1.55
HAMBURGER                $2.00   ❶
FLOWERS                 $15.38
HAMBURGER                $2.00   ❶
BOOK                    $24.89
MOVIE  TICKETS          $22.00
```

Example of duplicate rows that represent the same object

In this example, the duplicate rows in a table are redundant representations of a single object, event, or relationship. You are running an advertising campaign. You buy copies of several mailing lists and combine them into a single list. The duplicate rows have the same name and address. These duplicate rows are multiple representations of the same information. Here the duplicate row does not mean that there is another object. It only means that the same object is shown twice.

The two duplicate rows are a single piece of information (sec0615b table)

```
FIRST_NAME  LAST_NAME   ADDRESS
----------  ----------  --------------------
SUSAN       BROWN       512 ELM  STREET   ❶
JIM         KERN        837-9TH AVENUE
MARTHA      WOODS       169 PARK AVENUE
SUSAN       BROWN       512 ELM  STREET   ❶
ELLEN       OWENS       418 HENRY STREET
```

Notes

❶ These rows are duplicates.

6-16 How to eliminate duplicate rows

There are two ways to get rid of the duplicate rows in your tables. The method you use depends on the meaning you are giving to the duplicate rows. This section shows how to eliminate the duplicates if you consider them to be multiple representations of the same object. The next section shows how to add a new column that distinguishes between the duplicate rows. You use this method when you consider them to be representations of different objects.

If you want to keep only one row of each set of duplicate rows, you can create a new table using `select distinct`.

Task

Eliminate the duplicate rows from the `sec0615b` table. Keep only one copy of each row that has a duplicate.

Oracle SQL

```
create table sec0616_no_duplicate_rows as
select distinct *
from sec0615b;
```

Access SQL

```
select distinct *
into sec0616_no_duplicate_rows
from sec0615b;
```

Beginning table (sec0615b table)

```
FIRST_NAME  LAST_NAME   ADDRESS
----------  ----------  ------------------
SUSAN       BROWN       512 ELM STREET    ❶
JIM         KERN        837-9TH AVENUE
MARTHA      WOODS       169 PARK AVENUE
SUSAN       BROWN       512 ELM STREET    ❶
ELLEN       OWENS       418 HENRY STREET
```

Result table (sec0616_no_duplicate_rows table)

```
FIRST_NAME LAST_NAME  ADDRESS
---------- ---------- --------------------
ELLEN      OWENS      418 HENRY STREET
JIM        KERN       837-9TH AVENUE
MARTHA     WOODS      169 PARK AVENUE
SUSAN      BROWN      512 ELM STREET    ❶
```

Notes

❶ The beginning table has two rows that are duplicates. Every field in them has exactly the same value. The result table has just one of these rows.

Check your understanding

Eliminate the duplicate rows from the sec0616_duplicate_rows table.

6-17 How to distinguish between duplicate rows

Suppose you have a table containing duplicate rows and you consider each of these rows to represent a separate object. You can change this table to distinguish between the duplicate rows by adding a new column of meaningful data to the table. For example, you could add a date_purchased column to the first table in section 6-12. This would show that the two hamburgers were purchased on different dates. The two rows for hamburgers would thus no longer be duplicates.

There are no duplicate rows in this table (sec0617a table)

```
OBJECT_BOUGHT             PRICE DATE_PURCHASED
------------------------- --------- --------------
NEWSPAPER                 $0.75     14-JUN-2010
COFFEE                    $1.55     14-JUN-2010
HAMBURGER                 $2.00     14-JUN-2010
FLOWERS                   $15.38    14-JUN-2010
HAMBURGER                 $2.00     15-JUN-2010
BOOK                      $24.89    15-JUN-2010
MOVIE TICKETS             $22.00    15-JUN-2010
```

Although it is best to add a new column of meaningful data, this may require a lot of work. Another method is commonly used, which adds a column of numbers to the table. Each row is given a distinct number, ensuring that there will no longer be any duplicate rows in the table. This method is shown next.

Why would you want to distinguish between duplicate rows? For example, you might have four rows that are identical, but you only want to have three of them.

Task

Distinguish between the duplicate rows of the sec0612a table by adding a column of numbers to the table. Make this the first column of the table.

Oracle SQL

```
create table sec0617_with_line_numbers as  ❶
select rownum as row_id,  ❷
       object_bought,
       price
from sec0615a;
```

Access SQL

```
select *
into sec0617c  ❸
from sec0615a;

alter table sec0617c
add column row_id counter;  ❹

select row_id,  ❺
       object_bought,
       price
into sec0617_with_line_numbers
from sec0617c;
```

Beginning table (sec0615a table)

OBJECT_BOUGHT	PRICE
NEWSPAPER	$0.75
COFFEE	$1.55
HAMBURGER	$2.00
FLOWERS	$15.38
HAMBURGER	$2.00
BOOK	$24.89
MOVIE TICKETS	$22.00

Ending table (sec0617_with_line_numbers table)

```
   ROW_ID OBJECT_BOUGHT           PRICE
--------- -------------------- --------
        1 NEWSPAPER               $0.75
        2 COFFEE                  $1.55
        3 HAMBURGER               $2.00
        4 FLOWERS                $15.38
        5 HAMBURGER               $2.00
        6 BOOK                   $24.89
        7 MOVIE  TICKETS         $22.00
```

Notes

❶ In Oracle, when you add a column of numbers to a table, you can create either a new table or a new view.

❷ In Oracle, `rownum` generates the row numbers. It is a 0-parameter function that can be used within a `select` statement.

❸ In Access, when you add a column of numbers to a table, you must create a new table. You cannot create a new view because the `alter table` statement only works with tables.

❹ In Access, `counter` generates the row numbers. It is a sequence generator that is handled as a datatype. To add it to a table you must use an `alter table` statement, which will place the `row_id` column at the end of this table.

❺ This places the `row_id` column as the first column of the table, which is one of the requirements of this task.

Check your understanding

Assign a number to each row of the `sec0617_duplicate_rows` table.

Key Points

- You can create a new table with a `create table` statement. This allows you to see exactly what a table is and control every aspect of it.

- A table has a name and it has a sequence of columns in a specific order. Each column has a name and a datatype. That is what a table is. A table is a structure that can hold data, but it does not consist of the data it holds.

- When a table is first created, it contains no data. After a table is created rows of data can be put into it.

- The basic datatypes for columns are text, number, and date. Some SQL products have other datatypes for special kinds of data.

- You can make changes to a table after it has been created and even after data has been put into the table. You can add or change its primary key, add or delete columns, expand the size of a column, or make other changes.

- Duplicate rows in a table can cause confusion. Occasionally this cannot be avoided, However, you should almost always put a primary key on your data tables. This will prevent duplicate rows.

chapter 7

Formats, Sequences, and Indexes

You now know how to build your own tables and put data in them. This chapter discusses some other features you may want to add to your tables.

Formats affect the appearance of the data without changing its value. In Access, formats can be part of the definition of a table. In Oracle, they are used mostly within SQL statements to format dates.

Sequences provide a way to automatically number the rows of a table.

Indexes are used mostly to speed up the processing of `select` statements within large databases.

This chapter also discusses the Data Dictionary, which shows you how to find information about the tables you create.

Formats

People often confuse formats with functions. A ***format*** refers to the way a value is presented. For instance, "01-jan-10" and "January 1, 2010" are two formats for the same date. A function makes a change to the value. For instance, "01-jan-10 + 1" is "January 2, 2010".

7-1 Formats of dates

In both Oracle and Access, dates and times are stored together within a single datatype. Whenever you see a date, there is always a time stored with it. Whenever you see a time, there is always a date stored with it.

Inside the database a date is stored in a very compressed manner. If you saw one directly, you would not know what it was. When a date is displayed in a result table, it is always translated into a character string, such as "Jan 1, 2010", so that you can understand it. Several different translations are available to give different formats of the same date. Another format is "2010-01-01". The date format you specify tells the database how you want the dates to be displayed. If you do not specify a date format, the default date format is used.

In this section we discuss how to specify a format that is different than the default date format. In the following two sections, you will see how these formats can be applied to display dates in particular ways and how to enter times with dates.

The following table shows some of the most useful date formats. These can be combined together in any way you wish. These are used both for displaying dates and entering dates into tables.

In Oracle, there is one default format for dates. It is usually set to dd-mon-yy, which shows dates in the format 20-JAN-10 with a two-digit year. In the SQL Command Line environment, you can change this default format to dd-mon-yyyy with a four-digit year. To do this you can use the command:

alter session set nls_date_format = 'DD-MON-YYYY';

Whatever the default format is, if you want to display or enter dates in any other format, you must explicitly state what format you are using. In Oracle, dates and times are enclosed in single quotes. This is similar to text strings.

In Access, when you enter a date, you enclose it in pound signs (##) to set it apart from a text string. Access knows it is a date by the pound signs, and will attempt to automatically determine what format this date is in. Access can accept a date in many formats.

In Access, the default format for displaying a date is set by the Windows operating system, using the Regional Settings in the Windows Control Panel.

Oracle and Access date formats.

Oracle Format	Access Format	Example	Comment
YEAR			
yyyy	yyyy	1998	Four-digit year
yy	yy	98	Two-digit year
MONTH			
month	mmmm	October	Full name of the month
mon	mmm	Oct	Abbreviated name of the month
mm	mm	10	Number of the month, 01 to 12
DAY			
dd	dd	18	Date of the month, 01 to 31
day	dddd	Friday	Full name of the day
dy	ddd	Fri	Abbreviated name of the day
d	w	6	Numeric day of the week: 1 is Sunday, 2 is Monday, 7 is Saturday
TIME			
hh24	hh	14	24-hour time, 00 to 23
hh12	hh am/pm	02	12-hour time, 00 to 11
hh	hh am/pm	02	12-hour time, 00 to 11
mi	nn	30	Minute after the hour, 00 to 59
ss	ss	59	Second, 00 to 59
am	am/pm		AM or PM, whichever applies
pm	am/pm		AM or PM, whichever applies
OTHER			
q	q	4	Quarter of the year, 1 to 4
ww	ww	45	Week of the year, 1 to 54
JULIAN			
ddd	y	350	Number of days since January 1
j			Number of days since Dec. 31, 4713 BC
sssss			Number of seconds since midnight; used to calculate with times

Some combinations of date formats.

`mm-dd-yyyy  hh:mi:ss am`	`mm-dd-yyyy  hh:nn:ss am/pm`	10-18-1998 05:36:45 PM
`mm-dd-yyyy  hh:mi am`	`mm-dd-yyyy  hh:nn am/pm`	10-18-1998 05:36 PM
`day, month dd, yyyy`	`dddd, mmmm dd, yyyy`	Sunday, October 18, 1998
`dd-mon-yy`	`dd-mmm-yy`	18-Oct-98
`mm-dd-yyyy`	`mm-dd-yyyy`	10-18-1998
`hh:mi:ss am`	`hh:nn:ss am/pm`	05:36:45 PM
`hh:mi am`	`hh:nn am/pm`	05:36 PM
`hh24:mi`	`hh:nn`	17:36

7-2   Displaying formatted dates

In Oracle, the `to_char` function specifies the format to use when displaying a date. `To_char` means that we are converting a date datatype into a character datatype so it can be displayed. In Access, the `format` function is used the same way.

These functions have two parameters. The first is the name of the column containing the dates. The second is the format to be used in displaying the date. The format specification must be enclosed in single quotes. It is possible to add text to the format, such as "In the year of". This text must be enclosed in double quotes.

Task

From the `1_employees` table, list the `employee_id`, `first_name`, and `hire_date` of all the employees. Add another column showing the hire date formatted in the form `mm-dd-yyyy` followed by the time. Sort the rows of the result by the `employee_id`.

Oracle SQL

```
select employee_id,
       first_name,
       hire_date,
       to_char(hire_date, 'MM-DD-YYYY HH:MI AM') ❶
                          as formatted_date ❸
from 1_employees
order by employee_id;
```

Access SQL

```
select employee_id,
       first_name,
       hire_date,
       format(hire_date, 'MM-DD-YYYY HH:NN AM/PM') ❷
                          as formatted_date ❸
from 1_employees
order by employee_id;
```

Beginning table (1_employees table)

EMPLOYEE ID	FIRST_NAME	LAST_NAME	DEPT CODE	HIRE_DATE	CREDIT LIMIT	PHONE NUMBER	MANAGER ID
201	SUSAN	BROWN	EXE	01-JUN-1998	$30.00	3484	(null)
202	JIM	KERN	SAL	16-AUG-1999	$25.00	8722	201
203	MARTHA	WOODS	SHP	02-FEB-2009	$25.00	7591	201
204	ELLEN	OWENS	SAL	01-JUL-2008	$15.00	6830	202
205	HENRY	PERKINS	SAL	01-MAR-2006	$25.00	5286	202
206	CAROL	ROSE	ACT	(null)	(null)	(null)	(null)
207	DAN	SMITH	SHP	01-DEC-2008	$25.00	2259	203
208	FRED	CAMPBELL	SHP	01-APR-2008	$25.00	1752	203
209	PAULA	JACOBS	MKT	17-MAR-1999	$15.00	3357	201
210	NANCY	HOFFMAN	SAL	16-FEB-2007	$25.00	2974	203

Result table ❹

```
EMPLOYEE
      ID  FIRST_NAME  HIRE_DATE     FORMATTED_DATE
--------  ----------  ------------  --------------------
     201  SUSAN       01-JUN-1998   06-01-1998 12:00 AM
     202  JIM         16-AUG-1999   08-16-1999 12:00 AM
     203  MARTHA      02-FEB-2009   02-02-2004 12:00 AM
     204  ELLEN       01-JUL-2008   07-01-2003 12:00 AM
     205  HENRY       01-MAR-2006   03-01-2000 12:00 AM
     206  CAROL       (null)        (null)
     207  DAN         01-DEC-2008   12-01-2004 12:00 AM
     208  FRED        01-APR-2008   04-01-2003 12:00 AM
     209  PAULA       17-MAR-1999   03-17-1999 12:00 AM
     210  NANCY       16-FEB-2007   02-16-2004 12:00 AM
```

Notes

❶ In Oracle, the `to_char` function is used to control the format in which a date is displayed. The second parameter is the Oracle date format you want to use. It is enclosed in single quotes.

The `to_char` function is used, not the `to_date` function. When a date is stored in the database, it has a date datatype. You want to change the format to a text datatype, so that it can be displayed.

❷ In Access, the `format` function is used to control the format in which a date will be displayed. The second parameter is the Access date format you want to use. It is enclosed in single quotes.

❸ `as formatted_date` creates a column alias for the previous line. I would write it as part of that line if I had room to do so. I created the column alias on the next line and indented it to the far right to show that it is a continuation of the preceding line.

❹ The data in the table show that all the formatted dates have 12:00 AM (midnight) as their time. This is the default time that is set in Oracle and Access when no specific time is entered.

Check your understanding

Modify the `select` statement in this section to display the `hire_date` column in the format: January 10, 2012.

7-3   Entering formatted dates

This section shows you how to enter a time when you enter a date. All dates in SQL include a time, but the time is automatically set to midnight unless you enter a different time.

In Oracle, the DBAs have selected one default date format, which usually does not show the time. If you want to enter a time with a date, you must use the `to_date` function. It changes the text you enter for the date into a date datatype that can be stored in the database. This function has two parameters enclosed in single quotes. The first parameter is a character string, which expresses the date and the time. The second parameter tells Oracle how to format the first string into a date datatype. It gives the date format of the first parameter. The `to_date` function changes the character string you entered into a date with a time.

In Access the process is much simpler. You just enclose the date and time in pound signs, showing that what you enter is a date. Access will determine the format automatically.

Task

Insert a new row into the `sec0703_lunches` table. Use the following data:

```
lunch_id = 25
lunch_date = December 5, 2011 at 11:30 a.m.
employee_id = 202
date_entered = (use the current date and time)
```

Use a date format, if needed, to enter the date.

Oracle SQL

```
insert into sec0703_lunches
values (25,
to_date('12-05-2011 11:30 AM','MM-DD-YYYY HH:MI AM'),  ❶
        202, sysdate);  ❷
```

Access SQL

```
insert into sec0703_lunches
values (25, #DEC 5 2011 11:30 AM#,  ❸
        202, now());  ❹
```

Beginning table (`sec0703_lunches` table)

LUNCH_ID	LUNCH DATE	EMPLOYEE ID	DATE_ENTERE
1	16-NOV-2011	201	13-OCT-2011
2	16-NOV-2011	207	13-OCT-2011
3	16-NOV-2011	203	13-OCT-2011
4	16-NOV-2011	204	13-OCT-2011
6	16-NOV-2011	202	13-OCT-2011
7	16-NOV-2011	210	13-OCT-2011
8	25-NOV-2011	201	14-OCT-2011
9	25-NOV-2011	208	14-OCT-2011
12	25-NOV-2011	204	14-OCT-2011
13	25-NOV-2011	207	18-OCT-2011
15	25-NOV-2011	205	21-OCT-2011
16	05-DEC-2011	201	21-OCT-2011
17	05-DEC-2011	210	21-OCT-2011
20	05-DEC-2011	205	24-OCT-2011
21	05-DEC-2011	203	24-OCT-2011
22	05-DEC-2011	208	24-OCT-2011

New row ❺

25	05-DEC-2011	202	17-JUN-2011

Notes

❶ In Oracle, we use the `to_date` function to enter dates into tables. The date you write in an SQL statement is text because it is enclosed in single quotes. You need to change the text string into a date datatype to store it in the table. The `to_date` function does this.

Dates can be entered in any format, but the specific format of the text data must be explicitly specified. A time can be entered along with a date if the format includes a time.

If a time is entered, it is permanently stored in the table. However, it will only be displayed when it is explicitly requested. Dates containing times can cause errors if the users are not aware that the times are contained in the data.

❷ In Oracle, `sysdate` gives you the current date and time.

❸ In Access, a date is surrounded by pound signs (##), indicating that you want to enter a date. Most date formats are recognized automatically by Access. Their format does not need to be explicitly declared.

It is best to avoid ambiguous date formats. For example, does #7/4/99# mean April 7 or July 4? The meaning in America is different from the meaning in Europe.

❹ In Access, `now()` gives you the current date and time.

❺ The time, 11:30 AM, is present in the data, even though it is not displayed.

Check your understanding

Add a new row to a copy of the employees table, `sec0703_employees`. Set the hire date to show that the person was hired at 10:00 AM.

7-4   Other formats in Oracle

In Oracle, within the SQL Command Line environment, there are also formats for text and number fields. These are not set on the SQL level itself, rather they are set on the SQL*Plus level. For more information about this refer to the Oracle documentation about SQL*Plus.

7-5   Formats in Access

In Access, the format of a column is often specified in the field properties of the table design. It can also be specified within a `select` query using the `format` function. In addition to date formats, there are also formats for numbers, text, and yes/no datatypes.

Access offers a great variety of formats. There are two types of formats: predefined formats, which are ready-made for you and have names, and custom formats, which you specify yourself. A reference to all these formats is available in the Format Property Help.

In the following example, I create a custom format for the `phone_number` column, which has a text datatype. The format is:

```
"(415) 643-"@@@@
```

The characters within double quotes will be added as a literal value to each phone number. The @ represents a single character from the data in the `phone_number` column.

Oracle can also display the phone numbers this way, but it uses a different method. In Oracle, we could code a literal into the `select` statement and concatenate it to the phone number. For more details see section 9-12.

Task

Format the `phone_number` column entries of the `sec0705_employees` table. Give each phone number the area code (415) and the prefix 643-. Show two methods of doing this in Access: a GUI method and an SQL method. In the SQL method, show the `employee_id`, `first_name`, `last_name`, and the formatted `phone_number` columns.

Access GUI: Set field properties in the table design ❶

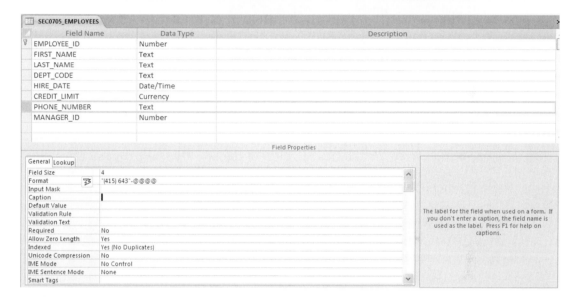

Access SQL: Use the `format` function

```
select employee_id,
       first_name,
       last_name,
       format(a.phone_number, '"(415) 643-"@@@@') ❷
                                as phone_number ❸
from sec0705_employees a; ❹
```

Result table

employee_id	first_name	last_name	phone_number
201	Susan	Brown	(415) 643-3484
202	Jim	Kern	(415) 643-8722
203	Martha	Woods	(415) 643-7591
204	Ellen	Owens	(415) 643-6830
205	Henry	Perkins	(415) 643-5286
206	Carol	Rose	
207	Dan	Smith	(415) 643-2259
208	Fred	Campbell	(415) 643-1752
209	Paula	Jacobs	(415) 643-3357
210	Nancy	Hoffman	(415) 643-2974

Notes

❶ This screen is the Design view of the sec0705_employees table. First select the phone_number field, which will be highlighted. Then set the field properties in the bottom half on the screen.

❷ In Access SQL, the same format is used as in the Access GUI. The difference is that it is placed as the second parameter within the format function and enclosed in single quotes. See notes ❸ and ❹ for an explanation of the "a" before the phone_number.

❸ When the format function is applied to the phone_number column, the result is an expression and is no longer named phone_number. To name the formatted expression phone_number it is necessary to give it a column alias. In Access, to give this expression the alias phone_number, I had to put an "a" before the column name phone_number. This is a table reference, and specifies that this is a column of the sec0705_employees table. In Oracle, this trick is not needed. The column alias can be phone_number without putting an "a" and a dot before the column name.

❹ This line assigns table alias "a" to the sec0705_employees table.

Sequences

A **sequence** is used to generate numbers sequentially. After the numbers are generated, their value is fixed and they are only numbers — there is no dynamic quality to them at all. If a row is deleted, the sequence numbers in the remaining rows do not change. The column with data generated by a sequence must have a numeric datatype.

The idea is that each row will be given a different number. Sequences are used in several ways: They can be used to put the rows in a specific order or to make sure that no two rows are identical. Sometimes a sequence is used as a "meaningless" primary key for a table. When several people are entering data into a table at the same time, a sequence may be used to show which record was entered first. It is up to the application to determine the meaning of the numbers generated by the sequence.

In the `Lunches` database, a sequence is used as the primary key of the `l_lunches` table. In this case, each time a person signs up to attend a lunch, that lunch is assigned the next number. So far, the numbers 1 through 22 have been used. A few numbers are missing, just like they would be in real life. These numbers were actually generated in sequence, but their rows have been deleted. The next row in this table will be assigned the number 23.

Both Oracle and Access offer sequences, but they implement them in different ways. In Oracle, a sequence is a database object, similar to a table. Oracle also has the `rownum` function to generate sequences. In Access, a sequence is implemented as a datatype.

7-6   Creating a sequence in Oracle

In Oracle, a sequence is a type of object in the database. This means that it exists within the database in the same way that a table or view exists. It can be created with the words `create sequence`, followed by the name of the new sequence. The starting number and the increment can be set in this command. I like to begin the names of all my sequences with `seq_` followed by an identification of the column it is used with.

A particular sequence is usually used to generate numbers for just one column, so if several columns in your tables use sequences, a separate sequence is set up for each one.

To delete a sequence enter `drop sequence`, followed by the name of the sequence.

Task

Create a sequence to use with the `lunch_id` column.

Oracle SQL: Create and drop a sequence

```
-- Delete command for a sequence ❶
-- This is a preventative delete for the sequence we
-- are about to create.
drop sequence sec0706_seq_lunch_id; ❷

-- Create a new sequence
create sequence sec0706_seq_lunch_id ❸
   start with 23
   increment by 1;
```

Result

After you create a sequence you can use it. See the next section.

Notes

❶ In Oracle and most other SQL products, a line that begins with two dashes is a comment line. In my opinion, all code should begin with at least one or two comment lines. In this book I usually do not include comment lines in the code because Access does not allow them and I am trying to write code that works in both Oracle and Access.

❷ This deletes the sequence, if it already exists. A preventative delete ensures that the name of the sequence is available for the `create sequence` command to use.

❸ This command creates the sequence.

Check your understanding

Create a new sequence named `seq0706_my_stuff`. Set the beginning value to 100.

7-7   Using sequences in Oracle

A sequence can do just two things: It can give you its current value or its next value. To get either of these you begin with the name of the sequence, followed by a period. Immediately after the period use `currval` to get the current value or `nextval` to get the next value. These can be used in a `select` statement, an `insert` statement, or any other SQL statement.

Task for example 1

Insert two rows into the sec0707_lunches table using the sec0707_seq_lunch_id sequence to assign the values in the lunch_id column.

Oracle SQL: Get the next value of a sequence

```
insert into sec0707_lunches
values (sec0707_seq_lunch_id.nextval, ❶
 '07-DEC-2011', 202, sysdate); ❷

insert into sec0707_lunches
values (sec0707_seq_lunch_id.nextval, ❸
 '07-DEC-2011', 204, sysdate);

select * from sec0707_lunches;
```

Result table: Example 1 — The new rows

```
          LUNCH        EMPLOYEE
 LUNCH_ID DATE             ID DATE_ENTERE
--------- ------------ -------- -----------
       23 07-DEC-2011      202 17-JUN-2011
       24 07-DEC-2011      204 17-JUN-2011
```

Task for example 2

Determine the most recent value that has been assigned by the seq_lunch_id sequence.

Oracle SQL: Get the current value of a sequence

```
select sec0707_seq_lunch_id.currval ❹
from dual; ❺
```

Result table: Example 2

```
CURRVAL
--------
      24
```

Notes

❶ This gets the next value from the sequence. We told it to start with 23 and that is the first value we get.

❷ In Oracle, `sysdate` supplies the current date and time.

❸ This gets the next value from the sequence. This time it gets the value 24.

❹ This gets the current value of the sequence.

❺ The `dual` table in Oracle is a dummy table used to print out values. For more details see section 9-7.

Check your understanding

Determine the current value of the sequence `seq_sec0707`. Then use its next three values to add new rows to the `sec0707_sequence` table. This table has only one column. It holds the value of the sequence number.

7-8 Sequences in Access

The Access way of generating sequences is called `autonumber` on the GUI level and `counter` on the JET engine level, and is treated as a datatype. It automatically assigns sequential numbers to new rows. If a new column is added to a table and that column is given the `counter` datatype, then all the rows currently in the table are assigned sequential numbers.

The JET engine level of Access is the level that processes the SQL. Access is a complex product with many levels. We are dealing with it on one particular level in this book — the level of the SQL view in the query mode.

Task

Add a new column to the `sec0708_suppliers` table that numbers all the rows sequentially. Show two methods to accomplish this, one using Access SQL and the other using Access GUI.

Access SQL

```
alter table sec0708_suppliers
add column new_num counter; ❶
```

Beginning table (sec0708_suppliers table)

SUPPLIER_ID	SUPPLIER_NAME
Arr	Alice & Ray'S Restaurant
Asp	A Soup Place
Cbc	Certified Beef Company
Frv	Frank Reed'S Vegetables
Fsn	Frank & Sons
Jbr	Just Beverages
Jps	Jim Parker'S Shop
Vsb	Virginia Street Bakery
*	

Ending table

SUPPLIER_ID	SUPPLIER_NAME	new_num
Arr	Alice & Ray'S Restaurant	1
Asp	A Soup Place	2
Cbc	Certified Beef Company	3
Frv	Frank Reed'S Vegetables	4
Fsn	Frank & Sons	5
Jbr	Just Beverages	6
Jps	Jim Parker'S Shop	7
Vsb	Virginia Street Bakery	8
*		(New)

Access GUI method ❷

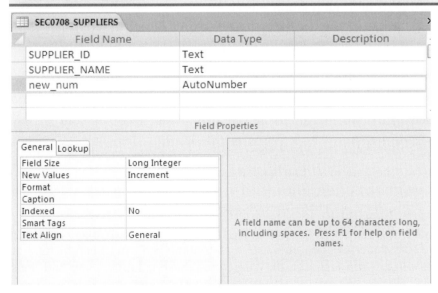

Field Name	Data Type	Description
SUPPLIER_ID	Text	
SUPPLIER_NAME	Text	
new_num	AutoNumber	

Field Properties

General | Lookup

Field Size	Long Integer
New Values	Increment
Format	
Caption	
Indexed	No
Smart Tags	
Text Align	General

A field name can be up to 64 characters long, including spaces. Press F1 for help on field names.

Notes

❶ On the SQL level, Access uses `counter` as the name of the special datatype of a sequence.

❷ On the GUI level, Access uses `autonumber` as the name of the special datatype of a sequence. Note that the field size is shown as `long integer`, which is the actual datatype of the column.

Check your understanding

Add a new column to the `sec0708_departments` table that numbers all the rows sequentially.

Indexes

Indexes are mysterious in SQL. They lurk behind the scenes, and you rarely work with them directly. An index is used to make SQL process more efficiently. It can make a `select` statement run much faster. Indexes are usually created by the DBA, so I do not discuss them in detail here. Application programmers and end users only need to have a slight awareness of indexes. The most important things to know are that indexes exist and you can talk to your DBA about them.

An index is always formed on certain columns of a particular table. It is something like a table, but it has an additional layer of organization that enables it to find information quickly by finding the correct rows of the table to use. It contains pointers that go directly into the table. It is a database object, it contains data drawn from the table, and it requires disk space. An index for a large table may require a considerable amount of disk space. All the indexes on a set of tables may require as much disk space as the tables themselves, which can be a large amount.

An index is a double-edged sword. Although it will speed up your `select` statements, it may also slow down changes that are being made to the data. The reason is that indexes in SQL are updated dynamically at runtime. Whenever the data in a table is changed, all the indexes on that table also must be changed. If this causes an index to be reorganized, a delay can occur while the reorganization takes place.

One way of "tuning" a database is to add an index to it. When an index is added to a database, certain `select` statements will run much faster, but others will not run faster at all. When a database is fairly young and does not contain much data, all queries run quickly and the database has a lot of flexibility. However, when the database ages and contains much more data, indexes must be built to keep it performing well. Because of these indexes some specific queries will still run quickly, but all other queries will run slowly, perhaps taking an hour or more. Then we say that the database has lost much of its flexibility.

You have already created some indexes, although you might not have known it. When you add a primary key to a table, an index is automatically built on the primary key columns. This all happens behind the scenes, without any messages to you. That is how elusive indexes can be.

7-9   Creating an index

It is very simple to create an index. The trick is to know which ones have more benefit than cost. Your DBA can help you determine this. In fact, your DBA may want to be the person responsible for building all of the indexes.

The command to create an index is:

```
CREATE INDEX name_of_the_new_index
ON table_name (ordered_list_of_columns_in_the_index)
```

I like to name indexes "ix" followed by the name of the table and then some indicator of the columns in the index. An index can be created even if there are several rows with the same values in the index columns. In the following example, it would be acceptable if there were several employees with the same first and last names.

Another kind of index, called a **unique index**, prevents such duplicate values. We discuss unique indexes in chapter 8. To delete an index, use the command `drop index` followed by the name of the index.

Task

Create an index on the names of the employees in the `l_employees` table. Include both the `last_name` and the `first_name` values in the index, in that order.

Oracle & Access SQL

```
create index ix_sec0709_employees_name
on sec0709_employees (last_name, first_name);
```

Result

An index is built, but you cannot see it. You can find entries for it in the Data Dictionary.

Check your understanding

Build an index on a copy of the departments table, `sec0709_departments`. Index the `department_name` field.

7-10 The Optimizer

You never use an index when you code a `select` statement. Instead, the Optimizer figures out the best way to process your `select` statement and it will make the best possible use of the indexes that have been built. The Optimizer is a very important component of database software.

Here is what goes on behind the scenes when you submit a `select` statement for a DBMS to run. First the statement is parsed. It is broken apart grammatically, so the computer understands what you want done. The next question is how to do it. This is where the Optimizer comes in.

The Optimizer makes a list of many different ways the `select` statement could be processed. It considers using many different indexes, searching and sorting the records in various ways. Then for each possible process it estimates how long it would take and how much computing power would be required. Then it decides which process is best, giving the fastest response and using the least amount of the computer's resources. This is the process the computer uses to create an answer to your `select` statement.

7-11 An example of how an index works

Here is an example of how an index works. This example is simplified to show the basic principle. Many complexities have been removed. First you need some background about the way computers work. Here I am speaking about one computer that is not networked with other computers.

The slowest operation in a computer is its input and output (I/O), which is reading and writing to the disk drive. It is approximately 1,000 times slower than any operation in the computer's central processing unit (CPU), which handles all the complex logic. You can have a good idea of how long a process will take if you can estimate how much I/O it requires; that is, how many times it will need to read and write to the disk.

One way to measure the size of a table is by the number of I/O operations it takes to read the entire table. Each read from the disk may get 100 rows, depending on the size of the rows in the table and many other factors. If a table contains 1,000,000 rows, it might require 10,000 reads to get the entire table. This might take 10 or 20 minutes or even longer, depending on the speed of the computer and how many other people are using the table.

As an example, suppose that this table is the l_employees table and it contains 1,000,000 rows. We are going to write a query to find all the people who were hired from 2009 to the end of 2010. First we examine how the query is processed if no indexes have been built on this table, or at least no indexes involving the hire_date column. Then we examine how it could be processed if an index has been created on that column. Here is the query:

```
select employee_id,
       last_name,
       first_name,
       hire_date
from l_employees
where hire_date >= '01-JAN-2009'
  and hire_date <= '31-DEC-2010'
order by last_name,
         hire_date,
         employee_id;
```

Before this query can be run, the Optimizer must determine how to process it. The primary factors are the from clause and the where clause, which indicate what table or tables the data will come from and which rows of those tables to use. This is what affects the amount of I/O. In this example, all the data comes from the l_employees table and only the hire_date column is used in the where clause.

If no indexes have been built on the l_employees table, the only way the computer can process this query is to read the whole table and test each row to see if the condition in the where clause is satisfied. Testing 1,000,000 rows may seem like a lot of work to you, but to the computer that is the easy part — reading all the rows of the table from the disk is the hard part. This process may take 20 minutes or more, as discussed earlier.

The processing of this select statement will be very different if an index has already been built on the hire_date column of the l_employees table. The Optimizer will use this index to determine which rows of the table are needed. This can greatly reduce the number of rows that need to be read from the disk. Instead of 10,000 I/O operations, perhaps only 100 are needed for the data of the result table. Using the index might require 10

I/O operations. Therefore, the total might be 110 I/O instead of 10,000. This would produce the result table 100 times quicker and use less of the computer's resources.

Using the Oracle Data Dictionary — Part 2

In chapter 5 you learned to use the Oracle Data Dictionary. You found information in it about all the database elements studied up to that point. Since then you have learned about datatypes, sequences, and indexes. We now want to see how to find information about these things in the Data Dictionary. I also show you how to use the two indexes for the Dictionary.

7-12 How to find information about the datatype of a column

This section shows you how to find detailed information about the datatypes of the columns in a table or view. We will use the table in the Oracle Data Dictionary called User Table Columns, which is spelled:

`user_tab_columns`

Note that this table contains information about the columns of both tables and views, even though its name mentions only tables. This table contains many columns of information, but we are only interested in a few of them. I have picked out the columns I want you to understand now. The following table provides a quick summary of what these columns mean.

Column	Meaning
`column_id`	Shows the order of the columns within the table or view — which column is first, second, etc.
`column_name`	Shows the name of the column.
`data_type`	Shows the datatype of the column. Of course, these are all Oracle datatypes.
`data_length`	For fixed length datatypes, such as numbers and dates, this shows the number of bytes of disk space required to store one cell of the column. For variable length datatypes, such as variable length character strings (`varchar2`), this shows the maximum length of the column.

Column	Meaning
`data_precision`	Used only with number columns. This is the maximum number of digits allowed for the number — both the digits before the decimal point and those after it.
`data_scale`	Used only with number columns. This is the number of digits after the decimal point.
`nullable`	Shows Y if a null can be entered into the column. Shows N if a null cannot be entered into the column.

I want to point out some things from the result table in the following example. The first line in the result table shows the first column of the `1_employees` table, which is the `employee_id` column. Its datatype is `number` and it allows a maximum of three digits with no digits after the decimal point. Nulls are not allowed in this column. You can guess that the reason nulls are not allowed in this column is because it is the primary key, although its status as the primary key is not shown here. Within each row, this column requires 22 bytes of disk space even though this number can only contain three digits.

The second row of the result table shows a text column, the `first_name` column. It is the second column within the `1_employees` table. Its datatype is `varchar2`, which is a variable length character string and it has a maximum length of ten characters. Nulls are allowed in this column.

The fifth row of the result table shows a date column, the `hire_date` column. Nulls are allowed in this column. Within each row, this column requires 7 bytes of disk space.

The sixth row of the result table shows a number with some digits after the decimal point. This is the `credit_limit` column. It can contain only numbers with a maximum of four digits, two before the decimal and two after.

In Access, much of this information is available on the GUI level from the `Design` view of the table. When you select a column, the field properties in the bottom part of the screen show details about the exact definition of the column.

Task

Find information about the datatypes of all the columns of the `l_employees` table.

Oracle SQL

```
-- Find information about the datatypes of columns ❶
select column_id,
       column_name,
       data_type,
       data_length,
       data_precision,
       data_scale,
       nullable
from user_tab_columns
where table_name = 'L_EMPLOYEES' ❷
order by column_id; ❸
```

Result table

COLUMN_ID	COLUMN_NAME	DATA_TYPE	DATA_LENGTH	DATA_PRECISION	DATA_SCALE	N
1	EMPLOYEE_ID	NUMBER	22	3	0	N
2	FIRST_NAME	VARCHAR2	10	(null)	(null)	Y
3	LAST_NAME	VARCHAR2	10	(null)	(null)	Y
4	DEPT_CODE	VARCHAR2	3	(null)	(null)	Y
5	HIRE_DATE	DATE	7	(null)	(null)	Y
6	CREDIT_LIMIT	NUMBER	22	4	2	Y
7	PHONE_NUMBER	VARCHAR2	4	(null)	(null)	Y
8	MANAGER_ID	NUMBER	22	3	0	Y

Notes

❶ This is a comment line. It may be omitted. Comment lines begin with two dashes.

❷ This `where` clause limits the result to showing the columns of a single table, the `l_employees` table.

❸ This `order by` clause sorts the columns into the same order they have within the `l_employees` table.

Access GUI

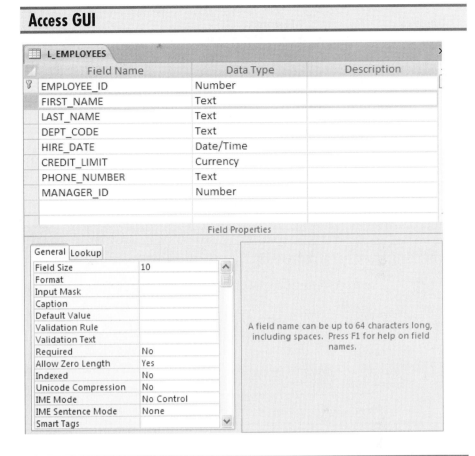

Check your understanding

Find information about the datatypes of all the columns of the l_foods table.

7-13 How to find information about sequences

In Oracle, we said that a sequence is a database object, so you should expect to find information about sequences in the Oracle Data Dictionary. The dictionary table to use is called user_sequences. By examining the columns in this table, you can learn exactly what an Oracle sequence is composed of. You can also make an educated guess about the options that are available when you create a sequence. The columns of this table are as follows:

Column	Meaning
`sequence_name`	Sequence name.
`min_value`	Minimum value of the sequence.
`max_value`	Maximum value of the sequence.
`increment_by`	Value by which sequence is incremented.
`cycle_flag`	Does sequence wrap around on reaching limit?
`order_flag`	Are sequence numbers generated in order?
`cache_size`	Number of sequence numbers to cache (hold in memory).
`last_number`	Last sequence number written to disk.

In Access, sequences are handled as if they were datatypes, so information about them is available on the GUI level from the `Design` view of the table. When you select a column with the `autonumber` datatype, the field properties in the bottom part of the screen show details about the sequence.

Task

Find all the information about your sequences in Oracle.

Oracle SQL

```
select *
from user_sequences;
```

Result table

```
SEQUENCE_NAME MIN_VAL MAX_VALUE  INCREMENT_BY C O CACHE_SIZE LAST_NUMBER
------------- ------- ---------  ------------ - - ---------- -----------
SEQ_EMPLOYEE_ID     1 1.000E+27             1 N N         20         211
SEQ_LUNCH_ID        1 1.000E+27             1 N N         20          43
SEQ_MENU_ITEM       1 1.000E+27             1 N N         20          11
```

Access GUI

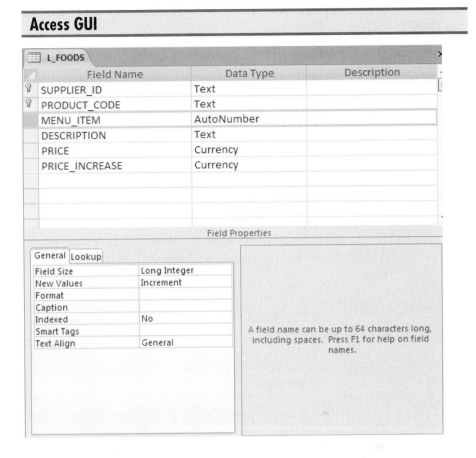

7-14 How to find information about indexes

In Oracle, you need to look at two tables in the Data Dictionary to find information about the indexes that have been built. This is similar to the way you found information about primary keys in section 5-15. An index, like a primary key, is a single database structure that may involve many columns in a particular order. All the columns must come from a single table. The two dictionary tables with information about indexes are as follows:

user_indexes
user_ind_columns

The user_indexes table contains one row for each index, even if several columns are involved in the index. This table has many columns, but we are only interested in a few of them. These columns are as follows:

Column	Meaning
index_name	Name of the index
table_name	Name of the table on which the index is formed
uniqueness	Whether two rows are allowed to have the same values in all of the columns of the index
tablespace_name	Name of the tablespace containing the index
status	Whether the index is valid or not

In the following example, you can see that there are two indexes on the l_employees table. They both are in the indx tablespace, which is where they should be. They are both valid, unique indexes.

The user_ind_columns table contains a row for every column involved with every index. This tells you all the columns involved with each index. We do not use the last two columns of this table, so you do not have to worry about what they mean. The columns of this table are as follows:

Column	Meaning
index_name	Name of the index
table_name	Name of the table on which the index is formed
column_name	Name of a column in the index
column_position	Position of the column within the index
column_length	Length of the column within the index
descend	Sort order — whether the index is in ascending or descending order

In Access, you can see the indexes on a table by opening the table in Design view. Then click Indexes in the Ribbon, which is within the Design tab. In the following example, you can see that there are two indexes on the l_employees table. Sometimes indexes are created automatically within Access as part of its "self-tuning" abilities.

Task

Find all the indexes on the `l_employees` table and which columns they contain.

Oracle SQL: Step 1

```
select index_name,
       table_name,
       uniqueness,
       tablespace_name,
       status
from user_indexes
where table_name = 'L_EMPLOYEES';
```

Result table

INDEX_NAME	TABLE_NAME	UNIQUENES	TABLESPACE_NAME	STATUS
PK_L_EMPLOYEES	L_EMPLOYEES	UNIQUE	INDX	VALID
UNIQUE_EMP_PHONE_NUM	L_EMPLOYEES	UNIQUE	INDX	VALID

Oracle SQL: Step 2

```
select *
from user_ind_columns
where table_name = 'L_EMPLOYEES';
```

Result table

INDEX_NAME	TABLE_NAME	COLUMN_NAME	COLUMN POSITION	COLUMN LENGTH	DESC
PK_L_EMPLOYEES	L_EMPLOYEES	EMPLOYEE_ID	1	22	ASC
UNIQUE_PHONE_NUM	L_EMPLOYEES	PHONE_NUMBER	1	4	ASC

Access GUI

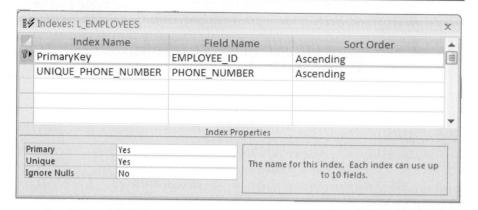

Check your understanding

Find out what indexes there are on the `l_departments` table.

7-15 How to find information about all your database objects

Most of the tables of the Oracle Data Dictionary are concerned with only a single type of database object, but there is one table that lists all of the objects you own regardless of what type of object they are. In addition to listing all of your objects, it also tells you when each object was created and the last time each object was changed. Sometimes this is very handy information to know. The name of this table is User Objects. Its most interesting columns are as follows:

Column	Meaning
object_name	The name of the object
object_type	The type of database object (table, view, sequence, index, etc.)
created	The date and time that the object was created
last_DDL_time	The last date and time that the object was changed
status	Valid or invalid

Task

List all the database objects you own in Oracle, the date each was created, and the most recent date each was changed.

Oracle SQL

```
select object_name,
       object_type,
       created,
       last_ddl_time,
       status
from user_objects;
```

Result table

```
OBJECT_NAME           OBJECT_TYPE  CREATED      LAST_DDL_TI STATUS
--------------------  -----------  -----------  ----------- -------
L_CONSTANTS           TABLE        06-JUN-2007  06-JUN-2007 VALID
L_DEPARTMENTS         TABLE        06-JUN-2007  06-JUN-2007 VALID
L_EMPLOYEES           TABLE        06-JUN-2007  20-JUN-2007 VALID
L_FOODS               TABLE        06-JUN-2007  06-JUN-2007 VALID
L_LUNCHES             TABLE        06-JUN-2007  06-JUN-2007 VALID
L_LUNCH_ITEMS         TABLE        06-JUN-2007  06-JUN-2007 VALID
L_SUPPLIERS           TABLE        06-JUN-2007  06-JUN-2007 VALID
NUMBERS_0_TO_9        TABLE        06-JUN-2007  06-JUN-2007 VALID
NUMBERS_0_TO_99       VIEW         06-JUN-2007  06-JUN-2007 VALID
PK_L_DEPARTMENTS      INDEX        06-JUN-2007  06-JUN-2007 VALID
PK_L_EMPLOYEES        INDEX        06-JUN-2007  06-JUN-2007 VALID
PK_L_FOODS            INDEX        06-JUN-2007  06-JUN-2007 VALID
PK_L_LUNCHES          INDEX        06-JUN-2007  06-JUN-2007 VALID
PK_L_LUNCH_ITEMS      INDEX        06-JUN-2007  06-JUN-2007 VALID
PK_L_SUPPLIERS        INDEX        06-JUN-2007  06-JUN-2007 VALID
SEQ_EMPLOYEE_ID       SEQUENCE     19-JUN-2007  19-JUN-2007 VALID
SEQ_LUNCH_ID          SEQUENCE     17-JUN-2007  17-JUN-2007 VALID
SEQ_MENU_ITEM         SEQUENCE     19-JUN-2007  19-JUN-2007 VALID
UNIQUE_PHONE_NUM      INDEX        20-JUN-2007  20-JUN-2007 VALID

(and many more)
```

7-16 How to use the index of Data Dictionary tables

The Oracle Data Dictionary contains more than 200 tables. It can be difficult to determine which table contains the information you are looking for. The Dictionary table solves this problem because it contains an entry for each of these tables, so it functions as an index to all the other tables. It contains two columns: column_name and comments. You can use like to search for patterns of letters in either of these columns.

Task

Find all the tables in the Oracle Data Dictionary that contain information about sequences. To do this, find the names of all the tables with the letters "SEQ" in them. Also list the comments about these tables.

Oracle SQL

```
select *
from dictionary
where table_name like '%SEQ%';
```

Result table

TABLE_NAME	COMMENTS
ALL_SEQUENCES	Description of SEQUENCEs accessible to the user
USER_SEQUENCES	Description of the user's own SEQUENCEs
SEQ	Synonym for USER_SEQUENCES

Check your understanding

Find all the tables in the Oracle Data Dictionary about views.

7-17 How to use the index of Data Dictionary columns

After you know the name of the dictionary table you want to look at, often the next problem is to learn the meanings of its columns. The Dictionary Columns table can give you this information, as the following example shows. This table contains three columns: `table_name`, `column_name`, and `comments`. Of course, these columns can also be used with `like` to search for patterns of letters.

Task

Find the meaning of all the columns of the `all_sequences` table.

Oracle SQL

```
select *
from dict_columns
where table_name = 'ALL_SEQUENCES';
```

Result table

TABLE_NAME	COLUMN_NAME	COMMENTS
ALL_SEQUENCES	SEQUENCE_OWNER	Name of the owner of the sequence
ALL_SEQUENCES	SEQUENCE_NAME	SEQUENCE name
ALL_SEQUENCES	MIN_VALUE	Minimum value of the sequence
ALL_SEQUENCES	MAX_VALUE	Maximum value of the sequence
ALL_SEQUENCES	INCREMENT_BY	Value by which sequence is incremented
ALL_SEQUENCES	CYCLE_FLAG	Does sequence wrap around on reaching limit?
ALL_SEQUENCES	ORDER_FLAG	Are sequence numbers generated in order?
ALL_SEQUENCES	CACHE_SIZE	Number of sequence numbers to cache
ALL_SEQUENCES	LAST_NUMBER	Last sequence number written to disk

Check your understanding

Find the meanings of all the columns of the `user_tables` table.

An Exercise Solved for You

7-18 Create a table of the days you want to celebrate

This section integrates the various topics discussed in this chapter. We create a table, put some data in it, and display it using a date format. I encourage you to make your own modifications to the following code and experiment with any variations that occur to you.

Task

Create a new table to keep track of events in your life you want to celebrate. Put three columns in the table: a sequence, a text column, and a date column. Put a primary key on the table using the sequence as a primary key. Put a few rows of data into the table and list them out, formatting the dates to show the day of the week, the full name of the month, and a four-digit year.

Oracle SQL

```
create table sec0718_my_days
(my_seq_id number,
my_event varchar2(25),
my_date date);

alter table sec0718_my_days
add constraint pk_sec0818_my_days
primary key (my_seq_id);

create sequence seq_sec0718_my_days
start with 1
increment by 1;

insert into sec0718_my_days
values (seq_sec0718_my_days.nextval,
'BIRTH DATE', '16-JAN-1971');

insert into sec0718_my_days
values (seq_sec0718_my_days.nextval,
'COLLEGE GRADUATION', '24-JUN-1993');
```

```
insert into sec0718_my_days
values (seq_sec0718_my_days.nextval,
'WEDDING', '14-FEB-1994');

commit;

select my_seq_id,
my_event,
to_char(my_date, 'DAY MONTH DD, YYYY') as my_date
from sec0718_my_days
order by my_seq_id;
```

Access SQL

```
create table sec0718_my_days
(my_seq_id counter,
my_event text(25),
my_date datetime);

alter table sec0718_my_days
add constraint pk_sec0718_my_days
primary key (my_seq_id);

insert into sec0718_my_days (my_event, my_date)
values ('Birth Date', #16-jan-1971#);

insert into sec0718_my_days (my_event, my_date)
values ('College Graduation', #24-jun-1993#);

insert into sec0718_my_days (my_event, my_date)
values ('Wedding', #14-feb-1994#);

select my_seq_id,
my_event,
format(my_date, 'DDDD MMMM DD, YYYY') as my_date2
from sec0718_my_days
order by my_seq_id;
```

Result table

```
MY_SEQ_ID MY_EVENT                        MY_DATE
--------- ------------------------------- ---------------------------
        1 BIRTH DATE                      SATURDAY   JANUARY   16, 1971
        2 COLLEGE GRADUATION              THURSDAY   JUNE      24, 1993
        3 WEDDING                         MONDAY     FEBRUARY  14, 1994
```

Key Points

- A format can change the appearance of a field, but cannot change its value. For example, "October 15, 2010" and "2010-10-15" are two formats for the same date. By specifying the date format you can control how your dates are displayed.

- A sequence is usually used to assign sequential numbers to the rows of a table. This can be used to create the primary key of a table.

- An index operates behind the scenes to make the database more efficient. Often indexes are created by DBAs, who are responsible for keeping the database healthy. However, when you create a table with a primary key, that primary key is implemented by creating an index.

chapter 8

DATA INTEGRITY

This chapter discusses the ways data can be validated before it is entered into the database. Validation is particularly important when many people are entering data and sharing the same database. Validation also ensures that the data meets a certain level of consistency.

In a relational database, *referential integrity* is one of the main techniques of data validation. It protects columns that contain codes. For example, a column for gender can only contain the codes M and F. Referential integrity can enforce that rule.

A `check` constraint is another type of validation. It can check that some statement is true; for example, "Price is less than $100.00." There is always validation on the primary key of a table to preserve its properties. A `not null` constraint is a way to say that the field is required. A `unique` constraint ensures that no two rows contain the same value.

The topics in this chapter are not needed to read the rest of this book. Readers may skip ahead to the next chapter and come back to this material later.

Constraints on One Table

8-1 A constraint keeps the data consistent

A constraint is a rule that ensures the data in the database meets a certain level of consistency. This consistency ensures that the data is meaningful and makes sense to all the people who use the database. The term "constraint" is a shortened form of the phrase "data integrity constraint."

A constraint works by allowing certain changes to the data in the database and not allowing other changes. The changes that are rejected would violate the rule that the constraint is trying to enforce.

A constraint can work when you use any of the SQL commands to change the data; that is, the `insert`, `update`, or `delete` command. First, the SQL command is checked to make sure it makes sense. Then the constraints are checked to make sure that the proposed changes do not violate any of the constraint rules. The data in the database is changed only after it has been shown that all the constraint rules are satisfied.

If you are only getting information from a database that has constraints and you are not changing any of that information, then you should be able to rely on the fact that the data is consistent and it obeys all the rules of the constraints.

There are many types of constraints, but the most important one is referential integrity (RI). It deals with the relationship between two different tables. It is one of the more complex constraints. That is why most of this chapter deals with RI.

Before we get into the details of RI, let's look at some of the simpler types of constraints that involve only one single table.

8-2 `check` constraints

A `check` constraint ensures that some statement about the data is true for every row of a table. Oracle supports `check` constraints, but Access does not. Access has **validation rules**, which are somewhat similar. They both validate data when it is being entered or updated. The change to the data is rejected when it does not pass the test.

A constraint always checks all the old data, so we know that all the data in the table passes the test. If the old data does not pass the test, the constraint is rejected. However, a validation rule does not check the old data unless we ask it to, so there may be old data in the table that would not pass the test. That is the main difference.

Another difference is that a `check` constraint in Oracle is part of Oracle SQL. It is a command that is issued like any other SQL. A validation rule in Access is a property and cannot be set through SQL. It can be set in the GUI, in a macro, or in a module, but not through the SQL window.

Task

In Oracle, set a constraint to check that all the prices in the `sec0802_foods` table are less than $10.00. In Access, set a validation rule to do this. (This constraint has already been set for the `1_foods` table.)

Oracle SQL

```
alter table sec0802_foods
add constraint sec0802_foods_max_price
check (price < 10.00);
```

Access GUI

Open the `sec0802_foods` table in `Design` view and highlight the `price` column. Within the General properties set the Validation Rule to be "<10", without the quotes, and set the Validation Text to be "Price exceeds $10.00". The Validation Text line is the error message to be displayed if the rule is not met.

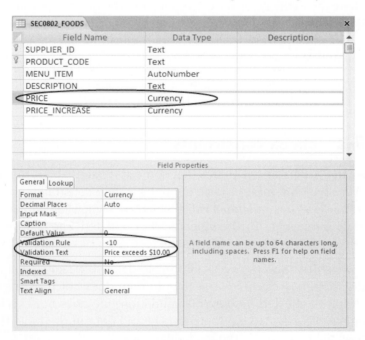

Check your understanding

Create a check constraint on the `hire_date` column of the `sec0802_employees` table. Check that the `hire_date` comes after 1995.

8-3 `unique` **constraints**

A **uniqueness constraint** on a table column ensures that every row of that table contains a different value. In other words, no two rows have the same value in that column. A null is always allowed in the column. Many rows of the table can have a null in the column, but all non-null values in the column can occur only once. A uniquess constraint is sometimes called a **unique constraint**. It can be created with an `alter table` statement.

A **unique index** is closely related to a uniqueness constraint and does almost the same thing. However, it is classified as a type of index rather than as a constraint. Like any other index, it can make some of the processing in the database more efficient. It can be created with a `create index` statement.

A uniqueness constraint or a unique index can be placed on a combination of several columns. Then each column itself could have duplicate values, but the combination of columns would be required to have a different value for every row of the table.

For example, if we put a uniqueness constraint on the `first_name` and `last_name` columns of the `1_employees` table, we could have several employees with the same first name or last name, but we could not have any two employees with both the same first name and also with the same last name.

Task

Place a uniqueness constraint on the `phone_number` column of the `sec0803_employees` table. This will ensure that each employee has his or her own phone number. Show two ways to do this. Use different tables so both SQL statements can be run.

Oracle SQL: Method 1 — Define a constraint

```
alter table sec0803_employees
add constraint unique_sec0803_emp_phone_num
unique (phone_number);
```

Oracle SQL: Method 2 — Define a unique index

```
create unique index uix_sec0803b_emp_phone
on sec0803b_employees (phone_number);
```

Access GUI method ❶

Open the sec0803_employees table in Design view, highlight the line for the phone_number column and set the Indexed line to the option that says "Yes (No Duplicates)", as in the screen shown here.

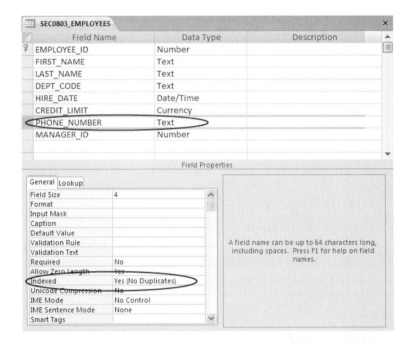

Notes

❶ The method shown can be used to put a uniqueness constraint in one field. To put a uniqueness constraint in a combination of fields, use:

```
Table design view → design tab → Indexes
```

Check your understanding

Put a uniqueness constraint on the department_name field of the sec0803_departments table.

8-4 `not null` **constraints**

A `not null` constraint on a column ensures that there are no nulls in that column. This is another way to say that data is required in that column. A `not null` constraint can only be placed on a single column. In Oracle this can be coded as a check constraint.

Task

Create a `not null` constraint for the `employee_id` column of the `sec0804_lunches` table.

Oracle SQL

```
alter table sec0804_lunches
add constraint nn_sec0804_lunches_employee_id
check (employee_id is not null);
```

Access GUI

Open the `sec0804_lunches` table in `Design` view, highlight the `employee_id` column, and set the Required line to Yes.

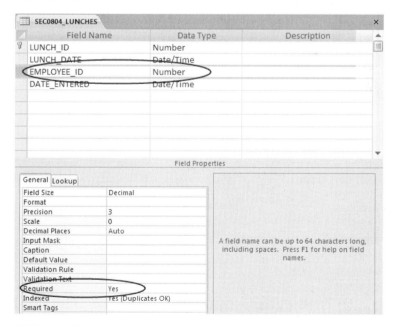

Check your understanding

Make the `last_name` column a required field in the `sec0804_employees` table.

8-5   `primary key` **constraints**

A `primary key` constraint is a combination of both a `unique` constraint and a `not null` constraint. A table is only allowed to have one `primary key` constraint. However it may have several `unique` constraints or `not null` constraints.

Task

Place a `primary key` constraint on the `employee_id` column of the `sec0805_employees` table.

Oracle & Access SQL

```
alter table sec0805_employees
add constraint pk_sec0805_employees
primary key (employee_id);
```

Access GUI

Open the `sec0805_employees` table in `Design` view and highlight the `employee_id` column. Click the button on the toolbar that shows a key, as shown on the following screen.

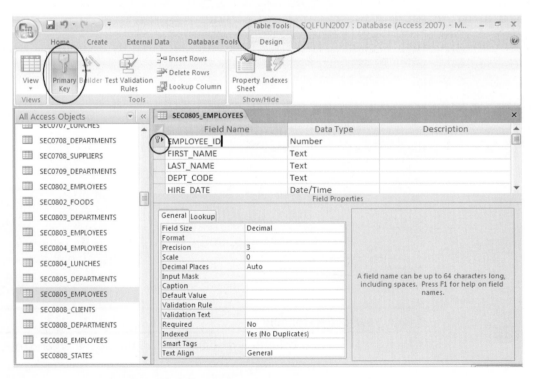

Check your understanding

Put a `primary key` constraint on the `sec0805_departments` table. Define the primary key to be the `dept_code` field.

8-6 Restrictions on the datatype and length of fields

The datatype definition for each column of a table functions as a constraint. That is, it limits the data that can be entered into that column. It limits the datatype of the data and also the length of the data. For example:

1. The value `Jane` cannot be entered into a numeric column.

2. The value `123456789` cannot be entered into a numeric column if the column is restricted to two-digit numbers.

These are restrictions on the data, and therefore they are constraints. However, most discussions of SQL do not list them as constraints.

Referential Integrity

RI is the main type of data validation within relational databases. It ensures that certain relationships are maintained between the data in one table and the data in another table. An RI constraint usually involves two different tables.

Usually this validation is done when the data is being changed; that is, during the processing of `insert`, `update`, and `delete` statements. These statements will fail if they would change the data in a way that does not conform to the requirements of RI.

During massive loads of thousands of rows of data, this validation is usually turned off temporarily. After the load is finished, the validation is turned on again. So what happens if faulty data is entered during these loads? We will not be able to turn on the validation until the data has been fixed. So whenever RI is active, we are assured that one table has a certain relationship to another table.

8-7   The concept of RI

The following illustration shows the concept of RI.

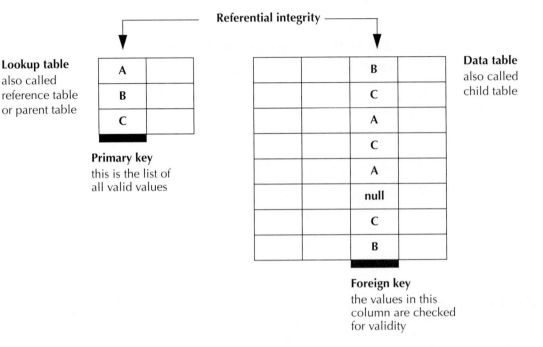

RI is a relationship between the data in two columns. These columns are usually in different tables. One column, called the **primary key**, contains a list of all the valid values for some field. The other column, the **foreign key**, contains data that is validated against this list. The table containing the list of valid values is called a **lookup table**. It is also called a **reference table** or the **parent table**. The other table is sometimes called the **data table** or the **child table**.

The valid values are often a set of codes containing two or three characters. The lookup table contains a list of these codes and their meanings. Sometimes it also contains additional data about them.

The data in both columns is allowed to change. However the rule must be maintained that the foreign key can only contain values that are also in the primary key column. The foreign key can also contain nulls.

The relationship between the data in these two columns has consequences for the way in which the data is allowed to change. In the lookup table, a new value can always be inserted into the primary key, but an `update` or `delete` statement is restricted if it would remove a value that is used in the foreign key.

In the data table, a value can always be deleted or set to null, but any new value introduced with an insert or update must pass validation, otherwise it is rejected.

The two columns often have the same or similar names. The database designers do this to suggest that the columns are related to each other. An index is usually built on each of the columns to keep the database running efficiently.

Before the RI relationship can be set up, you must create a primary key, or at least a unique index, in the lookup table. Access strictly enforces this rule, but Oracle allows some exceptions.

8-8 An example of RI

In this section we set up a relationship of RI between two tables. The `states` table is the lookup table and the `clients` table is the data table. More specifically, we create RI between the `state_code` columns of these tables.

The `states` table and the `clients` table are part of an application for a salesman. His sales region consists of three states: California, Oregon, and Washington. He is only allowed to have clients in those states.

In the following example, RI is set up using an `alter table` statement. The first line says `alter table`, and then gives the name of the data table, which is the table containing the column with data that will be validated.

The second line says `add constraint`, followed by the name of the con- straint. The naming convention used here begins all foreign key constraints with the letters `fk_`, followed by the names of the table and column that will be validated. This is one of several popular naming conventions.

The third line specifies that this is a foreign key constraint. This is followed by the name of the column to be validated, enclosed in parentheses.

The last line specifies the list of all the valid values. The word `references` is followed by the name of the lookup table. This implies that the primary key of the lookup table contains the list of all the valid values.

If the list of valid values is in a column that is different than the primary key of the lookup table, then the name of that column must be given, enclosed in parentheses.

Task

Show how to set up RI. Validate the `state_code` column of the `clients` table.

Oracle & Access SQL: Set up RI ❶

```
alter table sec0808_clients
add constraint fk_sec0808_clients_state_code
foreign key (state_code)
    references sec0808_states (state_code); ❷
```

Lookup table (`sec0808_states` table)

STATE CODE	STATE_NAME	STATE_CAPITAL
CA	CALIFORNIA	SACRAMENTO
OR	OREGON	SALEM
WA	WASHINGTON	OLYMPIA

Data table (`sec0808_clients` table)

CLIENT_ID	CLIENT_NAME	STATE CODE
100	LARRY COHEN	CA
200	ALICE WILLIAMS	CA
300	ROGER WOLF	OR
400	NANCY KERN	OR
500	CATHY LEE	WA
600	STEVEN LAKE	WA

Notes

❶ The `state_code` column is already the primary key of the lookup table, the `sec0808_states` table. This must be done before the RI relationship is created.

❷ Specifying the column with `(state_code)` is optional here because it is the primary key of the lookup table. I write the column name even when it is not required because I feel it makes the code easier for people to understand.

Check your understanding

Set up RI between the `sec0808_departments` table and the `sec0808_employees` table. The `sec0808_depatrments` table contains a list of all the valid values of the `dept_code` field.

8-9 Inserts and updates to the data table prevented by RI

This section shows that RI provides data validation within a foreign key column of the data table. It prevents a value from being entered into that column if it is not one of the valid values contained in the lookup table.

The SQL in the following example tries to put New York and Massachusetts into the state_code column of the clients table. These states are not part of the sales region, so they are not included in the states table. RI rejects these insert and update statements.

Task

On the clients table, write an insert and an update statement that will be rejected by RI.

Oracle & Access SQL

```
insert into sec0809_clients
values (700, 'GAIL HAUSER', 'NY');

update sec0809_clients
set state_code = 'MA'
where client_id = 200;
```

Result — An error message ❶

Notes

❶ Access will notify you that an error has occurred and ask you if you want to run the query anyway. Even if you choose Yes, no change is made to the tables.

Check your understanding

There is already an RI relation between the sec0809_departments table and the sec0809_employees table. Write an SQL insert statement and an update statement on the sec0809_employees table that will be rejected because of RI. Hint: Use a value of the dept_code field that is not one of the valid codes listed in the sec0809_departments table.

8-10 Inserts and updates to the data table allowed by RI

This section shows that RI allows an insert or update statement to occur in the foreign key column of the data table as long as it follows the rules. A value can be entered into that column if it is one of the valid values contained in the lookup table.

In the following example, the first two SQL commands are the same as in the previous section, except that the state codes are valid. These states are part of the sales region and they are included in the states table. RI allows these insert and update statements.

In the last insert statement, the state_code is null. This shows that we can enter a null in a foreign key column, even though there is no null in the list of valid values.

Task

On the clients table, write an insert and an update statement that will be allowed by RI.

Oracle & Access SQL

```
insert into sec0810_clients
values (700, 'GAIL HAUSER', 'OR');

update sec0810_clients
set state_code = 'WA'
where client_id = 200;

insert into sec0810_clients
values (800, 'CARL LOGAN', null);
```

Beginning table (sec0810_clients table)

| | | STATE CODE |
CLIENT_ID	CLIENT_NAME	CODE
100	LARRY COHEN	CA
200	ALICE WILLIAMS	CA
300	ROGER WOLF	OR
400	NANCY KERN	OR
500	CATHY LEE	WA
600	STEVEN LAKE	WA

Ending table

```
                                      STATE
CLIENT_ID  CLIENT_NAME                CODE
---------  --------------------------  ------
      100  LARRY COHEN                CA
      200  ALICE WILLIAMS             WA
      300  ROGER WOLF                 OR
      400  NANCY KERN                 OR
      500  CATHY LEE                  WA
      600  STEVEN LAKE                WA
      700  GAIL HAUSER                OR
      800  CARL LOGAN                 (null)
```

Check your understanding

There is already an RI relation between the sec0810_departments table and the sec0810_employees table. Write an SQL insert statement and an update statement on the sec0810_employees table that will be accepted by RI.

8-11 Updates and deletes to the lookup table prevented by RI

This section shows that RI prevents codes from being changed or deleted in the lookup table while those codes are being used in the foreign key column of the data table.

The SQL in the following example tries to change Oregon to Massachusetts and tries to delete California from the states table. These states are currently being referred to by rows in the clients table, so RI rejects these update and delete statements.

Here we are using RI with the restrict option, which is the default and most commonly used option. Later we look at some other ways to set up RI.

Task

On the states table, write an update and a delete statement that will be rejected by RI.

Oracle & Access SQL

```
update sec0811_states
set state_code = 'MA'
where state_code = 'OR';

delete from sec0811_states
where state_code = 'CA';
```

Result — An error message

Check your understanding

There is already an RI relation between the sec0811_departments table and the sec0811_employees table. Write an SQL update statement and a delete statement on the sec0811_departments table that will be rejected because of RI.

8-12 How to delete a code from the lookup table

To delete a value from the primary key of a lookup table, we must first ensure that the value is not being used in the foreign key column by any row of the data table.

In the following example, we want to remove California from the states table. Before we can do this, we must remove it from every row of the clients table. Instead of deleting these clients, we set their state_code values to null.

Task

Delete California from the states table.

Oracle & Access SQL

```
update sec0812_clients
  set state_code = null
where state_code = 'CA';

delete from sec0812_states
where state_code = 'CA';
```

Beginning table 1 (`sec0812_states` table)

```
STATE
CODE    STATE_NAME                       STATE_CAPITAL
------  -------------------------------  -------------------
CA      CALIFORNIA                       SACRAMENTO
OR      OREGON                           SALEM
WA      WASHINGTON                       OLYMPIA
```

Beginning table 2 (`sec0812_clients` table)

```
                                         STATE
CLIENT_ID CLIENT_NAME                    CODE
--------- ------------------------------ ------
      100 LARRY COHEN                    CA
      200 ALICE WILLIAMS                 CA
      300 ROGER WOLF                     OR
      400 NANCY KERN                     OR
      500 CATHY LEE                      WA
      600 STEVEN LAKE                    WA
```

Ending table 1 (`sec0812_states` table)

```
STATE
CODE    STATE_NAME                       STATE_CAPITAL
------  -------------------------------  ------------------
OR      OREGON                           SALEM
WA      WASHINGTON                       OLYMPIA
```

Ending table 2 (`sec0812_clients` table)

```
                                         STATE
CLIENT_ID CLIENT_NAME                    CODE
--------- ------------------------------ ------
      100 LARRY COHEN                    (null)
      200 ALICE WILLIAMS                 (null)
      300 ROGER WOLF                     OR
      400 NANCY KERN                     OR
      500 CATHY LEE                      WA
      600 STEVEN LAKE                    WA
```

Check your understanding

There is already an RI relation between the `sec0812_departments` table and the `sec0812_employees` table. Delete the shipping department from the `sec0812_departments` table. Hint: First you must change some data in the `sec0812_employees` table.

8-13 How to change a code in the lookup table

To change a value in the primary key of a lookup table, we use a three-step process. First, we enter the new code into the lookup table. Second, we change all the data in the data table from the old code to the new code. Third, we delete the old code from the lookup table.

In the following example, we want to change the code for California from CA to ZZ. The reason for doing this is to show the process of accomplishing it.

Task

Change the state_code for California to ZZ in both the states table and the clients table.

Oracle & Access SQL

```
insert into sec0813_states
values ('ZZ', 'CALIFORNIA', 'SACRAMENTO');

update sec0813_clients
    set state_code = 'ZZ'
where state_code = 'CA';

delete from sec0813_states
where state_code = 'CA';
```

Beginning table 1 (sec0813_states table)

```
STATE
CODE    STATE_NAME                          STATE_CAPITAL
------  ----------------------------------  --------------------
CA      CALIFORNIA                          SACRAMENTO
OR      OREGON                              SALEM
WA      WASHINGTON                          OLYMPIA
```

Beginning table 2 (sec0813_clients table)

```
                                            STATE
CLIENT_ID  CLIENT_NAME                      CODE
---------  ------------------------------   ------
      100  LARRY  COHEN                      CA
      200  ALICE  WILLIAMS                   CA
      300  ROGER  WOLF                       OR
      400  NANCY  KERN                       OR
      500  CATHY  LEE                        WA
      600  STEVEN  LAKE                      WA
```

Ending table 1 (sec0813_states table)

```
STATE
CODE    STATE_NAME                        STATE_CAPITAL
------  --------------------------------  ----------------
OR      OREGON                            SALEM
WA      WASHINGTON                        OLYMPIA
ZZ      CALIFORNIA                        SACRAMENTO
```

Ending table 2 (sec0813_clients table)

```
                                          STATE
CLIENT_ID CLIENT_NAME                     CODE
--------- ------------------------------  ------
      100 LARRY COHEN                     ZZ
      200 ALICE WILLIAMS                  ZZ
      300 ROGER WOLF                      OR
      400 NANCY KERN                      OR
      500 CATHY LEE                       WA
      600 STEVEN LAKE                     WA
```

Check your understanding

There is already an RI relation between the sec0813_departments table and the sec0813_employees table. Write SQL to change the code of the shipping department from SHP to ABC.

8-14 RI as a relationship between the tables

I said before that RI is a relationship between the data in two columns, but that is not quite the whole story. It is also a relationship between two tables: the lookup table and the data table. There are two parts to this:

1. We must insert rows into the lookup table before we can insert any rows into the data table.

2. We cannot drop either table until we drop the RI relationship.

These are the rules in general, but there are ways to get around them, which we discuss later.

8-15 Setting up RI in the Access GUI

This section shows how to set up RI in Access using GUI methods instead of SQL. The tables used here are called `sec0815_states` and `sec0815_clients`. These are separate copies of the `states` and `clients` tables.

Task

Set up RI between the `state_code` columns of the `sec0815_states` table and the `sec0815_clients` table. Use the Access GUI to do this.

Access GUI method

Step 1: Click the Database Tools tab on the Ribbon. Then click Relationships in the Show/Hide group. Then click Show Table in the Relationships group. Then scroll down the Show Table window until you find the `SEC0815_CLIENTS` table. Click on it to select it:

> Database Tools > Relationships > Show Table > select Tables tab > select SEC0815_CLIENTS > Add

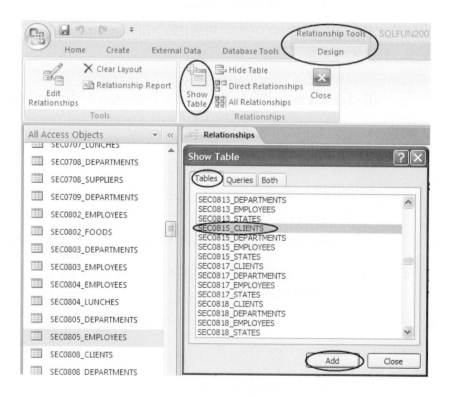

Step 2: Choose the tables you want and click Add for each of them. For this example, choose the SEC0815_STATES table and click Add. Then choose the SEC0815_CLIENTS table and click Add again. Then close the Show Table window. These tables will be shown in the Relationships window.

You can drag the tables by their title bars. Here I have rearranged the Relationships window so only these two tables are shown.

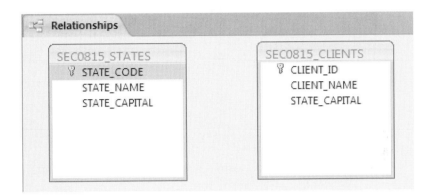

Step 3: Select the primary key. In this example, choose the STATE_CODE column of the SEC0815_STATES table. Hold the mouse down and drag from the primary key to the foreign key, then release the mouse button. In this example, drag from the STATE_CODE column of the SEC0815_STATES table to the STATE_CODE column of the SEC0815_CLIENTS table. The Edit Relationships window will open. Select the Enforce Referential Integrity checkbox.

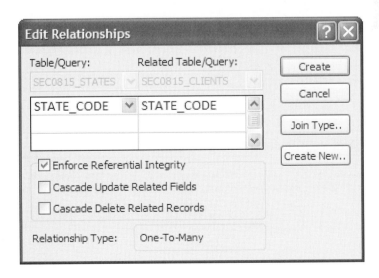

Step 4: Click the Create button. Now RI has been set up and you are done
The line between the two tables shows the RI relationship.

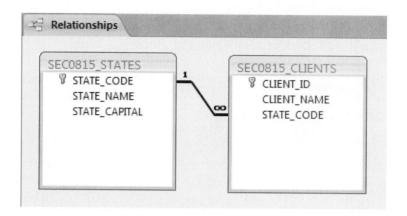

If, at a later time, you want to delete or change the relationship, right-click
the line between the two tables.

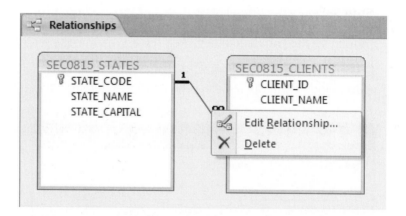

Check your understanding

Use the Access GUI to set up RI between the sec0815_departments table
and the sec0815_employees table.

The Delete Options and Update Options of RI

The previous sections showed you that a delete or an update to the lookup table can be disallowed by RI. This is the most common way RI is set up, but some other options are explained here.

8-16 The three options for deletes and updates to the lookup table

By default, we are not allowed to change or delete values in the primary key of the lookup table, when those values occur in the foreign key of the data table. Having RI operate this way is called the `restrict` option, because we are restricted from making these changes to the lookup table.

When we set up RI, we can choose one of three options for handling deletes from the lookup table. In Access, we can also choose one of three options for handling updates to the lookup table. This gives us nine ways to set up RI. The three options are:

- `restrict` (the default if we do not choose the other options)
- `set null`
- `cascade`

In describing RI up to now, I have been describing it with the `restrict` option, because this is the most common form. For some special purposes, we use the `set null` and `cascade` options, but they should always be used carefully.

The `set null` and `cascade` options for deletes say that we can always delete a value from the lookup table. These options for updates say that we can always change a value in the lookup table. Here are the effects of these options on the matching values within the foreign key column of the data table:

`set null`	All the matching values in the foreign key column are automatically changed to null. The rest of the data in the row is unchanged.
`cascade` deletes	The entire row is deleted from the data table when there is a matching value in the foreign key column.
`cascade` updates	All the matching values in the foreign key column are automatically changed to the new value. The rest of the data in the row is unchanged.

Delete options

Oracle supports all three delete options. From an SQL command, Access supports only the `restrict` deletes option. The `cascade` deletes option is available, but it must be set in the GUI.

Update options

Both Oracle and Access support the `restrict` updates option, which is the default. Access also supports the `cascade` updates option, which must be set in the GUI.

8-17 The delete rule: `set null`

In the next example, the first task sets up RI between the `sec0817_states` table and the `sec0817_clients` table using the `set null` option. The second task deletes California from the lookup table. In the foreign key all the references to California are automatically changed to null.

Task for example 1: Set up RI with set null for deletes

Set up RI between the `sec0817_states` table and the `sec0817_clients` table. Use the `set null` option for deletes.

Oracle SQL

```
alter table sec0817_clients
add constraint fk_sec0817_clients_state_code
foreign key (state_code)
  references sec0817_states (state_code)
  on delete set null; ❶
```

Access does not support this option.

Task for example 2: Show how RI works with set null for deletes

Delete California from the `sec0817_states` table. Do this when RI has been set up using the `set null` option.

Oracle SQL

```
delete from sec0817_states
where state_code = 'CA';
```

Access does not support the delete rule `set null`.

Beginning table 1 (`sec0817_states` table)

```
STATE
CODE      STATE_NAME                        STATE_CAPITAL
------    ----------------------------      ------------------
CA        CALIFORNIA                        SACRAMENTO
OR        OREGON                            SALEM
WA        WASHINGTON                        OLYMPIA
```

Beginning table 2 (`sec0817_clients` table)

```
                                            STATE
CLIENT_ID CLIENT_NAME                       CODE
--------- ----------------------------      ------
      100 LARRY COHEN                       CA
      200 ALICE WILLIAMS                    CA
      300 ROGER WOLF                        OR
      400 NANCY KERN                        OR
      500 CATHY LEE                         WA
      600 STEVEN LAKE                       WA
```

Ending table 1 (`sec0817_states` table)

```
STATE
CODE      STATE_NAME                        STATE_CAPITAL
------    ----------------------------      ------------------
OR        OREGON                            SALEM
WA        WASHINGTON                        OLYMPIA
```

Ending table 2 (`sec0817_clients` table)

```
                                            STATE
CLIENT_ID CLIENT_NAME                       CODE
--------- ----------------------------      ------
      100 LARRY COHEN                       (null) ❷
      200 ALICE WILLIAMS                    (null) ❷
      300 ROGER WOLF                        OR
      400 NANCY KERN                        OR
      500 CATHY LEE                         WA
      600 STEVEN LAKE                       WA
```

Notes

❶ This line creates the set null option.

❷ The state codes for California are automatically changed to nulls in the foreign key column.

Check your understanding

Set up RI between the `sec0817_departments` table and the `sec0817_employees` table. Handle deletes using the `set null` rule. Then show the effect of this rule by deleting the shipping department from the `sec0817_departments` table.

8-18 The delete rule: `cascade`

In the following example, the first task sets up RI between the `sec0818_states` table and the `sec0818_clients` table using the `cascade` option for deletes. The second task deletes California from the lookup table. In the data table all the rows that had `CA` in the foreign key column are deleted.

For emphasis, I want to say this again: It is not the values in the foreign key column that are deleted. It is the entire row of information that gets deleted automatically, so consider the consequences carefully before you set up this option.

Task for example 1: Set up RI with cascade for deletes

Set up RI between the `sec0818_states` table and the `sec0818_clients` table. Use the option to have cascading deletes.

Oracle SQL

```
alter table sec0818_clients
add constraint fk_sec0818_clients_state_code
foreign key (state_code)
   references sec0818_states (state_code)
   on delete cascade; ❶
```

Access GUI method

Follow the directions in section 8-15 to set up RI with the Access GUI. In the Edit Relationships dialog box, select two checkboxes:

- Enforce Referential Integrity
- Cascade Delete Related Records

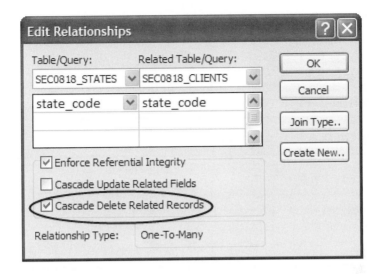

Task for example 2: Show how RI works with cascade for deletes

Delete California from the sec0818_states table. Do this when RI has been set up using the cascade deletes option.

Oracle & Access SQL

```
delete from sec0818_states
where state_code = 'CA';
```

Beginning table 1 (sec0818_states table)

STATE CODE	STATE_NAME	STATE_CAPITAL
CA	CALIFORNIA	SACRAMENTO
OR	OREGON	SALEM
WA	WASHINGTON	OLYMPIA

Beginning table 2 (sec0818_clients table)

CLIENT_ID	CLIENT_NAME	STATE CODE
100	LARRY COHEN	CA
200	ALICE WILLIAMS	CA
300	ROGER WOLF	OR
400	NANCY KERN	OR
500	CATHY LEE	WA
600	STEVEN LAKE	WA

Ending table 1 (sec0818_states table)

```
STATE
CODE    STATE_NAME                          STATE_CAPITAL
------  ----------------------------------  --------------------
OR      OREGON                              SALEM
WA      WASHINGTON                          OLYMPIA
```

Ending table 2 (sec0818_clients table) ❷

```
                                            STATE
CLIENT_ID  CLIENT_NAME                      CODE
---------  ----------------------------     ------
      300  ROGER WOLF                       OR
      400  NANCY KERN                       OR
      500  CATHY LEE                        WA
      600  STEVEN LAKE                      WA
```

Notes

❶ This line creates the `cascade` option.

❷ All the rows where the state codes were for California are automatically deleted.

Check your understanding

Set up RI between the `sec0818_departments` table and the `sec0818_employees` table. Handle deletes using the cascade rule. Then show the effect of this rule by deleting the shipping department from the `sec0818_departments` table.

8-19 The update rule: `cascade`

Access has the ability to cascade updates to the parent table and apply those updates to the child table.

In the following example, the first task sets up RI between the `sec0819_state` table and the `sec0819_clients` table using the `cascade` option for updates. The second task changes the abbreviation for California from CA to ZZ within the lookup table. In the data table, all the rows that had CA in the foreign key column now have the new value ZZ. This shows the process of changing codes, even if this example is a bit stretched.

Task for example 1: Set up RI with cascade for updates

Set up RI between the `sec0819_states` table and the `sec0819_clients` table. Use the option to have cascading deletes.

Access GUI method

Follow the directions in section 8-15 to set up RI with the Access GUI. In the Edit Relationships dialog box, select two checkboxes:

- Enforce Referential Integrity
- Cascade Update Related Fields

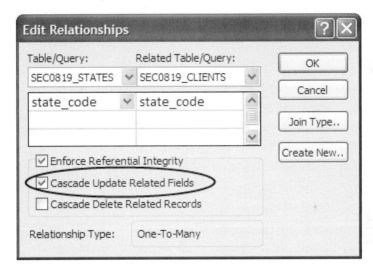

Task for example 2: Show how RI works with cascade for updates

Delete California from the `sec0819_states` table. Do this when RI has been set up using the `cascade` updates option.

Access SQL

```
update sec0819_states
  set state_code = 'ZZ'
where state_code = 'CA';
```

Oracle does not support cascaded updates.

Beginning table 1 (sec0819_states table)

STATE_CODE	STATE_NAME	STATE_CAPITAL	Add New Field
Ca	California	Sacramento	
Or	Oregon	Salem	
Wa	Washington	Olympia	

Beginning table 2 (sec0819_clients table)

CLIENT_ID	CLIENT_NAME	STATE_CODE	Add New Field
100	Larry Cohen	Ca	
200	Alice Williams	Ca	
300	Roger Wolf	Or	
400	Nancy Kern	Or	
500	Cathy Lee	Wa	
600	Steven Lake	Wa	

Ending table 1 (sec0819_states table)

STATE_CODE	STATE_NAME	STATE_CAPITAL	Add New Field
Or	Oregon	Salem	
Wa	Washington	Olympia	
ZZ	California	Sacramento	

Ending table 2 (sec0819_clients table) ❶

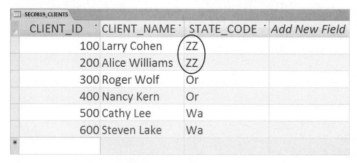

CLIENT_ID	CLIENT_NAME	STATE_CODE	Add New Field
100	Larry Cohen	ZZ	
200	Alice Williams	ZZ	
300	Roger Wolf	Or	
400	Nancy Kern	Or	
500	Cathy Lee	Wa	
600	Steven Lake	Wa	

Notes

❶ All the rows in the data table where the state codes were CA are automatically changed to ZZ.

Check your understanding

Set up RI between the `sec0819_departments` table and the `sec0819_employees` table. Handle updates using the cascade rule. Then show the effect of this rule by changing the shipping department code in the `sec0819_departments` table from SHP to ABC.

Variations of Referential Integrity

So far when I have described RI to you, the primary key was always a single column and the foreign key was always in a table that was different from the primary key. Some other options are presented in the following sections.

8-20 The two meanings of primary key

The term **_primary key_** is used with two different meanings. When we are talking about tables in general, we speak about the primary key as the unique identifier of each row. It is the noun or the subject of each row. A table is only allowed to have one primary key, although that key can consist of several columns.

When we are talking about RI, we speak about the primary key as the list of valid values, which is contained in the lookup table. A few years ago these were the same. That is, the list of valid values was always the primary key of the lookup table.

In the last few years a new option has become available that makes these two meanings different. The new option is that the list of valid values can be from a column that is different from the primary key of the lookup table. An example of this is shown later.

We cannot use just any column of the lookup table. The column must have a different value in every row and there must be a unique index defined on the column.

This feature is interesting and it is occasionally useful. But most of the time a lookup table is designed so that its primary key is its list of valid values. So we seldom need to distinguish between the two meanings of primary key.

The following example shows a case where the primary key of the table for the `sec0820_states` table is different from the primary key for RI, the list of valid values. We have two tables, `sec0820_states` and sec0820_clients, with RI between them. The state_capital column of the sec0820_clients table is validated from the column of the same name within the sec0820_states table.

Here we see that the state_code column is the primary key of the sec0820_states table. However, the state_capital column of the sec0820_states table provides the list of valid values for the RI.

Task

Set up RI between the sec0820_states table and the sec0820_clients table.

Oracle & Access SQL: Step 1, create a uniqueness constraint ❶

```
alter table sec0820_states
add constraint unique_sec0820_states_s_capital
   unique (state_capital);
```

Oracle & Access SQL: Step 2, create RI ❷

```
alter table sec0820_clients
add constraint fk_sec0820_clients_state_capital
foreign key (state_capital)
   references sec0820_states (state_capital);
```

Lookup table (sec0820_states table)

```
STATE
CODE     STATE_NAME                          STATE_CAPITAL
------   --------------------------------    ----------------
CA       CALIFORNIA                          SACRAMENTO
OR       OREGON                              SALEM
WA       WASHINGTON                          OLYMPIA
```

Data table (sec0820_clients table)

```
CLIENT_ID CLIENT_NAME                        STATE_CAPITAL
--------- --------------------------------   -------------------
      100 LARRY  COHEN                        SACRAMENTO
      200 ALICE  WILLIAMS                     SACRAMENTO
      300 ROGER  WOLF                         SALEM
      400 NANCY  KERN                         SALEM
      500 CATHY  LEE                          OLYMPIA
      600 STEVEN  LAKE                        OLYMPIA
```

Notes

❶ A uniqueness constraint must be put on the `state_capital` column of the `sec0820_states` table, which is the lookup table. This creates the restriction that each row of the table must have a different value in this column. This uniqueness constraint is required before the RI constraint can be created.

It is also possible to make the `state_capital` column the primary key of the `sec0820_states` table. This is another way to create the restriction that each row of the table must have a different value in this column and it allows the RI constraint to be created. However, in this example, this is not possible because the `state_code` column is already defined to be the primary key of the `sec0820_states` table.

This restriction is necessary so that when a specific value is "looked up" in the `sec0820_states` table, only a single row of that table can have a matching value.

❷ This `alter table` statement creates the RI constraint on the `state_capital` column. Now we might say that the `state_capital` column of the `sec0820_states` table is the "primary key of the RI relationship" even though it is not the primary key of the table.

8-21 Using two or more columns for the primary key

All of our examples so far have had a single column as the primary key. This is by far the most common situation when we are using a lookup table and RI. However it is also possible to have several columns in the primary key of the lookup table and within the data table to validate the combination of several columns together.

In fact, this is done in the `Lunches` database. We have RI between the `1_foods` table and the `1_lunch_items` table. The combination of the `supplier_id` and `product_code` columns is validated for every row of the `1_lunch_items` table.

Task

Show how RI is set up between the `1_foods` table and the `1_lunch_items` table. So this code will run, I use copies of these tables here.

Oracle & Access SQL

```
alter table sec0821_lunch_items
add constraint fk_sec0821_lunch_items_foods
foreign key (supplier_id, product_code) ❶
    references sec0821_foods (supplier_id, product_code); ❷
```

Lookup table (sec0821_foods table)

SUPPLIER ID	PRODUCT CODE	MENU ITEM	DESCRIPTION	PRICE	PRICE INCREASE
ASP	FS	1	FRESH SALAD	$2.00	$0.25
ASP	SP	2	SOUP OF THE DAY	$1.50	(null)
ASP	SW	3	SANDWICH	$3.50	$0.40
CBC	GS	4	GRILLED STEAK	$6.00	$0.70
CBC	SW	5	HAMBURGER	$2.50	$0.30
FRV	BR	6	BROCCOLI	$1.00	$0.05
FRV	FF	7	FRENCH FRIES	$1.50	(null)
JBR	AS	8	SODA	$1.25	$0.25
JBR	VR	9	COFFEE	$0.85	$0.15
VSB	AS	10	DESSERT	$3.00	$0.50

Data table (sec0821_lunch_items table)

LUNCH_ID	ITEM_NUMBER	SUPPLIER ID	PRODUCT CODE	QUANTITY
1	1	ASP	FS	1
1	2	ASP	SW	2
1	3	JBR	VR	2
2	1	ASP	SW	2
(and many more)				

Notes

❶ The foreign key consists of two columns, supplier_id and product_code, of the sec0821_lunch_items table. These two columns are in a specific order and are taken together to form a single unit, which is the foreign key, whose value needs to be verified. This is the same idea that allows the primary key of a table to consist of several columns, even though the primary key is considered to be a single entity.

❷ The list of all the valid values for the foreign key resides in the rows of the sec0821_foods table. Specifically, in the supplier_id column and product_code column of that table. Again, these two columns form a single unit, an ordered pair, in which the columns have a specific order.

8-22 The lookup and data tables can be the same table

It is possible for the lookup table and the data table to be the same table. That is, one column of a table is validated against another column from the same table. In fact this occurs within the Lunches database. The l_employees table has an employee_id column and a manager_id column. Each manager_id is required to be a valid employee_id.

Task

Show how RI is set up between the employee_id column and the manager_id column of the l_employees table.

Oracle & Access SQL

```
alter table sec0822_employees ❶
add constraint fk_sec0822_emp_manager_id
foreign key (manager_id)
    references sec0822_employees (employee_id); ❶
```

The lookup table and the data table are the same table(sec0822_employees table)

EMPLOYEE ID❷	FIRST NAME	LAST NAME	DEPT CODE	HIRE_DATE	CREDIT LIMIT	PHONE NUMBER	MANAGER ID❸
201	SUSAN	BROWN	EXE	01-JUN-1998	$30.00	3484	(null)
202	JIM	KERN	SAL	16-AUG-1999	$25.00	8722	201
203	MARTHA	WOODS	SHP	02-FEB-2009	$25.00	7591	201
204	ELLEN	OWENS	SAL	01-JUL-2008	$15.00	6830	202
205	HENRY	PERKINS	SAL	01-MAR-2006	$25.00	5286	202
206	CAROL	ROSE	ACT	(null)	(null)	(null)	(null)
207	DAN	SMITH	SHP	01-DEC-2008	$25.00	2259	203
208	FRED	CAMPBELL	SHP	01-APR-2008	$25.00	1752	203
209	PAULA	JACOBS	MKT	17-MAR-1999	$15.00	3357	201
210	NANCY	HOFFMAN	SAL	16-FEB-2007	$25.00	2974	203

Notes

❶ The same table, the sec0822_employees table, is named in both the alter table clause and the references clause. This creates the condition that the data table and the lookup table are both the same table.

❷ The employee_id column is the primary key of the table, so each row of the table must have a different value in this column. This column is also the primary key of the RI relationship. It is the list of all the valid values that may be entered into the manager_id column.

❸ Each time a new row is inserted into the table or a row within the table is changed, the value in the `manager_id` column is checked to verify that the value is valid. To be valid, that same value must be present in the `employee_id` column of some row already in the table. If the value in the `manager_id` column is not valid, then the new row or the changed row is not accepted into the table.

How to Code Constraints in a Create Table Statement

This section shows some examples of how to code constraints in the `create table` statement. You will often see this done in production code. The advantage to doing this is that it puts all the code in one place. It compacts the code into a single unt. This is great after the code has been fully developed and debugged.

However, when you first develop some new code, I suggest that you do not use this method of coding. Instead, write each constraint separately as I have done in this chapter up to now. This spreads the code out in small pieces so that errors are easier to isolate and fix.

8-23 Constraints are often coded in the `create table` statement

When you code a constraint within a `create table` statement, if the constraint affects only one column of this table, you can define the constraint at the same time that you define the column. You can often define them both on the same line of code. This is sometimes called a ***column constraint***.

However, if the constraint involves more than one column of this table, you are only allowed to code it after you have defined all the columns of the table. It goes in a separate section of the `create table` statement. This is sometimes called a ***table constraint***.

There are two variations of this coding. In the easiest method, you allow the database to assign all the names of the constraints. With a little more effort you can name the constraints yourself.

Constraint names are not used much, so many people feel that it is not important what the names are. However, they do appear in error messages. If you want the people using the database to understand the error messages when they occur, then it is best to assign names to the constraints that can be easily recognized.

Task

Show how to code the constraints on the `1_employees` table within the `create table` statement for that table.

Oracle SQL: Method 1 — Without naming the constraints

```
create table sec0823a_employees
(employee_id   number(3)      primary key, ❶
first_name     varchar2(10)   not null,
last_name      varchar2(20)   not null,
dept_code      varchar2(3)    references
                              sec0823a_departments(dept_code),
hire_date      date,
credit_limit   number(4,2)    check
                              (credit_limit < 50),
phone_number   varchar2(4)    unique,
manager_id     number(3)      references
                              sec0823a_employees(employee_id),
unique (first_name, last_name) ); ❷
```

Access SQL: Method 1 — Without naming the constraints

```
create table sec0823a_employees
(employee_id   integer        primary key, ❶
first_name     varchar(10)    not null,
last_name      varchar(20)    not null,
dept_code      varchar(3)     references
                              sec0823a_departments(dept_code),
hire_date      datetime,
credit_limit   money          check(credit_limit < 50),
phone_number   varchar(4)     unique,
manager_id     integer        references
                              sec0823a_employees(employee_id),
unique (first_name, last_name) );  ❷
```

Oracle SQL: Method 2 — Giving your own names to the constraints

```
create table sec0823b_employees
(employee_id   number(3)      constraint pk_employee_id  ❶
                              primary key,
first_name     varchar2(10)   constraint nn_first_name
                              check (first_name is not null),
last_name      varchar2(20)   constraint nn_last_name
                              check (last_name is not null),
dept_code      varchar2(3)    constraint fk_dept_code
                              references
                              sec0823b_departments(dept_code),
```

```
hire_date       date,
credit_limit    number(4,2)   constraint max_credit_limit
                              check (credit_limit < 50),
phone_number    varchar2(4)   constraint unique_phone_num
                              unique,
manager_id      number(3)     constraint fk_manager_id
                              references
                              sec0823b_employees(employee_id),
constraint      unique_full_name
                unique (first_name, last_name) );  ❷
```

Access SQL: Method 2 — Giving names to the constraints

```
create table sec0823b_employees
(employee_id    integer       constraint pk_employees    ❶
                              primary key,
first_name      varchar(10)   constraint nn_first_name
                              not null,
last_name       varchar(20)   constraint nn_last_name
                              not null,
dept_code       varchar(3)    constraint fk_dept_code
                              references
                              sec0823b_departments(dept_code),
hire_date       datetime,
credit_limit    money         constraint max_credit_limit
                              check (credit_limit < 50),
phone_number    varchar(4)    constraint unique_phone_num
                              unique,
manager_id      integer       constraint fk_manager
                              references
                              sec0823b_employees(employee_id),
constraint      unique_full_name
                unique (first_name, last_name) );  ❷
```

Notes

❶ The column constraints begin with the employee_id column and end with the manager_id column. Some columns of the table might not have a column constraint defined on them. In this example, the hire_date column does not have a column constraint.

❷ The table constraints begin here. A table constraint can involve more that one column. There can be many table constraints, although this example has only one. Note that there is a comma at the end of the definition of the last column of the table (the manager_id column) when table constraints are being defined.

Key Points

- The purpose of data integrity is to keep all the data in the database consistent so everyone can use it.

- The mechanism of data integrity is to define constraints, which are rules that sometimes do not allow you to add, change, or delete data. In a well designed database, the message is always clear about why this action is not allowed and what you can do to correct it. Unfortunately, many databases have messages that are somewhat confusing.

- An RI constraint restricts the values that can be entered into a specific column. The list of valid values is in the primary key column of another table. This ensures that the second table is a valid lookup table for the column. That is, for any value that is in the column, the lookup table has a match and can provide additional information, such as the meaning of a coded field.

- RI is a complex topic and there are several variations of it. The main issue is how you can change the list of valid values.

- A check constraint establishes a rule that the data must pass, for example, that a number must be between 10 and 50.

- A unique constraint says that every value in the column must be different. Any two rows must have different values.

- A not null constraint says that nulls are not allowed in the column; that is, the data value is required.

- A primary key constraint is a combination of a unique constraint and a not null constraint.

- The datatype of a column can restrict the size of a number that can be put into the column or the length of test that can be put into the column. In this way it is also a type of constraint.

chapter 9

Row
Functions

In all the `select` statements we have written so far, the data in the result was an exact copy of the data in some cell of the beginning table. In this chapter, we remove that limitation. Row functions can create new values that do not exist in the original table.

Introduction to Row Functions

Row functions calculate a new value based on the data in a single row of the table. The value can be based on the data in one column or several different columns. Some row functions operate on numbers, and others operate on text or on dates.

9-1　Getting data directly from the beginning table

In all the SQL we have done so far, the data in the result table came directly from the data in the original table. More specifically, the value in each cell of the result table was copied from some cell of the original table. No change at all was made to the value in the cell.

The following conceptual diagram shows this process. Data from a few rows and columns of the beginning table are gathered together to form the result table. All the other data in the beginning table is ignored.

Beginning table

Result table

The value in every cell comes from the beginning table.

9-2   What is a row function?

Row functions calculate or construct a new value that is not in the beginning table. This new value is constructed from the values in one or more cells of the original table. All these cells must be part of a single row within the table.

The following conceptual diagram shows a row function as seen from a point of view that considers one row of the beginning table. A single new value is constructed by the function from the values in one or more cells of the row.

Beginning table

New value
Created by a row
function from the
values in one or
more columns of
a single row.

The next conceptual diagram shows a row function as seen from the point of view that considers all the rows of the beginning table. A new value is created for each row. In effect, this adds a new column of data to the beginning table. Then the techniques you have already learned are applied to this enhanced table to create a final report from some of the rows and some of the columns.

The new values may appear in the result table, they may be used to pick rows from the beginning table, or they may be used to sort the rows of the result table. That is, the row function may be used in the select clause, the where clause, or the order by clause of a select statement.

The new column of information is not stored on the disk with the other data of the table. It does not become a permanent part of the table itself. Rather, it is held in memory while the select statement is being processed. The memory is released after the select statement has finished processing, so the new column of data exists only while one select statement is being processed.

Beginning table

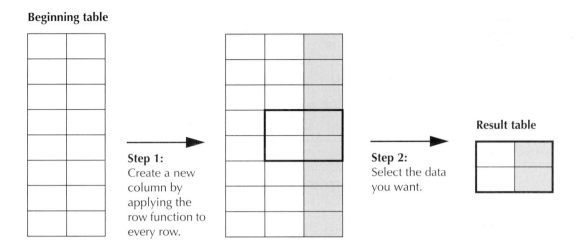

Step 1:
Create a new column by applying the row function to every row.

Step 2:
Select the data you want.

Result table

More precisely, the processing of the `select` statement occurs as if the new values were all stored in memory. Actually, the computer is allowed to take shortcuts as long as it obtains the correct result. The new values may be calculated for only a few of the rows, if that is sufficient to obtain the result table.

Of course, you can create a new table that stores the new column as data on the disk by using the `create table` statement you learned in section 4-1. An example of this is shown next.

Task

Create a new table that adds a new column to the `1_foods` table. Create the new column by using a row function that adds together the `price` and the `price_increase` columns. Name this column `new_price`.

Oracle SQL

```
create table sec0902_foods as
select 1_foods.*, ❶
       price + price_increase as new_price
from 1_foods;
```

Access SQL

```
select l_foods.*, ❶
       price + price_increase as new_price
into sec0902_foods
from l_foods;
```

Beginning table (1_foods table)

SUPPLIER ID	PRODUCT CODE	MENU ITEM	DESCRIPTION	PRICE	PRICE INCREASE
ASP	FS	1	FRESH SALAD	$2.00	$0.25
ASP	SP	2	SOUP OF THE DAY	$1.50	(null)
ASP	SW	3	SANDWICH	$3.50	$0.40
CBC	GS	4	GRILLED STEAK	$6.00	$0.70
CBC	SW	5	HAMBURGER	$2.50	$0.30
FRV	BR	6	BROCCOLI	$1.00	$0.05
FRV	FF	7	FRENCH FRIES	$1.50	(null)
JBR	AS	8	SODA	$1.25	$0.25
JBR	VR	9	COFFEE	$0.85	$0.15
VSB	AS	10	DESSERT	$3.00	$0.50

New table with a column created by a row function (seec0902_foods table)

SUPPLIER ID	PRODUCT CODE	MENU ITEM	DESCRIPTION	PRICE	PRICE INCREASE	NEW PRICE	
ASP	FS	1	FRESH SALAD	$2.00	$0.25	$2.25	
ASP	SP	2	SOUP OF THE DAY	$1.50	(null)	(null)	❷
ASP	SW	3	SANDWICH	$3.50	$0.40	$3.90	
CBC	GS	4	GRILLED STEAK	$6.00	$0.70	$6.70	
CBC	SW	5	HAMBURGER	$2.50	$0.30	$2.80	
FRV	BR	6	BROCCOLI	$1.00	$0.05	$1.05	
FRV	FF	7	FRENCH FRIES	$1.50	(null)	(null)	❷
JBR	AS	8	SODA	$1.25	$0.25	$1.50	
JBR	VR	9	COFFEE	$0.85	$0.15	$1.00	
VSB	AS	10	DESSERT	$3.00	$0.50	$3.50	

Notes

❶ In both Oracle and Access, when we follow `select *` with additional columns, we need to add the table name and a period before the asterisk.

❷ The `new_price` is null when the `price_increase` is null because a null is an unknown value. In general, when a null is added to another value the result is a null.

Check your understanding

Create a new table, named `sec0902_employees`, that adds two new columns to the `1_employees` table. Create the new columns by using the following row functions:

Column Name:	`full_name`
Oracle:	`first_name || ' ' || last_name`
Access:	`first_name & ' ' & last_name`

Column Name:	`new_credit_limit`
Oracle & Access:	`credit_limit + 10.00`

9-3 An example of a row function in the `select` clause

In the previous section I used a row function to create a new column in the table. This is step 1 in the diagram on page 325. In that example I did not go on to step 2, which would select some data from the new table I created. In this section I combine both steps in a single `select` statement. I use a row function, which defines a new column, and I also select data to display in the final report.

In this example the price increase is added to the price, which creates a new price. This is a function because a new value is obtained. This function uses two columns from the beginning table: `price` and `price_increase`. Other row functions can use a single column or multiple columns.

Task

From the `1_foods` table list the `menu_item`, `description`, and `new_price`. Calculate the `new_price` by adding together `price` and `price_increase`.

Oracle & Access SQL

```
select menu_item,
       description,
       price + price_increase as new_price ❶
from 1_foods
where menu_item < 15
order by menu_item;
```

Beginning table (1_foods table)

SUPPLIER ID	PRODUCT CODE	MENU ITEM	DESCRIPTION	PRICE	PRICE INCREASE
ASP	FS	1	FRESH SALAD	$2.00	$0.25
ASP	SP	2	SOUP OF THE DAY	$1.50	(null)
ASP	SW	3	SANDWICH	$3.50	$0.40
CBC	GS	4	GRILLED STEAK	$6.00	$0.70
CBC	SW	5	HAMBURGER	$2.50	$0.30
FRV	BR	6	BROCCOLI	$1.00	$0.05
FRV	FF	7	FRENCH FRIES	$1.50	(null)
JBR	AS	8	SODA	$1.25	$0.25
JBR	VR	9	COFFEE	$0.85	$0.15
VSB	AS	10	DESSERT	$3.00	$0.50

Result table

MENU ITEM	DESCRIPTION	NEW PRICE
1	FRESH SALAD	$2.25
2	SOUP OF THE DAY	(null)
3	SANDWICH	$3.90
4	GRILLED STEAK	$6.70
5	HAMBURGER	$2.80
6	BROCCOLI	$1.05
7	FRENCH FRIES	(null)
8	SODA	$1.50
9	COFFEE	$1.00
10	DESSERT	$3.50

Notes

❶ This is the row function.

Check your understanding

The following `select` statement lists all the employees hired before January 1, 2000 and shows their credit limits. Modify this statement to add $10.00 to their credit limits.

This change in the amount of the credit limits shows up in this one result table, but does not affect the data in the underlying table.

```
select employee_id,
       first_name,
       last_name,
       credit_limit
from l_employees
order by employee_id;
```

9-4 An example of a row function used in all the clauses of a `select` statement

This section shows an example of a row function used in several clauses of a `select` statement. In this example it is used in the `select` clause, `where` clause, and `order by` clause. Each time it is used we must write out the entire function. This is not ideal, and the next section shows you how to avoid writing out the function many times.

In this example, the function is fairly simple and writing it several times is not much of a problem. However, when a function is longer and more complex, having several copies of it can create a problem. When small changes are made to one instance of the function and not the others, it can be very difficult to debug.

In the following code, parentheses are put around the function when it is written in the `where` clause and the `order by` clause. These are optional, but I use them because I think it makes the code easier to read.

Task

From the 1_foods table list the menu_item, description, and new_price. Calculate the new_price by adding together the price and the price_increase. List only the foods where the new price is greater than $2.00. Sort the rows of the result table on the new_price column.

Oracle & Access SQL

```
select menu_item,
       description,
       price + price_increase as new_price ❶
from 1_foods
where (price + price_increase) > 2.00 ❷
order by (price + price_increase); ❸
```

Beginning table (1_foods table)

SUPPLIER ID	PRODUCT CODE	MENU ITEM	DESCRIPTION	PRICE	PRICE INCREASE
ASP	FS	1	FRESH SALAD	$2.00	$0.25
ASP	SP	2	SOUP OF THE DAY	$1.50	(null)
ASP	SW	3	SANDWICH	$3.50	$0.40
CBC	GS	4	GRILLED STEAK	$6.00	$0.70
CBC	SW	5	HAMBURGER	$2.50	$0.30
FRV	BR	6	BROCCOLI	$1.00	$0.05
FRV	FF	7	FRENCH FRIES	$1.50	(null)
JBR	AS	8	SODA	$1.25	$0.25
JBR	VR	9	COFFEE	$0.85	$0.15
VSB	AS	10	DESSERT	$3.00	$0.50

Result table ❹

MENU ITEM	DESCRIPTION	NEW PRICE
1	FRESH SALAD	$2.25
5	HAMBURGER	$2.80
10	DESSERT	$3.50
3	SANDWICH	$3.90
4	GRILLED STEAK	$6.70

Notes

❶ In the `select` clause the function is written for the first time.

❷ In the `where` clause the entire function must be written out again.

❸ In the `order by` clause the entire function must be written out again.

❹ Rows having a null in the `new_price` column do not satisfy the condition in the `where` clause, so they do not appear in the result table.

Check your understanding

From the `1_employees` table list the employee ID, first name, last name, and new credit limit (which is `credit_limit` + 10.00) for all employees whose new credit limit is above $20.00. Sort the rows by the new credit limit.

9-5   Defining a row function as the first step

This section shows you a technique that can be used when the same row function is used in several different clauses of a `select` statement. When this was done in the previous section, the function was written several times. We had no guarantee that the function was exactly the same each time it was used. A typing error could make one instance slightly different from another.

This technique prevents such differences from occurring. It also makes the code easier to write and understand. If the row function is complex, it ensures that all references to the function are defined in exactly the same way. I recommend using this technique in most situations.

The first step of this technique creates a table or view that defines the new column using the row function. The next step is able to use the name of the new column in several places without rewriting the entire definition of the row function.

Task

The task is the same as in the previous section.

Oracle SQL: Step 1 — Create a view ❶

```
create or replace view sec0905_step1_view as
select menu_item,
       description,
       price + price_increase as new_price ❷
from l_foods;
```

Access SQL: Step 1 — Create a view ❶

Part 1: Enter this in the SQL window:

```
select menu_item,
       description,
       price + price_increase as new_price
from l_foods;
```

Part 2: Save the query. Name it sec0905_step1_view.

Oracle & Access SQL: Step 2 — Use the new view ❷

```
select menu_item,
       description,
       new_price ❸
from sec0905_step1_view
where new_price > 2.00 ❹
order by new_price; ❺
```

Beginning table (l_foods table)

SUPPLIER ID	PRODUCT CODE	MENU ITEM	DESCRIPTION	PRICE	PRICE INCREASE
ASP	FS	1	FRESH SALAD	$2.00	$0.25
ASP	SP	2	SOUP OF THE DAY	$1.50	(null)
ASP	SW	3	SANDWICH	$3.50	$0.40
CBC	GS	4	GRILLED STEAK	$6.00	$0.70
CBC	SW	5	HAMBURGER	$2.50	$0.30
FRV	BR	6	BROCCOLI	$1.00	$0.05
FRV	FF	7	FRENCH FRIES	$1.50	(null)
JBR	AS	8	SODA	$1.25	$0.25
JBR	VR	9	COFFEE	$0.85	$0.15
VSB	AS	10	DESSERT	$3.00	$0.50

Result table produced by step 1

```
   MENU                         NEW
   ITEM DESCRIPTION            PRICE
------- --------------------   ------
      1 FRESH SALAD            $2.25
      2 SOUP OF THE DAY        (null)  ❻
      3 SANDWICH               $3.90
      4 GRILLED STEAK          $6.70
      5 HAMBURGER              $2.80
      6 BROCCOLI               $1.05
      7 FRENCH FRIES           (null)
      8 SODA                   $1.50
      9 COFFEE                 $1.00
     10 DESSERT                $3.50
```

Result table produced by step 2

```
   MENU                         NEW
   ITEM DESCRIPTION            PRICE
------- --------------------   ------
      1 FRESH SALAD            $2.25
      5 HAMBURGER              $2.80
     10 DESSERT                $3.50
      3 SANDWICH               $3.90
      4 GRILLED STEAK          $6.70
```

Notes

❶ The first step of this technique creates a view that defines the row function and gives a name to the column it creates. Step 1 could have created a table instead of a view, but using a view is usually more efficient.

Note that the row function is written only once with the new technique. However, with the previous technique, it had to be written several times.

❷ The second step is almost the same as the select statement in section 9-4. One difference is that the view created in step 1 is used in the from clause. Another difference is that the name of the new column is used in all the clauses instead of writing out the explicit definition of the function.

❸ Here, the new_price column is used in the select clause.

❹ Here, the new_price column is used in the where clause.

❺ Here, the new_price column is used in the order by clause.

❻ A null is an unknown number, so a null added to any other number is a null; at least this is the case for row functions. To prevent a null from occurring here, you can use the nvl function in Oracle or the nz function in Access. These functions can change the nulls in the price_increase column into zeros. Then the addition will work. I show you how to do this in chapter 10.

Check your understanding

Repeat the exercise in the previous section, but this time do it in two steps. In step 1, define a view that includes all the fields you need and defines the new credit limit field. In step 2 write a select statement based on that view.

Numeric Functions

Some row functions perform arithmetic on numbers. Others round or truncate numbers.

9-6   Functions on numbers

The row functions for arithmetic do exactly what you expect them to do. An asterisk is used for the multiplication sign, as it is in most computer languages. Null does not mean zero. It means an unknown value. So any row function that operates on a null produces a null as the result.

The following table shows some of the most frequently used functions on numbers. I omitted from this list the trigonometry functions and logarithms. Both Oracle and Access have them. Other, more specialized functions can be found in the technical reference.

Frequently used numerical functions.

Oracle	Access	Description	Examples
ARITHMETIC			
+	+	Addition	Oracle & Access: 3 + 2 = 5 Oracle & Access: 3 + null = null
–	–	Subtraction	Oracle & Access: 3 – 2 = 1 Oracle & Access: 3 – null = null
*	*	Multiplication	Oracle & Access: 3 * 2 = 6 Oracle & Access: 3 * null = null

Frequently used numerical functions. *(continued)*

Oracle	Access	Description	Examples
ARITHMETIC *(continued)*			
/	/	Division	Oracle & Access: `10 / 3 = 3.3333` Oracle & Access: `10 / null = null`
power	^	Value raised to an exponent	Oracle: `power(5, 2) = 25` Access: `5^2 = 25`
sqrt	sqr	Square root	Oracle: `sqrt(25) = 5` Access: `sqr(25) = 5`
(can be made)	\	Integer division	Access: `20 \ 3 = 6` Access: `20 \ null = null` Oracle equivalent: `floor(20 / 3) = 6`
mod	mod	Remainder after division	Oracle: `mod(10, 3) = 1` Access: `10 mod 3 = 1`
SIGN, ROUNDING, AND TRUNCATION			
sign	sgn	Sign indicator (1 if positive, −1 if negative, 0 if zero)	Oracle: `sign(-8) = -1` Access: `sgn(-8) = -1`
abs	abs	Absolute value	Oracle & Access: `abs(-8) = 8`
ceil	(can be made)	Smallest integer larger than or equal to a value	Oracle: `ceil(3.5) = 4` Access equivalent: `int(3.5 + 0.9) = 4`
floor	int	Largest integer less than or equal to a value	Oracle: `floor(3.5) = 3` Access: `int(3.5) = 3`
round	(can be made)	Round to a specified precision	Oracle: `round(3.4567, 2) = 3.46` Access equivalent: `int(3.4567 *(10^2)+0.5)/(10^2)= 3.46`
trunc	(can be made)	Truncate to a specified precision	Oracle: `trunc(3.4567, 2) = 3.45` Access equivalent: `int(3.4567 *(10^2))/(10^2)= 3.45`

9-7   How to test a row function

This section shows you one technique for testing a row function. This is a way to discover what a row function does by using it to calculate a value.

The problem with doing calculations in SQL is that everything in SQL must be done in terms of tables. You must begin with a table and end with a table. So how can you multiply two numbers?

You have to start with a table — any table. It does not matter what data is in the table. Oracle provides a special table set up for this purpose. It is called the ***dual table***. It has only one row and one column. In Access, I have created this table for you. In other Access databases you may have to create this table yourself. When you do this, be sure to put some data in the table. It does not matter what the values are, but they should not be a null. Actually, any table with only one row will work, so we could use the `1_constants` table here instead of the dual table.

This technique does not use the data in the beginning table. It only uses the table as a framework to get the `select` statement to process.

What I have just described is the traditional way that SQL worked — a table of some sort was always required in any SQL statement. However Access has created a new way to work around this problem. In Access you can write only the `select` clause and omit any reference to a table.

Task

Show how to test a row function. As an example, show   3 * 4 = 12.

Oracle & Access SQL ❶

```
select 3 * 4
from dual;
```

Access SQL ❷

```
select 3 * 4;
```

Beginning table (dual table with dummy data)

```
D
-
X
```

Result table

```
        3*4
---------
         12
```

Notes

❶ The dual table is used here as an empty vessel. It provides the structure of a table, but no content. It provides a framework to carry other content.

❷ No table name is required.

9-8 Another way to test a numeric row function

This section shows you another way to test a function on numbers. In the previous technique, we saw only one specific calculation. One of the significant features of numbers is that they form patterns. Using the previous technique, you could not see the pattern, but with this technique, you can.

This technique uses a table I set up for you containing all the numbers from −10 to +10. The numeric function is calculated on each of these numbers. The advantage is that you get to see how the function behaves over a range of values and the pattern that is created. If you want to see a larger range, you can use another table I set up for you called Numbers_0_to_99.

Task

Test the function MOD(x, 3) where x goes from −10 to +10.

Oracle SQL

```
select n,
       mod(n, 3)
from sec0908_test_numbers
order by n;
```

Access SQL

```
select n,
       n mod 3
from sec0908_test_numbers
order by n;
```

Beginning table (`sec0908_test_numbers` table)

```
        N
---------
      -10
       -9
       -8
       -7
       -6
       -5
       -4
       -3
       -2
       -1
        0
        1
        2
        3
        4
        5
        6
        7
        8
        9
       10
```

Result table ❶

```
        N   MOD(N,3)
---------   ---------
      -10          -1
       -9           0
       -8          -2
       -7          -1
       -6           0
       -5          -2
       -4          -1
       -3           0
       -2          -2
       -1          -1
        0           0
        1           1
        2           2
        3           0
        4           1
        5           2
        6           0
        7           1
        8           2
        9           0
       10           1
```

Notes

❶ The last column shows the pattern created by MOD 3. This pattern is 0, 1, 2, 0 ... on the positive numbers and it is 0, −1,−2, 0 ... on the negative numbers.

Check your understanding

Test the following numeric row functions over a range of values from −10 to +10, using the table sec0908_test_numbers.

Purpose	Oracle	Access
Multiplication	5 * n	5 * n
Division of *n*	n / 10	n / 10
Division by *n* ❷	10 / n	10 / n
Division by *n* ❸	10 / n	10 / n
Exponents	power(2, n)	2^n
Square root ❹	sqrt(n)	sqr(n)
Square root ❺	sqrt(n)	sqr(n)
Integer part of division	floor(n/3)	n\3
Remainder after division	mod(n,3)	n mod 3

Notes for "Check your understanding"

❷ Oracle handles this differently than Access. Oracle returns an error message and no result table. It refuses to process the query at all. Access produces a result table and calculates a result for all the values of *n* except when *n* = 0. It says "#Error" for the value of 10/n when *n* = 0.

❸ Add the condition: WHERE NOT (*n* = 0)

❹ Oracle handles this differently than Access. Oracle returns an error message and no result table. It refuses to process the query at all. Access produces a result table and calculates a result for all the values of *n* except when *n* < 0. It says "#Error" for the value of the square root when *n* < 0.

❺ Add the condition: WHERE *n* >= 0

Text Functions

Some row functions operate on text. Most of them produce text as output, but a few of them produce numbers. Text functions are also sometimes called *character functions* or *string functions*.

9-9   Functions on text

The table that follows shows the row functions on text that are used most often. Other ones can be found in the technical manuals. These row functions operate on both fixed length and variable length strings of characters.

The names of some of the Access functions here contain both uppercase and lowercase letters. This is done for readability, not because the names of these functions are case sensitive. It is a convention in Access that if the name is formed from two or more words, the first letter of each word is capitalized. For instance, the name of the function `StrConv` is a shortened form of String Conversion. The functions still work if you write them in all lowercase letters, but they are not as easy for people to understand.

Frequently used textual row functions.

Oracle	Access	Description	Examples
FUNCTIONS THAT RESULT IN TEXT			

concat or ||	& or +	Concatenation	Oracle:
			 `concat('sun', 'flower') = 'sunflower'`
			 Oracle:
			 `'sun' || 'flower' = 'sunflower'`
			 Access:
			 `'sun' & 'flower' = 'sunflower'`
			 Access:
			 `'sun' + 'flower' = 'sunflower'`
			 Parameters:
			 `first part = 'sun'`
			 `second part = 'flower'`
			 Notes: In Access, + and & are different in how they handle nulls.
			 `'sun' + null = null`
			 `'sun' & null = 'sun'`

Frequently used textual row functions. *(continued)*

Oracle	Access	Description	Examples
FUNCTIONS THAT RESULT IN TEXT *(continued)*			

substr	Mid	Substring	Oracle:
			`substr ('sunflower', 4, 3) = 'flo'`
			Access:
			`mid('sunflower', 4, 3) = 'flo'`
			Parameters:
			`beginning string = 'sunflower'`
			`starting position = 4`
			`length = 3`

replace	Replace	Replace string	Oracle & Access:
			`replace ('ABCABC', 'AB', '1234') =`
			`           '1234C1234C'`
			Parameters:
			`beginning string = 'ABCABC'`
			`substring to be replaced = 'AB'`
			`string used for replacement = '1234'`

rpad	(not available)	Right Pad	Oracle:
			`rpad('DOG', 10, '*-') = 'DOG*-*-*-*'`
			Parameters:
			`beginning string = 'DOG'`
			`ending length = 10`
			`padding string = '*-'`

lpad	(not available)	Left Pad	Oracle:
			`lpad('DOG', 10, '*-') = '*-*-*-*DOG'`
			Parameters:
			`beginning string = 'DOG'`
			`ending length = 10`
			`padding string = '*-'`

(can be made)	String	Create a string of specified length	Access: `string(5,'A') = 'AAAAA'`
			Parameters:
			`ending length = 5`
			`character to repeat = 'A'`
			Oracle equivalent: `rpad('A', 5, 'A')`

soundex	(not available)	Find names that sound similar but might be spelled differently	Oracle example:
			`select name`
			`from names_table`
			`where soundex(name)=soundex('John')`

Frequently used textual row functions. *(continued)*

Oracle	Access	Description	Examples
FUNCTIONS THAT CONTROL CAPITALIZATION			

upper	UCase
	or
	StrConv(,1)
		Uppercase
		or
		string conversion
			Oracle:
			`upper ('sunflower') = 'SUNFLOWER'`
			Access:
			`ucase('sunflower') = 'SUNFLOWER'`
			Access:
			`StrConv('sunflower',1) = 'SUNFLOWER'`

lower	LCase
	or
	StrConv(,2)
		Lowercase
		or
		string conversion
			Oracle:
			`lower ('SUNFLOWER') = 'sunflower'`
			Access:
			`lcase('SUNFLOWER') = 'sunflower'`
			Access:
			`StrConv('SUNFLOWER',2) = 'sunflower'`

initcap	StrConv(,3)	Initial capital
		for each word
			Oracle:
			`initcap ('sun flower') = 'Sun Flower'`
			Access:
			`StrConv('sun flower', 3)= 'Sun Flower'`

FUNCTIONS THAT CONTROL BLANK SPACES			

ltrim	LTrim	Left trim:
		remove spaces
		on left
			Oracle & Access:
			`ltrim('    hello world    ') =`
			`        'hello world    '`

rtrim	RTrim	Right trim:
		remove spaces
		on right
			Oracle & Access:
			`rtrim('    hello world    ') =`
			`        '    hello world'`

trim	Trim	Trim on both
		the left and
		right
			Oracle & Access:
			`trim('    hello world    ') =`
			`        'hello world'`

(can be
made)
	Space	Create a string
		of spaces of
		specified
		length
			Access:
			`space(5) ='        '`
			Parameters:
			`ending length = 5`
			Oracle equivalent: `rpad(' ', 5, ' ')`

Frequently used textual row functions. *(continued)*

FUNCTIONS THAT RESULT IN NUMBERS			
`length`	`Len`	Number of characters in a text string	Oracle: `length ('sunflower') = 9` Access: `len('sunflower') = 9`

`instr`	`InStr`	Starting position of one string occurring in another	Oracle & Access:
			`instr ('sunflower', 'low') = 5`
			Oracle & Access:
			`instr ('sunflower', 'zzz') = 0`
			Parameters:
			`base string = 'sunflower'`
			`string to find = 'low'`
			Note: Zero means that the second string does not occur in the first string.

Check your understanding

Test the following row functions using the dual table technique. (See section 9-7.) If you are using Access, you do not need to use the dual table.

Purpose	Oracle	Access
Concatenation	`'first' || 'second'`	`'first' & 'second'`
Substring	`substr('abcdefghij',3,4)`	`Mid('abcdefghij',3,4)`
Length of text	`length('abcdefg')`	`Len('abcdefg')`
Starting position, when the second string is part of the first string	`instr('abcdefg', cd')`	`InStr('abcdefg','cd')`
Starting position, when the second string is not part of the first string	`instr('abcdefg','zz')`	`InStr('abcdefg','zz')`
Uppercase	`upper('dog')`	`UCase('dog')`
Lowercase	`lower('CAT')`	`LCase('CAT')`
Trim spaces	`trim('   bird   ')`	`trim('   bird   ')`

9-10 Combining the first and last names

This section shows you an example that uses text functions. We combine the first name and the last name in a single column, placing one space between the two names.

A single space is then concatenated to the right of the first name. To code that single space, enclose one space within single quotes. Then the last name is concatenated to the end.

Oracle and Access use different signs for concatenation, but they mean the same thing. Access uses the ampersand (&). Oracle uses two double bars (||). On most keyboards the double bar is Shift + Backslash.

Variations of this technique can be used to put the name in other formats such as:

    Susan W. Brown
    Ms. Brown
    Brown, Susan W.

Task

List the `employee_id` and the full name of each employee. Create the full name by combining the first and last names separated by a single space.

Oracle SQL

```
select employee_id,
       first_name || ' ' || last_name as full_name  ❶
from 1_employees;
```

Access SQL

```
select employee_id,
       first_name & ' ' & last_name as full_name  ❷
from 1_employees;
```

Beginning table (1_employees table)

```
EMPLOYEE                           DEPT                     CREDIT PHONE   MANAGER
      ID FIRST_NAME  LAST_NAME  CODE HIRE_DATE           LIMIT NUMBER       ID
-------- ----------- ---------- ---- ------------      ------- ------  -------
     201 SUSAN       BROWN      EXE  01-JUN-1998       $30.00 3484    (null)
     202 JIM         KERN       SAL  16-AUG-1999       $25.00 8722       201
     203 MARTHA      WOODS      SHP  02-FEB-2009       $25.00 7591       201
     204 ELLEN       OWENS      SAL  01-JUL-2008       $15.00 6830       202
     205 HENRY       PERKINS    SAL  01-MAR-2006       $25.00 5286       202
     206 CAROL       ROSE       ACT  (null)            (null) (null)  (null)
     207 DAN         SMITH      SHP  01-DEC-2008       $25.00 2259       203
     208 FRED        CAMPBELL   SHP  01-APR-2008       $25.00 1752       203
     209 PAULA       JACOBS     MKT  17-MAR-1999       $15.00 3357       201
     210 NANCY       HOFFMAN    SAL  16-FEB-2007       $25.00 2974       203
```

Result table

```
EMPLOYEE
      ID FULL_NAME
-------- ---------------
     201 SUSAN BROWN
     202 JIM KERN
     203 MARTHA WOODS
     204 ELLEN OWENS
     205 HENRY PERKINS
     206 CAROL ROSE
     207 DAN SMITH
     208 FRED CAMPBELL
     209 PAULA JACOBS
     210 NANCY HOFFMAN
```

Notes

❶ In Oracle, the concatenation operator is ||, where | is the uppercase symbol on the Backslash key. I always put a space on both sides of the concatenation sign. In the middle of the concatenation, the single space between the names is formed by:

single quote — space — single quote

❷ In Access, the concatenation operator is &.

Check your understanding

List the employee ID and the names of all the employees. Write the names like "Brown, S." with the last name capitalized, then a comma and a space, then the first initial capitalized followed by a period.

9-11　Separating the first and last names

In the previous section we discussed how to combine the `first_name` and `last_name` to create the `full_name`. In this section we go in the opposite direction. We begin with the `full_name` and divide it into two parts: the `first_name` and the `last_name`.

Finding the position of the space that separates the `first_name` from the `last_name` is the central point of this technique. This is the first step and it can be done with the `instr` function. In the next step the `full_name` column can be divided into two parts: the part before the space and the part after the space, which become the `first_name` and the `last_name` columns, respectively.

In specifying the `last_name`, only two parameters are used: the beginning string and the starting position. The third parameter, which is the length, is not specified. When this is done the substring extends all the way to the end of the beginning string.

Task

The `sec0911_full_name` table contains one column, which contains the full name, both the first name and last name separated by a single space. From this table list the full name, the position of the space, the first name, and the last name.

Oracle SQL

```
create or replace view sec0911_step1_view as ❶
select full_name,
       instr(full_name, ' ') as position_of_space ❷
from sec0911_full_name;

select full_name,
       position_of_space,
       substr(full_name, 1, position_of_space - 1)
                                      as first_name, ❸
       substr(full_name, position_of_space + 1)
                                      as last_name ❹
from sec0911_step1_view;
```

Access SQL

Step 1: Enter the following query in the SQL window:

```
select full_name, ❺
       instr(full_name, ' ') as position_of_space ❷
from sec0911_full_name;
```

Save the query. Name it `sec0911_step1_view`.

Step 2:

```
select full_name,
       position_of_space,
       mid(full_name, 1, position_of_space - 1)
                                    as first_name, ❸
       mid(full_name, position_of_space + 1)
                                    as last_name ❹
from sec0911_step1_view;
```

Beginning table (sec0911 table)

```
FULL_NAME
----------------
SUSAN BROWN
JIM KERN
MARTHA WOODS
ELLEN OWENS
HENRY PERKINS
CAROL ROSE
DAN SMITH
FRED CAMPBELL
PAULA JACOBS
NANCY HOFFMAN
```

Result table

```
                 POSITION
FULL_NAME        OF SPACE  FIRST_NAME  LAST_NAME
---------------  --------- ----------  ----------
SUSAN BROWN             6  SUSAN       BROWN
JIM KERN               4  JIM         KERN
MARTHA WOODS           7  MARTHA      WOODS
ELLEN OWENS            6  ELLEN       OWENS
HENRY PERKINS          6  HENRY       PERKINS
CAROL ROSE             6  CAROL       ROSE
DAN SMITH              4  DAN         SMITH
FRED CAMPBELL          5  FRED        CAMPBELL
PAULA JACOBS           6  PAULA       JACOBS
NANCY HOFFMAN          6  NANCY       HOFFMAN
```

Notes

❶ In Oracle, the first step creates a view that defines the position of the space. Here I use the Oracle command `create or replace view`, which is one way to do a preventative delete.

❷ This is the definition of the position of the space.

❸ The `first_name` begins at the first character of the `full_name`. It extends until the character before the space.

❹ The `last_name` begins at the character after the space. It extends until the end of the `full_name`.

❺ In Access, I chose to have the first step create a new table, rather than a view. This does not create a problem because the amount of data is small.

Check your understanding

Table `sec0911_names` contains names of people in the format "Brown, Susan V." Create a new view in which you have separated the first name, middle initial, and last name into separate columns. Hint: This might be easier if you do it in a series of steps.

9-12 Formatting phone numbers

In section 7-5 we formatted the `phone_number` column of the `1_employees` table in Access. In the format we added an area code and the first three digits of the phone number. We could not use the same technique in Oracle because Oracle formats apply only to columns with a date or number datatype.

Now we are ready to format the phone numbers in Oracle by concatenating the `phone_number` with a literal. The same technique also works in Access.

When we use this technique we need to decide how we want to handle nulls in the data. There is one phone number that contains a null. To exclude it from the result table, we want to add a `where` clause to the code:

`where phone_number is not null;`

However if we do this, there is a price to pay — the entire row for Carol Rose disappears from the result table, so the listing of the employees is incomplete. We will be able to fix this problem when we discuss unions in chapter 15.

Task

List the employee ID, employee name, and the phone number of all the employees. Format the `phone_number` values to include the area code and the first three digits of the phone number.

Oracle SQL

```
select employee_id,
       first_name,
       last_name,
       '(415) 643-' || phone_number as phone_number2
from 1_employees;
```

Access SQL

```
select employee_id,
       first_name,
       last_name,
       '(415) 643-' & phone_number as phone_number2
from 1_employees;
```

Beginning table (1_employees table)

EMPLOYEE ID	FIRST_NAME	LAST_NAME	DEPT CODE	HIRE_DATE	CREDIT LIMIT	PHONE NUMBER	MANAGER ID
201	SUSAN	BROWN	EXE	01-JUN-1998	$30.00	3484	(null)
202	JIM	KERN	SAL	16-AUG-1999	$25.00	8722	201
203	MARTHA	WOODS	SHP	02-FEB-2009	$25.00	7591	201
204	ELLEN	OWENS	SAL	01-JUL-2008	$15.00	6830	202
205	HENRY	PERKINS	SAL	01-MAR-2006	$25.00	5286	202
206	CAROL	ROSE	ACT	(null)	(null)	(null)	(null)
207	DAN	SMITH	SHP	01-DEC-2008	$25.00	2259	203
208	FRED	CAMPBELL	SHP	01-APR-2008	$25.00	1752	203
209	PAULA	JACOBS	MKT	17-MAR-1999	$15.00	3357	201
210	NANCY	HOFFMAN	SAL	16-FEB-2007	$25.00	2974	203

Result table

EMPLOYEE ID	FIRST_NAME	LAST_NAME	PHONE NUMBER	
201	SUSAN	BROWN	(415) 643-3484	
202	JIM	KERN	(415) 643-8722	
203	MARTHA	WOODS	(415) 643-7591	
204	ELLEN	OWENS	(415) 643-6830	
205	HENRY	PERKINS	(415) 643-5286	
206	CAROL	ROSE	(415) 643-	❶
207	DAN	SMITH	(415) 643-2259	
208	FRED	CAMPBELL	(415) 643-1752	
209	PAULA	JACOBS	(415) 643-3357	
210	NANCY	HOFFMAN	(415) 643-2974	

Notes

❶ This incomplete phone number results from the null in the
`phone_number` column of the beginning table.

Check your understanding

Table `sec0912_phone_numbers` contains phone numbers in the format
"(415) 627-1445." These numbers do not all begin in the first column. Create a
new view with two columns in which you have separated the area code from
the rest of the phone number.

Date Functions

Some row functions operate on dates. Functions on dates are different
from the date formats you learned in chapter 7. Date formats change the
appearance of the date without changing its value. Date functions change
the value of the data to another date.

9-13 Functions on dates

This section shows you the date functions that are used most often. Date
calculations are usually made in terms of the number of days, rather than
months or years, because the number of days in a month or year can vary.

Both Oracle and Access can add a number of days to a date; subtract a
number of days from a date; and find the number of days between two
dates. These are the most important date functions.

Using the table of numbers from 0 to 99, you can add these numbers to any
date and create a calendar that is 100 days long. Although you can subtract
one date from another date, you cannot add one date to another date.

When you are working with dates, be sure to remember that each date also
has a time, even if the time is not being displayed. A fraction can be added
to a date to change the time.

In the table that follows, the Oracle dates are assumed to already be in
date format. This assumption works when they are in a column that has a
date datatype. If you are writing these dates directly into a `select` statement, the `to_date` function must be used to convert the text string within
quotes to a `date` datatype. For example, the first line in the table shows:

```
'20-jan-2015' + 3 = '23-jan-2015'
```

To use this function on a column of dates named `date_col`, we would write:

```
select date_col + 3
```

To use this function with the dual table and enter the date directly into the `select` clause, we would write:

```
select to_date('20-jan-2015') + 3
from dual;
```

Frequently used date functions.

Oracle	Access	Description and Examples

date + number	date + number
	or
	`DateAdd('d', )`
		Add a number of days to a date.
		Oracle:
		`'20-JAN-2015' + 3 = '23-JAN-2015'`
		Access:
		`#20-JAN-2015# + 3 = #23-JAN-2015#`
		Access:
		`DateAdd('d',3,#01-20-2015#) = #01-23-2015#`

date − number	date − number
	or
	`DateAdd('d', )`
		Subtract a number of days from a date.
		Oracle:
		`'20-JAN-2015' - 3 = '17-JAN-2015'`
		Access:
		`#20-JAN-2015# - 3 = #17-JAN-2015#`
		Access:
		`DateAdd('d',-3,#01-20-2015#) = #01-17-2015#`

date − date	date − date
	or
	`DateDiff('d', )`
		The number of days between two dates.
		Oracle:
		`'23-JAN-2015' - '20-JAN-2015' = 3`
		Access:
		`#23-JAN-2015# - #20-JAN-2015# = 3`
		Access:
		`DateDiff('d',#01-20-2015#,#01-23-2015#) = 3`

`extract(day )`	`Day`	Gets the day of the month from a date.
		Oracle:
		`extract(day from '20-JAN-2015') = 20`
		Access:
		`Day(#20-JAN-2015) = 20`

Frequently used date functions. *(continued)*

Oracle	Access	Description and Examples

extract(month)	Month	Gets the number of the month from a date.
		Oracle:
		`extract(month from '20-JAN-2015') = 1`
		Access:
		`Month(#20-JAN-2015) = 1`

extract(year)	Year	Gets the year from a date.
		Oracle:
		`extract(year from '20-JAN-2015') = 2015`
		Access:
		`Year(#20-JAN-2015) = 2015`

(can be made)	Weekday	Gets the day of the week from a date.
		Access:
		`Weekday(#20-JAN-2015) = 3`
		Notes:
		1 = Sunday
		2 = Monday
		3 = Tuesday
		4 = Wednesday
		5 = Thursday
		6 = Friday
		7 = Saturday
		Oracle equivalent:
		`to_char('20-JAN-2015', 'DAY') = 'TUESDAY'`

to_date	DateSerial	Creates a date.
		Oracle:
		`to_date('20-JAN-2015') = '20-JAN-2015'`
		Access:
		`DateSerial(2015, 1, 20) = #20-JAN-2015#`

trunc	DateValue	Sets the date/time to midnight, the beginning of the day. Optionally, may set the date/time to a different starting point such as the beginning of the hour, week, or century.
		Oracle:
		`trunc('20-JAN-2015 5:00 pm') =`
		`                '20-JAN-2015 12:00 am'`
		Access:
		`DateValue(#20-JAN-2015 5:00 pm#) =`
		`                #20-JAN-2015#`

Frequently used date functions. *(continued)*

Oracle	Access	Description and Examples

`round`	(can be made)	Rounds the date/time to midnight, the beginning of the day or optionally to another starting point.
		Oracle:
		`round('20-JAN-2015 5:00 pm') = '21-JAN-2015'`
		Access equivalent:
		`DateValue(#20-JAN-2015 5:00 pm# + .5) =`
		`                             #21-JAN-2015#`

`next_day`	(can be made)	Date of the next specified weekday.
		Oracle:
		`next_day ('20-JAN-2015', 'MON') =`
		`                              '26-JAN-2015'`
		Access equivalent:
		`#20-JAN-2015# - Weekday(#20-JAN-2015#) +`
		`iif(2 > Weekday(#20-JAN-2015#), 0, 7) + 2 =`
		`                              #26-JAN-2015#`
		Notes: 2 = Monday

`last_day`	(can be made)	Date of the last day of the month.
		Oracle:
		`last_day('20-FEB-2016') = '29-FEB-2016'`
		Oracle:
		`last_day('20-FEB-2015') = '28-FEB-2015'`
		Access equivalent:
		`DateSerial(Year(#20-FEB-2015#,`
		`           Month(#20-FEB-2015# + 1, 1) - 1`

`add_months`	`DateAdd('m', )`	Add a number of months to a date.
		Oracle:
		`add_months('21-JAN-2025', 3) = '21-apr-2025')`
		Access:
		`DateAdd('m', 3, #21-JAN-2025#) =`
		`                         #21-APR-2025#)`

`months_between`	`DateDiff('m', )`	Number of months between two dates.
		Oracle:
		`months_between('21-APR-2025','21-JAN-2025')`
		`                               = 3`
		Access:
		`DateDiff('m', #21-APR-2025#, #21-JAN-2025#)`
		`                               = 3`

Check your understanding

Test the following row functions using the dual table technique. (See section 9-7.) In Access, you do not need to use the dual table.

1. Add a number of days to a date.
   Oracle: `to_date('07-mar-2011') + 2`
   Access: `#07-mar-2011# + 2`

2. Subtract a number of days to a date.
   Oracle: `to_date('07-mar-2011') - 2`
   Access: `#07-mar-2011# - 2`

3. Add a number of months to a date.
   Oracle: `add_months(to_date('07-mar-2011'),2)`
   Access: `DateAdd('m',2,#07-mar-2011#)`

4. Add a number of years to a date (or 12 months for each year).
   Oracle: `add_months(to_date('07-mar-2011'),24)`
   Access: `DateAdd('y',2,#07-mar-2011#)`

5. Find the number of days between two dates.
   Oracle: `to_date('27-mar-2011')-to_date('07-mar-2011')`
   Access: `#27-mar-2011# - #07-mar-2011#`

9-14 An example of a date function

This section shows you an example of a date function. This function calculates the number of months each employee has worked for the company as of January 1, 2011. A month is not counted until a full month has been worked.

To count the months in an even way, I have decided to write the code as if all months are 30 days long. First I find the number of days between the person's hire date and January 1, 2011. Then I divide the number of days by 30 and throw away the fraction. This gives me the number of months.

When you are calculating with dates, it is usually best to do your calculation first in terms of the number of days and then, if you desire, convert the answer into weeks, months, or years. This strategy gives you the most control and the most accurate answers.

You might think this would be easier to do using the `months_between` function. However, this function often does not produce precise results. One reason is that the lengths of the months vary. When I tried using it in this example I found that Oracle and Access behave differently, and neither of them was as reliable as working directly with the number of days.

Here is an example of one of the problems with the `months_between` function. Using this function on the computer I found that between February 28 and March 28 there is one month, but between February 28 and March 29 there is less than one month.

Task

List all the employees, their hire dates, and the number of months each person will have worked for the company as of January 1, 2011.

Oracle SQL

```
select first_name, last_name, hire_date,
       floor((to_date('01-JAN-2011') - hire_date)/30) ❶
                        as months_with_the_company
from l_employees;
```

Access SQL

```
select first_name, last_name, hire_date,
       int((#01-JAN-2011# - hire_date)/30)
                        as months_with_the_company
from l_employees;
```

Beginning table (1_employees table)

EMPLOYEE ID	FIRST_NAME	LAST_NAME	DEPT CODE	HIRE_DATE	CREDIT LIMIT	PHONE NUMBER	MANAGER ID
201	SUSAN	BROWN	EXE	01-JUN-1998	$30.00	3484	(null)
202	JIM	KERN	SAL	16-AUG-1999	$25.00	8722	201
203	MARTHA	WOODS	SHP	02-FEB-2009	$25.00	7591	201
204	ELLEN	OWENS	SAL	01-JUL-2008	$15.00	6830	202
205	HENRY	PERKINS	SAL	01-MAR-2006	$25.00	5286	202
206	CAROL	ROSE	ACT	(null)	(null)	(null)	(null)
207	DAN	SMITH	SHP	01-DEC-2008	$25.00	2259	203
208	FRED	CAMPBELL	SHP	01-APR-2008	$25.00	1752	203
209	PAULA	JACOBS	MKT	17-MAR-1999	$15.00	3357	201
210	NANCY	HOFFMAN	SAL	16-FEB-2007	$25.00	2974	203

Result table

```
FIRST_NAME LAST_NAME   HIRE_DATE     MONTHS_WITH_THE_COMPANY
---------- ----------  ------------  -----------------------
SUSAN      BROWN       01-JUN-1998                       153
JIM        KERN        16-AUG-1999                       138
MARTHA     WOODS       02-FEB-2009                        23
ELLEN      OWENS       01-JUL-2008                        30
HENRY      PERKINS     01-MAR-2006                        58
CAROL      ROSE        (null)        (null)
DAN        SMITH       01-DEC-2008                        25
FRED       CAMPBELL    01-APR-2008                        33
PAULA      JACOBS      17-MAR-1999                       143
NANCY      HOFFMAN     16-FEB-2007                        47
```

Notes

❶ The `to_date` function is used to convert the character string `01-jan-2011` into a date. Subtracting the `hire_date` from this date gives the number of days the employee has worked for the company. Dividing this number by 30 gives the number of months. The `floor` function rounds down to get rid of the fraction.

9-15 Removing the time from a date

Every date in SQL includes a time, even though we do not always see it. Sometimes this can be a problem for us, depending on what we are doing. Sometimes we want to be able to use the date without the time.

This section shows you one way to remove the time from the date. Or rather, it sets all the times to midnight, so all the times have the same value. This technique is presented here because we will need to use it in chapter 11.

Task

List the `l_lunches` table. First, show the times that are in the beginning table. Then show how to remove these times.

Oracle SQL: Show the dates and times in the `1_lunches` table

```
select lunch_id, lunch_date,
       employee_id,
       to_char(date_entered,
               'DD-MON-YYYY HH:MI AM') as date_entered
from 1_lunches;
```

Access SQL: Show the dates and times in the `1_lunches` table

```
select lunch_id, lunch_date,
       employee_id,
       format(date_entered,
           'DD-MMM-YYYY HH:NN AM/PM') as date_entered2
from 1_lunches;
```

Oracle SQL: The `trunc` function removes the time

```
select lunch_id, lunch_date,
       employee_id,
       to_char(trunc(date_entered),
               'DD-MON-YYYY HH:MI AM') as date_entered
from 1_lunches;
```

Access SQL: The `datevalue` function removes the time

```
select lunch_id, lunch_date,
       employee_id,
       format(datevalue(date_entered),
           'DD-MMM-YYYY HH:NN AM/PM') as date_entered2
from 1_lunches;
```

Beginning table (1_lunches table)

LUNCH_ID	LUNCH DATE	EMPLOYEE ID	DATE_ENTERED
1	16-NOV-2011	201	13-OCT-2011 10:35 AM
2	16-NOV-2011	207	13-OCT-2011 10:35 AM
3	16-NOV-2011	203	13-OCT-2011 10:35 AM
4	16-NOV-2011	204	13-OCT-2011 10:35 AM
6	16-NOV-2011	202	13-OCT-2011 10:36 AM
7	16-NOV-2011	210	13-OCT-2011 10:38 AM
8	25-NOV-2011	201	14-OCT-2011 11:15 AM
9	25-NOV-2011	208	14-OCT-2011 02:23 PM
12	25-NOV-2011	204	14-OCT-2011 03:02 PM
13	25-NOV-2011	207	18-OCT-2011 08:42 AM
15	25-NOV-2011	205	21-OCT-2011 04:23 PM
16	05-DEC-2011	201	21-OCT-2011 04:23 PM
17	05-DEC-2011	210	21-OCT-2011 04:35 PM
20	05-DEC-2011	205	24-OCT-2011 09:55 AM
21	05-DEC-2011	203	24-OCT-2011 11:43 AM
22	05-DEC-2011	208	24-OCT-2011 02:37 PM

Result table

LUNCH_ID	LUNCH DATE	EMPLOYEE ID	DATE_ENTERED
1	16-NOV-2011	201	13-OCT-2011 12:00 AM
2	16-NOV-2011	207	13-OCT-2011 12:00 AM
3	16-NOV-2011	203	13-OCT-2011 12:00 AM
4	16-NOV-2011	204	13-OCT-2011 12:00 AM
6	16-NOV-2011	202	13-OCT-2011 12:00 AM
7	16-NOV-2011	210	13-OCT-2011 12:00 AM
8	25-NOV-2011	201	14-OCT-2011 12:00 AM
9	25-NOV-2011	208	14-OCT-2011 12:00 AM
12	25-NOV-2011	204	14-OCT-2011 12:00 AM
13	25-NOV-2011	207	18-OCT-2011 12:00 AM
15	25-NOV-2011	205	21-OCT-2011 12:00 AM
16	05-DEC-2011	201	21-OCT-2011 12:00 AM
17	05-DEC-2011	210	21-OCT-2011 12:00 AM
20	05-DEC-2011	205	24-OCT-2011 12:00 AM
21	05-DEC-2011	203	24-OCT-2011 12:00 AM
22	05-DEC-2011	208	24-OCT-2011 12:00 AM

Key Points

- A row function produces a single value based on the values in one or more columns of a single row. This is done for every row of the table. When a row function is used, you can think that a new column was added to the beginning table.

- There are many row functions. To learn about them you need to be able to use the reference material for the SQL product you are using. Each product is a little different. The next chapter shows you how to do this.

- There are row functions on text, number, and date columns. Sometimes there are also row functions on columns with other specialized datatypes.

- A column is often given a particular datatype so it is ready to handle certain row functions. For instance, a column may be given a numeric datatype if you intend to do arithmetic on it.

- Some of the row functions on numbers are addition, subtraction, multiplication, and division.

- Some of the row functions on text are concatenation, substring, and length.

- Some of the row functions on dates are adding or subtracting a given number of days to a date, calculating the number of days between two dates, and setting the time associated with a date to midnight.

chapter 10

USING ROW FUNCTIONS

In the last chapter, we discussed many of the most commonly used row functions. In this chapter, we discuss a few more row functions that are used for special purposes. We also discuss the documentation of row functions and show some of their applications.

Specialized Row Functions

A few other row functions also have special purposes.

10-1 Other row functions

Here is an overview of four other types of row functions. We discuss them in more detail in the following sections.

Other row functions.

Oracle	Access	Description and Examples
FUNCTIONS TO IDENTIFY THE USER AND THE DATE		
user	CurrentUser()	Name of the userID for the current session. Oracle: user = 'SQLFUN' Access: CurrentUser() = 'Admin'
sysdate	Now() Date() Time()	The current date and time. Oracle: sysdate = '20-DEC-2015' Access: Now() = '20-DEC-2015 10:30:25 AM' Access: Date() = '20-DEC-2015' Access: Time() = '10:30:25 AM'
systimestamp	(not available)	The current date and time to a fraction of a second. Also the time zone. Oracle: systimestamp = '20-DEC-2015 10.42.15.692000 AM -08:00' The meaning of this result is that for this computer the time is accurate to one-thousandth of a second. The time zone is 8 hours less than GMT, Greenwich Mean Time.
FUNCTIONS TO CHANGE NULLS TO OTHER VALUES		

nvl	nz	Converts nulls to another value.
		Oracle:
		nvl(col_1, 0) = col_1 if col_1 is not null
		          = 0 if col_1 is null
		Access:
		nz(col_1, 0) = 'col_1' if col_1 is not null
		         = '0' if col_1 is null

Other row functions. *(continued)*

Oracle	Access	Description and Examples
FUNCTIONS TO CHANGE NULLS TO OTHER VALUES *(continued)*		

nvl2	(can be made)	Converts nulls to another value.
		Oracle:
		`nvl2(col, val1, val2)`
		   `= val1  if col is not null`
		   `= val2  if col is null`
		Access equivalent:
		`iif(col is not null, val1, val2)`
		   `= val1  if col is not null`
		   `= val2  if col is null`

FUNCTIONS TO CHANGE THE DATATYPE		
to_char	CStr	Converts a number or date to a character string (text). Also used to control the formats of dates in Oracle. Oracle: `to_char(7) = '7'` Access: `CStr(7) = '7'`
to_date	CDate	Converts a number or character string to a date. Also used to control the input of dates with a specified format in Oracle. The first date Oracle and Access can handle: Oracle: `to_date(1, 'j') = '01-jan-4712 BC` Access: `CDate(1) = #12/31/1899#` A date closer to the present: Oracle: `to_date('03/10', 'mm/yy') = '01-mar-2010'` Access: `CDate('Jan 18, 2010') = #1/18/2010#`
to_number	CInt CDbl (others)	Converts a character string to a number. Oracle: `to_number('8') = 8` Access: `CInt('8') = 8`
FUNCTIONS TO PICK ONE VALUE		
greatest	(not available)	Chooses the greatest member of a list. Applies to numbers, text, and dates. Oracle: `greatest(1, 9, 2, 3) = 9`
least	(not available)	Chooses the least member of a list. Applies to numbers, text, and dates. Oracle: `least(1, 9, 2, 3) = 1`

10-2 Using a function to identify the user and the date

This section shows you how to use functions to identify the user, the date, and the time. The technique is similar in Oracle and Access, although the details are quite different.

In Oracle, the name of the userID is obtained from the User function. This is the name you use when you log on to Oracle. In Access, it is obtained from the `CurrentUser()` function. Unless you have set up special security for Access, the value of this function is set to `Admin`. The opening parenthesis, followed immediately by a closing parenthesis, might seem peculiar. This is an example of a **0-parameter function**. The pair of parentheses is retained to show that it is a function, but it does not require any input parameters. In effect, a 0-parameter function is a name for a constant value. Some people call this a **system variable**. Here that constant value depends on the userID you are logged on to.

In Oracle, the date and time are obtained from the `sysdate` function. In Access, they are obtained from the `Now()`, `Date()`, or `Time()` functions. In Oracle, if we want to see the time in addition to the date, we need to format `sysdate` with the `to_char` function. In Access, the time shows up automatically from the default formatting, so we do not need to use the `format` function. We discussed date formats in section 7-1.

Do not confuse the Oracle function `sysdate` with the Access function `Date()`. They both may show only the date and not the time. However, `sysdate` actually contains the time although it is not always shown. `Date()` does not include the time.

In Oracle, the following code uses the dual table in the `from` clause. In Oracle, this table is already built for us. In Access, we could build a dual table, but this is not required. This was discussed in section 9-7.

Task

Show how to identify the user, the date, and the time.

Oracle SQL

```
select user,
        to_char(sysdate, 'DAY MONTH DD, YYYY HH:MI AM')
                                              as date_time
from dual;
```

Oracle result table

```
USER                              DATE_TIME
--------------------------------  ------------------------------------
JPATRICK                          WEDNESDAY    DECEMBER 26,2007 02:13 PM
```

Access SQL

```
select CurrentUser() as user,
        format(Now(), 'DDDD MMMM DD, YYYY HH:NN AM/PM')
                                              as date_time;
```

Access result table

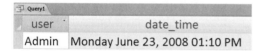

user	date_time
Admin	Monday June 23, 2008 01:10 PM

10-3 Using a function to change nulls to other values

The nvl (null value) function in Oracle and the nz (non-zero) function in Access change the nulls in some columns to another value, such as zero. When the original value in the column is not null, no change is made and the value stays the same. The original column can have any datatype — number, text, or date.

In Oracle, the nvl function does not change the datatype of the column, so the datatype of the replacement value must be the same as the one the column originally has. This restriction means that nulls in a numeric column can be changed to zero or some other number, but not to text or a date. The nulls in a text column must be replaced with text, or possibly with a string of blanks. The nulls in a date column can only be changed to a date.

In Access, the nz function always changes the column to a text datatype. Any data, including numbers and dates, can always be represented as text. The replacement value, which is substituted for nulls, can be any datatype. However, it is changed to text when it is output from the nz function.

Task

Show how to replace nulls with other values. Do this with a number column, a text column, and a date column.

Demonstrate two methods of doing this. In one method, the null is replaced with a value that has the same datatype as the column. In the other method, the null is replaced with text.

Oracle SQL: Oracle style — Replacement value has the same datatype as the column ❶

```
select pkey,
       nvl(num_col,0) as num_col2,
       nvl(text_col, 'ZILCH') as text_col2,
       nvl(date_col, '01-JAN-1900') as date_col2
from sec1003;
```

Access SQL: Oracle style — Replacement value has the same datatype as the column ❷

```
select pkey,
       nz(num_col,0) as num_col2,
       nz(text_col, 'ZILCH') as text_col2,
       nz(date_col, #01-JAN-1900#) as date_col2
from sec1003;
```

Beginning table (sec1003 table)

PKEY	NUM_COL	TEXT_COL	DATE_COL
A	1	M	(null)
B	2	(null)	20-JAN-2013
C	(null)	N	21-JAN-2013

Result table: Method 1

PKEY	NUM_COL2	TEXT_COL	DATE_COL2
A	1	M	01-JAN-1900
B	2	ZILCH	20-JAN-2013
C	0	N	21-JAN-2013

Oracle SQL:
Access style — Replacement value is text ❸

```
select pkey,
       nvl(to_char(num_col), 'NO NUMBER') as num_col2,
       nvl(text_col, 'NO TEXT') as text_col2,
       nvl(to_char(date_col), 'NO DATE') as date_col2
from sec1003;
```

Access SQL:
Access style — Replacement value is text ❹

```
select pkey,
       nz(num_col, 'NO NUMBER') as num_col2,
       nz(text_col, 'NO TEXT') as text_col2,
       nz(date_col, 'NO DATE') as date_col2
from sec1003;
```

Result table: Method 2

```
PKEY   NUM_COL2                                        TEXT_COL  DATE_COL2
-----  -------------------------------------------     --------  -----------
A      1                                               M         NO DATE
B      2                                               NO TEXT   20-JAN-2013
C      NO NUMBER                                       N         21-JAN-2013
```

Notes

❶ In Oracle, we use the `nvl` function to replace the null values. This example uses zero to replace the nulls in a column of numbers. It uses "zilch," a text string, to replace the nulls in a column of text. It uses January 1, 1900, a date, to replace the nulls in a column of dates. The datatype of the original column is not changed.

❷ In Access, we use the `nz` function to replace the null values. The same replacement values are used as in the Oracle example. The differences are that the name of the function is `nz`, and pound signs are used to enclose the date. In Access, the `nz` function converts all the columns to text, whereas in Oracle, the `nvl` function leaves the datatype of the column unchanged.

❸ In Oracle, if we want to replace the nulls with text, we must first convert the entire column to text using the `to_char` function. This is an unusual way to write the code in Oracle, but I am doing it here to show that it can be done.

❹ In Access, when you begin with a column of any datatype, you can change the nulls into text strings with the `nz` function.

10-4 Using a function to change the datatype

Functions that change datatypes keep the outer meaning of the data the same while changing the inner representation — the datatype — of the data. For instance, "8" as a character string differs from "8" as a number. They both mean 8 but if you could see the patterns of 1s and 0s inside the computer, you would see one binary pattern for the number and a different binary pattern for the character string.

Why do we care about this difference? One reason is that each row function works only with data that have a particular datatype. For example, consider addition. Addition is defined on numbers, but not on character strings. When 8 and 4 are numbers, then "8 + 4" makes sense, and is equal to the number 12. However, when 8 and 4 are character strings, "8 + 4" does not make sense. It is not equal to anything, and will give us an error message if we use it, or at least so says the theory. Things work a bit differently in practice, as we will see.

Oracle, Access, and most other SQL products do a certain amount of automatic datatype conversion. Some SQL products do more of this than other products. The idea is to make things easier for the user. A novice user might become confused and enraged if the database refuses to add 8 and 4 when they are text. An error message about the datatype might not calm the user. To make things work more smoothly, the 8 and 4 are automatically converted into numbers and then added together. This happens silently, behind the scenes. There is no message to indicate this is occurring.

The following example shows that automatic datatype conversion is used by both Oracle and Access to perform arithmetic on text strings. In this case, Oracle performs all the operations correctly. Access performs subtraction, multiplication, and division correctly, but it has a flaw when it performs addition. Access says that "8 + 4" = 84. Clearly, it is doing concatenation instead of addition. To obtain the correct result, we need to do the datatype conversion ourselves instead of relying on the automatic conversion. To do this we change the text datatype to an integer datatype, using the `cint` (convert to integer) function. This is one example of a time when the conversion must be done using the conversion functions.

Often when I first write some code, I assume that most of the datatype conversions will be done for me automatically. This works 99 percent of the time. If the results seem strange in some way, I have to debug and fix the code. It is during this process of debugging and fixing that I most often decide to control the datatype conversion myself using a datatype conversion function.

Task

Show the effects of automatic datatype conversion. Perform arithmetic on numbers that are in columns with a text datatype.

Oracle & Access SQL: This shows the problem in Access

```
select  pkey, ❶
        text_1,
        text_2,
        text_1 + text_2 as text_add, ❷
        text_1 - text_2 as text_subtract,
        text_1 * text_2 as text_multiply,
        text_1 / text_2 as text_divide
from sec1004;
```

Beginning table (sec1004 table)

```
PKEY  TEXT_1  TEXT_2
----  ------  ------
A     8       4
B     33      11
```

Oracle result table — Correct

PKEY	TEXT_1	TEXT_2	TEXT_ADD	TEXT_SUBTRACT	TEXT_MULTIPLY	TEXT_DIVIDE
A	8	4	12	4	32	2
B	33	11	44	22	363	3

Access result table — Addition is incorrect

pkey	text_1	text_2	text_add	text_subtract	text_multiply	text_divide
A	8	4	84	4	32	2
B	33	11	3311	22	363	3
*						

Access SQL: Correction

```
select pkey,
       text_1,
       text_2,
       cint(text_1) + cint(text_2) as text_add, ❸
       text_1 - text_2 as text_subtract,
       text_1 * text_2 as text_multiply,
       text_1 / text_2 as text_divide
from sec1004;
```

Access result table — Correct

pkey	text_1	text_2	text_add	text_subtract	text_multiply	text_divide
A	8	4	12	4	32	2
B	33	11	44	22	363	3

Notes

❶ This prints out the primary key and the two text items, so you can show them in the result table. Why is there a primary key? It does not do anything in this example. However, every table should have a primary key and most listings should display it.

❷ The next lines add, subtract, multiply, and divide the two text items. For these operations to make sense, the text must be automatically converted to numbers before the arithmetic can be done.

❸ The cint (convert to integer) function is used to convert the text to integers. Then Access can add them, giving 8 + 4 = 12.

There is a reason why Access says 8 + 4 = 84. In many of the early PC computer languages, the plus sign is used with text strings to mean concatenation. For example:

sun + flower = sunflower

Access has decided to preserve this legacy. Some computer code might need to be rewritten if they were to correct this mistake, so there is a reason for it, but I think that it is a bad reason!

Check your understanding

The following `select` statements show all the numbers from 0 to 99. One of the statements sorts these numbers in numeric order, the others sort the numbers in alphabetic order. Run these queries. Can you see the difference in the order of the numbers?

Oracle & Access:

```
select n as numeric_order
from numbers_0_to_99
order by n;
```

Oracle only:

```
select to_char(n) as alphabetic_order
from numbers_0_to_99
order by to_char(n);
```

Access only:

```
select cstr(n) as alphabetic_order
from numbers_0_to_99
order by cstr(n);
```

Using the Documentation of Row Functions

I have shown you the row functions I use the most. However, there are many more row functions available. Some SQL products have a few special row functions that other products do not have, so it is important to be able to find the list of row functions in the documentation.

Oracle and Access both have extensive online documentation that is easy to use. Google and other search engines are another good source of information. There are also blogs and online discussion groups available.

This documentation is not limited to row functions. All aspects of the products are included in this documentation. I do have to admit, however, that sometimes this documentation is difficult to read and to use. It is not always written at a level that matches your understanding. Sometimes it seems to give too much detail, and sometimes it seems not to give enough.

10-5 Using Oracle documentation

In Oracle, go to the home page and click Documentation. This opens the Oracle Database Documentation Library. From there you can use Search to find a term or use the Master Index.

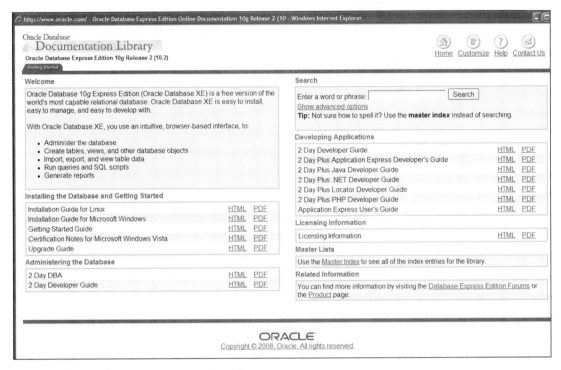

The Oracle Database Documentation Library.

Check your understanding

Find and read the documentation for the `replace` function. First use the Master Index in the Oracle documentation, as that will probably give you the best result. Then try using the Search facility.

10-6 Using Access documentation

In Access, all you need to do is press the F1 key to launch the online help.

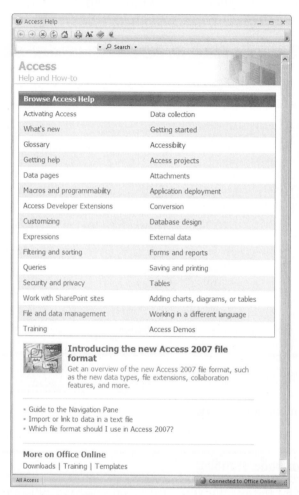

Press the F1 key to launch Access online help.

Check your understanding

Find and read the documentation for the `string` function.

10-7 Using the Access Expression Builder to find row functions

In Access, I use the Expression Builder as a reference document to tell me what row functions are available. This is not the only thing that Expression Builder is designed to do, but it is the way that I use it.

To start the Expression Builder and see the functions, follow these steps:

1. Click the Create tab on the Ribbon.

2. Click Query Design on the Ribbon.

3. Close the Show Table window.

4. Right-click a Field cell or a Criteria cell.

5. Click Build.

6. Double-click Functions.

7. Click Built-in Functions.

8. Select the type of function you want from the second column.

9. The third column shows you a list of the functions that are available.

Using the preceding steps to get to Expression Builder.

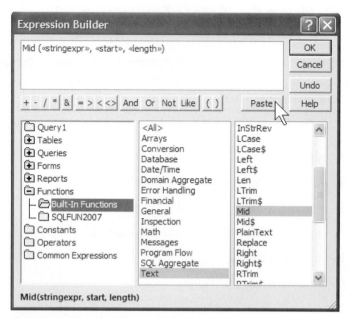

The Expression Builder opening screen.

Check your understanding

Find the list of all the text functions. See if you can understand most of them.

Creating Patterns of Numbers and Dates

Row functions can be used to create patterns of numbers or dates. These are useful in creating a variety of reports. When you create these patterns, the beginning table is usually a table of numbers. In this book, I have provided you with two tables of numbers: numbers_0_to_9 and numbers_0_to_99.

The technique shown here uses SQL to generate these patterns. SQL is able to do this, but other computer languages are designed to generate patterns and can do so more efficiently. Using another technique, we could generate the pattern of numbers in some other language, create a file, and then load that file into a database table.

Why would you want to create a pattern and put it in a database table? This can be useful in several ways. A pattern of dates can serve as a calendar. Often a pattern is the beginning point for adding other types of data. For instance, we might begin with a calendar and then add to it our plans for each day.

In another application a pattern can help us find flaws or imperfections in some other data. We might have some data that nearly fits into a pattern, but not quite. We might want to show explicitly where the data does not fit the pattern. One way to do this is to generate a perfect pattern and then compare it with the data we have.

10-8 Create a simple pattern of numbers

This section shows you how to create a simple pattern of numbers. The next section shows you how to create a complex pattern of numbers. The idea I want you to take away from these two sections is that we can create almost any pattern of numbers.

The example in this section shows how to list all the multiples of three between 50 and 250. The purpose of this is to show you how to create patterns of numbers. The particular patterns you need may vary. There is no particular significance to this pattern, except that it is easy to create.

The beginning table is the table `numbers_0_to_99`. I have created this table for you already. In chapter 16, we will discuss how to generate a table like this with as many numbers as you want. For now, 100 numbers are enough to handle.

To get the multiples of three, you multiply all the numbers in the table by three. To create other patterns, you could multiply the numbers in the beginning table by any number, M. Then you could add another number, A. If the numbers in the table are called T, this creates a table of numbers of the form (T * M) + A. You can also take any section from this table by setting a starting point and an ending point. Of course, any series of numbers you can list, you can also save in a new table or view.

Task

List all the numbers that are multiples of three between 50 and 250. To do this, begin with the table `numbers_0_to_99`.

Oracle SQL: Step 1

```
create or replace view sec1008_view as
select n,
       3 * n as multiple_of_3 ❶
from numbers_0_to_99; ❷
```

Access SQL: Step 1

Step 1, Part 1: Enter this in the SQL window:

```
select n,
       3 * n as multiple_of_3  ❶
from numbers_0_to_99;  ❷
```

Step 1, Part 2: Save the query and name it `sec1008_view`.

Oracle & Access SQL: Step 2

```
select multiple_of_3
from sec1008_view
where multiple_of_3 between 50 and 250
order by multiple_of_3;
```

Beginning table (numbers_0_to_99 table) ❸

```
        N
---------
        0
        1
        2
        3

(and many more)

       97
       98
       99
```

Result table

```
MULTIPLE_OF_3
-------------
           51
           54
           57
           60

(and many more)

          243
          246
          249
```

Notes

❶ This creates a new column called `multiple_of_3`.

❷ The beginning table contains all the numbers from 0 to 99. I have already created this table for you.

❸ The rows of this table are shown in their logical order so that this example is easy to understand. However, the rows in any table are in no particular order. If you display this table without an `order by` clause, the rows may be in a different order. To see them in this order you must include `order by` n.

Check your understanding

Create a view of the multiples of 7 between 700 and 900.

10-9 Create a complex pattern of numbers

In the previous section we created a simple pattern of numbers. Now I want to show you that you can create a very complex pattern of numbers. The prime numbers are one of the most complex sequences, so we'll use them as an example.

This section shows how to list the prime numbers between 10 and 99. We need to find the numbers that cannot be evenly divided by 2, 3, 5, or 7. This is done in the `where` clause. The `mod` function shows the remainder after division. If we enter

```
mod(x, y) = 0
```

this means that Y divides evenly into X. We want the opposite of that, so we want

```
not (mod(n, 2) = 0)
```

This gives us the numbers that are not divisible by 2. Similar logic is used with 3, 5, and 7.

In Access, this condition is written as follows:

```
not ((n mod 2) = 0)
```

Task

List all the prime numbers that are greater than 10 and less than 100.

Oracle SQL

```
select n as prime_number
from numbers_0_to_99
where n > 10
    and not (mod(n, 2) = 0)
    and not (mod(n, 3) = 0)
    and not (mod(n, 5) = 0)
    and not (mod(n, 7) = 0)
order by n;
```

Access SQL

```
select n as prime_number
from numbers_0_to_99
where n > 10
    and not ((n mod 2) = 0)
    and not ((n mod 3) = 0)
    and not ((n mod 5) = 0)
    and not ((n mod 7) = 0)
order by n;
```

Beginning table (numbers_0_to_99 table)

```
        N
---------
        0
        1
        2
(and many more)
       98
       99
```

Result table

```
PRIME_NUMBER
------------
          11
          13
          17
          19
          23
(and many more)
          83
          89
          97
```

10-10 List all the days of one week

This section shows you how to list all seven consecutive days of the week. The purpose is to show that we can create a pattern of dates, just like we can create a pattern of numbers. In fact, any pattern of numbers can also be made into a pattern of dates.

We do this in three steps. The first step creates what I call a table of constants, which is a table with only one row. It contains one column: the date on which we want the week to begin. There are several ways to create this table, but I use the method that gives me the most control over the process.

The second step creates a view containing seven consecutive days. We get the beginning date from the table of constants and then add the numbers 0 to 6 to it.

The third step formats these dates in three different ways. The date is actually presented three times with a different format each time.

Task

List all the days for one week beginning with February 24, 2010. For each date, also list the day of the week in both abbreviated form and fully spelled out.

Oracle SQL: Step 1 — Create a table of constants

```
create table sec1010_constants
(begin_date    date);

insert into sec1010_constants
values ('24-FEB-2010');
```

Access SQL: Step 1 — Create a table of constants

Remember, in Access, you can only run one statement at a time.

```
create table sec1010_constants
(begin_date    datetime);

insert into sec1010_constants
values (#24-FEB-2010#);
```

Result table: Step 1 (date_constants table)

```
BEGIN_DATE
----------
24-FEB-2010
```

Oracle SQL: Step 2 — Create a view containing seven dates

```
create or replace view sec1010_view as
select begin_date + digit as days
from numbers_0_to_9,
     sec1010_constants
where digit < 7;
```

Access SQL: Step 2 — Create a view containing seven dates

Step 2, Part 1: Enter the following query in the SQL window:

```
select cdate(begin_date + digit) as days ❶
from numbers_0_to_9,
     sec1010_constants
where digit < 7;
```

Step 2, Part 2: Save the query and name it sec1010_view.

Result table: Step 2 (sec1010_view)

```
DAYS
----------
24-FEB-2010
25-FEB-2010
26-FEB-2010
27-FEB-2010
28-FEB-2010
01-MAR-2010
02-MAR-2010
```

Oracle SQL: Step 3 — List the days formatted in three ways

```
select days,
       to_char(days, 'DY') as abbreviated_day,
       to_char(days, 'DAY') as full_day
from sec1010_view
order by days;
```

Access SQL: Step 3 — List the days formatted in three ways

```
select days,
       format(days, 'DDD') as abbreviated_day,
       format(days, 'DDDD') as full_day
from sec1010_view
order by days;
```

Result table: Step 3

DAYS	ABBREVIATED_DAY	FULL_DAY
24-FEB-2010	WED	WEDNESDAY
25-FEB-2010	THU	THURSDAY
26-FEB-2010	FRI	FRIDAY
27-FEB-2010	SAT	SATURDAY
28-FEB-2010	SUN	SUNDAY
01-MAR-2010	MON	MONDAY
02-MAR-2010	TUE	TUESDAY

Notes

❶ In Access, you need to use the CDate function to get dates in the result table. Otherwise, you will only get numbers.

Check your understanding

Create a calendar showing all the days of the current month.

10-11 Create a calendar of workdays

In this section we create a more complex pattern of dates. In the previous section we listed several consecutive days. In this section, we only list the days that are between Monday and Friday. We will also use a trick to put one blank line between the weeks.

We use four steps to create this calendar. The first two steps are similar to the technique we used in the previous section. This creates a table containing all the days between a beginning date and an end date. This table also contains a column, n, of whole numbers, which we use later. We create a table, rather than a view, because we want to modify some of these dates in step 3. We would be unable to make these modifications to a view.

In step 3, we delete all the dates on Sundays and we turn all the Saturday dates into nulls. These nulls become the blank lines separating one week from another.

In step 4, we list the dates in two different formats. The trick to positioning the blank lines is `order by n`. Think of N as another column in the result table, but it is hidden. It provides the framework that organizes the rows of the result table. An additional result table in step 4 shows the column that is hidden in the first result table.

Task

Create a calendar showing the workdays, Monday through Friday, for March, April, and May 2015. List the day of the week in one column and the date in the format MM/DD/YYYY in the next column. Leave one blank line between the weeks.

Oracle SQL: Step 1 — Create a table of constants

```
create table sec1011_boundaries
(start_date      date,
end_date         date);

insert into sec1011_boundaries
values ('01-MAR-2015', '01-JUN-2015');
```

Access SQL: Step 1 — Create a table of constants

```
create table sec1011_boundaries
(start_date      datetime,
end_date         datetime);

insert into sec1011_boundaries
values (#01-MAR-2015#, #01-JUN-2015#);
```

Result table: Step 1

START_DATE	END_DATE
01-MAR-2015	01-JUN-2015

Oracle SQL: Step 2 — Create a table containing all the consecutive days

```
create table sec1011_calendar as
select n, ❶
       start_date + n as date_1 ❷
from numbers_0_to_99,
     sec1011_boundaries
where start_date + n < end_date;
```

Access SQL: Step 2 — Create a table containing all the consecutive days

```
select n, ❶
       cdate(start_date + n) as date_1 ❷ ❸
into sec1011_calendar
from numbers_0_to_99,
     sec1011_boundaries
where start_date + n < end_date;
```

Result table: Step 2

```
        N DATE_1
--------- -----------
        0 01-MAR-2015
        1 02-MAR-2015
        2 03-MAR-2015
        3 04-MAR-2015
        4 05-MAR-2015
        5 06-MAR-2015
        6 07-MAR-2015
        7 08-MAR-2015

(and many more)

       90 30-MAY-2015
       91 31-MAY-2015
```

Notes

❶ We include the column, n, to use as a framework in step 4.

❷ We name this column date_1 instead of date to avoid the possibility of using a reserved word.

❸ In Access the cdate function is necessary to format this column as dates. Otherwise it appears only as numbers.

Oracle SQL: Step 3 —
Delete Sundays and change Saturdays to nulls to create a blank line

```
delete from sec1011_calendar
where to_char(date_1, 'DY') = 'SUN';

update sec1011_calendar
  set date_1 = null
where to_char(date_1, 'DY') = 'SAT';
```

Access SQL: Step 3 —
Delete Sundays and change Saturdays to nulls to create a blank line

```
delete from sec1011_calendar
where format(date_1, 'DDD') = 'SUN'; ❹

update sec1011_calendar
  set date_1 = null
where format(date_1, 'DDD') = 'SAT'; ❹
```

Result table: Step 3

```
       N DATE_1
-------- -----------
       1 02-MAR-2015
       2 03-MAR-2015
       3 04-MAR-2015
       4 05-MAR-2015
       5 06-MAR-2015
       6 (null)
       8 09-MAR-2015

(and many more)

      88 28-MAY-2015
      89 29-MAY-2015
      90 (null)
```

Notes

❹ Another way to write this condition in Access is:

```
where weekday(date_1) = 'SUN';
```

Oracle SQL: Step 4 — Display the report

```
select to_char(date_1, 'DAY') as day_of_the_week,
       to_char(date_1, 'MM/DD/YYYY') as work_day
from sec1011_calendar
order by n;
```

Access SQL: Step 4 — Display the report

```
select format(date_1, 'DDDD') as day_of_the_week,
       format(date_1, 'MM/DD/YYYY') as work_day
from sec1011_calendar
order by n;
```

Result table: Step 4

```
DAY_OF_THE_WEEK WORK_DAY
--------------- ----------
MONDAY          03/02/2015
TUESDAY         03/03/2015
WEDNESDAY       03/04/2015
THURSDAY        03/05/2015
FRIDAY          03/06/2015

MONDAY          03/09/2015
TUESDAY         03/10/2015
WEDNESDAY       03/11/2015
THURSDAY        03/12/2015
FRIDAY          03/13/2015

MONDAY          03/16/2015

(and many more)

FRIDAY          05/22/2015

MONDAY          05/25/2015
TUESDAY         05/26/2015
WEDNESDAY       05/27/2015
THURSDAY        05/28/2015
FRIDAY          05/29/2015
```

Result table: Step 4 — Showing the hidden column, N

```
   N DAY_OF_THE_WEEK WORK_DAY
---- --------------- ----------
   1 MONDAY          03/02/2015
   2 TUESDAY         03/03/2015
   3 WEDNESDAY       03/04/2015
   4 THURSDAY        03/05/2015
   5 FRIDAY          03/06/2015
   6
   8 MONDAY          03/09/2015

(and many more)

  82 FRIDAY          05/22/2015
  83
  85 MONDAY          05/25/2015
  86 TUESDAY         05/26/2015
  87 WEDNESDAY       05/27/2015
  88 THURSDAY        05/28/2015
  89 FRIDAY          05/29/2015
  90
```

10-12 How to find out how many days old you are

Do you know how old you are? How many **days** old? The date functions can tell you very easily. Just enter your birth date in the following code. The integer part of the answer is your age in days.

What does the decimal part of the answer mean? Two meanings are possible. If you enter the time you were born into the code, the decimal part shows you the fraction of the next day that has already gone by.

If you do not enter a time, the computer sees your birth date with the default time of midnight. It measures this against the current date and the current time, so the decimal represents the current time as of when you are running this code.

Task

Find out how many days old you are.

Oracle SQL

```
select sysdate - to_date('21-MAR-1978') as days_old ❶ ❷
from dual;
```

Access SQL

```
select now() - #21-MAR-1978# as days_old; ❶ ❸
```

Result table ❹

```
DAYS_OLD
---------
8509.3539
```

Notes

❶ Use your own birth date.

❷ In Oracle, we must use the to_date function to turn the text string '21-MAR-1978' into a date. We can subtract one date from another, but we cannot subtract a text string from a date.

❸ In Access, enclosing #21-MAR-1978# in pound signs makes it a date.

❹ Obviously, this number changes every day, so your result will be different from the one shown here.

Check your understanding

Create a table showing several significant dates in your life. Have a date field and a text field that says what happened on that date. Then write a select statement that shows how many days have passed since that time.

10-13 How to find the date when you will be 10,000 days old

Do you know on what date you will be 10,000 days old? Again, the date functions can easily tell you. Mark this date on your calendar so you can celebrate!

Task

Find the date when you will be (or were) 10,000 days old. Use your birth date in the following code.

Oracle SQL

```
select to_date('21-MAR-1978') + 10000
                              as celebration_day
from dual;
```

Access SQL

```
select #21-MAR-1978# + 10000 as celebration_day;
```

Result table

```
CELEBRATION
-----------
06-AUG-2011
```

Check your understanding

Find the date when the United States will be 100,000 days old.

10-14 Numbering the lines of a report in Oracle and Access

Sometimes you have a report in which the lines are sorted in a particular order. You may want to number these lines in the order in which they appear. To do this, you can create a new column that contains the line numbers.

Both Oracle and Access have special features to help you do this, but these features work differently.

The Oracle method

1. Create a new view from the beginning `select` statement. Oracle allows us to keep the `order by` clause in a view.

2. Use `rownum` to add a column of line numbers.

The Access method

1. Create a new table from the beginning `select` statement. Access allows us to keep the `order by` clause.

2. Add a new column with the `alter table` command. Give the new column the datatype `counter`. This assigns the numbers automatically.

Task

The following `select` statement creates a report. All the lines of the report are sorted in a particular order. We want to number the lines of this report sequentially, beginning with 1.

```
select price,
       description
from l_foods
where price > 1.75
order by price,
         description;
```

Beginning report

```
     PRICE DESCRIPTION
----------- ---------------
     $2.00 FRESH SALAD
     $2.50 HAMBURGER
     $3.00 DESSERT
     $3.50 SANDWICH
     $6.00 GRILLED STEAK
```

Oracle SQL:
Step 1 — Create a view that includes an `order by` clause

```
create or replace view sec1014_view as
select price,
       description
from l_foods
where price > 1.75
order by price,
         description;
```

Oracle SQL:
Step 2 — Use `rownum` to create the line numbers

```
select rownum as line_number,
       a.*
from sec1014_view a
order by rownum;
```

Access SQL:
Step 1 — Create a table that includes an `order by` clause

```
select price,
       description
into sec1014_table
from l_foods
where price > 1.75
order by price,
         description;
```

Access SQL:
Step 2 — Add a column of line numbers ❶

```
alter table sec1014_table
add column line_number counter;
```

Result table

```
LINE_NUMBER       PRICE DESCRIPTION
----------- ----------- ----------------
          1      $2.00 FRESH SALAD
          2      $2.50 HAMBURGER
          3      $3.00 DESSERT
          4      $3.50 SANDWICH
          5      $6.00 GRILLED STEAK
```

Notes

❶ In Access, this code will make the line numbers the last column. One more step is required if you want the line numbers in the first column: Just define another view and place the columns in the order you want.

10-15 Optional: An easy way to solve an algebraic equation

In this section I show you an easy way to solve an algebraic equation. I can hear the groans already. I know, you never wanted to do this again in your life. Well, give me a couple of minutes to show you that there is a much easier way than you learned in school. I'll do all the work. You can watch.

I use three steps to find the solution of the equation in the following task. The first step calculates the value of the function on the left side of the equation for every whole number between 0 and 99. Then I look at these values and I observe the following:

1. The value of the function at 0 is a negative value.

2. The value of the function at 99 is a positive value.

3. The value of the function changes from negative to positive only once.

4. This change occurs between 90 and 91.

So I have found that this function equals zero somewhere between 90 and 91. Next, I want to refine this solution and make it accurate to two decimal places.

Step 2 generates all the numbers with two decimal places between 90.00 and 90.99. Step 3 calculates the value of the function for each of these numbers. I look at these values and I observe that they change from negative to positive between 90.33 and 90.34, so this is the solution to the equation.

I could repeat this process more times to get additional accuracy.

Task

Find a solution to the following equation:

$$x^4 - 91x^3 + 66x^2 - 451x - 5913 = 0$$

Find a solution between 0 and 99, if there is one. Make the solution accurate to two decimal places.

Oracle & Access SQL:
Step 1 — Calculate the value of the function between 0 and 99

```
select n,
        ((n * n * n * n) - 91 * (n * n * n) +66 * (n * n)
        -451 * n -5913) as value_of_function
from numbers_0_to_99
order by n;
```

Beginning table (numbers_0_to_99 table)

```
         N
---------
         0
         1

(and many more)

        98
        99
```

Result table: Step 1

```
       N VALUE_OF_FUNCTION
-------- -----------------
       0             -5913
       1             -6388

(all negative values)

      89           -933204
      90           -240903
      91            499592
      92           1289907
      93           2131692

(all positive values)

      98           7172097
      99           8358696
```

Step 1 — Conclusion

There is a solution to the equation between 90 and 91.

Oracle SQL: Step 2 — Generate the numbers between 90.00 and 90.99

```
create or replace view sec1015_view as
select n,
       90 + (n/100) as m
from numbers_0_to_99
order by n;
```

Access SQL: Step 2 — Generate the numbers between 90.00 and 90.99

Step 2, Part 1: Enter this query in the SQL window:

```
select n,
       90 + (n/100) as m
from numbers_0_to_99
order by n;
```

Step 2, Part 2: Save this query and name it sec1015_view.

Result table: Step 2

```
       N         M
--------- ---------
       0        90
       1     90.01
       2     90.02

(and many more)

      98     90.98
      99     90.99
```

Oracle & Access SQL:
Step 3 — Calculate the value of the function between 90.00 and 90.99

```
select m,
       ((m * m * m * m) -91 * (m * m * m) +66 * (m * m)
       -451 * m -5913) as value_of_function
from sec1015_view
order by (m * 100); ❶
```

Beginning table (`sec1015 view`)

```
         N         M
--------- ---------
         0        90
         1     90.01
         2     90.02

(and many more)

        97     90.97
        98     90.98
        99     90.99
```

Result table: Step 3

```
         M VALUE_OF_FUNCTION
--------- -----------------
        90          -240903
     90.01        -233739.3
     90.02        -226570.8

(all negative values)

     90.32        -9265.465
     90.33        -1946.697
     90.34        5376.9437
     90.35        12705.458

(all positive values)

     90.98        484299.32
     90.99        491943.17
```

Step 3 — Conclusion

There is a solution to the equation between 90.33 and 90.34.

Notes

❶ Why do I multiply M by 100 in the `order by` clause? I can write `order by m`, in Oracle, which is a more logical way to write the code. However, this does not work in Access. A bug in Access puts the rows in the wrong order. To work around this problem, I multiply M by 100.

Key Points

- This chapter shows you some specialized row functions and gives a few examples.

- The online documentation for Oracle and Access is easy to use.

- You can change nulls to other values with a row function.

- You can identify the user with a row function.

- You can get the current date and time with a row function.

- You can change the datatype of a column to another datatype with row functions.

- You can number the rows of a result table with a row function.

chapter 11

SUMMARIZING DATA

In the previous chapters, the data in the result table came directly from the beginning table or was a function of a single row of that table. In this chapter, the data in the result table can summarize the data in an entire column of the beginning table. This is done using a column function. The seven types of column functions provide different ways to summarize the data in a column.

In the next chapter, you will see how to control the level of summarization. In this chapter, the summarization always produces a single row in the result table.

Introduction to the Column Functions

The data in a table is summarized using **column functions**, which examine all the data in a column. Column functions are also called **aggregate functions**.

Every row of the table is involved. Within this chapter, we consider the case when this summarization produces a single row in the result table. In the next chapter I will show you how to get several rows of summarization. The following sections provide an overview of the column functions.

11-1 Summarizing all the data in a column

The conceptual diagram that follows shows the way a column function works when it is applied to the whole table. All the data in a single column is summarized and produces one result. For example, the result might be the sum of all the numbers in the column.

The column can be a row function as well as a column of data stored on the disk. Any of the row functions you studied in chapter 9 can create a new column. A column function can then operate on it.

Several different column functions exist, and each one summarizes the data in a different way. One gets the maximum value, one gets the average, one gets the minimum, and there are several others, all listed in section 11-2.

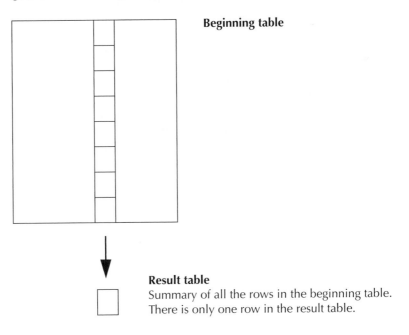

Beginning table

Result table
Summary of all the rows in the beginning table.
There is only one row in the result table.

11-2 A list of the column functions

This section is an overview of the column functions. Each one produces a different type of summarization. They are explained in detail on the next few pages. Column functions are also called **aggregate functions** or **group functions**.

Compared with the row functions, only a few column functions exist — seven main ones, to be exact. Of course, some SQL products extend the list and define other column functions for special purposes. For instance, both Oracle and Access have defined Standard Deviation and Variance. These are not usually considered parts of standard SQL.

Nulls are ignored by all the column functions except one

The column functions ignore nulls in the data. Nulls are treated as if they did not exist. The one exception is the count(*) function, which does count nulls and treats them like any other type of data.

Nulls are treated this way because this is how summarization usually deals with unknown values. For example, suppose you have data for 1,000 people, such as which political candidates they like. There are two people who are supposed to be in this sample, but you do not have any data for them yet. Now you are asked to summarize the data. Would you reply that you cannot summarize the data, because you do not have all the data yet? Or would you summarize the data you have for 1,000 people and ignore the two people for whom you do not have any data?

Most people would do the latter: They would summarize the 1,000 pieces of data they have and ignore the two pieces of data they do not have. This process of ignoring the unknown data is exactly what SQL does. When SQL summarizes data, it completely ignores the nulls and treats them as if they were not even there. SQL has not created any new rules here. It has only followed the standard method of summarization.

Overview of the column functions.

Oracle SQL	Access SQL	Meaning
Column functions for text, number, and date columns		
max	max	Maximum value in the column.
min	min	Minimum value in the column.
count(*)	count(*)	Total number of rows in the table.
count(*column*)	count(*column*)	Number of rows in the column that are not null.
count(distinct *column*)	Not available as a column function, but the same result can be achieved by a workaround.	Number of distinct values in the column where *column* is the name of a column in the table.
Column functions for numeric columns only		
sum	sum	Sum of all values in a column.
avg	avg	Average of all values in a column.
stddev (two Ds)	stdev (one D)	Standard deviation.
variance	var	Variance.

Examples of column functions.

Column Function	Text Column	Number Column	Date Column
(Data)	Apple	1	25-jan-2055
	Banana	2	null
	Cherry	null	21-jan-2033
	null	2	17-jan-1999
	Peach	3	19-jan-2015
max	Peach	3	25-jan-2055
min	Apple	1	17-jan-1999
sum	n/a	8	n/a
avg	n/a	8/4 = 2	n/a
count(*)	5	5	5
count(*column*)	4	4	4
count(distinct *column*)	4	3	4

Maximum and Minimum

11-3 Finding the maximum and minimum values

This section shows you how to use a column function. It uses the minimum (min) and maximum (max) column functions, and shows them applied to three columns with the datatypes of text, number, and date.

The datatype of a column determines the sort order that is applied to its data: Text columns are sorted in alphabetic order, number columns are sorted in numeric order, and date columns are sorted in date order. This can affect which values are chosen to be the minimum and maximum values.

When the query does not contain a where clause, the column function applies to all the rows in the table. The next section shows the effect of a where clause.

The result of a column function is always a single value. In the next chapter, I introduce the group by clause. Then the column function will result in more than one value. When you don't have a group by clause, the entire table is one group, and therefore you have only one row in the result.

Note that the result table in this example contains only a single row. This single value summarizes all the values in the entire column within all the rows of the table.

Each column of the result table is calculated separately and the row in the result table contains columns that may not be closely related to each other. In the following example, there is no employee named "Susan Woods," but that name appears in the result table. "Susan" is the maximum value in the first_name column. "Woods" is maximum value in the last_name column. However, "Susan" and "Woods" are not related to each other.

Nulls and column functions

Column functions ignore nulls, so where they are placed in the sort order doesn't matter — whether they come first, as in Access, or last, as in Oracle. The maximum or minimum value is not affected by any nulls the column may contain. The maximum and minimum are never a null, unless the entire column is null.

A few people get upset about this. They argue that if a column contains even one null, which is an unknown value, then the maximum or minimum is unknown, so it should be a null. For these people, I make the following points:

1. Summarization always deals with the known data and ignores the unknown data. This approach is part of the process of summarization. It is not a feature that is unique to SQL.

2. If summarization handled nulls in the way these people suggest, then almost all summarized values would be nulls. A single null would be more important than thousands of known values, making summarization itself ineffective. So the process of summarization cannot treat nulls in the way these people suggest. A person can object to all summarization, but that is another matter.

3. The result of every SQL query is based on the data we have right now. We can never obtain some "ultimately perfect" database. We almost never can know every detail we would like to know about any topic.

Task

Find the following:

- The minimum credit limit given to any employee
- The maximum credit limit given to any employee
- The first name of an employee that comes last alphabetically
- The last name of an employee that comes last alphabetically
- The latest date when any of the employees was hired

Oracle & Access SQL

```
select min(credit_limit), ❶
       max(credit_limit),
       max(first_name),
       max(last_name), ❷
       max(hire_date) ❸
from l_employees;
```

Beginning table (1_employees table)

```
EMPLOYEE                        DEPT               CREDIT PHONE  MANAGER
      ID FIRST_NAME LAST_NAME  CODE HIRE_DATE      LIMIT NUMBER      ID
-------- ---------- ---------  ---- ------------   ------- ------ -------
     201 SUSAN      BROWN      EXE  01-JUN-1998    $30.00 3484   (null)
     202 JIM        KERN       SAL  16-AUG-1999    $25.00 8722      201
     203 MARTHA     WOODS      SHP  02-FEB-2009    $25.00 7591      201
     204 ELLEN      OWENS      SAL  01-JUL-2008    $15.00 6830      202
     205 HENRY      PERKINS    SAL  01-MAR-2006    $25.00 5286      202
     206 CAROL      ROSE       ACT  (null)         (null) (null) (null)
     207 DAN        SMITH      SHP  01-DEC-2008    $25.00 2259      203
     208 FRED       CAMPBELL   SHP  01-APR-2008    $25.00 1752      203
     209 PAULA      JACOBS     MKT  17-MAR-1999    $15.00 3357      201
     210 NANCY      HOFFMAN    SAL  16-FEB-2007    $25.00 2974      203
```

Result table ❹

```
MIN(CREDIT_LIMIT) MAX(CREDIT_LIMIT) MAX(FIRST_ MAX(LAST_N MAX(HIRE_DA
----------------- ----------------- ---------- ---------- -----------
          $15.00            $30.00 SUSAN      WOODS      01-DEC-2008
```

Notes

❶ The min function is applied to the credit_limit column, a numeric column. The numeric order is used to decide the minimum value.

❷ The max function is applied to the last_name column, a text column. The alphabetic order is used to decide the maximum value.

❸ The max function is applied to the hire_date column, a date column. The date order is used to decide the maximum value.

❹ The result table contains only one row. Note that in Oracle the column headings for the text and date columns are truncated.

Check your understanding

Table sec1103 contains two columns, row_ID and num_1. (It also contains a column named num_2, but we are not going to use that column now.) Find the minimum and maximum values of the num_1 column. Name these values "minimum" and "maximum."

11-4 Using a where clause with a column function

When a where clause is used in a query that contains a column function, the where clause is applied first. The column function is then applied only to the rows that satisfy the where condition, not to all the rows of the table.

This section shows the same query we used in the previous section with the addition of a where clause. This changes some of the values in the result table.

Task

Perform the same task as in the previous section, but only for some of the rows of the table. For employees 202 to 206, find the following:

- The minimum credit limit given to any employee

- The maximum credit limit given to any employee

- The first name of an employee that comes last alphabetically

- The last name of an employee that comes last alphabetically

- The latest date when any of the employees was hired

Oracle & Access SQL

```
select min(credit_limit),
       max(credit_limit),
       max(first_name),
       max(last_name),
       max(hire_date)
from l_employees
where employee_id between 202 and 206; ❶
```

Beginning table (1_employees table)

EMPLOYEE ID	FIRST_NAME	LAST_NAME	DEPT CODE	HIRE_DATE	CREDIT LIMIT	PHONE NUMBER	MANAGER ID
201	SUSAN	BROWN	EXE	01-JUN-1998	$30.00	3484	(null)
202	JIM	KERN	SAL	16-AUG-1999	$25.00	8722	201
203	MARTHA	WOODS	SHP	02-FEB-2009	$25.00	7591	201
204	ELLEN	OWENS	SAL	01-JUL-2008	$15.00	6830	202
205	HENRY	PERKINS	SAL	01-MAR-2006	$25.00	5286	202
206	CAROL	ROSE	ACT	(null)	(null)	(null)	(null)
207	DAN	SMITH	SHP	01-DEC-2008	$25.00	2259	203
208	FRED	CAMPBELL	SHP	01-APR-2008	$25.00	1752	203
209	PAULA	JACOBS	MKT	17-MAR-1999	$15.00	3357	201
210	NANCY	HOFFMAN	SAL	16-FEB-2007	$25.00	2974	203

First, the where clause is applied to the beginning table ❷

EMPLOYEE ID	FIRST_NAME	LAST_NAME	DEPT CODE	HIRE_DATE	CREDIT LIMIT	PHONE NUMBER	MANAGER ID
202	JIM	KERN	SAL	16-AUG-1999	$25.00	8722	201
203	MARTHA	WOODS	SHP	02-FEB-2009	$25.00	7591	201
204	ELLEN	OWENS	SAL	01-JUL-2008	$15.00	6830	202
205	HENRY	PERKINS	SAL	01-MAR-2006	$25.00	5286	202
206	CAROL	ROSE	ACT	(null)	(null)	(null)	(null)

Then the column functions are calculated to create the result table

MIN(CREDIT_LIMIT)	MAX(CREDIT_LIMIT)	MAX(FIRST_	MAX(LAST_N	MAX(HIRE_DA
$15.00	$25.00	MARTHA	WOODS	02-FEB-2009

Notes

❶ The where clause limits the scope of the column functions to consider only employees 202 to 206.

❷ The where clause is applied first. In effect, this reduces the number of rows in the beginning table.

Check your understanding

Repeat the exercise in the previous section, except this time add a where clause that limits the row_ID column to values less than 8. Is there any change in the minimum and maximum values?

11-5 Finding the rows that have the maximum or minimum value

Often, finding the maximum or minimum value in a column is not enough. You want to find more information about the row or rows where the maximum or minimum value occurs.

Several rows may have the minimum or maximum value. Asking, "Which row has the maximum value?" is okay, but two rows have the minimum value. So, the question, "Which row has the minimum value?" contains an incorrect assumption that only one such row exists.

Incidentally, you can see that no column function is able to display this additional information. The result table of a column function is always one single row, but the result table in the following example contains three rows.

You can write SQL in two ways to accomplish this goal. These two methods are very similar. In the first method, you run two separate queries. The first `select` statement finds the correct value of the maximum or minimum. In this example, you want to find the minimum credit limit, which is $15.00. You enter this value into the `where` clause of the second query. This method relies on you to transfer the information from the result table of the first query to the SQL code of the second query.

The second method uses a subquery to get the minimum value. A subquery is a `select` statement embedded within another `select` statement. In this case, the inner `select` statement is evaluated first. It obtains the minimum value for `credit_limit`, which is $15.00. The computer substitutes this result in the outer `select` statement, replacing the inner `select` statement. Then the outer query is evaluated, giving the result table. The benefit of this method is that it uses only one query. It does not rely on the person running the query to transfer information, so it provides a more packaged solution.

Task

Find all the employees who have the minimum credit limit.

Oracle & Access SQL: Method 1, Step 1 ❶

```
select min(credit_limit)
from l_employees;
```

Oracle & Access SQL: Method 1, Step 2 ❷

```
select employee_id,
       first_name,
       last_name,
       credit_limit
from 1_employees
where credit_limit = 15.00 ❸
order by employee_id;
```

Oracle & Access SQL: Method 2 ❹

```
select employee_id,
       first_name,
       last_name,
       credit_limit
from 1_employees
where credit_limit = (select min(credit_limit) ❹
                             from 1_employees)
order by employee_id;
```

Beginning table (1_employees table)

EMPLOYEE ID	FIRST_NAME	LAST_NAME	DEPT CODE	HIRE_DATE	CREDIT LIMIT	PHONE NUMBER	MANAGER ID
201	SUSAN	BROWN	EXE	01-JUN-1998	$30.00	3484	(null)
202	JIM	KERN	SAL	16-AUG-1999	$25.00	8722	201
203	MARTHA	WOODS	SHP	02-FEB-2009	$25.00	7591	201
204	ELLEN	OWENS	SAL	01-JUL-2008	$15.00	6830	202
205	HENRY	PERKINS	SAL	01-MAR-2006	$25.00	5286	202
206	CAROL	ROSE	ACT	(null)	(null)	(null)	(null)
207	DAN	SMITH	SHP	01-DEC-2008	$25.00	2259	203
208	FRED	CAMPBELL	SHP	01-APR-2008	$25.00	1752	203
209	PAULA	JACOBS	MKT	17-MAR-1999	$15.00	3357	201
210	NANCY	HOFFMAN	SAL	16-FEB-2007	$25.00	2974	203

Result table

EMPLOYEE ID	FIRST_NAME	LAST_NAME	CREDIT LIMIT
204	ELLEN	OWENS	$15.00
209	PAULA	JACOBS	$15.00

Notes

❶ This finds the smallest credit limit of any of the employees, $15.00.

❷ A second query gets additional information about the employees who have the minimum credit limit.

❸ The value "15.00" is obtained from the result of the first query. The dollar sign is dropped. Numbers within SQL code cannot contain dollar signs or commas. The decimal point and two zeros are optional. They are written here to show that this is a currency value. It could also be written as "15" without the decimal point and zeros.

❹ This is the subquery.

Check your understanding

Repeat the exercise in section 11-3. Then find the row_IDs for the minimum and maximum values.

Count

11-6 Counting rows and counting data

SQL has two different methods of counting the data in a column. These methods differ in how they count nulls. Later we discuss a third method of counting that counts the number of different values in the column.

This section shows two varieties of the count column function. The count(*) function counts the number of rows in the table. The count(*column*) function counts the amount of data in a specific column, ignoring all the nulls.

Counting all the rows in a table

The count(*) function counts all the rows in the table. The result is the same as if all the values in any column were counted, including the nulls. This is the only column function that treats nulls the same way it treats other values.

You can think of this function in two ways. If you think of it as counting all the rows in a table, then any nulls in the table do not get involved in this. If you think of it as counting all the values in a column, then all the nulls are included in the count. No matter which column is counted, the result is the same for every column. You are free to think about the function in either way.

Counting all the values in a column, excluding nulls

The count(*column*) function counts all the values in the specified column that are not nulls. It tells you how much data is entered in the column. Clearly, each column can have a different count because each column can contain a different number of nulls. The column can have any datatype — text, number, or date.

Task

Count the number of rows in the 1_employees table. Also, count the number of non-null values in these three columns:

  last_name

  hire_date

  manager_id

Oracle & Access SQL

```
select count(*), ❶
       count(last_name), ❷
       count(hire_date), ❸
       count(manager_id) ❹
from 1_employees;
```

Beginning table (1_employees table)

EMPLOYEE ID	FIRST_NAME	LAST_NAME	DEPT CODE	HIRE_DATE	CREDIT LIMIT	PHONE NUMBER	MANAGER ID
201	SUSAN	BROWN	EXE	01-JUN-1998	$30.00	3484	(null)
202	JIM	KERN	SAL	16-AUG-1999	$25.00	8722	201
203	MARTHA	WOODS	SHP	02-FEB-2009	$25.00	7591	201
204	ELLEN	OWENS	SAL	01-JUL-2008	$15.00	6830	202
205	HENRY	PERKINS	SAL	01-MAR-2006	$25.00	5286	202
206	CAROL	ROSE	ACT	(null)	(null)	(null)	(null)
207	DAN	SMITH	SHP	01-DEC-2008	$25.00	2259	203
208	FRED	CAMPBELL	SHP	01-APR-2008	$25.00	1752	203
209	PAULA	JACOBS	MKT	17-MAR-1999	$15.00	3357	201
210	NANCY	HOFFMAN	SAL	16-FEB-2007	$25.00	2974	203

Result table ❺

COUNT(*)	COUNT(LAST_NAME)	COUNT(HIRE_DATE)	COUNT(MANAGER_ID)
10	10	9	8

Notes

❶ Count(*) finds the number of rows in the table.

❷ This applies the count(*column*) function to a text column — the last_name column. The result is 10 because there are no nulls in this column.

❸ This applies the count(*column*) function to a date column — the hire_date column. The result is 9 because there is one null in this column.

❹ This applies the count(*column*) function to a column of numbers — the manager_id column. The result is 8 because there are two nulls in this column.

❺ The result table contains only one row.

Check your understanding

In table sec1106, find the following information:

■ The number of rows in the table

■ The number of rows that have a non-null value in the Num_1 column

■ The number of rows that have a null value in the Num_1 column

11-7 Counting to zero, part 1

Sometimes you want zeros to appear in your result. When you want this, the way to get it is to apply the count(*column*) function to a column of nulls. The count(distinct *column*) function can also create a zero.

No other column function can do this. When any other column function is applied to a column of nulls, the result is a null. The one exception is the count(*) function. It counts the number of rows in the table, so it never results in a zero.

Now you are probably thinking that it is unusual for a table to have a column that contains only nulls. That is true. However, in the next chapter we won't be summarizing an entire column at once. Instead, we will divide the rows into several groups and separately summarize each group. A column often contains only nulls for a group of rows.

We use this later, but right now I am trying to show you how each column function works.

Task for example 1

In Oracle and Access, apply all the column functions to the column that contains only nulls. Show that the count(*column*) function results in a zero, but the max, min, sum, and avg functions result in a null.

Oracle & Access SQL

```
select count(col_2) as count_col,
       count(*) as count_rows,
       max(col_2) as max,
       min(col_2) as min,
       sum(col_2) as sum,
       avg(col_2) as avg
from sec1107;
```

Beginning table (sec1107 table)

```
PK_1 COL_2
---- ------
A    (null)
B    (null)
C    (null)
D    (null)
E    (null)
```

Result table

COUNT_COL	COUNT_ROWS	MAX	MIN	SUM	AVG
0	5	(null)	(null)	(null)	(null)

Task for example 2

In Oracle, apply count(distinct *column*) to the column of nulls. Show that this also results in a zero.

Oracle SQL

```
select count(distinct col_2) as count_distinct
from sec1107;
```

Access does not support count(distinct *column*).

Result table

```
COUNT_DISTINCT
--------------
             0
```

Check your understanding

Repeat the exercise in the previous section, except add a `where` clause that limits the `row_id` to the value 1. Note the zero in the result.

11-8 Counting the number of distinct values in a column

This section shows you how to count the number of different values in a column. Nulls are not counted as values. If the column contains codes, such as the `dept_code` column, you can use this technique to find out how many different codes are used within that column. Oracle and Access use different methods for this.

In Oracle, the column function `count(distinct column)` produces this result. In Access, this column function does not exist. You can get around this problem by using two steps.

The first step uses `select distinct` to create a table or a view that contains all the distinct values within the column. If there is a null in the column, it is included in the result table produced by `select distinct`. The second step counts the values in this table without counting the null. This gives the correct result.

Task

Find the number of different values in the `manager_id` column of the `1_employees` table.

Oracle SQL ❶

```
select count(distinct manager_id)
from 1_employees;
```

Beginning table (1_employees table)

```
EMPLOYEE                               DEPT                    CREDIT  PHONE   MANAGER
      ID FIRST_NAME LAST_NAME  CODE HIRE_DATE         LIMIT NUMBER      ID
-------- ---------- ---------- ---- ------------    ------- ------  -------
     201 SUSAN      BROWN      EXE  01-JUN-1998     $30.00 3484    (null)
     202 JIM        KERN       SAL  16-AUG-1999     $25.00 8722       201
     203 MARTHA     WOODS      SHP  02-FEB-2009     $25.00 7591       201
     204 ELLEN      OWENS      SAL  01-JUL-2008     $15.00 6830       202
     205 HENRY      PERKINS    SAL  01-MAR-2006     $25.00 5286       202
     206 CAROL      ROSE       ACT  (null)          (null) (null)  (null)
     207 DAN        SMITH      SHP  01-DEC-2008     $25.00 2259       203
     208 FRED       CAMPBELL   SHP  01-APR-2008     $25.00 1752       203
     209 PAULA      JACOBS     MKT  17-MAR-1999     $15.00 3357       201
     210 NANCY      HOFFMAN    SAL  16-FEB-2007     $25.00 2974       203
```

Result table

```
COUNT(DISTINCTMANAGER_ID)
-------------------------
                        3
```

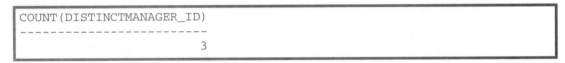

Access SQL (workaround): Step 1 ❷

```
select distinct manager_id ❸
into sec1108_step1
from 1_employees;
```

Access table: Step 1

| sec1108_step1 |
| manager_id |
| |
| 201 |
| 202 |
| 203 |
| * |

Access SQL (workaround): Step 2 ❷

```
select count(manager_id) ❹
from sec1108_step1;
```

Access result table

| Query1 |
| Expr1000 |
| 3 |

Notes

❶ In Oracle, you can use the `count(distinct column)` function.

❷ In Access, you must write two separate queries and run each query separately.

❸ In Access, the first query creates a table containing all the different values, including the null. If there are several nulls in the `manager_id` column of the beginning table, there is still only one null in the `step1` table. That is, `select distinct` treats all nulls as though they have the same value, even though they are all unknown values.

❹ In Access, the second query uses the function `count(column)`.

Check your understanding

In table `sec1103`, find the number of distinct values in the `num_1` column.

11-9 Counting the number of distinct values in two or more columns

This section shows you how to use `count distinct` to find the number of different values of two or more columns. Here I mean that the columns are taken in combination with each other, so a new combination occurs whenever any one of the columns has a new value.

This combination of the columns into a single unit of data is similar to the way that `select distinct` works with rows. With `select distinct`, two rows are considered identical only when all the columns have the same values.

There is a technical difference between `count distinct` and `select distinct`. `Count distinct` is a column function. Here, `distinct` eliminates duplicate values of a single column. `Select distinct` is an entire `select` statement. Here `distinct` eliminates duplicate rows of the result table.

To get these two structures to work the same way, you need to use a trick: Concatenate all the columns together into a single column before applying `count distinct` to them. The one column that `count distinct` applies to then actually contains the values of all the columns.

A second trick should also be used. A separator should be placed between the columns of the concatenation. The separator is usually a one-character literal. It is often a punctuation character or special character that you know does not appear in the data. If the data might contain any character, you may need to use a separator containing a string of two or three characters. In the following SQL code, an asterisk is used for the separation character.

By using a separator, we prevent the possibility that different values in two columns will produce the same value when they are concatenated. For example:

Column 1	Column 2	Concatenation without a Separator	Concatenation with a Separator
A	BCD	ABCD	A*BCD
AB	CD	ABCD	AB*CD
ABC	D	ABCD	ABC*D

Nulls are counted when the `count distinct` function is applied to two or more columns and a separator is used. Even if there are nulls in all the columns that are concatenated together, it is still counted. The separators are not nulls, so the concatenation is not a null and it is counted.

Column 1	Column 2	Concatenation without a Separator	Concatenation with a Separator
null	null	null	*

In Access, we need to use the same workaround to get `count distinct` that we used in the previous section.

Task

Count the number of distinct combinations of `manager_id` and `credit_limit`.

Oracle SQL

```
select count(distinct (manager_id || '*' || credit_limit))
from l_employees;
```

Beginning table (1_employees table)

EMPLOYEE ID	FIRST_NAME	LAST_NAME	DEPT CODE	HIRE_DATE	CREDIT LIMIT	PHONE NUMBER	MANAGER ID
201	SUSAN	BROWN	EXE	01-JUN-1998	$30.00	3484	(null)
202	JIM	KERN	SAL	16-AUG-1999	$25.00	8722	201
203	MARTHA	WOODS	SHP	02-FEB-2009	$25.00	7591	201
204	ELLEN	OWENS	SAL	01-JUL-2008	$15.00	6830	202
205	HENRY	PERKINS	SAL	01-MAR-2006	$25.00	5286	202
206	CAROL	ROSE	ACT	(null)	(null)	(null)	(null)
207	DAN	SMITH	SHP	01-DEC-2008	$25.00	2259	203
208	FRED	CAMPBELL	SHP	01-APR-2008	$25.00	1752	203
209	PAULA	JACOBS	MKT	17-MAR-1999	$15.00	3357	201
210	NANCY	HOFFMAN	SAL	16-FEB-2007	$25.00	2974	203

Result table

```
COUNT(DISTINCT(MANAGER_ID||'*'||CREDIT_LIMIT))
-----------------------------------------------
                                              7
```

Access SQL (workaround): Step 1 ⓘ

```
select distinct manager_id,
                credit_limit
into sec1109_manager_credit
from 1_employees;
```

Access temporary table: Step 1

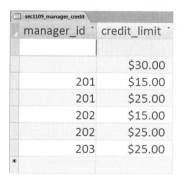

manager_id	credit_limit
	$30.00
201	$15.00
201	$25.00
202	$15.00
202	$25.00
203	$25.00

Access SQL (workaround): Step 2

```
select count(*) ❷
from sec1109_manager_credit;
```

Access result table: Step 2

Expr1000
7

Notes

❶ This two-step method also works in Oracle, and it avoids the trick of using a separator character.

❷ When you are counting more than one column, use count(*) instead of count(column) as you did in section 11-8. The row with the null in both columns is counted.

Check your understanding

In table sec1103, find the number of distinct values in the num_1 and num_2 columns, taken together.

Sum and Average

11-10 The sum and average functions

This section shows an example using the sum (sum) and average (avg) column functions. These functions can be applied only to a column of numbers. Text and date columns cannot be used with these functions.

Nulls are ignored by both of these functions. The next section shows how this can sometimes cause a problem for the sum function. For the avg function, nulls are ignored both in adding up the column and in counting the number of items to set the divisor.

Task

Find the sum and average of all the credit limits in the 1_employees table.

Oracle & Access SQL

```
select sum(credit_limit), ❶
       avg(credit_limit) ❷
from 1_employees;
```

Beginning table (1_employees table)

```
EMPLOYEE                        DEPT                 CREDIT  PHONE   MANAGER
      ID FIRST_NAME LAST_NAME  CODE HIRE_DATE        LIMIT   NUMBER       ID
-------- ---------- ---------  ---- ------------     -------  ------  -------
     201 SUSAN      BROWN      EXE  01-JUN-1998      $30.00  3484    (null)
     202 JIM        KERN       SAL  16-AUG-1999      $25.00  8722        201
     203 MARTHA     WOODS      SHP  02-FEB-2009      $25.00  7591        201
     204 ELLEN      OWENS      SAL  01-JUL-2008      $15.00  6830        202
     205 HENRY      PERKINS    SAL  01-MAR-2006      $25.00  5286        202
     206 CAROL      ROSE       ACT  (null)           (null)  (null)  (null)
     207 DAN        SMITH      SHP  01-DEC-2008      $25.00  2259        203
     208 FRED       CAMPBELL   SHP  01-APR-2008      $25.00  1752        203
     209 PAULA      JACOBS     MKT  17-MAR-1999      $15.00  3357        201
     210 NANCY      HOFFMAN    SAL  16-FEB-2007      $25.00  2974        203
```

Result table ❸

```
SUM(CREDIT_LIMIT)  AVG(CREDIT_LIMIT)
-----------------  -----------------
              210         23.333333
```

Notes

❶ This is an example of the sum(column) function. The result, 210, is the sum of the nine values in the credit_limit column.

❷ This is an example of the avg(column) function. It finds the average of the numbers. The result is 210 / 9 = 23.33, where 210 is the sum of the values in the credit_limit column and 9 is the number of values in that column, excluding nulls.

❸ The result table contains only one row.

Check your understanding

In table sec1103, find the sum and average of the num_1 column.

11-11 The problem with nulls in addition and how to solve it

SQL sometimes has a problem with addition when both of the following conditions exist:

1. Two or more columns are added together.

2. There are nulls in some of those columns.

One of the basic properties of addition is that the order in which you add the numbers does not matter. The sum is always the same. Sometimes addition in SQL violates this property, as the example in this section shows.

The problem is that SQL has two kinds of addition, row addition and column addition, which have different ways of handling nulls. Row addition adds numbers within one row. It is a row function. Row addition handles a null as an unknown value. So, for example:

3 + null = null

Column addition adds numbers within one column. It is one of the functions used for summarization. All summarization functions ignore nulls. So, for example:

$$
\begin{array}{r}
3 \\
+ \; \text{null} \\
\hline
3
\end{array}
$$

To solve this problem, you need to replace all the nulls with zeros. You can do this by using the row functions `nvl` in Oracle and `nz` in Access. Another method uses the `update` statement to make the change. This method changes the data in the beginning table. If you do not want to change the data permanently, you can do a `rollback` after you perform the calculation.

The following example shows two columns of numbers, and these columns contain some nulls. When all the numbers are added together, you get one result if you add the columns first and you get a different result if you add the rows first.

When the columns are added first, using column addition, you get the result that the sums of the columns are 6 and 15. Adding these together with row addition, you get the following:

6 + 15 = 21

When the rows are added first, using row addition, you get the result that the sums of the rows are 5, null, 8, and null. Adding these together with column addition, you get the following:

```
    5
+ null
+   8
+ null
  ─────
   13
```

The solution

Several solutions are available. The easiest is to always add the columns first. This works, but it is sometimes tricky to implement. You need to be aware of columns that are defined as row functions of other columns and that information may get hidden.

A better solution is to stay aware of numeric columns in your database that allow nulls. Whenever you use one of these columns, use it with the `nvl` or `nz` function.

Task

Add all the numbers in columns 2 and 3 of the following beginning table. Show that in SQL we get two different answers, depending on the order in which we add the numbers. If we add each of the columns first, the resulting sum is 21. If we add across the rows first, the resulting sum is 13.

Then show that when the nulls are changed to zeros, the problem with addition is solved: The result is the same whether the columns or the rows are added first.

Oracle & Access SQL: An example of the problem with addition

```
select sum(col_2)+sum(col_3) as columns_added_first, ❶
       sum(col_2 + col_3) as rows_added_first ❷
from sec1111;
```

Beginning table (sec1111 table)

```
PK_1         COL_2      COL_3
------ --------- ---------
A                1          4
B          (null)          5
C                2          6
D                3 (null)
```

Result table — Without changing the nulls to zeros ❸

```
COLUMNS_ADDED_FIRST ROWS_ADDED_FIRST
------------------- ----------------
              21               13
```

Notes

❶ This line adds the columns first.

❷ This line adds the rows first.

❸ This shows that the sums are different.

Explanation

Add columns first:

Col_2	Col_3
1	4
null	5
2	6
3	null
———	———
Sum 6	15

Then $6 + 15 = 21$.

Add rows first:

Col_2	Col_3	Sum
1	4	= 5
null	5	= null
2	6	= 8
3	null	= null

Then 5 + 8 = 13.

Oracle SQL: Method 1 — Using a row function   CORRECT

```
select sum(nvl(col_2, 0)) + sum(nvl(col_3, 0)) ❹ ❻
                        as columns_added_first,
       sum(nvl(col_2, 0) + nvl(col_3, 0)) ❹
                        as rows_added_first
from sec1111;
```

Access SQL: Method 1 — Using a row function   CORRECT

```
select sum(nz(col_2, 0)) + sum(nz(col_3, 0)) ❺ ❻
                        as columns_added_first,
       sum(nz(col_2, 0) + nz(col_3, 0)) ❺
                        as rows_added_first
from sec1111;
```

Result table — With the nulls changed to zeros ❼

```
COLUMNS_ADDED_FIRST  ROWS_ADDED_FIRST
-------------------  ----------------
               21                  21
```

Notes

❹ In Oracle, the nvl function is applied to both columns to change the nulls into zeros.

❺ In Access, the nz function is applied to both columns to change the nulls into zeros.

❻ If you remember to always add the columns first, you do not need to use the `nvl` or `nz` functions. This makes the code:

```
select sum(col_2) + sum(col_3)
```

In a way, this is the easiest solution. However, sometimes it can leave a trap in your code that someone else may fall into. The next programmer who works on the code might write:

```
sum(col_2 + col_3)
```

This would give the wrong answer.

❼ This shows that the sums are the same.

Explanation

Add columns first:

Col_2	Col_3
1	4
0	5
2	6
3	0
——	——
Sum 6	15

Then 6 + 15 = 21.

Add rows first:

Col_2	Col_3	Sum
1	4	= 5
0	5	= 5
2	6	= 8
3	0	= 3

Then 5 + 5 + 8 + 3 = 21.

Oracle SQL: Method 2 — Changing the data temporarily   CORRECT

Step 1: In the Home Page interface, clear the Autocommit checkbox. In the SQL Command Line interface, set Autocommit off.

Step 2: Change the nulls to zeros in any columns used in the calculation.

```
update sec1111
   set col_2 = 0
where col_2 is null;
```

```
update sec1111
   set col_3 = 0
where col_3 is null;
```

Step 3: Run your report.

```
select sum(col_2)+sum(col_3) as columns_added_first,
       sum(col_2 + col_3) as rows_added_first
from sec1111;
```

Step 4: Undo the temporary changes to the data.

```
rollback;
```

In Access, we could use a similar process, but Access does not have a `roll-back` statement, so the changes to the data would be permanent.

One last thought

As long as you are comfortable interpreting all the nulls in your numeric columns as zeros, all you need to do is add up the columns first. This works because column addition ignores the nulls, which is similar to treating them as zeros.

Check your understanding

In table `sec1103`, show the problem with nulls in addition and how to solve it.

1. Add columns `num_1` and `num_2`, adding each row first.

2. Add columns `num_1` and `num_2`, adding each column first.

3. Add columns `num_1` and `num_2`, changing all the nulls to zeros first.

Other Topics

The next three sections discuss some details that are important in many applications that use summarization.

11-12 Nulls are not always changed to zero

In the previous section, all the nulls were changed to zeros, which is the usual procedure. Ninety percent of the time the nulls in numeric columns are changed to zeros, if their value is changed at all. Sometimes, however, you might want to change the nulls to some other value, perhaps an estimate of what the value will eventually be. This section gives an example.

In this example, a store receives orders for merchandise that it will ship to customers. At the end of each day, the store wants to know the total value of all the invoices. Each invoice is calculated with the formula:

(Price * Quantity) + Tax + Shipping = Invoice

The problem is that sometimes the `tax` or `shipping` columns contain nulls, meaning that it is an unknown amount. In this situation, you need to carefully control how the calculation is performed and how the rows that contain nulls are counted.

There are three choices:

1. Bill all the amounts you know and estimate an amount for the nulls.
2. Bill all the amounts you know and nothing for the nulls.
3. Ignore any invoice with incomplete data.

This section shows the SQL code for the first choice, which is the best one.

Task

Find the total for all the invoices in the table. Calculate an invoice as:

(Price * Quantity) + Tax + Shipping = Invoice

Estimate values for the nulls that occur in the `tax` and `shipping` columns by applying these rules:

1. Replace a null in the `tax` column with:

    `0.07 * price * quantity`

2. Replace a null in the `shipping` column with:

    `0.12* price * quantity`

Oracle SQL

```
select sum((price * quantity)
          + nvl(tax, 0.07 * price * quantity) ❶
          + nvl(shipping, 0.12 * price * quantity)) ❷
                                    as total_invoices
from sec1112_shipping;
```

Access SQL

```
select sum((price * quantity)
          + nz(tax, 0.07 * price * quantity) ❶
          + nz(shipping, 0.12 * price * quantity)) ❷
                                    as total_invoices
from sec1112_shipping;
```

Beginning table (sec1112_shipping table)

PK_1	PRICE	QUANTITY	TAX	SHIPPING
A	$211.00	3	$48.00	$63.00
B	$138.00	7	(null)	$72.00
C	$592.00	1	$51.00	$76.00
D	$329.00	2	$54.00	(null)

Result table

TOTAL_INVOICES
$3,359.58

Notes

❶ Change the null in the tax column to an estimate of the tax.

❷ Change the null in the shipping column to an estimate of the shipping charge.

11-13 Counting the number of nulls in a column

How can you count the number of nulls in a column? This goal may seem to be a problem because all the column functions ignore nulls. This section shows the technique. The where clause limits the rows to the ones we want to count. Then the count(*) function counts them.

Often we are most interested in knowing if a column contains any nulls at all and less interested in getting the exact count.

Task

Find the number of nulls in the manager_id column of the l_employees table.

Oracle & Access SQL

```
select count(*) as number_of_nulls
from l_employees
where manager_id is null;
```

Beginning table (l_employees table)

EMPLOYEE ID	FIRST_NAME	LAST_NAME	DEPT CODE	HIRE_DATE	CREDIT LIMIT	PHONE NUMBER	MANAGER ID
201	SUSAN	BROWN	EXE	01-JUN-1998	$30.00	3484	(null)
202	JIM	KERN	SAL	16-AUG-1999	$25.00	8722	201
203	MARTHA	WOODS	SHP	02-FEB-2009	$25.00	7591	201
204	ELLEN	OWENS	SAL	01-JUL-2008	$15.00	6830	202
205	HENRY	PERKINS	SAL	01-MAR-2006	$25.00	5286	202
206	CAROL	ROSE	ACT	(null)	(null)	(null)	(null)
207	DAN	SMITH	SHP	01-DEC-2008	$25.00	2259	203
208	FRED	CAMPBELL	SHP	01-APR-2008	$25.00	1752	203
209	PAULA	JACOBS	MKT	17-MAR-1999	$15.00	3357	201
210	NANCY	HOFFMAN	SAL	16-FEB-2007	$25.00	2974	203

Result table

NUMBER_OF_NULLS
2

11-14 Counting distinct dates

When you use count distinct on a date column, you may not get the
result you expect. This happens because the data in a date column may
contain a time, which is often not shown. Thus two rows that appear to
have the same date may in fact be different because the times are different.

Task

Count the number of different dates in the date_entered column of the
l_lunches table.

Oracle SQL: The problem

```
select count(distinct date_entered)  ❶
from l_lunches;
```

Beginning table (l_lunches table) ❷

```
              LUNCH         EMPLOYEE
LUNCH_ID DATE                    ID DATE_ENTERE
-------- ------------- -------- -----------
       1 16-NOV-2011        201 13-OCT-2011
       2 16-NOV-2011        207 13-OCT-2011
       3 16-NOV-2011        203 13-OCT-2011
       4 16-NOV-2011        204 13-OCT-2011
       6 16-NOV-2011        202 13-OCT-2011
       7 16-NOV-2011        210 13-OCT-2011
       8 25-NOV-2011        201 14-OCT-2011
       9 25-NOV-2011        208 14-OCT-2011
      12 25-NOV-2011        204 14-OCT-2011
      13 25-NOV-2011        207 18-OCT-2011
      15 25-NOV-2011        205 21-OCT-2011
      16 05-DEC-2011        201 21-OCT-2011
      17 05-DEC-2011        210 21-OCT-2011
      20 05-DEC-2011        205 24-OCT-2011
      21 05-DEC-2011        203 24-OCT-2011
      22 05-DEC-2011        208 24-OCT-2011
```

Result table — The problem ❸

```
COUNT(DISTINCTDATE_ENTERED)
---------------------------
                         16
```

Oracle SQL: The solution

```
select count(distinct trunc(date_entered)) ❹
from l_lunches;
```

Result table — The solution ❺

```
COUNT(DISTINCTTRUNC(DATE_ENTERED))
----------------------------------
                                 5
```

Access SQL: The solution ❻

Step 1:

```
select distinct format(date_entered, 'YYYY-MM-DD') ❼
                                 as date_entered2
into temp_date
from l_lunches;
```

Step 2:

```
select count(date_entered2)
from temp_date;
```

Beginning table (1_lunches table as shown in Access) ❽

LUNCH	LUNCH_DATE	EMPLOYEE_ID	DATE_ENTERED	Add New Field
1	16-Nov-2011	201	13-Oct-2011 10:35:24 AM	
2	16-Nov-2011	207	13-Oct-2011 10:35:39 AM	
3	16-Nov-2011	203	13-Oct-2011 10:35:45 AM	
4	16-Nov-2011	204	13-Oct-2011 10:35:58 AM	
6	16-Nov-2011	202	13-Oct-2011 10:36:41 AM	
7	16-Nov-2011	210	13-Oct-2011 10:38:52 AM	
8	25-Nov-2011	201	14-Oct-2011 11:15:37 AM	
9	25-Nov-2011	208	14-Oct-2011 2:23:36 PM	
12	25-Nov-2011	204	14-Oct-2011 3:02:53 PM	
13	25-Nov-2011	207	18-Oct-2011 8:42:11 AM	
15	25-Nov-2011	205	21-Oct-2011 4:23:50 PM	
16	05-Dec-2011	201	21-Oct-2011 4:23:59 PM	
17	05-Dec-2011	210	21-Oct-2011 4:35:26 PM	
20	05-Dec-2011	205	24-Oct-2011 9:55:27 AM	
21	05-Dec-2011	203	24-Oct-2011 11:43:13 AM	
22	05-Dec-2011	208	24-Oct-2011 2:37:32 PM	

Access result table: Step 1

temp_date
date_entered
2011-10-13
2011-10-14
2011-10-18
2011-10-21
2011-10-24

Access result table: Step 2

Query1
Expr1000
5

Notes

❶ You need to be careful when you use `count distinct` with a date field. You need to remember that a date always includes a time.

❷ Only the dates are shown in this listing of the `l_lunches` table. The times are not shown, even though they are actually in the data.

❸ The result shows there are 16 different values in this column. The date in each row is different because the times are different.

❹ The solution is to apply the `trunc` function to the date column. This truncates the time and leaves only the date.

❺ Now we get the answer we expected.

❻ Because Access does not support `count distinct`, you must use the workaround given in section 11-9.

❼ Here the `format` function is used to remove the time from the data in the `date_entered` column. There are other ways to achieve the same thing. In Oracle you can use the `trunc` function and in Access you can use the `DateValue` function.

❽ In Access the default date format does show the time, so the problem described in this section is less likely to happen.

Key Points

- Column functions summarize all the data in a single column of a table. This can be either the data table or a result table. In this chapter, the summarization extends over all the rows of the table and it produces a single number, text string, or date. In the next chapter, you will see how to modify this summarization process to produce several numbers, text strings, or dates.

- There are only seven column functions and two more that are fairly new. They are: maximum, minimum, sum, average, and three types of counting. Recently, many SQL products have added variance and standard deviation to deal with statistical data.

- All of the column functions, except `count(*)`, completely ignore any nulls that are in the summarized column.

- `Max` and `min` return the values you expect. To find the rows that have these values, it is best to use a separate `select` statement.

- `Sum` and `avg` can apply only to columns of numbers. Often, you will want to use a row function to change the nulls in the column to zeros before you apply the `sum` or `avg` column functions.

- `Count(column_name)` counts the number of rows in the table that have a non-null value in the column.

- `Count(distinct column_name)` counts the number of different values that are in the column. To find the number of different values in two or more columns, first combine those columns into a single column, then apply the `count(distinct)` column function to that combined column.

- `Count(*)` counts the number of rows in the table. It is not bound to one specific column.

chapter 12

CONTROLLING THE LEVEL OF SUMMARIZATION

In chapter 11, we summarized all the data in a column of a table. The result was a single value. In this chapter, we divide the rows of the table into *groups*, which are nonoverlapping sets of rows. Each group is summarized separately, resulting in a summary value for each of the groups.

At our discretion, we can either summarize a column into a single value or divide it into 100 pieces and summarize each piece. This gives us control over the level of detail we want to see.

Dividing a Table into Groups of Rows

You can divide the rows of a table into separate groups. The `group by` clause in a `select` statement can do this. Then each group of rows is summarized into one line (row) of the summary.

The column functions summarize each group of rows. This allows you to control the level of summarization and detail.

12-1 Summary of groups of data within a column

This section shows a conceptual diagram of the way a column function works when it is applied to groups of rows within a table. Each row of the table is assigned to a group. Each row can be part of only a single group.

The column function produces a summary of each group of rows, which is a single value for each group. The result of the column function has one row for every group of rows in the beginning table.

The number of groups that the beginning table is divided into determines how detailed and fine-grained the summarization is. At one extreme, each row of the beginning table can be a separate group. Then no summarization occurs at all. At the other extreme, all the rows of the beginning table can be put into a single group. This was the case when we summarized the entire table in the previous chapter. Then all the data within the column is condensed down to a single value — a single number, text item, or date.

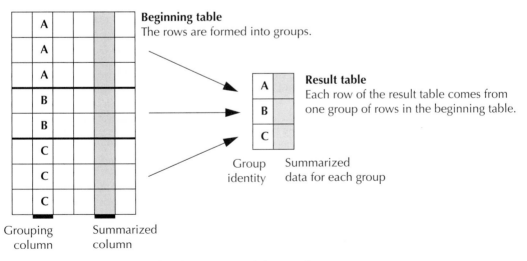

Beginning table
The rows are formed into groups.

Result table
Each row of the result table comes from one group of rows in the beginning table.

Group identity   Summarized data for each group

Grouping column   Summarized column

Grouping the rows of a table, then summarizing each group.

12-2 The group by **clause**

The example in this section shows how you can control the level of summarization using a group by clause. In this example a single column is used in the group by clause. This is the simplest case.

Each group is formed from all the rows of the table that have the same value in the grouping column. This means that each row of the table is placed in a group along with all the other rows that have the same value in that column. No row is placed in more than one group.

The columns are then summarized separately for each group. The result table contains one row for each group along with the summarized data for that group.

All the rows with a null in the grouping column are placed within a single group called the **null group**. The null group is similar to the Other category that is often used when data is summarized. This may seem a little unusual because nulls are unknown values and normally we do not consider one null to be equal to another. But what would the alternative be?

It would not work well if SQL formed a separate group from each null value. Each of these groups would contain only one row. There would be too many groups with only a single row and the summarization would not work well. Therefore the only effective solution is to form a single group from all the rows with a null in the grouping column.

We often say that every table should have a primary key, although we allow some exceptions. However, in this example you could not put a primary key on the manager_id column. Because of the null group, there is a null value in this column and a primary key column must not contain a null. You often cannot put a primary key on the result table of a grouped query.

Task

For each manager_id, list the number of employees each one manages. Also list the range of their employees' credit limits by showing the minimum and maximum. Omit employee 202.

Oracle & Access SQL

```
select manager_id, ❸
       count(employee_id) as number_of_employees,
       min(credit_limit) as minimum_credit,
       max(credit_limit) as maximum_credit
from l_employees
where not (employee_id = 202) ❶
group by manager_id ❷
order by manager_id;
```

Beginning table (l_employees table)

EMPLOYEE ID	FIRST_NAME	LAST_NAME	DEPT CODE	HIRE_DATE	CREDIT LIMIT	PHONE NUMBER	MANAGER ID
201	SUSAN	BROWN	EXE	01-JUN-1998	$30.00	3484	(null)
202	JIM	KERN	SAL	16-AUG-1999	$25.00	8722	201
203	MARTHA	WOODS	SHP	02-FEB-2009	$25.00	7591	201
204	ELLEN	OWENS	SAL	01-JUL-2008	$15.00	6830	202
205	HENRY	PERKINS	SAL	01-MAR-2006	$25.00	5286	202
206	CAROL	ROSE	ACT	(null)	(null)	(null)	(null)
207	DAN	SMITH	SHP	01-DEC-2008	$25.00	2259	203
208	FRED	CAMPBELL	SHP	01-APR-2008	$25.00	1752	203
209	PAULA	JACOBS	MKT	17-MAR-1999	$15.00	3357	201
210	NANCY	HOFFMAN	SAL	16-FEB-2007	$25.00	2974	203

First the where clause is applied and the row for employee_id = 202 is removed ❹

EMPLOYEE ID	FIRST_NAME	LAST_NAME	DEPT CODE	HIRE_DATE	CREDIT LIMIT	PHONE NUMBER	MANAGER ID
201	SUSAN	BROWN	EXE	01-JUN-1998	$30.00	3484	(null)
203	MARTHA	WOODS	SHP	02-FEB-2009	$25.00	7591	201
204	ELLEN	OWENS	SAL	01-JUL-2008	$15.00	6830	202
205	HENRY	PERKINS	SAL	01-MAR-2006	$25.00	5286	202
206	CAROL	ROSE	ACT	(null)	(null)	(null)	(null)
207	DAN	SMITH	SHP	01-DEC-2008	$25.00	2259	203
208	FRED	CAMPBELL	SHP	01-APR-2008	$25.00	1752	203
209	PAULA	JACOBS	MKT	17-MAR-1999	$15.00	3357	201
210	NANCY	HOFFMAN	SAL	16-FEB-2007	$25.00	2974	203

Then the rows of the table are divided into groups that have the same value in the manager_id column ❺

EMPLOYEE ID	FIRST_NAME	LAST_NAME	DEPT CODE	HIRE_DATE	CREDIT LIMIT	PHONE NUMBER	MANAGER ID
203	MARTHA	WOODS	SHP	02-FEB-2009	$25.00	7591	201
209	PAULA	JACOBS	MKT	17-MAR-1999	$15.00	3357	201
204	ELLEN	OWENS	SAL	01-JUL-2008	$15.00	6830	202
205	HENRY	PERKINS	SAL	01-MAR-2006	$25.00	5286	202
207	DAN	SMITH	SHP	01-DEC-2008	$25.00	2259	203
208	FRED	CAMPBELL	SHP	01-APR-2008	$25.00	1752	203
210	NANCY	HOFFMAN	SAL	16-FEB-2007	$25.00	2974	203
201	SUSAN	BROWN	EXE	01-JUN-1998	$30.00	3484	(null)
206	CAROL	ROSE	ACT	(null)	(null)	(null)	(null)

Result table ❻

MANAGER ID	NUMBER_OF_EMPLOYEES	MINIMUM_CREDIT	MAXIMUM_CREDIT
201	2	$15.00	$25.00
202	2	$15.00	$25.00
203	3	$25.00	$25.00
(null)	2	$30.00	$30.00

Notes

❶ ❹ First, the where clause is applied to the rows of the beginning table. It eliminates some of the rows. In this example, employee 202 is deleted from further consideration.

❷ ❺ Second, the remaining rows of the table are divided into groups by their value in the manager_id column. This creates four groups:

  • The two rows with a manager_id of 201

  • The two rows with a manager_id of 202

  • The three rows with a manager_id of 203

  • The two rows with a null value in the manager_id column

❸ ❻ Third, the column functions summarize the data in each of the groups. They produce one row in the result table for each of the groups.

The result table is usually structured to identify each group and then give summary information about that group. It does not need to be structured this way, but that is usually the most logical way to present the data. To achieve this, the `select` clause lists the grouping column(s) first, followed by column functions. The `select` clause here is organized that way.

Last, the `order by` clause sorts the rows of the result table into a logical order. Usually the `order by` clause contains the same columns as the `group by` clause.

Check your understanding

Table `sec1202` has four columns: `row_id`, `col_1`, `col_2`, and `col_3`. Write a `select` statement that groups the rows by the value in `col_1` and for each group determines the sum of the values in `col_3`.

12-3 Groups formed on two or more columns

This section shows a `group by` clause that uses two grouping columns. Each group is formed from all the rows that have identical values in both of these columns. If two rows have different values in either of these columns, they belong to different groups. The groups are the same regardless of the order in which the columns are listed in the `group by` clause.

A `group by` clause can list any number of columns. When a new column is added to the `group by` clause, each prior group may split into two or more new groups.

Drill down is a term that is used to describe the process of beginning with a high level of summarization and progressing to finer levels of detail. You can compare the result table of this section with the one from the previous section to see an example of a drill down.

The usual SQL technique behind a drill down is to add another column to the `group by` clause. This further divides each of the groups of rows. The same column is also added to the `select` clause and the `order by` clause. In the following example, the `dept_code` column is added to these clauses. I highlighted this change in the code.

Task

From the code in section 12-2, drill down by adding the department code. Omit employee 202.

Oracle & Access SQL

```
select manager_id, ❸
       dept_code,
       count(employee_id) as number_of_employees,
       min(credit_limit) as minimum_credit,
       max(credit_limit) as maximum_credit
from l_employees
where not (employee_id = 202) ❶
group by manager_id, ❷
         dept_code
order by manager_id, ❹
         dept_code;
```

Beginning table (l_employees table)

EMPLOYEE ID	FIRST_NAME	LAST_NAME	DEPT CODE	HIRE_DATE	CREDIT LIMIT	PHONE NUMBER	MANAGER ID
201	SUSAN	BROWN	EXE	01-JUN-1998	$30.00	3484	(null)
202	JIM	KERN	SAL	16-AUG-1999	$25.00	8722	201
203	MARTHA	WOODS	SHP	02-FEB-2009	$25.00	7591	201
204	ELLEN	OWENS	SAL	01-JUL-2008	$15.00	6830	202
205	HENRY	PERKINS	SAL	01-MAR-2006	$25.00	5286	202
206	CAROL	ROSE	ACT	(null)	(null)	(null)	(null)
207	DAN	SMITH	SHP	01-DEC-2008	$25.00	2259	203
208	FRED	CAMPBELL	SHP	01-APR-2008	$25.00	1752	203
209	PAULA	JACOBS	MKT	17-MAR-1999	$15.00	3357	201
210	NANCY	HOFFMAN	SAL	16-FEB-2007	$25.00	2974	203

First the where clause is applied and the row for employee_id = 202 is removed ❺

EMPLOYEE ID	FIRST_NAME	LAST_NAME	DEPT CODE	HIRE_DATE	CREDIT LIMIT	PHONE NUMBER	MANAGER ID
201	SUSAN	BROWN	EXE	01-JUN-1998	$30.00	3484	(null)
203	MARTHA	WOODS	SHP	02-FEB-2009	$25.00	7591	201
204	ELLEN	OWENS	SAL	01-JUL-2008	$15.00	6830	202
205	HENRY	PERKINS	SAL	01-MAR-2006	$25.00	5286	202
206	CAROL	ROSE	ACT	(null)	(null)	(null)	(null)
207	DAN	SMITH	SHP	01-DEC-2008	$25.00	2259	203
208	FRED	CAMPBELL	SHP	01-APR-2008	$25.00	1752	203
209	PAULA	JACOBS	MKT	17-MAR-1999	$15.00	3357	201
210	NANCY	HOFFMAN	SAL	16-FEB-2007	$25.00	2974	203

Then the rows of the table are divided into groups that have the same values in both the `manager_id` and `dept_code` columns ❻

EMPLOYEE ID	FIRST_NAME	LAST_NAME	DEPT CODE	HIRE_DATE	CREDIT LIMIT	PHONE NUMBER	MANAGER ID
203	MARTHA	WOODS	SHP	02-FEB-2009	$25.00	7591	201
209	PAULA	JACOBS	MKT	17-MAR-1999	$15.00	3357	201
204	ELLEN	OWENS	SAL	01-JUL-2008	$15.00	6830	202
205	HENRY	PERKINS	SAL	01-MAR-2006	$25.00	5286	202
207	DAN	SMITH	SHP	01-DEC-2008	$25.00	2259	203
208	FRED	CAMPBELL	SHP	01-APR-2008	$25.00	1752	203
210	NANCY	HOFFMAN	SAL	16-FEB-2007	$25.00	2974	203
201	SUSAN	BROWN	EXE	01-JUN-1998	$30.00	3484	(null)
206	CAROL	ROSE	ACT	(null)	(null)	(null)	(null)

Result table

MANAGER ID	DEPT CODE	NUMBER_OF_EMPLOYEES	MINIMUM_CREDIT	MAXIMUM_CREDIT
201	MKT	1	$15.00	$15.00
201	SHP	1	$25.00	$25.00
202	SAL	2	$15.00	$25.00
203	SAL	1	$25.00	$25.00
203	SHP	2	$25.00	$25.00
(null)	ACT	1	(null)	(null)
(null)	EXE	1	$30.00	$30.00

Notes

❶ ❺ The `where` clause is applied first. In this example it eliminates the row for employee 202 from further consideration.

❷ ❻ Groups of rows are formed that have identical values in both the `manager_id` and `dept_code` columns.

❸ Then the column functions in the `select` clause are evaluated separately for each group. The result table contains one row for each group. The department code is added to the `select` clause to fully identify each group in the listing of the result table.

❹ As a last step, the rows of the result table are sorted on the two columns used to create the groups. Although the order of these columns does not matter in the `group by` clause, it does matter in the `order by` clause. Because the `manager_id` is listed first in the `order by` clause, the primary sort is done on that column.

12-4 Null groups when there are two or more grouping columns

This section shows what happens when the rows of a table are grouped on two or more columns and several of those columns contain nulls. In this situation, the nulls are handled as if "null" was a specific value, like any other value. That is, if two nulls occur within a single grouping column, they are handled as if they have the same value and they are placed within the same group. If they occur in different grouping columns, they are handled separately, as any other values would be. Actually, this occurred in the previous section, but this section emphasizes the point.

In effect, this can create several Other categories within the summarization, but all the nulls are not placed into a single Other category. That is how the process is sometimes described, and that description is wrong. It is correct only when there is a single grouping column.

If you are grouping by more than one column and you truly want an Other category, you will need to create it yourself as a separate step. SQL will not create it for you. Usually you will not need to do this. However, you should pay careful attention to the sort order of the rows if they have any nulls in the grouping columns.

A null in the data is handled in two different ways within a grouped summarization. A null in a grouping column is handled as if it is a specific value and it is placed in a null group. However, a null in a column that is being summarized is ignored by the column functions that do the summarization.

In the following example, the groups are formed on col_2 and col_3. Both of these columns contain nulls. There are five separate groups that contain a null group in one of the two grouping columns. In the result table, each of these groups creates a separate row. In effect, this gives five Other categories.

Then the data in col_4 and col_5 are summarized for each of the groups. When the data is summarized with the count(*) function, we could think that the nulls are being counted, although it is really the rows that are being counted for each group. When the data are summarized with the count(*column*) function, the nulls are completely ignored.

Within this example we can see that nulls in grouping columns are handled differently from nulls in summarized columns.

Task

Group the following table on the two columns, col_2 and col_3. For each group of rows, calculate

- The number of rows in the group
- The number of rows that have data in column col_4
- The number of rows that have data in column col_5

Oracle & Access SQL

```
select col_2, ❶
       col_3, ❶
       count(*),
       count(col_4),
       count(col_5)
from sec1204
group by col_2,
         col_3 ❷
order by col_2,
         col_3;
```

Beginning table (sec1204 table) divided into groups

PK_1	COL_2	COL_3	COL_4	COL_5
1	A	Y	M	(null)
2	A	Y	(null)	(null)
3	A	Z	M	(null)
4	A	Z	(null)	(null)
5	A	(null)	M	(null)
6	A	(null)	(null)	(null)
7	B	Y	M	(null)
8	B	Y	(null)	(null)
9	B	Z	M	(null)
10	B	Z	(null)	(null)
11	B	(null)	M	(null)
12	B	(null)	(null)	(null)
13	(null)	Y	M	(null)
14	(null)	Y	(null)	(null)
15	(null)	Z	M	(null)
16	(null)	Z	(null)	(null)
17	(null)	(null)	M	(null)
18	(null)	(null)	(null)	(null)

Result table ❸

COL_2	COL_3	COUNT(*)	COUNT(COL_4)	COUNT(COL_5)
A	Y	2	1	0
A	Z	2	1	0
A	(null)	2	1	0
B	Y	2	1	0
B	Z	2	1	0
B	(null)	2	1	0
(null)	Y	2	1	0
(null)	Z	2	1	0
(null)	(null)	2	1	0

This is what does *not* happen when the beginning table (sec1204 table) is divided into groups. Here all the rows with a null in either grouping column form a single group. If SQL worked this way, there would be only one Other category.

	PK_1	COL_2	COL_3	COL_4	COL_5
	1	A	Y	M	(null)
	2	A	Y	(null)	(null)
	3	A	Z	M	(null)
	4	A	Z	(null)	(null)
	7	B	Y	M	(null)
	8	B	Y	(null)	(null)
	9	B	Z	M	(null)
	10	B	Z	(null)	(null)
	5	A	(null)	M	(null) ❹
	6	A	(null)	(null)	(null)
	11	B	(null)	M	(null)
	12	B	(null)	(null)	(null)
	13	(null)	Y	M	(null)
	14	(null)	Y	(null)	(null)
	15	(null)	Z	M	(null)
	16	(null)	Z	(null)	(null)
	17	(null)	(null)	M	(null)
	18	(null)	(null)	(null)	(null)

Notes

❶ col_2 and col_3 are used to group the data from the beginning table. They are listed in the select clause so that the result table makes sense.

❷ The group by clause lists both col_2 and col_3.

❸ The highlighted rows in the result table show the five separate null groups. In more general terms, these are five separate Other categories.

❹ This is what does not happen. SQL does not form a single group out of all the rows that have a null in one of the grouping columns.

Check your understanding

Use table sec1202. Write a select statement that groups the rows by the value in col_1 and col_2. For each group determine the sum of the values in col_3.

12-5 Summarized data cannot be mixed with nonsummarized data in the same select statement

A select statement cannot list both summarized data and detail data because the output of a select statement must be like a table. I have been calling this the result table. It must have columns and rows. In particular, each of the columns must have the same number of rows.

The example in this section shows a select statement that does not work and produces an error message because this select statement is mixing summarized data with detail data.

The second and third columns of the select clause are detail data. They are first_name and last_name. No column functions are applied to these columns and they are not listed in the group by clause. That is why they yield detail data. If the select clause listed only these columns, the result table would have 10 rows. Each row of the result table would come from a single row in the beginning table. The result table would be similar to the following:

```
FIRST_NAME      LAST_NAME
----------      ---------

(10 rows of detail data)
```

The first and fourth columns of the `select` clause are summarized data. The first column is `manager_id`. This column is also listed in the `group by` clause, so it is a grouping column, which is summarized data. The fourth column uses the `max` column function, so it is also summarized data. If the `select` clause listed only these columns, the result table would have four rows. Each of these rows would summarize all the rows with a particular `manager_id`. There are four different values in the `manager_id` column, so the result table would be similar to the following:

```
MANAGER_ID      MAX(CREDIT_LIMIT)
----------      -----------------

(4 rows of summarized data)
```

These two tables cannot be combined to form a single table because the columns contain different numbers of rows. For this reason, you are not allowed to mix summarized data and detail data in the same `select` statement.

Error messages

This section also shows that the error messages produced by Oracle and Access do not always tell you specifically what the error is or how to fix it. This is a problem with almost all computer software, not just Oracle and Access. It is very difficult for any type of computer software to tell you what the problems are in your code. Often when the computer detects a problem, it is genuinely confused, so it gives you a confused error message. It may point to the wrong location of the error — often the error actually occurs on the line above or below where the error message says it occurs. The error message may say that one thing is wrong, when the problem is something else entirely. The one thing you can count on is that when an error message appears, there is actually an error of some sort somewhere in your code. This is one of the basic problems you must learn to deal with in any type of computer programming.

The error messages shown in this section illustrate another difficulty. These error messages are specific to the problem and they do indicate accurately where the error first occurs. However, they are worded in a manner that is difficult to understand.

How to solve the problem

At times, you will attempt to mix summarized data with detail data. It happens to everyone. You will receive the error messages shown here. The question is, how do you move on and deal with the problem?

On a technical level, there are two main techniques you can use. The one you choose depends on what you are trying to do. The next two sections show these techniques with the SQL code used in this section. The techniques are as follows:

1. Add more columns to the group by clause. Add all the columns that contain detail data.

2. Separate your query into two separate select statements, one for summarized data and the other for detail data.

Task

Show the error that occurs when a summarized column and a nonsummarized column both occur within the same select statement.

Oracle & Access SQL: This contains an error

```
select manager_id, ❶
       first_name, ❷
       last_name, ❷
       max(credit_limit) ❸
from 1_employees
group by manager_id
order by manager_id;
```

Beginning table (1_employees table)

EMPLOYEE ID	FIRST_NAME	LAST_NAME	DEPT CODE	HIRE_DATE	CREDIT LIMIT	PHONE NUMBER	MANAGER ID
201	SUSAN	BROWN	EXE	01-JUN-1998	$30.00	3484	(null)
202	JIM	KERN	SAL	16-AUG-1999	$25.00	8722	201
203	MARTHA	WOODS	SHP	02-FEB-2009	$25.00	7591	201
204	ELLEN	OWENS	SAL	01-JUL-2008	$15.00	6830	202
205	HENRY	PERKINS	SAL	01-MAR-2006	$25.00	5286	202
206	CAROL	ROSE	ACT	(null)	(null)	(null)	(null)
207	DAN	SMITH	SHP	01-DEC-2008	$25.00	2259	203
208	FRED	CAMPBELL	SHP	01-APR-2008	$25.00	1752	203
209	PAULA	JACOBS	MKT	17-MAR-1999	$15.00	3357	201
210	NANCY	HOFFMAN	SAL	16-FEB-2007	$25.00	2974	203

Oracle error message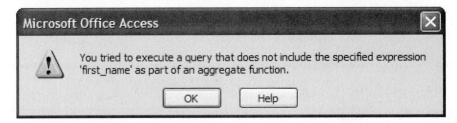

```
      FIRST_NAME,
      *
ERROR at line 2:
ORA-00979: not a GROUP BY expression
```

Access error message ❺

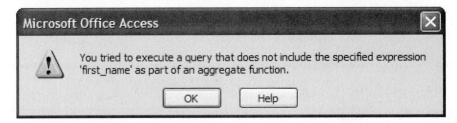

Notes

❶ The `manager_id` column is a grouping column because it is listed in the `group by` clause.

❷ The `first_name` and `last_name` columns are detail data. They are not summarized.

❸ The `maximum_credit_limit` column is summarized data because it applies a column function.

❹ In Oracle the asterisk under `first_name` indicates that this is the location of the first error. The message, "not a GROUP BY expression," is meant to suggest that you should put `first_name` in the `group by` clause.

Sometimes Oracle displays a more cryptic message, "not a single-group group function," to indicate that you are trying to mix summarized data with detail data.

❺ In Access, the error message can also be confusing.

12-6 Solution 1: Add more columns to the group by clause

This section shows one technique for dealing with the error that occurred in the SQL code of section 12-5. In this technique, all the columns of the select clause that are not column functions are placed in the group by clause.

This technique works, in the sense that it produces SQL code that runs. However, it might or might not produce the result you want. It can add many more groups to your result, which can affect the level of summarization.

In this example several new groups have been formed by adding the first_name and last_name columns to the group by clause. In fact a separate group has been created for each employee, because there are no two employees with the same name. Each of these groups has only one row, so the column function max(credit_limit) produces the same result as simply listing the credit_limit column. It is up to you to decide if this is the result you want.

Task

Show one technique to deal with the error in the SQL code of section 12-5. This technique adds more columns to the group by clause. (I highlighted the changes to the code.)

Oracle & Access SQL

```
select manager_id,
       first_name, ❶
       last_name, ❶
       max(credit_limit)
from l_employees
group by manager_id,
         first_name, ❷
         last_name ❷
order by manager_id;
```

Beginning table (1_employees table)

EMPLOYEE ID	FIRST_NAME	LAST_NAME	DEPT CODE	HIRE_DATE	CREDIT LIMIT	PHONE NUMBER	MANAGER ID
201	SUSAN	BROWN	EXE	01-JUN-1998	$30.00	3484	(null)
202	JIM	KERN	SAL	16-AUG-1999	$25.00	8722	201
203	MARTHA	WOODS	SHP	02-FEB-2009	$25.00	7591	201
204	ELLEN	OWENS	SAL	01-JUL-2008	$15.00	6830	202
205	HENRY	PERKINS	SAL	01-MAR-2006	$25.00	5286	202
206	CAROL	ROSE	ACT	(null)	(null)	(null)	(null)
207	DAN	SMITH	SHP	01-DEC-2008	$25.00	2259	203
208	FRED	CAMPBELL	SHP	01-APR-2008	$25.00	1752	203
209	PAULA	JACOBS	MKT	17-MAR-1999	$15.00	3357	201
210	NANCY	HOFFMAN	SAL	16-FEB-2007	$25.00	2974	203

Result table

MANAGER ID	FIRST_NAME	LAST_NAME	MAX(CREDIT_LIMIT)
201	JIM	KERN	25
201	MARTHA	WOODS	25
201	PAULA	JACOBS	15
202	ELLEN	OWENS	15
202	HENRY	PERKINS	25
203	DAN	SMITH	25
203	FRED	CAMPBELL	25
203	NANCY	HOFFMAN	25
(null)	CAROL	ROSE	(null)
(null)	SUSAN	BROWN	30

Notes

❶ First_name and last_name were detail data in the select statement in the previous section. Here they are summarized data because they appear in the group by clause.

❷ First_name and last_name are added to the group by clause.

12-7 Solution 2: Divide the query into two separate select statements

This section shows another technique for dealing with the error that occurred in the SQL code of section 12-5. In this technique, the query is divided into two separate select statements, one statement for summarized data and one for detail data.

In the statement for summarized data all the columns of detail data are removed from the select clause. No other clause needs to be changed. In the statement for the detail data all the column functions are removed and the group by clause is removed. This gets both of the select statements to run and produce results. Then it is up to you to decide how to put those results together to express your meaning.

Task

Show another technique to deal with the error in the SQL code of section 12-5. This technique divides the select statement into two separate select statements — one for summarized data and one for detail data.

Oracle & Access SQL: Statement 1 — For summarized data

```
select manager_id,
       max(credit_limit)
from l_employees
group by manager_id
order by manager_id;
```

Beginning table (l_employees table)

EMPLOYEE ID	FIRST_NAME	LAST_NAME	DEPT CODE	HIRE_DATE	CREDIT LIMIT	PHONE NUMBER	MANAGER ID
201	SUSAN	BROWN	EXE	01-JUN-1998	$30.00	3484	(null)
202	JIM	KERN	SAL	16-AUG-1999	$25.00	8722	201
203	MARTHA	WOODS	SHP	02-FEB-2009	$25.00	7591	201
204	ELLEN	OWENS	SAL	01-JUL-2008	$15.00	6830	202
205	HENRY	PERKINS	SAL	01-MAR-2006	$25.00	5286	202
206	CAROL	ROSE	ACT	(null)	(null)	(null)	(null)
207	DAN	SMITH	SHP	01-DEC-2008	$25.00	2259	203
208	FRED	CAMPBELL	SHP	01-APR-2008	$25.00	1752	203
209	PAULA	JACOBS	MKT	17-MAR-1999	$15.00	3357	201
210	NANCY	HOFFMAN	SAL	16-FEB-2007	$25.00	2974	203

Result table

MANAGER ID	MAX(CREDIT_LIMIT)
201	25
202	25
203	25
(null)	30

Oracle & Access SQL: Statement 2 — For detail data

```
select manager_id,
       first_name,
       last_name
from l_employees
order by manager_id;
```

Result table

```
MANAGER
     ID FIRST_NAME LAST_NAME
------- ---------- ----------
    201 JIM        KERN
    201 MARTHA     WOODS
    201 PAULA      JACOBS
    202 ELLEN      OWENS
    202 HENRY      PERKINS
    203 DAN        SMITH
    203 FRED       CAMPBELL
    203 NANCY      HOFFMAN
 (null) SUSAN      BROWN
 (null) CAROL      ROSE
```

Check your understanding

Suppose you wanted to show all the data in table `sec1202` and you also wanted to show the total for `col_3`. Could you do this with SQL?

The answer is no. The best you can do is to run two queries. One would show the data with:

```
select *
from sec1202;
```

The other would show the total with:

```
select sum(col_3) as grand_total
from sec1202;
```

Then, if you were desperate, you could paste the two pieces of paper together. Or you could do the same thing in SQL using a `union`.

Fortunately, most SQL products give you a better way. There is usually some sort of report level to the software that will do totals and subtotals for you.

12-8 How to create a report with subtotals and a grand total

A common type of report shows details and also has subtotals and a grand total. How can SQL produce a report like this? The previous sections have stated that you cannot get both detail data and summarized data from a single `select` statement, so it will take more than a single `select` statement to produce such a report.

The usual way to produce a report like this is to have SQL work together with another layer of reporting software. SQL supplies the detail data sorted in the correct order. The other layer of software takes care of the control breaks (where the subtotals are placed), the subtotals, and the grand total.

This arrangement, having SQL work together with another layer of software, goes back to the idea of using SQL as part of a back-end data server. The plan is for SQL to deal with the information level while the other layer of software deals with the presentation level.

What can you use for this other layer of software? There are many options. Oracle SQL*Plus, which is used in the SQL Command Line environment, can create a report with totals and subtotals. Access can also, using its reports. Another option is a software package called Crystal Reports.

Oracle has some special features for totals and subtotals

Oracle has developed two special functions for doing totals and subtotals on the SQL level. They are called `rollup` and `cube`. I do not explain them here because they are not part of standard SQL. If you want to find out about them you can find information in the documentation or on the Web.

12-9 Counting to zero, part 2

This is part two of a series. We want to count the number of lunches each employee will attend and list all the employees, even the two who are not attending any lunches. For those two, we want to put a zero in the `number_of_lunches` column. We will achieve this goal in chapter 14. Right now we are building up to it.

Section 11-7 is part one of this series. There we showed that the `count(column)` function is capable of counting to zero. In this part we use the `l_lunches` table and that column function to count the number of lunches for each employee who is listed in that table. This is a good first try that gets most of the answer.

When we examine the result table we see some success and also that some improvement is needed. The success is that it counts the number of lunches for the employees who are attending at least one lunch. The changes we want to make are to list the two employees who are not attending any lunches and to list the names of all the employees.

Task

From the `1_lunches` table, count the number of lunches each employee will attend.

Oracle & Access SQL

```
select employee_id,
       count(lunch_id) as number_of_lunches
from 1_lunches
group by employee_id
order by employee_id;
```

Beginning table (1_lunches table)

```
            LUNCH        EMPLOYEE
 LUNCH_ID  DATE               ID  DATE_ENTERE
---------  ------------  --------  -----------
        1  16-NOV-2011        201  13-OCT-2011
        2  16-NOV-2011        207  13-OCT-2011
        3  16-NOV-2011        203  13-OCT-2011
        4  16-NOV-2011        204  13-OCT-2011
        6  16-NOV-2011        202  13-OCT-2011
        7  16-NOV-2011        210  13-OCT-2011
        8  25-NOV-2011        201  14-OCT-2011
        9  25-NOV-2011        208  14-OCT-2011
       12  25-NOV-2011        204  14-OCT-2011
       13  25-NOV-2011        207  18-OCT-2011
       15  25-NOV-2011        205  21-OCT-2011
       16  05-DEC-2011        201  21-OCT-2011
       17  05-DEC-2011        210  21-OCT-2011
       20  05-DEC-2011        205  24-OCT-2011
       21  05-DEC-2011        203  24-OCT-2011
       22  05-DEC-2011        208  24-OCT-2011
```

Result table ❶

```
EMPLOYEE
      ID NUMBER_OF_LUNCHES
-------- -----------------
     201                 3
     202                 1
     203                 2
     204                 2
     205                 2
     207                 2
     208                 2
     210                 2
```

Notes

❶ There are no rows for employees 206 or 209.

12-10 Counting to zero, part 3

To get to the final result of this "Counting to zero" series, you need to use two techniques: summarization and outer join. Because we have talked about summarization in this chapter, I want you to see the summarization part of the solution, so for now I am giving you the outer join part. In chapter 14, I show you how to create it yourself. This outer join adds two rows to the `l_lunches` table, one for employee 206 and one for employee 209. These rows have a null in the `lunch_id` and `lunch_date` columns.

The one thing that is a bit tricky is the `group by` clause. You might think it is enough to have just the `employee_id` column in this clause because that is what really forms the groups. However, then we would be mixing summarized data (`employee_id` and `number_of_lunches`) with detail data (`first_name` and `last_name`), which we are not allowed to do.

You might say that we know that there is only one first name and one last name for each employee ID because `employee_id` is the primary key of the `l_employees` table. There is some validity to that point, but that level of intelligence is not built into SQL.

The computer does not know that there is only one first name and one last name for each employee ID, or at least it is not thinking about that fact when it processes this `select` statement. SQL requires you to put `first_name` and `last_name` into the `group by` clause. Then all the columns in the `select` clause are summarized data.

Task

Count the number of lunches each employee will attend. List the employee IDs and names of all the employees.

Oracle & Access SQL

```
select employee_id,
       first_name, ❶
       last_name, ❶
       count(lunch_id) as number_of_lunches
from sec1210
group by employee_id,
         first_name,
         last_name
order by employee_id;
```

Beginning table (sec1210)

EMPLOYEE ID	FIRST_NAME	LAST_NAME	LUNCH_ID	LUNCH DATE	
201	SUSAN	BROWN	1	16-NOV-2011	
201	SUSAN	BROWN	8	25-NOV-2011	
201	SUSAN	BROWN	16	05-DEC-2011	
202	JIM	KERN	6	16-NOV-2011	
203	MARTHA	WOODS	3	16-NOV-2011	
203	MARTHA	WOODS	21	05-DEC-2011	
204	ELLEN	OWENS	12	25-NOV-2011	
205	HENRY	PERKINS	15	25-NOV-2011	
205	HENRY	PERKINS	20	05-DEC-2011	
206	CAROL	ROSE	(null)	(null)	❷
207	DAN	SMITH	2	16-NOV-2011	
207	DAN	SMITH	4	16-NOV-2011	
207	DAN	SMITH	13	25-NOV-2011	
208	FRED	CAMPBELL	9	25-NOV-2011	
208	FRED	CAMPBELL	22	05-DEC-2011	
209	PAULA	JACOBS	(null)	(null)	❷
210	NANCY	HOFFMAN	7	16-NOV-2011	
210	NANCY	HOFFMAN	17	05-DEC-2011	

Result table

```
EMPLOYEE  FIRST       LAST
      ID  NAME        NAME        NUMBER_OF_LUNCHES
--------  ----------  ----------  ------------------
     201  SUSAN       BROWN                        3
     202  JIM         KERN                         1
     203  MARTHA      WOODS                        2
     204  ELLEN       OWENS                        2
     205  HENRY       PERKINS                      2
     206  CAROL       ROSE                         0  ❸
     207  DAN         SMITH                        2
     208  FRED        CAMPBELL                     2
     209  PAULA       JACOBS                       0  ❸
     210  NANCY       HOFFMAN                      2
```

Notes

❶ We must add the first_name and last_name to the group by clause.

❷ These new rows are created by an outer join.

❸ All the employees are shown. A zero is created for the two people who are not attending any lunches.

Eliminating Some of the Summarized Data

After data have been summarized, it is possible to eliminate some of the rows of the result. This is done with the having clause of a select statement. We might do this if we only want to see the largest categories or the most relevant portion of the data.

Often by the time data are grouped and summarized, the result table is only a few pages long and we do not object to looking at the whole thing. In that case, we do not need a having clause.

When there are many groups in the summarization, the having clause can be a convenient way to focus on the ones in which we are most interested.

12-11 The `having` clause

There is one more clause in the `select` statement that we have not yet discussed: the `having` clause. When the result table contains data that are grouped and summarized, the `having` clause can eliminate some of the groups from the result table. The groups are still formed and all the calculations and summarizations are done, but they are deleted at the end of the process.

The example in this section shows a query with a `having` clause that eliminates the foods for which fewer than 10 servings have been ordered.

For the data shown here, only a few rows are eliminated from the result table. The `having` clause is usually used with a larger amount of data. For instance, out of 100 employees, most of them would only attend one lunch. The `having` clause can help you find the few people who are attending two or more lunches. This clause is often used to find exceptions in the data.

The `having` clause is always used with a `group by` clause, but a `group by` clause is often used alone. As the following code shows, the `having` clause is written directly after the `group by` clause and before the `order by` clause.

Task

From the `1_lunch_items` table, list the supplier ID and product code (these identify a food) of all the foods for which 10 servings or more have been ordered.

Oracle & Access SQL

```
select supplier_id,
       product_code,
       sum(quantity) as total_servings
from 1_lunch_items
group by supplier_id,
         product_code
having sum(quantity) >= 10 ❶
order by supplier_id,
         product_code;
```

Beginning table (`1_lunch_items` table) ❷

```
                          SUPPLIER PRODUCT
LUNCH_ID ITEM_NUMBER ID          CODE     QUANTITY
-------- ----------- -------- ------- ---------
       1           1 ASP      FS             1
       1           2 ASP      SW             2
       1           3 JBR      VR             2
       2           1 ASP      SW             2
       2           2 FRV      FF             1
       2           3 JBR      VR             2
       2           4 VSB      AS             1
       3           1 ASP      FS             1
       3           2 CBC      GS             1
       3           3 FRV      FF             1
       3           4 JBR      VR             1
       3           5 JBR      AS             1
(and many more rows)
```

Result table before the `having` clause is applied

```
SUPPLIER PRODUCT
ID       CODE    TOTAL_SERVINGS
-------- ------- --------------
ASP      FS                   9
ASP      SP                  11
ASP      SW                   7
CBC      GS                  10
CBC      SW                   5
FRV      FF                  10
JBR      AS                  11
JBR      VR                  17
VSB      AS                   6
```

Result table after the `having` clause is applied ❸

```
SUPPLIER PRODUCT
ID       CODE    TOTAL_SERVINGS
-------- ------- --------------
ASP      SP                  11
CBC      GS                  10
FRV      FF                  10
JBR      AS                  11
JBR      VR                  17
```

Notes

❶ This is the `having` clause. You often write a column function within this clause.

❷ The rows of the beginning table are grouped and processed in the same way, as if the `having` clause were not present.

❸ The `having` clause eliminates rows from the result table.

Check your understanding

Table `sec1211` has three columns: `row_id`, `col_1`, and `col_2`. Group on `col_1` and get the sum of `col_2`. Add a `having` clause to show only the rows of the result table where the sum is greater than 20.

12-12 The `having` clause contrasted with the `where` clause

The `having` clause is similar to the `where` clause in the following ways:

1. They both eliminate data from the result table.
2. They both set conditions that some data will pass and other data will not pass.
3. A null in the data can never satisfy a condition in either a `having` clause or a `where` clause. The only exception occurs with the `is null` condition.

The `having` clause is different from the `where` clause in the following ways:

1. The `where` clause can only eliminate rows from the beginning table, the raw data, before any other processing occurs.
2. The `having` clause can eliminate data that have been grouped and summarized, after most of the processing has already taken place.
3. The `where` clause cannot use column functions in the conditions it sets.
4. The `having` clause can use column functions in its conditions.

12-13 The whole process of the `select` statement on a single table

Here is a summary of the entire process that a `select` statement describes when it operates on a single table. All six clauses of the `select` statement are shown here. This is an idealized model of the processing. The computer is allowed to use shortcuts in its processing as long as it gets the same result that this idealized model would produce.

Step 1: The `from` clause chooses the beginning table.

Step 2: The row functions are calculated. In effect, this adds new columns to the beginning table.

Step 3: The `where` clause chooses which rows of data to process from the table. Any rows that do not satisfy its condition are eliminated.

Step 4: The `select` clause chooses which columns of data to process and list in the result table. The process also includes other columns used in the `group by`, `having`, and `order by` clauses. Any other columns are eliminated.

Step 5: The `group by` clause separates the rows into different groups.

Step 6: The column functions summarize the data in each group.

Step 7: The `having` clause chooses which rows of summarized data to put in the result table.

Step 8: The `order by` clause chooses which columns are used to sort the rows of the result table for its presentation.

12-14 The `having` clause does not add any more power to the `select` statement

The `having` clause is sometimes convenient to use, but it is never required. At best it can save us one step, one SQL statement. To eliminate a `having` clause use the following procedure:

Step 1: Create a view or a table from all the data after they are grouped and summarized. Do not include the `having` clause.

Step 2: Write a `select` statement from that view. In this `select` statement a `where` clause can be used to do the same work that the `having` clause did before.

Task

Show an example of replacing a `having` clause with a two-step process. Rewrite the SQL code of section 12-11 and eliminate the `having` clause.

Oracle SQL:
Step 1 — Create a view from the grouped and summarized data

```
create or replace view sec1214_view as
select supplier_id,
       product_code,
       sum(quantity) as total_servings
from l_lunch_items
group by supplier_id,
         product_code;
```

Access SQL:
Step 1 — Create a view from the grouped and summarized data

Step 1, Part 1: Enter this `select` statement in the SQL window:

```
select supplier_id,
       product_code,
       sum(quantity) as total_servings
from l_lunch_items
group by supplier_id,
         product_code;
```

Step 1, Part 2: Save this query. Name it `sec1214_view`.

Beginning table (`l_lunch_items` table)

LUNCH_ID	ITEM_NUMBER	SUPPLIER ID	PRODUCT CODE	QUANTITY
1	1	ASP	FS	1
1	2	ASP	SW	2
1	3	JBR	VR	2
2	1	ASP	SW	2
2	2	FRV	FF	1
2	3	JBR	VR	2
2	4	VSB	AS	1
3	1	ASP	FS	1
3	2	CBC	GS	1
3	3	FRV	FF	1
3	4	JBR	VR	1
3	5	JBR	AS	1

(and many more rows)

View created by step 1

```
SUPPLIER  PRODUCT
ID        CODE     TOTAL_SERVINGS
--------  -------  --------------
ASP       FS                    9
ASP       SP                   11
ASP       SW                    7
CBC       GS                   10
CBC       SW                    5
FRV       FF                   10
JBR       AS                   11
JBR       VR                   17
VSB       AS                    6
```

Oracle & Access SQL: Step 2

```
select *
from sec1214_view
where total_servings >= 10 ❶
order by supplier_id,
         product_code;
```

Result table from step 2

```
SUPPLIER  PRODUCT
ID        CODE     TOTAL_SERVINGS
--------  -------  --------------
ASP       SP                   11
CBC       GS                   10
FRV       FF                   10
JBR       AS                   11
JBR       VR                   17
```

Notes

❶ This where clause does the same work that the having clause is doing in section 12-11

12-15　Use a where clause to eliminate raw data

Sometimes you can use either a where clause or a having clause to eliminate the data you do not want to see. When you have a choice like this, it is always better to use a where clause. This will let your query process more efficiently because the data are eliminated earlier in the process.

You should only use a having clause to eliminate data that are summarized, not raw data from the beginning table.

In theory, it should not make a difference whether we code a condition in the where clause or in the having clause. People should specify only the result. The optimizer is responsible for determining the most efficient way to obtain the result. However, optimizers are not always perfect and most do not even attempt to make a change of this type.

The code in this section shows an example of a having clause that can be replaced by a where clause.

Task

For each manager_id between 201 and 203, show the number of employees the manager supervises.

Oracle & Access SQL: Using a having clause

```
select manager_id,
       count(*)
from l_employees
group by manager_id
having manager_id between 201 and 203; ❶
```

Oracle & Access SQL:
Gets the same result more efficiently by using a where clause

```
select manager_id,
       count(*)
from l_employees
where manager_id between 201 and 203 ❷
group by manager_id;
```

Beginning table (1_employees)

EMPLOYEE ID	FIRST_NAME	LAST_NAME	DEPT CODE	HIRE_DATE	CREDIT LIMIT	PHONE NUMBER	MANAGER ID
201	SUSAN	BROWN	EXE	01-JUN-1998	$30.00	3484	(null)
202	JIM	KERN	SAL	16-AUG-1999	$25.00	8722	201
203	MARTHA	WOODS	SHP	02-FEB-2009	$25.00	7591	201
204	ELLEN	OWENS	SAL	01-JUL-2008	$15.00	6830	202
205	HENRY	PERKINS	SAL	01-MAR-2006	$25.00	5286	202
206	CAROL	ROSE	ACT	(null)	(null)	(null)	(null)
207	DAN	SMITH	SHP	01-DEC-2008	$25.00	2259	203
208	FRED	CAMPBELL	SHP	01-APR-2008	$25.00	1752	203
209	PAULA	JACOBS	MKT	17-MAR-1999	$15.00	3357	201
210	NANCY	HOFFMAN	SAL	16-FEB-2007	$25.00	2974	203

Result table — Both select statements give the same result

MANAGER ID	COUNT(*)
201	3
202	2
203	3

Notes

❶ This shows a condition limiting the data written in the having clause.

❷ This shows the same condition written in the where clause.

12-16 How to apply one column function to another column function and get around other restrictions

Some people say you cannot apply one column function to another column function. I say you can do it, but it requires a series of steps. In most SQL products it cannot be done in a single select statement.

The problem SQL in the following example does not run in either Oracle or Access. What I am trying to do in this code is to find the most popular food, the one that been ordered the most. The problem seems to be that I cannot apply the max column function to the sum column function.

To get around this restriction I will solve the problem in three steps. First, I will create a view showing the total quantity of each food item that has been ordered for the lunches. The sum column function will be used in creating this view.

In step 2, I find the maximum value in that sum column. In step 3 I find all the rows of the view I created in step 1 that have the maximum value. In this example there is only one row that has the maximum value, but in other examples there could be several rows that all have the same maximal value.

How to work around other restrictions on column functions

You might encounter other "restrictions" on what you can do with column functions. In my experience, I have been able to get around all the restrictions by just dividing the problem into two or more steps.

Task

Show how to divide the following problem SQL into a series of steps that will run. The problem area is highlighted.

Problem SQL

```
select supplier_id,
       product_code,
       max(sum(quantity))
from l_lunch_items
group by supplier_id,
         product_code,
         sum(quantity);
```

Oracle SQL: Step 1 — Create a view using one column function

```
create or replace view sec1216_view as
select supplier_id,
       product_code,
       sum(quantity) as total_quantity
from l_lunch_items
group by supplier_id,
         product_code;
```

Access SQL: Step 1 — Create a view using one column function

Step 1, Part 1: Enter this in the SQL window:

```
select supplier_id,
       product_code,
       sum(quantity) as total_quantity
from l_lunch_items
group by supplier_id,
         product_code;
```

Step 1, Part 2: Save the query. Name it `sec1216_view`.

Beginning table (`l_lunch_items` table)

```
                         SUPPLIER PRODUCT
  LUNCH_ID ITEM_NUMBER ID       CODE    QUANTITY
  -------- ----------- -------- ------- ---------
         1           1 ASP      FS             1
         1           2 ASP      SW             2
         1           3 JBR      VR             2
         2           1 ASP      SW             2
         2           2 FRV      FF             1
         2           3 JBR      VR             2
         2           4 VSB      AS             1
         3           1 ASP      FS             1
         3           2 CBC      GS             1
         3           3 FRV      FF             1
         3           4 JBR      VR             1
         3           5 JBR      AS             1

(and many more rows)
```

View created in step 1 (`sec1216_view`)

```
SUPPLIER PRODUCT
ID       CODE    TOTAL_QUANTITY
-------- ------- --------------
ASP      FS                   9
ASP      SP                  11
ASP      SW                   7
CBC      GS                  10
CBC      SW                   5
FRV      FF                  10
JBR      AS                  11
JBR      VR                  17
VSB      AS                   6
```

Oracle & Access SQL: Step 2 — Apply the other column function to the view created in step 1

```
select max(total_quantity)
from sec1216_view;
```

Result table of step 2

```
MAX(TOTAL_QUANTITY)
-------------------
                 17
```

Oracle & Access SQL: Step 3 — Finish the report

```
select supplier_id,
       product_code,
       total_quantity
from sec1216_view
where total_quantity = 17;
```

Result table of step 3

```
SUPPLIER PRODUCT
ID       CODE    TOTAL_QUANTITY
-------- ------- --------------
JBR      VR                  17
```

Key Points

- You can divide the rows of a table into several separate groups, then summarize the rows in each group. The result table will have one row for each group that is summarized.

- The table can be either a data table or a view. Each row of the table can belong to only one group.

- If a single column of the table is used to group the rows, all the nulls in that column are put into a single group. That is, all the nulls in that column are handled as if they all had the same value. This one group for all the unknown values is a true Other group.

- If two or more columns are used to group the rows, all the nulls in a single grouping column are put into a single group and handled as if they were the same, but the nulls in different columns are kept separate. This creates several different groups for the unknown values.

- A result table that contains summarized data will contain only summarized data. It cannot also contain raw data that are not summarized. However, many SQL products have reports that can do this and Oracle has the functions `rollup` and `cube` to do totals and subtotals.

- Some rows can be dropped from a result table containing summarized data. To do this you use the `having` clause of the `select` statement. This clause can be a convenience, but it does not add any more power to the `select` statement.

chapter 13

INNER JOINS

So far, we have obtained data from one table or view, sometimes adding a table of constants. In the next four chapters, we discuss seven different ways to combine two tables. On a conceptual level, the tables are combined first, which creates a single table. Then the techniques we have discussed so far are applied to get a final report from that table.

This chapter discusses inner joins, the most common way to combine two tables.

Introduction to Joins

An inner join combines the data from two or more tables. The result of this is a single table that is often quite large. The techniques you have learned in previous chapters are then used to extract a small amount of data from this large table.

An inner join used to just be called a **join** and many people still speak this way, but now the terminology is changing. **Outer joins** have become an official part of SQL. To distinguish what we used to call a join from an outer join, we now use the term **inner join**. We discuss outer joins in the next chapter.

13-1 A query can use data from several tables

Often, several different tables are used together in a `select` statement. This is necessary when the data you need do not all exist in one table or view. On a conceptual level, this process has two steps: First, the separate tables are combined into a single table. Then the `select` statement operates on this table using any of the techniques we have discussed so far.

The following diagram shows these two steps. In the first step, four separate tables of data are combined to form a single table that can be very large. It may contain several copies of the four beginning tables in different permutations and combinations. One row of any of the beginning tables can be matched with many combinations of rows from the other tables.

In the second step, a report is extracted from the single table. It gathers a few of the rows and a few of the columns of the table, applies row functions and column functions to them, and sorts the result.

The single table that combines all the data might exist only in theory. It might never be formed physically within the computer, either in memory or on the disk. It might be too large for the computer to handle. However, the final report that is produced must be the same as if this table were formed. The computer is allowed to take shortcuts in the process, as long as they do not affect the result.

The two steps shown here may be coded in SQL as a single `select` statement, or each step can be a separate `select` statement. There are many different ways to write the SQL statements, but the process is always fundamentally the same as the one shown in the following diagram.

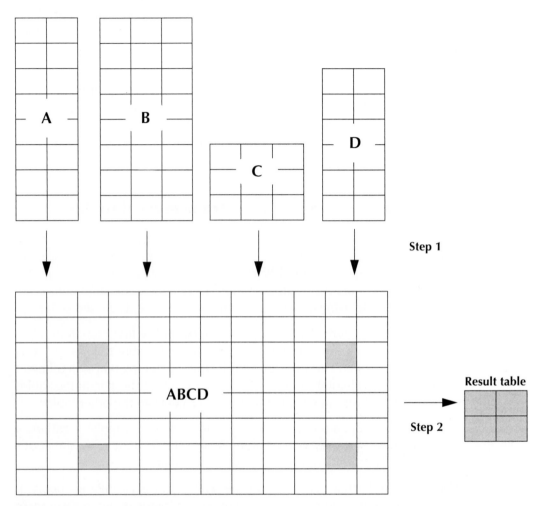

A query can use data from several tables.

In this model, in step 1 all the tables are joined at once into a single large table. Then, in step 2, we extract a small amount of information from this large table using the techniques described in the previous chapters.

13-2 The best approach is to join two tables at a time

You can combine several tables at one time, as shown in the previous section. However, this process often becomes difficult to control and it is prone to errors.

Often, the best technique is to combine the beginning tables two at a time. The first step of this process combines two of the tables and each step after that adds one additional table.

The following diagram shows this process with four beginning tables. This shows the way the SQL code can be written. Each step in the diagram is a separate SQL statement and the process is written as a series of three SQL statements, each of which creates a table or view. Creating views is usually more efficient.

Step 1a combines tables A and B. This can be coded as one `select` statement and saved as a view.

Step 1b combines the result of step 1 with table C. This can also be coded as a `select` statement and saved as a view.

Step 1c combines the result of step 2 with table D. The view this creates combines the data from all four of the beginning tables. Together, the three steps of this process are equivalent to the first step of the diagram in the previous section.

Step 2 extracts a small amount of data using all the techniques we have discussed so far.

You can understand a join of several tables as a series of steps that each join two tables at a time. The presentation in the next few chapters is focused on the process of combining just two tables.

A query can use data from several tables. In this model, in step 1 the tables are joined two at a time to form a single large table. Then, in step 2, we extract a small amount of information from this large table.

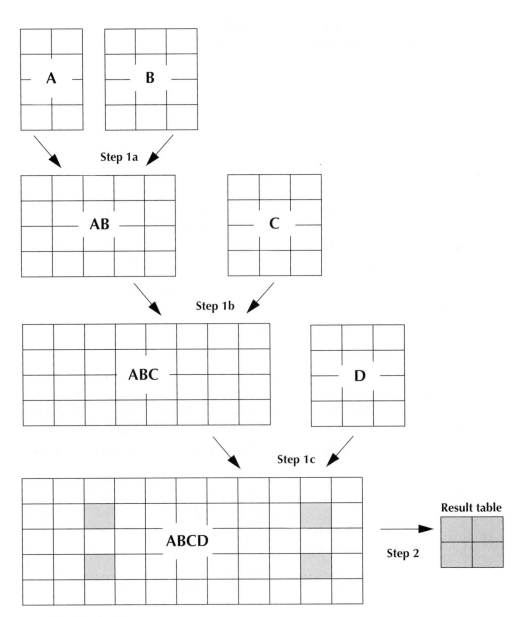

Combining tables two at a time.

Inner Joins of Two Tables

The most common way to combine two tables is with an inner join. An inner join strictly enforces the join condition. Any row without a matching row in the other table is dropped from the result. Because of this, an inner join may lose information.

13-3 A one-to-one relationship

This section shows a model case of combining two tables with an inner join. This shows the technique that is always used, but avoids the complexities, which we discuss later. For now, just focus on this simple example.

Rows from one table are matched with rows from the other table. There are no hidden links between the two tables. The data in the tables determine how to combine the rows. One column is chosen from each table. When these columns have the same value, the rows are combined.

The Data

In the example that follows, the fruit number column (f_num) is chosen from the fruits table and the color number column (c_num) is chosen from the colors table. These are sometimes called the *matching columns*. A row of the fruits table is matched with a row of the colors table when the matching columns have the same value. The apple is matched with red because both the matching columns contain a 1. The banana is matched with yellow because both matching columns contain a 2, and so on.

Each row of the fruits table matches with one and only one row of the colors table. Likewise, each row of the colors table matches with one and only one row of the fruits table. This is sometimes called a *one-to-one relationship* between the two tables. It is a special condition that can occur only when both tables have the same number of rows. (Some people use the term one-to-one relationship with a slightly different meaning, but that is another story.)

The data in the chosen columns create this relationship. The tables are seemingly being "zipped together" by the values of the data in the matching columns. Note that the color red occurs in rows 1 and 3 of the colors table. This is allowed; there is no rule that every row has to have a different value.

Task

Join the `fruits` table and the `colors` table with an inner join. Match the `f_num` column of the `fruits` table with the `c_num` column of the `colors` table. Combine a row of the `fruits` table with a row of the `colors` table when the values in these matching columns are equal. Because of the data in the beginning tables, this creates a one-to-one relationship between the two beginning tables.

Oracle & Access SQL — Explained below

```
select a.fruit,
       a.f_num,
       b.c_num,
       b.color
from sec1303_fruits a,
     sec1303_colors b
where a.f_num = b.c_num
order by a.fruit;
```

Beginning table 1 sec1303_fruits table		Relationship f_num = c_num	Beginning table 2 sec1303_colors table	
FRUIT	F_NUM		C_NUM	COLOR
----------	---------		-----	----------
APPLE	1	<-------------->	1	RED
BANANA	2	<-------------->	2	YELLOW
CHERRY	3	<-------------->	3	RED
GRAPE	4	<-------------->	4	PURPLE
ORANGE	5	<-------------->	5	ORANGE

Result table

FRUIT	F_NUM	C_NUM	COLOR
----------	---------	---------	----------
APPLE	1	1	RED
BANANA	2	2	YELLOW
CHERRY	3	3	RED
GRAPE	4	4	PURPLE
ORANGE	5	5	ORANGE

The SQL for this inner join

The SQL statement in this example needs some explanation. The `from` clause lists both beginning tables. It also assigns a ***table alias*** to each table. This is an alternative name or short name for the table, which only applies within the context of a single `select` statement. The `fruits` table is assigned the table alias a and the `colors` table is assigned the table alias b. The table alias follows the name of the table. A comma separates the entry for the first table from the one for the second table.

When table aliases have been assigned in the `from` clause, they can be used in all the other clauses of the `select` statement. When there is more than one beginning table, it is a good idea to identify the table to which each column belongs. This is done whenever the column is used throughout the `select` statement. To do this, write the table alias and a period before the name of each column. For example, in the first line of the following code, a.fruit means the `fruit` column from the `fruits` table.

The `select` clause in this code includes all the columns of both beginning tables. I want to show you how the two tables join together, which is step I in the diagram on page 476. At this time, I am not doing any selection from these data, which is step 2 in this same diagram. In section 13-16 I show how both steps can be combined in a single `select` statement.

The `where` clause contains the ***join condition***, which is a statement. When that statement is true, a row from one table is matched with a row from the other table. Here the join condition is that the fruit number (`f_num`) column of the `fruits` table is equal to the color number (`c_num`) column of the `colors` table. This is written as follows:

a.f_num = b.c_num

In every row of the result table, we see that the fruit number column has the same value as the color number column because of the join condition we have used. With a more complex join condition, they might not always have the same value.

The `order by` clause is not usually included as part of the join, but I wrote it here so that the rows of the result table would be in a logical order.

Two definitions of a one-to-one relationship — A sad story

It is very nice when a term for a fundamental concept such as a "one-to-one relationship" has a single meaning that everyone agrees on. It is sad when a term like this becomes compromised by having two different definitions.

This term was first used in mathematics to talk about sets. In mathematics, two sets have a one-to-one relationship when you can match every member of the first set with a member from the second set and vice versa. No member of either set is allowed to be unmatched.

About 100 years later, database designers decided to use this same term and give it a different meaning. In database design, unmatched rows are allowed. The only thing that is not allowed is having a row of one table matched with several rows from the other table.

What database designers really mean is a "(zero-or-one)-to-(zero-or-one) relationship," but that is a very clumsy phrase.

SQL uses both these concepts, although the context is a little different. The inner join is based on the exact matching that mathematics requires. The outer join allows for unmatched rows.

Check your understanding

Do these joins by hand, without a computer. Join a row of Table 1 with a row of Table 2 if the first letters are the same. Show all the rows of both tables, even if they do not have a matching row in the other table. Create the result table and state if this is a one-to-one relationship in the mathematical sense or in the database design sense.

1.

Table 1
Active
Busy
Crafty
Determined
Eccentric

Table 2
Cat
Dog
Ape
Eel
Bird

2.

Table 1
Active
Busy
Crafty
Determined
Eccentric

Table 2
Cat
Dog
Ape
Fish
Bird
Rabbit

13-4 A many-to-one relationship

The next five sections, including this one, all use the same SQL statement as the previous section. What differs is the data in the beginning tables. The changing data give us an opportunity to discuss other aspects of this inner join.

In this section a strawberry has now been added to the `fruits` table. The row of the `strawberry` has a 1 in the `f_num` column, which matches with the 1 in the `c_num` column for the color red.

The result shows that there is a red apple and a red strawberry. Therefore, two rows of the `fruits` table are matched with a single row of the `colors` table.

In effect, the row 1 RED is duplicated within the result table. It occurs twice in the result table, even though it occurs only once in the beginning `colors` table.

This section shows a ***many-to-one relationship*** between the two tables. Some colors are matched with many fruits. In this context, ***many*** means more than one. However, each fruit is matched with only one color.

Task

Join the `fruits` table and the `colors` table with an inner join. Use the same join condition as the previous section. The data here show a many-to-one relationship between the tables.

Oracle & Access SQL

```
select a.fruit,
       a.f_num,
       b.c_num,
       b.color
from sec1304_fruits a,
     sec1304_colors b
where a.f_num = b.c_num
order by a.fruit;
```

Beginning tables

sec1304_fruits table

```
FRUIT            F_NUM
----------   ----------
APPLE              1
BANANA             2
CHERRY             3
GRAPE              4
ORANGE             5
STRAWBERRY         1
```

sec1304_colors table

```
          C_NUM  COLOR
      ----------  ----------
           1  RED
           2  YELLOW
           3  RED
           4  PURPLE
           5  ORANGE
```

Result table

```
FRUIT            F_NUM       C_NUM  COLOR
----------   ----------  ----------  ----------
APPLE              1          1  RED
BANANA             2          2  YELLOW
CHERRY             3          3  RED
GRAPE              4          4  PURPLE
ORANGE             5          5  ORANGE
STRAWBERRY         1          1  RED
```

Check your understanding

Do this join by hand, without a computer. Join a row of Table 1 with a row of Table 2 if the first letters are the same. Create the result table and state if this is a many-to-one relationship.

Table 1
Active
Busy
Crafty
Determined
Eccentric
Blissful
Careless
Cautious
Eerie

Table 2
Cat
Dog
Ape
Eel
Bird

13-5 A one-to-many relationship

In this section the color green has been added to the `colors` table and the strawberry has been temporarily removed. The color `green` has `1` as its color number (`c_num`), which is the same as the color number value for `red`.

This is an example of a ***one-to-many relationship***. It is the same as the previous section, except the roles of the tables are reversed. Here some fruits match with many colors, although each color is matched with only one fruit.

The result table shows that the `apple` row in the beginning `fruits` table is matched with both the `red` and `green` rows of the `colors` table. This results in a red apple and a green apple. The `apple` row occurs once in the beginning tables, but twice in the result table.

This shows that inner joins are symmetric. The principles work the same way regardless of the order of the tables.

Task

Join the `fruits` table and the `colors` table with an inner join. Use the same join condition as in the previous sections.

Oracle & Access SQL

```
select a.fruit,
       a.f_num,
       b.c_num,
       b.color
from sec1305_fruits a,
     sec1305_colors b
where a.f_num = b.c_num
order by a.fruit;
```

Beginning tables

sec1305_fruits table   **sec1305_colors table**

FRUIT	F_NUM
APPLE	1
BANANA	2
CHERRY	3
GRAPE	4
ORANGE	5

C_NUM	COLOR
1	RED
1	GREEN
2	YELLOW
3	RED
4	PURPLE
5	ORANGE

Result table

FRUIT	F_NUM	C_NUM	COLOR
APPLE	1	1	RED
APPLE	1	1	GREEN
BANANA	2	2	YELLOW
CHERRY	3	3	RED
GRAPE	4	4	PURPLE
ORANGE	5	5	ORANGE

Check your understanding

Do this join by hand, without a computer. Join a row of Table 1 with a row of Table 2 if the first letters are the same. Create the result table and state if this is a one-to-many relationship.

Table 1
Active
Busy
Crafty
Determined
Eccentric

Table 2
Cat
Dog
Ape
Eel
Bird
Armadillo
Butterfly
Camel
Crocodile

13-6 A many-to-many relationship

In this section we combine the changes in the last two sections. Here we have both the strawberry in the `fruits` table and green in the `colors` table. The `strawberry` has a 1 in the fruit number (`f_num`) column and green has a 1 in the color number (`c_num`) column.

This is an example of a ***many-to-many relationship*** between the tables. Here, two fruits, the apple and the strawberry, have a 1 in the matching column of the `fruits` table. Also two colors, red and green, have a 1 in the matching column of the `colors` table.

The result table shows all the possible combinations and permutations of these matches. There is a red apple, a green apple, a red strawberry, and a green strawberry.

If there were 10 fruits and 10 colors that all matched, these would create 100 rows in the result table, so you can see that the result table can easily become very large.

Task

Join the `fruits` table and the `colors` table with an inner join. Use the same join condition as in the previous sections.

Oracle & Access SQL

```
select a.fruit,
       a.f_num,
       b.c_num,
       b.color
from sec1306_fruits a,
     sec1306_colors b
where a.f_num = b.c_num
order by a.fruit;
```

Beginning tables

sec1306_fruits table   **sec1306_colors table**

FRUIT	F_NUM
APPLE	1
BANANA	2
CHERRY	3
GRAPE	4
ORANGE	5
STRAWBERRY	1

C_NUM	COLOR
1	RED
1	GREEN
2	YELLOW
3	RED
4	PURPLE
4	GREEN
5	ORANGE

Result table ❶

FRUIT	F_NUM	C_NUM	COLOR
APPLE	1	1	RED
APPLE	1	1	GREEN
BANANA	2	2	YELLOW
CHERRY	3	3	RED
GRAPE	4	4	PURPLE
GRAPE	4	4	GREEN
ORANGE	5	5	ORANGE
STRAWBERRY	1	1	RED
STRAWBERRY	1	1	GREEN

Notes

❶ The result of a join includes all the possible combinations of rows from the first table and second table that satisfy the join condition. Here we have a red apple, a green apple, a red strawberry, and a green strawberry.

In this example I have kept the tables small. However, when you are handling larger tables, you might be surprised at the number of rows in the result table. For instance, if the beginning tables each contain 100 rows, the result table could contain 10,000 rows.

Check your understanding

Do this join by hand, without a computer. Join a row of Table 1 with a row of Table 2 if the first letters are the same. Create the result table and state if this is a many-to-many relationship.

Table 1
Active
Busy
Crafty
Determined
Eccentric
Blissful
Careless
Cautious
Eerie

Table 2
Cat
Dog
Ape
Eel
Bird
Armadillo
Butterfly
Camel
Crocodile

13-7 Unmatched rows are dropped

This section shows that rows are dropped if they do not have a matching row in the other table — they do not appear in the result table. This situation occurs whether the rows are in the first table or the second table.

The only rows that appear in the result tables are those that have a matching row in the other table. It is somewhat like a dance where you must bring your partner — singles are not allowed. This feature distinguishes an inner join. Outer joins, discussed in the next chapter, provide an alternative and restore some of the rows that have been dropped.

The inner join applies a strict interpretation to the join condition. All the rows of the result table must satisfy the join condition. This requires a matching pair of rows with one coming from each beginning table.

With an inner join, many rows from the beginning tables can be dropped, so information that is in the beginning tables may not be in the result table. That is, information may be lost. There is no warning message when this occurs.

In the beginning tables that follow, the highlighted rows are the ones dropped from the result table.

Task

Join the `fruits` table and the `colors` table with an inner join with the join condition used in the previous sections. The data here show that rows in beginning tables may not appear at all in the result table.

Oracle & Access SQL

```
select a.fruit,
       a.f_num,
       b.c_num,
       b.color
from sec1307_fruits a,
     sec1307_colors b
where a.f_num = b.c_num
order by a.fruit;
```

Beginning tables

sec1307_fruits table

FRUIT	F_NUM	
APPLE	1	
BANANA	2	
CHERRY	3	❶
GRAPE	4	❶
ORANGE	5	
STRAWBERRY	1	

sec1307_colors table

C_NUM	COLOR		
1	RED		
2	YELLOW		
1	GREEN		
5	ORANGE		
6	WHITE	3	❶

Result table

FRUIT	F_NUM	C_NUM	COLOR
APPLE	1	1	GREEN
APPLE	1	1	RED
BANANA	2	2	YELLOW
ORANGE	5	5	ORANGE
STRAWBERRY	1	1	GREEN
STRAWBERRY	1	1	RED

Notes

❶ These rows do not have a matching row in the other table, so they disappear from the result table.

13-8 Rows with a null in the matching column are dropped

This section shows a detail from the previous section. If there is a null in one of the matching columns, then the entire row that contains that null will be dropped from the result table. This is because a null can never satisfy any join condition in the where clause that combines two tables.

In the following data, the kiwi has a null in the matching column. The color brown also has a null in the matching column. The join condition says the values in the two matching columns must be equal before a pair of rows can be combined in the result table.

However, a null is an unknown value and the two nulls are not considered to be equal, so both these rows are dropped from the result table.

Task

Join the fruits table and the colors table with an inner join using the join condition from the previous sections. Note that there is no brown kiwi in the result table.

Oracle & Access SQL

```
select a.fruit,
       a.f_num,
       b.c_num,
       b.color
from sec1308_fruits a,
     sec1308_colors b
where a.f_num = b.c_num
order by a.fruit;
```

Beginning tables

sec1308_fruits table   **sec1308_colors table**

```
FRUIT          F_NUM                    C_NUM  COLOR
----------  ----------              ----------  ----------
APPLE            1                        1   RED
BANANA           2                        2   YELLOW
CHERRY           3                        3   RED
GRAPE            4                        4   PURPLE
ORANGE           5                        5   ORANGE
KIWI          (null)              (null)      BROWN
```

Result table

```
FRUIT          F_NUM       C_NUM  COLOR
----------  ----------  ----------  ----------
APPLE            1           1   RED
BANANA           2           2   YELLOW
CHERRY           3           3   RED
GRAPE            4           4   PURPLE
ORANGE           5           5   ORANGE
```

Check your understanding

Which rows from each table are unmatched and would be dropped from the inner join? Assume a row of Table 1 would be joined with a row of Table 2 if the first letters are the same.

Table 1
Active
Busy
Crafty
Determined
Eccentric
(null)

Table 2
Cat
Dog
Ape
Fly
Bird
(null)

13-9 Five ways to write the SQL for an inner join

This section shows five variations of the SQL code used in the previous sections. There is no difference in what these variations do in terms of the result tables they produce. They are just different ways to write the same code. Which one you choose is just a matter of style and what you find easiest to read and understand.

Variation 1 is the one I usually like best. Each table alias is a single letter and the names of all the columns are spelled out.

Variation 2 is similar, except that `select *` is used instead of spelling out the names of the columns. This emphasizes that all the columns from both tables are being included. It is also easier to write than variation 1 when the tables have many columns. Note that the table alias must precede the asterisk. In the `select` clause `a.*` means "all the columns of the `fruits` table" and `b.*` means "all the columns of the `colors` table."

Variation 3 uses table aliases that are longer than a single letter, allowing them to be more descriptive of the beginning table they stand for.

Variation 4 does not use table aliases. The `from` clause lists the beginning tables, but it does not assign table aliases to them. Within the other clauses of the `select` statement, the full name of each table is written before each column. So, instead of

Table_Alias.Column_Name

we write

Table_Name.Column_Name

Variation 5 also does not use any table aliases. It makes use of the fact that there is no column in the first table with exactly the same name as any column in the second table. When this is true, the computer is able to figure out which table each column belongs to, just from the column name itself, so we are not required to identify the table. The computer can understand this SQL code, but it is kinder to the other people who might read it if we identify the beginning table of each column. I always try to write my code so that both computers and people can easily understand. I do not recommend using this variation.

Task

Show the five ways of writing the SQL for the inner join used in the previous sections.

Oracle & Access SQL: Variation 1 — This is the best solution

```
select a.fruit,
       a.f_num,
       b.c_num,
       b.color
from sec1309_fruits a,
     sec1309_colors b
where a.f_num = b.c_num
order by a.fruit;
```

Oracle & Access SQL: Variation 2

```
select a.*,
       b.*
from sec1309_fruits a,
     sec1309_colors b
where a.f_num = b.c_num
order by a.fruit;
```

Oracle & Access SQL: Variation 3

```
select fru.fruit,
       fru.f_num,
       col.c_num,
       col.color
from sec1309_fruits fru,
     sec1309_colors col
where fru.f_num = col.c_num
order by fru.fruit;
```

Oracle & Access SQL: Variation 4

```
select sec1309_fruits.fruit,
       sec1309_fruits.f_num,
       sec1309_colors.c_num,
       sec1309_colors.color
from sec1309_fruits,
     sec1309_colors
where sec1309_fruits.f_num = sec1309_colors.c_num
order by sec1309_fruits.fruit;
```

Oracle & Access SQL: Variation 5
Fine for computers, confusing for people — Not recommended

```
select fruit,
       f_num,
       c_num,
       color
from sec1309_fruits,
     sec1309_colors
where f_num = c_num
order by fruit;
```

Check your understanding

Write a `select` statement to create the inner join of these tables. Join a row of Table 1 with a row of Table 2 if the first letters are the same. Write the SQL in the recommended way, using variation 1.

Sec1309_Table1
Adjective
Active
Busy
Crafty
Determined
Eccentric
(null)

Sec1309_Table2
Animal
Cat
Dog
Ape
Fly
Bird
(null)

Variations of the Join Condition

The preceding examples all showed the most common type of join condition: using just one matching column from each table and requiring the two matching columns to have the same value. This section shows examples of the many other types of inner join conditions.

13-10 A join using two or more matching columns

This section shows an example of a join condition that uses two matching columns from each table. This contrasts with the previous sections, which used a single column from each table to form the inner join. The same principle shown here can be used to join tables on any number of columns.

Here, a color is matched with a fruit only when both sets of matching columns have the same values:

fruits.f_num_1 = colors.c_num_1

and

fruits.f_num_2 = colors.c_num_2

The first row of the `fruits` table matches with the first row of the `colors` table, giving a red apple. This match occurs because the first column of each row has the value 1 and the second column of each row has the value 5. However, the first row of the `fruits` table does not match with the second row of the `colors` table. That is, no yellow apple exists because the second columns of these rows have different values — the `fruits` table has the value 5 and the `colors` table has the value 6.

Task

Join the `fruits` table and the `colors` table with an inner join. Use a join condition that matches rows when the first two columns of each table are equal.

Oracle & Access SQL

```
select  a.f_num_1, ❶
        a.f_num_2,
        a.fruit,
        b.c_num_1,
        b.c_num_2,
        b.color
from sec1310_fruits a,
     sec1310_colors b
where a.f_num_1 = b.c_num_1 ❷
  and a.f_num_2 = b.c_num_2
order by a.fruit; ❸
```

Beginning tables
sec1310_fruits table   **sec1310_colors table**

F_NUM_1	F_NUM_2	FRUIT
1	5	APPLE
1	6	BANANA
2	5	CHERRY
2	6	GRAPE
2	7	ORANGE

C_NUM_1	C_NUM_2	COLOR
1	5	RED
1	6	YELLOW
2	5	RED
2	6	PURPLE
2	7	ORANGE

Result table

F_NUM_1	F_NUM_2	FRUIT	C_NUM_1	C_NUM_2	COLOR
1	5	APPLE	1	5	RED
1	6	BANANA	1	6	YELLOW
2	5	CHERRY	2	5	RED
2	6	GRAPE	2	6	PURPLE
2	7	ORANGE	2	7	ORANGE

Notes

❶ All the columns are listed from both tables.

❷ The join condition is written in the where clause. Here there are two conditions combined together with the word and.

❸ The order by clause is not really part of the join, but it is included here to make the result table easier to read.

Check your understanding

Write a select statement to create the inner join of tables sec1310_table1 and sec1310_table2. The join condition should say that the first three columns of these tables are equal.

13-11 A join using between to match on a range of values

This section shows an example of using the between condition in a join, rather than a condition of equality. Three columns are involved in this join condition, and the value in one column must lie between the values in the other two.

In this example, test scores between 90 and 100 get an A, those between 80 and 89 get a B, and so on. The grade ranges must not overlap.

Task

Assign grades to students by placing their individual test scores within one of the grading ranges.

Oracle & Access SQL

```
select a.student_name, ❶
       a.test_score,
       b.letter_grade
from sec1311_student_scores a,
     sec1311_grade_ranges b
where a.test_score between b.beginning_score
                      and b.ending_score ❷
order by a.student_name; ❸
```

Beginning tables

sec1311_student_scores table

STUDENT_NAME	TEST_SCORE
CATHY	85
FRED	60
JOHN	95
MEG	92

sec1311_grade_ranges table ❹

BEGINNING SCORE	ENDING SCORE	LETTER GRADE
90	100	A
80	89	B
70	79	C
60	69	D
0	59	F

Result table

STUDENT_NAME	TEST_SCORE	LETTER_GRADE
CATHY	85	B
FRED	60	D
JOHN	95	A
MEG	92	A

Notes

❶ Here, only three columns are listed in the select clause because that is enough to understand this join and that is all I wanted in the result.

❷ The join condition is written in the where clause. Note that this condition uses between. The test score is placed between the beginning score and the ending score.

❸ The order by clause makes the result table easier to read. It is not part of the join.

❹ You must set up the grade ranges so there are no overlaps. Each score must correspond to only one letter grade.

Check your understanding

A large dictionary has four volumes. Table `sec1311_dictionary` shows the range of words that are in each volume. Table `sec1311_words` contains some words that are in the dictionary. Write SQL to determine which volume of the dictionary contains each of these words.

13-12 A join using the Greater Than condition

This section shows an example of using a *Greater Than* condition to form a join, rather than an equality. Variations of this type of join can use:

- Less Than
- Less Than or Equal to
- Greater Than or Equal to

In this example, each row of one table is paired with many rows of the other table. For example, row 6 from the `bigger_numbers` table is matched with rows 1 to 5 from the `smaller_numbers` table.

Task

Join the `bigger_numbers` table with the `smaller_numbers` table. Create a join condition that pairs each bigger number with all the smaller numbers that are less than it.

Oracle & Access SQL

```
select a.*,  ❶
       b.*
from sec1312_bigger_numbers a,
     sec1312_smaller_numbers b
where a.larger_number > b.smaller_number  ❷
order by a.larger_number,  ❸
         b.smaller_number;
```

Beginning tables

sec1312_bigger_numbers table

```
LARGER_NUMBER  WORD
-------------  ---------------
            1  ONE
            2  TWO
            3  THREE
            4  FOUR
            5  FIVE
            6  SIX      ❹
```

sec1312_smaller_numbers table

```
SMALLER_NUMBER  WORD
--------------  ---------------
             1  ONE
             2  TWO
             3  THREE
             4  FOUR
             5  FIVE
             6  SIX
```

Result table

```
LARGER_NUMBER  WORD             SMALLER_NUMBER  WORD
-------------  ---------------  --------------  ---------------
            2  TWO                           1  ONE
            3  THREE                         1  ONE
            3  THREE                         2  TWO
            4  FOUR                          1  ONE
            4  FOUR                          2  TWO
            4  FOUR                          3  THREE
            5  FIVE                          1  ONE
            5  FIVE                          2  TWO
            5  FIVE                          3  THREE
            5  FIVE                          4  FOUR
            6  SIX                           1  ONE     ❹
            6  SIX                           2  TWO     ❹
            6  SIX                           3  THREE   ❹
            6  SIX                           4  FOUR    ❹
            6  SIX                           5  FIVE    ❹
```

Notes

❶ All the columns are listed from both tables.

❷ The `where` clause contains the join condition, which says that one column is greater than another column.

❸ The `order by` clause makes the result table easier to read.

❹ The one row, 6, in the `bigger_numbers` table, combines with each row of the `smaller_numbers` table and generates five rows within the result table.

Check your understanding

List all the letters that are greater than S. Use the `alphabet` table. Put these letters in order.

13-13 A join using a row function

This section shows a row function being used to create a join condition. In the following example, the values of two columns are added together. Each of the beginning tables contains one of these columns. Rows from the two beginning tables are joined together whenever the sum is equal to six.

Oracle & Access SQL

```
select a.fruit,
       a.f_num,
       b.c_num,
       b.color
from sec1313_fruits a,
     sec1313_colors b
where a.f_num + b.c_num = 6
order by a.fruit;
```

Beginning tables

sec1313_fruits table

FRUIT	F_NUM
APPLE	1
BANANA	2
CHERRY	3
GRAPE	4
ORANGE	5
STRAWBERRY	1

sec1313_colors table

C_NUM	COLOR
1	RED
1	GREEN
2	YELLOW
3	RED
4	PURPLE
4	GREEN
5	ORANGE

Result table

FRUIT	F_NUM	C_NUM	COLOR
APPLE	1	5	ORANGE
BANANA	2	4	PURPLE
BANANA	2	4	GREEN
CHERRY	3	3	RED
GRAPE	4	2	YELLOW
ORANGE	5	1	RED
ORANGE	5	1	GREEN
STRAWBERRY	1	5	ORANGE

Check your understanding

Tables `sec1313_words1` and `sec1313_words2` contains words. Join these tables together when the words end in the same letter.

13-14 Writing the join condition in the `from` clause

This section shows a newer way of writing the join of the `fruits` table with the `colors` table. This method of writing a join is part of the new SQL standard, called SQL-92. This syntax places the join condition within the `from` clause, rather than in the `where` clause. The older syntax is still valid, and will remain valid in the future. Access and Oracle support this newer syntax.

The newer syntax writes the join condition in an `on` clause within the `from` clause. This allows the `where` clause to be focused on the rows of data we want to use for the final report. It does not need to handle the join condition.

There is no comma after the `a`, which is the table alias for the first table. Instead of a comma, the words `inner join` are placed between the two tables.

Task

Show the syntax for joining two tables in the `from` clause. Join the `fruits` table and the `colors` table as we have done before.

Oracle & Access SQL: Older syntax

```
select a.fruit,
       a.f_num,
       b.c_num,
       b.color
from sec1314_fruits a,   ❶
     sec1314_colors b
where a.f_num = b.c_num   ❷
order by a.fruit;
```

Oracle & Access SQL: Newer syntax

```
select a.fruit,
       a.f_num,
       b.c_num,
       b.color
from sec1314_fruits a    ❸
     inner join sec1314_colors b
     on a.f_num = b.c_num   ❹
order by a.fruit;
```

Beginning tables
sec1314_fruits table   **sec1314_colors table**

```
FRUIT           F_NUM                 C_NUM  COLOR
----------      ---------             ---------  ----------
APPLE               1                     1  RED
BANANA              2                     1  GREEN
CHERRY              3                     2  YELLOW
GRAPE               4                     3  RED
ORANGE              5                     4  PURPLE
STRAWBERRY          1                     4  GREEN
                                          5  ORANGE
```

Result table

```
FRUIT           F_NUM      C_NUM  COLOR
----------      ---------  ---------  ----------
APPLE               1          1  RED
APPLE               1          1  GREEN
BANANA              2          2  YELLOW
CHERRY              3          3  RED
GRAPE               4          4  PURPLE
GRAPE               4          4  GREEN
ORANGE              5          5  ORANGE
STRAWBERRY          1          1  RED
STRAWBERRY          1          1  GREEN
```

Notes

❶ The `from` clause lists the tables and assigns aliases (short names) to the tables. There is a comma between the names of the tables.

❷ The join condition is written in the `where` clause.

❸ The `from` clause specifies that this is an inner join, in addition to listing the tables and assigning the aliases. There is no comma between the names of the tables.

❹ The join condition is written within the `from` clause. The word `on` precedes the join condition.

Check your understanding

Change this SQL, writing the join condition in the `from` clause.

```
select a.student_name,
       a.test_score,
       b.letter_grade
from sec1311_student_scores a,
     sec1311_grade_ranges b
where a.test_score between b.beginning_score
                      and b.ending_score
order by a.student_name;
```

Applications of Joins

Now let's look at a few applications of inner joins.

13-15 Lookup tables

A *lookup table* is also known as a ***table of codes***. It is a table that contains a set of codes and their meanings. In the `Lunches` database, the `l_departments` table is a lookup table because it contains a row for each valid department code and the full name of that department. Because this is a typical lookup table, let's look at it while I explain more about this type of table.

An example of a lookup table (`l_departments` table)

```
DEPT
CODE  DEPARTMENT_NAME
----  -------------------
ACT   ACCOUNTING
EXE   EXECUTIVE
MKT   MARKETING
PER   PERSONNEL
SAL   SALES
SHP   SHIPPING
```

A lookup table often has only two columns: a column of the codes and a column of their meanings. There can be additional columns of information that, when present, contain further information about the code. For example in the `l_departments` table, additional columns could include department budget, department staff level, or department manager.

The column of codes is the primary key of the table. This column contains a row for each code that is a valid value. Referential integrity, a form of data validation, is set up between the lookup table and any other table that uses the code. In this example, the first column, `dept_code`, of the `l_departments` table is the list of all the valid values of the department code.

The `l_employees` table also contains a `dept_code` column, and a data validation rule is applied to that column. Whenever a new row is inserted into the `l_employees` table, the value in the `dept_code` column must be one of the valid values. Otherwise the row is rejected and we get an error message.

The same data validation rule also applies to updates. In a row that already exists in the `l_employees` table, we can change the value of the `dept_code` column to any valid value. If we try to change it to an invalid value, the update is rejected and we get an error message.

There is a many-to-one relationship between a lookup table and another table that makes use of its codes. In our example, a code can occur only once in the `l_departments` table, which is the lookup table, but the code can occur many times in the `l_employees` table, which uses the codes.

Lookup tables are often used in database design to make the database self-documenting. The very large tables in a database use codes to save disk space and to validate the data. The lookup tables provide the meanings of those codes and a complete list of all their valid values.

Inner joins and lookup tables

An inner join can be used to look up the meanings of the codes from a lookup table. The following example shows the department name for each employee. The `l_employees` table contains only the `dept_code` column. The `department_name` column is looked up from the `l_departments` table.

When we use an inner join we must remember that some of the rows of data could be dropped. We need to sit down and analyze this in detail to see if anything important may have been lost. In the following example, we want all the employees to appear in the result table. An employee will be dropped if there is no matching row in the `l_departments` table. In this example, no employees are dropped because the `dept_code` column of the `l_employees` table:

1. Has Referential integrity with the `l_departments` table.

2. Contains no nulls.

Referential integrity assures us that every value within the dept_code column of the 1_employees table has a matching row in the 1_departments table, so no employee will be dropped.

Task

For each employee show the employee_id, first_name, last_name, dept_code, and department_name. Sort the rows by the employee_id. Use an inner join to get the department_name from the 1_departments table.

Oracle & Access SQL

```
select a.employee_id,
       a.first_name,
       a.last_name,
       a.dept_code,
       b.department_name
from 1_employees a,
     1_departments b
where a.dept_code = b.dept_code
order by a.employee_id;
```

Beginning table 1 (1_employees table)

EMPLOYEE ID	FIRST_NAME	LAST_NAME	DEPT CODE	HIRE_DATE	CREDIT LIMIT	PHONE NUMBER	MANAGER ID
201	SUSAN	BROWN	EXE	01-JUN-1998	$30.00	3484	(null)
202	JIM	KERN	SAL	16-AUG-1999	$25.00	8722	201
203	MARTHA	WOODS	SHP	02-FEB-2009	$25.00	7591	201
204	ELLEN	OWENS	SAL	01-JUL-2008	$15.00	6830	202
205	HENRY	PERKINS	SAL	01-MAR-2006	$25.00	5286	202
206	CAROL	ROSE	ACT	(null)	(null)	(null)	(null)
207	DAN	SMITH	SHP	01-DEC-2008	$25.00	2259	203
208	FRED	CAMPBELL	SHP	01-APR-2008	$25.00	1752	203
209	PAULA	JACOBS	MKT	17-MAR-1999	$15.00	3357	201
210	NANCY	HOFFMAN	SAL	16-FEB-2007	$25.00	2974	203

Beginning table 2 (`1_departments` table)

```
DEPT
CODE DEPARTMENT_NAME
---- ----------------
ACT  ACCOUNTING
EXE  EXECUTIVE
MKT  MARKETING
PER  PERSONNEL
SAL  SALES
SHP  SHIPPING
```

Result table

```
EMPLOYEE                            DEPT
      ID FIRST_NAME LAST_NAME       CODE DEPARTMENT_NAME
-------- ---------- ----------      ---- ----------------
     201 SUSAN      BROWN           EXE  EXECUTIVE
     202 JIM        KERN            SAL  SALES
     203 MARTHA     WOODS           SHP  SHIPPING
     204 ELLEN      OWENS           SAL  SALES
     205 HENRY      PERKINS         SAL  SALES
     206 CAROL      ROSE            ACT  ACCOUNTING
     207 DAN        SMITH           SHP  SHIPPING
     208 FRED       CAMPBELL        SHP  SHIPPING
     209 PAULA      JACOBS          MKT  MARKETING
     210 NANCY      HOFFMAN         SAL  SALES
```

Check your understanding

Write a `select` statement to list all the foods on the lunch menu and show the full name of the supplier of each food.

13-16 Combining a join and selection of data

The SQL code in section 13-15 combined the inner join and the selection of data from that join. A `select` statement often does both of these things.

Now, I want to show you that there are two steps going on here, even though we wrote only one SQL statement. The first step forms the inner join of the `1_employees` table and the `1_departments` table. This creates a table or view that contains all the columns of both tables: eight columns from the `1_employees` table and two from the `1_departments` table, for a total of 10 columns.

In the second step only part of those data are selected to be in the result table. In this case, five of the columns are retained and the other five are dropped.

Each of these steps can have a `where` clause. In step 1 the `where` clause is the join condition used to combine the two tables. In step 2 the `where` clause selects the rows we want to appear in the result table. When both steps are combined into a single `select` statement, the `where` clause performs both of these roles.

Task

Modify the SQL in section 13-15 so that only employees 201 to 205 appear in the result table. This is an example of a `where` clause that performs two roles.

Then rewrite this SQL to show the two separate steps: the inner join and the selection of data.

Oracle & Access SQL: The `where` clause performs two functions

```
select a.employee_id,
       a.first_name,
       a.last_name,
       a.dept_code,
       b.department_name
from 1_employees a,
     1_departments b
where a.dept_code = b.dept_code ❶
  and a.employee_id < 206 ❷
order by a.employee_id;
```

The `where` clause performs two functions:

- It joins several beginning tables together into one combined table
- It selects some rows of the combined table and rejects other rows

Oracle SQL: Step 1 — Create the inner join of the tables

```
create or replace view sec1316_view as
select a.*,
       b.dept_code as dept_code2,
       b.department_name
from 1_employees a,
     1_departments b
where a.dept_code = b.dept_code; ❸
```

Access SQL: Step 1 — Create the inner join of the tables

Step 1, Part 1: Enter this query in the SQL window:

```
select a.*,
       b.dept_code as dept_code2,
       b.department_name
from 1_employees a,
     1_departments b
where a.dept_code = b.dept_code; ❸
```

Step 1, Part 2: Save the query. Name it `sec1316_view`.

Step 1 result table (`sec1316_view`)

EMPLOYEE ID	FIRST_NAME	LAST_NAME	DEPT CODE	HIRE_DATE	CREDIT LIMIT	PHONE NUMBER	MANAGER ID	DEP	DEPARTMENT NAME
201	SUSAN	BROWN	EXE	01-JUN-1998	$30.00	3484	(null)	EXE	EXECUTIVE
202	JIM	KERN	SAL	16-AUG-1999	$25.00	8722	201	SAL	SALES
203	MARTHA	WOODS	SHP	02-FEB-2009	$25.00	7591	201	SHP	SHIPPING
204	ELLEN	OWENS	SAL	01-JUL-2008	$15.00	6830	202	SAL	SALES
205	HENRY	PERKINS	SAL	01-MAR-2006	$25.00	5286	202	SAL	SALES
206	CAROL	ROSE	ACT	(null)	(null)	(null)	(null)	ACT	ACCOUNTING
207	DAN	SMITH	SHP	01-DEC-2008	$25.00	2259	203	SHP	SHIPPING
208	FRED	CAMPBELL	SHP	01-APR-2008	$25.00	1752	203	SHP	SHIPPING
209	PAULA	JACOBS	MKT	17-MAR-1999	$15.00	3357	201	MKT	MARKETING
210	NANCY	HOFFMAN	SAL	16-FEB-2007	$25.00	2974	203	SAL	SALES

Oracle & Access SQL:
Step 2 — Select part of the data from the `sec1316_view`

```
select employee_id,
       first_name,
       last_name,
       dept_code,
       department_name
from sec1316_view
where employee_id < 206 ❹
order by employee_id;
```

Step 2 result table

```
EMPLOYEE                        DEPT
     ID FIRST_NAME LAST_NAME   CODE DEPARTMENT_NAME
-------- ---------- ---------- ---- ----------------
    201 SUSAN      BROWN       EXE  EXECUTIVE
    202 JIM        KERN        SAL  SALES
    203 MARTHA     WOODS       SHP  SHIPPING
    204 ELLEN      OWENS       SAL  SALES
    205 HENRY      PERKINS     SAL  SALES
```

Notes

❶ This is the join condition. It refers to both tables.

❷ This is a selection condition. It refers to only one table.

❸ In step 1, this is the join condition. It combines the two tables.

❹ In step 2, this is the selection condition. It selects the rows for the result table.

Check your understanding

Demonstrate that a `select` statement can be separated into two parts: The first part joins the tables and creates a new table, and the second part restricts the amount of data that is shown. For the following `select` statement, write two SQL statements to separate these two steps.

```
select a.description,
       b.supplier_name
from l_foods a,
     l_suppliers b
where a.supplier_id = b.supplier_id
order by a.description;
```

13-17 Using a join with summarization

The example in this section shows all six clauses of the `select` statement and an inner join, all working together. The `where` clause contains a join condition and also a condition that selects the data for the result table. The `group by` clause needs to contain three columns of data to make every column a summarized column.

Task

List all the employees who are attending more than one lunch, except employee 208. Show the following columns: employee_id, first_name, last_name, and number_of_lunches.

Oracle & Access SQL

```
select a.employee_id,
       a.first_name,
       a.last_name,
       count(*) as number_of_lunches
from l_employees a,
     l_lunches b
where a.employee_id = b.employee_id
  and not (a.employee_id = 208)
group by a.employee_id,
         a.first_name,
         a.last_name
having count(*) > 1
order by a.employee_id;
```

Result table

```
EMPLOYEE
      ID FIRST_NAME LAST_NAME  NUMBER_OF_LUNCHES
-------- ---------- ---------- -----------------
     201 SUSAN      BROWN                      3
     203 MARTHA     WOODS                      2
     204 ELLEN      OWENS                      2
     205 HENRY      PERKINS                    2
     207 DAN        SMITH                      2
     210 NANCY      HOFFMAN                    2
```

Check your understanding

List all the foods on the menu and the total number of orders for each food item. Note that broccoli does not show up in the result because no one has ordered it.

13-18 How to find the primary key in the Oracle Data Dictionary

In section 5-15 I showed you how to find the columns of the primary key of a table using two steps. I promised to show you how to do it in a single step, and now that you understand an inner join I can fulfill that promise.

Task

Find all the columns in the primary key of the `l_foods` table.

Oracle SQL: Two-step method

Step 1:

```
select table_name,
       constraint_type,
       constraint_name
from user_constraints
where table_name = 'L_FOODS';
```

Step 2:

```
select *
from user_cons_columns
where table_name = 'L_FOODS';
```

Oracle SQL: One-step method using an inner join

```
select b.column_name,
       b.position
from user_constraints a, ❶
     user_cons_columns b
where a.table_name = b.table_name ❷
  and a.constraint_name = b.constraint_name
  and a.table_name = 'L_FOODS' ❸
  and a.constraint_type = 'P'; ❹
order by b.position;
```

Result table ❺

COLUMN_NAME	POSITION
SUPPLIER_ID	1
PRODUCT_CODE	2

Notes

❶ Both Data Dictionary tables are used in the `from` clause.

❷ The first two lines of the `where` clause join the two tables.

❸ This line gives the name of the table. We want to find whether this table has a primary key. If so, this code will show which columns are part of that key.

❹ A constraint type of `'p'` is a primary key constraint. The other values of this column are:

   `r` — Referential integrity constraint

   `u` — Uniqueness constraint

   `c` — Check constraint

❺ The primary key of the `l_foods` table has these two columns in this order.

13-19 Combining three or more tables with inner joins

You can combine three or more tables with inner joins. You can join several tables together all at the same time, as I do in this section, or you can join the tables together two at a time in a series of steps.

When you combine several tables at once, the `where` clause can become quite long and complex. You must be sure to put all the join conditions into the `where` clause and relate each table to every other table.

When you combine several tables together with inner joins, you need to keep in mind that some of the information from the beginning tables may be dropped. The rows of the result table will only be the perfectly matched combinations of rows from all the beginning tables. In other words, if four tables are being joined, a matching row from each of those four tables is required to produce one row in the result table. If any of these rows is missing, data will be dropped.

Sometimes that is not a problem, because that is exactly what you want to happen. At other times, it is a problem.

Task

Show information about all the lunches ordered by people in the shipping department. Show the employee ID, names of the employees, the lunch date, and the descriptions and quantities of the foods they will eat. Sort the result by the `employee_id` and the `lunch_date` columns. To do this you need to join four tables.

Oracle & Access SQL

```
select a.employee_id,
       a.first_name,
       a.last_name,
       b.lunch_date,
       d.description,
       c.quantity
from l_employees a, ❶
     l_lunches b,
     l_lunch_items c,
     l_foods d
where a.employee_id = b.employee_id ❷
  and b.lunch_id = c.lunch_id
  and c.supplier_id = d.supplier_id
  and c.product_code = d.product_code
  and a.dept_code = 'SHP' ❸
order by a.employee_id,
         b.lunch_date;
```

Result table

EMPLOYEE ID	FIRST NAME	LAST NAME	LUNCH DATE	DESCRIPTION	QUANTITY
203	MARTHA	WOODS	16-NOV-2011	FRESH SALAD	1
203	MARTHA	WOODS	16-NOV-2011	GRILLED STEAK	1
203	MARTHA	WOODS	16-NOV-2011	COFFEE	1
203	MARTHA	WOODS	16-NOV-2011	SODA	1
203	MARTHA	WOODS	16-NOV-2011	FRENCH FRIES	1
203	MARTHA	WOODS	05-DEC-2011	SOUP OF THE DAY	1
203	MARTHA	WOODS	05-DEC-2011	DESSERT	1
203	MARTHA	WOODS	05-DEC-2011	COFFEE	2
203	MARTHA	WOODS	05-DEC-2011	GRILLED STEAK	1
207	DAN	SMITH	16-NOV-2011	SANDWICH	2
207	DAN	SMITH	16-NOV-2011	FRENCH FRIES	1
207	DAN	SMITH	16-NOV-2011	COFFEE	2
207	DAN	SMITH	16-NOV-2011	DESSERT	1
207	DAN	SMITH	25-NOV-2011	SOUP OF THE DAY	2
207	DAN	SMITH	25-NOV-2011	SANDWICH	2
207	DAN	SMITH	25-NOV-2011	SODA	1
207	DAN	SMITH	25-NOV-2011	FRENCH FRIES	1
208	FRED	CAMPBELL	25-NOV-2011	FRESH SALAD	1
208	FRED	CAMPBELL	25-NOV-2011	SOUP OF THE DAY	1
208	FRED	CAMPBELL	25-NOV-2011	HAMBURGER	2
208	FRED	CAMPBELL	25-NOV-2011	FRENCH FRIES	1
208	FRED	CAMPBELL	25-NOV-2011	COFFEE	1
208	FRED	CAMPBELL	25-NOV-2011	SODA	1
208	FRED	CAMPBELL	05-DEC-2011	FRESH SALAD	1
208	FRED	CAMPBELL	05-DEC-2011	GRILLED STEAK	1
208	FRED	CAMPBELL	05-DEC-2011	FRENCH FRIES	1
208	FRED	CAMPBELL	05-DEC-2011	COFFEE	1
208	FRED	CAMPBELL	05-DEC-2011	SODA	1

Notes

❶ The `from` clause must list all the tables being joined, even if no column from the table appears in the `select` clause.

❷ The first four lines of the `where` clause make up the join condition that relates each table to all of the other tables.

❸ The last line of the `where` clause limits the data that appear in the final result table. It is not part of the join condition.

Check your understanding

Join all the tables of the `lunches` database together. Show all the columns of each table. To do this, modify the `select` statement in this section and add the three other tables to it. How many rows and columns are in this table?

Key Points

- You can write a `select` statement that uses data from several tables. When you are joining the tables, first the tables are combined together to form a new larger table. Then data are selected or summarized from this new table. Inside the computer, SQL is allowed to use shortcuts to get to the result more efficiently, but the result must be the same as if the steps had been done in this order.

- The inner join is the most frequently used method to combine several tables together. Other methods include outer joins and unions. These are presented in the next two chapters.

- When you are combining more than two tables, the best approach is to join only two tables at a time. You can repeat this process to combine as many tables as you want.

- The join condition is the rule that is used to match rows of one table with rows of another table. It can be written in either the `from` clause or the `where` clause. Often a database is designed so that its tables are joined together in certain fixed ways.

- Unmatched rows are always dropped from an inner join. This can cause a loss of information in the result. This is an important issue to be aware of.

- When you are combining several tables together, if a row from one table does not have a match in just one of the other tables, that row will be dropped from the result. Therefore, the more tables you combine with an inner join, the greater the potential for lost information.

- Lookup tables are often used in database design to show the meaning of codes and other standardized information. When you are using a lookup table, there should be no possibility of unmatched rows or lost information.

chapter 14

OUTER JOINS

An inner join may drop some of the rows from the beginning tables. An outer join puts back some of those rows. There are three types of outer joins, each type adding back a different set of the dropped rows.

Introduction to Outer Joins

Inner joins often drop some of the rows of the beginning tables if they do not have a matching row in the other table. If we want to keep these unmatched rows instead of dropping them, we need to use an outer join.

14-1 Outer joins are derived from inner joins

An outer join is derived from an inner join by adding back some of the rows that the inner join dropped from the beginning tables. Each of the three types of outer joins adds back a different set of rows. However, all three types of outer joins begin by forming the inner join.

Most of this discussion of outer joins is based on two tables named `twos` and `threes`. The `twos` table contains a column of numbers that consists of all the multiples of two up to 20, with the addition of one null. This table also contains a column of words that describe the numbers and the null.

The `threes` table is similar, except that it contains the multiples of three up to 20. The joins will be done on the columns of numbers. The columns of words are there to show that the tables have columns other than those used in the joins. Often, many such columns exist. We always join these tables on the columns of numbers, matching the number column from the `twos` table with the number column from the `threes` table.

In both tables, the number column contains a null and the word column for that row does not contain a null. It contains a word with four letters: N, U, L, and L. These are meant to be a description of what is in the number column.

The inner join of these tables contains three rows — 6, 12, and 18. All the other rows of the beginning tables are dropped from the result table.

Task

Show the inner join of the `twos` table and the `threes` table. Make a list of the rows of the beginning tables that are dropped from the result table.

Oracle & Access SQL

```
select a.*,
       b.*
from twos a,
     threes b
where a.number_2 = b.number_3
order by a.number_2;
```

Beginning tables

twos table

```
NUMBER_2 WORD_2
-------- ---------------
       2 TWO
       4 FOUR
       6 SIX
       8 EIGHT
      10 TEN
      12 TWELVE
      14 FOURTEEN
      16 SIXTEEN
      18 EIGHTEEN
      20 TWENTY
(null)    NULL
```

threes table

```
NUMBER_3 WORD_3
-------- ---------------
       3 THREE
       6 SIX
       9 NINE
      12 TWELVE
      15 FIFTEEN
      18 EIGHTEEN
(null)    NULL
```

Result table (inner join)

```
NUMBER_2 WORD_2            NUMBER_3 WORD_3
-------- --------------- -------- --------------
       6 SIX                    6 SIX
      12 TWELVE                12 TWELVE
      18 EIGHTEEN              18 EIGHTEEN
```

Rows dropped from the twos table

```
NUMBER_2      WORD_2
------------ ---------------
           2 TWO
           4 FOUR
           8 EIGHT
          10 TEN
          14 FOURTEEN
          16 SIXTEEN
          20 TWENTY
(null)        NULL
```

Rows dropped from the threes table

```
NUMBER_3      WORD_3
------------ ---------------
           3 THREE
           9 NINE
          15 FIFTEEN
(null)        NULL
```

14-2 The three types of outer joins

There are three types of outer joins: the left outer join, the right outer join, and the full outer join. They all begin with the inner join, and then they add back some of the rows that have been dropped.

The left outer join adds back all the rows that are dropped from the first table. Nulls are placed in the columns that come from the other table. For instance, in the first row of the following table, the row 2 TWO is added back to the result table. The columns for the matching row of the threes table, number_3 and word_3, are set to null.

The right outer join adds back all the rows that are dropped from the second table. In all the rows that are added back, the columns for the matching rows of the twos table are set to null.

The full outer join adds back all the rows dropped from both tables.

Task

For the twos table and the threes table, show the results of the three types of outer joins.

Result table — Left outer join (has all the rows from the first table)

NUMBER_2	WORD_2	NUMBER_3	WORD_3
2	TWO	(null)	(null)
4	FOUR	(null)	(null)
6	SIX	6	SIX
8	EIGHT	(null)	(null)
10	TEN	(null)	(null)
12	TWELVE	12	TWELVE
14	FOURTEEN	(null)	(null)
16	SIXTEEN	(null)	(null)
18	EIGHTEEN	18	EIGHTEEN
20	TWENTY	(null)	(null)
(null)	NULL	(null)	(null)

Result table — Right outer join (has all the rows from the second table)

NUMBER_2	WORD_2	NUMBER_3	WORD_3
(null)	(null)	3	THREE
6	SIX	6	SIX
(null)	(null)	9	NINE
12	TWELVE	12	TWELVE
(null)	(null)	15	FIFTEEN
18	EIGHTEEN	18	EIGHTEEN
(null)	(null)	(null)	NULL

Result table — Full outer join (has all the rows from both tables)

NUMBER_2	WORD_2	NUMBER_3	WORD_3
2	TWO	(null)	(null)
(null)	(null)	3	THREE
4	FOUR	(null)	(null)
6	SIX	6	SIX
8	EIGHT	(null)	(null)
(null)	(null)	9	NINE
10	TEN	(null)	(null)
12	TWELVE	12	TWELVE
14	FOURTEEN	(null)	(null)
(null)	(null)	15	FIFTEEN
16	SIXTEEN	(null)	(null)
18	EIGHTEEN	18	EIGHTEEN
20	TWENTY	(null)	(null)
(null)	NULL	(null)	(null)
(null)	(null)	(null)	NULL

14-3 The left outer join

A left outer join keeps all of the rows from the first table, but has only the rows from the second table that match with a row from the first table. You write the join condition in the from clause. Oracle also has another way to write a left outer join that puts the join condition in the where clause. This is an older syntax that you should be able to recognize, but it is best not to use it anymore.

In the following example, the rows of the result table are sorted on the number column from the first table to put them in a logical order. In Oracle, the null is sorted at the end of the table. In Access, it is sorted at the beginning. The order by clause in this example is not needed to join the two tables together. It is used here to display the rows of the result in a logical order.

Task

Show the syntax to write a left outer join in Oracle and in Access.

Oracle & Access SQL

```
select a.*,
       b.*
from twos a
     left outer join threes b ❶
     on a.number_2 = b.number_3 ❷
order by a.number_2; ❸
```

Oracle SQL — Older syntax, Oracle 8 or earlier, do not use it anymore

```
select a.*,
       b.*
from twos a,
     threes b
where a.number_2 = b.number_3 (+) ❹
order by a.number_2; ❸
```

Beginning tables
twos table   **threes table**

```
NUMBER_2 WORD_2                    NUMBER_3 WORD_3
-------- ---------------          -------- ---------------
       2 TWO                             3 THREE
       4 FOUR                            6 SIX
       6 SIX                             9 NINE
       8 EIGHT                          12 TWELVE
      10 TEN                            15 FIFTEEN
      12 TWELVE                         18 EIGHTEEN
      14 FOURTEEN                 (null)    NULL
      16 SIXTEEN
      18 EIGHTEEN
      20 TWENTY
(null)    NULL
```

Result table — Left outer join

```
NUMBER_2 WORD_2           NUMBER_3 WORD_3
-------- ---------------  -------- ---------------
       2 TWO              (null)   (null)
       4 FOUR             (null)   (null)
       6 SIX                     6 SIX
       8 EIGHT            (null)   (null)
      10 TEN              (null)   (null)
      12 TWELVE                 12 TWELVE
      14 FOURTEEN         (null)   (null)
      16 SIXTEEN          (null)   (null)
      18 EIGHTEEN                18 EIGHTEEN
      20 TWENTY           (null)   (null)
(null)    NULL            (null)   (null)
```

Notes

❶ "Left outer join" is written in the `from` clause. The word "outer" is optional, so you can also write "left join" here.

❷ The join condition is written in the `on` subclause of the `from` clause.

❸ The `order by` clause puts the rows in a logical order. It is not required in a left outer join.

❹ In the older syntax of Oracle, the join condition is written in the `where` clause. A plus sign in parentheses, `(+)`, is written to the right of the join condition. This specifies a left outer join. When several clauses are in the join condition, the plus sign must be written to the right of each of them.

Putting the plus sign on the right might not seem to make sense to write a left outer join. One way to think about this is that the plus sign is written on the side where the nulls are added to the incomplete rows that are added back.

Check your understanding

The following `select` statement shows all the employees who are in each department. First run this code as it is — as an inner join. Then change it to a left outer join. What is the difference in the result tables?

```
select a.department_name,
       b.first_name,
       b.last_name
from l_departments a,
     l_employees b
where a.dept_code = b.dept_code;
```

14-4 The right outer join

The right outer join is similar to the left outer join, except it is the reverse: The rows dropped from the second table are added back instead of the rows from the first table. The syntax is also similar. The difference between the syntax for Oracle and Access is the same for both the left and right outer joins.

A right outer join keeps all of the rows from the second table, but has only the rows from the first table that match with a row from the second table.

Task

Show the syntax to write a right outer join in Oracle and in Access.

Oracle & Access SQL

```
select a.*,
       b.*
from twos a
     right outer join threes b ❶
     on a.number_2 = b.number_3 ❷
order by b.number_3; ❸
```

Oracle SQL — Older syntax, Oracle 8 or earlier, do not use it anymore

```
select a.*,
       b.*
from twos a,
     threes b
where a.number_2 (+) = b.number_3 ❹
order by b.number_3; ❸
```

Beginning tables
twos table

NUMBER_2	WORD_2
2	TWO
4	FOUR
6	SIX
8	EIGHT
10	TEN
12	TWELVE
14	FOURTEEN
16	SIXTEEN
18	EIGHTEEN
20	TWENTY
(null)	NULL

threes table

NUMBER_3	WORD_3
3	THREE
6	SIX
9	NINE
12	TWELVE
15	FIFTEEN
18	EIGHTEEN
(null)	NULL

Result table — Right outer join

NUMBER_2	WORD_2	NUMBER_3	WORD_3
(null)	(null)	3	THREE
6	SIX	6	SIX
(null)	(null)	9	NINE
12	TWELVE	12	TWELVE
(null)	(null)	15	FIFTEEN
18	EIGHTEEN	18	EIGHTEEN
(null)	(null)	(null)	NULL

Notes

❶ The phrase "right outer join" is written in the `from` clause. The word "outer" is optional, so you can also write "right join" here.

❷ The join condition is written in the `on` subclause of the `from` clause.

❸ The `order by` clause puts the rows in a logical order. It is not required in a right outer join.

❹ In the older syntax of Oracle, the join condition is written in the `where` clause. A plus sign in parentheses, `(+)`, is written to the left of the equal sign. This specifies a right outer join. When several clauses are in the join condition, the plus sign must be written on the left side of each of them.

Check your understanding

This is a modification of the exercise in section 14-3. The only thing that has been changed is the order of the tables in the `from` clause. First run this code as it is — as an inner join. Then change this `select` statement to a right outer join. What is the difference in the result tables?

```
select a.department_name,
       b.first_name,
       b.last_name
from l_employees b,
     l_departments a
where a.dept_code = b.dept_code;
```

14-5 The full outer join

The full outer join adds back all the rows dropped from both tables by the inner join. It keeps all the rows from both tables and makes as many matches as the data and the join condition allow.

Oracle has direct support for the full outer join. That is, you can do it with a single command. However, in Access you need to construct it yourself as a union of two one-sided outer joins.

You can create a full outer join by writing a `union` of the left outer join and the right outer join. The next two sections of this chapter tell you as much as you need to know about the `union` to understand it when it is used in a full outer join. For now, you can think of it as a way to combine a left outer join and a right outer join. We discuss the `union` in more detail in the next chapter.

The SQL may look complicated, but it is only:

- Left outer join
- union
- Right outer join

The order of the left and right outer joins does not matter and can be reversed, so the full outer join can also be written:

- Right outer join
- union
- Left outer join

Task

Show the syntax to write a full outer join in Oracle and in Access.

Oracle SQL ❶

```
select a.*,
       b.*
from twos a
     full outer join threes b
     on a.number_2 = b.number_3;
```

Access SQL (This also works in Oracle)

```
select a.*,
       b.*
from twos a
     left outer join threes b
     on a.number_2 = b.number_3
union
select c.*,
       d.*
from twos c ❷
     right outer join threes d ❷
     on c.number_2 = d.number_3;
```

Beginning tables — twos table and threes table, shown in the previous sections

Result table — Full outer join ❸

```
NUMBER_2 WORD_2              NUMBER_3 WORD_3
-------- ---------------    -------- ---------------
       2 TWO                  (null)    (null)
  (null)    (null)                 3 THREE
       4 FOUR                 (null)    (null)
       6 SIX                       6 SIX
       8 EIGHT                (null)    (null)
  (null)    (null)                 9 NINE
      10 TEN                  (null)    (null)
      12 TWELVE                   12 TWELVE
      14 FOURTEEN             (null)    (null)
  (null)    (null)                15 FIFTEEN
      16 SIXTEEN              (null)    (null)
      18 EIGHTEEN                 18 EIGHTEEN
      20 TWENTY               (null)    (null)
  (null)    NULL              (null)    (null)
  (null)    (null)            (null)    NULL
```

Notes

❶ Oracle has direct support for a full outer join.

❷ In this example I use a and b for the table aliases in the first select statement and then I use c and d for the table aliases in the second select statement. I do this for clarity, so anyone who looks at the code can tell immediately what is going on. To the computer the two select statements are independent of each other and the table aliases do not need to be different. So many people would write a and b again in the second select statement instead of c and d.

❸ I have put the rows of this table in a logical order so you can see what is going on. When you run the code you will probably see the rows in a different order.

Check your understanding

This is a modification of the exercise in section 14-3. The only thing that has changed is that table sec1405_employees replaces table 1_employees. The new table contains one new employee who has not been assigned to any department yet. First run this code as it is — as an inner join. Then change this select statement to a full outer join. What is the difference in the result tables?

```
select a.department_name,
       b.first_name,
       b.last_name
from l_departments a,
     sec1405_employees b
where a.dept_code = b.dept_code;
```

14-6 An introduction to the `union`

This section introduces the `union` because we have used it in creating a full outer join. At this time, I limit the discussion to its use in this context. The next chapter discusses the `union` in more detail.

A `union` of two tables adds the rows of one table to the other table, and the two beginning tables are combined to form a single table, as shown in the following diagram. The rows of the two tables must be identical or nearly identical in structure, so that they can all fit together within the framework of a single table. This means that they must have the same number of columns and the datatypes of these columns must be in the same order. Otherwise, a `union` cannot be formed.

Duplicate rows are eliminated from a `union`. If two rows have the same values in every column, the `union` keeps only one of them and drops the other one. This action is taken whether both rows come from the same table or whether they come from different tables.

The definition of a `union` of tables is similar to the way a union of sets is defined in mathematics. In a union of sets no duplicate elements are allowed. This is why duplicate rows are not allowed in a `union` of tables.

We have formed a `union` of two tables before. The method we used was to insert the rows from one table into the other table and then to use `select distinct` to eliminate the duplicate rows.

When a `union` is written within SQL code, the word `union` is placed between two `select` statements. Each `select` statement stands for a table — the result table it produces.

In the case of a full outer join, the `union` is placed between the `select` statements for the left outer join and the right outer join. These two tables always have the same number of columns and the datatypes of those columns are always in the same order, so the `union` can always be formed.

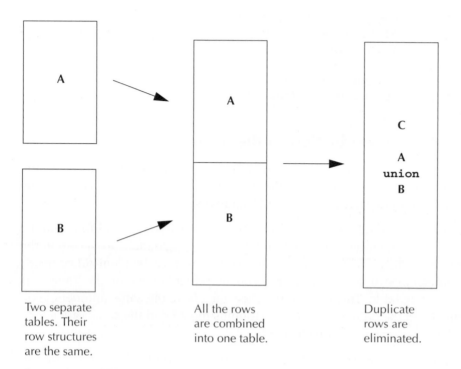

Two separate tables. Their row structures are the same.

All the rows are combined into one table.

Duplicate rows are eliminated.

The process of forming a union.

Task for example 1: Write a union

Show how to write a union in SQL. Show the select statement for the preceding diagram. Write the select statement so that its result table is table C in the diagram.

Oracle & Access SQL: select statement for the preceding diagram

```
select *
from A
union
select *
from B;
```

Task for example 2: Another procedure to form a `union`

Show another way to write the SQL for the preceding diagram. Write this SQL to create table C as a new table.

Oracle & Access SQL: Step 1

```
insert into B
   select *
   from A;
```

Oracle SQL: Step 2

```
create table C as
   select distinct *
   from B;
```

Access SQL: Step 2

```
select distinct *
into C
from B;
```

Notes

This is a model of the SQL code for the diagram. This SQL does not actually run.

14-7 An example of a `union` of two tables with matching columns

This section shows an example of a `union`. The two beginning tables have the same structure. That is, they both have three columns and the datatypes of these columns in order are as follows:

- Numeric

- Text

- Date/time

These are the three main types of columns that are used in relational databases. This example shows they can all be used in a `union`.

The result table contains all the rows from both beginning tables. We can call these rows 1 through 7. Rows 1 and 2 come only from the first beginning table. Rows 6 and 7 come only from the second beginning table. Rows 3, 4, and 5 come from both beginning tables; however, only a single copy of these rows is kept in the result table, because the duplicate copies of rows are eliminated.

Look at the column headings of the result table. The first `select` statement sets them. The column headings of the first beginning table are used, unless a column alias is assigned. The `word_1` column in this example is assigned to the column alias `text_1`.

The `order by` clause is the last line and it is placed after the second `select` statement. A union can have only one `order by` clause, and it must be the last line of the `union`. This clause sorts all the rows of the `union` into a designated order.

After you examine this example of a `union`, turn back to section 14-2 and look at the tables for the three types of outer joins. Can you see how the full outer join is the result of a `union` between the left outer join and the right outer join?

Task

Show an example of a `select` statement that uses a `union`.

Oracle & Access SQL

```
select a.number_1, ❶
       a.word_1 as text_1, ❷
       a.date_1
from sec1407_first a
union ❸
select b.number_2, ❹
       b.word_2,
       b.date_2
from sec1407_second b
order by number_1; ❺
```

Beginning tables

sec1407_first table   **sec1407_second table**

NUMBER_1	WORD_1	DATE_1
1	ONE	01-DEC-2001
2	TWO	02-DEC-2002
3	THREE	03-DEC-2003
4	FOUR	04-DEC-2004
5	FIVE	05-DEC-2005

NUMBER_2	WORD_2	DATE_2
3	THREE	03-DEC-2003
4	FOUR	04-DEC-2004
5	FIVE	05-DEC-2005
6	SIX	06-DEC-2006
7	SEVEN	07-DEC-2007

Result table ❻

NUMBER_1	TEXT_1	DATE_1
1	ONE	01-DEC-2001
2	TWO	02-DEC-2002
3	THREE	03-DEC-2003
4	FOUR	04-DEC-2004
5	FIVE	05-DEC-2005
6	SIX	06-DEC-2006
7	SEVEN	07-DEC-2007

Notes

❶ The first `select` statement lists three columns. It determines the heading for the columns. It cannot have an `order by` clause.

❷ In a `union`, a column alias is assigned within the first `select` statement. Aliases cannot be assigned in the second `select` statement.

❸ The word `union` is placed between the two `select` statements.

❹ The second `select` statement must have the same number of columns as the first `select` statement and the datatypes of the matching columns must be compatible.

❺ The `order by` clause is placed at the end of the `union`.

❻ Even though both beginning tables have rows 3, 4, and 5, the result table contains only a single copy of these rows. This shows that duplicate rows are eliminated.

Check your understanding

The table `sec1407_departments` has the same format as the `1_departments` table. Write a `select` statement that shows the union of the two tables.

Applications of Outer Joins

The following sections provide some applications of outer joins and the last section shows why left and right outer joins can be difficult to handle.

14-8 Counting to zero, part 4

This section shows the full SQL solution in our continuing discussion of how to count the number of lunches each employee will attend. The new aspect shown here is the outer join between the 1_employees table and the 1_lunches table.

Task

Show the number of lunches each employee will attend. Include all the employees. Show a zero if the employee is not attending any lunches.

Oracle & Access SQL

```
select a.employee_id,
       a.first_name,
       a.last_name,
       count(b.lunch_id) as number_of_lunches ❶
from 1_employees a
     left outer join 1_lunches b
     on a.employee_id = b.employee_id
group by a.employee_id,
         a.first_name,
         a.last_name
order by a.employee_id;
```

Beginning table 1 (1_employees table)

EMPLOYEE ID	FIRST_NAME	LAST_NAME	DEPT CODE	HIRE_DATE	CREDIT LIMIT	PHONE NUMBER	MANAGER ID
201	SUSAN	BROWN	EXE	01-JUN-1998	$30.00	3484	(null)
202	JIM	KERN	SAL	16-AUG-1999	$25.00	8722	201
203	MARTHA	WOODS	SHP	02-FEB-2009	$25.00	7591	201
204	ELLEN	OWENS	SAL	01-JUL-2008	$15.00	6830	202
205	HENRY	PERKINS	SAL	01-MAR-2006	$25.00	5286	202
206	CAROL	ROSE	ACT	(null)	(null)	(null)	(null)
207	DAN	SMITH	SHP	01-DEC-2008	$25.00	2259	203
208	FRED	CAMPBELL	SHP	01-APR-2008	$25.00	1752	203
209	PAULA	JACOBS	MKT	17-MAR-1999	$15.00	3357	201
210	NANCY	HOFFMAN	SAL	16-FEB-2007	$25.00	2974	203

Beginning table 2 (1_lunches table)

```
          LUNCH          EMPLOYEE
LUNCH_ID  DATE                 ID  DATE_ENTERE
--------  ------------  --------  -----------
       1  16-NOV-2011        201  13-OCT-2011
       2  16-NOV-2011        207  13-OCT-2011
       3  16-NOV-2011        203  13-OCT-2011
       4  16-NOV-2011        204  13-OCT-2011
       6  16-NOV-2011        202  13-OCT-2011
       7  16-NOV-2011        210  13-OCT-2011
       8  25-NOV-2011        201  14-OCT-2011
       9  25-NOV-2011        208  14-OCT-2011
      12  25-NOV-2011        204  14-OCT-2011
      13  25-NOV-2011        207  18-OCT-2011
      15  25-NOV-2011        205  21-OCT-2011
      16  05-DEC-2011        201  21-OCT-2011
      17  05-DEC-2011        210  21-OCT-2011
      20  05-DEC-2011        205  24-OCT-2011
      21  05-DEC-2011        203  24-OCT-2011
      22  05-DEC-2011        208  24-OCT-2011
```

Result table

```
EMPLOYEE_ID  FIRST_NAME  LAST_NAME   NUMBER_OF_LUNCHES
-----------  ----------  ----------  -----------------
        201  SUSAN       BROWN                       3
        202  JIM         KERN                        1
        203  MARTHA      WOODS                       2
        204  ELLEN       OWENS                       2
        205  HENRY       PERKINS                     2
        206  CAROL       ROSE                        0
        207  DAN         SMITH                       2
        208  FRED        CAMPBELL                    2
        209  PAULA       JACOBS                      0
        210  NANCY       HOFFMAN                     2
```

Notes

❶ Here the count(*column*) function is being applied to the lunch_id column from the 1_lunches table. Why did I choose this column? To get the zeros, I could have used any column from the 1_lunches table, because the outer join sets all the columns to nulls when an employee is not attending any lunches.

Check your understanding

The following `select` statement shows the number of orders for each food on the menu. Modify the SQL so the result table shows that there are no orders for broccoli.

```
select a.description as food_item,
       sum(b.quantity) as number_of_orders
from l_foods a,
     l_lunch_items b
where a.supplier_id = b.supplier_id
  and a.product_code = b.product_code
group by a.description
order by a.description;
```

14-9 Combining an outer join with a selection of the data

The SQL code in the previous section combined two steps into a single `select` statement. In theory, the first step creates the outer join of the two beginning tables. The result of this step is a table that has all the columns from both tables and all the rows that the outer join creates.

The second step selects some of the data from this table, groups it, and summarizes it. This creates the result table.

The following example solves the same problem as in the previous section, but shows each of these steps separately. When the problem is more complex than the one shown here, this method of coding is easier to create and less prone to errors.

Task for example 1

Create an outer join of the `l_employees` table and the `l_lunches` table. Retain all the rows of data from both tables.

Oracle SQL

```
create table sec1409 as
select a.*,
       b.lunch_id,
       b.lunch_date,
       b.employee_id as employee_id2,
       b.date_entered
from l_employees a
     left outer join l_lunches b
     on a.employee_id = b.employee_id;
```

Access SQL

```
select a.*,
       b.lunch_id,
       b.lunch_date,
       b.employee_id as employee_id2,
       b.date_entered
into sec1409
from l_employees a
     left outer join l_lunches b
     on a.employee_id = b.employee_id;
```

Beginning tables —

The `l_employees` table and the `l_lunches` table are shown in the previous section.

Result table —

`Sec1409` table, except for the last column, `date_entered`, which does not fit here.

EMP ID	FIRST NAME	LAST NAME	DEPT CODE	HIRE_DATE	CREDIT LIMIT	PHONE NUMBER	MANAGER ID	LUNCH ID	LUNCH DATE	EMP ID2
201	SUSAN	BROWN	EXE	01-JUN-1998	$30.00	3484	(null)	1	16-NOV-2011	201
201	SUSAN	BROWN	EXE	01-JUN-1998	$30.00	3484	(null)	8	25-NOV-2011	201
201	SUSAN	BROWN	EXE	01-JUN-1998	$30.00	3484	(null)	16	05-DEC-2011	201
202	JIM	KERN	SAL	16-AUG-1999	$25.00	8722	201	6	16-NOV-2011	202
203	MARTHA	WOODS	SHP	02-FEB-2009	$25.00	7591	201	3	16-NOV-2011	203
203	MARTHA	WOODS	SHP	02-FEB-2009	$25.00	7591	201	21	05-DEC-2011	203
204	ELLEN	OWENS	SAL	01-JUL-2008	$15.00	6830	202	4	16-NOV-2011	204
204	ELLEN	OWENS	SAL	01-JUL-2008	$15.00	6830	202	12	25-NOV-2011	204
205	HENRY	PERKINS	SAL	01-MAR-2006	$25.00	5286	202	15	25-NOV-2011	205
205	HENRY	PERKINS	SAL	01-MAR-2006	$25.00	5286	202	20	05-DEC-2011	205
206	CAROL	ROSE	ACT	(null)	(null)	(null)	(null)	(null)	(null)	(null)
207	DAN	SMITH	SHP	01-DEC-2008	$25.00	2259	203	2	16-NOV-2011	207
207	DAN	SMITH	SHP	01-DEC-2008	$25.00	2259	203	13	25-NOV-2011	207
208	FRED	CAMPBELL	SHP	01-APR-2008	$25.00	1752	203	9	25-NOV-2011	208
208	FRED	CAMPBELL	SHP	01-APR-2008	$25.00	1752	203	22	05-DEC-2011	208
209	PAULA	JACOBS	MKT	17-MAR-1999	$15.00	3357	201	(null)	(null)	(null)
210	NANCY	HOFFMAN	SAL	16-FEB-2007	$25.00	2974	203	7	16-NOV-2011	210
210	NANCY	HOFFMAN	SAL	16-FEB-2007	$25.00	2974	203	17	05-DEC-2011	210

Task for example 2

Show the number of lunches each employee will attend. Start with the `sec1409` table. Then select these columns: `employee_id`, `first_name`, and `last_name`. Group these data and summarize them to count the number of lunches each employee will attend.

This code is almost identical to the SQL in section 12-10.

Oracle & Access SQL

```
select employee_id,
       first_name,
       last_name,
       count(lunch_id) as number_of_lunches
from sec1409
group by employee_id,
         first_name,
         last_name
order by employee_id;
```

Result table

```
EMPLOYEE
      ID FIRST_NAME LAST_NAME  NUMBER_OF_LUNCHES
-------- ---------- ---------- -----------------
     201 SUSAN      BROWN                      3
     202 JIM        KERN                       1
     203 MARTHA     WOODS                      2
     204 ELLEN      OWENS                      2
     205 HENRY      PERKINS                    2
     206 CAROL      ROSE                       0
     207 DAN        SMITH                      2
     208 FRED       CAMPBELL                   2
     209 PAULA      JACOBS                     0
     210 NANCY      HOFFMAN                    2
```

14-10 A full outer join in sorted order

This section shows a full outer join of the twos table with the threes table. The rows of the result table are sorted into their logical order. This order may not seem surprising to you, but a trick is required to achieve it.

The difficulty in sorting the rows of a full outer join is that they need to be sorted on a combination of the two columns, number_2 and number_3. If it is sorted on a single column, all the rows that contain a null in that column are sorted together. In Oracle, all of these rows go to the bottom. In Access, they all go to the top. Both the number_2 column and the number_3 column contain many nulls because this is a full outer join. Sorting on either of these columns does not give us the result we want.

The trick is to use a row function that combines the values of the number_2 and number_3 columns. In Oracle, we can use the nvl (null value) function:

NVL(number_2, number_3)

In Access, we can use the nz (nonzero) function and multiply the result by one:

NZ(number_2, number_3) * 1

The resulting value from both of these functions is as follows:

number_2 if it is not null

number_3 if number_2 is null, even if number_3 is a null

In Access, we multiply the nz function by one to convert it into a number. Otherwise, it would be a text field and would sort the rows in alphabetic order rather than numeric order. Because a union requires the columns of each select statement to match, these functions must be placed within each of the select statements.

Task

Create a full outer join of the twos table and the threes table. Create a column that will sort the rows in numeric order.

Oracle SQL

```
select a.*, ❶
       b.*,
       nvl(a.number_2,b.number_3) as sort_order ❷
from twos a
     full outer join threes b
     on a.number_2 = b.number_3
order by sort_order; ❸
```

Access SQL

```
select a.*, ❶
       b.*,
       nz(a.number_2,b.number_3) * 1 as sort_order ❹
from twos a
     left outer join threes b
     on a.number_2 = b.number_3
union
select c.*,
       d.*,
       nz(c.number_2,d.number_3) * 1   ❺
from twos c
     right outer join threes d
     on c.number_2 = d.number_3
order by sort_order;   ❸
```

Beginning tables

twos table		threes table	

```
 NUMBER_2 WORD_2                    NUMBER_3 WORD_3
--------- ---------------         --------- --------------
        2 TWO                             3 THREE
        4 FOUR                            6 SIX
        6 SIX                             9 NINE
        8 EIGHT                          12 TWELVE
       10 TEN                            15 FIFTEEN
       12 TWELVE                         18 EIGHTEEN
       14 FOURTEEN               (null)     NULL
       16 SIXTEEN
       18 EIGHTEEN
       20 TWENTY
(null)     NULL
```

Result table ❻

```
NUMBER_2 WORD_2           NUMBER_3 WORD_3            SORT_ORDER
-------- ----------------  -------- ----------------  ----------
       2 TWO               (null)   (null)                     2
(null)   (null)                   3 THREE                      3
       4 FOUR              (null)   (null)                     4
       6 SIX                      6 SIX                         6
       8 EIGHT             (null)   (null)                     8
(null)   (null)                   9 NINE                       9
      10 TEN               (null)   (null)                    10
      12 TWELVE                  12 TWELVE                     12
      14 FOURTEEN          (null)   (null)                    14
(null)   (null)                  15 FIFTEEN                    15
      16 SIXTEEN           (null)   (null)                    16
      18 EIGHTEEN                18 EIGHTEEN                   18
      20 TWENTY            (null)   (null)                    20
(null)   NULL              (null)   (null)            (null)
(null)   (null)            (null)   NULL              (null)
```

Notes

❶ The `select` clause includes all the columns of both tables and an additional column to determine the sort order.

❷ The null value function, `nvl`, is used in Oracle to determine the sort order. This is equal to the `number_2` column, except if that column contains a null, in which case it is equal to the `number_3` column. The column alias `sort_order` is given to this column.

❸ The full outer join is sorted by the `sort_order` column.

❹ In Access, the `nz` function is used to determine the sort order. This is equal to `number_2`, except when `number_2` is null then it is equal to `number_3`. It is multiplied by one to give it a numeric datatype.

❺ The `nz` function to create the `sort_order` column must also be included in the second `select` statement.

❻ Often the `sort_order` column is not displayed. This makes the sort order just "naturally appear." To use this trick, you could create a view from the `select` statement in this section and then not display the `sort_order` column, but still use it for sorting.

Comment

You can force a full other join, or any other result table, to be in the order you want by adding a new column to specify the sort order. Special tricks are sometimes used to assign numbers to rows when a particular order is required.

14-11   Finding the defects in a pattern

In this section we compare two tables using a single column from each table. In this particular example each table has only one column, but in a more general setting the tables could have any number of columns.

The idea is that one table contains a pattern of numbers that has some defects. The other table contains the same pattern without any defects. Our job is to find all the defects in the first table.

The SQL does an outer join between these tables, keeping all the rows of the perfect pattern and listing the columns from both tables. If a number, such as 5, is missing from the defective table, the join shows it by producing the row <5, null>. If a number is repeated several times in the defective table, it is also repeated that many times in the join. An example is that 3 occurs twice in the defective table, and the outer join contains the row <3, 3> twice.

Then the SQL groups the rows of the join, making a separate group for each number. It counts each group on the column that comes from the defective table. Most numbers have a count of 1. When these are eliminated, only the defects are shown in the result table.

Task

The table `sec1411_numbers` contains the numbers from 1 to 1,000. A few numbers are missing and a few numbers are repeated. Find all the missing numbers and all the repeated numbers. Count the number of times each of these numbers occurs. For the missing numbers, count that they occur zero times.

Oracle & Access SQL

```
select a.n,
       b.n,
       count(b.n)
from numbers_1_to_1000 a
     left outer join sec1411_numbers b
     on a.n = b.n
group by a.n,
         b.n
having not (count(b.n) = 1)
order by a.n;
```

Beginning table (ex1203a table)

```
        N
---------
        1
        2
        3
        3
        4
        6
        7
        8
        9
       10
       11
       12
       13
       13
       13
       13
       14
(and many more)
```

Result table

```
        N         N COUNT(B.N)
--------- --------- ----------
        3         3          2
        5 (null)              0
       13        13          4
       48        48          4
       67        67          2
       72        72          3
      103       103          2
      113       113          5
      123 (null)              0
      148       148          4
      167       167          2
      172       172          3
      248       248          2
      267       267          2
      275 (null)              0
      367 (null)              0
      460 (null)              0
      503       503          2
      548       548          2
      555 (null)              0
      619 (null)              0
      713       713          2
      748       748          2
      778 (null)              0
      821 (null)              0
      872       872          2
      913       913          2
      972       972          2
      998 (null)              0
```

Comment

When you need to look for repeated rows or values in a large amount of data, the trick that we employed here is often useful. First, group the data together and count them in a way that most of the data will get a count of one. Then use a having clause to hide these data so you can focus on the exceptions.

14-12 Comparing tables using two or more columns

This section shows you how to compare two tables that contain two or more columns by finding the rows in one table that do not exist in another table. This can be done in several ways.

The technique shown here lists all the columns from both tables. It forms a left outer join between the first table and the second table. This join retains all the rows in the first table, and when the second table does not have a matching row, nulls are placed in the columns of the second table.

The second part of this technique selects all the rows that have a null in a column of the second table. This shows the rows of the first table that do not exist in the second table.

You can also perform this process in two steps. It may be easier to understand that way. In the first step, form the left outer join and examine the results. In the second step, select the rows that have a null in one of the columns of the second table.

Task

Find the rows in the sec1412a table that do not exist in the sec1412b table.

Oracle & Access SQL

```
select a.first_col,
       a.second_col,
       b.first_col,
       b.second_col
from sec1412a a
     left outer join sec1412b b
     on a.first_col = b.first_col
     and a.second_col = b.second_col
where b.first_col is null ❶
order by a.first_col,
         a.second_col;
```

Beginning table 1 (sec1412a table)

FIRST_COL	SECOND_COL
11101	22201
11101	22202
11101	22203
11102	22201
11102	22202
11102	22203
11103	22201
11103	22202
11103	22203
11104	22201
11104	22202
11104	22203
11105	22201
11105	22202
11105	22203

Beginning table 2 (sec1412b table)

FIRST_COL	SECOND_COL
11101	22201
11101	22202
11101	22203
11102	22201
11102	22203
11103	22202
11103	22203
11104	22201
11104	22202
11105	22201
11105	22202
11105	22203

Result table

FIRST_COL	SECOND_COL	FIRST_COL	SECOND_COL
11102	22202	(null)	(null)
11103	22201	(null)	(null)
11104	22203	(null)	(null)

Notes

❶ Eliminate this `where` condition if you want to perform the process in two steps. That creates the first step, which forms the left outer join. In the second step, apply this `where` condition.

Comment

In this section we found the rows from the first table that do not exist in the second table. If you want to fully compare the tables you will need to run this `select` statement again to find the rows of the second table that do not exist in the first table.

Check your understanding

The table `sec1412_departments` is similar to the `l_departments` table, except that a few rows have been added, deleted, or changed. Find all the differences between the two tables.

14-13 Comparing two different full outer joins

People sometimes talk as if there were only one way to form a full outer join between two tables. However, there are many ways to create the join. Every join condition you can write can be used to form a different full outer join. In this section we compare two full outer joins of the same tables to see how they are similar and how they are different. For this example, we return to the `fruits` and `colors` tables from chapter 13.

Task

Use the two tables `sec1413_fruits` and `sec1413_colors`. Form the full outer join of these tables using the join condition:

`f_num = c_num`

Then form the full outer join using the join condition:

`fruit = color`

Examine the result tables. State what is similar and what is different about these full outer joins.

Oracle & Access SQL (Oracle also has another method)

In Oracle, the full outer join can be written directly, without using a union. I use a union here to make the Oracle SQL the same as the Access SQL.

First full outer join:

```
select a.*,
       b.*
from sec1413_fruits a
     left outer join sec1413_colors b
     on a.f_num = b.c_num
union
select a.*,
       b.*
from sec1413_fruits a
     right outer join sec1413_colors b
     on a.f_num  = b.c_num;
```

Second full outer join:

```
select a.*,
       b.*
from sec1413_fruits a
     left outer join sec1413_colors b
     on a.fruit = b.color
union
select a.*,
       b.*
from sec1413_fruits a
     right outer join sec1413_colors b
     on a.fruit = b.color;
```

Beginning tables
`sec1413_fruits` table   `sec1413_colors` table

FRUIT	F_NUM		C_NUM	COLOR
APPLE	1		1	RED
BANANA	2		2	YELLOW
CHERRY	3		1	GREEN
GRAPE	4		5	ORANGE
ORANGE	5		6	WHITE
STRAWBERRY	1			

First full outer join using the join condition: `f_num = c_num`

```
FRUIT           F_NUM      C_NUM COLOR
----------  ---------  --------- ----------
APPLE             1          1 GREEN
APPLE             1          1 RED
BANANA            2          2 YELLOW
CHERRY            3 (null)      (null)
GRAPE             4 (null)      (null)
ORANGE            5          5 ORANGE
STRAWBERRY        1          1 GREEN
STRAWBERRY        1          1 RED
(null)     (null)          6 WHITE
```

Second full outer join using the join condition: `fruit = color`
This looks completely different to me.

```
FRUIT           F_NUM      C_NUM COLOR
----------  ---------  --------- ----------
APPLE             1 (null)      (null)
BANANA            2 (null)      (null)
CHERRY            3 (null)      (null)
GRAPE             4 (null)      (null)
ORANGE            5          5 ORANGE
STRAWBERRY        1 (null)      (null)
(null)     (null)          1 GREEN
(null)     (null)          1 RED
(null)     (null)          2 YELLOW
(null)     (null)          6 WHITE
```

Similarities between the two full outer joins

- They both contain all the rows from the beginning tables.
- They both contain all the columns from the beginning tables.

Differences between the two full outer joins

	First Full Outer Join	Second Full Outer Join
Total number of rows in the result table	9	10
Number of rows in the result table that match a fruit and a color	6	1
Number of rows in the result table with an unmatched fruit or color	3	9

	First Full Outer Join	Second Full Outer Join
Number of fruits from the beginning table that are matched with at least one color	4	1
Number of fruits from the beginning table that are not matched with any color	2	5
Number of colors from the beginning table that are matched with at least one fruit	4	1
Number of colors from the beginning table that are not matched with any fruit	1	4

14-14 Problem: Left and right outer joins can be difficult to handle

In this section I want to tell you about one of the main problems with left and right outer joins. They are okay when there is only one of them and you use it to join two tables together, but things become subtle and complex the moment you use two of them to join three tables together. You can get this to work, but you have to be extremely careful or you will get a result that is different than what you expect it to be.

This is one of the more difficult sections of the book. Don't get hung up on it. You can safely move on and skip this section entirely if you want.

I want to make this point by showing you an example. I picked an example where almost everything is the same so you might expect the difference to have no effect at all. However, I show you that in the result there is a difference you might not anticipate.

In this example we join three tables together using two left outer joins. We keep the tables in the same order relative to each other and keep the join conditions as similar as possible. There is just one difference. In case one, tables 1 and 2 are joined together first, then the result is joined with table 3. In case two, tables 2 and 3 are joined together first, then the result is joined with table 1. Expressing this mathematically, we show

`(A x B) x C    is not equal to    A x (B x C)`

where:

    A, B, and C   are tables

    x   is a left outer join

Next we need to agree on some details for this test. I have tried to be fair. I picked three tables without any hidden relationships to each other. I picked:

Table A = multiples of 2 from 0 to 100

Table B = multiples of 3 from 0 to 100

Table C = multiples of 5 from 0 to 100

The numbers 2, 3, and 5 are prime numbers. This keeps the tables independent from each other.

The first left outer join on each side is between two tables with one column each; let's call them R and S. The simplest join condition is R = S.

The second left outer join on each side is between a table with one column — let's call it T — and the previous result table, which has two columns, R and S. Which of these columns should T be equal to? To be fair, let's allow a join when T is equal to either R or S.

Putting this all together, I wrote the following code. Note that for clarity I write each left outer join in a separate step. I also save the result of each step in a new table. After creating the two tables, I compare them to show that they are different.

The Access SQL and the Oracle SQL differ slightly. I show only the Access SQL here. The notes tell you how to modify it for Oracle.

Access SQL: Create (A × B)   (Modify this for Oracle ❶)

```
select a.*,
       b.*
into sec1414_AxB ❶
from sec1414_twos a
    left outer join sec1414_threes b
    on a.multiple_of_2 = b.multiple_of_3;
```

Access SQL: Create (A × B) × C   (Modify this for Oracle ❶)

```
select a.*,
       b.*
into sec1414_AxB_xC ❶
from sec1414_AxB a
    left outer join sec1414_fives b
    on (a.multiple_of_2 = b.multiple_of_5
        or a.multiple_of_3 = b.multiple_of_5);
```

Access SQL: Create (B × C)   (Modify this for Oracle ❶)

```
select a.*,
       b.*
into sec1414_BxC ❶
from sec1414_threes a
     left outer join sec1414_fives b
     on a.multiple_of_3 = b.multiple_of_5;
```

Access SQL: Create A × (B × C)   (Modify this for Oracle ❶)

```
select a.*,
       b.*
into sec1414_Ax_BxC ❶
from sec1414_twos a
     left outer join sec1414_BxC b
     on (a.multiple_of_2 = b.multiple_of_3
         or a.multiple_of_2 = b.multiple_of_5);
```

Oracle & Access SQL: Compare (A × B) × C with A × (B × C)

To compare these two tables I use a technique from the next chapter because I think it shows the result more clearly. I label the rows from each table and combine the tables with a `union all`. Follow along with me for now. You can come back later and check how I did this.

```
select a.*,
       '(AxB)xC' as source
from sec1414_AxB_xC a
union all
select b.*,
       'Ax(BxC)'
from sec1414_Ax_BxC b
order by 1, 2, 3, 4;
```

Result table (the first few rows show the difference)

```
MULTIPLE_OF_2    MULTIPLE_OF_3    MULTIPLE_OF_5    SOURCE
---------------  ---------------  ---------------  -----------
0                0                0                (AxB)xC
0                0                0                Ax(BxC)
2                (null)           (null)           (AxB)xC
2                (null)           (null)           Ax(BxC)
4                (null)           (null)           (AxB)xC
4                (null)           (null)           Ax(BxC)
6                6                (null)           (AxB)xC
6                6                (null)           Ax(BxC)
8                (null)           (null)           (AxB)xC
8                (null)           (null)           Ax(BxC)
10               (null)           10               (AxB)xC      ❷
10               (null)           (null)           Ax(BxC)      ❷
12               12               (null)           (AxB)xC
12               12               (null)           Ax(BxC)
14               (null)           (null)           (AxB)xC
14               (null)           (null)           Ax(BxC)
...
(102 rows total)

(90 more rows)
```

Notes

❶ Here is how to create the Oracle SQL: Remove the line

```
into new_table
```

that comes after the select clause in the Access SQL. Replace it with the line

```
create new_table as
```

Put this line before the select clause in the Oracle SQL. This has been done for you in the script file containing all the Oracle SQL for chapter 14. It is available from the Web site.

❷ These rows are different. They show part of the differences between (A × B) × C and A × (B × C).

Key Points

There are three types of outer joins:

Type of Outer Join	Effect on First Table	Effect on Second Table
Left outer join	Keeps all the rows	Keeps only the matching rows
Right outer join	Keeps only the matching rows	Keeps all the rows
Full outer join	Keeps all the rows	Keeps all the rows

- An outer join is similar to an inner join, except it retains some of the unmatched rows that an inner join drops.

- An outer join requires more processing by the computer than an inner join. For this reason they are used less than inner joins. They are often reserved for situations in which they are specifically needed.

- There are three types of outer joins: left outer join, right outer join, and full outer join.

- A left outer join and a right outer join of two tables retain all the unmatched rows from one table, but do not retain the unmatched rows from the other table. These are sometimes called one-sided outer joins.

- A full outer join of two tables retains all the unmatched rows from both tables. This is sometimes called a two-sided outer join.

- When three or more tables are combined with outer joins, the tables should be joined two at a time in a series of steps. If any of these joins is a left outer join or a right outer join, the result depends on the specifics of how the join is done — the specific sequence in which the tables are joined and types of joins used. Unless you are very careful, this can lead to inaccurate results.

- When three or more tables are combined with only inner joins, the order of the joins is not important.

- When three or more tables are combined with only full outer joins, the order of the joins is not important, but this is best avoided because of the additional expense and processing required.

- Outer joins are often used with summarization to include zeros in the result.

- Outer joins are also used to compare two tables.

chapter 15

UNION
AND
UNION ALL

The union was introduced in the last chapter because it was needed to code a full outer join. In this chapter, we discuss the union in detail. Union and union all provide two more ways to combine tables.

Forming a union can be a very powerful technique. Unfortunately, many people do not understand it or use it very well. Skillful use of unions can replace many more complex features of SQL, such as outer joins or if-then-else logic.

Union Basics

A union of tables combines the rows of two tables together in a single table without making any changes to those rows. For all the rows to fit into one table, the rows of both tables must have the same structure. That is, they must have the same number of columns and the datatypes of corresponding columns must be the same.

15-1 The difference between a union and a join

A union and a join are similar in that they are both ways of combining two tables to form another table. However, they do this combining in very different ways. The geometry is different, as shown in the following diagram.

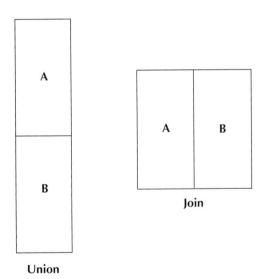

Join

Union

The differing geometry of a union and a join.

In a union, the rows of one table must fit into the other table. The number of columns in the result table is the same as the number in both of the beginning tables. No new columns are added. The rows of all the tables have the same sequence of datatypes for their columns.

In a join, the rows of one table may be very different from the rows of the other table. The result table can contain columns from both the first and second tables. It can contain all the columns of the first table and all the columns of the second table.

In a `union`, the maximum number of rows is the **sum** of the number of rows in the two tables. In a join, the maximum number of rows is the **product** of them.

Neither a join nor a `union` automatically gets a primary key. If you want to create a primary key for them, you must use an `alter table` statement. We did this in section 6-9.

Task

Show an example of the difference between a `union` and a join. Here, we use the same tables we used in chapter 14.

Oracle & Access SQL — For a `union`

```
select number_1,
       word_1,
       date_1
from sec1501_first
union
select number_2,
       word_2,
       date_2
from sec1501_second
order by number_1;
```

Beginning tables

sec1501_first table

NUMBER_1	WORD_1	DATE_1
1	ONE	01-DEC-2001
2	TWO	02-DEC-2002
3	THREE	03-DEC-2003
4	FOUR	04-DEC-2004
5	FIVE	05-DEC-2005

sec1501_second table

NUMBER_2	WORD_2	DATE_2
3	THREE	03-DEC-2003
4	FOUR	04-DEC-2004
5	FIVE	05-DEC-2005
6	SIX	06-DEC-2006
7	SEVEN	07-DEC-2007

Result table — A union

NUMBER_1	WORD_1	DATE_1
1	ONE	01-DEC-2001
2	TWO	02-DEC-2002
3	THREE	03-DEC-2003
4	FOUR	04-DEC-2004
5	FIVE	05-DEC-2005
6	SIX	06-DEC-2006
7	SEVEN	07-DEC-2007

Oracle & Access SQL — For an inner join

```
select a.*,
       b.*
from sec1501_first a,
     sec1501_second b
where a.number_1 = b.number_2
order by a.number_1;
```

Result table — An inner join

NUMBER_1	WORD_1	DATE_1	NUMBER_2	WORD_2	DATE_2
3	THREE	03-DEC-2003	3	THREE	03-DEC-2003
4	FOUR	04-DEC-2004	4	FOUR	04-DEC-2004
5	FIVE	05-DEC-2005	5	FIVE	05-DEC-2005

Check your understanding

1. Here is some information about the size of two tables:

   Table 1:   10 columns   100,000 rows

   Table 2:   10 columns   50,000 rows

   What is the maximum size of the union of these two tables? What is the maximum size of the inner join of the tables? By "maximum size" I mean the maximum number of columns and rows.

2. Write a select statement to form the union of the twos table and the threes table.

15-2 The difference between a union and a union all

Union all is another way to combine tables. It is very similar to a union. The only difference is that duplicate rows are not eliminated and the rows are not automatically sorted. In a union the rows get sorted as part of the process of eliminating duplicate rows.

A union all requires fewer computing resources than a union, so use it when you can, particularly when you are handling large tables. In most situations you should use a union. The following are situations when you should use union all:

- You know you have duplicate rows and you want to keep them.

- You know there cannot be any duplicate rows.

- You do not care whether there are any duplicate rows.

The rules that apply to a union also apply to union all, so as I discuss the details of a union, I am usually discussing them both.

In the following example, the union all has two identical rows numbered 3. As the previous section shows, a union has one of these rows. Except for duplicate rows, the result tables of the union and the union all are the same.

Task

Show an example of a union all.

Oracle & Access SQL — For a union all

```
select number_1,
       word_1,
       date_1
from sec1502_first
union all
select number_2,
       word_2,
       date_2
from sec1502_second
order by number_1;
```

Beginning tables
sec1502_first table   **sec1502_second table**

NUMBER_1	WORD_1	DATE_1
1	ONE	01-DEC-2001
2	TWO	02-DEC-2002
3	THREE	03-DEC-2003
4	FOUR	04-DEC-2004
5	FIVE	05-DEC-2005

NUMBER_2	WORD_2	DATE_2
3	THREE	03-DEC-2003
4	FOUR	04-DEC-2004
5	FIVE	05-DEC-2005
6	SIX	06-DEC-2006
7	SEVEN	07-DEC-2007

Result table — Showing a union all

```
NUMBER_1  WORD_1        DATE_1
--------- ----------    -----------
        1 ONE           01-DEC-2001
        2 TWO           02-DEC-2002
        3 THREE         03-DEC-2003
        3 THREE         03-DEC-2003
        4 FOUR          04-DEC-2004
        4 FOUR          04-DEC-2004
        5 FIVE          05-DEC-2005
        5 FIVE          05-DEC-2005
        6 SIX           06-DEC-2006
        7 SEVEN         07-DEC-2007
```

Check your understanding

Write a `select` statement to form a union of the `twos` table and the `threes` table. Use `union all`. How does this differ from using a regular `union`?

15-3 The `select` statements within a `union`

The `select` statements within a `union` can be quite complex. They are allowed to contain all six clauses, except for the `order by` clause. They are allowed to contain row functions, grouped summarization, inner joins, and outer joins.

If we want to assign a new name to a column — a column alias — then we must do this in the first `select` statement within the `union`.

In the following example, the first `select` statement contains an inner join and grouped summarization. It contains all five clauses of the `select` statement that it can use: `select`, `from`, `where`, `group by`, and `having`. The `select` clause lists three columns: The first two are text and the third is a number. That sets the structure of the rows of the result table. The rows from the second `select` statement must have the same structure. The first `select` clause also assigns the column alias `number_of_lunches`.

The second `select` statement may seem to be entirely different. It is as simple as it can be. The `select` clause contains literals and the dual table is used in the `from` clause. The `order by` clause is not part of the second `select` statement, it is part of the `union`. The `select` clause does have three columns with the datatypes: text, text, and number. That is as similar as it needs to be to the first `select` statement.

Some people consider this a sneaky way to put more data into the result table.

Task

From the `l_lunches` table, count the number of lunches each employee will attend. Get the last name and first name of each employee from the `l_employees` table using an inner join. Do not try to include employees who are not attending any lunches. Use a `union` to include a row showing that you will not attend any of the lunches.

Oracle & Access SQL

```
select a.last_name,
       a.first_name,
       count(b.lunch_id) as number_of_lunches
from l_employees a,
     l_lunches b
where a.employee_id = b.employee_id
group by a.first_name,
         a.last_name
having count(b.lunch_id) < 5
union all  ❶
select 'PATRICK',
       'JOHN',
        0
from dual
order by last_name;
```

Beginning tables — The `l_lunches` table and the `l_employees` table from the Lunches database

Result table

LAST_NAME	FIRST_NAME	NUMBER_OF_LUNCHES
BROWN	SUSAN	3
CAMPBELL	FRED	2
HOFFMAN	NANCY	2
KERN	JIM	1
OWENS	ELLEN	2
PATRICK	JOHN	0
PERKINS	HENRY	2
SMITH	DAN	2
WOODS	MARTHA	2

Notes

❶ Here I am using a union all instead of a union because I already know that there are no duplicate rows.

Check your understanding

1. What is wrong with this select statement?

```
select number_2
from twos
union
select number_3,
       word_3
from threes;
```

2. Goal 1: Show that a union is similar to an insert statement in that it can add new data to the result table.

3. Goal 2: Show a union that uses more than two select statements. The following select statement shows the number of lunches that each employee will attend, but it does not account for Carol Rose or Paula Jacobs because they are not attending any lunches. Modify this statement to show that these two people will not attend any lunches.

```
select a.first_name,
       a.last_name,
       count(b.lunch_id) as number_of_lunches
from l_employees a
     inner join l_lunches b
     on a.employee_id = b.employee_id
group by a.first_name,
         a.last_name;
```

15-4 The order by clause in a union

A union can have only one order by clause and it must be placed at the end of the statement. It provides the sort order for all the rows of the union from both select statements.

There are some choices about what kind of items we can sort by. There is also some confusion here. The order by clause in a union can seem to be a bit temperamental. In some SQL products you might have to try several options before you find one that works. In some circumstances we may find that only some of these options work. Here is a list of possibilities to try:

1. A column name from the first `select` clause, without a table reference

2. A column alias from the first `select` clause, without a table reference

3. A column name or column alias from the first `select` clause, with a table reference

4. A number that is the position of the column within the `union`

The first three options are preferred because they make the code easier to read and understand. They are shown in tasks 1, 2, and 3. Task 3 shows that in Access we can specify which table the column name or column alias comes from. The last option, shown in task 4, almost always works, even when the first three options do not.

Task for example 1

Show a `union` that uses a column name in its `order by` clause.

Oracle & Access SQL: Use a column name in the `order by` clause

```
select number_1,
       word_1,
       date_1
from sec1504_first
union
select *
from sec1504_second
order by word_1;
```

Beginning tables

sec1504_first table   **sec1504_second table**

NUMBER_1	WORD_1	DATE_1
1	ONE	01-DEC-2001
2	TWO	02-DEC-2002
3	THREE	03-DEC-2003
4	FOUR	04-DEC-2004
5	FIVE	05-DEC-2005

NUMBER_2	WORD_2	DATE_2
3	THREE	03-DEC-2003
4	FOUR	04-DEC-2004
5	FIVE	05-DEC-2005
6	SIX	06-DEC-2006
7	SEVEN	07-DEC-2007

Result table — Sorted on the second column

```
NUMBER_1  WORD_1      DATE_1
--------- ----------  -----------
        5 FIVE        05-DEC-2005
        4 FOUR        04-DEC-2004
        1 ONE         01-DEC-2001
        7 SEVEN       07-DEC-2007
        6 SIX         06-DEC-2006
        3 THREE       03-DEC-2003
        2 TWO         02-DEC-2002
```

Task for example 2

Show a union that uses a column alias in its order by clause.

Oracle & Access SQL: Use a column alias in the order by clause

```
select number_1,
       word_1 as text_1,
       date_1
from sec1504_first
union
select *
from sec1504_second
order by text_1;
```

Beginning tables — Same as in task 1

Result table — Same as in task 1

Task for example 3

Show that in Access we can use a table alias in an order by clause of a union.

Access SQL: Include a table reference in the order by clause

```
select a.number_1,
       a.word_1,
       a.date_1
from sec1504_first a
union
select *
from sec1504_second
order by a.word_1;
```

Oracle does not support using a table alias in an order by clause of a union.

Beginning tables — Same as in task 1

Access result table

number_1	word_1	date_1
5	Five	05-Dec-2005
4	Four	04-Dec-2004
1	One	01-Dec-2001
7	Seven	07-Dec-2007
6	Six	06-Dec-2006
3	Three	03-Dec-2003
2	Two	02-Dec-2002

Task for example 4

Show a union that uses a column position number in its order by clause.

Oracle & Access SQL: Use a column number in the order by clause

```
select *
from sec1504_first
union
select *
from sec1504_second
order by 2;  ❶
```

Beginning tables — Same as in task 1

Result table — Same as in task 1

Notes

➊ This says to sort the rows of the result table on its second column.

Check your understanding

Modify the following `union`. Add an `order by` clause to it to sort the rows by the last name. Try all four methods. Which ones work?

```
select a.first_name,
       a.last_name,
       count(b.lunch_id) as number_of_lunches
from l_employees a
     inner join l_lunches b
     on a.employee_id = b.employee_id
group by a.first_name,
         a.last_name
union all
select 'Carol',
       'Rose',
       0
from dual
union all
select 'Paula',
       'Jacobs',
       0
from dual;
```

15-5 Creating a table or view that includes a `union`

A few years ago, in earlier versions of SQL, people were not allowed to create a view that contained a `union`. This restriction no longer applies to most SQL products, so we do not need to worry about it. If you have inherited some SQL code written years ago, you might find that code had to work around this restriction.

Although this feature is available now, it does not work perfectly in most SQL products. It can still give you a few surprises. The following examples show you how to create a table and a view that includes a `union`. The notes discuss the surprises I found.

Task for example 1

Create a view in Oracle that is defined using a union. Show that you can also include an order by clause.

Oracle SQL: Create a view using a union with an order by clause

```
create or replace view sec1505a_view as
select *
from sec1505_first
union
select *
from sec1505_second
order by 2;
```

Beginning tables — sec1505_first table and sec1505_second table; same as the sec1504 tables in the preceding listing

Result view (sec1505a_view)

```
NUMBER_1 WORD_1     DATE_1
-------- ---------- -----------
       5 FIVE       05-DEC-2005
       4 FOUR       04-DEC-2004
       1 ONE        01-DEC-2001
       7 SEVEN      07-DEC-2007
       6 SIX        06-DEC-2006
       3 THREE      03-DEC-2003
       2 TWO        02-DEC-2002
```

Task for example 2

Create a table in Oracle that is defined using a union. Show that you can also include an order by clause.

Oracle SQL: Create a table using a union with an order by clause

```
create table sec1505b_table as
select *
from sec1505_first
union
select *
from sec1505_second
order by 2;
```

Result table — Same as in task 1

Task for example 3

Create a view in Access that is defined using a `union`. Show that you can also include an `order by` clause.

Access SQL: Create a view using a `union` with an `order by` clause

Step 1: Enter this query in the SQL window:

```
select *
from sec1505_first
union
select *
from sec1505_second
order by 2;
```

Step 2: Save the query. Name it `sec1505a_view`.

Task for example 4

Create a table in Access that is defined using a `union`. Show that you can also include an `order by` clause.

Access SQL: Create a table using a `union` with an `order by` clause ❶

You cannot do this directly. The workaround is to create the table from a saved query.

```
select *
into sec1505b_table
from sec1505a_view;
```

Notes

❶ In Access, we cannot directly create a table from a `union` query. The workaround is to first create a saved query containing the `union` and then create a table from the saved query.

Check your understanding

Goal: Show that a `union` can add new rows of data to a table. This is similar to what an `insert` statement does.

First, create a `select` statement that lists all the columns and rows of the `l_employees` table and uses a `union all` to add the following new employee. Then save the result table as a new table called `sec1505_employees`.

Employee_id:	301
First_Name:	Gail
Last_Name:	Jones
Dept_code:	Sal
Hire_date:	Feb 15, 2011
Credit_limit:	$25.00
Phone_number	(null)
Manager_id	202

15-6 Automatic datatype conversion in a `union`

The result table of a `union` contains all the rows from both beginning tables. Each column of this result table has one specific datatype, like any column of any other table. Does this mean that we can only form a `union` when both beginning tables have columns with exactly the same datatypes in all their columns? No.

All that is required is that the matching columns are compatible with each other. They could both be text, or they could both be numbers, or they could both be dates. Beyond that, any difference in the datatypes will be handled by automatic datatype conversion.

Text columns

First, consider text columns. Suppose the first column of one beginning table contains text strings that are 10 characters long. Suppose the first column of the other beginning table contains text strings that are 20 characters long. I am speaking about the first columns because it is convenient, but this applies to any matching set of columns from each table.

Under the strictest definition of a union, this small difference in the datatype of these columns would mean that the data from one cannot be put into the other column. In our example, the data of a text string that is 20 characters long would not be able to fit into a space that is only 10 characters long, so it might seem that a `union` cannot be formed.

However, all SQL products resolve this difference to make the `union` possible. This is done by automatically changing the datatype of one or both columns to make them the same. In our example, the data of the first table, the 10-character-long text strings, are automatically converted into 20-character-long text strings. Then all the data have precisely the same datatype, so all the data can be put into a single column. This permits the `union`.

When two columns of text strings have different lengths, this difference in their datatypes is resolved by making the length of all the data equal to the length of the longest column. This is the shortest possible length to use without losing any part of the data.

Numeric columns

Next, consider numeric columns. Suppose the first column of one beginning table contains numbers that are two digits long and the first column of the other beginning table contains numbers that are seven digits long.

Under the strictest definition of a `union`, we would not be able to create a `union`. That is, the seven-digit numbers would not be able to fit into a space that allowed for only two digits.

However, all SQL products are able to resolve this difference by changing the datatypes automatically in the process of forming the `union`.

When two columns of numbers have different lengths, this difference in their datatypes is usually resolved by giving all the numbers the maximum length allowed to any number. Different SQL products will differ on the exact details of what that maximum length is.

Date columns

Last, consider date columns. There is only one datatype for dates, so all columns of dates have will always have precisely the same datatype.

Compatibility of columns

Because of this automatic datatype conversion, we say that any two columns of text are compatible and any two columns of numbers are compatible. By extension, we also say that any two columns of dates are compatible. In conclusion, we can always form a `union` of two tables if they have the same number of columns and the matching columns from each table are compatible.

Task

Show an example of automatic datatype conversion taking place in a `union`.

Oracle SQL ❶

```
create or replace view sec1506_union_view as
select number_column_with_length_7 as number_column,
       text_column_with_length_7 as text_column
from sec1506_with_long_columns
union
select number_column_with_length_2,
       text_column_with_length_2
from sec1506_with_short_columns
order by 1;
```

Access SQL ❶

Step 1: Enter this query in the SQL window:

```
select number_column_with_length_7 as number_column,
       text_column_with_length_7 as text_column
from sec1506_with_long_columns
union
select number_column_with_length_2,
       text_column_with_length_2
from sec1506_with_short_columns
order by 1;
```

Step 2: Use the GUI to save the query. Name it sec1506_union_view.

Oracle & Access SQL

```
select *
from sec1506_union_view;
```

Beginning table: sec1506_with_long_columns

```
NUMBER_COLUMN_WITH_LENGTH_7 TEXT_COLUMN_WITH_LENGTH_7
--------------------------- -------------------------
                    1111111 AAAAAAA
                    2222222 BBBBBBB
                    3333333 CCCCCCC
                    4444444 DDDDDDD
                    5555555 EEEEEEE
```

Beginning table: sec1506_with_short_columns

```
NUMBER_COLUMN_WITH_LENGTH_2 TEXT_COLUMN_WITH_LENGTH_2
--------------------------- -------------------------
                         33 CC
                         44 DD
                         55 EE
                         66 FF
                         77 GG
```

Result table

```
NUMBER_COLUMN   TEXT_COLUMN
------------- -----------
           33 CC
           44 DD
           55 EE
           66 FF
           77 GG
      1111111 AAAAAAA
      2222222 BBBBBBB
      3333333 CCCCCCC
      4444444 DDDDDDD
      5555555 EEEEEEE
```

Notes

❶ The reason the Oracle SQL differs from the Access SQL here has nothing to do with the automatic datatype conversion that takes place in a union. Instead, Oracle and Access have different ways of saving the result in a new view.

Check your understanding

Run the code from this section. Use the methods of section 7-12 to examine the datatypes of the columns of the beginning tables and of the new view created by the union. Have any of the datatypes changed in the process of forming the union?

Unconventional Unions

It is common knowledge that we can only create a union of two tables if they have the same number of columns and the datatypes of the matching columns are compatible. That common knowledge is wrong!

These rules are only true on the most detailed level, which is the most trivial level. They are false on the broader level, which is the level of handling information, In the next two sections, I break both these rules and create unions of tables that have different numbers of columns and where the columns do not seem to match.

I end up with the opinion that I can perform a union of any two tables. The one limitation is that the columns of the result table must have some consistent meaning. I impose that rule myself because I want the result to make sense on one level or another.

15-7 A union of tables with different datatypes

This section shows a union that matches a numeric column with a text column. Some people think this cannot be done.

The reason it can be done is that all types of data can be converted to text. After all the columns have been converted to text, they all have the same datatype, so they all fit together in a union. In this example, I use a row function to explicitly convert the datatype of each column to text, rather than relying on automatic datatype conversion. However, in many SQL products this conversion is done automatically for you.

In the following example, numeric data are changed into text data so that they can be combined in the union with other text data. In Oracle, the to_char row function changes numeric data and date/time data to text data. In Access you can use the format row function.

Task

Show how to use datatype conversion functions in a union to make every column into a text column.

Oracle SQL

```
create or replace view sec1507_union_view as
select to_char(number_column_with_length_7 as first_column,
       text_column_with_length_7 as second_column
from sec1507_with_long_columns
union
select text_column_with_length_2,
       to_char(number_column_with_length_2
from sec1507_with_short_columns
order by 1;
```

Access SQL

Step 1: Enter this query in the SQL window:

```
select format(number_column_with_length_7) as first_column,
       text_column_with_length_7 as second_column
from sec1507_with_long_columns
union
select text_column_with_length_2,
       format(number_column_with_length_2)
from sec1507_with_short_columns
order by 1;
```

Step 2: Use the GUI to save the query. Name it sec1507_union_view.

Oracle & Access SQL

```
select *
from sec1507_union_view;
```

Beginning table: sec1507_with_long_columns

```
NUMBER_COLUMN_WITH_LENGTH_7 TEXT_COLUMN_WITH_LENGTH_7
--------------------------- -------------------------
                    1111111 AAAAAAA
                    2222222 BBBBBBB
                    3333333 CCCCCCC
                    4444444 DDDDDDD
                    5555555 EEEEEEE
```

Beginning table: sec1507_with_short_columns

```
NUMBER_COLUMN_WITH_LENGTH_7 TEXT_COLUMN_WITH_LENGTH_7
--------------------------- -------------------------
                         33 CC
                         44 DD
                         55 EE
                         66 FF
                         77 GG
```

Created view (sec1507_union_view)

```
FIRST_COLUMN                             SECOND_COLUMN
---------------------------------------- -------------------------
1111111                                  AAAAAAA
2222222                                  BBBBBBB
3333333                                  CCCCCCC
4444444                                  DDDDDDD
5555555                                  EEEEEEE
CC                                       33
DD                                       44
EE                                       55
FF                                       66
GG                                       77
```

Check your understanding

Modify the following `select` statement. Convert the datatypes of all the columns to text. (Actually, sometimes this code will work as it is and the conversion of the datatypes is done automatically for you behind the scenes.)

```
select date_1,
       date_1,
       date_1
```

```
from sec1507_first
union
select number_2,
       word_2,
       date_2
from sec1507_second;
```

15-8 A union of two tables with different numbers of columns

This section shows a union of two tables that have different numbers of columns. Some people think this cannot be done. It can be done because we can add extra columns to one table to give both tables the same number of columns.

In the following example, I do a union of a table that has two columns with a table that has three columns. To do this I add a column of nulls to the first table. Both tables have three columns when the union is performed.

Task

Show how to form a union of two tables that have different numbers of columns.

Oracle & Access SQL

```
select a.number_col,
       a.text_col,
       a.date_col
from sec1508_more_columns a
union
select b.number_col,
       b.text_col,
       null ❶
from sec1508_less_columns b;
```

Beginning tables

sec1508_more_columns

NUMBER_COL	TEXT_COL	DATE_COL
1111111	AAAAAAA	01-DEC-2015
2222222	BBBBBBB	02-DEC-2015
3333333	CCCCCCC	03-DEC-2015
4444444	DDDDDDD	04-DEC-2015
5555555	EEEEEEE	05-DEC-2015

sec1508_less_columns

NUMBER_COL	TEXT_COL
3333333	CCCCCCC
4444444	DDDDDDD
5555555	EEEEEEE
6666666	FFFFFFF
7777777	GGGGGGG

Result table

```
NUMBER_COL TEXT_COL DATE_COL
---------- -------- -----------
   1111111 AAAAAAA  01-DEC-2015
   2222222 BBBBBBB  02-DEC-2015
   3333333 CCCCCCC  03-DEC-2015
   3333333 CCCCCCC  (null)
   4444444 DDDDDDD  04-DEC-2015
   4444444 DDDDDDD  (null)
   5555555 EEEEEEE  05-DEC-2015
   5555555 EEEEEEE  (null)
   6666666 FFFFFFF  (null)
   7777777 GGGGGGG  (null)
```

Notes

❶ This is where the extra column is added. It is also possible to use a literal to create a new column. For example, you could use the literal 'This value is unknown' to replace the null in the SQL statement.

Check your understanding

Modify the following `select` statement to make it work. Add one more columns to the second `select` statement. You can use either a null or a literal value.

```
select number_1,
       word_1,
       date_1
from sec1508_more_columns
union
select number_2,
       word_2
from twos;
```

Applications of a Union

A union has some very useful applications. It gives us a lot of power that we have not had until now. Two analogies come to mind when I think of the applications of a union. The first is the saying from ancient Rome, "Divide and conquer." We are able to divide the rows of a table into separate groups, apply a different type of processing to each group, and then use a union to put all the rows back into one table.

The other analogy is "management by exception." This contrasts with "management by handling all the details," which can overwhelm us with the volume of details. We are able to isolate the exceptional cases and flag them so we can see and handle the special circumstances they present. Using a union, we can merge these exceptional cases with the majority of the data to again create a unified view of all the data.

15-9 Determining if two tables are identical

When two tables have the same number of columns and rows, they might appear to be identical, but perhaps one of the cells has a different value in one table than in the other. How can we be certain about this?

One way is to form the union of the two tables. This method works if the tables have primary keys or if you know that they do not have any duplicate rows, which is the case for most tables.

If the two tables are identical, the union will have the same number of rows as the beginning tables. All the rows of the second table will be eliminated as duplicates. If they are not identical, the union will have more rows.

If there is a difference between the tables, this technique does not help us find out what it is. We have other ways of finding that information. This technique only determines whether there is a difference.

Task

Test whether two tables are identical. We already know that these tables have the same number of columns and that the datatypes of those columns are compatible.

Oracle & Access SQL:
Step 1 — Determine if the tables have the same number of rows

```
select count(*) from l_foods;
select count(*) from sec1509_foods;
```

Beginning table 1 (1_foods table)

SUPPLIER ID	PRODUCT CODE	MENU ITEM	DESCRIPTION	PRICE	PRICE INCREASE
ASP	FS	1	FRESH SALAD	$2.00	$0.25
ASP	SP	2	SOUP OF THE DAY	$1.50	(null)
ASP	SW	3	SANDWICH	$3.50	$0.40
CBC	GS	4	GRILLED STEAK	$6.00	$0.70
CBC	SW	5	HAMBURGER	$2.50	$0.30
FRV	BR	6	BROCCOLI	$1.00	$0.05
FRV	FF	7	FRENCH FRIES	$1.50	(null)
JBR	AS	8	SODA	$1.25	$0.25
JBR	VR	9	COFFEE	$0.85	$0.15
VSB	AS	10	DESSERT	$3.00	$0.50

Beginning table 2 (sec1509_foods table)

SUPPLIER ID	PRODUCT CODE	MENU ITEM	DESCRIPTION	PRICE	PRICE INCREASE
ASP	FS	1	FRESH SALAD	$2.00	$0.25
ASP	SP	2	SOUP OF THE DAY	$1.50	(null)
ASP	SW	3	SANDWICH	$3.50	$0.40
CBC	GS	4	GRILLED STEAK	$6.00	$0.70
CBC	SW	5	HAMBURGER	$2.50	$0.30
FRV	BR	6	BROCCOLI	$1.00	$0.05
FRV	FF	7	FRENCH FRIES	$1.50	(null)
JBR	AS	8	SODA	$1.25	$0.25
JBR	VR	9	COFFEE	$0.85	$0.15
VSB	AS	10	DESSERT	$3.00	$0.50

**The result table is the same for both `select` statements in step 1.
This shows that both tables have the same number of rows.**

COUNT(*)
10

Oracle SQL:
Step 2 — Create a view that is the union of both tables

```
create or replace view sec1509_union_view as
select * from 1_foods
union
select * from sec1509_foods;
```

Access SQL:
Step 2 — Create a view that is the union of both tables

Step 2, Part 1: Enter this query in the SQL window:

```
select * from 1_foods
union
select * from sec1509_foods;
```

Step 2, Part 2: Save this query. Name it sec1509_union_view.

Oracle & Access SQL:
Step 3 — Count the number of rows in the view

```
select count(*)
from sec1509_union_view;
```

Result table

```
COUNT(*)
---------
       10
```

Conclusion

The tables are identical.

Check your understanding

One of the two tables, sec1509a_lunches or sec1509b_lunches, is identical to the 1_lunches table. The other table is different. Determine which table is the same and which one is different.

15-10 Using a literal in a union to identify the source of the data

In this section we add a new column to each of the beginning tables using a literal. That column identifies the table that the data come from. After we perform the union, the source of each row of data is identified.

If both tables contain an identical row, the duplicate is not eliminated. Rather, it is shown to come from both tables. This might be what we want to happen.

The new column ensures that no row from the first table can be identical to a row from the second table, so we should use a union all instead of a union.

Task

Show a select statement that uses a union with literals to identify the source of each row.

Oracle & Access SQL

```
select number_1, ❶
       word_1,
       date_1,
       'from the first table' as source_of_the_data ❷
from sec1510_first
union all
select number_2, ❸
       word_2,
       date_2,
       'from the second table' ❹
from sec1510_second
order by number_1;
```

Beginning tables

sec1510_first table   **sec1510_second table**

```
NUMBER_1 WORD_1      DATE_1          NUMBER_2 WORD_2      DATE_2
-------- ----------  -----------     -------- ----------  -----------
       1 ONE         01-DEC-2001            3 THREE       03-DEC-2003
       2 TWO         02-DEC-2002            4 FOUR        04-DEC-2004
       3 THREE       03-DEC-2003            5 FIVE        05-DEC-2005
       4 FOUR        04-DEC-2004            6 SIX         06-DEC-2006
       5 FIVE        05-DEC-2005            7 SEVEN       07-DEC-2007
```

Result table

```
NUMBER_1 WORD_1      DATE_1          SOURCE_OF_THE_DATA
-------- ----------  -----------     ---------------------
       1 ONE         01-DEC-2001 FROM THE FIRST  TABLE
       2 TWO         02-DEC-2002 FROM THE FIRST  TABLE
       3 THREE       03-DEC-2003 FROM THE FIRST  TABLE
       3 THREE       03-DEC-2003 FROM THE SECOND TABLE
       4 FOUR        04-DEC-2004 FROM THE FIRST  TABLE
       4 FOUR        04-DEC-2004 FROM THE SECOND TABLE
       5 FIVE        05-DEC-2005 FROM THE FIRST  TABLE
       5 FIVE        05-DEC-2005 FROM THE SECOND TABLE
       6 SIX         06-DEC-2006 FROM THE SECOND TABLE
       7 SEVEN       07-DEC-2007 FROM THE SECOND TABLE
```

Notes

❶ The first `select` statement lists the rows from the first table. It attaches a literal to each of these rows.

❷ The literal is text placed within quotation marks. A column alias gives this column a name. Every row of the first table has the same value in this new column.

❸ The second `select` statement lists the rows from the second table. It attaches a different literal to each of these rows.

❹ This is the text that is added to each row of the second table.

Check your understanding

The following `select` statement creates a `union` of the `twos` table with the `threes` table. Add a new column to show the table from which each row comes.

```
select number_2,
       word_2
from twos
union
select number_3,
       word_3
from threes;
```

15-11 Attaching messages to flag exceptions, warnings, and errors

This section shows you how to attach messages to rows of data. The rows of a table are divided into two groups: a small group that will be flagged with a message and a much larger group that will receive no message.

This technique is useful for finding exceptional conditions in the data and for attaching warning messages and error messages.

The `where` clauses in the two `select` statements divide the rows of data into two groups. One group receives a message and the other group gets a blank space instead of a message. Then the `union` puts all these rows back into a single table.

When we divide the rows into two separate groups, it is important to remember that SQL uses three-valued logic. It is not enough to use a condition, A, in one `where` clause and its opposite, NOT A, in the other. We must always consider the possibility that there are nulls in the data and handle that case.

Task

List the foods and their prices. Add the message "expensive item" to the foods that cost more than $2.00. List the foods in alphabetical order.

Oracle & Access SQL

```
select description,
       price,
       'EXPENSIVE ITEM' as message
from l_foods
where price > 2.00
union all
select description,
       price,
       ' '
from l_foods
where not (price > 2.00)
   or price is null
order by description;
```

Beginning table (l_foods table)

```
SUPPLIER PRODUCT   MENU                                    PRICE
ID       CODE      ITEM DESCRIPTION             PRICE INCREASE
-------- -------   ------ -------------------- -------- --------
ASP      FS           1 FRESH SALAD             $2.00     $0.25
ASP      SP           2 SOUP OF THE DAY         $1.50    (null)
ASP      SW           3 SANDWICH                $3.50     $0.40
CBC      GS           4 GRILLED STEAK           $6.00     $0.70
CBC      SW           5 HAMBURGER               $2.50     $0.30
FRV      BR           6 BROCCOLI                $1.00     $0.05
FRV      FF           7 FRENCH FRIES            $1.50    (null)
JBR      AS           8 SODA                    $1.25     $0.25
JBR      VR           9 COFFEE                  $0.85     $0.15
VSB      AS          10 DESSERT                 $3.00     $0.50
```

Result table

```
DESCRIPTION            PRICE MESSAGE
-------------------- -------- --------------
BROCCOLI              $1.00
COFFEE                $0.85
DESSERT               $3.00 EXPENSIVE ITEM
FRENCH FRIES          $1.50
FRESH SALAD           $2.00
GRILLED STEAK         $6.00 EXPENSIVE ITEM
HAMBURGER             $2.50 EXPENSIVE ITEM
SANDWICH              $3.50 EXPENSIVE ITEM
SODA                  $1.25
SOUP OF THE DAY       $1.50
```

List all the rows and columns of the `l_employees` table. Add a new column that says "Old Timer" for any employee that was hired before the year 2000 and is blank for all other employees. Sort this by the `employee_id` column.

15-12 Dividing data from one column into two different columns

This section shows you how to divide one column of data into two or more columns. This technique can be useful in making some types of data stand out or in sorting the data into several categories.

This technique is similar to the ones we have used before. The `where` clauses of the `select` statements divide the rows of the beginning table into separate groups. Then the data are listed in the desired column and a blank is placed in the other columns. A `union` puts all these pieces back together.

Task

Divide the `cost` column from the beginning table into two columns: `debits` and `credits`.

Oracle & Access SQL

```
select item,
       null as debits,
       cost as credits
from sec1512_finances
where cost > 0
union all
select item,
       cost,
       null
from sec1512_finances
where cost < 0
   or cost is null
order by item;
```

Beginning table (`sec1512_finances` table)

```
ITEM                         COST
--------------------  -----------
SAMSONITE SUITCASE        -$248.13
RENT FOR APRIL            $700.00
OPERA TICKET             -$145.00
LUNCH                     -$15.62
DEBT REPAID BY JIM         $20.00
CAR REPAIR               -$622.98
HAIRCUT                   -$22.00
BIRTHDAY GIFT FROM MOM    $200.00
```

Result table

```
ITEM                    DEBITS   CREDITS
--------------------  --------  --------
BIRTHDAY GIFT FROM MOM            $200.00
CAR REPAIR            -$622.98
DEBT REPAID BY JIM                 $20.00
HAIRCUT               -$22.00
LUNCH                 -$15.62
OPERA TICKET          -$145.00
RENT FOR APRIL                    $700.00
SAMSONITE SUITCASE    -$248.13
```

Check your understanding

List the last name, first name, and hire date of all the people in the `1_employees` table. Divide the hire date column into two columns: one called "old timers" for people hired before the year 2000, and one called "newer hires" for people hired after that year. Sort the result table by last name and then by first name.

15-13 Applying two functions to different parts of the data

This section shows you how to apply several different calculations to the data in different rows. First, we use the where clauses in the select statements to divide the rows into groups. We make a separate group for each calculation and perform the calculations on all the rows within each group. Then we use a union to combine all the groups again.

Task

Show how to make two different calculations, depending on the data in a row. Increase the price of all foods costing more than $2.00 by 5 percent. Increase the price of all other foods by 10 percent. Ignore the existing price_increase column.

Oracle & Access SQL

```
select menu_item,
       description,
       price + (price * .05) as new_price
from l_foods
where price > 2.00
   or price is null
union all
select menu_item,
       description,
       price + (price * .10)
from l_foods
where price <= 2.00
order by menu_item;
```

Beginning table (1_foods table)

SUPPLIER ID	PRODUCT CODE	MENU ITEM	DESCRIPTION	PRICE	PRICE INCREASE
ASP	FS	1	FRESH SALAD	$2.00	$0.25
ASP	SP	2	SOUP OF THE DAY	$1.50	
ASP	SW	3	SANDWICH	$3.50	$0.40
CBC	GS	4	GRILLED STEAK	$6.00	$0.70
CBC	SW	5	HAMBURGER	$2.50	$0.30
FRV	BR	6	BROCCOLI	$1.00	$0.05
FRV	FF	7	FRENCH FRIES	$1.50	
JBR	AS	8	SODA	$1.25	$0.25
JBR	VR	9	COFFEE	$0.85	$0.15
VSB	AS	10	DESSERT	$3.00	$0.50

Result table

MENU ITEM	DESCRIPTION	NEW PRICE
1	FRESH SALAD	$2.20
2	SOUP OF THE DAY	$1.65
3	SANDWICH	$3.68
4	GRILLED STEAK	$6.30
5	HAMBURGER	$2.63
6	BROCCOLI	$1.10
7	FRENCH FRIES	$1.65
8	SODA	$1.38
9	COFFEE	$0.94
10	DESSERT	$3.15

Check your understanding

The numbers_0_to_9 table contains the numbers from zero to nine. Multiply all the even numbers by two and multiply all the other numbers by three.

15-14 A union of three or more tables

You can code a union of as many tables as you wish, as many as 10 or more. The union operation works the same way. If you want to use column aliases, you must assign them in the first select statement. The code may be long, but it is not complex.

Task

List the letters from `'A'` to `'G'`. Do this as a union of seven tables.

Oracle & Access SQL

```
select 'A' as letters
from dual
union
select 'B'
from dual
union
select 'C'
from dual
union
select 'D'
from dual
union
select 'E'
from dual
order by 1;
```

Beginning table

```
DUMMY
-------
X
```

Result table

```
LETTERS
-------
A
B
C
D
E
```

Set Intersection and Set Difference in Oracle

Oracle has created extensions to standard SQL that provide direct support for finding the intersection and difference between two tables. These operations can be done in any brand of SQL, but the Oracle extensions make them easier. These methods provide a good way to compare two tables to determine which rows are identical and which rows are different.

15-15 Set intersection

The intersection of two tables consists of all the rows that are identical in both tables. In Oracle, we can find the intersection of two tables with the `intersect` operation. This works much like a `union` in that the word goes between two `select` statements. These `select` statements define the tables that we are intersecting.

You can perform the same operation in other brands of SQL by writing an inner join of the tables, listing all the rows that are identical in both tables. This method is shown in the Access code.

Task

Find the intersection of two tables. That is, find all the rows that occur in both tables.

Oracle SQL ❶

```
select number_1,
       word_1,
       date_1
from sec1515_first
intersect
select number_2,
       word_2,
       date_2
from sec1515_second
order by number_1;
```

Access does not support this method.

Access SQL ❷

```
select a.number_1,
       a.word_1,
       a.date_1
from sec1515_first a,
     sec1515_second b
where a.number_1 = b.number_2
  and a.word_1 = b.word_2
  and a.date_1 = b.date_2
order by a.number_1;
```

Beginning tables
sec1515_first table   **sec1515_second table**

NUMBER_1	WORD_1	DATE_1
1	ONE	01-DEC-2001
2	TWO	02-DEC-2002
3	THREE	03-DEC-2003
4	FOUR	04-DEC-2004
5	FIVE	05-DEC-2005

NUMBER_2	WORD_2	DATE_2
3	THREE	03-DEC-2003
4	FOUR	04-DEC-2004
5	FIVE	05-DEC-2005
6	SIX	06-DEC-2006
7	SEVEN	07-DEC-2007

Result table

NUMBER_1	WORD_1	DATE_1
3	THREE	03-DEC-2003
4	FOUR	04-DEC-2004
5	FIVE	05-DEC-2005

Notes

❶ This method works even when there are nulls in several of the columns.

❷ This method works only when there are no nulls in any of the columns. To compare tables that contain nulls, one method is to temporarily change all the nulls to some other value, doing a `rollback` at the end to return them to nulls. Another method is to change the join condition on each column to include the possibility of nulls. Using this method, instead of writing

```
a.column1 = b.column1
```

I would write

```
(a.column1 = b.column1
or (a.column1 is null and b.column1 is null))
```

Check your understanding

Use the method of this section to find the intersection of the `twos` table and the `threes` table.

15-16   Set difference

Oracle supports the `minus` operation to find all the rows in one table that are not present in another table. The word `minus` is placed between two `select` statements, similar to the way the word `union` is placed.

This is a very nice feature that Oracle has created. It is not part of standard SQL. Rather, it is an extension to standard SQL that Oracle has added. Few, if any, other types of SQL have a feature like this.

Clearly, this operation is one-sided; that is, it makes a difference which table is the first table and which one is second. To find all the differences between two tables, A and B, we must look at both:

- A minus B
- B minus A

Another way to produce this result uses an outer join. The Access code shows this technique.

Task

Find all the rows that are in one table and not in the other table. Do this both ways to find all the differences between the two tables.

Oracle SQL: Step 1 ❶

```
select number_1,
       word_1,
       date_1
from sec1516_first
minus
select number_2,
       word_2,
       date_2
from sec1516_second
order by number_1;
```

Access does not support the `minus` operation.

Access SQL: Step 1 ❷

```
select a.number_1,
       a.word_1,
       a.date_1
from sec1516_first a
     left outer join sec1516_second b
     on a.number_1 = b.number_2
     and a.word_1 = b.word_2
     and a.date_1 = b.date_2
where b.number_2 is null
order by a.number_1;
```

Beginning tables

sec1516_first table   **sec1516_second table**

NUMBER_1	WORD_1	DATE_1
1	ONE	01-DEC-2001
2	TWO	02-DEC-2002
3	THREE	03-DEC-2003
4	FOUR	04-DEC-2004
5	FIVE	05-DEC-2005

NUMBER_2	WORD_2	DATE_2
3	THREE	03-DEC-2003
4	FOUR	04-DEC-2004
5	FIVE	05-DEC-2005
6	SIX	06-DEC-2006
7	SEVEN	07-DEC-2007

Result table — Step 1

NUMBER_1	WORD_1	DATE_1
1	ONE	01-DEC-2001
2	TWO	02-DEC-2002

Oracle SQL: Step 2 ❶

```
select number_2,
       word_2,
       date_2
from sec1516_second
minus
select number_1,
       word_1,
       date_1
from sec1516_first
order by number_2;
```

Access does not support the minus operation.

Access SQL: Step 2 ❷

```
select  b.number_2,
        b.word_2,
        b.date_2
from  sec1516_first a
      right outer join sec1516_second b
      on a.number_1 = b.number_2
      and a.word_1 = b.word_2
      and a.date_1 = b.date_2
where a.number_1 is null
order by b.number_2;
```

Result table — Step 2

```
NUMBER_2  WORD_2        DATE_2
--------- ----------    -----------
      6 SIX           06-DEC-2006
      7 SEVEN         07-DEC-2007
```

Notes

❶ This method works even when there are nulls in several of the columns.

❷ This method works only when there are no nulls in any of the columns. To compare tables that contain nulls, one method is to temporarily change all the nulls to some other value, doing a `rollback` at the end to return them to nulls. Another method is to change the join condition on each column to include the possibility of nulls. Using this method, instead of writing

```
a.column1 = b.column1
```

we would write

```
(a.column1 = b.column1
or (a.column1 is null and b.column1 is null))
```

Check your understanding

Use the method of this section to find the difference of the `twos` table and the `threes` table.

Key Points

- A union is different from a join. In a join, the data tables are combined before the selection or summarization takes place. In a union, the selection or summarization is done before the result tables are combined.

- In a union, the rows of two or more result tables are merged into a single result table and then duplicate rows are eliminated. To make this possible, the result tables from the select statements must be created with the same number of columns. Also, for every N, the Nth columns of all the result tables must have compatible datatypes.

- A union all is similar to a union, except the duplicate rows are not eliminated. They are left in the final result table.

- There can only be one order by clause in a union or union all. It must be placed at the end of the statement.

- Union and union all have many applications. They can be used to compare tables and add missing data to reports. They can replace outer joins and if-then-else logic.

- Unfortunately, many of the graphical (GUI) tools that generate SQL do not support the union. This is one of their major failings.

- Oracle has added two special operations, extensions to SQL, that are similar to a union: intersect and minus.

chapter 16

CROSS JOINS, SELF JOINS, AND CROSSTAB QUERIES

This chapter finishes the discussion of techniques used to join two tables. You will not use these techniques very often, but knowing them will add depth to your understanding of all joins. They will also enable you to get results that would be almost impossible to obtain otherwise.

A cross join is used to define an inner join. It is also important in detecting errors in your code. Cross joins of small tables are acceptable and useful at times, but cross joins of large tables should be avoided.

A self join involves joining a table with itself. This is necessary when you need information from several rows of the same table at the same time.

Cross Joins

A **cross join** is another way to combine two tables. It should only be used with small tables.

Cross joins are important to understand because they provide the foundation for both inner and outer joins. The properties of inner joins are derived from the properties of cross products.

16-1 Definition of a cross join

This section shows an example of a cross join, which is also called a **cross product** and a **Cartesian product**. A cross join matches each row of the first table with each row of the second table. This results in all possible combinations of the rows. A cross join often generates a lot of data, so it should be used infrequently and with great care.

The number of columns and rows in a cross join are as follows:

Columns in cross join = Sum of the number of columns in the beginning tables. (Add)

Rows in cross join = Product of the number of rows in the beginning tables. (Multiply)

In the following example, the cross join is written by putting both of the beginning tables in the `from` clause. This may look similar to an inner join. The difference is that there is no join condition at all.

When there is no join condition, SQL forms the cross product of the beginning tables.

The first table has four rows and the second table has five, so the result table has 20 rows. The first table has two columns and the second table has three, so the result table has five columns.

Task

Show an example of a cross join.

Oracle & Access SQL ❶

```
select a.*,
       b.*
from   sec1601_columns_1_to_2 a,
       sec1601_columns_3_to_5 b;
```

Beginning tables

sec1601_columns_1_to_2 table   **sec1601_columns_3_to_5 table**

NUM_COL_1	TEXT_COL_2
1	A
2	B
3	C
4	D

NUM_COL_3	TEXT_COL_4	DATE_COL_5
25	VV	05-AUG-2025
26	WW	06-SEP-2026
27	XX	07-OCT-2027
28	YY	08-NOV-2028
29	ZZ	09-DEC-2029

Result table

NUM_COL_1	TEXT_COL_2	NUM_COL_3	TEXT_COL_4	DATE_COL_5
1	A	25	VV	05-AUG-2025
2	B	25	VV	05-AUG-2025
3	C	25	VV	05-AUG-2025
4	D	25	VV	05-AUG-2025
1	A	26	WW	06-SEP-2026
2	B	26	WW	06-SEP-2026
3	C	26	WW	06-SEP-2026
4	D	26	WW	06-SEP-2026
1	A	27	XX	07-OCT-2027
2	B	27	XX	07-OCT-2027
3	C	27	XX	07-OCT-2027
4	D	27	XX	07-OCT-2027
1	A	28	YY	08-NOV-2028
2	B	28	YY	08-NOV-2028
3	C	28	YY	08-NOV-2028
4	D	28	YY	08-NOV-2028
1	A	29	ZZ	09-DEC-2029
2	B	29	ZZ	09-DEC-2029
3	C	29	ZZ	09-DEC-2029
4	D	29	ZZ	09-DEC-2029

Notes

❶ There is no `where` clause to create a join condition between the two beginning tables. This is how a cross join is coded.

Check your understanding

By hand, without a computer, write the cross join of the following two tables:

Table 1
U
V
W
X
Y
Z

Table 2
10
20
30
40
50

16-2 Why are cross joins important?

A cross join is such a simple concept that people sometimes ask, "What is its purpose? What is it good for?"

As the following sections show, cross joins are important for several reasons:

1. The definition of an inner join is based on a cross join.
2. Sometimes errors show up as cross joins.
3. A cross join of small tables can be used to show all combinations.
4. We need to avoid cross joins of large tables.

16-3 An inner join is derived from a cross join

A inner join is defined from a cross join. Here is the exact definition of the process that creates an inner join of two tables:

1. Create the cross join of the beginning tables.
2. Evaluate the join condition for each row of the cross join. The join condition is a statement. (Some people prefer to call it an ***expression*** or a ***logical expression***.) For every row of the cross join, that statement will be either True, False, or Unknown.
3. Keep only the rows that evaluate to True. Drop all the rows that evaluate to False or Unknown.
4. Remove the evaluation column.

Task

Show each step of the process to create an inner join of the `fruits` and `colors` tables. Use the join condition `f_num = c_num`.

Oracle & Access SQL

```
select a.*,
       b.*
from sec1603_fruits a,
     sec1603_colors b
where a.f_num = b.c_num;
```

Beginning tables

sec1603_fruits table   **sec1603_colors table**

FRUIT	F_NUM
APPLE	1
BANANA	2
STRAWBERRY	1
GRAPE	4
KIWI	(null)

5 rows

C_NUM	COLOR
1	RED
2	YELLOW
1	GREEN
5	WHITE
(null)	BROWN

5 rows

Step 1 — Form the cross join of the two tables

FRUIT	F_NUM	C_NUM	COLOR
APPLE	1	1	RED
APPLE	1	1	GREEN
APPLE	1	2	YELLOW
APPLE	1	5	WHITE
APPLE	1	(null)	BROWN
BANANA	2	1	RED
BANANA	2	1	GREEN
BANANA	2	2	YELLOW
BANANA	2	5	WHITE
BANANA	2	(null)	BROWN
GRAPE	4	1	RED
GRAPE	4	1	GREEN
GRAPE	4	2	YELLOW
GRAPE	4	5	WHITE
GRAPE	4	(null)	BROWN
KIWI	(null)	1	RED
KIWI	(null)	1	GREEN
KIWI	(null)	2	YELLOW
KIWI	(null)	5	WHITE
KIWI	(null)	(null)	BROWN
STRAWBERRY	1	1	RED
STRAWBERRY	1	1	GREEN
STRAWBERRY	1	2	YELLOW
STRAWBERRY	1	5	WHITE
STRAWBERRY	1	(null)	BROWN

25 rows

Step 2 — Evaluate the join condition in each row of the cross join

Assign an evaluation to each row: True, False, or Unknown.

Here, the join condition is f_num = c_num.

FRUIT	F_NUM	C_NUM	COLOR	EVALUATION
APPLE	1	1	GREEN	TRUE
APPLE	1	1	RED	TRUE
APPLE	1	2	YELLOW	FALSE
APPLE	1	5	WHITE	FALSE
APPLE	1	(null)	BROWN	UNKNOWN
BANANA	2	1	GREEN	FALSE
BANANA	2	1	RED	FALSE
BANANA	2	2	YELLOW	TRUE
BANANA	2	5	WHITE	FALSE
BANANA	2	(null)	BROWN	UNKNOWN
GRAPE	4	1	GREEN	FALSE
GRAPE	4	1	RED	FALSE
GRAPE	4	2	YELLOW	FALSE
GRAPE	4	5	WHITE	FALSE
GRAPE	4	(null)	BROWN	UNKNOWN
KIWI	(null)	1	GREEN	UNKNOWN
KIWI	(null)	1	RED	UNKNOWN
KIWI	(null)	2	YELLOW	UNKNOWN
KIWI	(null)	5	WHITE	UNKNOWN
KIWI	(null)	(null)	BROWN	UNKNOWN
STRAWBERRY	1	1	GREEN	TRUE
STRAWBERRY	1	1	RED	TRUE
STRAWBERRY	1	2	YELLOW	FALSE
STRAWBERRY	1	5	WHITE	FALSE
STRAWBERRY	1	(null)	BROWN	UNKNOWN

Step 3 — Keep only the rows that evaluate as True

FRUIT	F_NUM	C_NUM	COLOR	EVALUATION
APPLE	1	1	RED	TRUE
APPLE	1	1	GREEN	TRUE
BANANA	2	2	YELLOW	TRUE
STRAWBERRY	1	1	RED	TRUE
STRAWBERRY	1	1	GREEN	TRUE

Step 4 — Remove the evaluation; this is the inner join

```
FRUIT            F_NUM        C_NUM  COLOR

----------    ----------   ----------  ----------
APPLE               1            1  RED
APPLE               1            1  GREEN
BANANA              2            2  YELLOW
STRAWBERRY          1            1  RED
STRAWBERRY          1            1  GREEN
```

Check your understanding

By hand, without a computer, write the cross join of the following two tables:

Table 1
2
4
6
8
10
12

Table 2
(null)
3
6
9
12

16-4 The properties of an inner join

This section shows you how the properties of an inner join, which we discussed in chapter 13, are derived from the definition of an inner join given in the previous section.

■ **An inner join contains all valid combinations of rows. Each row of one table can match with many rows of the other table.**

This occurs because the first step of forming an inner join is to form a cross join. The cross join creates all possible combinations of the rows. Every possible combination that passes the validity test of the succeeding steps becomes part of the inner join.

■ **Rows are dropped from the join if there is no matching row in the other table.**

In step 2 of the definition in the previous section, for each row of the cross join, the statement of the join condition was evaluated. If there is no matching row in the other table, this evaluation is never True. It is always False or Unknown.

In step 3 we only keep the rows of the cross join that evaluate to True. This drops all the rows from one of the beginning tables that do not have a match in the other beginning table.

- **Rows are dropped from the join if any matching column(s) contains a null.**

In step 2, the join condition statement always evaluates to Unknown if any of the matching columns contains a null because a null is always handled as an unknown value when we evaluate row functions.

In step 3, all of these rows of the cross join are dropped.

- **Inner joins are symmetric. The order in which the tables are joined does not matter. Expressed mathematically:**
  $$A \times B = B \times A$$
  and $\quad (A \times B) \times C = A \times (B \times C)$

The symmetry of inner joins occurs because each of the steps in the definition is symmetric.

In step 1, the cross join is symmetric. That is, "A cross join B" is equal to "B cross join A." This is because a cross join creates all possible combinations of the rows. It does not consider the order of the tables.

Step 2 evaluates the join condition statement. It does not know or care which table came first.

Step 3 drops all the rows of the cross join that do not evaluate to True. This has no reference to the order of the tables.

Step 4 drops the evaluation column. The order of the tables plays no role here.

16-5 An error in the join condition can appear to be a cross join

One frequent type of error that occurs in SQL is omission of one of the join conditions within the `where` clause. The result often resembles a cross product. You may see the data you expected, but then see it repeated many times. For example, if you were expecting to have 100 rows in the result, you might find that you have 2,000, with each of the rows you wanted repeated 20 times.

If you see this, do not panic. Just examine your `where` clause carefully to be sure it contains all the conditions it needs. Sometimes you might not be sure if a condition is needed or not. It may seem redundant and unnecessary. Putting extra conditions in the where clause may cause more processing to occur, but at least the results are accurate. Putting too few conditions in the where clause can produce the wrong results. When in doubt, add extra conditions to the where clause.

As you write SQL, you should pay attention to the size of your tables and know approximately how much data to expect. If your results do not meet your expectations, you can search for possible coding errors.

In the following example, there is a mistake in the first version of the SQL. The join between the 1_lunch_items table and the 1_foods table is incorrect. This join should match on two columns, supplier_id and product_code, but the condition that the product codes are equal has been left out of the where clause.

The effect of the mistake in this example is subtle. When we look at the result table, we might notice that the values in the supplier_id column are repeated several times. That gives us a hint that there could be an error.

The repetition is due to a cross join, which occurs because we have left one of the join conditions out of the where clause. To confirm our suspicions, we could ask how many items are expected in lunch 2. By looking at the 1_lunch_items table, we would find that there should be four items in this lunch, but the result table lists eight items, so we know there is an error somewhere.

The first thing I would do in this situation would be to review all the join conditions in the where clause. In this case, that would solve the problem.

The effect of the error is that when someone orders one item from a supplier, they get all the items offered by that supplier.

Task

Show an example of SQL that contains an error. Leave one of the join conditions out of the where clause. Show how we might detect this error.

For lunch 2, list the lunch_id, supplier_id, product_code, description, price, and quantity columns. Use the 1_foods table and the 1_lunch_items table.

Oracle & Access SQL: Join is incorrect

```
select a.lunch_id,
       b.supplier_id,
       b.product_code,
       b.description,
       b.price,
       a.quantity
from l_lunch_items a,
     l_foods b
where a.supplier_id = b.supplier_id
  and a.lunch_id = 2;
```

Incorrect result table

```
         SUPPLIER PRODUCT
LUNCH_ID ID       CODE    DESCRIPTION              PRICE   QUANTITY
-------- -------- ------- ------------------------ ------- --------
       2 ASP      FS      FRESH SALAD              $2.00         2
       2 ASP      SP      SOUP OF THE DAY          $1.50         2
       2 ASP      SW      SANDWICH                 $3.50         2
       2 FRV      BR      BROCCOLI                 $1.00         1
       2 FRV      FF      FRENCH FRIES             $1.50         1
       2 JBR      AS      SODA                     $1.25         2
       2 JBR      VR      COFFEE                   $0.85         2
       2 VSB      AS      DESSERT                  $3.00         1
```

Oracle & Access SQL: Join is correct

```
select a.lunch_id,
       b.supplier_id,
       b.product_code,
       b.description,
       b.price,
       a.quantity
from l_lunch_items a,
     l_foods b
where a.supplier_id = b.supplier_id
  and a.product_code = b.product_code
  and a.lunch_id = 2;
```

Correct result table

LUNCH_ID	SUPPLIER ID	PRODUCT CODE	DESCRIPTION	PRICE	QUANTITY
2	ASP	SW	SANDWICH	$3.50	2
2	FRV	FF	FRENCH FRIES	$1.50	1
2	JBR	VR	COFFEE	$0.85	2
2	VSB	AS	DESSERT	$3.00	1

Check your understanding

Suppose you are developing a new `select` statement. It is fairly complex and you are using several tables. You are expecting a result with about 400 rows, but the result you get is about 2,000 rows. What part of your `select` statement would you examine first?

16-6 Using a cross join to list all the possible combinations

Sometimes we might want to list all the possible combinations of several factors. This occurs mostly when we are trying to analyze a complex situation or when we just want to be sure we have considered all the possibilities.

For example, suppose I have decided to buy a new car. I plan to spend some time shopping for it, so I get exactly the one I want. I know that salespeople are going to try to get me to make a purchase before I have completed all my shopping, so I want to set up a framework, a checklist, for myself.

I have decided to look at four types of cars: Ford, Toyota, Volkswagen, and Chevy. I want to look at three colors: white, red, and green. I could make two lists:

Car Type
Ford
Toyota
Volkswagen
Chevy

Color
White
Red
Green

Then I could arrange the options as a two-dimensional grid:

	White	Red	Green
Ford			
Toyota			
Volkswagen			
Chevy			

Or I could use a cross join to create a table of all the combinations. This table has 12 rows. The first few are as follows:

Car Type	Color
Ford	White
Ford	Red
Ford	Green
Toyota	White
Toyota	Red

It might seem that the two-dimensional layout is the easiest to use. It is more compact than the format generated by the cross join. The problem is that it is limited to handling only two factors and it cannot easily handle additional factors. In contrast, the cross join layout is able to handle any number of factors without any changes.

For example, suppose I also decide to look at two-door cars and four-door cars. I want to add this factor into my shopping. With the cross join approach, this is easy to do.

I get 24 rows in the table I create with the cross join. The first few are as follows:

Car Type	Color	Doors
Ford	White	2
Ford	White	4
Ford	Red	2
Ford	Red	4
Ford	Green	2

The power of using a cross join in a situation like this is that the cross join will continue to work without any rearrangement even if you have 20 or more factors that you want to consider.

Task

Use a cross join to list all the combinations of the following factors: car_type and color.

Oracle & Access SQL

```
select a.car_type,
       b.color
from sec1606_car_types a,
     sec1606_colors b
order by a.car_type,
         b.color;
```

Beginning tables

sec1606_car_types table

CAR_TYPE
FORD
TOYOTA
VOLKSWAGEN
CHEVY

sec1606_colors table

COLOR
WHITE
RED
GREEN

Result table

CAR_TYPE	COLOR
CHEVY	GREEN
CHEVY	RED
CHEVY	WHITE
FORD	GREEN
FORD	RED
FORD	WHITE
TOYOTA	GREEN
TOYOTA	RED
TOYOTA	WHITE
VOLKSWAGEN	GREEN
VOLKSWAGEN	RED
VOLKSWAGEN	WHITE

16-7 Other layouts when there are three or more dimensions

Let's continue the example from the previous section. We have three dimensions we are considering: car type, color, and number of doors. In the last section we saw that the layout of the result table produced by a cross join can handle this easily and it can continue to handle the situation even if many more dimensions are added. So the layout of a cross join is fine for the computer and all analysis tasks.

However, a two-dimensional layout is very attractive and can make a nice presentation for people view. A two-dimensional layout can be best, therefore, when your aim is to communicate with other people, or even just to understand the data yourself.

How are we going to deal with having three dimensions, but having only two dimensions in which to present them? There are two solutions to this problem.

Layout 1: Several two-dimensional tables

Table 1: Two-door cars

	White	Red	Green
Ford			
Toyota			
Volkswagen			
Chevy			

Table 2: Four-door cars

	White	Red	Green
Ford			
Toyota			
Volkswagen			
Chevy			

Here two separate tables are being used. If you can picture one of these tables stacked on top of the other, you will see that this is essentially a three-dimensional layout. Only two dimensions are shown at a time and all other dimensions become labels for for the variety of tables.

Layout 2: One table

	Doors	White	Red	Green
Ford	2			
Toyota	2			
Volkswagen	2			
Chevy	2			
Ford	4			
Toyota	4			
Volkswagen	4			
Chevy	4			

Here the layout uses one single table. One dimension goes across the page. All the other dimensions are kept in a cross join layout on the left side of the page.

16-8 Avoid a cross join of large tables

Never perform a cross join of two large tables! This can bring even a large computer to its knees. It can use up a large amount of the computer's resources and cost a lot of money. It probably will not give you anything useful anyway.

There have been a few times in my career as a programmer when I considered doing a cross join on some large tables. Usually I was searching for something, I had been working on a problem for several days, and using a cross join seemed to be the only solution.

In every one of those cases, after a bit more thought, I was able to avoid the cross join or at least limit it to a few small tables. Before you do a cross join take a good look at the tables you are going to join. If there are any rows you can eliminate from these tables, you should do so. I have always found that I only needed a small part of the entire table.

If you first create new tables that have only a few rows of the original large table, it is okay to perform a cross join on those small tables.

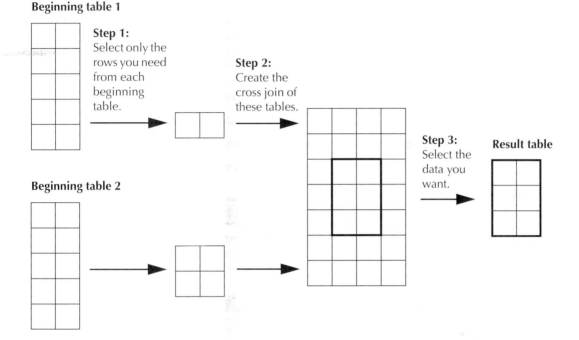

Beginning table 1

Step 1: Select only the rows you need from each beginning table.

Step 2: Create the cross join of these tables.

Step 3: Select the data you want.

Result table

Beginning table 2

Avoiding a cross join of large tables.

Self Joins

A self join is any inner, outer, or cross join in which a table is joined with itself. Many database designers consider self joins to be confusing and unintuitive, so they try to avoid them. Most databases are designed so that self joins are rarely needed for everyday tasks. However, using a self join can provide information that cannot be obtained in any other way.

16-9 Why would you ever join a table with itself?

It does not seem to make sense to join a table with itself

When we work on a problem, one of the first things we decide is which tables are needed. To make this decision, we think about the tables as containing certain kinds of information — one table contains information about food, another table contains information about employees. Joining a table with itself seems to just give us two copies of the same thing. It does not seem to give us any more information, so it does not seem to make any sense.

Why it does make sense

All databases, Oracle and Access included, process one row of a table at a time. You can access all the columns within a row, but only within one row. If we need information from two different rows at the same time, then it is necessary to join the table with itself.

How it is done

We can think about a self join as if we have two separate tables; they just happen to be identical. In the `from` clause, the table is listed twice. The two copies are distinguished by giving each one a separate table alias.

We only need to have one copy of the table stored on the disk. The computer software is able to behave as if we had two separate copies of it. If we are using a view instead of a table, that view only needs to be defined once.

In the following example, the beginning table contains a G and an H in column 1 (`col_1`). They are in different rows, so the computer cannot use both of them at the same time. However, in the result table of the cross join, there are two rows containing both G and H. From this table the computer can use both G and H at the same time.

Within the SQL, we see that the same table is listed twice in the `from` clause. Each time it is listed we give it a different table alias. The first table alias is A and the second one is B.

Task

Form a cross join of a table with itself.

Oracle & Access SQL

```
select a.col_1,
       a.col_2,
       b.col_1 as col_3,
       b.col_2 as col_4
from sec1609 a,
     sec1609 b;
```

Beginning table (sec1609 table)

```
COL_1          COL_2
---------- ---------
G                  1
H                  2
I                  3
J                  4
```

Result table (Cross join of the sec1609 table with itself)

```
COL_1          COL_2 COL_3          COL_4
---------- --------- ---------- ---------
G                  1 G                  1
H                  2 G                  1 ❶
I                  3 G                  1
J                  4 G                  1
G                  1 H                  2 ❶
H                  2 H                  2
I                  3 H                  2
J                  4 H                  2
G                  1 I                  3
H                  2 I                  3
I                  3 I                  3
J                  4 I                  3
G                  1 J                  4
H                  2 J                  4
I                  3 J                  4
J                  4 J                  4
```

Notes

❶ These two lines both include G and H.

16-10 An example of a self join

This section shows you an example of a self join. We want to list information about the employee and the manager on the same row of a report. The problem is that the information about the manager is in a different row from the information about the employee. So, we need to use two different rows of the table at the same time. We might picture the situation like this:

Employee ID	Last Name	Phone	Manager ID
XXXXX	XXXXX	XXXXX	◯	← employee information
◯	XXXXX	XXXXX		← manager information

Next, we change the picture to a different form. The next depiction shows two tables being joined. They are placed side by side and the join condition is shown. The join condition is that the value in the Manager ID column of the first table equals the value in the Employee ID column of the second table. These two tables just happen to be identical. That is what makes this a self join. Now all the information we need is in a single row.

Employee Information table (emp):
First copy of 1_employees table

Employee ID	Last Name	Phone	Manager ID
XXXXX	XXXXX	XXXXX	◯

Manager Information table (boss):
Second copy of 1_employees table

Employee ID	Last Name	Phone	Manager ID
◯	XXXXX	XXXXX	

In the SQL, the l_employees table is joined to itself. The first copy is given the table alias emp, meaning that employee information is taken from this copy of the table. The second copy is given the table alias boss, meaning that manager information is taken from this copy of the table. The computer only needs a single copy of the table, but it acts as if it has two separate copies.

The preceding depiction shows that the join condition is:

emp.manager_id = boss.employee_id

A left outer join is used because we want to include all the employees, even those who do not currently have a manager.

Task

From the l_employees table, list the employee ID, last name, and phone number of each employee with the name and phone number of his or her manager. Include a row for each employee, even those who do not have a manager. Sort the rows by the employee_id column.

Oracle & Access SQL

```
select  emp.employee_id,
        emp.last_name,
        emp.phone_number,
        boss.last_name as manager_name,
        boss.phone_number as manager_phone
from l_employees emp
     left outer join l_employees boss
     on emp.manager_id = boss.employee_id
order by emp.employee_id;
```

Beginning table (1_employees table)

EMPLOYEE ID	FIRST_NAME	LAST_NAME	DEPT CODE	HIRE_DATE	CREDIT LIMIT	PHONE NUMBER	MANAGER ID
201	SUSAN	BROWN	EXE	01-JUN-1998	$30.00	3484	(null)
202	JIM	KERN	SAL	16-AUG-1999	$25.00	8722	201
203	MARTHA	WOODS	SHP	02-FEB-2009	$25.00	7591	201
204	ELLEN	OWENS	SAL	01-JUL-2008	$15.00	6830	202
205	HENRY	PERKINS	SAL	01-MAR-2006	$25.00	5286	202
206	CAROL	ROSE	ACT	(null)	(null)	(null)	(null)
207	DAN	SMITH	SHP	01-DEC-2008	$25.00	2259	203
208	FRED	CAMPBELL	SHP	01-APR-2008	$25.00	1752	203
209	PAULA	JACOBS	MKT	17-MAR-1999	$15.00	3357	201
210	NANCY	HOFFMAN	SAL	16-FEB-2007	$25.00	2974	203

Result table

EMPLOYEE ID	LAST_NAME	PHONE NUMBER	MANAGER_NAME	MANAGER_PHONE
201	BROWN	3484	(null)	(null)
202	KERN	8722	BROWN	3484
203	WOODS	7591	BROWN	3484
204	OWENS	6830	KERN	8722
205	PERKINS	5286	KERN	8722
206	ROSE	(null)	(null)	(null)
207	SMITH	2259	WOODS	7591
208	CAMPBELL	1752	WOODS	7591
209	JACOBS	3357	BROWN	3484
210	HOFFMAN	2974	WOODS	7591

16-11 Handling a sequence of events

Here is another example of using a self join. Sometimes a table in a database is used to show a sequence of events. A table like this has an order to its rows. This order might be achieved by including a timestamp field to indicate when each row was created or changed. Another method uses a primary key that is a sequence or an AutoNumber field. Each row shows one event. To determine the time between events, you can use a self join.

For example, suppose we set up a database for a package pickup and delivery service. One table in the database might keep track of each stop the truck makes. This could be done in a number of ways, but I will keep the example here fairly simple.

The beginning table shows several stops made by one truck. These data have already been conditioned for our task. Probably your raw data will not look like this. To get the data in a form like this you will probably need to extract these data from a larger table, sort them by the date and time fields, and add a sequence number field. We discussed how to add a sequence number field in section 10-14.

In this section we want to determine the time between events. That is, we want to determine the time that elapsed between the time shown on one row and the time shown on the next row. To do this, I will match each row with the next row in a self join. Then I can subtract one time field from the other to find the elapsed time.

Task

Find the amount of time that has elapsed between one event and the next event.

Oracle SQL

```
select b.event,
       to_char(a.time_done, 'HH:MI') as start_time,  ❶
       to_char(b.time_done, 'HH:MI') as end_time,    ❶
       ((b.time_done - a.time_done) * 60 * 24)  ❷
                              as minutes_elapsed_time
from sec1611_events a,  ❸
     sec1611_events b  ❸
where a.sequence_number + 1 = b.sequence_number  ❹
order by a.sequence_number;
```

Access SQL

```
select b.event,
       a.time_done as start_time,  ❶
       b.time_done as end_time,  ❶
       format((b.time_done - a.time_done),'HH:NN')  ❷
                              as elapsed_time
from sec1611_events a,  ❸
     sec1611_events b  ❸
where a.sequence_number + 1 = b.sequence_number  ❹
order by a.sequence_number;
```

Beginning table (sec1611_events table)

```
SEQUENCE_NUMBER   TRUCK_ID  EVENT                                    TIME_DONE
---------------   --------  ------------------------------------     ---------
              1         41  DELIVERED PACKAGE 391                    11:27 AM
              2         41  DELIVERED PACKAGE 392                    11:33 AM
              3         41  PICKED UP PACKAGE 572                     11:42 AM
              4         41  STARTED LUNCH BREAK                      11:54 AM
              5         41  ENDED LUNCH BREAK                        12:23 PM
              6         41  DELIVERED PACKAGE 393                    12:37 PM
              7         41  PICKED UP PACKAGE 573                     12:44 PM
              8         41  PICKED UP PACKAGE 574                     01:02 PM
              9         41  DELIVERED PACKAGE 394                    01:08 PM
             10         41  DELIVERED PACKAGE 395                    01:12 PM
```

Result table

```
EVENT                    START_TIME  END_TIME  MINUTES_ELAPSED_TIME
--------------------     ----------  --------  ----------------------------
DELIVERED PACKAGE 392    11:27 AM    11:33 AM                          6
PICKED UP PACKAGE 572    11:33 AM    11:42 AM                          9
STARTED LUNCH BREAK      11:42 AM    11:54 AM                         12
ENDED LUNCH BREAK        11:54 AM    12:23 PM                         29
DELIVERED PACKAGE 393    12:23 PM    12:37 PM                         14
PICKED UP PACKAGE 573    12:37 PM    12:44 PM                          7
PICKED UP PACKAGE 574    12:44 PM    01:02 PM                         18
DELIVERED PACKAGE 394    01:02 PM    01:08 PM                          6
DELIVERED PACKAGE 395    01:08 PM    01:12 PM                          4
```

Notes

❶ What I want to show here is a time without a date. The data implies that all the dates are the same, so there is no point in showing them. When I entered the data, I entered only the time without a date. However, both Oracle and Access used the current date when I loaded the data and they both stored both the time and date in the time_done field. To show only the time requires some special tricks.

In Oracle, I use the to_char function and a date format that shows only the time.

In Access, I do not need to apply any function. Access remembers that I entered the data as a time without a date. Therefore, it automatically displays the data in the form in which I entered it.

❷ Here I want to show the number of minutes that have elapsed between events. Oracle and Access have different ways to do this.

In Oracle, when I subtract one date from another date, I get a number. This is the number of days between the events. To translate this into minutes I need to multiply this number by 60 * 24, which is the number of minutes in a day.

In Access, I can simply format the number as an elapsed time.

❸ Here the table is joined with itself.

❹ This is the join condition. It matches each row with the row that comes after it in the sequence.

Check your understanding

Table `sec1611_prime_numbers` contains the first 50 prime numbers. Use a self join to determine the difference between each prime and the next one.

16-12 Generating the numbers from 0 to 999

This section shows you how to create a table containing all the numbers from 0 to 999. To do this we will use both a self join and a cross join. We will cross join a table with itself. With this technique, you can create as many numbers as you want.

First, we create a table of all the digits, all the numbers from 0 to 9. Then, we create another table from this by using a `select` statement.

We have already been using a table of numbers from 0 to 99. I created this table for you. Here you will see how to create a table like this for yourself whenever you want one.

In the first step, a table is created to contain all the digits. Oracle and Access must use their own datatypes, `number` for Oracle and `smallint` for Access. Otherwise, the SQL is the same. At this point, the table contains no data.

In the second step, the data are put into the table. There are only 10 records, so this is easy. The SQL is exactly the same in Oracle and Access.

In the third step, this table of digits is used to create a new table containing the numbers from 0 to 999. The table, `numbers_0_to_9`, is cross joined with itself. You can see this self join in the `from` clause, which lists the table three times. The first copy of the table is given the table alias `a`, the second copy is given the table alias `b`, and the third copy is given the table alias `c`. The result of this join is every combination of three digits.

The `select` clause turns each combination of three digits into a single, three-digit number. It multiplies the first digit by 100, and the second digit by 10. Then it adds up all the numbers to get a single three-digit number.

For example,

three digits: 3,   4,   5

become one number: $(3 \times 100) + (4 \times 10) + 5 = 345$

This much of the third step is the same in both Oracle and Access. However, they differ in their techniques to save these results in a table.

Task

Create a table with all the numbers from 0 to 999. First, create a table of the numbers from 0 to 9. Then cross join it with itself.

We already have a table named `numbers_0_to_9` containing all the digits. We want to leave that table alone. We create a new table with a slightly different name so I can show you how this all works.

Oracle SQL: Step 1 — Create a table to contain all 10 digits

```
create table numbers_0_to_9
(digit     number(1));
```

Access SQL: Step 1 — Create a table to contain all 10 digits

```
create table my_numbers_0_to_9
(digit     smallint);
```

Oracle & Access SQL: Step 2 — Put data in the table

```
insert into my_numbers_0_to_9 values (0);
insert into my_numbers_0_to_9 values (1);
insert into my_numbers_0_to_9 values (2);
insert into my_numbers_0_to_9 values (3);
insert into my_numbers_0_to_9 values (4);
insert into my_numbers_0_to_9 values (5);
insert into my_numbers_0_to_9 values (6);
insert into my_numbers_0_to_9 values (7);
insert into my_numbers_0_to_9 values (8);
insert into my_numbers_0_to_9 values (9);
commit;
```

Created table (`my_numbers_0_to_9` table)

```
     DIGIT
---------
        0
        1
        2
        3
        4
        5
        6
        7
        8
        9
```

Oracle SQL: Step 3 — Create a table of numbers from 0 to 999

```
create table numbers_0_to_999 as
select ((a.digit * 100) + (b.digit * 10) + c.digit) as n
from my_numbers_0_to_9 a,
     my_numbers_0_to_9 b,
     my_numbers_0_to_9 c;
order by 1;
```

Access SQL: Step 3 — Create a table of numbers from 0 to 999

```
select ((a.digit * 100) + (b.digit * 10) + c.digit) as n
into numbers_0_to_999
from my_numbers_0_to_9 a,
     my_numbers_0_to_9 b,
     my_numbers_0_to_9 c;
order by 1;
```

Created table (`numbers_0_to_999` table)

```
         N
---------
         0
         1
etc
       999
```

CrossTab Queries in Access

16-13 CrossTab queries when there are two dimensions

Access has a way to display one dimension (column) of a result table in columns across the page. Every value in that column then creates a separate column in the new result table. This is called a **CrossTab query** or a **Pivot query**. Oracle also has a way to do this, but the code is more difficult in Oracle. I show the Oracle method later in this chapter.

In this section I want to create this table:

	White	Red	Green
Ford			
Toyota			
Volkswagen			
Chevy			

A CrossTab query works best when the data have only two dimensions. That is what we discuss in this section. In the next sections we discuss a CrossTab query when the data have more than two dimensions.

Access has two new clauses of the `select` statement, **Transform** and **Pivot**, which are special extensions to SQL to support CrossTab queries. You could learn how to code those clauses, but there is a much easier way. It is easier to use the CrossTab Query Wizard and that is what I use in this and the next section.

Access designs the wizard to ask you a series of questions. It is hoped that each question is narrowly focused and easy to answer. This does mean that there are several steps to the process. I like to have some guidance on my first time through a wizard, so I try to provide that guidance to you.

Task

Create a CrossTab query that shows two dimensions — car types going down the left side of the page and colors going across the top of the page.

Step 1: Create three columns of data

The first step is to create a view (saved query) with three columns. Two of the columns are the two dimensions of the table that you see displayed on the edges. In our example, they are the type of car and the color. The third column is the data that you will see in the middle part of the table. In our example, that is just blanks. Here is the SQL:

```
select a.car_type,
       b.color,
       null as blank_field
from sec1613_car_types a,
     sec1613_colors b
order by a.car_type,
         b.color;
```

I will save this query and I name it `sec1613_data_view`.

Step 2: Start the CrossTab Query Wizard

1. Click the Create tab.
2. Click Query Wizard, shown as follows.
3. Select CrossTab Query Wizard.
4. Click OK.

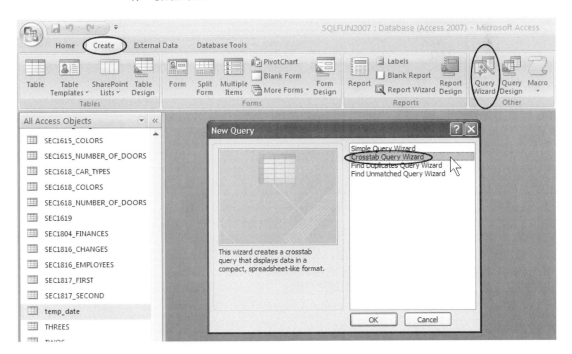

Step 3: Select the table or view that contains the data

5. Choose to view the queries, because I saved the data as a query.

6. Select sec1613_data_view.

7. Click Next.

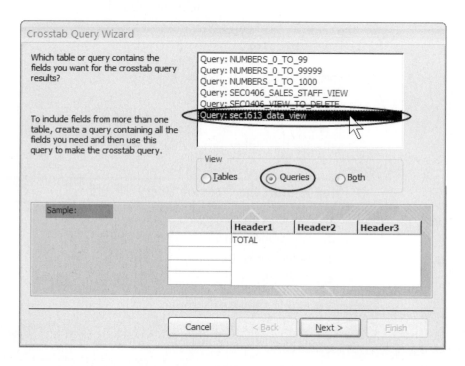

Step 4: Select the column to go down the left edge of the page

8. Highlight `car_type` in available fields.

9. Click the > button to select it. This moves the `car_type` to the list of selected fields and removes it from the list of available fields. It sets the vertical dimension of the report. In the sample report, this places the `car_type` as the first column.

10. Click Next.

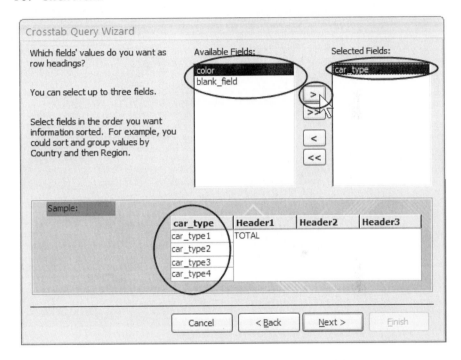

Step 5: Select the column to go across the top of the page

11. Highlight `color`. It may already be highlighted for you. This sets the horizontal dimension of the report. In the sample report, this places the values of the color field as the headers of the remaining columns.

12. Click Next.

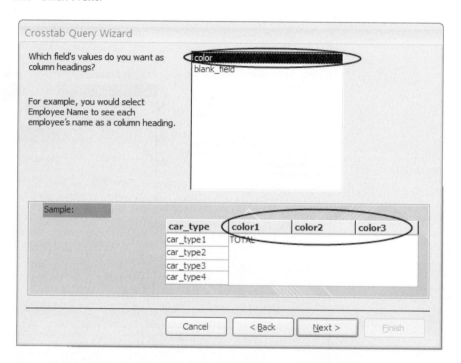

Step 6: Select the column of data to display in the table

13. The `blank_field` is already highlighted. It is highlighted because it is the only field left. I set things up to work this way when I created a view with only three fields. If you start with more than three fields, this step allows you to select which field will go in the body of the report.

14. Select Max in the Functions list. You could also select First, Last, or Min, but not Count.

This says that if there is more than one blank field for any combination of a color and a body type, then the blank field with the maximum value will be used within the body of the report.

Again, I already set things up so this will work easily. I set things up so that there is only one blank field for any combination of a color and a body type. That is why it does not matter in this example if you choose First, Last, Max, or Min. However, if you select Count, the body of the report will contain only zeros. In the sample report, this places Max(blank_field) in the body of the report.

15. Clear the Yes, Include row sums checkbox. We do not want row sums in this report.

16. Click Next.

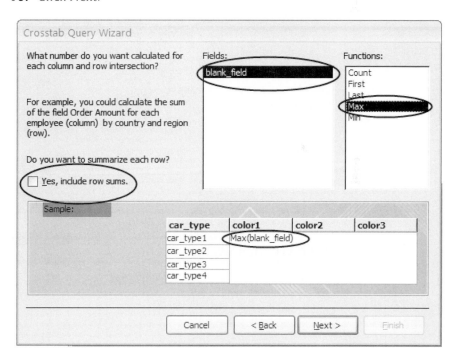

Step 7: Finish

17. Name the query. I am naming mine `Sec1613_Crosstab`, but you can use any name you want.

18. Select View the query.

19. Click Finish.

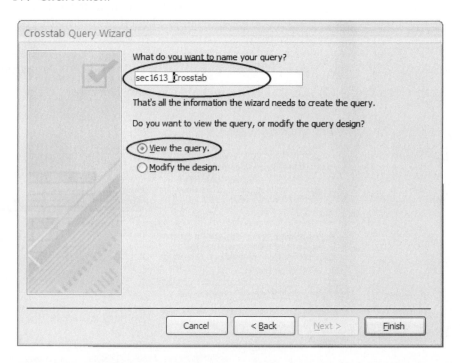

Result: CrossTab Query

car_type	Green	Red	White
Chevy			
Ford			
Toyota			
Volkswagen			

16-14   CrossTab queries with up to four dimensions

In this section we continue our example and add the number of doors as the third dimension. Here, we continue to use the CrossTab Query Wizard. We lay out the result as one table, where two dimensions go down the page and one goes across, as explained in section 16-7.

The process here is very similar to the previous section. Because the procedure has many steps, I only show you the parts that are different.

Task

Create a CrossTab query that shows three dimensions — car types and number of doors going down the left side of the page and colors going across the top of the page.

Step 1: Create the data

In this example we create four columns of data — one for each of the three dimensions and one for the body of the table. Here is the SQL:

```
select a.car_type,
       b.color,
       c.doors,
       null as blank_field
from sec1614_car_types a,
     sec1614_colors b,
     sec1614_number_of_doors c
order by a.car_type,
         b.color,
         c.doors;
```

Save this query and name it `sec1614_data_view`. Steps 2 and 3 are similar to the previous section.

Step 4: Select the columns to go down the left edge of the page

In this step we select two columns to go down the page, `car_type` and `doors`.

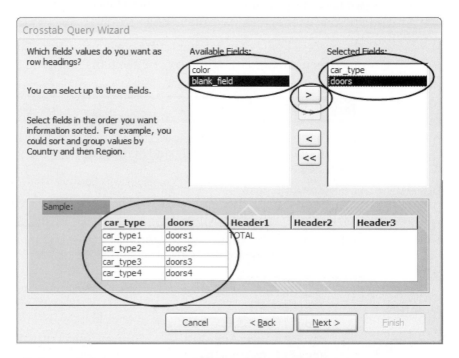

All the rest of the steps are similar to the previous section.

Result: CrossTab query

car_type	doors	Green	Red	White
Chevy	2			
Chevy	4			
Ford	2			
Ford	4			
Toyota	2			
Toyota	4			
Volkswagen	2			
Volkswagen	4			

16-15 CrossTab queries with more dimensions

In this section I show you another method to do the same thing we did in the previous section. The reason for using another method is that the Access wizard we used in the last section is limited in what it can do. It has a built-in restriction that only allows you to put three columns on the left edge of the page.

Sometimes you might need a more flexible tool. That is what I show you here. This method uses the Access GUI tool for query design.

This section shows a simple example of this technique. Later in this chapter I show you a more complex example.

Task

This is the same as the previous section. Create a CrossTab query that shows three dimensions — car types and number of doors going down the left side of the page and colors going across the top of the page.

Step 1: Create the data

This step is almost the same as the previous section. I could have used the same code here, but to make this example easier to understand I spelled out the full names of the tables instead of using the table aliases a, b, and c. Also, I do not save the query in this step. I modify it before I save it.

```
select sec1615_car_types.car_type,
       sec1615_colors.color,
       sec1615_number_of_doors.doors,
       null as blank_field
from sec1615_car_types,
     sec1615_colors,
     sec1615_number_of_doors
order by sec1615_car_types.car_type,
         sec1615_colors.color,
         sec1615_number_of_doors.doors;
```

Step 2: Change from SQL view to design view

After you run the query, click the Design View icon in the bottom right corner of the screen. You will get something like this:

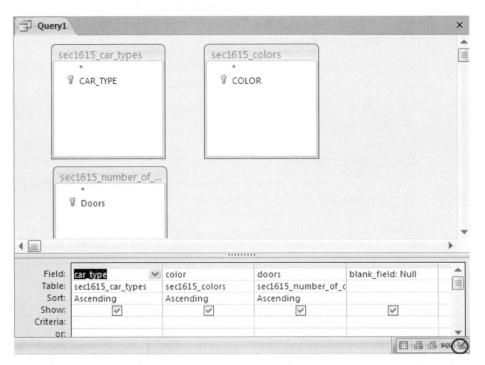

Step 3: Adjust the GUI

Make several adjustments to the GUI:

1. Rearrange the tables on top. Drag them by their header bars.

2. Shorten the length of the tables. Place the mouse pointer at the bottom of each table. When it turns into a double-headed arrow, hold down the mouse button and drag the bottom of the table upward.

3. Move the bottom panel up. Place the mouse pointer between the top part of the screen and the bottom part. When it turns into a double-headed arrow, hold down the mouse button and drag the bottom part of the screen upward.

4. Expand the width of the doors field. Place the mouse pointer at the right edge of the doors field and one row up. When it turns into a double-headed arrow, hold down the mouse button and drag the edge of the field to the right.

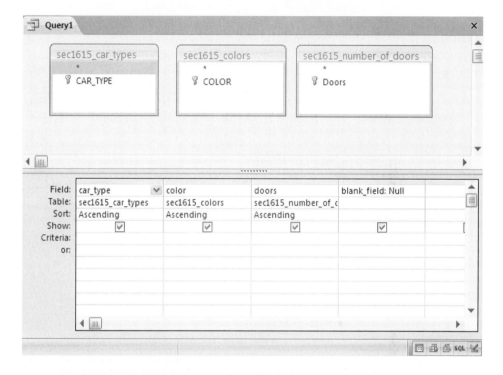

Step 4: Make this a CrossTab query

In the Query Type section of the Ribbon, click the CrossTab Query button.

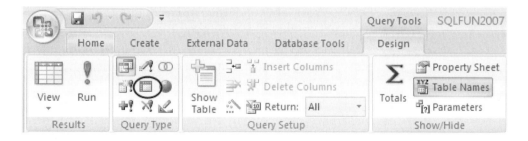

This creates two new rows in the query grid, Total and Crosstab. The query grid will now look something like this:

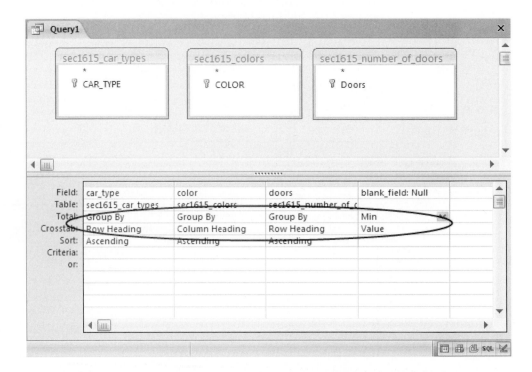

Step 5: Specify which columns are row headings, etc.

1. Set the CrossTab line of the `car_type` column to Row Heading. To do this, click the mouse in the cell of the CrossTab row and the `car_type` column. Click the selection button and select Row Heading.

2. Set the CrossTab line of the `doors` column to Row Heading. You can have any number of columns set to Row Heading.

3. Set the CrossTab line of the `color` column to Column Heading. You must have only one column set to Column Heading. This is the column that will be displayed across the top of the page.

4. Set the CrossTab line of the `blank_field` column to Value. You must have one column set to Value. This will provide the values inside the cells of the result table.

5. Set the totals line of the `blank_field` column to Min. The totals line for all the other columns is automatically set to Group By.

The query grid will now look something like this:

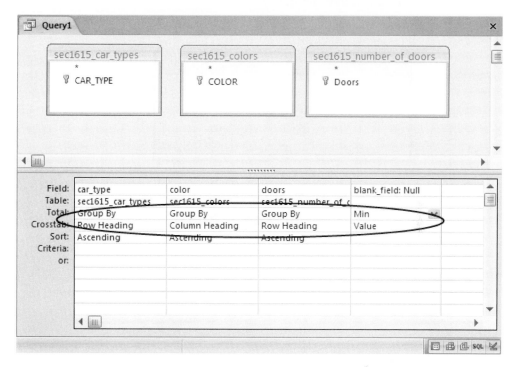

Step 6: Run the query

Click the Run button on the Ribbon or click the Datasheet View button in the bottom right corner of the screen.

Step 7: Save the query

Press Ctrl + S. Name it `sec1615_crosstab`.

16-16 CrossTab to show who is attending each lunch

In this section I create a CrossTab query in Access to show which lunches each employee has signed up for. In particular, what I want to create is a CrossTab query that shows the following:

- Down the left side of the page

    All employees (`employee_id`, `first_name`, `last_name`)

- Across the top of the page

    All lunch dates

- Within the body of the CrossTab

    An X if the employee has signed up for that lunch

I will do this task as if I am dealing with a large production database. I am allowing you to look over my shoulder and see exactly what I am doing.

First, I make a list of all the entries in each dimension. I list all the employees, then I list all the lunch dates.

Next, I form the cross product of these dimensions.

- All employees × all lunch dates

This gives me the framework for the CrossTab I want to create. It shows all the possibilities.

Then, I will get the specific data from the `1_lunches` table that shows which lunches each employee has signed up for. At this point I have three types of data and I am ready to do the CrossTab procedure. The three types of data are: employee data, lunch dates, and an X if the employee signed up for the lunch

In the last step I form the CrossTab query with the lunch dates going across the top of the page.

Step 1: List all employees

```
select employee_id,
       first_name,
       last_name
from l_employees;
```

Save the query. Name it `sec1616_step1_employee_dimension_view`.

I do not need to be concerned about duplicate rows here because I know `employee_id` is the primary key of the table.

I note that the number of rows is 10.

Step 2: List all lunch dates

```
select distinct lunch_date
from l_lunches;
```

Save the query. Name it `sec1616_step2_lunch_date_dimension_view`.

I need to use `select distinct` here because I want each date to occur only once.

I note that the number of rows is three.

Step 3: Create the framework

```
select a.*,
       b.*
from sec1616_step1_employee_dimension_view a,
     sec1616_step2_lunch_date_dimension_view b;
```

Save the query. Name it `sec1616_step3_framework_view`.

I use a cross product to show every possible combination of an employee and a lunch date.

I note that there are 30 rows. This is correct because $30 = 10 \times 3$.

As I add data to this framework, I want to make sure that this framework remains complete. To do this, I use an outer join to add the data so no row of the framework can be deleted. I also check that I always retain all 30 rows.

Step 4: Add data from the `1_lunches` table

```
select a.*,
       format(b.lunch_date, 'X') as signed_up
from sec1616_step3_framework_view a
     left outer join l_lunches b
     on a.employee_id = b.employee_id
        and a.lunch_date = b.lunch_date;
```

Save the query. Name it `sec1616_step4_view`.

Now all the data have been placed within the framework. All the data I need are completely integrated. I am ready to display the lunch dates across the top of the page with a CrossTab query.

Step 5: Make the CrossTab query

I have already explained most of the steps to do this, but here are the steps if you need them:

1. Click the Create tab on the Ribbon.
2. Click Query Design on the Ribbon.
3. Click the Queries tab in the Show Table window.
4. Add the `sec1616_step4_view`.
5. Close the Show Table window.
6. Drag each column from the `sec1616_step4_view` to the grid below.
7. On the Ribbon, click the button to create a crosstab query.
8. Set the values in the Total, Crosstab, and Sort rows as shown next.

Save the query. Name it `sec1616_step5_crosstab`. Here is the design view for the query.

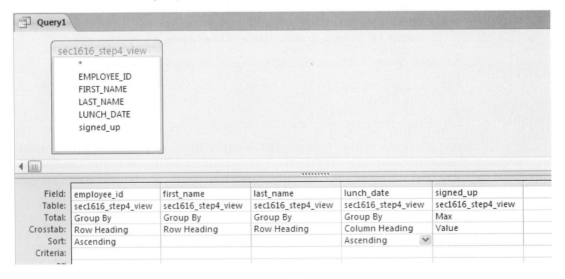

Field:	employee_id	first_name	last_name	lunch_date	signed_up	
Table:	sec1616_step4_view	sec1616_step4_view	sec1616_step4_view	sec1616_step4_view	sec1616_step4_view	
Total:	Group By	Group By	Group By	Group By	Max	
Crosstab:	Row Heading	Row Heading	Row Heading	Column Heading	Value	
Sort:	Ascending			Ascending		
Criteria:						

Result table

employee_id	first_name	last_name	16-Nov-2011	25-Nov-2011	05-Dec-2011
201	Susan	Brown	X	X	X
202	Jim	Kern	X		
203	Martha	Woods	X		X
204	Ellen	Owens	X	X	
205	Henry	Perkins		X	X
206	Carol	Rose			
207	Dan	Smith	X	X	
208	Fred	Campbell		X	X
209	Paula	Jacobs			
210	Nancy	Hoffman	X		X

16-17   CrossTab to show the foods for each lunch

In this section I create a CrossTab query in Access for the foods that have been ordered for each lunch. In particular, I want to create a CrossTab query that shows the following:

- Down the left side of the page

    All employees (`employee_id`, `first_name`, `last_name`)

    All lunch dates

    An X if the employee will attend that lunch

- Across the top of the page

    All foods (shown as menu item number)

- Within the body of the CrossTab

    Quantity ordered (1 or 2)

To fit the result in this book I have to use menu item number instead of the name of the food. I would prefer to show the full names of the foods, but that would take up too much space. I would do that if I did not have to fit the result in a confined space.

First, I make the framework:

- All employees   ×   all lunch dates   ×   all foods

Next, I will get put specific data in the framework from two tables: `1_lunches` and `1_lunch_items`. I use a separate step to add the data from each of these tables.

The last step will be to turn this table into a CrossTab query with the foods going across the top of the page.

Step 1: List all foods

```
select supplier_id,
       product_code,
       menu_item,
       description as food
from 1_foods;
```

Save the query. Name it `sec1617_step1_food_dimension_view`.

Why do I use so many columns? I need the `menu_item` column for the CrossTab query. I need the `supplier_id` and `product_code` to use in the join when I get data from the `1_lunch_items` table. The `description` column is optional, but I like to have it because it contains the name of the food.

I know that I will not have any duplicate rows because the `supplier_id` and `Product_code` form the primary key of the `1_foods` table.

I note that the number of rows is 10.

Step 2: Create the framework

```
select a.*,
       b.*,
       c.*
from sec1616_step1_employee_dimension_view a,
     sec1616_step2_lunch_date_dimension_view b,
     sec1617_step1_food_dimension_view c
```

Save the query. Name it `sec1617_step2_framework_view`.

This is the cross product of the three dimensions I want for this query.

I note that the number of rows is 300. This is correct because 300 = 10 (employees) × 3 (lunch dates) × 10 (foods).

As data is added to this framework, none of the rows should be deleted. There should always be 300 rows.

Step 3: Add data from the `1_lunches` table

```
select a.*,
       format(b.lunch_date, 'X') as signed_up,
       b.lunch_id
from sec1617_step2_framework_view a
     left outer join 1_lunches b
     on a.employee_id = b.employee_id
        and a.lunch_date = b.lunch_date;
```

Save the query. Name it `sec1617_step3_view`.

In this step I get two pieces of information. I get the indicator to say that the employee has signed up for the lunch. I also get the `lunch_id`. I will need to use this in the join condition when I get data from the `1_lunch_items` table.

I am using a left outer join to make sure that this does not delete any rows from the framework.

There are 300 rows. This is correct.

Step 4: Add data from the `1_lunch_items` table

```
select a.*,
       b.quantity
from sec1617_step3_view a
     left outer join 1_lunch_items b
     on a.supplier_id = b.supplier_id
        and a.product_code = b.product_code
        and a.lunch_id = b.lunch_id;
```

Save the query. Name it `sec1617_step4_view`.

In this step I get the quantity of each food that has been ordered. I know the value must be 1 or 2. Again, I use a left outer join to make sure I preserve all the rows of the framework.

I still have 300 rows. That is correct.

Now all the information is integrated. If I wanted, I could go directly to the CrossTab process from here. But there are several columns I will not use in the CrossTab. I added those columns to use them in join conditions and for other reasons.

In the next step I clean up the data so that they match the CrossTab as closely as possible. Here that means I keep the columns for the CrossTab and drop all the others.

Step 5: Select the columns for the CrossTab query

```
select a.employee_id,
       a.first_name,
       a.last_name,
       a.lunch_date,
       a.menu_item,
       a.signed_up,
       a.quantity
from sec1617_step4_view a;
```

Save the query. Name it `sec1617_step5_view`.

I still have 300 rows. That is correct.

This step just drops some columns from the previous view.

Step 6: Make the CrossTab query

I have already explained most of the steps to do this, for a reminder see the previous section. Save the query. Name it `sec1617_step6_crosstab`. Here is the design view for the query:

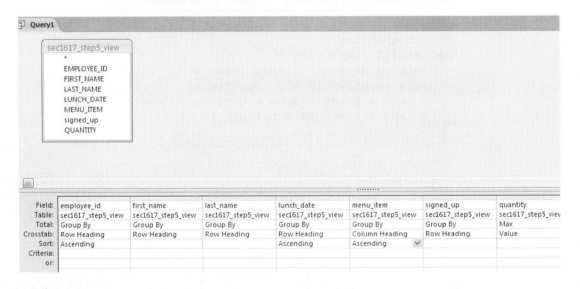

Result table

employee_id	first_name	last_name	lunch_date	signed_up	1	2	3	4	5	6	7	8	9	10
201	Susan	Brown	16-Nov-2011	X	1		2						2	
201	Susan	Brown	25-Nov-2011	X	1			1				1		
201	Susan	Brown	05-Dec-2011	X	1		1		1			1	1	
202	Jim	Kern	16-Nov-2011	X			1		1			1	2	1
202	Jim	Kern	25-Nov-2011											
202	Jim	Kern	05-Dec-2011											
203	Martha	Woods	16-Nov-2011	X	1			1			1	1	1	
203	Martha	Woods	25-Nov-2011											
203	Martha	Woods	05-Dec-2011	X			1		1				2	1
204	Ellen	Owens	16-Nov-2011	X			2			2	1	2		
204	Ellen	Owens	25-Nov-2011	X	1			1					2	1
204	Ellen	Owens	05-Dec-2011											
205	Henry	Perkins	16-Nov-2011											
205	Henry	Perkins	25-Nov-2011	X			1		1			1	2	
205	Henry	Perkins	05-Dec-2011	X	1	1			1			1	1	
206	Carol	Rose	16-Nov-2011											
206	Carol	Rose	25-Nov-2011											
206	Carol	Rose	05-Dec-2011											
207	Dan	Smith	16-Nov-2011	X				2				1	2	1
207	Dan	Smith	25-Nov-2011	X			2	2				1	1	
207	Dan	Smith	05-Dec-2011											
208	Fred	Campbell	16-Nov-2011											
208	Fred	Campbell	25-Nov-2011	X	1	1				2		1	1	1
208	Fred	Campbell	05-Dec-2011	X	1			1				1	1	1
209	Paula	Jacobs	16-Nov-2011											
209	Paula	Jacobs	25-Nov-2011											
209	Paula	Jacobs	05-Dec-2011											
210	Nancy	Hoffman	16-Nov-2011	X	1	1		1					1	1
210	Nancy	Hoffman	25-Nov-2011											
210	Nancy	Hoffman	05-Dec-2011	X			1		1			1	2	1

CrossTab Queries in Oracle

16-18   CrossTab queries in Oracle — Part 1

In general, it is difficult to create CrossTab queries in Oracle. It can be done, but it requires a lot of effort. When I want to write a CrossTab query, I usually use Access rather than Oracle because it is easier.

What I show you here are two fairly simple examples, just to give you the flavor of the code. First, I continue the preceding example. I get the same result table, but I write the code in Oracle. In the next section I add some data to the table, so you can see the technique involved in handling those data.

In this section, I again produce a three-dimensional grid with no data in it, just as I did in the last section. However, there is one important difference between Oracle and Access that is shown in this code. In Oracle, you often choose the column that will go across the top of the page so you know in advance all the values that the column could possibly contain. Those values are hard-coded into the SQL. In the following example, those are the values of the color column: Green, Red, and White. These become the column headings that go across the page.

In Access, it is not necessary to hard-code those values. The column headings are obtained from the data that are in the column.

Task

Create the same CrossTab query result that we had in the previous section; that is, create a three-dimensional grid. Car type and number of doors will go down the left edge of the page. Color will go across the top of the page.

Oracle SQL

```
select a.car_type, ❶
       b.doors, ❶
       ' ' as green, ❷
       ' ' as red, ❷
       ' ' as white ❷
from sec1618_car_types a,
     sec1618_number_of_doors b,
     sec1618_colors c
group by a.car_type, ❶
         b.doors ❶
order by a.car_type,
         b.doors;
```

Result table

CAR_TYPE	DOORS	GREEN	RED	WHITE
CHEVY	2			
CHEVY	4			
FORD	2			
FORD	4			
TOYOTA	2			
TOYOTA	4			
VOLKSWAGEN	2			
VOLKSWAGEN	4			

Notes

❶ Usually, you need to `group by` all the columns that go down the left side of the page.

❷ In this code, I needed to know all the possible colors and hard-code those values into the column headings. Access does not require this.

16-19 CrossTab queries in Oracle — Part 2

This section continues the example of the previous section, but this time there are data to display. The beginning table has 24 rows. The first three columns create a three-dimensional structure. They are a cross product of four car types, three colors, and two different styles of doors.

The fourth column contains data that will be displayed in the CrossTab query. This is the new factor that I focus on. To handle it, I need to use the `decode` row function and the `max` column function. The `decode` row function is explained in chapter 18. All you need to see here is that it can distribute data into several different columns.

This code runs as a single SQL statement. However, I can explain it better if I divide what I say into two parts. The first part uses the `decode` row function to distribute the data into the three color columns, but it leaves many nulls in the result table. The second part uses the `max` column function to get rid of the null values.

Task

Create a CrossTab query in Oracle that displays data.

Oracle SQL:
First version — Showing just the effect of the `decode` function

```
select car_type,
       doors,
       decode(color, 'GREEN', to_char(my_data), null)
                                         as green,
       decode(color, 'RED', to_char(my_data), null) as red,
       decode(color, 'WHITE', to_char(my_data), null)
                                         as white
from sec1619
order by car_type,
         doors;
```

Beginning table (sec1619)

```
CAR_TYPE        DOORS COLOR          MY_DATA
----------  ---------  ----------  ----------
CHEVY           2 GREEN              1
CHEVY           2 RED                2
CHEVY           2 WHITE              3
CHEVY           4 GREEN              4
CHEVY           4 RED                5
CHEVY           4 WHITE              6
FORD            2 GREEN              7
FORD            2 RED                8
FORD            2 WHITE              9
FORD            4 GREEN             10
FORD            4 RED               11
FORD            4 WHITE             12
TOYOTA          2 GREEN             13
TOYOTA          2 RED               14
TOYOTA          2 WHITE             15
TOYOTA          4 GREEN             16
TOYOTA          4 RED               17
TOYOTA          4 WHITE             18
VOLKSWAGEN      2 GREEN             19
VOLKSWAGEN      2 RED               20
VOLKSWAGEN      2 WHITE             21
VOLKSWAGEN      4 GREEN             22
VOLKSWAGEN      4 RED               23
VOLKSWAGEN      4 WHITE             24
```

Result table: First version — data are distributed into three columns

CAR_TYPE	DOORS	GREEN	RED	WHITE
CHEVY	2	(null)	2	(null)
CHEVY	2	1	(null)	(null)
CHEVY	2	(null)	(null)	3
CHEVY	4	4	(null)	(null)
CHEVY	4	(null)	5	(null)
CHEVY	4	(null)	(null)	6
FORD	2	7	(null)	(null)
FORD	2	(null)	8	(null)
FORD	2	(null)	(null)	9
FORD	4	(null)	11	(null)
FORD	4	10	(null)	(null)
FORD	4	(null)	(null)	12
TOYOTA	2	(null)	14	(null)
TOYOTA	2	13	(null)	(null)
TOYOTA	2	(null)	(null)	15
TOYOTA	4	(null)	17	(null)
TOYOTA	4	16	(null)	(null)
TOYOTA	4	(null)	(null)	18
VOLKSWAGEN	2	19	(null)	(null)
VOLKSWAGEN	2	(null)	20	(null)
VOLKSWAGEN	2	(null)	(null)	21
VOLKSWAGEN	4	22	(null)	(null)
VOLKSWAGEN	4	(null)	23	(null)
VOLKSWAGEN	4	(null)	(null)	24

Oracle SQL:
Complete and final version — This is the only SQL you need

```
select car_type,
       doors,
       max(decode(color, 'GREEN', to_char(my_data), null))
                                       as green,
       max(decode(color, 'RED', to_char(my_data), null))
                                       as red,
       max(decode(color, 'WHITE', to_char(my_data), null))
                                       as white
from sec1619
group by car_type,
         doors
order by car_type,
         doors;
```

Result table: Final version

CAR_TYPE	DOORS	GREEN	RED	WHITE
CHEVY	2	1	2	3
CHEVY	4	4	5	6
FORD	2	7	8	9
FORD	4	10	11	12
TOYOTA	2	13	14	15
TOYOTA	4	16	17	18
VOLKSWAGEN	2	19	20	21
VOLKSWAGEN	4	22	23	24

Key Points

- A cross join of two tables is an inner join without a join condition. The result is that every row of the first table is combined with every row of the second table.

- An inner join, in theory, is defined from a cross join.

- If you are developing a query that involves a join and you get many more rows in the result than you expected, your problem is probably that you left out one of the join conditions. You should carefully examine the `from` clause and the `where` clause.

- When you are handling large tables be careful about the join conditions. If you leave out the join conditions completely you will get a cross join. This can cause the computer to do a lot of processing, it can be expensive, and will not produce the result you want. In a regulated environment your query may be removed from the computer before it finishes.

- It is okay to do a cross join of a few small tables if that is what you need to do. In a self join a table is joined to another copy of itself. The join can be either an inner join or an outer join. You can use a self join when you need information from two or more rows at the same moment to perform a row function or check a condition.

- In a CrossTab query, the values of one column are displayed across the top of the page. This gives a more compact presentation of the data. Often this can make the data easier to understand.

COMBINING TABLES IN A PRODUCTION DATABASE

Congratulations! If you have read this far, you have finished all the topics that I cover in detail. The last four chapters of this book round out the discussion and place that material in context. The viewpoint changes here to a broader perspective and less detail.

Chapter 17 discusses some of the challenges in combining tables within a production-sized system, which is a much larger system than those we have discussed until now.

Chapter 18 discusses the `if-then-else` functions, parameter queries, and subqueries. These are important topics that I have not covered yet because they did not fit into the framework of our discussion so far.

Chapter 19 discusses the multiuser environment. Most databases are shared environments that many people use at the same time. This environment is set up by the DBAs, but you can work more effectively if you understand how it is done.

Chapter 20 discusses the design of SQL and what the language is attempting to achieve. It also discusses forms and reports, which have become the way many people interact with a database.

Methods of Joining Three or More Tables

When you need to join three or more tables for a query, the method I recommend is to use a series of steps and combine the tables two at a time. The first step combines two of the tables and saves the result as a view. The next step combines that view with one more table and creates another view. This is repeated as many times as necessary.

This method gives you maximum control. It is less prone to errors than other methods. If errors do occur, they are easier to find and fix. If your query takes a long time to run, you can time and monitor each step individually.

To keep this process as efficient as possible for the computer, particularly if you run some of the steps individually, you should select the data you want as early in the process as possible. The idea is to keep the size of your tables as small as possible so the computer does not have to handle a lot of rows that you will later discard.

That is my recommendation, but there is another school of thought. Some people like to write a single `select` statement that joins all their tables and selects all their data at the same time.

There is sometimes some logic to this other point of view. If you can tell the computer what you want to do all at one time, then the optimizers in the database might be able to find a more efficient way to process your query. If you have production code that you know is completely debugged and correct, it makes sense to combine the steps together into a single SQL statement.

However, I have usually been a person who develops new code for the database. I know that errors and inefficiencies can creep into the code in many unexpected ways. I try to write code so that I can find the errors and fix them as easily as possible. Also, I like to keep things simple so I make fewer errors to begin with. That is why I like to divide any problem into a series of steps.

17-1 Joining several tables in a series of steps

Here is an example of code that joins two tables at a time in a series of steps. This is the technique I recommend.

Task

For the lunch on November 16, 2011, list all the foods served, the quantities, the total price of each food, and who will be eating the lunches. The price increases will be in effect and 10 cents will be added to the price when the price increase is null. List the following columns:

```
employee_id

first_name

last_name

food

quantity

total_price
```

Oracle SQL

```
create or replace view sec1701a_view as
select a.employee_id,
       a.first_name,
       a.last_name,
       b.lunch_id
from l_employees a,
     l_lunches b
where a.employee_id = b.employee_id
  and b.lunch_date = '16-NOV-2011';

create or replace view sec1701b_view as
select a.*,
       b.supplier_id,
       b.product_code,
       b.quantity
from sec1701a_view a,
     l_lunch_items b
where a.lunch_id = b.lunch_id;

create or replace view sec1701c_view as
select a.*,
       b.description as food,
       b.price+nvl(b.price_increase,.10) as new_price
from sec1701b_view a,
     l_foods b
where a.supplier_id = b.supplier_id
  and a.product_code = b.product_code;
```

```
select employee_id,
       first_name,
       last_name,
       food,
       quantity,
       new_price * quantity as total_price
from sec1701c_view
order by employee_id,
         food;
```

Access SQL

The Access code is very similar, and I encourage you to write your own. Remember that Access does not have create view, so you have to create saved queries using the GUI.

Result table

EMPLOYEE ID	FIRST NAME	LAST NAME	FOOD	QUANTITY	TOTAL_PRICE
201	SUSAN	BROWN	COFFEE	2	$2.00
201	SUSAN	BROWN	FRESH SALAD	1	$2.25
201	SUSAN	BROWN	SANDWICH	2	$7.80
202	JIM	KERN	COFFEE	2	$2.00
202	JIM	KERN	DESSERT	1	$3.50
202	JIM	KERN	FRENCH FRIES	1	$1.60
202	JIM	KERN	GRILLED STEAK	1	$6.70
202	JIM	KERN	SOUP OF THE DAY	1	$1.60
203	MARTHA	WOODS	COFFEE	1	$1.00
203	MARTHA	WOODS	FRENCH FRIES	1	$1.60
203	MARTHA	WOODS	FRESH SALAD	1	$2.25
203	MARTHA	WOODS	GRILLED STEAK	1	$6.70
203	MARTHA	WOODS	SODA	1	$1.50
204	ELLEN	OWENS	FRENCH FRIES	1	$1.60
204	ELLEN	OWENS	HAMBURGER	2	$5.60
204	ELLEN	OWENS	SODA	2	$3.00
204	ELLEN	OWENS	SOUP OF THE DAY	2	$3.20
207	DAN	SMITH	COFFEE	2	$2.00
207	DAN	SMITH	DESSERT	1	$3.50
207	DAN	SMITH	FRENCH FRIES	1	$1.60
207	DAN	SMITH	SANDWICH	2	$7.80
210	NANCY	HOFFMAN	COFFEE	1	$1.00
210	NANCY	HOFFMAN	DESSERT	1	$3.50
210	NANCY	HOFFMAN	FRESH SALAD	1	$2.25
210	NANCY	HOFFMAN	GRILLED STEAK	1	$6.70
210	NANCY	HOFFMAN	SOUP OF THE DAY	1	$1.60

17-2 Joining several tables at once in the `where` clause

This section shows all the tables being joined within one `select` statement. This is a style of coding that I do not recommend, because it can get too complex.

Task

The task here is the same as in section 17-1.

Oracle SQL

```
select a.employee_id,
       a.first_name,
       a.last_name,
       d.description as food,
       c.quantity,
       ((d.price + nvl(d.price_increase,.10))
          * c.quantity)             as total_price
from l_employees a,
     l_lunches b,
     l_lunch_items c,
     l_foods d
where a.employee_id = b.employee_id
  and b.lunch_date = '16-NOV-2011'
  and b.lunch_id = c.lunch_id
  and c.supplier_id = d.supplier_id
  and c.product_code = d.product_code
order by a.employee_id,
         d.description;
```

Access SQL

For Access, just change the `nvl` function to an `nz` function and enclose the date in pound signs.

17-3 Joining several tables at once in the `from` clause

This is a variation of the code in section 17-2. The difference here is that the join condition is written in the `from` clause rather than the `where` clause. The syntax itself forces you to join two tables at a time. This is done in a nesting arrangement, which you can see in the code.

Task

The task here is the same as in section 17-1.

Oracle SQL

```
select a.employee_id,
       a.first_name,
       a.last_name,
       d.description as food,
       c.quantity,
       ((d.price + nvl(d.price_increase,.10))
        * c.quantity)                    as total_price
from ((l_employees a
     inner join l_lunches b
     on a.employee_id = b.employee_id)
        inner join l_lunch_items c
        on b.lunch_id = c.lunch_id)
           inner join l_foods d
           on c.supplier_id = d.supplier_id
           and c.product_code = d.product_code
where b.lunch_date = '16-NOV-2011'
order by a.employee_id,
         d.description;
```

Access SQL

```
select a.employee_id,
       a.first_name,
       a.last_name,
       d.description as food,
       c.quantity,
       ((d.price + nz(d.price_increase,.10))
          * c.quantity)                  as total_price
from ((l_employees a
     inner join l_lunches b
     on a.employee_id = b.employee_id)
        inner join l_lunch_items c
        on b.lunch_id = c.lunch_id)
           inner join l_foods d
           on c.supplier_id = d.supplier_id
           and c.product_code = d.product_code
where b.lunch_date = #16-NOV-2011#
order by a.employee_id,
         d.description;
```

Result table — Same as in section 17-1

Losing Information

One of the things we need to think carefully about when we join several tables together is what data might be lost in the process. Inner joins, left outer joins, and right outer joins can all lose information. Only a full outer join always preserves all the information.

17-4 Be careful with an inner join

An inner join can lose more data than any other type of join. A row from one of the beginning tables is lost unless there is a matching row in **every** other table. If any of the tables has a null in a column used in the join condition, then some data may be lost. The only time we can be certain an inner join will not lose any information is when referential integrity protects the join condition between the tables. The more tables you use in an inner join, the greater the chance of losing data.

Some aspects of inner joins do make them easy to use. When we use an inner join we do not need to be concerned about which table comes first and which comes second. The same result is produced either way. This is sometimes expressed as:

A inner join B = B inner join A

Also, when we combine three or more tables with inner joins, the order in which we combine them does not matter. The result is always the same. This is sometimes expressed as:

(A inner join B) inner join C = A inner join (B inner join C)

17-5 Be careful with a left and right outer join

A left and right outer join restores some of the information lost by an inner join, but it does not restore all of the lost data. Of course, a left outer join and a right outer join are the same thing except for the order of the tables, so I am talking about one type of join here, not two different types. This means that we can turn all right outer joins into left outer joins by changing the order of the tables.

A left (or right) outer join of two tables is fairly straightforward and easy to understand. However, things get trickier when we use left outer joins to combine three or more tables. The order in which we combine the tables can make a difference — which two tables are joined first, which one is third, which one is fourth, and so on. This subtle difference can cause errors that are not easy to detect.

17-6 A full outer join preserves all the information

A full outer join does not lose any information. It keeps all the information in all of the tables. This is nice from the perspective of the application programmer. On the other hand, it requires more computing resources, so use it only when you need to.

Full outer joins also have the nice properties of inner joins. We do not need to be concerned about which table comes first and which one comes second. That is:

A full outer join B = B full outer join A

Also, when we combine three or more tables with full outer joins, the order in which we combine them does not matter. The result is always the same. That is:

(A full outer join B) full outer join C = A full outer join (B full outer join C)

17-7 A full outer join of several tables

Because full outer joins preserve all of the information, why don't we use them all of the time? Some people do. This can be a good practice, particularly when you are working with several small tables that are often not completely consistent with each other.

In general, we are discouraged from using full outer joins all the time, particularly when we are working with large tables. Why? A full outer join requires more computer resources to process than an inner join. Sometimes people are trying to protect the computer when they tell you not to use a full outer join.

When I am developing new code and working with tables with which I am not completely familiar, I use a full outer join whenever I think I might need one. When I create code that will run frequently — every day, every week, or even once a month, then I try to use inner joins whenever I can.

People sometimes ask me how to combine three or more tables with full outer joins. If you do it as a series of steps, it is simple and easy to do, as shown in the following task. If you try to do it all in one `select` statement, it will be quite difficult.

Task

Join three tables: 1_employees, 1_departments, and 1_lunches. Join all the tables with full outer joins.

The point here is the technique of writing the SQL code, so I do not show you the beginning tables and result table.

Oracle SQL

```
-- step 1: create a full outer join from two of the tables
create or replace view sec1707a_view as
select a.*,
       b.lunch_id,
       b.lunch_date,
       b.date_entered
from l_employees a
     full outer join l_lunches b
     on a.employee_id = b.employee_id;

/* step 2: create a full outer join from the results of
step 1 and the third table
*/

create or replace view sec1707b_view as
select a.*,
       b.department_name
from sec1707a_view a
     full outer join l_departments b
     on a.dept_code = b.dept_code;
```

Access SQL

Step 1: Enter this code in the SQL window:

```
select a.*,
       b.lunch_id,
       b.lunch_date,
       b.date_entered
from l_employees a
     left outer join l_lunches b
     on a.employee_id = b.employee_id
```

```
union
select a.*,
       b.lunch_id,
       b.lunch_date,
       b.date_entered
from l_employees a
     right outer join l_lunches b
     on where a.employee_id = b.employee_id;
```

Save this query. Name it `sec1707a_view`.

Step 2: Enter this query in the SQL window:

```
select a.*,
       b.department_name
from sec1707a_view a
     left outer join l_departments b
     on a.dept_code = b.dept_code
union
select a.*,
       b.department_name
from sec1707a_view a,
     right outer join l_departments b
     on a.dept_code = b.dept_code;
```

Save this query. Name it `sec1707b_view`.

Caring about the Efficiency of Your Computer

If you are going to combine several large tables together, you should be aware of the effect this might have on your computer. If you are running on your own computer, your query might take a long time to run. Some queries can run for several hours.

If you are running on a shared computer, a long-running query can affect the other people using the computer and it can cost a lot of money.

17-8 Monitor your queries

It is a good idea to monitor your queries in some way, particularly when you are handling several large tables. I consider a table to be large when it has more than 100,000 rows.

It is good to have an approximate idea of the number of rows of the beginning tables, the number of rows you expect in the result, and how long you expect the query to run. If you expected a result in less than two minutes and your query has been running for more than 20 minutes, you might want to stop the processing and examine your code.

In many shops you can also monitor the cost of your queries. This is an approximate measure of the amount of computer resources required to process the query. Do not try to be too precise about the cost, because the accounting procedures that produce the cost are usually not very accurate.

Sometimes you might want to ask for help from another programmer or your DBA. The next sections may also give you some hints.

17-9 Use the indexes

One way to improve the efficiency of your queries is to use the indexes that the database has. You need to find out which columns have indexes on them. Try to use those columns in your join conditions and when you place selection conditions in the `where` clause. Most databases already have indexes on all the columns intended for use in join conditions.

Here is one of my experiences involving indexes. Once I was writing some queries at a large company and every time I wrote a query using a particular table, the query would time out. When a query times out, this means that the query has processed in the computer for the maximum time allowed, which was about an hour at that shop. When I submitted one of these queries, it would run for an hour, then I would get an error message from the operating system, no result table, and a bill for $3,000.

I investigated this by going to the Data Dictionary and looking for the indexes on the table. I found that an index was missing. I told the DBA, and within two days the index was built. Then my queries ran in just a few minutes.

17-10   Select the data you want early in the process

Another way to improve the efficiency of your queries is to select the data you want early in the process. Make the beginning tables as small as possible before you join them. In other words, don't ask the computer to handle rows of data that you know you will not use.

This is fairly simple to do if you organize your code as a series of steps. Just put steps at the beginning that eliminate some of the rows from each beginning table.

If the optimizer always worked perfectly, it would do this for you automatically. However, most optimizers are not that smart yet, so it is worthwhile for you to try doing it yourself.

17-11 Use a table to save summarized data

Sometimes we may develop a small amount of data, perhaps a few thousand rows, from several tables that are much larger, using a query that runs for an hour. If we anticipate using this information several times or if we intend to do some complex manipulations on it, we might want to save it in a table rather than a view.

If we saved it as a view, the information would need to be created afresh each time we wanted to use it. By saving it in a table we know that it only needs to be created once.

We did this at a company I worked for. The company had more than 10,000 employees and an accounting system that kept track of every penny each person spent. There were 2 million rows of data generated each month. Once a month we would summarize these expenses into 500 categories and save the data in a table. Then we would run all the monthly budgeting reports from the summarized data in that table, instead of running them from the raw data.

17-12 Try several ways of writing the SQL

Suppose you have a long-running query that is scheduled to process regularly — daily, weekly, or even monthly. You might try to write the SQL in several different ways to see if you can find one way that is more efficient than the others. For instance, you might try combining the tables in a different order, or you might try using a subquery instead of a join. This type of experimentation is not worth doing if the query is only run occasionally, but it can pay off when the query is run many times.

Standardizing the Way That Tables Are Joined

You should seldom have to invent ways to join tables. You should just follow the pattern that has already been set up by the designers of the database. If a view has been created that joins all the tables together, then you can use that view to get information as if it were a single table.

17-13   The joins are part of the database design

Usually the people who design the database tables also design a way for those tables to be joined. You should almost always follow their design. You should not have to guess or make things up yourself. However, this information is not always communicated very clearly.

Sometimes the names of the columns suggest how to make the join. All the columns with identical names should be joined. Sometimes you can look at code other people have written to see what join conditions they used. Your DBA may be able to help. Rarely will it be worthwhile to try to find the documents from the database design team. Occasionally, the database may have changed and evolved, which could mean that you will need to use a different join condition.

17-14   A view can standardize the way tables are joined

If the tables in a database are fairly small, we can set up one view that combines the data from all of the tables. Then anyone who wants information from the database can select it from this one view. It is as if the whole database were one table. The following example creates a view like this for the Lunches database.

If the database contains several large tables, we usually do not combine them into a single view because that could consume too much of the computer's resources. However, we might create a few views that combine two or three of the tables at a time.

The view created in this section contains all the employees, even the ones who are not attending any of the lunches. It also contains all the foods, even the one that has not been ordered. However, it contains only the departments that have employees in them and only the suppliers that are supplying foods on the current menu.

Task

Create a single view that combines all the tables of the Lunches database. Name this view all_lunches_view.

Oracle SQL

```
create or replace view sec1714a_view as
select a.*,
       b.department_name
from l_employees a,
     l_departments b
where a.dept_code = b.dept_code;


create or replace view sec1714b_view as
select a.*,
       b.business_name,
       b.business_start_date,
       b.lunch_budget,
       b.owner_name
from sec1714a_view a,
     l_constants b;


create or replace view sec1714c_view as
select a.*,
       b.lunch_id,
       b.lunch_date,
       b.date_entered
from sec1714b_view a
     left outer join l_lunches b
     on a.employee_id = b.employee_id;


create or replace view sec1714d_view as
select a.*,
       b.supplier_name
from l_foods a
     left outer join l_suppliers b
     on a.supplier_id = b.supplier_id;
```

```
create or replace view sec1714e_view as
select a.*,
       b.lunch_id,
       b.item_number,
       b.quantity
from sec1714d_view a
     left outer join l_lunch_items b
     on a.supplier_id = b.supplier_id
        and a.product_code = b.product_code;


create or replace view sec1714_all_lunches_view as
select a.*,
       b.supplier_id,
       b.product_code,
       b.menu_item,
       b.description,
       b.price,
       b.price_increase,
       b.supplier_name,
       b.item_number,
       b.quantity
from sec1714c_view a
     full outer join sec1714e_view b
     on a.lunch_id = b.lunch_id;
```

Access SQL

Step 1: Enter this query in the SQL window:

```
select a.*,
       b.department_name
from l_employees a,
     l_departments b
where a.dept_code = b.dept_code;
```

Save the query. Name it `sec1714a_view`.

Step 2: Enter this query in the SQL window:

```
select a.*,
       b.business_name,
       b.business_start_date,
       b.lunch_budget,
       b.owner_name
from sec1714a_view a,
     l_constants b;
```

Save the query. Name it `sec1714b_view`.

Step 3: Enter this query in the SQL window:

```
select a.*,
       b.lunch_id,
       b.lunch_date,
       b.date_entered
from sec1714b_view a
     left outer join l_lunches b
     on a.employee_id = b.employee_id;
```

Save the query. Name it `sec1714c_view`.

Step 4: Enter this query in the SQL window:

```
select a.*,
       b.supplier_name
from l_foods a
     left outer join l_suppliers b
     on a.supplier_id = b.supplier_id;
```

Save the query. Name it `sec1714d_view`.

Step 5: Enter this query in the SQL window:

```
select a.*,
       b.lunch_id,
       b.item_number,
       b.quantity
from sec1714d a
     left outer join l_lunch_items b
     on a.supplier_id = b.supplier_id
        and a.product_code = b.product_code;
```

Save the query. Name it `sec1714e_view`.

Step 6: Enter this query into the SQL window:

```
select a.*,
       b.supplier_id,
       b.product_code,
       b.menu_item,
       b.description,
       b.price,
       b.price_increase,
       b.supplier_name,
       b.item_number,
       b.quantity
from sec1714c_view a
     left outer join sec1714e_view b
     on a.lunch_id = b.lunch_id
```

```
union
select a.*,
       b.supplier_id,
       b.product_code,
       b.menu_item,
       b.description,
       b.price,
       b.price_increase,
       b.supplier_name,
       b.item_number,
       b.quantity
from sec1714c_view a
     right outer join sec1714e_view b
     on a.lunch_id = b.lunch_id;
```

Save the query. Name it `sec1714_all_lunches_view`.

Result table — The result table has 25 columns and 74 rows

17-15 Ad hoc reporting

Sometimes a database is called on to do things that it was never designed to do. Sometimes a business needs to respond to unforeseen changes. Maybe the currency rate has changed. Maybe Congress is considering a new law and we need to estimate how it will affect the business. At such times the database can be looked on as a resource, a vast collection of data. People try to use the database to fill their immediate needs, even if it was not designed for that purpose. This is always a bit unreliable, but it can provide some information.

An ad hoc report is meant to run only once. The database can be used in some very creative ways. One of the features of a relational database that is supposed to help with ad hoc reporting is that it is possible to join tables together in ways that the designers never imagined.

Key Points

- If you have a complex project, try to break it up into a series of simpler steps, instead of trying to do it all at once. Then each piece will be easier to do. Also, if you make some mistakes like I do, they will be easier to find and correct. If you create a view from each step, you will only need to run the last step and all the preceding steps will run automatically. If you are looking for possible errors, you can run each step individually.

- Try to join just two tables together at a time. Lookup tables can be an exception to this if you are sure that the lookup table always has a matching row. You can be sure of this when the lookup table is protected by referential integrity.

- If you combine tables with an inner join, be aware that some information could be dropped from the result. This is also a concern with left and right outer joins.

- If you combine tables with left and right outer joins, be aware that your result depends on the specific order in which the tables are combined.

- If you combine tables with full outer joins, be aware of how much computer processing this requires.

- Usually the tables of a database are designed to be joined together in one specific way. It is usually best to follow the method that other people are using.

- When you deal with a large database you should often monitor your query. You should have some rough idea of how long it will take to run and how many rows it will produce. If it takes too long to run or produces too many rows, investigate why this happened.

- The tables may be combined in many ways. You can use an inner join, three types of outer join, union, cross join, or self join. All the reporting that comes later depends on the way the tables have been combined, so it is important to make sure it has been done correctly. Because the data in the tables changes, it is important to write code that can deal with any data that could be put into the tables, not just the data that is there right now.

- The two major problems when combining several tables are loss of data and use of excessive computer resources. Loss of data can occur if the tables are not combined correctly. This is sometimes difficult to detect. The data just seem to disappear. It requires careful checking to make sure that you are getting all the data you think you should have.

- Databases have often been accused of requiring excessive computer resources. It is hard to know if that is true or not. However, certainly if a query is to be run daily, we should pay attention to the amount of resources it consumes. Sometimes a small change can make a query run much more efficiently.

chapter 18

If-Then-Else, Parameter Queries, and Subqueries

This chapter discusses three important topics that do not fit into the framework of the rest of the book. The first topic discusses `if-then-else` logic. Oracle implements this with the `decode` function. Access uses the Immediate If (`iif`) function. These functions do not introduce any new power into SQL, but they make some queries easier to write.

The second topic is parameter queries. This type of query asks you some questions before it runs. For example, it might ask, "What are the beginning and ending dates?" The answers you provide are used to modify the SQL, so the result is tailored to your needs.

The last topic is subqueries. When one query is written inside another query, it is called a subquery. This was once considered to be the most important feature of SQL, but now its use has diminished and it is only used occasionally.

In this chapter some of the Oracle code contains SQL*Plus commands. You need these when you run in the Oracle SQL Command Line environment. However, the Oracle Home Page environment does not support SQL*Plus and will usually ignore these commands.

If-Then-Else Logic

The original design of SQL intentionally omitted the `if-then-else` and `goto` constructs. They were considered to add too much complexity. The objective was to keep the SQL language very simple and straightforward.

Sometimes people say that the `case` and `decode` functions in Oracle introduces `if-then-else` logic into SQL. The examples in this section show what they mean by this statement. They imply that this makes SQL more powerful and capable of doing new things.

Actually, most things that can be done using these functions can also be done using a `union`. No new capabilities are added. However, the `case` and `decode` function does make many SQL statements easier to write.

In Access, the Immediate If (`iif`) function can do many of the things that the Oracle functions can do.

18-1 The `case` and `decode` functions in Oracle

The `decode` function is an extension that Oracle has added to standard SQL. It names some specific values that will be turned into other values. It performs a series of tests to determine whether the data in the column are equal to one of a few specific values. If one of these values is matched, it places a new value in the column. Otherwise, if none of the specific values is matched, it places a default value (else-value) in the column.

This is based on a series of tests for an Equal condition. It can also test for a Less Than or Greater Than condition by using a trick with the `sign` function that I show you in section 18-3.

Oracle syntax for the `decode` function

```
DECODE(tested_value,
       if_1, then_1,
       if_2, then_2,
       ...
       default_value)
```

where

  `tested_value` = a column of a table or a row function.

  If `tested_value` equals `if_1`, then the `decode` function equals `then_1`.

  If `tested_value` equals `if_2`, then the `decode` function equals `then_2`.

And so on.

If `tested_value` is not equal to any of the `if` values, then the `decode` function equals the last value, in the `default_value` position.

The `if` value, the `then` value, and the `default_value` may be:

- A literal (of any data type)
- A null
- A column
- A row function, using one or several columns in a single row

Oracle `case` function

The `case` function is a more modern version of the `decode` function. It works in a similar way. I think you will be able to understand the examples without any more explanation, because the logic is very similar to the logic of the `decode` function.

The syntax of the `case` function is cleaner and easier to understand. It also has more power and capabilities. What I show you here is just part of what it can do.

Task for example 1

Show an example using the `decode` function in Oracle. Substitute carrots for broccoli in the menu of lunch foods.

Oracle SQL using the `decode` function

```
-- Override a value in one column.
select decode(description, ❶
              'BROCCOLI', 'CARROTS', ❷
              description) as new_menu, ❸
       price
from l_foods;
```

Oracle SQL using the `case` function

```
-- Override a value in one column.
select case when description = 'BROCCOLI' then 'CARROTS' ❶❷
            else description ❸
       end as new_menu, ❹
       price
from l_foods;
```

Beginning table (1_foods table)

SUPPLIER ID	PRODUCT CODE	MENU ITEM	DESCRIPTION	PRICE	PRICE INCREASE
ASP	FS	1	FRESH SALAD	$2.00	$0.25
ASP	SP	2	SOUP OF THE DAY	$1.50	(null)
ASP	SW	3	SANDWICH	$3.50	$0.40
CBC	GS	4	GRILLED STEAK	$6.00	$0.70
CBC	SW	5	HAMBURGER	$2.50	$0.30
FRV	BR	6	BROCCOLI	$1.00	$0.05
FRV	FF	7	FRENCH FRIES	$1.50	(null)
JBR	AS	8	SODA	$1.25	$0.25
JBR	VR	9	COFFEE	$0.85	$0.15
VSB	AS	10	DESSERT	$3.00	$0.50

Result table

NEW_MENU	PRICE
FRESH SALAD	$2.00
SOUP OF THE DAY	$1.50
SANDWICH	$3.50
GRILLED STEAK	$6.00
HAMBURGER	$2.50
CARROTS	$1.00 ❺
FRENCH FRIES	$1.50
SODA	$1.25
COFFEE	$0.85
DESSERT	$3.00

Notes

❶ The change is based on the data in the description column.

❷ If the value in the description column is broccoli, then change it to carrots.

❸ Otherwise, if the value in the description column is not broccoli, the value of this function is equal to the value in the description column.

❹ The case statement must finish with the word end.

❺ This is the row that was changed.

Task for example 2

The decode function in task 1 changed the value in a single column. To change several columns, we must use the functions several times, once for each column. In addition to the changes we made in task 1, change the price of the carrots to $1.20.

Oracle SQL using the decode function

```
-- Override the values in two columns.
select decode(description,
              'BROCCOLI', 'CARROTS',
              description) as new_menu,
       decode(description, ❶
              'BROCCOLI', 1.20, ❷
              price) as price ❸
from l_foods;
```

Oracle SQL using the case function

```
-- Override the values in two columns.
select case when description = 'BROCCOLI' then 'CARROTS'
            else description
       end as new_menu,
       case when description = 'BROCCOLI' then 1.20  ❶❷
            else price ❸
       end as price
from l_foods;
```

Result table

```
NEW_MENU                PRICE
-------------------- --------
FRESH SALAD             $2.00
SOUP OF THE DAY         $1.50
SANDWICH               $3.50
GRILLED STEAK          $6.00
HAMBURGER              $2.50
CARROTS                $1.20 ❹
FRENCH FRIES           $1.50
SODA                   $1.25
COFFEE                  $.85
DESSERT                $3.00
```

Notes

❶ To determine which row will receive the changed value, we test the `description` column, even though it is the `price` column that is being changed. We do this because we only want to change one price of one item and it is the value in the `description` column that tells the computer which row to change.

❷ If the `description` column is equal to `broccoli`, then we change the price to $1.20. You might think that because we want to change the price of the carrots, we should use `carrots` in this test, but the data comes from the beginning table, and there the value is `broccoli`.

❸ Otherwise, for all rows except the one for `broccoli`, the value of this function is equal to the value in the `price` column.

❹ This is the row that has been changed. Only the value in the result table is changed. The value in the beginning table is not changed.

Check your understanding

One of the ways that `if-then-else` logic is often used is to replace a lookup table. This can be handy when a lookup table is not available and you do not have permission to create a new table.

For example, suppose you are working with the data in the `l_employees` table. Suppose the lookup table `l_departments` does not exist or you have not been given permission to use it. Suppose you want to translate the `dept_code` fields into departments' names. You might find yourself in a position where the only way you have to do this is to use `if-then-else` logic.

Write an SQL query from the `l_employees` table (without using the `l_departments` table) that shows the `employee_id`, `first_name`, `last_name`, and `department` name. Get the department name from the `dept_code` field by using `if-then-else` logic.

18-2 The Immediate If (`iif`) function in Access

The Immediate If (`iif`) function is used to create an `if-then-else` condition in Access. This is an extension to standard SQL that Access has added. It tests a statement to determine whether it is true or false. It assigns one value to the function if the statement is true and a different value if the statement is false.

The condition used in the test can be any SQL condition, including:

- Equal
- Less Than
- Greater Than
- In
- Between
- Like
- Is null

Access syntax for the `immediate if` function (`iif`)

`iif(true_or_false_expression, true_value, false_value)`

where

> `true_or_false_expression` is any statement resulting in a value of True or False. In Access, False is the value 0 and True is any other value. The value used most frequently for True is −1.

> `true_value` is the final value of the iif function when the statement in the first parameter is True.

> `false_value` is the final value of the iif function when the statement in the first parameter is False or Unknown.

Task for example 1

Show an example of an SQL statement using the `iif` function. Substitute carrots for broccoli in the menu of lunch foods.

Access SQL

```
select iif(description = 'BROCCOLI', 'CARROTS',
           description) as new_menu,
       price
from l_foods;
```

Beginning table (1_foods table)

SUPPLIER_ID	PRODUCT_CODE	MENU_ITEM	DESCRIPTION	PRICE	PRICE_INCREASE	Add New Field
Asp	Fs	1	Fresh Salad	$2.00	$0.25	
Asp	Sp	2	Soup Of The Day	$1.50		
Asp	Sw	3	Sandwich	$3.50	$0.40	
Cbc	Gs	4	Grilled Steak	$6.00	$0.70	
Cbc	Sw	5	Hamburger	$2.50	$0.30	
Frv	Br	6	Broccoli	$1.00	$0.05	
Frv	Ff	7	French Fries	$1.50		
Jbr	As	8	Soda	$1.25	$0.25	
Jbr	Vr	9	Coffee	$0.85	$0.15	
Vsb	As	10	Dessert	$3.00	$0.50	
		(New)		$0.00	$0.00	

Result table

new_menu	price
Fresh Salad	$2.00
Soup Of The Day	$1.50
Sandwich	$3.50
Grilled Steak	$6.00
Hamburger	$2.50
CARROTS	$1.00
French Fries	$1.50
Soda	$1.25
Coffee	$0.85
Dessert	$3.00
	$0.00

Task for example 2

In addition to the changes you made in task 1, change the price of the carrots to $1.20.

Access SQL

```
select iif(description = 'BROCCOLI',
              'CARROTS', description) as new_menu,
        iif(description = 'BROCCOLI',
              1.20, a.price) as price ❶
from 1_foods a;
```

Result table

new_menu	price
Fresh Salad	$2.00
Soup Of The Day	$1.50
Sandwich	$3.50
Grilled Steak	$6.00
Hamburger	$2.50
CARROTS	$1.20
French Fries	$1.50
Soda	$1.25
Coffee	$0.85
Dessert	$3.00

Notes

❶ In Access, I write "a.price" to say it is a column from the beginning table. The "a" is a table alias for the 1_foods table, which is assigned in the from clause. This distinguishes it from the column alias price, which is assigned in the select clause of this SQL statement and determines the heading for the column in the result table.

If you do not make this distinction, Access becomes confused, and cannot run the SQL.

Check your understanding

Do the same task as "Check your understanding" for the previous section. This time perform the task in Access, rather than Oracle.

18-3 Attaching messages to rows

The decode, case, and iif functions can be used to attach messages to certain rows. These messages might convey information, flag exceptions, issue warnings, or show errors. This can also be done with a union.

The task of this section is the same as in section 15-11 in which the SQL code was written with a union. Here it is written using the decode, case, and iif functions.

Which way of writing the code is best? In this example, I like the Oracle code using the case function. It says what it is doing most clearly in simple words. The code for the Oracle decode function seems tricky and difficult to understand.

Task

List the foods and their prices. Add the message "expensive item" to the foods that cost more than $2.00. List the foods in alphabetical order.

Oracle SQL — Using decode

```
select description,
       price,
       decode(sign(price - 2.00), ❶
                      +1, 'EXPENSIVE ITEM',
                       0, '     ',
                      -1, '     ',
                    null, '     ') as message
from 1_foods
order by description;
```

Oracle SQL — Using case

```
select description,
       price,
       case when price > 2.00 then 'EXPENSIVE ITEM'
            else '  '
       end as message
from 1_foods
order by description;
```

Access SQL — Using `iif`

```
select description,
       price,
       iif (price > 2.00, 'EXPENSIVE ITEM', '   ')
                                        as message
from l_foods
order by description;
```

Beginning table (l_foods table)

SUPPLIER ID	PRODUCT CODE	MENU ITEM	DESCRIPTION	PRICE	PRICE INCREASE
ASP	FS	1	FRESH SALAD	$2.00	$0.25
ASP	SP	2	SOUP OF THE DAY	$1.50	(null)
ASP	SW	3	SANDWICH	$3.50	$0.40
CBC	GS	4	GRILLED STEAK	$6.00	$0.70
CBC	SW	5	HAMBURGER	$2.50	$0.30
FRV	BR	6	BROCCOLI	$1.00	$0.05
FRV	FF	7	FRENCH FRIES	$1.50	(null)
JBR	AS	8	SODA	$1.25	$0.25
JBR	VR	9	COFFEE	$0.85	$0.15
VSB	AS	10	DESSERT	$3.00	$0.50

Result table

DESCRIPTION	PRICE	MESSAGE
BROCCOLI	$1.00	
COFFEE	$0.85	
DESSERT	$3.00	EXPENSIVE ITEM
FRENCH FRIES	$1.50	
FRESH SALAD	$2.00	
GRILLED STEAK	$6.00	EXPENSIVE ITEM
HAMBURGER	$2.50	EXPENSIVE ITEM
SANDWICH	$3.50	EXPENSIVE ITEM
SODA	$1.25	
SOUP OF THE DAY	$1.50	

Notes

❶ In Oracle, the `sign` function allows `decode` to cover a range of values, rather than just a few specific values. This is a trick. We take the price and subtract $2.00 from it. Then we test the result to see if it is positive or negative. The result is positive when the price is greater than $2.00.

The value of the `sign` function is +1 for all positive numbers. It is -1 for all negative numbers. Otherwise, it is 0 or `null`. In this example, the `sign` function creates a +1 when the price is more than $2.00, a 0 when the price is equal to $2.00, a -1 when the price is less than $2.00, and a `null` when the price is null.

This trick reduces a range of values to four distinct possibilities.

Check your understanding

List all the employees from the `1_employees` table. Include their `hire_date`. Use `if-then-else` logic to define a message field. When the hire date is before the year 2000, add the message "Old Guard." When the hire date is after the year 2005, add the message "Young Turk."

18-4 Dividing data from one column into two different columns

The `decode`, `case`, and `iif` functions can be used to divide the data in one column into two columns. This is done to make the information easier for people to absorb. The task in this section is the same as in section 15-12, where the SQL was written using a `union`.

Task

Divide the `cost` column from the beginning table into two columns: `debits` and `credits`.

Oracle SQL — Using the `decode` function

```
set null ' '; ❶

select item,
       decode (sign(cost),
                    +1, null,
                     0, null,
                    -1, cost,
                    null, null) as debits,
       decode (sign(cost),
                    +1, cost,
                     0, cost,
                    -1, null, ❷
                    null, null) as credits
from sec1804_finances
order by item;
```

Oracle SQL — Using the `case` function

```
set null ' ';  ❶

select item,
       case when cost < 0 then cost
            else null   ❷
       end as debits,
       case when cost >= 0 then cost
       else null   ❷
       end as credits
from sec1804_finances
order by item;
```

Access SQL — Using the `iif` function

```
select item,
       iif(cost < 0, cost, '   ') as debits,
       iif(cost >=0, cost, '   ') as credits
from sec1804_finances
order by item;
```

Beginning table (sec1804_finances table)

```
ITEM                               COST
------------------------    ------------
SAMSONITE SUITCASE              -$248.13
RENT FOR APRIL                   $700.00
OPERA TICKET                    -$145.00
LUNCH                            -$15.62
DEBT REPAID BY JIM                $20.00
CAR REPAIR                      -$622.98
HAIRCUT                          -$22.00
BIRTHDAY GIFT FROM MOM           $200.00
```

Result table

```
ITEM                            DEBITS       CREDITS
------------------------    ------------   ------------
BIRTHDAY GIFT FROM MOM                        $200.00
CAR REPAIR                    -$622.98
DEBT REPAID BY JIM                             $20.00
HAIRCUT                        -$22.00
LUNCH                          -$15.62
OPERA TICKET                  -$145.00
RENT FOR APRIL                                $700.00
SAMSONITE SUITCASE            -$248.13
```

Notes

❶ In Oracle, this command tells SQL*Plus to display nulls as blank spaces. After running this query, you may want to see the nulls as (null) again. If you do, you can use this command:

```
set null '(null)';
```

❷ In Oracle, the null here cannot be replaced with a space enclosed in single quotes because the credits column is numeric, as cost is a number. We are not allowed to enter text values into a numeric column.

Check your understanding

List all the employees from the l_employees table. Include their hire_date. Use if-then-else logic to divide the hire dates into two different columns. One column will contain all the hire dates before the year 2000. The other column will contain all the hire dates after the year 2000.

18-5 Applying two functions to different parts of the data

The decode, case, and iif functions can be used to apply one function to part of the data and another function to the rest of the data. The task in this section is the same as in section 15-13, where the SQL code was written using a union.

Task

Increase the price of all foods costing more than $2.00 by 5 percent. Increase the price of all other foods by 10 percent. Ignore the price_increase column.

Oracle SQL — Using decode

```
select menu_item,
       description,
       decode (sign(price - 2.00),
                   +1, price * 1.05,
                    0, price * 1.10,
                   -1, price * 1.10,
                   null, null)          as new_price
from 1_foods
order by menu_item;
```

Oracle SQL — Using case

```
select menu_item,
       description,
       case when price > 2.00 then price * 1.05
            else price * 1.10
       end as new_price
from 1_foods;
```

Access SQL — Using iif

```
select description,
       iif(price > 2.00, price * 1.05, price * 1.10)
                                       as new_price
from 1_foods;
```

Beginning table (1_foods table)

SUPPLIER ID	PRODUCT CODE	MENU ITEM	DESCRIPTION	PRICE	PRICE INCREASE
ASP	FS	1	FRESH SALAD	$2.00	$0.25
ASP	SP	2	SOUP OF THE DAY	$1.50	
ASP	SW	3	SANDWICH	$3.50	$0.40
CBC	GS	4	GRILLED STEAK	$6.00	$0.70
CBC	SW	5	HAMBURGER	$2.50	$0.30
FRV	BR	6	BROCCOLI	$1.00	$0.05
FRV	FF	7	FRENCH FRIES	$1.50	
JBR	AS	8	SODA	$1.25	$0.25
JBR	VR	9	COFFEE	$0.85	$0.15
VSB	AS	10	DESSERT	$3.00	$0.50

Result table

```
    MENU                                NEW
    ITEM DESCRIPTION                  PRICE
 ------- --------------------      --------
       1 FRESH SALAD                 $2.20
       2 SOUP OF THE DAY             $1.65
       3 SANDWICH                    $3.68
       4 GRILLED STEAK               $6.30
       5 HAMBURGER                   $2.63
       6 BROCCOLI                    $1.10
       7 FRENCH FRIES                $1.65
       8 SODA                        $1.38
       9 COFFEE                       $.94
      10 DESSERT                     $3.15
```

Check your understanding

List all the employees from the `l_employees` table. Include their `hire_date` and `credit_limit`. Use `if-then-else` logic to increase the credit limits. For employees hired before the year 2000, double their credit limits. For other employees, increase their credit limits by 50 percent.

Parameter Queries

There are no variables in SQL. Everything about an SQL query must be specific — the literal values, the column names, and the table names. The state of the data can be an unknown, because the data may be constantly changing, but there are no unknowns within an SQL query or command.

In this chapter, we discuss two methods that take a step toward introducing variables into SQL — parameter queries and subqueries. We have already discussed another method, using a table of constants. In that method, many of the literal values are put as data into a table instead of being coded directly into the SQL. Usually a table of constants has only one row.

In a parameter query, the variables do not belong to the SQL itself; rather, they belong to the environment that people use to submit SQL queries.

- In Oracle Database Home Page, the environment is PL/SQL. Variables are written with a colon before the name of the variable. For example:

  `:dog`

- In Oracle SQL Command Line, the environment is SQL*Plus. Variables are written with one or two ampersands before the name of the variable. For example:

  &dog or &&dog

- In Access, the environment is the GUI layer, before the SQL query is sent to the JET database engine for processing. Variables are written enclosed in square brackets. For example:

  [Enter the name of the dog]

You usually write a parameter query for an end user to run. At runtime, the end user is asked to provide specific values for all the variables. These values are placed into the SQL statement before it is sent to the DBMS.

In the next few sections I mostly discuss the SQL Command Line environment for Oracle.

18-6 A parameter query in Oracle

A parameter query in Oracle is a `select` statement that contains variables. These variables begin with an ampersand, such as `&employee_id`. When SQL*Plus finds a variable beginning with `&`, it asks you for the value of the variable. It substitutes the value you give to the variable into the `select` statement, so that the `select` statement no longer contains any variables. Then it sends that statement to the SQL level for processing.

In this section, you cannot type the commands directly into SQL*Plus. To write a parameter query in Oracle, you must write it in Notepad and save it as a file. This is called an Oracle script file. To run this file, enter "start" within SQL*Plus, followed by the name of the file. An example of this follows.

Parameter queries are used to make the SQL code more flexible. The person running the code can enter the values they need. Oracle allows you to use parameters with all types of SQL statements.

Task

Write an Oracle script file containing a parameter query. Make the query prompt for a value of the `employee_id` number and have it return the row for that employee from the `l_employees` table.

Oracle SQL: Step 1 — Create a file using Notepad

Save this code in a file named c:\temp\sec1806a.txt.

```
-- Prepare SQL*Plus to run a parameter query
set echo off; ❶
set scan on; ❷
set define on;

-- Run the parameter query
select *
from l_employees
where employee_id = &employee_num; ❸

-- Return SQL*Plus to the standard settings
set scan off;
set define off;
set echo on;
```

Oracle SQL: Step 2 — Run the parameter query

```
start c:\temp\sec1806a.txt
```

When the code is run, the computer asks for information.
I enter 210 for the value of the employee_num field.

```
Enter value for employee_num: 210
```

Result table

EMPLOYEE ID	FIRST NAME	LAST NAME	DEPT CODE	HIRE_DATE	CREDIT LIMIT	PHONE NUMBER	MANAGER ID
210	NANCY	HOFFMAN	SAL	16-FEB-2007	$25.00	2974	203

Notes

❶ This prevents detail messages from appearing on the screen. They are irrelevant in this context.

❷ The next two lines set up the SQL*Plus environment to accept parameter queries.

The set scan on tells SQL*Plus to scan SQL statements for variables, which begin with an ampersand. The set define on allows SQL*Plus to define variables.

❸ &employee_num is a variable. SQL*Plus will ask you what value you want this variable to have.

Oracle SQL: Enter this parameter query on the SQL Commands page

```
select *
from l_employees
where employee_id = :employee_num;
```

You can get to the SQL Commands page from the Oracle Database Home Page. This query will not work as an SQL Script because a script is not allowed to ask the user for parameter values.

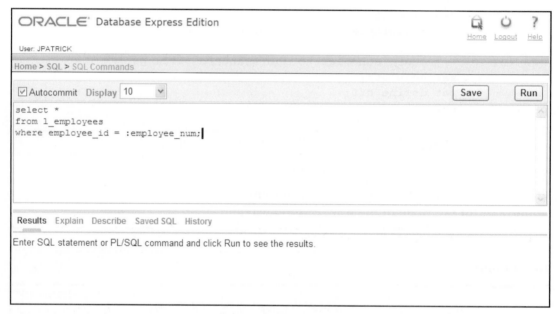

The parameter query is entered into the SQL Commands page.

After you click the Run button, a new screen is shown to collect the values of the parameters. Here I entered the value 202.

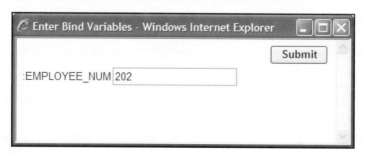

Then you click the Submit button in the Enter Bind Variables window and the query will run.

The SQL Commands page now shows both the SQL statement and the result table.

Check your understanding

Write a parameter query that asks the user to enter a department code and then gives the user the full name of the department.

18-7 Using a parameter more than once in Oracle

In an Oracle script file, we might want to use the same variable several times. To do this, we begin the name of the variable with two ampersands (&&) the first time it occurs. When SQL*Plus encounters a variable beginning with &&, it asks for a value of the variable and remembers the value you have given to that variable. Then it will use that value whenever it finds the variable again.

Task

Write an Oracle script file containing a parameter query. Have the query prompt for a value of the employee_id number and have it return all the rows for that employee from the l_employees table and the l_lunches table.

Oracle SQL: Step 1 — Create a file using Notepad

Save this code in a file named `c:\temp\sec1807.txt`.

```
-- Prepare SQL*Plus to run a parameter query
set echo off;
set scan on;
set define on;

-- Run the first parameter query
select *
from l_employees
where employee_id = &&employee_num; ❶

-- Run the second parameter query
-- without asking the user again for the Employee ID
select *
from l_lunches
where employee_id = &employee_num; ❷

-- Return SQL*Plus to the standard settings
undefine employee_num; ❸
set scan off;
set define off;
set echo on;
```

Oracle SQL: Step 2 — Run the parameter query

```
start c:\temp\sec1807.txt
```

When the code is run, the computer asks for information.
I enter 210 for the value of the `employee_num` field.

```
Enter value for employee_num: 210
```

Result table

EMPLOYEE ID	FIRST NAME	LAST NAME	DEPT CODE	HIRE_DATE	CREDIT LIMIT	PHONE NUMBER	MANAGER ID
210	NANCY	HOFFMAN	SAL	16-FEB-2007	$25.00	2974	203

1 row selected.

LUNCH_ID	LUNCH DATE	EMPLOYEE ID	DATE_ENTERE
7	16-NOV-2011	210	13-OCT-2011
17	05-DEC-2011	210	21-OCT-2011

Notes

❶ `&&employee_num` prompts for the value, remembers it, and uses this value whenever it encounters `&employee_num` again.

❷ The value of `&employee_num` has already been set, so you will not be prompted for the value of this variable.

❸ This resets the SQL*Plus environment so that the value of the `&employee_num` variable is no longer defined. Notice that in this statement there is no `&` before the name of the variable.

The Oracle Database Home Page method cannot do this task

Actually, this task cannot be done using the Oracle Home Page environment. This task runs two queries with two different tables. In the SQL Command environment, you can only run a single query. In the SQL Script environment, you can run two queries, but parameter queries do not work in this environment because there is no interaction with the user.

Check your understanding

Write a parameter query that asks the user to enter a department code and then gives the user the full name of the department and the names of all the employees in that department.

18-8 More ways to define parameters in Oracle

There are two other ways to define a parameter in an Oracle script file. One way uses the define command:

```
define my_dog = jimmy;
```

The word `define` is followed by the name of the variable, an equal sign, and the value of the variable. The semicolon is optional. This is useful if you want to have variables in your code for your own use. You can use a variarble this way to keep the code flexible. However, if another person runs the code, that person will not be asked for the value of the variable at runtime.

The other way to define a parameter prompts the person who runs the code for the value of the variable. It requires two commands. The prompt command asks a question. Then the accept command takes the response and stores that response in a variable. For example:

```
prompt Enter the name of your dog;
accept my_dog char;
```

The `accept` command creates the variable. The word `char` at the end of the command tells it to create a character variable to hold a text value. The other options that can be used at the end of an `accept` command are `num-ber` and `date`.

When the variable is used where the substitution is intended to occur, the name of the variable must be preceded with an ampersand. For example,

`&my_dog`

Oracle SQL: Step 1 — Create a file using Notepad

Save this code in a file named `c:\temp\sec1808.txt`.

```
-- Prepare the SQL*Plus environment
set echo off;
set scan on;
set define on;

-- Have SQL*Plus define three SQL*Plus variables. The value
-- of one variable is set here in the SQL*Plus script file.
-- The user is asked for values of the other two variables.
define table = l_employees; ❶
prompt Enter a valid Employee ID number; ❷
accept employee_num number; ❸
prompt Enter a valid Department code using uppercase letters; 
accept depart_code char; ❹

-- Run two SQL queries using those variables
select *
from &table ❺
where employee_id = &employee_num;
select *
from &table
where dept_code = '&depart_code'; ❻

-- Return SQL*Plus to the standard settings
undefine table;
undefine employee_num;
undefine depart_code;
set scan off;
set define off;
set echo on;
```

Step 2: Oracle SQL*Plus — Run the parameter query

```
start c:\temp\sec1808.txt
```

When the code is run, the computer asks for information.
I enter 210 and then `SAL`.

```
Enter a valid Employee ID number
210
Enter a valid Department code using uppercase letters
SAL
```

Result table

EMPLOYEE ID	FIRST NAME	LAST NAME	DEPT CODE	HIRE_DATE	CREDIT LIMIT	PHONE NUMBER	MANAGER ID
210	NANCY	HOFFMAN	SAL	16-FEB-2007	$25.00	2974	203

EMPLOYEE ID	FIRST NAME	LAST NAME	DEPT CODE	HIRE_DATE	CREDIT LIMIT	PHONE NUMBER	MANAGER ID
202	JIM	KERN	SAL	16-AUG-1999	$25.00	8722	201
204	ELLEN	OWENS	SAL	01-JUL-2008	$15.00	6830	202
205	HENRY	PERKINS	SAL	01-MAR-2006	$25.00	5286	202
210	NANCY	HOFFMAN	SAL	16-FEB-2007	$25.00	2974	203

Notes

❶ This `define` command creates a variable called `table` and gives it the value `1_employees`. Notice that there is no ampersand at the beginning of the word `table` when the variable is defined. However, there is an ampersand in `&table` when the variable is used.

❷ This `prompt` command displays the message "Enter a valid Employee ID number". It does not have single quotes around the message. If you use single quotes, they will appear in the message. The message is case sensitive.

❸ This `accept` command takes the value that has been entered and assigns it to the variable `employee_num`. The variable is defined as a numeric datatype.

❹ This `accept` command takes the value that has been entered and assigns it to the variable `depart_code`. The variable is defined as a text datatype.

❺ This line uses the `&table` variable, the value of which has already been set by the `define` command.

❻ This line uses the `&depart_code` variable, the value of which has already been set by the `accept` command. Notice that single quotes are placed around the variable. These are required because it is a text item. Without the quotes, after substitution, this line would read:

```
where dept_code = SAL
```

This would result in an error message. With the quotes, after substitution, this line reads:

```
where dept_code = 'SAL'
```

This is correct code.

Check your understanding

Repeat the problem of the previous section, but use the methods shown in this section.

Write a parameter query that asks the user to enter a department code and then gives the user the full name of the department and the names of all the employees in that department.

18-9 A parameter query in Access

Access automatically prompts you for the value of any variable it does not recognize. It is tuned to prompt for parameter values. You may have encountered this already. If you misspell the name of a column, it prompts you to enter a value for that column. Usually, that is not what you want to do, and this can create some strange error messages.

When you want to create a parameter query in Access, it is easy to do. Access is always ready to accept parameters.

Task

Write a procedure in Access that will ask for an employee ID number. After the user enters this number, the procedure finds the information about that employee in the `l_employees` table.

Access SQL

```
select *
from l_employees
where dept_code = [Enter a valid Department Code]; ❶
```

Prompt for information

Result table

EMPLOYEE_ID	FIRST_NAME	LAST_NAME	DEPT_CODE	HIRE_DATE	CREDIT_LIMIT	PHONE_NUMBER	MANAGER_ID
202	Jim	Kern	Sal	16-Aug-1999	$25.00	8722	201
204	Ellen	Owens	Sal	01-Jul-2008	$15.00	6830	202
205	Henry	Perkins	Sal	01-Mar-2006	$25.00	5286	202
210	Nancy	Hoffman	Sal	16-Feb-2007	$25.00	2974	203

Notes

❶ The text within the square brackets indicates a single parameter. The actual text is used to prompt for the information. This technique will work even without the square brackets, as long as the text contains no spaces

Check your understanding

Write a parameter query that asks the user to enter a department code and then gives the user the full name of the department.

18-10 A query in Access with two parameters

When there are two or more parameters within a query in Access, the same value is placed in all the parameters with the same name. If you want to put different values in two parameters, you must give them different names. The name of a parameter comes from the text that it prompts for.

Task

Ask the person running the query for a beginning date and an ending date. Then show the rows from the 1_employees table for all the people hired between those two dates.

Access SQL — Incorrect

```
select *
from 1_employees
where hire_date between [date] and [date]
order by hire_date;
```

With this code, there will be only one prompt for date. The same value will be placed into both parameters. The query returns only the rows for the people hired on that one date.

Access SQL — Correct

```
select *
from l_employees
where hire_date between [Enter beginning date]
                    and [Enter ending date]
order by hire_date;
```

Check your understanding

Write a parameter query that asks the user to enter a department code and then gives the user the full name of the department and the names of all the employees in that department.

18-11 Limitations on parameters in Access

In Access, you can only use a parameter in a query to hold the place for a specific value, such as "102," "Bob," or "March 4, 1906." You cannot use a parameter in the place of a column name or a table name. In contrast, Oracle allows you to use a parameter for any word within a query.

Within an Oracle script file, the same parameter can be used in several related queries. You cannot do this in Access, because the SQL window only allows you to enter one query at a time.

Subqueries

A select statement that is embedded within another select statement is called a **subquery**. In the following sections I discuss several variations on this idea. Most of the time you do not have to use subqueries. There are still a few places where you have to use them, and you may have to understand code that was written 10 years ago when outer joins were not available and inner joins were less efficient than they are today.

18-12 Introduction to subqueries

When SQL was first created, people thought that subqueries would be the most important feature of the language. One style of coding SQL, found in older code, makes extensive use of subqueries. Some people still write code this way, but this style has now fallen out of favor.

It has largely been replaced by a style that prefers to use joins when there is a choice. There are three reasons for this change. One reason is that the processing of joins has become much more efficient. Originally it was thought that subqueries would always process much more quickly than joins. In the past few years many improvements have been made to the Optimizer that make joins more efficient. Now joins are often just as efficient as subqueries, and sometimes even more efficient.

The second reason is that outer joins have now become a standard part of the language. The early SQL standards, SQL-86 and SQL-89, did not include outer joins. Subqueries were used to write them. Now most products support outer joins and they are included in the newest standard, SQL-92. Now we can write an outer join without using a subquery.

The third reason is that code written with many subqueries is difficult to understand and maintain. Code written with joins is often easier to understand and modify when changes are needed, and other people can work with the code more easily.

Task

Show an example of a subquery. List the foods that cost less than the average price of all the items on the menu. List the descriptions and prices of these foods. Sort the rows in ascending order on the `description` column.

Oracle & Access SQL

```
select a.description,
       a.price
from l_foods a
where a.price < (select avg(b.price)
                 from l_foods b)
order by a.description;
```

Beginning table (1_foods table)

SUPPLIER ID	PRODUCT CODE	MENU ITEM	DESCRIPTION	PRICE	PRICE INCREASE
ASP	FS	1	FRESH SALAD	$2.00	$0.25
ASP	SP	2	SOUP OF THE DAY	$1.50	(null)
ASP	SW	3	SANDWICH	$3.50	$0.40
CBC	GS	4	GRILLED STEAK	$6.00	$0.70
CBC	SW	5	HAMBURGER	$2.50	$0.30
FRV	BR	6	BROCCOLI	$1.00	$0.05
FRV	FF	7	FRENCH FRIES	$1.50	(null)
JBR	AS	8	SODA	$1.25	$0.25
JBR	VR	9	COFFEE	$0.85	$0.15
VSB	AS	10	DESSERT	$3.00	$0.50

How the computer processes this query

Step 1: The subquery is processed first.

```
select avg(b.price)
from 1_foods b;
```

Result table: Step 1

AVG(B.PRICE)
2.31

Step 2: The result is placed in the outer query.

```
select a.description,
       a.price
from 1_foods a
where a.price < 2.31
order by a.description;
```

Step 3: The outer query is processed.

Result table

DESCRIPTION	PRICE
BROCCOLI	$1.00
COFFEE	$0.85
FRENCH FRIES	$1.50
FRESH SALAD	$2.00
SODA	$1.25
SOUP OF THE DAY	$1.50

Check your understanding

Write an SQL query using a subquery. List all the employees who have a credit limit that is greater than the average credit limit.

18-13 Subqueries that result in a list of values

Some subqueries result in a single value and others return a list of values. Those are the only options. A subquery is not allowed to return any more values than that. For example, it cannot return a table with several rows and several columns. The reason is that the result of the subquery must fit into the statement of the outer query. Within the context of an SQL statement, only a single value or a list of values can make sense.

This section shows a subquery that results in a list of values. To make this list work with the syntax of the outer join, the condition in the `where` clause must be:

    IN

or   **NOT IN**

Task for example 1

Find all the rows from the `twos` table where the `number_2` column matches a value in the `number_3` column of the `threes` table.

Oracle & Access SQL: Using the `in` condition

```
select number_2,
       word_2
from twos
where number_2 in (select number_3 ❶
                   from threes);
```

Beginning tables

twos table   **threes table**

```
NUMBER_2 WORD_2              NUMBER_3 WORD_3
-------- ------------        -------- ------------
       2 TWO                        3 THREE
       4 FOUR                       6 SIX
       6 SIX                        9 NINE
       8 EIGHT                     12 TWELVE
      10 TEN                       15 FIFTEEN
      12 TWELVE                    18 EIGHTEEN
      14 FOURTEEN         (null)     NULL
      16 SIXTEEN
      18 EIGHTEEN
      20 TWENTY
(null)     NULL
```

Result table ❷

```
NUMBER_2 WORD_2
-------- ---------------
       6 SIX
      12 TWELVE
      18 EIGHTEEN
```

Notes

❶ The result of this subquery is the list (3, 6, 9, 12, 15, 18, null). When this list is substituted in the main query, the `select` statement is:

```
select number_2,
       word_2
from twos
where number_2 in (3, 6, 9, 12, 15, 18, null);
```

❷ The result of this subquery is the same as an inner join.

Task for example 2

Find all the rows from the `twos` table where the `number_2` column does not match any value in the `number_3` column of the `threes` table.

Oracle & Access SQL: Using the `not in` condition

```
select number_2,
       word_2
from twos
where number_2 not in (select number_3 ❶
                       from threes
                       where number_3 is not null);
```

Result table ❷

```
NUMBER_2 WORD_2
-------- --------------
       2 TWO
       4 FOUR
       8 EIGHT
      10 TEN
      14 FOURTEEN
      16 SIXTEEN
      20 TWENTY
```

Notes

❶ The result of this subquery is the list (3, 6, 9, 12, 15, 18). The null has been removed because the `not in` condition is used (see section 18-15). When this list is substituted in the main query, the `select` statement is:

```
select number_2,
       word_2
from twos
where number_2 not in (3, 6, 9, 12, 15, 18);
```

❷ The row with a null in the `number_2` column does not appear in the result table.

Check your understanding

First write an SQL query that results in a list of values. List the `employee_ids` from the `l_employees` table where the hire date is after the year 2000.

Next use that query as a subquery within another query. List all the lunches from the `l_lunches` table for those employees.

18-14   Subqueries that result in a single value

This section shows a subquery that results in a single value. One way to ensure that there is only one value is to use a column function such as max or sum. Here, the condition in the where clause can be any of the following:

- = (Equal)
- <> (Not Equal)
- < (Less Than) or <= (Less Than or Equal)
- > (Greater Than) or >= (Greater Than or Equal)
- IN
- NOT IN
- BETWEEN

Task for example 1

Find the row of the twos table where the number_2 column is equal to the maximum value in the number_3 column of the threes table.

Oracle & Access SQL: Using the Equal condition

```
select number_2,
       word_2
from twos
where number_2 = (select max(number_3) ❶
                  from threes);
```

Beginning tables — Same as in the previous section

Result table

```
NUMBER_2 WORD_2
-------- ---------------
      18 EIGHTEEN
```

Notes

❶ This subquery results in the value 18. When this value is substituted in the main query, the select statement is

```
select number_2,
       word_2
from twos
where number_2 = 18;
```

Task for example 2

Find all the rows of the `twos` table where the `number_2` column is not equal to the maximum value in the `number_3` column of the `threes` table.

Oracle & Access SQL: Using the Not Equal condition

```
select number_2,
       word_2
from twos
where number_2 <> (select max(number_3) ❶
                        from threes);
```

Result table ❷

```
NUMBER_2 WORD_2
--------- ------------
       2 TWO
       4 FOUR
       6 SIX
       8 EIGHT
      10 TEN
      12 TWELVE
      14 FOURTEEN
      16 SIXTEEN
      20 TWENTY
```

Notes

❶ This subquery results in the value 18.

❷ The row with a null in the `number_2` column does not appear in the result table.

Check your understanding

First write an SQL query that results in a single value. List the average credit limit for all the employees from the `l_employees` table.

Next, use that query as a subquery within another query. List all the employees who have a credit limit above that value.

18-15 Avoid using not in with nulls

If you use a subquery that generates a list of values and the subquery is used in a where clause with the not in condition, you need to make sure that the subquery excludes nulls from its list.

The SQL code for example 2 shows that no rows are selected when both of the following conditions apply: The result of a subquery is a list that includes a null, and the list is used with a not in condition. This makes sense because a null is an unknown value. There are not any rows that we can say are definitely not in a list, when the list contains an unknown value. The following example shows how this works.

Task for example 1

Find all the rows of the twos table where the number_2 column is equal to one of the values in the number_3 column of the threes table. This SQL code shows that the in condition is not affected by nulls.

Oracle & Access SQL

```
select number_2,
       word_2
from twos
where number_2 in (select number_3 ❶
                   from threes);
```

Result table

```
NUMBER_2 WORD_2
-------- --------------
       6 SIX
      12 TWELVE
      18 EIGHTEEN
```

Task for example 2

Find all the rows of the twos table where the number_2 column is not equal to any of the values in the number_3 column of the threes table. You need to be careful here because the number_3 column contains a null. The SQL code here shows that nulls are critical when you are using the not in condition with a subquery.

Oracle & Access SQL: Incorrect

```
select number_2,
       word_2
from twos
where number_2 not in (select number_3 ❷
                       from threes);
```

Result — The query runs, but there are no data in the result

Oracle & Access SQL: Correct

```
select number_2,
       word_2
from twos
where number_2 not in (select number_3 ❸
                       from threes
                       where number_3 is not null);
```

Result table

```
NUMBER_2 WORD_2
--------- ---------------
       2 TWO
       4 FOUR
       8 EIGHT
      10 TEN
      14 FOURTEEN
      16 SIXTEEN
      20 TWENTY
```

Notes

❶ This subquery results in the list (3, 6, 9, 12, 18, null). The null in this list does not cause a problem when it is used with an in condition.

❷ This subquery results in the list (3, 6, 9, 12, 18, null). The null in this list causes a major problem when it is used with a not in condition. The query runs, but it produces a message that says "no rows selected."

❸ This subquery results in the list (3, 6, 9, 12, 18). The null is removed by the where condition in the subquery. This list works with a not in condition.

Applications of Subqueries

The sections that follow show you some of the ways in which subqueries are most useful. You often have to use them in update statements, to compare tables, or to select the most current data from your tables.

18-16   Subqueries used in an update command

Often you may be given several changes to make in the data of a large table. If you use an update statement to make these changes, you will need to use a subquery. In fact, you will need to use two subqueries: one in the set clause and one in the where clause.

The subquery in the set clause gives new values to the column that is being changed. The subquery in the where clause specifies which rows to change. Without this second subquery, every value in the column is changed. Many of these values are set to null.

Task

Apply the updates given in the following table to change the manager_id column of the sec1816_employees table.

I am going to show you two methods of coding this. Each method will change the data in the table. I will use two different copies of the employees table so that you can run both SQL statements and compare the results.

Beginning tables to be updated
(sec1816a_employees table and sec1816bb_employees table)

EMPLOYEE ID	FIRST NAME	LAST NAME	DEPT CODE	HIRE_DATE	CREDIT LIMIT	PHONE NUMBER	MANAGER ID
201	SUSAN	BROWN	EXE	01-JUN-1998	$30.00	3484	(null)
202	JIM	KERN	SAL	16-AUG-1999	$25.00	8722	201
203	MARTHA	WOODS	SHP	02-FEB-2009	$25.00	7591	201
204	ELLEN	OWENS	SAL	01-JUL-2008	$15.00	6830	202
205	HENRY	PERKINS	SAL	01-MAR-2006	$25.00	5286	202
206	CAROL	ROSE	ACT	(null)	(null)	(null)	(null)
207	DAN	SMITH	SHP	01-DEC-2008	$25.00	2259	203
208	FRED	CAMPBELL	SHP	01-APR-2008	$25.00	1752	203
209	PAULA	JACOBS	MKT	17-MAR-1999	$15.00	3357	201
210	NANCY	HOFFMAN	SAL	16-FEB-2007	$25.00	2974	203

Beginning table of updates (`sec1816_changes` table)

```
   EMP_ID NEW_MANAGER
--------- -----------
      206         204
      207         204
      209         205
      210         205
```

Oracle & Access SQL: Incorrect

```
update sec1816a_employees a
set a.manager_id = (select b.new_manager
                    from sec1816_changes b
                    where a.employee_id = b.emp_id);
```

Result table — Incorrect

EMPLOYEE ID	FIRST NAME	LAST NAME	DEPT CODE	HIRE_DATE	CREDIT LIMIT	PHONE NUMBER	MANAGER ID
201	SUSAN	BROWN	EXE	01-JUN-1998	$30.00	3484	(null)❶
202	JIM	KERN	SAL	16-AUG-1999	$25.00	8722	(null)❶
203	MARTHA	WOODS	SHP	02-FEB-2009	$25.00	7591	(null)❶
204	ELLEN	OWENS	SAL	01-JUL-2008	$15.00	6830	(null)❶
205	HENRY	PERKINS	SAL	01-MAR-2006	$25.00	5286	(null)❶
206	CAROL	ROSE	ACT	(null)	(null)	(null)	204
207	DAN	SMITH	SHP	01-DEC-2008	$25.00	2259	204
208	FRED	CAMPBELL	SHP	01-APR-2008	$25.00	1752	(null)❶
209	PAULA	JACOBS	MKT	17-MAR-1999	$15.00	3357	205
210	NANCY	HOFFMAN	SAL	16-FEB-2007	$25.00	2974	205

Notes

❶ The incorrect SQL code placed nulls in the `manager_id` column of these rows.

Oracle & Access SQL: Correct

```
update sec1816b_employees a
set a.manager_id = (select b.new_manager
                    from sec1816_changes b
                    where a.employee_id = b.emp_id)
where a.employee_id in (select c.emp_id ❶
                        from sec1816_changes c);
```

Result table

```
EMPLOYEE  FIRST     LAST      DEPT                    CREDIT  PHONE   MANAGER
      ID  NAME      NAME      CODE    HIRE_DATE        LIMIT  NUMBER       ID
--------  -------   --------  ------  ------------    -------  ------  -------
     201  SUSAN     BROWN     EXE     01-JUN-1998     $30.00  3484    (null)
     202  JIM       KERN      SAL     16-AUG-1999     $25.00  8722        201
     203  MARTHA    WOODS     SHP     02-FEB-2009     $25.00  7591        201
     204  ELLEN     OWENS     SAL     01-JUL-2008     $15.00  6830        202
     205  HENRY     PERKINS   SAL     01-MAR-2006     $25.00  5286        202
     206  CAROL     ROSE      ACT     (null)          (null)  (null)      204  ❷
     207  DAN       SMITH     SHP     01-DEC-2008     $25.00  2259        204  ❷
     208  FRED      CAMPBELL  SHP     01-APR-2008     $25.00  1752        203
     209  PAULA     JACOBS    MKT     17-MAR-1999     $15.00  3357        205  ❷
     210  NANCY     HOFFMAN   SAL     16-FEB-2007     $25.00  2974        205  ❷
```

Notes

❶ A second subquery is required to specify which rows to change.

❷ Changes are made only to the desired rows.

18-17   Finding the difference between two tables

This section shows you how to find the differences between two tables. This method uses a subquery to remove all the rows that are identical in the two tables, so only the rows that are different remain. Two tricks are involved in this process.

The first trick concatenates all the columns of a table to form a single value. A separator is placed between the columns. We used a similar trick in section 11-9. This is necessary because a subquery is able to compare one list of single values with another, but it cannot compare rows of values.

The second trick is to use two SQL queries. Each query finds all the rows in one table that are not present in the other table. Therefore, two queries are needed to find all the rows that do not match.

The Access code is very similar to the Oracle code, but you need to use & for concatenation instead of ||.

Task for example 1

Find all the rows of the sec1817_first table that are not identical to any row of the sec1817_second table.

Oracle SQL

```
select *
from sec1817_first
where (number_1||'*'||word_1||'*'||date_1)
    not in (select (number_2||'*'||word_2||'*'||date_2)
            from sec1817_second);
```

Beginning tables

sec1817_first table   **sec1817_second table**

NUMBER_1	WORD_1	DATE_1
1	ONE	01-DEC-2001
2	TWO	02-DEC-2002
3	THREE	03-DEC-2003
4	FOUR	04-DEC-2004
5	FIVE	05-DEC-2005

NUMBER_2	WORD_2	DATE_2
3	THREE	03-DEC-2003
4	FOUR	04-DEC-2004
5	FIVE	05-DEC-2005
6	SIX	06-DEC-2006
7	SEVEN	07-DEC-2007

Result table

NUMBER_1	WORD_1	DATE_1
1	ONE	01-DEC-2001
2	TWO	02-DEC-2002

Task for example 2

Find all the rows of the sec1817_second table that are not identical to any row of the sec1817_first table.

Oracle SQL

```
select *
from sec1817_second
where (number_2||'*'||word_2||'*'||date_2)
    not in (select (number_1||'*'||word_1||'*'||date_1)
            from sec1817_first);
```

Result table

NUMBER_2	WORD_2	DATE_2
6	SIX	06-DEC-2006
7	SEVEN	07-DEC-2007

18-18   Using the most current data

Sometimes you may need to use a subquery to get the most current data out of a table. Some tables contain historic data as well as current data.

I had to do this when I was working with a table that received new data every month. The old data were retained in the table. It would have been a cleaner database design if the current data had been kept separate from the historic data, but in this case the database tables were not designed that way. I could not change the design, so I had to code around it.

I used a subquery to make sure the most current data was being used. My SQL code looked something like this:

```
select ...
from historic_data
where data_date = (select max(data_date)
                      from historic_data)
```

Older Features of Subqueries

I suggest you do not use the features shown in the following sections. You need to understand them because they might be used in code that you inherit, but they show an older way of using SQL that is rarely used today.

18-19   Correlated subqueries

A correlated subquery is a subquery that contains a reference to the table in the outer query. Because of this, a correlated subquery cannot be evaluated before the outer query. In the following SQL code, the twos table is named in the from clause of the outer query. The threes table is named in the from clause of the subquery. However, the where clause of the subquery references both the twos table and the threes table.

Because of this reference, the subquery cannot be evaluated separately from the outer query. They must be evaluated together. This is a complex process and you might want to skip this section unless you need to know it.

Step 1: A row is obtained from the `twos` table, which is the table of the outer `select` statement. This could be any row, but we suppose it is the row for the number 2. Next, the number 2 is placed into the subselect, resulting in:

```
(select b.number_3
 from threes b
 where 2 = b.number_3)
```

This results in no values, so a list containing no values is plugged into the outer `select` statement, which becomes:

```
select a.number_2,
       a.word_2
from twos a
where a.number_2 = null
order by a.number_2;
```

This `select` results in no values, so the number 2 does not become part of the final result table.

Step 2: Another row is obtained from the `twos` table. This could be any row, but we suppose it is the row for the number 6. Next, the number 6 is placed into the subselect, resulting in:

```
(select b.number_3
 from threes b
 where 6 = b.number_3)
```

The result table of this subselect is the number 6, so the value 6 is plugged into the outer `select` statement, which becomes:

```
select a.number_2,
       a.word_2
from twos a
where a.number_2 = 6
order by a.number_2;
```

This `select` results in the number 6, which comes from the `twos` table. So the number 6 does become part of the final result table.

Step 3 through Step 10,000: This process is repeated for every row of the `twos` table, however many there are.

Task

Use a correlated subquery to find all the rows of the `twos` table that match with a row of the `threes` table. Use the `number` columns of both tables to do the match.

Oracle & Access SQL

```
select  a.number_2,
        a.word_2
from twos a
where a.number_2 = (select b.number_3
                    from threes b
                    where a.number_2 = b.number_3)
order by a.number_2;
```

Result table

```
NUMBER_2 WORD_2
-------- ---------------
       6 SIX
      12 TWELVE
      18 EIGHTEEN
```

18-20 Subqueries using `exists`

The word `exists` can be used in the `where` clause with a subquery. This is always a correlated subquery. As shown earlier, the process of evaluating this query goes through a separate step for every row of the table in the outer query. A row of the outer query becomes part of the result table only if there is at least one row when the subquery is evaluated.

Task

Use a correlated subquery with `exists` to find all the rows of the `twos` table that match with a row of the `threes` table. Use the `number` columns of both tables to do the match.

Oracle & Access SQL

```
select  a.number_2,
        a.word_2
from twos a
where exists (select b.number_3
              from threes b
              where a.number_2 = b.number_3)
order by a.number_2;
```

Result table

```
NUMBER_2 WORD_2
--------- ---------------
      6 SIX
     12 TWELVE
     18 EIGHTEEN
```

18-21   Using a subquery to write an outer join

It used to be that if you wanted to use an outer join you had to write it yourself using a subquery with not exists. You would not write code like this today. The following example shows you how this used to be done. We will form a left outer join of the twos table and the threes table.

There are two select statements that are combined with a union. The first select statement forms the inner join of the two tables. The second select statement adds back all the rows from the twos table that were dropped by the inner join.

Task

Form the left outer join of the twos table and the threes table. Show how this code used to be written before outer joins were included in SQL.

Oracle & Access SQL

```
select a.number_2, ❶
       a.word_2,
       b.number_3,
       b.word_3
from twos a,
     threes b
where a.number_2 = b.number_3
union all ❷
select a.number_2, ❸
       a.word_2,
       null, ❹
       null
from twos a
where not exists (select b.number_3 ❺
                  from threes b
                  where a.number_2 = b.number_3)
order by 1;
```

Result table

```
NUMBER_2  WORD_2            NUMBER_3  WORD_3
--------- ----------------  --------- ----------------
        2 TWO               (null)    (null)
        4 FOUR              (null)    (null)
        6 SIX                       6 SIX
        8 EIGHT             (null)    (null)
       10 TEN               (null)    (null)
       12 TWELVE                   12 TWELVE
       14 FOURTEEN          (null)    (null)
       16 SIXTEEN           (null)    (null)
       18 EIGHTEEN                 18 EIGHTEEN
       20 TWENTY            (null)    (null)
(null)    NULL              (null)    (null)
```

Notes

❶ This `select` is an inner join of the `twos` table and the `threes` table.

❷ A `union all` can be used instead of `union` because no rows from the first `select` will be duplicated by a row of the second `select`.

❸ This `select` lists the rows from the `twos` table that were dropped by the inner join.

❹ In Oracle8i, replace this null with `to_number (null)`. Oracle requires the null to be declared as a numeric datatype. This is a workaround for a problem in Oracle8i. Oracle9i has fixed this problem.

❺ A `not exists` is used with a correlated subquery to find the rows of the `twos` table that were dropped by the outer join.

18-22　Nested subqueries

The SQL language allows you to nest subqueries 15 levels deep, but you should never do this. I could not even bring myself to make an example for you to see. It is acceptable to have one or two levels of subqueries. Beyond that, the code is almost impossible to understand, change, and maintain. If you find code like this, I recommend that you rewrite it.

18-23 Subqueries can be used in limited locations

It is sometimes said that subqueries can act as variables. However, they are not very good variables because they have a limitation: They can only be used in the `where` clause and the `having` clause. For instance, they cannot be used in the `select` clause as a variable name for a column. They cannot be used in the `from` clause as a variable name for a table.

18-24 Many subqueries can also be written as a join

The subqueries in the previous sections could also be written as joins. See chapters 13 and 14 if you would like to compare the two methods. In most cases I recommend you use joins because the code they produce is easier to understand, maintain, and change.

If a query is run frequently, such as every day, the performance of the query might be the most important issue. In some cases a subquery will run faster than a join. In other cases, the join will run faster. You might have to code a query both ways and test them to see which is faster.

Key Points

- You can use `if-then-else` logic in a `select` statement. Many people prefer this to using a `union`. I like to use a `union` because it is the same in every type of SQL product. On the other hand, many people find that `if-then-else` logic is easier to think about. The choice is yours.

- Parameter queries are useful if you want to make some decisions about a query at the moment you are running it. They are also useful if you are designing a query for someone else to run and you want them to make some decisions at runtime. I often like to use a table of constants instead of parameters. I feel that I have better control that way. But some people like parameters better. Again, the choice is up to you and your users.

- Most of the time I avoid using subqueries by using outer joins instead. But there are time when you may need a subquery. The most common use of a subquery is in an `update` statement.

chapter 19

THE
MULTIUSER
ENVIRONMENT

One of the most important features of a database is its ability to coordinate the work of many people who are all using its data at the same time. Many people can change the data and many other people can run queries simultaneously. Each person can work independently, as if he or she is working alone. The database coordinates all the work and prevents conflicts.

In this chapter, I discuss only Oracle, so we can cover more material more quickly. Access also has a way to implement many of these same concepts and to set up a secure multiuser environment. However, many of the details are different, so it would be too complex to discuss both products at the same time.

This chapter is an introduction to this topic. It covers the most important points. If you need more detail, you can refer to the Oracle or Access technical reference manuals.

Database Configurations

A database can be set up and configured in many ways. It can be set up to be used by a single person, or it can be set up for thousands of people to use with computers located in many different places. This configuration is performed by the DBAs. As an end user or application programmer, you simply use the computers you are given and many of the details of the configuration are hidden from you. However, it is my experience that the details are never completely hidden and understanding some of the basics of the configuration is important for everybody using the database.

19-1 The single-user environment

So far in this book we have not discussed how the computer and database are configured. That is what we discuss in this chapter. When you use SQL, you may have pictured yourself working alone on your own computer. In this configuration the database belongs to you, it runs on your own personal computer, and you are the only user.

This is one way a database can be set up. It is the default configuration for Access. It is rare for Oracle to run this way, but it is possible. In fact, you probably have run Oracle with this configuration as you studied this book. The following illustration shows a single-user configuration.

Bob

One person working alone on his own computer. So far, this is the configuration we have been working with throughout this book.

19-2 The multiuser environment

In a multiuser configuration many people use the database at the same time. The database is on a server. Each user has his or her own personal computer. A network connects all the PCs to the server. Most of this chapter discusses issues involved in this configuration.

Usually the database is installed on a userID that belongs to the application, rather than to a particular user. Each user has his or her own userID. All of these userIDs are installed on the same server.

Most of SQL works the same in this configuration as it does in the single-user configuration. The main difference is in the names of the tables. To refer to a table that belongs to a different userID, we use the format:

`Owner_Name.Table_Name`

For example, suppose the `Lunches` database has been installed on a userID named "Lunches". Suppose I am logged onto a different userID named "John". If I want to list all the data in the `l_employees` table, I would write:

```
select *
from lunches.l_employees;
```

Similarly, I could refer to any table that belonged to another user, if I had permission to do so. The following illustration shows a multiuser configuration.

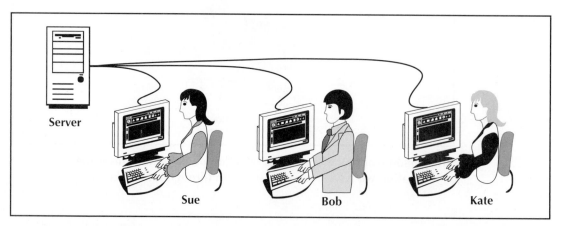

Server　　　　　Sue　　　　　Bob　　　　　Kate

Several people working together using a database on a shared server. This configuration is often used in medium-sized companies.

19-3 The distributed environment

In the previous configuration the database resided on a single server. Sometimes the database can be distributed across several servers connected in a network. The servers are often in diverse locations. Perhaps one is in London, another is in San Francisco, and a third is in Tokyo. This is a complex configuration and it can have many variations. We discuss it only briefly in this section.

The distribution of data can take several forms. Usually some tables are on one server and other tables are on another server. In Access, we use **linked tables**. In Oracle, the servers are connected together on the software level using **database links**. Again, the table names show this difference. In Oracle, the format of the table names is:

`Owner_Name.Table_Name@Database_Link`

The server that you are logged onto is called your **local server**. Any other server is called a **remote server**. If you have the right permissions, you can access all the data in the distributed database this way. Database links allow you to handle a distributed database as if it were a single integrated database.

However, there is a serious problem: A query can be very inefficient if it is getting a lot of data from a remote server. Moving a large amount of data across the network can be very slow. There are two solutions to this problem.

One solution is to design your queries so they only bring small amounts of data across the network. This requires careful design and programming, which can be a lot of work.

Another solution makes local copies of many of the tables that are on the remote servers. In Oracle, these are called **snapshots** or **materialized views**. In Access, they are called **replicas** and the process is called **replication**. These copies are often set up to be read-only, but they can also be set up to be updateable so you can do an `insert`, `update`, or `delete` to modify the data.

This solves one problem, but it creates another. When you have two copies of the same table, they may start to diverge, so you have the problem of synchronization and setting a refresh rate.

Designing a distributed database is complex because you must consider the network, the number of servers, the distribution of the data, which tables to replicate, and how often to synchronize them. The following illustration shows a distributed database.

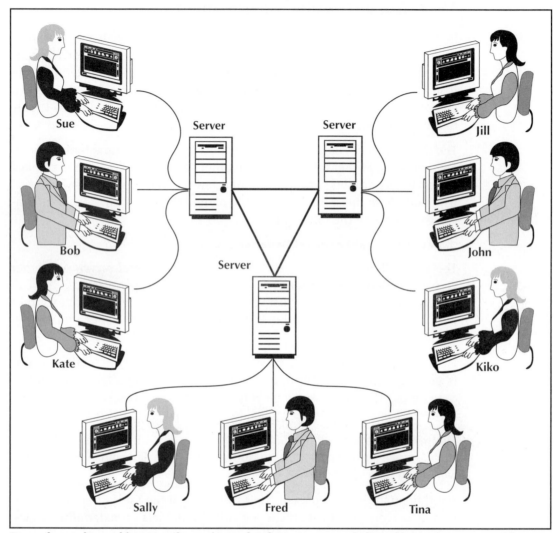

Several people working together using a database on several shared servers connected by a network. This configuration is often used in large companies.

19-4 Connecting via the Internet

How are the servers connected to each other? And how are the users connected to their local servers? There are many possibilities. It used to be that this was always done on a private high-speed network. Now the Internet can be used by some systems to connect to the users. You probably noticed that the new user interface in Oracle uses your browser and takes you to the Database Home Page.

Operating in a Multiuser Environment

When you work in a multiuser environment, you often need to use tables you do not own. These tables may be in a remote location. You might develop your own names for them, called **synonyms**, or you might find that many of these complexities are hidden from you. Sometimes when a table is in a remote location, you work with a local version of it called a **snapshot**.

19-5 How to use a table you do not own

So far you have owned all the tables you have used. When you create a table, view, or other database object, you are the owner of it. This gives you the exclusive right to use it, change it, or delete it. You can also share it with other people by giving them permission to use it. There are many different levels of permission you can grant to others.

When you have permission to use a table you do not own, you can refer to it by writing the owner name and a period before the table name, in the following format:

`owner_name.table_name`

This section provides an example of using such a table name. Usually when Oracle is installed, a demonstration userID is set up called `HR` and a table called `regions` is created on it. You will list all the data in this table. First, I must show you how to set this up.

Task

In Oracle, list all the data in the table `regions` owned by HR. On your first try, you will not be able to do this because HR has not shared the table with you. Then you will log on as HR and give yourself permission to use this table. Finally, you will go back to your own ID and show that you can now list the data in this table.

Oracle SQL

Step 1: Log on to your own userID as usual. Then try to list the table.

```
select * from hr.regions;
```

You will get an error message saying that the table does not exist In fact, the table does exist, but you do not yet have permission to use it.

Step 2: Log on to hr. The password is what you set it to after you installed Oracle. Show that the table does exist by listing it. Then give yourself permission to run a `select` statement with the table.

```
select * from regions;
grant select on regions to your_userid;
```

Replace `your_userid` with the name of your own userID in the `grant` statememt.

Step 3: Log on to our own userID again and show that you can now list the table.

```
select * from hr.regions;
```

Result table

```
REGION_ID REGION_NAME
---------- ------------------------
        1 Europe
        2 Americas
        3 Asia
        4 Middle East and Africa
```

19-6 Synonyms

In Oracle, a synonym is an alternate name for a table or view. It can also be an alternate name for many other types of database objects, such as a sequence or snapshot. A synonym itself is a database object. It is permanent until you drop it. This contrasts with a table alias, which is also an alternate name for a table or view. However, a table alias exists only while a single `select` statement is running. It vanishes when the `select` statement ends.

A synonym can be private or public. A private synonym can be used only by the person (userID) who created it or owns it. A public synonym can be used by anyone on any userID.

Synonyms are often used in a multiuser configuration or a distributed database configuration. They are used to make the names of the tables or other database objects simpler and easier to remember. Synonyms can hide the owner name or the name of the database link. They can create the illusion that you are working in a single-user configuration by hiding the complex names of objects in the other configurations.

Task for example 1

Create a synonym for the l_employees table on the lunches userID of the denver server. Give it the name d_employees.

Oracle SQL: This shows an idea. It is not meant to work ❶

```
create synonym d_employees
for lunches.employees@denver;
```

Notes

❶ You can run this code and create the synonym, but you will not be able to use it unless you happen to have a remote server named denver.

Task for example 2

Create a synonym for the regions table owned by HR. Give this synonym the name my_regions. You already have permission to use a select statement with this table. A synonym will allow you to use a simpler name for this table, as if it were your own table.

Then list all the data in this table using the synonym in the select statement.

Oracle SQL

Log in to your own userID. Then enter:

```
create synonym my_regions for hr.regions;
select * from my_regions; ❶
```

Result table ❷

```
REGION_ID REGION_NAME
---------- -------------------------
         1 Europe
         2 Americas
         3 Asia
         4 Middle East and Africa
```

Notes

❶ `my_regions` is a synonym for `hr.regions` which is the `regions` table owned by `hr`.

❷ This is the same table we listed in the previous section.

19-7 Snapshots

A snapshot is a copy of a table made at a particular time. To an end user, it might appear exactly like a table. A snapshot is frequently used in a distributed database to create a local copy of a remote table. This speeds up the processing of queries that use that table, because it saves the time of transferring the data across the network. A snapshot is also called a ***materialized view*** or a ***replica***.

Snapshots are used mostly to "tune" a database and get it to perform more quickly. Only DBAs create snapshots, but you need to know what they are because you might use them.

A snapshot can be set up in a number of different ways. Most snapshots are read-only. This means they can be used in queries, but you cannot modify the data.

A few snapshots can be updated. Updateable snapshots allow you to make changes to the data by using `insert`, `update`, and `delete`. However, updateable snapshots are more complex and they are used less frequently.

A major issue with any snapshot is how often it is refreshed. It needs to be synchronized with the table it has copied. When you are using snapshots, you will need to be aware of the timing of this synchronization. The data you see may not be completely current, and when you change the data, people at other locations may not see those changes immediately.

Task

Create a snapshot and use it in a query. You will need DBA authority to perform this task. You can do this on your own computer, but you will not be able to do it on a computer you share with others at work or school.

Oracle SQL

Log in to the `system` userID or another userID that has DBA privileges.

```
create snapshot snap_countries as
select * from hr.countries;

grant select on snap_countries to public;
```

Then log in to your own userID.

```
select * from snap_countries;
```

Result table

CO	COUNTRY_NAME	REGION_ID
AR	Argentina	2
AU	Australia	3
BE	Belgium	1
BR	Brazil	2
CA	Canada	2
CH	Switzerland	1
CN	China	3
DE	Germany	1
DK	Denmark	1
EG	Egypt	4
FR	France	1
HK	HongKong	3
IL	Israel	4
IN	India	3
IT	Italy	1
JP	Japan	3
KW	Kuwait	4
MX	Mexico	2
NG	Nigeria	4
NL	Netherlands	1
SG	Singapore	3
UK	United Kingdom	1
US	United States of America	2
ZM	Zambia	4
ZW	Zimbabwe	4

Security and Privileges

When many people are working with the same database, there are usually restrictions on which data each person is allowed to change. There are also restrictions on which data they can access. These rules are often defined for a group of people, such as for the payroll department, and each person within that department is given the privileges of that group.

19-8 Identifying the user

Each user should have his or her own userID and password. You must use them to identify yourself when you log on to the database. From a computer's point of view, a human is a userID. That is the basis for the security of the database. This may seem obvious, but Access, for instance, does not usually require you to log on to the database.

Sometimes a computer is set up so that the userID and password you supply when you log on to the operating system are automatically passed to Oracle. These replace the userID and password for the Oracle login.

19-9 Privileges

When you create a table, view, or other database object on your userID, you are the owner of that object and you are the only person who can use it (although DBAs can access anything in the database). You can allow other people to use your table by granting them the privilege to use it in a `select` statement, or you can grant them the privilege to use an `insert` statement, `update`, `delete`, or any combination of these. Using a view, you can limit their access to certain rows and certain columns. You can also revoke privileges any time you wish.

The privileges you can grant are very fine-grained. That means you have a high degree of control. You can be very specific about what you allow people to do and what you do not allow.

You can grant a privilege to one particular userID or grant it to the public. When you grant a privilege to the public, you are granting it to every userID.

Up to now, we have discussed object privileges. There are also system privileges that a DBA can grant to a userID to control the operations that it can do. For example there is a Create Table privilege. Without it, you cannot create a table. There is also a Connect privilege. Without it, you cannot log on to the userID.

Why would someone set up a userID and not allow anyone to log on to it? This is a common practice for an application userID. For example, suppose we set up the Lunches database so that three people, Bob, Jill, and Mary, can use it. Suppose that we do not want any of these people to own the database. They are just allowed to use it.

We would set up three individual userIDs for Bob, Jill, and Mary. We would also set up an application userID for the Lunches database. It would own all the tables, views, and other database objects of the application. No one would be allowed to log on directly to the Lunches userID. People could only log on to their individual userIDs and use the privileges they have been granted to the Lunches database.

Task for example 1

Grant to hr the privilege to insert new rows into the l_lunches table.

Oracle SQL

```
grant insert on l_lunches to hr;
```

Task for example 2

Revoke the privilege granted in task 1.

Oracle SQL

```
revoke insert on l_lunches from hr;
```

Task for example 3

Allow anyone to use the l_employees table in a select statement.

Oracle SQL

```
grant select on l_employees to public;
```

19-10　Roles

Privileges can control access to the database, but they are difficult to manage because they are so fine-grained. A privilege usually authorizes one userID to perform one operation. In many applications there are thousands of privileges that must be granted. That can be a lot of work!

Roles provide a more organized way to manage privileges. A role is a set of privileges and it has a name. To use a role, you first create it and give it a name. DBA authority is required to create a role, so you will need to use the system userID. If you are not running your own copy of Oracle, you might not be allowed to create a role.

After the role is created, you grant a set of privileges to the role. When you grant the role to a userID, it gets all the privileges assigned to the role. This makes it easy to assign the same set of privileges to many userIDs.

Task 1: Create the role and give it a name

Create a role named sales_dept_role.

Oracle SQL ❶

Log in to the system userID or another userID that has DBA privileges.

```
create role sales_dept_role;
```

Task 2: Grant privileges you own to the role

Grant to the sales_dept_role the privilege to run a select, insert, update, or delete statement on the job_history table owned by hr. Grant this role to your own userID.

Oracle SQL

Log in to the HR userID.　❷

```
grant select, insert, update, delete
on job_history to sales_dept_role;

grant sales_dept_role to your_userid; ❸
```

Task 3: Use the role

From your own userID, you can now display all the rows and columns of the `job_history` table owned by `hr`.

Oracle SQL

Log in to your own userID. ❹

```
select * from hr.job_history;
```

Result table

```
EMPLOYEE
      ID START_DATE        END_DATE     JOB_ID      DEPARTMENT_ID
-------- ----------------  -----------  ----------  -------------
     102 13-JAN-1993       24-JUL-1998  IT_PROG                60
     101 21-SEP-1989       27-OCT-1993  AC_ACCOUNT            110
     101 28-OCT-1993       15-MAR-1997  AC_MGR               110
     201 17-FEB-1996       19-DEC-1999  MK_REP                20
     114 24-MAR-1998       31-DEC-1999  ST_CLERK              50
     122 01-JAN-1999       31-DEC-1999  ST_CLERK              50
     200 17-SEP-1987       17-JUN-1993  AD_ASST               90
     176 24-MAR-1998       31-DEC-1998  SA_REP                80
     176 01-JAN-1999       31-DEC-1999  SA_MAN                80
     200 01-JUL-1994       31-DEC-1998  AC_ACCOUNT            90
```

Notes

❶ Log on to the `system` userID. This has DBA authority, which is needed to create a role. The role created here has no privileges yet. It only has a name.

❷ Log on to the `hr` userID and grant privileges to the role.

❸ Grant all the privileges of the role to your own userID.

❹ Log on to your own userID and view the `job_history` table that belongs to `hr`. You are allowed to view this table because `hr` has given you permission to do so.

19-11 Several people can use the same table at the same time

The database is designed to allow several people to use the same table at the same time. Some people may be looking at the data. Other people may be changing the data.

There is only a conflict when two people want to change the same row of the table at the same time. When this happens, the database makes one person wait until changes by the other person are finished and committed.

The Oracle Data Dictionary and the Multiuser Environment

You can find all the information about your multiuser environment in the Data Dictionary.

19-12 ALL versus USER

The names of the tables in the Oracle Data Dictionary begin with ALL, USER, or DBA. Most tables have all three versions. To see what this means, consider an example:

Table Name	Information in the Data Dictionary Table
USER_TABLES	Information about all the tables you own; that is, all the tables created on your userID.
ALL_TABLES	Information about all the tables you own and all the tables on other userIDs that you have been granted the privilege to use.
DBA_TABLES	Information about all the tables in the database. To use this table you must have DBA privileges. If you have Oracle installed on your home computer, you can use this table from the system userID or any other userID you create with DBA privileges.

19-13   How to find the tables you want in the Data Dictionary

In the Data Dictionary you can find information about the multiuser environment — synonyms, snapshots, privileges, and roles. You will have to look in several tables. Use the `dictionary` table to find the names of the tables you want. Here is how to get started.

Task

Find the names of the Data Dictionary tables containing information about synonyms.

Oracle SQL

```
select *
from dictionary
where table_name like '%SYN%';
```

Result table

TABLE_NAME	COMMENTS
ALL_SYNONYMS	All synonyms accessible to the user
USER_SYNONYMS	The user's private synonyms
SYN	Synonym for USER_SYNONYMS

19-14   How to find the meaning of the columns

Once you know the name of a Data Dictionary table, you can find the meaning of all of its columns using the `dict_columns` table.

Task

Find the meanings of all the columns of the `all_synonyms` table.

Oracle SQL

```
select *
from dict_columns
where table_name = 'ALL_SYNONYMS';
```

Result table

```
TABLE_NAME      COLUMN_NAME     COMMENTS
-------------   -------------   ---------------------------------------
ALL_SYNONYMS    OWNER           Owner of the synonym
ALL_SYNONYMS    SYNONYM_NAME    Name of the synonym
ALL_SYNONYMS    TABLE_OWNER     Owner of the object referenced by the
                                synonym
ALL_SYNONYMS    TABLE_NAME      Name of the object referenced by the
                                synonym
ALL_SYNONYMS    DB_LINK         Name of the database link referenced in
                                a remote synonym
```

Key Points

- Databases are designed so that many people can use them at the same time. Some databases can have hundreds or thousands of people using them at the same moment.

- Each person using a database is allowed to think that he or she is the only person using it at that moment. The database is carefully engineered to handle any conflicts and give you that illusion. You are actually in a protected environment. You do not need to think about what anyone else might be doing with the database. On rare occasions the database may not be able to fully resolve a conflict and you might be asked to wait until another person has completed some work.

- Several people can make changes to the same table at the same time. There is only a conflict when two people try to change the same row at the same time. Then one person will have to wait until the other person is done changing that row. That could be some time if the person is doing a long transaction.

- To use a table owned by someone else, you put the owner name before the table name. To use a table at another location, you put the database link name after the table name. The full format is:

  `owner_name.table_name@database_link`

- You can use synonyms to give tables names that are more convenient.

- You can use `grant` and `revoke` to control the access other people have to your tables. The privileges you can grant or revoke include `select`, `insert`, `update`, and `delete`.

chapter 20

THE DESIGN
OF SQL

SQL lies at the heart of most information systems today. The main objective of SQL is to find the correct information for you. It relies on other software to present that information to you in a polished manner. A variety of software can provide that polish.

SQL is often used with software that can produce forms and reports. A form displays one record at a time. Data in a single row can be entered, viewed, changed, or deleted. Most people find this easier than entering SQL commands.

A report displays many records. It is always based on a query. It cleans up the result table; puts in page numbers, column headings, and totals; and adds other elements that make the report easier to read.

Original SQL Design Objectives

In the early 1970s people were devising ways to handle very large amounts of information. Solving that problem was the original motivation that led to relational databases and SQL. Essential aims of the design are to make the handling of information as simple as possible and to make the information accessible to a large number of people.

20-1 Do one thing and do it well

SQL was designed to handle a large amount of information and to coordinate the use of that information by a group of people. That is all it was designed to do. It was never intended to be a complete application in itself or to replace other types of software. It was designed to be an information repository and to work in cooperation with other types of software. It was designed to do one thing and do it well.

Until now in this book I have focused the discussion on SQL itself. I have invited you to imagine that the database is already built and you are sitting alone at a computer trying to get some information out of it or perhaps making a few modifications to the data. I have invited you to imagine that you are the only person using the database, that it belongs to you, and that SQL is the only software you will use. That has been a useful illusion for teaching you SQL, but in the real world you will usually be sharing the database with many other people. SQL will provide an important part of what you need, but it may leave a few gaps for you to fill with other tools.

20-2 Focus on information

SQL makes a distinction between the **information level** and the **presentation level**. Within that dichotomy, SQL focuses primarily on the information level and leaves the presentation level to other software. This is not meant to suggest that the presentation is less important than the information. The presentation may be very important, but it is not what SQL is designed to do well.

For example, SQL does not put page numbers on a report. It might produce a report of 100 pages without any page numbers. If you want page numbers on the report, and I would want them, you might pull the report into Microsoft Word. There you could choose among several types of page numbers, in several sizes and typefaces, placed on the page in a variety of ways. It is important to have these options and to use them. However, it is not the job of SQL to give them to you.

SQL is designed to work hand-in-hand with other programming languages such as Java, C#, COBOL, and Visual Basic. The idea is that SQL will provide some specialized services and these other languages will do all the other things that need to be done. Some of those other things are:

- Presenting the data in a polished form

- Interacting with the end user

- Interfacing and integrating with other programming systems

- Providing complex rules for data validation

In fact, when we used SQL in this book, we always had another level of software between SQL and us. When we used Oracle with the Home Page environment, we reached SQL through the browser and an Oracle SQL interface embedded within the browser. If you used Oracle with the SQL Command Line environment, you reached SQL through the system Command Line software and through SQL*Plus. Another language that is frequently used with Oracle is PL/SQL. When we used Access, we reached the JET engine, which processes SQL, through GUI screens that actually communicate with JET using a language called Data Access Objects (DAO). Another language that can be used to communicate with Jet SQL is ActiveX Data Objects (ADO).

20-3 Keep it simple

SQL is designed to avoid the things that make many computer languages complex. Because of this, sometimes programmers feel that SQL is missing some important parts. It does not have all the things that programmers are used to having in a computer language. In particular, SQL does not have:

- Variables

- Loops or `goto` statements

- Mixing of detail data with summarized data (although Oracle does have `cube` and `rollup`)

- An object model with objects, properties, events, and methods

This is not a mistake. The design of SQL intentionally avoids these things. The idea is to keep the handling of information as simple as possible. These structures can lead to excessive complexity, so they are not included in SQL.

The issue we discussed in the previous section is also a part of the strategy to keep the design simple. That is, SQL is intended to do one thing well — handle information. It is not intended to do other things, and that is a major part of what keeps it simple.

Variables, loops, and the other things listed are available in most programming languages. Because SQL is designed to work along with one of these languages, there is no reason to also have these things within SQL itself. If you need a variable or a loop, you can get it from the other programming language.

As SQL has evolved over a few decades, an effort has been made to make it even simpler. When SQL was first developed it was designed so that subqueries would be used extensively. The original design allowed subqueries to be nested 15 levels deep. This produced code that was hard to understand and maintain even if you had written it yourself.

In the past few years outer joins have become an official part of SQL. To a large extent, an outer join can be used to replace a subquery. This makes the code much easier to understand and maintain, taking SQL one step further toward its goal of being simple.

20-4 Coordinate people to work together

One of the strengths of SQL is that it allows a large group of people to work together using current information. People at all levels of an organization can work on the same project. In this aspect, SQL is a tool for coordinating a large workforce and getting everyone to pull in the same direction, as we discussed in chapter 19.

In the world today, databases lie at the heart of most large businesses and government agencies. The database plays a role in coordinating the people as well as providing a store of information.

Newer Interfaces

When SQL was first designed, the idea was that everybody from vice presidents to secretaries would write `select` queries. That would be the way they would interact with the database. However, experience has shown that most vice-presidents do not want to write their own `select` queries, so new interfaces are needed.

Forms provide a universal language that everyone feels comfortable with. They are used a lot in business and government, so forms were adopted as a front end to databases. Forms deal primarily with data at the lowest level of detail.

Reports provide formatting to make larger collections of information easier to read. Web tools are in the process of being integrated into many databases so that forms and reports can be accessed over the Internet. Databases also interface with programming languages such as Java or Visual Basic to provide a bridge to other software applications.

20-5 Forms

Forms can be used to enter, modify, and delete data and to find individual records in a database. This is equivalent to writing an `insert`, `update`, `delete`, or `select` statement in SQL. Forms usually handle one row at a time. Some forms show a few records together. An example of a form is shown here.

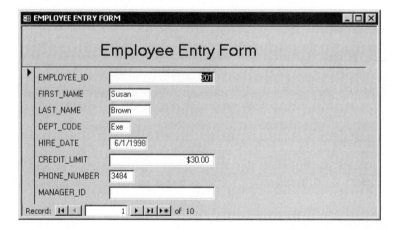

20-6 Reports

Whereas forms handle individual records, reports handle many records at a time. The example in the next section shows the detail of every lunch, along with subtotals and a grand total. It has a title for the report, a date when the report was run, page numbers, and the data in the first three columns is not repeated on every line.

20-7 Web tools

Oracle and Access have developed the ability to use forms and reports over the Internet. This is one of the major features that has been added in the past few years.

Employee Lunches

Employee ID	First Name	Lunch Date	Description	Quantity	Total Price
201	Susan	Nov 16, 2011	Sandwich	2	$7.00
			Coffee	2	$1.70
			Fresh Salad	1	$2.00
		Summary for 'Lunch Date' = Nov 16, 2011 (3 detail records)			
		Sum		**5**	**$10.70**
201	Susan	Nov 25, 2011	Fresh Salad	1	$2.00
			Grilled Steak	1	$6.00
			Soda	1	$1.25
		Summary for 'Lunch Date' = Nov 25, 2011 (3 detail records)			
		Sum		**3**	**$9.25**
201	Susan	Dec 05, 2011	Hamburger	1	$2.50
			Soda	1	$1.25
			Sandwich	1	$3.50
			Fresh Salad	1	$2.00
			Coffee	1	$0.85
		Summary for 'Lunch Date' = Dec 05, 2011 (5 detail records)			
		Sum		**5**	**$10.10**
Summary for 'Employee ID' = 201 (11 detail records)					
Sum				**13**	**$30.05**
202	Jim	Nov 16, 2011	Soup Of The Day	1	$1.50
			Grilled Steak	1	$6.00
			French Fries	1	$1.50
			Coffee	2	$1.70
			Dessert	1	$3.00
		Summary for 'Lunch Date' = Nov 16, 2011 (5 detail records)			
		Sum		**6**	**$13.70**
Summary for 'Employee ID' = 202 (5 detail records)					
Sum				**6**	**$13.70**
203	Martha	Nov 16, 2011	Fresh Salad	1	$2.00
			Coffee	1	$0.85
			Soda	1	$1.25
			French Fries	1	$1.50
			Grilled Steak	1	$6.00
		Summary for 'Lunch Date' = Nov 16, 2011 (5 detail records)			
		Sum		**5**	**$11.60**
203	Martha	Dec 05, 2011	Soup Of The Day	1	$1.50
			Grilled Steak	1	$6.00
			Coffee	2	$1.70
			Dessert	1	$3.00

Employee ID	First Name	Lunch Date	Description	Quantity	Total Price
		Summary for 'Lunch Date' = Dec 05, 2011 (4 detail records)			
		Sum		*5*	*$12.20*
Summary for 'Employee ID' = 203 (9 detail records)					
Sum				*10*	*$23.80*
204	Ellen	Nov 16, 2011	Hamburger	2	$5.00
			French Fries	1	$1.50
			Soup Of The Day	2	$3.00
			Soda	2	$2.50
		Summary for 'Lunch Date' = Nov 16, 2011 (4 detail records)			
		Sum		*7*	*$12.00*
204	Ellen	Nov 25, 2011	Fresh Salad	1	$2.00
			Grilled Steak	1	$6.00
			Coffee	2	$1.70
			Dessert	1	$3.00
		Summary for 'Lunch Date' = Nov 25, 2011 (4 detail records)			
		Sum		*5*	*$12.70*
Summary for 'Employee ID' = 204 (8 detail records)					
Sum				*12*	*$24.70*
205	Henry	Nov 25, 2011	Soda	2	$2.50
			Soup Of The Day	1	$1.50
			Grilled Steak	1	$6.00
			French Fries	1	$1.50
		Summary for 'Lunch Date' = Nov 25, 2011 (4 detail records)			
		Sum		*5*	*$11.50*
205	Henry	Dec 05, 2011	Fresh Salad	1	$2.00
			Soup Of The Day	1	$1.50
			Grilled Steak	1	$6.00
			French Fries	1	$1.50
			Soda	1	$1.25
		Summary for 'Lunch Date' = Dec 05, 2011 (5 detail records)			
		Sum		*5*	*$12.25*
Summary for 'Employee ID' = 205 (9 detail records)					
Sum				*10*	*$23.75*
207	Dan	Nov 16, 2011	French Fries	1	$1.50
			Coffee	2	$1.70
			Sandwich	2	$7.00
			Dessert	1	$3.00
		Summary for 'Lunch Date' = Nov 16, 2011 (4 detail records)			
		Sum		*6*	*$13.20*
207	Dan	Nov 25, 2011	Soup Of The Day	2	$3.00
			Sandwich	2	$7.00
			French Fries	1	$1.50

Employee ID	First Name	Lunch Date	Description	Quantity	Total Price
207	Dan	Nov 25, 2011	Soda	1	$1.25

Summary for 'Lunch Date' = Nov 25, 2011 (4 detail records)

			Sum	6	$12.75

Summary for 'Employee ID' = 207 (8 detail records)

			Sum	12	$25.95

Employee ID	First Name	Lunch Date	Description	Quantity	Total Price
208	Fred	Nov 25, 2011	Hamburger	2	$5.00
			Coffee	1	$0.85
			French Fries	1	$1.50
			Fresh Salad	1	$2.00
			Soup Of The Day	1	$1.50
			Soda	1	$1.25

Summary for 'Lunch Date' = Nov 25, 2011 (6 detail records)

			Sum	7	$12.10

Employee ID	First Name	Lunch Date	Description	Quantity	Total Price
208	Fred	Dec 05, 2011	Fresh Salad	1	$2.00
			Grilled Steak	1	$6.00
			French Fries	1	$1.50
			Soda	1	$1.25
			Coffee	1	$0.85

Summary for 'Lunch Date' = Dec 05, 2011 (5 detail records)

			Sum	5	$11.60

Summary for 'Employee ID' = 208 (11 detail records)

			Sum	12	$23.70

Employee ID	First Name	Lunch Date	Description	Quantity	Total Price
210	Nancy	Nov 16, 2011	Fresh Salad	1	$2.00
			Dessert	1	$3.00
			Coffee	1	$0.85
			Soup Of The Day	1	$1.50
			Grilled Steak	1	$6.00

Summary for 'Lunch Date' = Nov 16, 2011 (5 detail records)

			Sum	5	$13.35

Employee ID	First Name	Lunch Date	Description	Quantity	Total Price
210	Nancy	Dec 05, 2011	Dessert	1	$3.00
			Soup Of The Day	1	$1.50
			Grilled Steak	1	$6.00
			French Fries	1	$1.50
			Coffee	2	$1.70

Summary for 'Lunch Date' = Dec 05, 2011 (5 detail records)

			Sum	6	$13.70

Summary for 'Employee ID' = 210 (10 detail records)

			Sum	11	$27.05
Grand Total				86	$192.70

Typical Applications

20-8 Smaller databases

SQL and relational databases were originally developed to handle very large amounts of data. It was considered overkill to use them for smaller amounts of data. It used to be said that if you used a relational database for your address book, it would be like using a bulldozer to crack a peanut.

Today, SQL and relational databases are being used for much smaller databases, such as for a lawyer's office. I even use a database to balance my checkbook and organize my address book. Once you start thinking in terms of representing information in tables, you see how you can use this framework to organize many things, big or small. One of the leading SQL products for developing smaller databases is Access.

20-9 OLTP

Online transaction processing (OLTP) systems focus mostly on inputting data. There may also be a few small reports. Often, OLTP systems use forms and handle only a few records at a time.

There is no "typical" OLTP system. Every application is different, but here is a sketch of one such system:

- 25,000,000 rows of data
- 200 users who can simultaneously enter and retrieve data
- Two-second response time on most transactions

20-10 Data warehouses

Data warehouses emphasize the collection and analysis of even larger amounts of data. These systems often focus on reports that perform a detailed analysis of the data.

Again, there is no "typical" data warehouse system, but here is a sketch of one such system:

- 500,000,000 rows of data
- One report is run at a time to analyze the data
- Three hours is a typical time to run a report

Key Points

- Relational databases were originally designed to store and handle large amounts of data. People would obtain that data by using SQL.

- SQL was originally designed with the goal that it would be simple and easy to use.

- It has succeeded, to a large extent, in meeting that goal, but things are not always as easy as we would like them to be,

- Today forms, reports, and Web tools are used in addition to SQL to make it easy to use the information in a database.

Oracle Is Free: How to Get Your Copy

This appendix shows you how to obtain and install your free copy of Oracle. This is not an evaluation copy. It does not limit your use to only a few days. It is free for you to use forever for your learning as long as you use it in a noncommercial manner. It is also fast to download and easy to administer.

The topics in this appendix are as follows:

- Getting current information.
- Which version of Oracle should you get?
- System requirements.
- Downloading Oracle from the Internet.
- Installing Oracle.
- Setup to run the examples in this book.
- How to stop running Oracle.
- What to do if Oracle slows down your computer.

Getting Current Information

The information in this appendix is subject to change because, from time to time, Oracle Corporation changes its policies and the way it markets its products. To obtain the most current information, please visit the Web site for this book:

`http://groups.google.com/group/sqlfun`

Links to the Oracle Web pages will be available there.

Which Version of Oracle Should You Get?

To run the examples of SQL code in this book on your computer(s), you will need Oracle Database 10g Express Edition, which is also called Oracle Database XE. It comes in two versions using different character sets. One is for English and a few other languages of Western Europe. The other version is for international languages. In this book I use the English version.

You will be asked if you want to install a client or a server. You must install the server of this database, not just a client. If you have a network of computers at home, you could install the server on one computer and install only the client on the other computers. When you install the server, a client will automatically be installed on the same computer.

If you use Oracle at work or at school, you might have a different product or version. All the examples in this book should run there, too, so use the version you have available. Be aware, however, that you might have restrictions on what you can do when you are using an Oracle database that you do not control. For example, you might not be allowed to create your own tables.

Because Oracle Database XE is free, I recommend that you install it on your home computer even if you can use Oracle at work or at school.

System Requirements

Most modern computers running a Microsoft Windows or Linux operating system will be able to run Oracle Database XE. Having sufficient hard drive space is the biggest problem I've seen, so you might consider adding an external hard drive that uses a USB connection, if you don't have one already.

Here are the computer specifications I recommend. For more exact requirements, consult the Oracle documentation.

- Operating system: Microsoft Windows 2000 or later (32-bit version)
- Broadband connection to the Internet (to download Oracle)
- Network protocol: TCP/IP
- Web browser: Microsoft IE 6.0 or later (or some others)
- Memory: 512 megabytes of RAM
- Disk space: 2 gigabytes (not using disk compression)

To install Oracle, you must be an Administrator on your computer. If it is your own computer, you are already the administrator.

If you have an Apple computer you might be able to find ways to get Oracle and other Windows software to work on your computer.

Downloading Oracle from the Internet

First, you will need to register as a member of OTN (Oracle Technology Network). This is free. You must provide your name, address, and some other information. You will also need to accept the license for the software.

If you have a broadband connection to the Internet, you can download Oracle Database 10g Express Edition. It is about 170 megabytes, so this could take a few hours.

If you have a 56k modem, you should use a download manager so you can recover if the connection is lost. Another alternative is to find a friend or a shop with a DSL connection.

Installing Oracle

Oracle is fairly easy to install: Just follow the documentation. The link to this documentation is on the Web site for this book. You may need to make a few adjustments to your operating system, Web browser, and firewall.

During the installation, you will be asked to set a password for the Database Administrator named "System." Be sure to remember this password.

After Oracle is installed, you can find the program from your Start menu, as shown here:

Initially, two database users are set up: System and HR. System is a database administrator with an unlocked account. HR is an ordinary database user with a locked account.

You should follow the directions under "Get Started" for at least the first three steps. This shows you how to set a password for the HR user, unlock the account, and log in as that user.

Setup to Run the Examples in This Book

There are a few more steps you need to perform before you are ready to run the examples in this book. First you will create a new database user. Then you will run an SQL script to build the Oracle tables. Follow each of these next steps.

A-1 Create a new database user

You should set up a new user to run the examples in this book. Here is how to do that:

1. Open the Database Home Page login window: Start > All Programs > Oracle Database 10g Express Edition > Go To Database Home Page. (If you get a "Page Not Found" message, see Appendix B.) This actually takes you to the Database Login page. You will get to the Database Home Page after you log in.

2. Log in to the database administrator's account: Username = System, Password = [the password you set up when Oracle was installed]. Click Login.

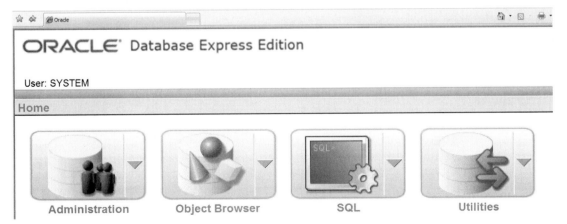

3. Open the window to create a new user: Click the arrow on the right side of Administration > Manage Database Users > Create Database User.

4. Enter information for the new user: Username = your_name or sql-fun (I recommend not putting spaces in the username), Password = your_password, Expire Password = [leave this blank unless you want your password to expire], Account Status = Unlocked, User Privileges: Roles = [check all roles], Direct Grant System Privileges = [give yourself all these privileges].

5. Click the Create button.

6. Click Logout.

A-2   Download the files to build the Oracle tables

Download the file SQLFUN_Build_Oracle_Tables.txt from the Web site. This file is an SQL script. It is a sequence of SQL commands.

A-3   Build the Oracle tables by running an SQL script

1. Open the Database Home Page login window: Start > All Programs > Oracle Database 10g Express Edition > Go To Database Home Page.

2. Log in to the user account you created to use with this book: Username = your_name or sqlfun, Password = your_password, click Login.

3. Open the window to upload an SQL script: Click the arrow on the right of SQL > SQL Scripts > Upload Script. The window shown here will appear:

ORACLE Database Express Edition

User: JPATRICK

Home > SQL > SQL Scripts > Upload Script

Upload Script		Cancel	Upload
* File		Browse...	
Script Name			
File Character Set	Unicode UTF-8		

4. Enter all the information for the upload: File = |browse to find the file you downloaded from the Web site|, Script Name = SQLFUN_Build_Oracle_Tables |or any other name you want to call it|, File Character Set = Unicode UTF-8 .

ORACLE® Database Express Edition

User: JPATRICK

Home > SQL > SQL Scripts > Upload Script

Upload Script		Cancel	Upload
# File	I:\SQL_Code\SQLFUN_Build_Oracle_Tables.sql	Browse...	
Script Name	SQLFUN_Build_Oracle_Tables		
File Character Set	Unicode UTF-8		

5. Click Upload. Wait until you get the "Script Uploaded" message and then change the View from Icons to Details.

ORACLE® Database Express Edition

User: JPATRICK

Home > SQL > SQL Scripts

Script | Owner JPATRICK ∨ View Details ∨ Display 15 ∨ Go | Delete Checked | Upload >

	Edit	Owner	Name	Updated By	Last Updated ▼	Bytes	Results	Run
☐	📝	JPATRICK	SQLFUN_Build_Oracle_Tables	JPATRICK	38 seconds ago	85,320	0	

row(s) 1 - 1 of 1

6. Open the Script Editor: Click the Edit icon, shown in the previous image, in the detail line for SQLFUN_Build_Oracle_Tables. Doing so will bring you to the following screen:

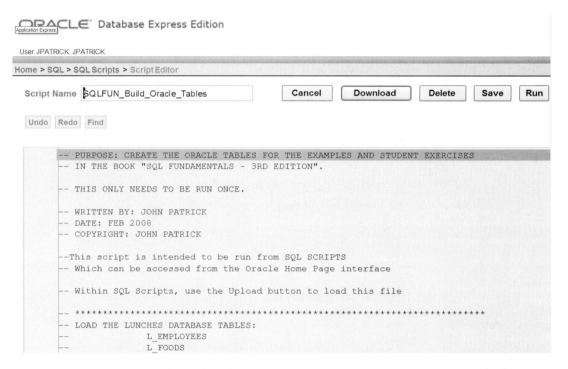

7. Click the Run button. You will be shown some information about the script and asked to confirm that you want to run it.

8. Click Run again to confirm your request. Your script will now run. It might take two or three minutes to complete the process.

At first, the Status will say "Submitted." You can press the F5 key whenever you want to refresh the Web page and see the progress of the script. The Status will change to "Executing." When the script is done, the Status will say "complete."

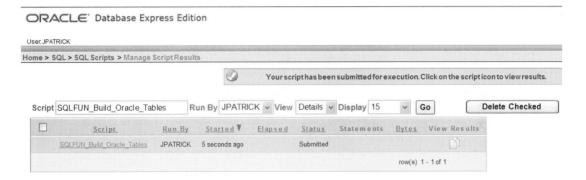

9. View the results: Click the View Results icon. Each line shows the result of one SQL command.

10. Select View = Summary (not Detail), Display = 5000, and click the Go button.

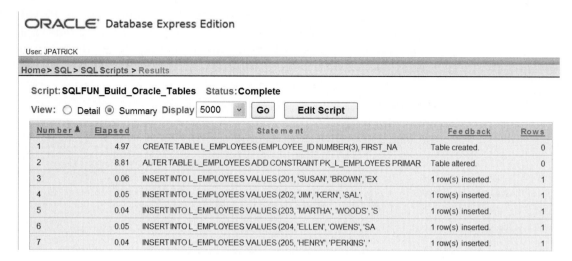

ORACLE® Database Express Edition

User: JPATRICK

Home > SQL > SQL Scripts > Results

Script: **SQLFUN_Build_Oracle_Tables**   Status: **Complete**

View: ○ Detail ◉ Summary Display 5000 ⌄ Go   Edit Script

Number ▲	Elapsed	Statement	Feedback	Rows
1	4.97	CREATE TABLE L_EMPLOYEES (EMPLOYEE_ID NUMBER(3), FIRST_NA	Table created.	0
2	8.81	ALTER TABLE L_EMPLOYEES ADD CONSTRAINT PK_L_EMPLOYEES PRIMAR	Table altered.	0
3	0.06	INSERT INTO L_EMPLOYEES VALUES (201, 'SUSAN', 'BROWN', 'EX	1 row(s) inserted.	1
4	0.05	INSERT INTO L_EMPLOYEES VALUES (202, 'JIM', 'KERN', 'SAL',	1 row(s) inserted.	1
5	0.04	INSERT INTO L_EMPLOYEES VALUES (203, 'MARTHA', 'WOODS', 'S	1 row(s) inserted.	1
6	0.05	INSERT INTO L_EMPLOYEES VALUES (204, 'ELLEN', 'OWENS', 'SA	1 row(s) inserted.	1
7	0.04	INSERT INTO L_EMPLOYEES VALUES (205, 'HENRY', 'PERKINS', '	1 row(s) inserted.	1

11. Scroll to the bottom of the page. At the bottom you should see a report showing the number of objects the SQL script created. The rightmost column should always read OK. The last number on the With Errors line at the bottom of the page is the number of errors. It should be 0.

OBJECT_TYPE	ACTUAL_COUNT	EXPECTED_COUNT	COMPARE_COUNTS
INDEX	49	49	OK
SEQUENCE	2	2	OK
TABLE	228	228	OK
VIEW	8	8	OK
CHECK CONSTRAINT	2	2	OK
PRIMARY KEY CONSTRAINT	48	48	OK
REFERENTIAL INTEGRITY CONSTRAII	20	20	OK
UNIQUENESS CONSTRAINT	1	1	OK

8 rows selected. 2.23 seconds

Run By	JPATRICK
Parsing Schema	JPATRICK
Script Started	Tuesday, June 10, 2008
	8 minutes ago
Elapsed time	159.00 seconds
Statements Processed	1302
Successful	1302
With Errors	0

12. If With Errors = 0, you are done. You can log out.

13. Otherwise you need to identify the errors. Scroll to the top of the page. Use CTRL+F to open the Find window in the browser. Search for "ORA-". That is the prefix for all the errors. (At this point you might not know how to deal with the errors very well. Check for a few obvious things: Did you run out of memory or disk space? Did you run this script more than once? If there are errors you cannot resolve, send me a message on the Web site.)

Note: Later you can use this technique of running an SQL script to run all the SQL examples for a single chapter.

A-4 Disaster recovery if you need it

In case you created the Oracle tables on a production ID, you can drop all the tables and other database objects created by the preceding SQL scripts. Just download and run the SQLFUN_Delete_Oracle_Tables.txt file.

How to Stop Running Oracle

When you are done with your Oracle session, you can log out and close your browser. You might also want to stop the Oracle database with: Start > All Programs > Oracle Database 10g Express Edition > Stop Database.

What to Do if Oracle Slows Down Your Computer

When Oracle is installed, the default configuration automatically starts the Oracle database each time you start up your computer. This is fine if you use Oracle all the time or if your computer is so strong that you do not miss the resources that Oracle consumes. But some people (like me) use their computers for many other things and don't have extra resources to waste.

There are two solutions to this problem. You can pick the one you like better.

A-5 The official Oracle solution

You can stop the database: Start > All Programs > Oracle Database 10g Express Edition > Stop Database.

If you do this and later you decide you want to use Oracle, you must start the database again: Start > All Programs > Oracle Database 10g Express Edition > Start Database.

This technique works perfectly.

The problem with it from my perspective is that you must remember to stop the database each time you start up your computer. To me that is a nuisance.

A-6   My own solution

Oracle uses services to start the database. I change the startup type property of the OracleServiceXE service from Automatic to Manual. This prevents the database from starting automatically and it keeps the resources of my computer available for other uses.

To do this: Start > Control Panel > Administrative Tools > Services > right-click on the OracleServiceXE service > Properties > change the Startup Type from Automatic to Manual > click Apply > click OK.

If you do this and later you decide you want to use Oracle, you must start the database. Use the preceding procedure. The downside to this method is it may not be possible to run Oracle from a User Limited account on the computer.

Quick Start with Oracle

This appendix contains a sample session that shows you how to use Oracle with this book. This demonstration shows you all the tricks you need to know. To keep things simple I assume you have installed Oracle on a single computer running Windows XP.

The topics in this appendix are as follows:

- Log in to your computer.
- Go to the Database Home Page.
- Log in to the Oracle database.
- Go to the SQL Commands page.
- Enter and run an SQL query.
- Optional: Print your query and the results.

Log in to Your Computer

Log in to your computer with the same account you used when you installed Oracle. This will be an Administrator account.

Here I am being conservative. You might also be able to get other accounts to work. But let's keep things simple for now. You can be sure that the account that installed Oracle is set up correctly for Oracle to run.

If you only have one user set up on your computer, you do not need to worry about this issue.

Go to the Database Home Page

Oracle uses your Web browser to interact with you. This will start your browser and display a Web page that allows you to log in to the database. Here you will be logging on as a client of the Database. Usually the server part of the database starts automatically when you start your computer.

Here is the procedure:

1. Start > All Programs > Oracle Database 10g Express Edition > Go To Database Home Page. This displays the Login page.

2. If you get to this screen, skip ahead to "Log in to the Oracle Database" on the next page. If you do not get this, you might get a "Page Not Found" message instead:

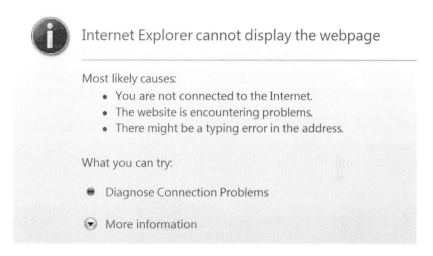

3. This means the server part of the database has not started yet. To start it: Start > All Programs > Oracle Database 10g Express Edition > Start Database. This runs in a command window and takes a minute or two. Here is what you will see:

4. When that finishes, you can close the Start Database window and the browser window. Then try again to go to the Database Home Page.

Log in to the Oracle Database

Enter the Username and Password for the user account you set up to use with this book. (See Appendix A.) Then click the Login button.

Do not use the System or HR user. My username is JPATRICK. Yours might be your name, or you might have used SQLFUN.

This displays the home page for the user account that logged in.

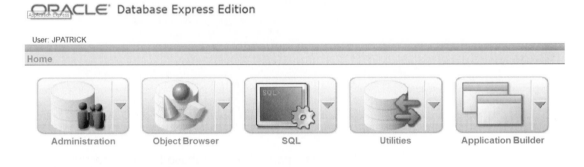

Go to the SQL Commands Page

The SQL Commands page will allow you to run one SQL command at a time. That is what you usually want to do.

There are two ways to get to the SQL Commands page:

1. Click the SQL icon > Click the SQL Commands icon.

2. Click the arrow on the right side of the SQL icon > Click SQL Commands > Click Enter Command.

This displays the following page:

ORACLE Database Express Edition

User: JPATRICK

Home > SQL > SQL Commands

☑ Autocommit   Display   10 ▾

Results   Explain   Describe   Saved SQL   History

Enter SQL statement or PL/SQL command and click Run to see the results.

Enter and Run an SQL Query

Type in an SQL query. Or, if you have your query in a Notepad file, you can copy and paste it into this page.

```
select first_name,
       last_name
from l_employees;
```

Then click the Run button. The result of the SQL query is displayed in the bottom part of the page:

10 rows returned in 0.44 seconds   CSV Export

If you get an error message instead of a result table, the error message does not always accurately tell you what the problem is. Sometimes you will need to figure out the cause of the error yourself.

Note: To run all the SQL queries for a chapter, run an SQL script. This method is shown in Appendix A.

Optional: Print Your Query and the Results

You can print your results using CTRL+P, just as you would with any other Web page.

QUICK START WITH ACCESS

Here is a sample session that shows you how to use Access. I begin by showing you how to start the program. Then I show you how to enter a query, run it, and print the result.

The topics in this appendix are as follows:

- You may use Access 2007, 2003, 2002, or 2000.
- How to start Access.
- Entering an SQL query.
- Dealing with errors in Access.
- Printing from Access.
- Using the Access Trust Center.

You May Use Access 2007, 2003, 2002, or 2000

The Web site for this book has Access databases in four formats: Access 2007, Access 2003, Access 2002, and Access 2000. You need to use the one that matches the version of Access installed on your computer. The images and procedures in this appendix are from Access 2007. If you have a different version, the images and procedures will be a little different, but the functions will be the same.

How to Start Access

There are several ways to open Access. I recommend this method:

1. Right-click the Start button.

2. Click Explore (or use another method to open Windows Explorer).

3. Find the database you want to open, which will have the file type ACCDB (for older versions of Access, the file type is MDB). Then Double-click it.

Another way to open Access is:

1. Left-click the Start button.

2. Click All Programs.

3. Click Microsoft Access (it might be in the Microsoft Office folder).

If you get a message that the database is read-only, you will need to make some corrections and start again. You need the database to be read-write in order to enter SQL queries. If you find that it is read-only, there are two major things to check.

The most common cause is that the read-only property is set. To change this:

1. Open Windows Explorer.

2. Locate the Access database file and right-click it.

3. Select Properties and clear the checkbox for Read-only, shown in the following image.

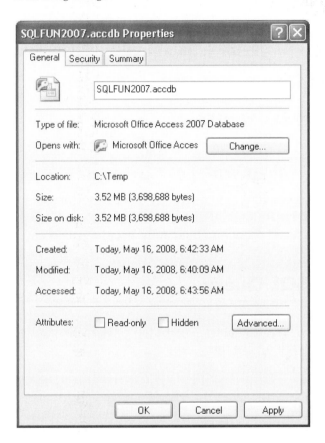

4. Click Apply, then Click OK.

Another reason some Access databases are read-only is that they are on a read-only disk drive. This occurs in the computer labs of many schools where the teacher has placed some files on a server for the students to copy. To use the database, you must make a personal copy of the Access database file onto your local read-write drive, which is usually the C drive.

When you have successfully started Access, you will see something like the following image.

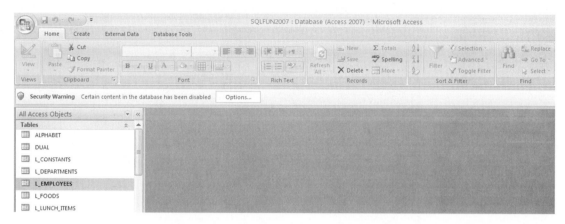

In Access 2007, you might get a Security Warning like the one shown here. To elminate the warning for this session: Options > Enable this content > OK. To get rid of it permanently, use the Trust Center.

Entering an SQL Query

1. Begin a query: Create tab > Query Design icon. You will see something like this:

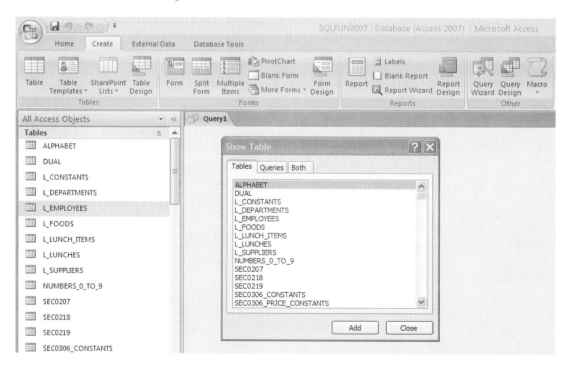

2. Close the Show Table window. Enter SQL view by clicking the SQL button in the bottom right corner of the screen.

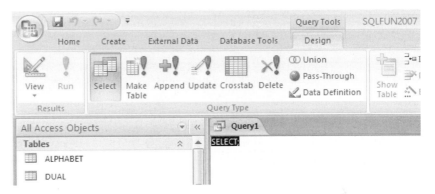

3. You can type in your SQL query. The method that I prefer is to copy the query from a Notepad file and paste it into this screen.

I recommend that you enter your query into Notepad, rather than directly into Access, so you have more control over it. Access reformats a query when it is saved, but in Notepad your query will retain the format you give it. Notepad provides an easy way to edit and print your queries.

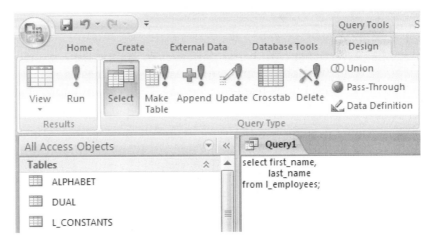

4. Run the SQL query. To do this, click the Run icon, shown as an exclamation point in the preceding image.

Optional: Adjust the width of the columns so that the column name appears completely. You can adjust the width of a column with the mouse. Run the mouse over the top line of the table. Between columns the mouse icon will change. Then you can hold the mouse button down and drag to change the width of the column.

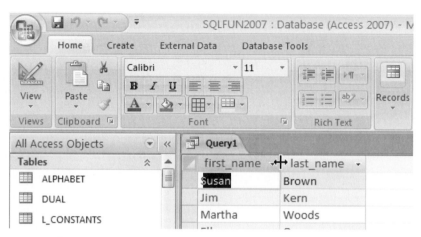

5. **Optional:** You can print the result table from the query with CTRL+P. You cannot print the SQL query itself this way. That is another reason you should keep your SQL in a Notepad file when you are working with Access.

Dealing with Errors in Access

Some of the error messages in Access are very helpful and others are less so. Some of the error messages in Access are so strange that they do not even look like error messages Once you know what they are, it is easy to deal with them. I will show you an example of this.

We can use the same query we used earlier, but this time we will put an error in it. The error is that we will leave the second letter A out of the name of the `last_name` field. Here is the SQL:

```
select first_name,
       last_nme
from l_employees;
```

Now here is the message that Access uses to tell you about this error:

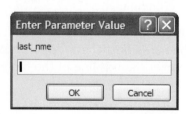

It doesn't look much like an error message. In fact, it is not an error message at all. Rather, it is asking you to enter a value for the unknown called last_nme.

When Access comes across something it does not recognize, it often treats the unknown as a parameter and it asks you what value you want to enter in that parameter. This is a case where Access is getting seriously confused.

However, once you understand that Access has this quirk, then the message is helpful. You look at the "parameter" that Access wants you to enter. In this case it is "Last_nme" and you can immediately tell what the problem is.

For people who want to know more about this particular error message, here is an explanation: Access assumes that anything it does not recognize is a parameter, which is a type of variable value that is entered when the query is run. In this case, Access is asking you for the value of last_nme. If you responded to the message by entering "Smith", Access would replace last_nme in the query with Smith, which is equivalent to placing the literal Smith in the query. The result table would look like this:

first_name	last_nme
Susan	Smith
Jim	Smith
Martha	Smith
Ellen	Smith
Henry	Smith
Carol	Smith
Dan	Smith
Fred	Smith
Paula	Smith
Nancy	Smith

Printing from Access

You can print your result tables directly from Access by using File > Print.

The one thing you cannot print this way is your SQL code. That is one of the reasons you should put your SQL code into Notepad. You can print it from there.

Using the Access Trust Center

Each time you open the Access database, you might see a message that reads,

Security Warning   Certain content in the database has been disabled

and gives you an Options button to click.

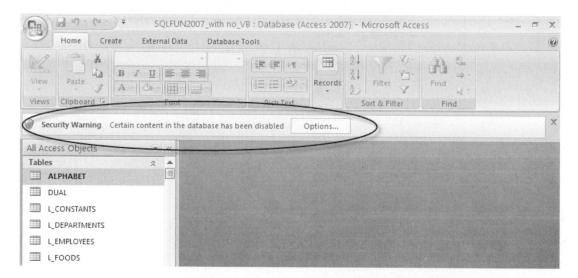

If you do not see this message, don't worry. You are okay and do not need the informtion in this section.

If you do see this message and you want to get rid of it permanently, then this section is for you. First, you must have administrative privileges on your computer. Usually, this means that the computer belongs to you and you log into the computer as an administrator.

If you do not have administrative privileges, then you can only get rid of this message for one session at a time and you must repeat the process in each session. That is annoying, but there is no way around it. I have already showed you what you need to do at the end of the "How to Start Access" section of this appendix.

Before you decide to get rid of this message permanently, you need to understand what it means. Does it mean that Access has scanned this database and has found some horrible virus that is just waiting to destroy your computer? No, the message does not mean that, though it seems to want to imply this. The message is vague and scary. I think it is intended to be that way.

What it actually means is that Access will disable Visual Basic modules and certain macro commands, unless you say it is okay to run them. Those things could potentially harm your computer. If some malicious stranger sends you an Access database by e-mail, don't open it. At least, don't open it in Enabled mode. When an Access database is opened, it can be set to run some code automatically and that code could possibly harm your computer.

The database you use with this book doesn't have any Visual Basic modules or any macros. Then why are you still getting this message? The message doesn't mean that Access has scanned the database and found something that might damage your comuter. Rather, it means that Access has not scanned the database and Microsoft wants you to assume all the responsibility in case something goes wrong. That is rather weak in my opinion. I think they could have done better.

Now that you understand the message, if you still want to turn it off permanently, here is how:

1. Click the Options button. The Microsoft Office Security Options window will open.

2. Click Open The Trust Center. This opens the Trust Center window. It will probably open to the Message Bar settings. One way to turn the message off is to change the Message Bar Settings to the option "Never show information about blocked content," but that is not the best way. It might block too much.

3. Click Trusted Locations on the left side of the window.

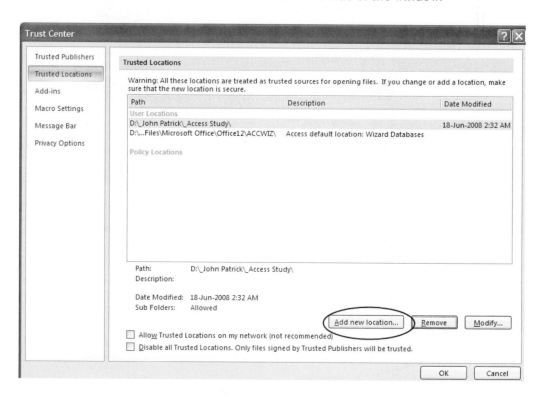

4. Click the Add new location button. This opens the Microsoft Office Trusted Location window. There is a warning that asks you to make sure the new trusted location is secure. I am not sure how you are expected to be able to do that. I suppose if it is your own computer, you can say that certain folders in it it will be secure.

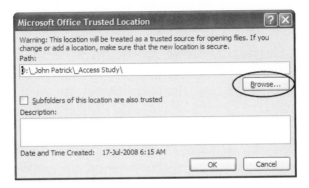

5. Click the Browse button, then choose the folder where you have installed the database or one of its parent folders. Then click OK.

6. If you decide to, select the checkbox "Subfolders of this location are also trusted." Enter a description if you want. Then click the OK button in the Microsoft Trusted Location window.

7. Click OK in the Trust Center window and click OK again in the Microsoft Office Security Options window. Now you are done.

Diagram of the Lunches Database

This appendix contains a diagram of the Lunches database that shows all the tables in the database and how they are related to each other. It contains a list of the join conditions to use when you are obtaining data from more than one table. The data validation rules are also shown here.

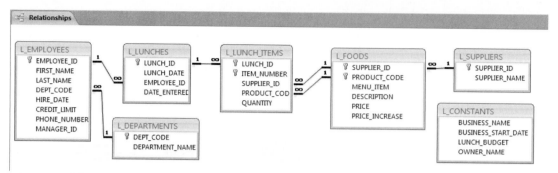

Diagram of the Lunches database.

The columns of the primary key are shown with a key symbol next to them.

The names of all the tables in the Lunches database begin with the prefix l_. This prefix shows that these tables are related and that they are all parts of a single system.

The lines between the tables show the join conditions.

The lines containing a one (1) and an infinity sign (∞) show join conditions that are also referential integrity constraints.

Join Conditions

The relationships between the tables.

Tables to Be Joined	SQL Code Showing the Join Condition (The join condition is shown in the **where** clause.)
| l_employees<br>l_departments | ```
select a.*,
       b.*
from l_employees a,
     l_departments b
where a.dept_code = b.dept_code;
``` |
| l_employees<br>l_lunches | ```
select a.*,
       b.*
from l_employees a,
     l_lunches b
where a.employee_id = b.employee_id;
``` |
| l_lunches<br>l_lunch_items | ```
select a.*,
       b.*
from l_lunches a,
     l_lunch_items b
where a.lunch_id = b.lunch_id;
``` |
```

The relationships between the tables. *(continued)*

Tables to Be Joined	SQL Code Showing the Join Condition (The join condition is shown in the `where` clause.)
`l_lunch_items` `l_foods`	```select a.*, b.* from l_lunch_items a, l_foods b where a.supplier_id = b.supplier_id and a.product_code = b.product_code;```
`l_foods` `l_suppliers`	```select a.*, b.* from l_foods a, l_suppliers b where a.supplier_id = b.supplier_id;```
`l_constants` Any other table	```select a.*, b.* from l_constants a any_other_table b;``` (No join condition is needed between the `l_constants` table and any other table because this table contains only one row.)

Data Validation Rules

Primary key constraints are not shown here.

Table	Column	Validation Rule
Validation Rule 1: Not Null Constraint		
`l_employees`	`first_name`	`first_name` is a required field.
Validation Rule 2: Not Null Constraint		
`l_employees`	`last_name`	`last_name` is a required field.
Validation Rule 3: Not Null Constraint		
`l_lunches`	`employee_id`	`employee_id` is a required field.
Validation Rule 4: Uniqueness Constraint		
`l_employees`	`phone_number`	Each employee must have a distinct phone number.

Table	Column	Validation Rule
Validation Rule 5: Uniqueness Constraint		
l_employees	first_name, last_name	No two employees can have both the same first name and the same last name.
Validation Rule 6: Check Constraint		
l_foods	price	The price must be less than $10.00.
Validation Rule 7: Referential Integrity Constraint		
l_employees	manager_id	Data is checked. It must have a valid value.
l_employees	employee_id	List of all the valid values.
Validation Rule 8: Referential Integrity Constraint		
l_employees	dept_code	Data is checked. It must have a valid value.
l_departments	dept_code	List of all the valid values.
Validation Rule 9: Referential Integrity Constraint		
l_lunches	employee_id	Data is checked. It must have a valid value.
l_employees	employee_id	List of all the valid values.
Validation Rule 10: Referential Integrity Constraint		
l_lunch_items	lunch_id	Data is checked. It must have a valid value.
l_lunches	lunch_id	List of all the valid values.
Validation Rule 11: Referential Integrity Constraint		
l_lunch_items	supplier_id, product_code	Data is checked. It must have a valid value.
l_foods	supplier_id, product_code	List of all the valid values.
Validation Rule 12: Referential Integrity Constraint		
l_foods	supplier_id	Data is checked. It must have a valid value.
l_suppliers	supplier_id	List of all the valid values.

INDEX

Symbols and Numbers

' (single quote):
  apostrophe, 105, 107, 127
  single quote, 52, 66, 103, 107
- (dash):
  subtract a date from another date,
    351
  subtract a number from a date, 351
  subtract numbers, 334
-- (double dash), comment line, 109
! (exclamation mark), 109
!= (not equal), 60, 111
" (double quote), 40, 103, 106
(pound sign):
  date indicator, 55, 103, 108, 247, 252
  wildcard character, 66, 112
$ (dollar sign), 36, 57, 110
% (percent), wildcard character, 66, 112
& (ampersand):
  concatenate, 110, 340, 344, 348
  variable in SQL*Plus, 109, 689, 690,
    693
&& (variable in SQL*Plus), 693
@ (at sign), 725
* (asterisk):
  count all rows, 403, 411
  multiply, 111, 334
  select all columns, 37, 111
  wildcard character, 66, 112
, (comma), 36, 57, 102, 106, 110
. (period):
  decimal point, 36, 57, 110
  in table names, 109, 724, 725, 727

/ (forward slash):
  divide numbers, 111, 335
  statement end in Oracle, 111
/* */ (multiline comment), 111
\ (backslash), integer divide, 335
: (colon), prefix creating a variable, 110, 689
; (semicolon), end of SQL statement, 104, 110
? (question mark), wildcard character, 66, 112
[ ] (square brackets):
  handling spaces in names, 40, 106, 111
  variable in Access, 689
  in wildcard, 66, 112
^ (caret, Shift + 6, exponent), 335
^= (not equal), 60, 111
_ (underscore):
  in names, 36, 40, 106
  wildcard character, 66, 12
|| (two double bars or two pipe symbols),
    concatenate, 110, 340, 344, 349
+ (plus):
  add a number to a date, 351
  add numbers, 334
< (less than), 51, 56, 499
<= (less than or equal to), 51, 56, 499
<> (not equal), 51, 60, 111
= (equal):
  do not use with null, 69
  equal condition, 51, 52
  = null (okay in update), 296
> (greater than), 51, 56, 499
>= (greater than or equal to), 51, 499
0-parameter function, 365
3-valued logic, 60, 120

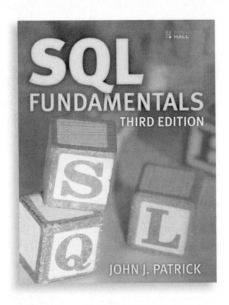

FREE Online Edition

Your purchase of **SQL Fundamentals, Third Edition,** includes access to a free online edition for 120 days through the Safari Books Online subscription service. Nearly every Prentice Hall book is available online through Safari Books Online, along with over 5,000 other technical books and videos from publishers such as Addison-Wesley Professional, Cisco Press, Exam Cram, IBM Press, O'Reilly, Que, and Sams.

SAFARI BOOKS ONLINE allows you to search for a specific answer, cut and paste code, download chapters, and stay current with emerging technologies.

Activate your FREE Online Edition at
www.informit.com/safarifree

> **STEP 1:** Enter the coupon code: PPGR-5PME-1GTD-PAE5-TDX9.

> **STEP 2:** New Safari users, complete the brief registration form.
> Safari subscribers, just log in.

If you have difficulty registering on Safari or accessing the online edition,
please e-mail customer-service@safaribooksonline.com